NINTH EDITION

Theories
of Personality

Duane P. Schultz
University of South Florida

Sydney Ellen Schultz

WADSWORTH
CENGAGE Learning™

Australia • Brazil • Japan • Korea • Mexico • Singapore • Spain • United Kingdom • United States

WADSWORTH
CENGAGE Learning

Theories of Personality, **Ninth Edition**
Duane P. Schultz
Sydney Ellen Schultz

Publisher: Michele Sordi

Assistant Editor: Rachel Guzman

Technology Project Manager: Amy Cohen

Marketing Manager: Kim Russell

Marketing Assistant: Melanie Cregger

Marketing Communications Manager:
Linda Yip

Sr. Project Manager, Editorial Production:
Pat Waldo

Creative Director: Rob Hugel

Art Director: Vernon Boes

Print Buyer: Becky Cross

Text Permissions Editor: Bob Kauser

Image Permissions Editor: Deanna Ettinger

Production Service: Ruchika Vij,
ICC Macmillan Inc.

Text Designer: John Edeen

Photo Researcher: Charlotte Goldman

Copy Editor: Carol Noble

Illustrator: Graphic World Illustration Studio

Cover Designer: Gopa & Ted2, Inc.

Cover Images: From top left to bottom right:
© Flint/Corbis, © Banana Stock/Jupiterimages,
© Image Source/Jupiterimages, © Thinkstock
Images/Jupiterimages, © Blend Images/
Jupiterimages, © Image Source Black/
Jupiterimages, © Larry Williams/Corbis,
© Heide Benser/zefa/Corbis, © Corbis,
© Thinkstock Images/Jupiterimages, © Nea
Frisk Photography/Corbis, and © Photo Alto
Agency/Jupiterimages

Compositor: ICC Macmillan Inc.

For product information and technology assistance, contact us at
Cengage Learning Customer & Sales Support, 1-800-354-9706.

For permission to use material from this text or product, submit all requests online at **cengage.com/permissions.** Further permissions questions can be e-mailed to **permissionrequest@cengage.com.**

Library of Congress Control Number: 2007942486

ISBN-13: 978-0-495-50625-6
ISBN-10: 0-495-50625-7

Wadsworth
10 Davis Drive
Belmont, CA 94002-3098
USA

Cengage Learning is a leading provider of customized learning solutions with office locations around the globe, including Singapore, the United Kingdom, Australia, Mexico, Brazil, and Japan. Locate your local office at **international.cengage.com/region.**

Cengage Learning products are represented in Canada by Nelson Education, Ltd.

For your course and learning solutions, visit **academic.cengage.com.** Purchase any of our products at your local college store or at our preferred online store **www.ichapters.com.**

Printed in the United States of America
1 2 3 4 5 6 7 12 11 10 09 08

For Albert F. Green and June B. Green, in admiration.

Brief Contents

Contents

CHAPTER 8

Raymond Cattell, Hans Eysenck, and Other Trait Theorists   263

PART FIVE
The Humanistic Approach   297

CHAPTER 9
Abraham Maslow: Needs-Hierarchy Theory   299

CHAPTER 10
Carl Rogers: Self-Actualization Theory   324

Preface to the Ninth Edition

Each edition of a textbook must be as vital, dynamic, and responsive to change as the field it covers. To remain an effective teaching instrument, it must reflect the development of the field and continue to challenge its readers. We have seen the focus of personality study shift from global theories, beginning with Sigmund Freud's 19th-century psychoanalytic theory of neuroses, to 21st-century explorations of more limited personality dimensions. And we have seen the basis of personality exploration change from case studies of emotionally disturbed persons to more scientifically based research with diverse populations. Contemporary work in the field reflects differences in gender, age, and sexual orientation as well as ethnic, racial, religious, and cultural heritage.

New and Expanded Coverage

Major changes for this edition include new biographical material for the theorists, to suggest, where warranted, how the development of their theory may have been influenced by events in their personal and professional lives. This approach shows students that the development of science through theory and research is not always totally objective. It may also derive from intuition and personal experience later refined and extended by more rational, analytic processes. Social and cultural influences on the theorists' beliefs about human nature are described.

The sections on personality research have been updated with more than 300 new references to maintain the emphasis on current issues. Considerable material has been added on the effects of gender, ethnicity, and culture on the issues of personality development, test performance, and the broader conceptions of human nature. We present the results of cross-cultural research and a diversity of samples of research participants from more than 45 nations throughout the world, not only English-speaking countries but also countries in Europe, Asia, the Middle East, Africa, and South America. We have expanded coverage of ethnic issues in personality assessment among African American, Asian American, Hispanic American, and Native American populations.

There is new material on personality assessment including computerized test taking and the use of personal electronic devices as diaries for recording samples of thoughts and behaviors. We describe the increasing use of the Internet as a psychology laboratory to sample a greater number and variety of subjects online.

For Freudian theory, we have added more than two dozen new studies on concepts such as the influence of the unconscious, ego control, ego resiliency, displaced aggression, repressors and non-repressors, and dream content. For Jung, we discuss research on the development of the Myers-Briggs Type Indicator and on behavioral differences as a function of psychological type. We have added research on the midlife crisis in women, a stage of life Jung considered to be particularly important. And we include more description of Jung's psychotherapy sessions with his patients. For Adler, we present new findings on early memories, birth order and social interest. For Horney, we have expanded the coverage of neurotic competitiveness.

For the chapter on Murray there is additional material on the needs for achievement and affiliation. For Erikson there is extensive biographical material from a new book by his daughter. In addition, we offer more coverage of psychosocial stages of identity, ethnic identity, gender preference identity, cultural differences in the search for identity, and the role of the Internet in creating a virtual identity. As the general population ages, we have more research available on the issues of generativity in middle age and ego integrity in old age.

For Allport, we discuss more research on expressive behavior, computer recognition of facial expressions and emotions, and the computer transmission of facial expressions through the use of "emoticons."

To reinforce findings on the genetic basis of personality, we present new research growing out of Eysenck's work and the five-factor model. The Maslow chapter contains additional work on self-esteem, and the Skinner chapter includes research with human subjects on superstitious behavior and on self-control. The Bandura chapter contains more material on self-efficacy, on the relationship between video games and aggressive behavior, and on the effect of rap music on aggressive behavior. The Rotter chapter has new biographical material and updated research on locus of control.

The chapter on limited-domain approaches, or the study of specific facets of personality, evaluates new forms of sensation seeking, such as tattooing, body piercing, and Internet addiction. Cultural differences in optimism/pessimism are reported as well as cross-cultural research on positive psychology and the different types of happiness.

Organization of the Text

The ninth edition of *Theories of Personality* retains its orientation toward undergraduate students who have had little previous exposure to personality theories. Our purpose is to reach out to beginning students and ease their task of learning about the study of personality. We have chosen theorists who represent psychoanalytic, neopsychoanalytic, life-span, trait, humanistic, cognitive, behavioral, and social-learning approaches, as well as clinical and experimental work. The concluding chapter reviews the seven major perspectives from which to view personality development and suggests ways to help students draw conclusions and achieve closure from their studies.

Each theory in the text is discussed as a unit. Although we recognize the value of an issues or problems approach that compares theories on specific points, we believe that the issues-oriented book is more appropriate for higher-level students. The theories-oriented text makes it easier for beginning students to grasp a theory's essential concepts and overall flavor. We try to present each theory clearly, to convey its most important ideas, assumptions, definitions, and methods. We discuss each theorist's methods of assessment and empirical research, and we offer our evaluations and reflections. The Questions About Human Nature section for each theorist deals with six fundamental issues: free will versus determinism, nature versus nurture, childhood experiences, uniqueness versus universality, goals, and optimism versus pessimism.

Except for placing Freud first in recognition of his chronological priority, we have not arranged the theories in order of perceived importance. They are presented in nine parts, placing each theory in the perspective of competing viewpoints.

A Note on Diversity

The first person to propose a comprehensive theory of the human personality was Sigmund Freud, a clinical neurologist who formulated his ideas while treating patients in Vienna, Austria, in the 19th century. His work, known as "psychoanalysis," was based largely on sessions with wealthy White European females who came to him complaining of emotional distress and disturbing thoughts and behaviors. From his observations of their progress, or lack of it, he offered a theory to explain the personalities of everybody.

Freud's system was important for the concepts he proposed—many of which are now part of popular culture—as well as for the opposition he provoked, inspiring other theorists to examine and promote their own ideas to explain personality.

Today, personality theorists and researchers recognize that an explanation based on a small, homogeneous segment of the population cannot be applied to the many diverse groups of people sharing living space in our world. The situation is similar in medicine. Doctors and researchers are recognizing that some medications and treatments appropriate for young adults are not suitable for children or elderly people. Some diseases prevalent in certain ethnic groups are rare in others, requiring differences in medical screening and testing for diverse populations.

Contemporary personality theory and research strives to be inclusive, studying the influences of age, gender, race, ethnic origin, religious beliefs, sexual orientation, and child-rearing practices. We see examples of this diversity throughout the text.

Features

For the student, we offer chapter outlines, summaries, review questions, annotated reading lists, margin glossary terms, a cumulative glossary, tables and figures, a reference list, and referrals to relevant Web sites. Students can also log on to the book companion Web site located at http:/academic.cengage.com/psychology/schultz for tutorial quizzes and other resources.

For instructors, the instructor's manual with test bank has been thoroughly revised by Ken Pearce of California Baptist University and offers lecture outlines, ideas for class discussion, projects, useful Web links, and test items. The test bank is available both in print and computerized formats. The instructors can also create, deliver, and customize tests and study guides (both print and online) in minutes with ExamView®, an easy-to-use assessment and tutorial system. ExamView offers both a Quick Test Wizard and an Online Test Wizard that guide users step-by-step through the process of creating tests, while its unique WYSIWYG capability previews the test on the screen exactly as it will print or display online. Instructors can build tests of up to 250 questions using up to 12 question types. With ExamView's complete word-processing capabilities, instructors can also enter an unlimited number of new questions or edit existing questions. New to this edition is WebTutor Toolbox on WebCT and Blackboard, an online course management system that also offers supplementary study materials for students. PowerPoint Lecture Slides and electronic transparencies are available on eBank. The transparencies feature selects figures and tables from the text loaded into Microsoft PowerPoint. Contact your local sales representative for details.

Acknowledgments

We would like to thank the many colleagues and students who have written to us about the book and have offered suggestions for this edition. We are especially grateful to the following reviewers: Charisse Chappell, Salisbury University; Travis Langley, Henderson State University; Pamela Mulder, Marshall University; Ken Pearce, California Baptist University; Linda Rangell, New York Institute of Technology.

Duane P. Schultz
Sydney Ellen Schultz

The Study of Personality: Assessment, Research, and Theory

You are about to begin a fascinating journey that covers the various ideas psychologists and other scientists have advanced to explain the human personality—your personality. It also tells the story of the great theorists' lives and how their own experiences may have influenced the explanations they proposed. You already know how important personality is. Everything you have achieved so far, your expectations for the future and even your general health are influenced by your personality and the personalities of the people with whom you interact.

We have organized the theories by their outlook on human nature, beginning with Sigmund Freud. We consider extensions of his theory of psychoanalysis and discuss the men and women who revised his ideas or rebelled against his system. These chapters are followed by a life-span approach, tracking personality development from birth to old age. We then discuss theories that focus on individual personality traits, on psychological health, on predetermined behavior patterns, and on cognitive learning from social situations. We also introduce an idea for the 21st century, the happy personality type. The book's final chapter offers conclusions from our exploration of personality.

We also recognize that theorists from the last century rarely considered the importance of ethnic and cultural diversity. You can readily see that it is not appropriate to generalize to all people from, for example, ideas that one theorist based on clinical observations of neurotic European women or that another theorist based on tests given to American college men. Therefore, when we discuss research conducted on these theories, and describe their use for real-world problems of diagnosis and therapy, we show the influence of age, gender, race, ethnic and national origin, religious beliefs, and sexual orientation.

To make your study easier, we include chapter outlines, summaries, review questions, and reading lists. Important words are defined in the margin, and these definitions are also listed in the back of the book. Also, you may want to check out the Web sites in our "Log On" features included in each chapter. They contain a wealth of information on personality.

The Study of Personality

Everybody Has One

Everybody has one—a personality, that is—and yours will help determine the boundaries of your success and life fulfillment. It is no exaggeration to say that your personality is one of your most important assets. It has already helped shape your experiences and certainly will continue to do so. All your achievements to date, your expectations for the future, whether you will be a good spouse or parent, even your health can be influenced by your personality and the personalities of the people with whom you interact. Your personality can limit or expand your options and choices, prevent you from sharing certain experiences or enable you to take advantage of them. It restricts or constrains some people and opens up the world to others.

How often have you described someone as having a *terrific* personality? By that you typically mean the person is affable, pleasant, nice to be around, and easy to get along with—the kind of person you might select for a friend, roommate, or colleague at work. If you are a manager, you might choose to hire this person. If you are ready to make a commitment to a personal relationship, you might want to marry this person, basing your decision on your perception of his or her personality. You have also known people you would describe as having a *terrible* personality. Such persons may be aloof, hostile, aggressive, unfriendly, unpleasant, or difficult to get along with. You would not hire them or want to associate with them, and they may be similarly shunned, rejected, and isolated by others.

While you are making judgments about the personalities of other people, they are making similar judgments about you. These mutual decisions that shape the lives of both the judged and the judges are made countless times, every time we encounter a social situation that requires us to interact with new people. Of course, the number and variety of social situations you willingly participate in are also determined by your personality—for example, your relative sociability or shyness. You know where you rate on that factor, just as you no doubt have a reasonably clear picture of your overall personality.

Describing Your Personality

Of course, it is glib and facile to attempt to sum up the total constellation of someone's personality characteristics by using such fuzzy terms as *terrific* and *terrible*. The subject of personality is too complex for such a simplified description, because humans are too complex and changeable in different situations and with different people. We need to be more precise in our language to adequately define and describe personality. For that reason, psychologists have devoted considerable effort to developing tests to evaluate, or assess, personality.

You may believe you don't need any psychological test to tell you what your personality is like, and, in general, you may be correct. After all, you probably know yourself better than anyone else. If you were asked to list the words that best describe your personality, no doubt you could do it without too much thought.

Table i.1 Adjective checklist

Make a check mark next to the words you believe apply to your personality.

✓ affectionate	___ ambitious	___ assertive
___ boastful	___ cheerful	✓ cynical
___ demanding	___ dominant	✓ fearful
___ forceful	✓ generous	___ high-strung
___ impatient	✓ insightful	✓ meek
✓ moody	___ optimistic	✓ opinionated
___ persistent	___ prudish	___ relaxed
✓ sarcastic	✓ sensitive	___ sociable
✓ submissive	___ tolerant	✓ trusting
___ uninhibited	✓ vindictive	✓ withdrawn

OK. Try it. Take a piece of paper and write down as many adjectives as you can to describe what you are really like—not how you would like to be, or what you want your teachers or parents or friends to think you are like—but the real you. Try not to use the word *terrific*, even if it does apply in your case. How many words did you select? Six? Ten? A few more? A widely used personality test, the Adjective Checklist, offers an astonishing 300 adjectives to describe personality. People taking the test choose the ones that best describe themselves. No, we're not going to ask you to review all 300 adjectives, only the 30 we have listed in Table i.1. Place a check mark next to the ones you believe apply to you. Now you have a description of your personality in greater detail, but remember that in the actual test, you would have an additional 270 items to pick from.

How Does Personality Develop?

Our focus here is not what *your* personality is like. You don't need a psychology course to learn that. What we will be studying are the forces and factors that shape your personality. Later in this chapter, and throughout the book, we consider some basic questions about the nature of personality—for example, whether we are born with a certain type of personality or learn it from our parents, whether personality is influenced by unconscious forces, or whether personality can change after our childhood years.

In this book, we describe a variety of theories that have been proposed to help answer these and related questions about human nature. After we have discussed them—what they are, how they developed, and what their current status is—we will evaluate their usefulness in answering our questions and contributing to our understanding of how personality develops. We may think of each of these theorists as contributing pieces to a grand puzzle, which is why we study their ideas, even though some of their concepts are decades old. Psychologists continue to try to fit these pieces together to bring forth a clearer image, a more complete picture of what makes us the way we are and determines how we look at the world.

The Place of Personality in the History of Psychology

Because the study of personality is so central to an understanding of human nature, you might assume it has always occupied a prominent position in psychology. For more than half of psychology's history as a science, however, psychologists paid relatively little attention to personality.

Psychology emerged as an independent and primarily experimental science from an amalgam of ideas borrowed from philosophy and physiology. The birth of psychology took place in the late 19th century in Germany and was largely the work of Wilhelm Wundt, who established psychology's first laboratory in 1879 at the University of Leipzig.

The Study of Consciousness

The new science of psychology focused on the analysis of conscious experience into its elemental parts. The methods of psychology were modeled on the approach used in the natural sciences. Physics and chemistry appeared to be unlocking the secrets of the physical universe by reducing all matter to its basic elements and analyzing them. If the physical world could be understood by breaking it down into elements, why couldn't the mind or the mental world be studied in the same way?

Wundt and other psychologists of his day who were concerned with studying human nature were greatly influenced by the natural science approach, and they proceeded to apply it to the study of the mind. Because these researchers limited themselves to the experimental method, they studied only those mental processes that might be affected by some external stimulus that could be manipulated and controlled by the experimenter. There was no room in this experimental psychology approach for such a complex, multidimensional topic as personality. It was not compatible with either the subject matter or the methods of the new psychology.

The Study of Behavior

behaviorism
The school of psychology, founded by John B. Watson, that focused on psychology as the study of overt behavior rather than of mental processes.

In the early decades of the 20th century, the American psychologist John B. Watson, at Johns Hopkins University in Baltimore, Maryland, sparked a revolution against the work of Wilhelm Wundt. Watson's movement, called **behaviorism**, opposed Wundt's focus on conscious experience. More devoted than Wundt to a natural science approach, Watson argued that if psychology was to be a science, it had to focus only on the tangible aspects of human nature—that which could be seen, heard, recorded, and measured. Only overt behavior—not consciousness—could be the legitimate topic of psychology.

Consciousness, Watson said, cannot be seen or experimented upon. Therefore, like the philosophers' concept of the soul, consciousness is meaningless for science. Psychologists must deal only with what they can see, manipulate, and measure—that is, external stimuli and the subject's behavioral responses to them. According to

Watson, whatever happens inside the person after the stimulus is presented and before the response is made cannot be seen. Because we can only speculate about it, it is of no interest or value to science.

Behaviorism presents a mechanistic picture of human beings as well-ordered machines that respond automatically to external stimuli. It has been said that behaviorists see people as a kind of vending machine. Stimuli are put in, and appropriate responses, learned from past experience, spill out. In this view, personality is nothing more than the accumulation of learned responses or habit systems, a definition later offered by B. F. Skinner. Thus, behaviorists reduced personality to what could be seen and observed objectively, and there was no place in their conception for consciousness or for unconscious forces. However, the more recent social-learning theorists, who offer explanations derived from Watson's and Skinner's versions of behaviorism, have restored to personality some measure of consciousness.

If Watson and the early behavioral psychologists dismissed all those notions, feelings, and complexities that come to mind when we use the word *personality*, then where were they? What happened to the consciousness you know you experience every moment you are awake? Where were those unconscious forces that sometimes seem to compel us to act in ways over which we feel we have no control?

The Study of the Unconscious

Those aspects of human nature were dealt with by a third line of inquiry, one that arose independently of Wundt and Watson. They were investigated by Sigmund Freud, beginning in the 1890s. Freud, a physician in Vienna, Austria, called his system **psychoanalysis**.

Psychoanalysis and *psychology* are not synonymous or interchangeable terms. Freud was not a psychologist but a physician in private practice, working with persons who suffered from emotional disturbances. Although trained as a scientist, Freud did not use the experimental method. Rather, he developed his theory of personality based on clinical observation of his patients. Through a lengthy series of psychoanalytic sessions, Freud applied his creative interpretation to what patients told him about their feelings and past experiences, both actual and fantasized. His approach was thus quite different from the rigorous experimental laboratory investigation of the elements of conscious experience or of behavior.

Inspired by Freud's psychoanalytic approach, a group of personality theorists developed unique conceptions of human nature outside the mainstream of experimental psychology. These theorists, the neopsychoanalysts, focused on the whole person as he or she functions in the real world, not on elements of behavior or stimulus-response units as studied in the psychology laboratory. The neopsychoanalysts accepted the existence of conscious and unconscious forces, whereas the behaviorists accepted the existence only of that which they could see. As a result, the early personality theorists were speculative in their work, relying more on inferences based on observations of their patients' behavior than on the quantitative analysis of laboratory data.

psychoanalysis
Sigmund Freud's theory of personality and system of therapy for treating mental disorders.

The Scientific Study of Personality

We see, then, that experimental psychology and the formal study of personality began in two separate traditions, using different methods and pursuing different aims. We should note that experimental psychology in its formative years did not totally ignore personality—some limited aspects of personality were studied—but there did not exist within psychology a distinct specialty area known as personality as there was child psychology or social psychology.

It was not until the late 1930s that the study of personality became formalized and systematized in American psychology, primarily through the work of Gordon Allport at Harvard University. Allport's landmark book, *Personality: A Psychological Interpretation*, is generally considered to mark the formal beginning of the study of personality. Following his initial efforts, other professional books appeared, journals were founded, universities offered courses, and research was undertaken. These activities signaled a growing recognition that some areas of concern to the psychoanalysts and neopsychoanalysts could be incorporated into psychology. Academic psychologists came to believe that it was possible to develop a scientific study of personality.

From the 1930s to the present day, a variety of approaches to the study of personality have emerged. In this book, in addition to the psychoanalytic and behavioristic viewpoints noted above, we discuss several others. These include the life-span approach, which argues that personality continues to develop throughout the course of our life; the trait approach, which contends that much of our personality is inherited; the humanistic approach, which emphasizes human strengths, virtues, aspirations, and the fulfillment of our potential; and the cognitive approach, which deals with conscious mental activities.

Finally, we explore the work of theorists who have focused on narrower issues in personality such as the need for achievement, locus of control, sensation-seeking behavior, learned helplessness, and optimism/pessimism. We then examine what each approach can teach us about personality and conclude on a cheerfully positive note with a description of the so-called happy personality.

 LOG ON

The Personality Project

A large, informative Web site from the psychology department at Northwestern University. Contains discussions of the major approaches to personality theory, recommended readings, academic and nonacademic links, advice for students, and information about personality tests.

Personality Theories

A personality theories e-text with chapters to download. Includes links to other sites on personality.

Great Ideas of Personality

Includes information on research programs, journals, and professional societies, as well as a glossary and self-quiz for students.

Society for Personality and Social Psychology

The Web site of the Society for Personality and Social Psychology. Contains information for students and links to other relevant sites.

For direct links to these sites, log on to the student companion site for this book at http://www.academic.cengage.com/psychology/Schultz and choose Chapter Introduction.

Definitions of Personality

We often use the word *personality* when we are describing other people and ourselves, and we all believe we know what it means. Perhaps we do. One psychologist suggested that we can get a good idea of its meaning if we examine our intentions whenever we use the word *I* (Adams, 1954). When you say *I*, you are, in effect, summing up everything about yourself—your likes and dislikes, fears and virtues, strengths and weaknesses. The word *I* is what defines you as an individual, separate from all others.

As Others See Us

In our effort to define the word more precisely, we can look to its source. *Personality* derives from the Latin word *persona*, which refers to a mask used by actors in a play. It is easy to see how persona came to refer to outward appearance, the public face we display to the people around us. Based on its derivation, then, we might conclude that personality refers to our external and visible characteristics, those aspects of us that other people can see. Our personality would then be defined in terms of the impression we make on others—that is, what we appear to be. One definition of

Our personality may be the mask we wear when we face the outside world.

© Jeff Greenberg/PhotoEdit

personality in a standard dictionary agrees with this reasoning. It states that personality is the visible aspect of one's character, as it impresses others.

But is that all we mean when we use the word *personality?* Are we talking only about what we can see or how another person appears to us? Does personality refer solely to the mask we wear and the role we play? Surely, when we speak of personality, we refer to more than that. We mean to include many attributes of an individual, a totality or collection of various characteristics that goes beyond superficial physical qualities. The word encompasses a host of subjective social and emotional qualities as well, ones that we may not be able to see directly, that a person may try to hide from us, or that we may try to hide from others.

Enduring and Stable Characteristics

We may also, in our use of the word *personality*, refer to enduring characteristics. We assume that personality is relatively stable and predictable. Although we recognize, for example, that a friend may be calm much of the time, we know that he or she can become excitable, nervous, or panicky at other times. Thus, our personality can vary with the situation. Yet although it is not rigid, it is generally resistant to sudden changes.

In the 1960s a debate erupted within psychology about the relative impact on behavior of such enduring personal variables as traits and needs, versus variables relating to the situation (see Mischel, 1968, 1973). The controversy continued for some 20 years and concluded with the realization that the "longstanding and controversy-generating dichotomy between the effect of the situation versus the effect of the person on behavior…is and always was a fake" (Funder, 2001, p. 200). And so the issue was resolved by accepting an interactionist approach, agreeing that enduring and stable personal traits, changing aspects of the situation, and the interaction between them must all be considered in order to provide a full explanation for human nature.

Unique Characteristics

personality
The unique, relatively enduring internal and external aspects of a person's character that influence behavior in different situations.

Our definition of personality may also include the idea of human uniqueness. We see similarities among people, yet we sense that each of us possesses special properties that distinguish us from all others. Thus, we may suggest that **personality** is an enduring and unique cluster of characteristics that may change in response to different situations.

Even this, however, is not a definition with which all psychologists agree. To achieve more precision, we must examine what each personality theorist means by the term. Each offers a unique version, a personal vision, of the nature of personality, and that viewpoint has become his or her definition. And that is what this book is all about: reaching an understanding of the different versions of the concept of personality and examining the various ways of defining the word *I*.

Ethnic and Gender Issues in Personality

The personality theorists we discuss in this book offer diverse views of the nature of the human personality. Despite their disagreements and divergences, however, they share certain defining characteristics: All are White, of European or American heritage, and almost all are men. There was nothing unusual about this situation, given the period during which most of these researchers and theorists were developing their ideas. At the time, nearly all of the great advances in the arts, philosophy, literature, and the sciences, including the development of the scientific method, were propounded and promoted by White men of European or American background. In most fields, educational and professional opportunities for women, people of color, and people of other ethnic groups were limited.

In addition, in the field of personality theory, virtually all of the patients, clients, and subjects on whom the theories are based were also White. Even the laboratory rats were white. Further, the majority of the patients and subjects were men. Yet the personality theorists confidently offered theories that, by implication, were supposed to be valid for all people, regardless of gender, race, or ethnic origin.

None of the theorists stated explicitly that his or her views applied only to males or to Whites or to U.S. citizens, or that their ideas might not be useful for explaining personality in people of other backgrounds. Although the theorists accepted, to some degree, the importance of social and environmental forces in shaping personality, they tended to ignore or minimize the influence of gender and ethnic background.

Our own experiences tell us that our brothers and sisters were exposed to different childhood influences than we were and that, as a result, they grew up to have different personalities. We also know from research in social psychology and sociology that children from different environments—such as a predominantly White Midwestern town, an Asian immigrant community, a Los Angeles barrio, an Appalachian mountain village, a Native-American reservation, or an affluent Black suburb—are exposed to vastly different social and cultural influences. If the world in which people live and the factors that affect their upbringing are so different, then surely as a result their personalities can be expected to differ.

They do, as demonstrated by a rapidly growing body of research. For example, consider a classic study comparing the personalities of Chinese college students in Hong Kong with Chinese students in Canada. Those living in Hong Kong, an Eastern culture, were more introverted than those living in Canada, a Western culture, a finding that supports earlier research showing that Eastern societies, in general, are more introverted than Western societies.

In the same study, recent Chinese immigrants to Canada demonstrated a similarly low level of introversion as the Hong Kong Chinese. However, Chinese immigrants who had lived in Canada at least 10 years, and thus had greater exposure to Western culture, scored significantly higher in extraversion than did more recent immigrants or the Hong Kong subjects. In this instance, cultural forces had exerted an impact on this basic personality characteristic (McCrae, Yi, Trapnell, Bond, & Paulhus, 1998).

Boys and girls are still typically reared according to traditional stereotypes, and this upbringing influences personality in different ways. Research has documented many instances of differences between men and women on specific personality factors. Let us note a few examples. One large-scale study of the intensity of emotional awareness and expression compared male and female college undergraduates at two U.S. universities and male and female students at medical schools in the United States and in Germany. The results showed that women from both cultures displayed greater emotional complexity and intensity than did men (Barrett, Lane, Sechrest, & Schwartz, 2000). A study of more than 7,000 college students in 16 Islamic nations found that women measured significantly higher in anxiety than men did in 11 of the 16 samples studied (Alansari, 2006).

A study of stress on the job found that women managers reported more frequent headaches, anxiety, depression, sleep disturbances, and eating disorders than did men managers. Women also reported a higher incidence of smoking and of alcohol and drug use in response to workplace stress (Nelson & Burke, 2000).

Another study compared the death rates of men and women 45 years after they took various psychological tests. The tests, given in the year 1940, measured vocational interests, degree of masculinity-femininity, and occupational preferences. The average age of the subjects when they were tested was approximately 30. The results showed clearly that those who selected occupations that in 1940 were considered "masculine," such as airline pilot, engineer, judge, chemist, or lawyer, had a higher mortality rate than those who selected other occupations. The researchers concluded that certain typical gender-related traits correlated highly with death rates (Lippa, Martin, & Friedman, 2000).

Cross-Cultural Psychology

The influence of cultural forces on personality is now widely recognized in psychology. A specialty area called cross-cultural psychology developed in the late 1960s, as reflected in new publications such as the *Cross-Cultural Psychology Bulletin* and the *Directory of Cross-Cultural Psychological Research*. In 1970, the *Journal of Cross-Cultural Psychology* began, and in 1980, the *Handbook of Cross-Cultural Psychology* first appeared, revised in 1997. In 2002, an article entitled "Cultural influences on personality" was published in the influential *Annual Review of Psychology*. The authors noted that "personality is shaped by both genetic and environmental influences. Among the most important of the latter are cultural influences" (Triandis & Suh, 2002, p. 135).

All this attention sounds impressive and it does represent a major advance after years of neglect. However, comparatively less research has been conducted on personality in African and in South American nations than in English-speaking countries or many of the countries of Europe and Asia. Also, much of the research that has been conducted among these populations has not been widely published in English-language sources. Another problem limiting the applicability of cross-cultural personality research is that the majority of studies use college students as subjects; it is questionable whether we can generalize results obtained from college students in the United States to the population as a whole. In this text we offer research results from a more diverse selection of people. Studies are cited from more than 40 countries and from a variety of age groups, cultures, religions, and ethnic backgrounds.

LOG ON

Social Psychology Network

Provides links to diverse sites related to racial, ethnic, and multicultural issues, especially African, Asian, Hispanic, Jewish, and Native-American cultures.

For a direct link to this site, log on to the student companion site for this book at http://www.academic.cengage.com/psychology/Schultz and choose Chapter Introduction.

Assessment in the Study of Personality

To assess something means to evaluate it. The assessment of personality is a major area of application of psychology to real-world concerns. Consider a few everyday examples. Clinical psychologists try to understand the symptoms of their patients or clients by attempting to assess their personalities, by differentiating between normal and abnormal behaviors and feelings. Only by evaluating personality in this way can clinicians diagnose disorders and determine the best course of therapy. School psychologists evaluate the personalities of the students referred to them for treatment in an attempt to uncover the causes of adjustment or learning problems. Industrial/organizational psychologists assess personality to select the best candidate for a particular job. Counseling psychologists measure personality to find the best job for a particular applicant, matching the requirements of the position with the person's interests and needs. Research psychologists assess the personalities of their subjects in an attempt to account for their behavior in an experiment or to correlate their personality traits with other measurements.

No matter what you do in your life or your working career, it is difficult to avoid having your personality assessed in some way. Indeed, much of your success in the workplace will be determined by your performance on various psychological tests. Therefore, it is important that you have some understanding of what they are and how they work.

reliability
The consistency of response to a psychological assessment device. Reliability can be determined by the test-retest, equivalent-forms, and split-halves methods.

validity
The extent to which an assessment device measures what it is intended to measure. Types of validity include predictive, content, and construct.

Reliability and Validity

Assessment techniques differ in their degree of objectivity or subjectivity; some techniques are wholly subjective and therefore open to bias. The results obtained by subjective techniques may be distorted by the personality characteristics of the person making the assessment. The best techniques of personality assessment adhere to the principles of **reliability** and **validity**.

Reliability. Reliability involves the consistency of response to an assessment device. If you took the same test on two different days and received two widely different scores, the test could not be considered reliable because its results were so inconsistent. No one could depend on that test for an adequate assessment of your personality. It is common to find some slight variation in scores when a test is retaken, but if the variation is large, then it is likely that something is wrong with the test or with the method of scoring it.

Several procedures are available to determine the reliability of a test before it is used for assessment or research. The test-retest method involves giving the test twice to the same people and statistically comparing the two sets of scores by calculating the correlation coefficient. The closer the two sets of scores are to each other (the higher the correlation coefficient), the greater the test's reliability.

In the equivalent-forms method, instead of taking the test a second time, the subjects take two equivalent forms of the test. The higher the correlation between the two sets of scores, the greater the test's reliability. This approach is more expensive and time-consuming than the test-retest method because it requires that psychologists develop two equal forms of the test.

In the split-halves method, the test is administered once, and the scores on half the test items are compared with the scores of the other half. This is the fastest approach because the test is given only one time. Also, there is no opportunity for learning or memory to influence performance.

Validity. Validity refers to whether an assessment device measures what it is intended to measure. Does an intelligence test truly measure intelligence? Does a test of anxiety actually evaluate anxiety? If a test does not measure what it claims to, then it is not valid and its results cannot be used to predict behavior. For example, your score on an invalid intelligence test, no matter how high, will be useless for predicting how well you will do in college or in any other situation that requires a high level of intelligence. A personality test that is not valid may provide a misleading portrait of your emotional strengths and weaknesses.

As with reliability, validity must be determined precisely before a test is applied. Psychologists use several kinds of validity, including predictive validity, content validity, and construct validity. From a practical standpoint, the most important kind of validity is predictive validity—how well a test score predicts future behavior. Suppose you apply for flight training to become an astronaut. As part of the selection process, you are given a lengthy paper-and-pencil test to complete. If the majority of the applicants over the last 10 years who scored above, let us say, 80 percent on the test became successful astronauts, and the majority of those who scored below 80 percent failed as astronauts, then the test can be considered a valid predictor of performance in that situation. In establishing predictive validity, we must determine the correlation between a test score and some objective measure of behavior, such as job performance. The higher the correspondence between the two, the greater the test's predictive validity.

Content validity refers to the test's individual items or questions. To determine content validity, psychologists evaluate each item to see if it relates to what the test is supposed to measure. For example, the Sensation-Seeking Scale is a test designed to measure the need for stimulation and excitement. One of the test items is the statement "I would like to try parachute jumping." A content analysis would ascertain how well this statement (and all other statements) distinguishes between people high in sensation-seeking behavior and people low in sensation-seeking behavior.

Construct validity relates to a test's ability to measure a construct—a hypothetical or theoretical component of behavior, such as a trait or motive. Anxiety is one example of a construct. How can we tell if a new test that promises to measure anxiety really does so? A standard way to determine this is to correlate the scores on the new test with other established and validated measures of anxiety, such as other psychological tests or some behavioral measure. If the correlation is high, then we can assume that the new test truly measures anxiety.

Methods of assessment. The personality theorists discussed in this book devised unique methods for assessing personality, ways that were appropriate for their theories. By applying these methods, they derived the data on which they based their formulations. Their techniques vary in objectivity, reliability, and validity, and they range from dream interpretation and childhood recollections to paper-and-pencil and computer-administered tests. In psychology today, the major approaches to personality assessment are:

- Self-report or objective inventories
- Projective techniques
- Clinical interviews
- Behavioral assessment procedures
- Thought- and experience-sampling procedures

It is important to note that assessment for diagnostic and therapeutic purposes should not be based solely on a single approach. Ideally, multiple assessment measures are used to provide a range of information about a person.

Self-Report Inventories

self-report inventory
A personality assessment technique in which subjects answer questions about their behaviors and feelings.

The **self-report inventory** approach involves asking people to report on themselves by answering questions about their behavior and feelings in various situations. These tests include items dealing with symptoms, attitudes, interests, fears, and values. Test-takers indicate how closely each statement describes their characteristics or how much they agree with each item. Two widely used self-report inventories are the Minnesota Multiphasic Personality Inventory (MMPI) and the California Psychological Inventory (CPI).

Minnesota Multiphasic Personality Inventory (MMPI). The MMPI has been translated into more than 140 languages and may be the world's most widely used psychological test. First published in 1943, the MMPI was revised in 1989 to make the language more contemporary and nonsexist. Items were also rewritten to eliminate words that over the years had acquired alternative meanings or interpretations. The 1989 revision, the MMPI-2, is a true-false test that consists of 567 statements. These items cover physical and psychological health; political and social attitudes; educational, occupational, family, and marital factors; and neurotic and psychotic behavior tendencies. The test's clinical scales measure such personality characteristics as gender role, defensiveness, depression, hysteria, paranoia, hypochondriasis, and schizophrenia. Some items can be scored to determine if the test-taker was faking or careless, or misunderstood the instructions. Examples of the types of statements in the MMPI can be found in Table i.2.

Table i.2 **Simulated items from the Minnesota Multiphasic Personality Inventory (MMPI)**

Answer "true" or "false."
At times I get strong cramps in my intestines.
I am often very tense on the job.
Sometimes there is a feeling like something is pressing in on my head.
I wish I could do over some of the things I have done.
I used to like to do the dances in gym class.
It distresses me that people have the wrong ideas about me.
The things that run through my head sometimes are horrible.
There are those out there who want to get me.
Sometimes I think so fast I can't keep up.
I give up too easily when discussing things with others.

The MMPI-2 is used with adults in research on personality, as a diagnostic tool for assessing personality problems, and for vocational and personal counseling. In 1992, the MMPI-A was developed for use with adolescents. The number of questions was decreased from 567 to 478, to reduce the time and effort needed to administer it.

Both forms of the test have their shortcomings, however, one of which is length. It takes considerable time to respond diligently to the large number of items. Some people lose interest and motivation long before they finish. Also, some of the items on this and other self-report personality tests deal with highly personal characteristics, and some people consider the questions an invasion of privacy, particularly when someone is required to take the test to get a job. Nevertheless, despite the length and privacy issues, the MMPI-2 is a valid test that discriminates between neurotics and psychotics and between emotionally healthy and emotionally disturbed persons. Thus, it remains a highly valuable diagnostic tool.

California Psychological Inventory (CPI). Developed in 1957 and revised in 1987, this test is designed for use with normal people ages 12 to 70. It consists of 434 items that call for a true or false response. The CPI has three scales to measure test-taking attitudes and provides scores on 17 personality dimensions, including sociability, dominance, self-control, self-acceptance, and responsibility. The CPI has been successful in profiling potential delinquents and high school dropouts and in predicting success in various occupations, such as medicine, dentistry, nursing, and teaching.

Assessment of self-report inventories. Although there are self-report inventories to assess many facets of personality, the tests are not always appropriate for people whose level of intelligence registers below normal, or for people with limited reading skills. Research has shown that even minor changes in the wording of the questions or the response alternatives on self-report measures can lead to major changes in the results. For example, when adults were asked what they thought was the most important thing for children to learn, 61.5 percent chose the alternative "to think for themselves." But when adult subjects were asked to supply the answer—when no list of alternatives was provided—only 4.6 percent made that or a similar response (Schwarz, 1999).

This is also the tendency for test-takers to give answers that appear to be more socially desirable or acceptable, particularly when they are taking tests as part of a job application process. Consider the MMPI-type question: I am often very tense on the job. If you were taking the test for a job you really wanted, wouldn't you answer "no" to that question? When a group of 161 college students took a self-report test with the instructions to make themselves appear as good, or as socially acceptable, as possible, they were more careful with their answers and took longer to complete the test than did students who were not deliberately trying to appear good (Holtgraves, 2004).

Despite these problems, self-report inventories remain the most objective approach to personality assessment. Their greatest advantage is that they are designed to be scored objectively. Virtually anyone with the proper answer key can score these tests accurately. The test results do not depend on the scorer's personal or theoretical biases. This objectivity in scoring, combined with the widespread use of computers, has led to automated personality assessment programs for the MMPI-2, the CPI, and dozens of other tests. Computerized scoring provides a complete diagnostic profile of the test-taker's responses.

Computerized Test Administration

Most self-report inventories can be taken on your PC or laptop at home, in your dormitory room, or at your local Wifi-equipped coffee shop. Many organizations prefer that job applicants take tests in this way as a prescreening method, rather than taking up time and space at the company's office. The advantages of computerized test administration include the following:

- It is less time consuming for the application and the organization
- It is less expensive
- The scoring is more objective
- The method is readily accepted by younger members of the workforce
- It prevents test-takers from looking ahead at questions (which they can do with a traditional paper-and-pencil test), and it prevents them from changing answers already given

A sizable body of research has confirmed the usefulness of this approach. No significant differences in responses to self-report inventories have been found between paper-and-pencil tests and the same tests administered online (see, for example, Chuah, Drasgow, & Roberts, 2006; Luce, Winzelberg, Das, Osborne, Bryson, & Taylor, 2007).

Other research has shown that people are significantly more likely to reveal sensitive, even potentially embarrassing information when responding to computerized self-report inventories than to paper-and-pencil tests given by a live test administrator. Apparently, many people feel a greater sense of anonymity and privacy when interacting with a computer and so will reveal more personal information.

Projective Techniques

Clinical psychologists developed **projective tests** of personality for their work with emotionally disturbed persons. Inspired by Sigmund Freud's emphasis on the importance of the unconscious, projective tests attempt to probe that invisible portion of our personality. The theory underlying projective techniques is that when we are presented with an ambiguous stimulus, such as an inkblot or a picture that can be understood or interpreted in more than one way, we will project our needs, fears, and values onto the stimulus when asked to describe it.

Because the interpretation of the results of projective tests is so subjective, these tests are not high in reliability or validity. It is not unusual for different test administrators to form different impressions of the same person, based on the results of a projective test; in such a case, the interscorer reliability of the test is considered to be low. Nevertheless, such tests are widely used for assessment and diagnostic purposes. Two popular projective tests are the Rorschach Inkblot Technique and the Thematic Apperception Test (TAT).

Rorschach Inkblot Technique. The Rorschach was developed in 1921 by the Swiss psychiatrist Hermann Rorschach (1884–1922), who had been fascinated by inkblots since childhood. As a youngster he had played a popular game called *klecksographie,* or *blotto,* in which children gave their interpretations of various inkblot designs. Rorschach was known to be so intensely interested in inkblots that as a teenager, he acquired the nickname *Klecks,* which means, in German, blot of ink. Later, when Rorschach was serving a hospital residency in psychiatry after receiving his M.D., he and a friend played *blotto* with patients to pass the time. Rorschach noticed consistent differences between the responses of patients and the responses offered by school children to the same inkblots.

In developing his inkblot test, Rorschach created the inkblots by dropping blobs of ink on blank paper and folding the paper in half (see Figure i.1). After trying numerous patterns, he settled on 10 blots because he could not afford to have more than 10 printed. He wrote about his work with inkblots, but the publication was a failure. Few copies were sold, and the few reviews it received were negative. Although the test eventually became immensely popular, Rorschach became depressed and died nine months after his work was published.

The inkblot cards (some black, others using color) are shown one at a time, and test-takers are asked to describe what they see. Then the cards are shown a second time, and the psychologist asks specific questions about the earlier answers. The examiner also observes behavior during the testing session, noting test-takers' gestures, reactions to particular inkblots, and general attitude. Responses can be interpreted in several ways, depending on whether the subject or patient reports seeing movement, human or animal figures, animate or inanimate objects, and partial or whole figures. Attempts have been made to standardize the administration, scoring, and interpretation of the Rorschach. The most successful of these, the Comprehensive System, claims, on the basis of considerable research, to lead to improved reliability and validity (see Exner, 1993).

It should be noted that there is not universal agreement about the Rorschach's usefulness and validity, even with the Comprehensive System for scoring. Some

Figure i.1
An inkblot similar to a
Rorschach inkblot

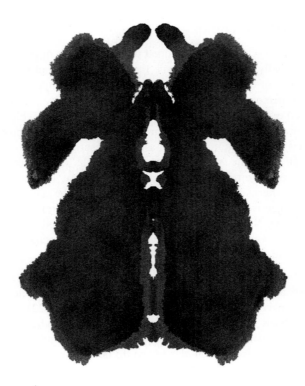

researchers have concluded that there is no scientific basis for the Rorschach; others insist that the test is as valid as any other personality assessment measure. A good overview of the problem was published in a special issue of *Psychological Assessment* (2001, volume 13, number 4). Nevertheless, the Rorschach remains the second most frequently used assessment technique in personality research and clinical practice; only the MMPI is more popular (Ganellen, 2002; Meyer, 2001). The Rorschach is also widely used in research in Europe and South America. The International Rorschach Society has more than 2,400 members; over 7,000 articles have been published about the test (Allen & Dana, 2004). Overall, validity research is generally more supportive of the MMPI than of the Rorschach. Thus, the MMPI can be used with greater confidence, especially for ethnic minority groups and diverse cultural groups (see, for example, Wood, Garb, Lilienfeld, & Nezworski, 2002).

 LOG ON

The Classical Rorschach

Serious information sources about Hermann Rorschach and the Rorschach test.

For a direct link to this site, log on to the student companion site for this book at http://www.academic.cengage.com/psychology/Schultz and choose Chapter Introduction.

Thematic Apperception Test (TAT). Henry Murray and Christiana Morgan developed the TAT (Morgan & Murray, 1935). The test consists of 19 ambiguous pictures, showing one or more persons, and 1 blank card. The pictures are vague about the events depicted and can be interpreted in several ways. A sample TAT picture and a possible interpretation are shown on page 194. Persons taking the test are asked to construct a story about the people and objects in the picture, describing what led up to the situation shown, what the people are thinking and feeling, and what the outcome is likely to be. In clinical work, psychologists consider several factors in interpreting these stories, including the kinds of personal relationships involved, the motivations of the characters, and the degree of contact with reality shown by the characters.

There are no objective scoring systems for the TAT, and its reliability and validity are low when used for diagnostic purposes. However, the TAT has proven highly valid for research; for that purpose, scoring systems have been devised to measure specific aspects of personality, such as the needs for achievement, affiliation, and power.

Other projective techniques. Word association and sentence completion are additional projective techniques that psychologists use to assess personality. In the word-association test, a list of words is read to the subject, and he or she is asked to respond with the first word that comes to mind. Response words are analyzed for their commonplace or unusual nature, for their possible indication of emotional tension, and for their relationship to sexual conflicts. Speed of response is considered important. The sentence-completion test also requires verbal responses. Subjects are asked to finish such sentences as "My ambition is . . ." or "What worries me . . ." Interpretation of the responses with both of these approaches can be highly subjective. However, some sentence-completion tests, such as the Rotter Incomplete Sentence Blank, provide for more objective scoring.

Clinical Interviews

In addition to the specific psychological tests used to measure an individual's personality, the assessment procedure often includes clinical interviews. After all, it is reasonable to assume that valuable information can be obtained by talking to the person being evaluated and asking relevant questions about past and present life experiences, social and family relationships, and the problems that led the person to seek psychological help. A wide range of behaviors, feelings, and thoughts can be investigated in the interview, including general appearance, demeanor, and attitude; facial expressions, posture, and gestures; preoccupations; degree of self-insight; and level of contact with reality.

Armed with the results of psychological tests such as the MMPI, which are usually administered before or during a series of interview sessions, the psychologist can focus on problems indicated by the test results and explore those areas in detail. Interpretation of interview material is subjective and can be affected by the interviewer's theoretical orientation and personality. Nevertheless, clinical interviews remain a widely used technique for personality assessment and a useful tool when supplemented by more objective procedures.

Table i.3 **Sample items from the Buss and Plomin EASI Temperament Survey**

Child tends to cry easily.
Child has a quick temper.
Child cannot sit still long.
Child makes friends easily.
Child tends to be shy.
Child goes from toy to toy quickly.

Behavioral Assessment

In the behavioral assessment approach, an observer evaluates a person's behavior in a given situation. The better the observers know the person being assessed, the more accurate their evaluations are likely to be. Psychologists Arnold Buss and Robert Plomin developed a questionnaire to assess the degree of various temperaments present in twins of the same sex (Buss & Plomin, 1984). The mothers of the twins were asked, on the basis of their observations of their children, to check those items on the questionnaire that best described specific and easily discernible instances of their children's behavior. Sample items from the questionnaire are listed in Table i.3.

As we noted in the section on clinical interviews, counselors routinely observe their clients' behavior—considering, for example, facial expressions, nervous gestures, and general appearance—and use that information in formulating their diagnoses. Such observations are less systematic than formal behavioral assessment procedures, but the results can provide valuable insights.

Thought and Experience Sampling

In the behavioral approach to personality assessment described in the preceding paragraphs, specific behavioral actions are monitored by trained observers. In the thought-sampling approach to assessment, a person's thoughts are recorded systematically to provide a sample over a period of time. Because thoughts are private experiences and cannot be seen, the only person who can make this type of observation is the individual whose thoughts are being studied. In this procedure, then, the observer and the person being observed are the same.

In one study, 88 men and women college students recorded their most positive and negative experiences at intervals every day for 2 weeks. The students, along with two trained judges, then grouped the experiences around common themes. These themes were compared with the results of objective and projective tests administered to the same subjects. The validity of the thought-sampling procedure was found to be as high or higher than the other assessment techniques and to uncover material that was difficult (or impossible) to obtain by other methods (Hanson, 1992).

The thought-sampling assessment procedure is typically used with groups, but it has also been applied to individuals to aid in diagnosis and treatment. A client can be asked to write or tape-record thoughts and moods for later analysis by the psychologist.

A variation of thought sampling is the experience sampling method. This is conducted similarly to thought sampling, but the participants are asked also to describe the social and environmental context in which the experience being sampled occurs. For example, subjects might be asked to note whether they were alone or with other people when the electronic beeper sounded, alerting them to record their experiences. Or they might be asked precisely what they were doing or where they were. The goal of this method is to determine how one's thoughts or moods may be influenced by the context in which they occur.

Thought-sampling research relies on technological developments such as pagers and smart wristwatches that emit a signal when subjects are supposed to record their thoughts, experiences, or moods. Handheld computer devices such as personal digital assistants (PDAs), BlackBerrys, and electronic diaries also allow participants to record their assessments quickly and easily. Electronic entries can be timed and dated. Thus, researchers can determine whether assessments are being recorded as requested; if they are entered too late, they could be influenced by the vagaries of memory (see, for example, Bolger, Davis, & Rafaeli, 2003; Tennen, Affleck, & Armeli, 2005). A comparison of electronic formats versus paper-and-pencil techniques for thought and experience sampling found no differences in the data obtained (Green, Rafaeli, Bolger, Shrout, & Reis, 2006).

Let us consider an example of the experience sampling approach to personality assessment. A group of 190 college students kept a daily Internet diary for 28 days, describing their moods as well as stressful events and how they coped with these difficulties. The primary type of negative event related to academic matters. The second most reported type of negative event dealt with interpersonal issues—getting along with others (Park, Armeli, & Tennen, 2004). Other approaches to personality assessment might not have uncovered this information so easily.

Gender and Ethnic Issues in Assessment

Gender. The assessment of personality can be influenced by a person's gender. For example, women tend to score lower than do men on tests measuring assertiveness, a difference that may result from cultural sex-role training that traditionally teaches girls and young women not to assert themselves. Whatever the cause, however, personality test data do show differences between males and females on a number of characteristics and at every age. For example, a study of 474 children, median age 11, reported that girls showed a higher level of depression and a greater concern with what other people thought of them than boys did (Rudolph & Conley, 2005).

In addition, considerable data from personality tests, clinical interviews, and other assessment measures indicate differential rates of diagnosis based on gender for various emotional disorders. Women are more often diagnosed with and treated for depression, anxiety, and related disorders than are men. Several explanations have been offered. There actually may be a higher incidence of these disorders among women, or the differential rate may be related to gender bias or gender stereotyping in interpreting the assessment results. Also, the therapists who recommend treatment options based on the assessment results may exhibit a bias against women. The average course of therapy for women tends to be longer than that for men, and doses of psychoactive medications prescribed for women tend to be higher than those for men (Pilkington & Lenaghan, 1998).

Asians. The Asian-American population in the United States is a complex, heterogeneous group and includes people of Chinese, Japanese, Filipino, Thai, Korean, and Vietnamese extraction, among others. A psychological test such as the MMPI, which has been validated in a major city in China, may not be valid for Chinese people living in the United States, or even for Chinese people living in other parts of China. Although the MMPI and other personality tests have been translated into Asian languages, little research has been conducted on their reliability and validity for use with Asian Americans.

We know there are substantial and consistent cultural differences between people of Asian and non-Asian background. For example, research has shown that people of Asian heritage tend to hold strong beliefs about the common good of society as a whole. When 108 American and Chinese adults, ages 30 to 60, were asked to recall events in their past, Americans remembered more individual or personal experiences and focused more on their own behaviors and feelings. The Chinese adults, in contrast, reported more memories of group and historical events and focused more on the roles of other significant people in these situations rather than on themselves (Wang & Conway, 2004).

Individual competitiveness and assertiveness are often seen as undesirable and contrary to Asian cultural standards. Western cultures are typically depicted as the opposite. For example, when 206 college students in Australia were compared with 253 college students in Japan, the Australians were found to emphasize the importance of individuality much more than the Japanese, whereas the Japanese students were more oriented toward the collective or the group (Kashima, Kokubo, Kashima, Boxall, Yamaguchi, & Macrae, 2004). In another example, an Asian-American job applicant who is a recent immigrant to the United States and not yet fully acculturated to American values and beliefs is likely to score low on a personality test measuring such factors as competitiveness, assertiveness, and self-promotion. This person would probably be judged as deficient—as not measuring up to American standards—and thus unlikely to be offered a job.

Research on the personality factors of self-effacement and self-enhancement has supported such ethnic differences. Self-enhancement has been defined as the tendency to promote oneself aggressively and make one conspicuous. Self-effacement, the opposite of self-enhancement, is considered to be more in agreement with the cultural values of Asian societies. This was supported in a laboratory study comparing Canadian and Japanese college students. Self-enhancement was far more prevalent among the Canadian students; self-criticism was significantly more evident among the Japanese students (Heine, Takata, & Lehman, 2000).

Similar results were obtained in two additional studies comparing self-ratings and questionnaire responses in collectivist versus individualistic cultures. The subjects in these instances were Japanese college students compared with American college students, and Chinese high school and college students in Singapore compared with Jewish high school and college students in Israel. The results from both studies showed that those from collectivist cultures (Japan and China) showed significantly greater self-criticism and significantly lower self-enhancement than those from individualistic cultures (the United States and Israel) (Heine & Renshaw, 2002; Kurman, 2001).

A review of related research supported the contention that Western peoples, in general, and Americans, in particular, exhibited greater optimism and viewed themselves and their future more positively. They even considered their sports teams, cities, and friends to be superior, when compared to those of Asian cultures (Endo, Heine, & Lehman, 2000). Thus, whether personality was assessed by self-report inventory, questionnaire, self-rating, or laboratory experiment, the personality variable of self-enhancement was consistently related to cultural differences.

Anxiety and other negative emotions may also be related to cultural differences. When the experiences of 45 Asian-American students were compared with those of 38 European-American students in a daily diary study, it was found that the Asian Americans reported a far greater number of negative emotions in social situations than the European Americans did (Lee, Okazaki, & Yoo, 2006).

A study using a self-report inventory assessing a person's view or conception of the nature of depression found a wide difference between Chinese-American and non-Chinese White college students in the United States and a group of adults in the Chinese-American community born and educated in China. Both groups of college students accepted the typical Western view that depression is predominantly a mental or mood disorder. The community group was more likely to accept the typical Eastern view that depression is a physical rather than a mental or emotional disorder (Ying, Lee, Tsai, Yeh, & Huang, 2000).

Asian Americans tend to view any form of mental disorder as a shameful condition that they are embarrassed to admit and thus they are less likely to seek treatment from a therapist or counselor for emotional problems. They also tend to wait until the disturbance is severe before seeking help and are less likely to benefit from it (Hwang, 2006).

A psychologist in New York City reported that her immigrant Chinese patients initially complained only about physical symptoms such as backache or stomachache, and never about depression. Several sessions were required before they built up sufficient trust to venture to describe a problem such as depression. Some Asian languages, such as Korean, do not have a specific word for depression. The psychologist reported that one Korean client finally struck his chest with his fist and said he had a "down heart," thus describing the mental condition in physical terms (Kershaw, 2003).

With such contrasting beliefs about the nature of a particular disorder, it is easy to understand why people of diverse cultural backgrounds may score differently on tests of personality variables. In addition, the practice of using American values, beliefs, and norms as the standard by which everyone is judged may help explain much research that shows that Asian Americans tend to receive different psychiatric diagnoses than American patients of European heritage.

Blacks. Research conducted in the 1990s showed generally consistent differences between Black and White subjects on self-report personality tests. In one study, Black men scored significantly higher than White men on the factors of alienation, vigilance, impulsivity, and cynicism (Hamberger & Hastings, 1992). In a study using the MMPI, Black women demonstrated higher energy and self-esteem, as well as more elated moods, than did White women (McNulty, Graham, Ben-Porath, & Stein, 1997).

Based on test score differences such as these, some psychologists concluded that popular and frequently used personality tests, such as the MMPI, are biased against African Americans and should not be used to assess their personalities. One wrote that "Psychological tests used for clinical diagnosis and personality description were developed for a mainstream, largely middle-class European American population . . . and may be pejorative and pathologizing" to Blacks because of different cultural and racial identities (Dana, 2002, p. 5).

Evidence to support this viewpoint was contradicted by later research using the MMPI. For example, in a study of psychiatric patients (both Blacks and Whites) who were hospitalized at a Veterans Administration (VA) center, no significant differences were found on any of the test's scales (Arbisi, Ben-Porath, & McNulty, 2002). A review of other recent research studies also found no significant racial differences on performance on the MMPI (see Wood, Garb, Lilienfeld, & Nezworski, 2002). However, Black and White college students were found to differ on a test designed to measure paranoia. Black students scored significantly higher on items measuring a lack of trust in other people, a suspicion of their motives, and a tendency to be on guard with others. Do these findings mean that Blacks are more paranoid than Whites? No. We must evaluate and interpret these and similar findings within the appropriate racial and ethnic context. Thus, the researchers noted that "the group differences may reflect mistrust or interpersonal wariness caused by pervasive discrimination and perceived racism" (Combs, Penn, & Fenigstein, 2002, p. 6).

A similar conclusion was reached in interpreting the higher than usual scores on some MMPI-2 scales for members of two Native American tribes. The researchers concluded that these results for Native Americans may reflect "the possibility of psychological distress spurred by historical oppression and present adversity" (Pace, Robbins, Choney, Hill, Lacey, & Blair, 2006, p. 320).

Research on the effects of counseling and therapy conducted with two groups of Black college students showed that they rated Black therapists more favorably than they did White therapists. The students were also more accepting and understanding of the treatment options when they were presented by Black therapists and more likely to believe that the therapy would benefit them (Thompson & Alexander, 2006; Want, Parham, Baker, & Sherman, 2004).

Hispanics. Hispanics are the largest minority group in the United States. In fewer than 50 years they are predicted to constitute one-fourth of the population. Studies show that scores obtained on the MMPI by people of Hispanic origin are similar to those obtained by Whites (see, for example, Handel & Ben-Porath, 2000). With projective techniques, however, the situation is different. Rorschach scores for subjects from Mexico and from Central American and South American countries differ significantly from the norms of the comprehensive scoring system. Thus, it is questionable whether these norms should be used with Hispanic populations (Wood, Garb, Lilienfeld, & Nezworski, 2002).

Hispanics are less likely than other minority groups to seek psychological counseling or treatment. Among Hispanics who do seek counseling, half never follow up on their first visit by returning for additional sessions (Dingfelder, 2005). One reason may be the shortage of Spanish-speaking clinical psychologists and other mental health personnel. This is important because, as we noted, nearly 40 percent of the Hispanic population in the United States is not fluent in the English language.

Studies show that Hispanic Americans are more satisfied with mental health personnel who understand their culture, which typically is highly collectivist in nature and thus more group-oriented than individual-oriented (see, for example, Malloy, Albright, Diaz-Loving, Dong, & Lee, 2004). And they are more likely to benefit from therapy with Hispanic psychologists, who, unfortunately, account for only 1 percent of the psychologists in the United States.

The collectivist orientation may help explain the higher rates of post-traumatic stress disorder (PTSD) found in a study of Hispanic police officers when compared with Black officers and non-Hispanic White officers. The Hispanic officers reported receiving significantly less social support following critical incidents on the job that lead to PTSD. The researchers noted that for the Hispanic officers, "their culturally valued collectiveness may have left these officers particularly sensitive to social isolation, thus exacerbating their symptoms" (Pole, Best, Metzler, & Marmar, 2005, p. 257).

It is obvious, then, that in the development of personality assessment techniques, cultural differences must be considered. Yet until recently, relatively few personality tests, other than the MMPI, had been published in Spanish-language versions. That situation is changing as specific tests to assess anxiety, panic, phobias and fears, and post-traumatic stress disorders are now available. The English and Spanish versions of these tests have been shown to correlate highly with each other (see, for example, Novy, Stanley, Averill, & Daza, 2001).

Cross-cultural issues. Hermann Rorschach was one of the first to recognize the effects of cultural differences in performance on personality assessment techniques. In 1921 he recorded differences in responses to his inkblot test from people living in two culturally distinct areas of Switzerland. He wrote that such responses "should be very different in various people and races" (quoted in Allen & Dana, 2004, p. 192).

Although some personality tests have been translated for use in other cultures, there are potential problems with their cross-cultural application. This is particularly crucial when a test designed for the population of a Western culture is administered to people in a non-Western culture, such as China or the Philippines. For example, among traditional Chinese people, important personality characteristics include being gracious, having a family orientation, emphasizing harmony with others, and showing frugality in everyday behavior. None of these factors is typical of those measured by American personality inventories.

When the MMPI-2 was translated into Arabic, the issue arose of how to treat questions about one's sex life. In Arab countries, any open discussion of sex is considered inappropriate, even offensive. The researchers decided to retain the sex questions in the test but to specify in the instructions that the subjects' responses to these items were optional.

The TAT cannot be used in Islamic cultures because of the Muslim prohibition against representing humans in pictorial form. When groups of European women and Muslim women were asked to make up stories in response to the TAT pictures, the European women did so readily and easily, whereas the Muslim women hesitated. The researcher noted that the Muslim women "consistently refused to give coherent interpretations. They refused to invent or fictionalize [the pictures]" (Bullard, 2005, p. 235).

Translators of American personality tests for use in other cultures also face the problem of American slang and colloquial expressions. Phrases such as "I often get the blues," or "I like to keep up with the Joneses" might have little meaning or relevance when translated into another language. Some test questions will also be meaningless because they lack reference to everyday experience. The phrase "I like to ski fast" would have no personal meaning to people who have always lived in the desert or the tropics and therefore would reveal little about their personality.

Even the manner in which people in the United States answer test questions may differ from other cultures. Responding to items in a true-false format or multiple-choice format seems natural to American college students, who have been taking these types of tests since childhood. To others, it may be an awkward and alien way of answering questions. When the MMPI was first introduced in Israel in the 1970s, many people there found it difficult to respond because they were unfamiliar with the true-false answer format. The test instructions had to be rewritten to explain to the respondents how they were supposed to record their answers (Butcher, 2004). The reworking of personality tests to ensure that they accurately reflect and measure relevant personality variables is difficult and requires knowledge of and sensitivity to cultural differences.

Research in the Study of Personality

One criterion for a useful personality theory is that it must stimulate research. In other words, a theory must be testable. Psychologists must be able to conduct research on its propositions to determine which to accept and which to reject. Ideally, a theory will be shaped, modified, and elaborated on—or discarded—on the basis of the research it generates.

Psychologists study personality in different ways. The method used depends on the aspect of personality under investigation. Some psychologists are interested only in overt behavior—what we do and say in response to certain stimuli. Other psychologists are concerned with feelings and conscious experiences as measured by tests and questionnaires. Such self-report inventories are among the most frequently used research techniques. Still other investigators try to understand the unconscious forces that may motivate us. A method useful for examining one aspect of personality may be inappropriate for another aspect.

As we discuss the various theories throughout this book, you will see examples of all these expressions of personality—behavior, conscious processes, and unconscious processes—and the techniques used to study them. The number of subjects used and the ways in which they are studied may also categorize personality

idiographic research
The intensive study of a relatively small number of subjects using a variety of assessment techniques.

nomothetic research
The study of the statistical differences among large groups of subjects.

research. For example, the **idiographic research** approach involves the intensive study of a small number of subjects—in some cases, only a single subject. Typically, the goal in the idiographic approach is therapeutic, in which the knowledge gained about a subject is used to aid in treatment. An additional goal is gaining general insights into the human personality.

The **nomothetic research** approach involves comparing and analyzing statistical differences among large samples of subjects. The goal in the nomothetic approach is to obtain data that can be generalized to a broad range of people. We will describe examples of both approaches throughout this book.

Three major methods used in personality research are the clinical method, the experimental method, and the correlational method. Although different in their specifics, these methods rely on objective observation, which is the fundamental defining characteristic of scientific research in any discipline.

The Clinical Method

case study
A detailed history of an individual that contains data from a variety of sources.

The primary clinical method is the **case study** or case history, in which psychologists search their patients' past and present for clues that might point to the source of the patients' emotional problems. Undertaking a case study is similar to writing a mini-biography of a person's emotional life from the early years to the present day, including feelings, fears, and experiences.

Freud used case studies extensively in developing his theory of psychoanalysis. He probed into his patients' childhood years, seeking those events and conflicts that may have caused their present neuroses. One such patient was Katharina, an 18-year-old woman suffering from anxiety attacks and shortness of breath. In reconstructing what he considered to be the relevant experiences in her childhood, Freud traced Katharina's symptoms to several early sexual experiences she reported, including a seduction attempt by her father when she was 14. With another patient, Lucy, Freud linked her reported hallucinations to events in her past that related to her love for her employer, a love that had been rebuffed.

It was through such case studies that Freud developed his theory of personality, with its focus on sexual conflicts or traumas as causal factors in neurotic behavior. Freud and later theorists who used the case study method searched for consistencies in their patients' lives. On the basis of what they perceived as similarities among the reports of their patients, these theorists generalized their findings to everyone.

To investigate personality, psychologists use a variety of clinical methods in addition to case studies. These methods include tests, interviews, and dream analysis, all of which can also be used for assessment. Although the clinical method attempts to be scientific, it does not offer the precision and control of the experimental and correlational methods. The data obtained by the clinical method are more subjective, relating to mental and largely unconscious events and early life experiences. Such data are open to different interpretations that may reflect the therapist's personal biases, more so than data obtained by other methods. Further, memories of childhood events may be distorted by time, and their accuracy cannot easily be verified. However, the clinical method can provide a window through which to view the depths of the personality, and we shall see many examples of its use, especially by the psychoanalytic and neopsychoanalytic theorists.

The Experimental Method

As we noted, the fundamental defining characteristic of research in any scientific discipline is objective observation. The clinical method does not meet that requirement very well. Two other requirements of scientific research are even more difficult to fulfill by using the clinical method but are satisfied by the experimental method. One of these requirements is that observations be well controlled and systematic. Such control is not possible when dealing with a person's past life events or unconscious phenomena. The other requirement involves duplication and verification. With careful control of experimental conditions, a researcher working at another time and in another place can duplicate precisely the conditions under which the earlier research was conducted. Events in a person's life cannot be repeated or duplicated so exactly.

An experiment is a technique for determining the effect of one or more variables or events on behavior. We are constantly exposed to stimuli in our everyday world, such as lights, sounds, sights, odors, instructions, demands, and trivial conversations. If a psychologist wants to determine the effect of just one stimulus variable, he or she can arrange an experimental situation in which only that variable is allowed to operate. All other variables must be eliminated or held constant during the experiment. Then, if the behavior of the subjects changes while only the stimulus variable is in operation, we can be certain that it alone is responsible for any change in behavior. The change could not have been caused by another variable because no other variable was allowed to influence the subjects during the experiment.

Scientists distinguish two kinds of variables in an experiment. One is the **independent** or stimulus **variable**, which is manipulated by the experimenter. The other is the **dependent variable**, which is the subjects' behavior or response to that manipulation. To be sure no variable other than the independent variable can affect the results, researchers must study two groups of subjects: the experimental group and the control group. Both groups are chosen at random from the same population of subjects.

The **experimental group** includes those subjects to whom the experimental treatment is given. This is the group exposed to the stimulus or independent variable. The **control group** is not exposed to the independent variable. Measures of the behavior being studied are taken from both groups before and after the experiment. In this way, researchers can determine if any additional variables have influenced the subjects' behavior. If some other variable was operating, then both groups would show the same changes in behavior. But if no other variable was in operation—if the independent variable alone influenced the subjects—then only the behavior of the experimental group would change. The behavior of the control group would remain the same.

independent variable
In an experiment, the stimulus variable or condition the experimenter manipulates to learn its effect on the dependent variable.

dependent variable
In an experiment, the variable the experimenter desires to measure, typically the subjects' behavior or response to manipulation of the independent variable.

experimental group
In an experiment, the group that is exposed to the experimental treatment.

control group
In an experiment, the group that does not receive the experimental treatment.

Applying the experimental method. Let us follow the experimental method in action, using data from psychologist Albert Bandura's social-learning theory of personality. Bandura wanted to determine whether children would imitate the aggressive behavior they observed in adults. What was the best way to study this problem? Bandura could have observed children on neighborhood streets or at a playground, hoping to catch their reactions if they happened to witness a violent incident. He could then have waited to see whether the children would imitate the aggressive behavior they had seen.

This approach is unsystematic and uncontrolled, and it does not allow for duplication and verifiability; it is unlikely that the identical conditions would recur. Also, observing children who happened to be present on a street corner would not necessarily provide an appropriate sample of subjects. Some of these children might already possess the tendency to behave aggressively, regardless of the adult behavior they observed. Therefore, it would be impossible to decide whether their behavior resulted from witnessing a violent act or from some factor that had long been part of their personality.

Further, observing children at random would not allow the researcher to control the type of aggressive act to which the subjects might be exposed. Children see many kinds of violence—television actors in a gun battle, teenagers in a fistfight, drive-by shootings, parental brawling, action figures in video games. Each form of aggression would have to be studied individually before its effects on behavior could be determined reliably. For Bandura to study the phenomenon, then, it was necessary that all the children he observed be exposed to the same instance of aggressive behavior. He approached the problem systematically by designing an experiment in which children whose pre-experiment levels of aggression had been measured were exposed to the same display of adult aggression. Children in the control group witnessed nonaggressive adults in the same setting. Both groups of children were watched by trained observers to see how they would behave.

Children who watched the aggressive adult behaved aggressively; children in the control group exhibited no change in aggressiveness. Bandura concluded that aggressiveness can be learned by imitating the aggressive behavior of others.

Limitations of the experimental method. The experimental method, whether applied online or in a laboratory, has the potential for being the most precise research method, but it has several limitations. There are situations in which it cannot be used; some aspects of behavior and personality cannot be studied under rigorously controlled laboratory conditions because of safety and ethical considerations. For example, psychologists might be better able to treat emotional disturbances if they had data from controlled experiments on different child-rearing techniques to determine what kinds of early experiences might lead to problems in adulthood. Obviously, however, we cannot take groups of children from their parents at birth and expose them to various child-rearing manipulations to see what happens.

Another difficulty with the experimental method is that the subjects' behavior may change not because of the experimental treatment (the manipulation of the independent variable) but because the subjects are aware that they are being observed. They might behave differently if they thought no one was observing their responses. When people know they are participating in an experiment, they sometimes try to guess the purpose and behave accordingly, either to please or to frustrate the experimenter. This kind of response defeats the purpose of the experiment because the resulting behavior (the dependent variable) has been influenced by the subjects' attitudes rather than by the experimental treatment. This is quite a different response from what the researcher intended to study.

Experimental research has its limitations, but when it is well controlled and systematic, it provides excellent data. We will see examples throughout the book of how the experimental method applies to understanding aspects of personality.

The Virtual Research Method

Psychologists routinely conduct research online, including administering psychological tests, taking opinion surveys, and presenting experimental stimuli and recording the subjects' responses. A review of articles published in journals of the American Psychological Association for 2003–2004 found that

> the majority of studies in our sample were straightforward translations of the traditional psychological measures and methods for use on the Web. These studies were designed to ask the same kinds of questions and to employ methods that one typically uses in the psychological laboratory. (Skitka & Sargis, 2006, p. 535)

Virtual research offers certain advantages over traditional experimental research. Studies conducted on the Web produce faster responses, are less costly, and have the potential to reach a broader range of subjects of different ages, levels of education, types of employment, income levels, social class, and ethnic origin. Thus, in theory, broader populations can be sampled than are typically found on a college campus.

However, this research method also has disadvantages. Research has shown that Web users tend to be younger, more affluent, and better educated than nonusers, thus limiting the chances that an online sample will be truly representative of the population as a whole (though still likely to be more representative than a typical group of college student subjects). Also, responders may differ from nonresponders on important personality characteristics. Research conducted in Germany found that people who failed to respond to an online survey were judged—on the basis of their personal Web sites—to be more introverted, more disagreeable, and less open to new experiences than those who did respond to the survey (Marcus & Schutz, 2005).

It is also impossible to determine how honest and accurate online subjects will be when they provide personal information on factors such as age, gender, ethnic origin, education, or income. Nevertheless, a significant number of studies comparing online and traditional laboratory research methods shows that the results are, in general, consistent and similar (see, for example, Birnbaum, 2004; Gosling, Vazire, Srivastava, & John, 2004).

 LOG ON

Hanover College: Psychological Research on the Net

PsychEperiments: Psychology Experiments on the Internet

Visit these sites to learn more about Web-based research, including how to do it and how to participate as a subject, as well as results from research in several areas of psychology.

For direct links to these sites, log on to the student companion site for this book at http://www.academic.cengage.com/psychology/Schultz and choose Chapter Introduction.

The Correlational Method

correlational method
A statistical technique that measures the degree of the relationship between two variables, expressed by the correlation coefficient.

In the **correlational method**, researchers investigate the relationships that exist among variables. Rather than manipulating an independent variable, the experimenters deal with the variable's existing attributes. For example, instead of experimentally creating stress in subjects in the psychology laboratory and observing the effects, researchers can study people who already function in stressful situations—such as police officers, race car drivers, or college students suffering from test anxiety.

Another way the correlational method differs from the experimental method is that in the correlational approach subjects are not assigned to experimental and control groups. Instead, the performance of subjects who differ on an independent variable—such as age, gender, order of birth, level of aggressiveness, or degree of neuroticism—is compared with their performance on some dependent variable, such as personality test responses or job performance measures.

Applying the correlational method. Researchers applying the correlational method are interested in the relationship between the variables—in how behavior on one variable changes or differs as a function of the other variable. For example, is birth order related to aggressiveness? Do people who score high on an IQ test make better computer scientists than people who score low? Do people who score high in optimism process certain stimuli differently from people who score high in pessimism? The answers to such questions are useful not only in research but also in applied situations where predictions must be made about a person's chances of success. The college entrance examinations you took are based on correlational studies that show the relationship between the variables of standardized test scores and classroom success.

A great deal of correlational research has been conducted on various facets of the human personality. Consider the need for achievement, a concept formulated by Henry Murray and subsequently studied by David McClelland. Much of the research on that topic compared the measured level of the achievement need with performance on a number of other variables.

Let us say, for example, that researchers want to determine whether people high in the need for achievement earn higher grades in college than people low in the need for achievement. The researchers could apply the experimental method and design an experiment in which children would be separated from their parents and reared by adults specially trained in techniques known to increase the motivation to achieve. Years later, when the children attended college, the grades of those high in the achievement need could be compared with the grades of those low in the achievement need. You can see, of course, that such an experiment is too ridiculous to contemplate.

Using the correlational method, psychologists measured the achievement-need levels of a group of college students and compared them with the students' grades. The independent variable (the different levels of the need for achievement, from high to low) was not manipulated or changed in this case. These researchers worked with existing data and found that students high in the need for achievement did earn higher grades than students low in the need for achievement (Atkinson, Lens, & O'Malley, 1976).

Figure i.2
Graphs of high positive and high negative correlations

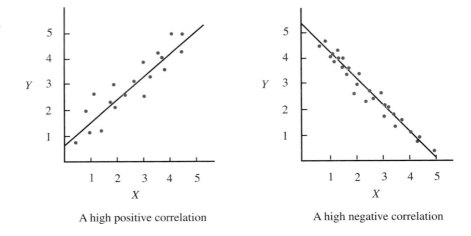

A high positive correlation   A high negative correlation

We will see many examples of the correlational method in personality research throughout the book, especially in discussions of the development and application of assessment techniques. The reliability and validity of assessment devices are typically determined through the correlational method. In addition, many facets of personality have been studied by correlating them with other variables.

The correlation coefficient. The primary statistical measure of correlation is the correlation coefficient, which provides precise information about the direction and strength of the relationship between two variables. The direction of the relationship can be positive or negative. If high scores on one variable accompany high scores on the other variable, the direction is positive. If high scores on one variable accompany low scores on the other variable, the direction is negative. (See Figure i.2.)

Correlation coefficients range from $+1.00$ (a perfect positive correlation) to -1.00 (a perfect negative correlation). The closer the correlation coefficient is to $+1.00$ or -1.00, the stronger the relationship and the more confidently we can make predictions about one variable from the other.

Cause and effect. The primary limitation of the correlational method relates to cause and effect. Just because two variables show a high correlation, it does not necessarily follow that one has caused the other. There may indeed be such a relationship, but researchers cannot automatically conclude that one exists, as they can with a well-controlled, systematic experiment.

Suppose a psychologist applied the correlational method and found a strong negative relationship between the two personality variables of shyness and self-esteem: the higher the level of shyness, the lower the level of self-esteem. Conversely, the lower the level of shyness, the higher the level of self-esteem. The relationship is clear: People who are shy tend to score low on measures of self-esteem. We cannot conclude with certainty, however, that being shy causes people to have low self-esteem. It could be the other way around—that low self-esteem causes people to be shy. Or some other variable, such as physical appearance or parental rejection, could cause both shyness and low self-esteem.

This restriction on drawing conclusions from correlational research presents difficulties for researchers, whose goal is to identify specific causes. However, for practitioners, whose goal is to predict behavior in the real world, the correlational method is more satisfactory. To be able to predict success in college on the basis of the need for achievement, for example, we need only establish that the two variables have a high correlation. If a college applicant scores high on a test of the need for achievement, we can predict that he or she will earn good grades in college. In this case, we are not concerned with determining whether the level of the achievement need causes good academic performance, only with whether the two variables are related and whether one can be predicted from the other.

Theory in the Study of Personality

Theories are sometimes referred to in contemptuous terms. "After all," people may say, "it's only a theory!" It is popular to assume that a theory is vague, abstract, and speculative—really no more than a hunch or a guess and quite the opposite of a fact. It is true that a theory without research evidence to support it is speculation. However, a mass of research data can be meaningless unless it is organized in some sort of explanatory framework or context. A theory provides the framework for simplifying and describing empirical data in a meaningful way. A theory can be considered a kind of map that represents the data in their interrelationships. It attempts to bring order to the data, to fit them into a pattern.

Theories are sets of principles used to explain a particular class of phenomena (in our case, the behaviors and experiences relating to personality). If personality theories are to be useful, they must be testable, capable of stimulating research on their various propositions. Researchers must be able to conduct experiments to determine whether aspects of the theory should be accepted or rejected. Personality theories must be able to clarify and explain the data of personality by organizing those data into a coherent framework. Theories should also help us understand and predict behavior. Those theories that can be tested and can explain, understand, and predict behavior may then be applied to help people change their behaviors, feelings, and emotions from harmful to helpful, from undesirable to desirable.

Formal Theories and Personal Theories

Scientists are not the only people who use theories; nor are all theories formal proposals containing numerous postulates and corollaries. We all use implicit personal theories in our everyday interactions with other people. We have some idea of the concept of personality, and we make suppositions about the personalities of those with whom we interact. Many of us speculate about human nature in general. For example, we may believe that all people are basically good or that people care only about themselves.

These suppositions are theories. They are frameworks within which we place the data of our observations of others. We usually base our personal theories on data that we collect from our perceptions of the behavior of those around us. In that respect—that our theories derive from our observations—personal theories are similar to formal theories.

However, formal theories in psychology, as well as in other sciences, have certain characteristics that set them apart from our personal theories. Formal theories are based on data from observations of large numbers of people of diverse natures, whereas personal theories are derived from our observations of a limited number of persons—usually our small circle of relatives, friends, and acquaintances, as well as ourselves. Because a broader range of data supports formal theories, they are more comprehensive. We can generalize more effectively from formal theories to explain and predict the behavior of more kinds of people.

A second characteristic is that formal theories are likely to be more objective because scientists' observations are, ideally, unbiased by their needs, fears, desires, and values. In contrast, our personal theories are based as much on observations of ourselves as of others. We tend to interpret the actions of other people in terms of our thoughts and feelings, evaluating their reactions to a situation on the basis of what we would do or how we would feel. We view others in personal and subjective terms, whereas scientists try to observe more objectively and dispassionately.

Another characteristic is that formal theories are tested repeatedly against reality, often by a scientist other than the one who proposed the theory. A formal theory may be put to many objective experimental tests and, as a consequence, be supported, modified, or rejected in light of the results. Personal theories are not so tested by us or by a neutral party. Once we develop a personal theory about people in general or about one person in particular, we tend to cling to it, perceiving only those behaviors that confirm our theory and failing to attend to those that contradict it.

In principle, scientists can recognize and evaluate data that do not support their theories. Unfortunately, in reality, this is not always true. Many examples exist in both the history of science and the history of psychology of scientists who were so prejudiced by their theory, so emotionally committed to it, that their objectivity was compromised. However, the ideal of objectivity remains the goal toward which scientists strive.

Subjectivity in Personality Theories

We noted that the intent of formal theories is greater objectivity and that personal theories tend to be more subjective. We might assume that personality theories, because they belong to a discipline that calls itself a science, are exclusively of the formal and objective variety but that is not always the case. Psychologists recognize that some personality theories have a subjective component and may reflect events in the theorist's life as a sort of disguised autobiography. The theorist may draw on these events as a source of data to describe and support his or her theory. No matter how hard scientists try to be impartial and objective, their personal viewpoint is likely to influence their perception to some degree. This should not surprise us. Personality theorists are human, too, and like most of us they sometimes find it difficult to accept ideas that diverge from their own experience.

The distinction between formal and personal theories may not be as pronounced in personality as it is in other branches of psychology. This does not mean that all personality theories are personal theories. Personality theories have the characteristics of formal theories. Some are based on the observation of a large number and variety of persons. Some are tested against reality either by the theorist who proposed it or by others. These scientists attempt to be objective in making their observations and in analyzing their data, which may or may not support the theory. Ultimately, the theories are as objective as their subject matter—the complex human personality—permits, but their propositions may owe much to the personalities and life experiences of their originators.

The first stage in constructing a theory may be based primarily on intuition, but in later stages these intuitively based ideas may be modified and refined by the theorist's rational and empirical knowledge. Thus, through the application of reason and data analysis, what began as a personal theory assumes the characteristics of a formal theory. Whatever level of objectivity is found in personality theories (and we will see that some are more objective than others), there is no denying that they are also partly subjective, reflecting the experiences and needs of the theorist.

If we want to understand a theory fully, we should learn as much as we can about the person who proposed it. It is important to consider how the development of a theory may have been influenced by specific events in a theorist's life. In cases where sufficient biographical information is available, we suggest how a theory reflects those events. At least initially, the theorist may have been describing himself or herself. Later, the theorist may have sought appropriate data from other sources to support the generalization of that personal view to others.

The significance of personal events in a theorist's life has long been recognized, as we noted. William James (1842–1910), considered by many scholars to have been the greatest American psychologist, believed that biography was a crucial subject for anyone who attempts to study human nature. He argued that it was even more important to understand eminent persons' lives than it was to know their theories or systems if we wanted to learn about the different ways people approach human experience (Simon, 1998). One historian noted:

> More than any other professional discipline, psychologists have sought to publish biographical and autobiographical sketches of those in their calling. . . . At some level, at least, they seem to have acknowledged that their lives and values are the key to their "scientific knowledge." (Friedman, 1996, p. 221)

We shall see throughout this book many examples of the autobiographical nature of personality theory, but we must also introduce a note of caution into this intriguing relationship between theory and real life. Perhaps it is not the life experiences that influence the development of the theory. Instead, maybe the theory influences what the theorists recall and choose to tell us about their lives. Much of our information about a theorist's life comes from autobiographical recollections. These accounts are usually written late in life, after the person has proposed and defended the theory. The time spent developing the theory and affirming a commitment to it may distort the theorist's memories of earlier years. Does the person recall only those events that support the theory? Are contradictory or troublesome events conveniently forgotten? Are experiences invented to enhance a theory's credibility? Although we cannot always answer these questions, we should keep them in mind while we explore the notion that personality theory may be partly autobiographical.

Questions About Human Nature

An important aspect of any personality theory is the image of human nature formulated by the theorist. Each theorist has a conception of human nature that addresses the basic issues of what it means to be human. For centuries, poets, philosophers, and artists have phrased and rephrased these questions, and we see their attempts at answers in our great books and paintings. Personality theorists, too, have addressed these troubling questions and have reached no greater consensus than artists or writers.

The various conceptions of human nature offered by the theorists allow for a meaningful comparison of their views. These ideas are not unlike personal theories; they are frameworks within which the theorists perceive themselves and other people and then construct their theories. The issues that define a theorist's image of human nature are described below. As we discuss each theory, we will consider how the theorist deals with these fundamental questions.

Free Will or Determinism?

A basic question about human nature concerns the age-old controversy between free will and determinism. Theorists on both sides of the issue ask, do we consciously direct the course of our actions? Can we spontaneously choose the direction of our thoughts and behavior, rationally selecting among alternatives? Do we have a conscious awareness and a measure of self-control? Are we masters of our fate or are we victims of past experience, biological factors, unconscious forces, or external stimuli—forces over which we have no conscious control? Have external events so shaped our personality that we are incapable of changing our behavior? Some personality theorists take extreme positions on this issue. Others express more moderate views, arguing that some behaviors are determined by past events and some can be spontaneous and under our control.

Nature or Nurture?

A second issue has to do with the nature–nurture controversy. Which is the more important influence on behavior: inherited traits and attributes (our nature or genetic endowment) or features of our environment (the nurturing influences of our upbringing, education, and training)? Do the abilities, temperaments, and predispositions we inherit determine our personality, or are we shaped more strongly by the conditions under which we live? Personality is not the only topic affected by this issue. Controversy also exists about the question of intelligence: Is intelligence affected more by genetic endowment (nature) or by the stimulation provided by home and school settings (nurture)?

As with the free will–determinism issue, the alternatives are not limited to extreme positions. Many theorists assume that personality is shaped by both sets of forces. To some, inheritance is the predominant influence and environment of minor importance; others hold the opposite view.

Past or Present?

A third issue involves the relative importance of past events, such as our early childhood experiences, compared with events that occur later in life. Which is the more powerful shaper of personality? If we assume, as some theorists do, that what happens to us in infancy and childhood is critical to personality formation, we must consequently believe that our later development is little more than an elaboration of the basic themes laid down in the early years of life. This view is known as **historical determinism**. Our personality (so this line of thought goes) is mostly fixed by the age of five or so and is subject to little change over the rest of our life. The adult personality is determined by the nature of these early experiences.

The opposite position considers personality to be more independent of the past, capable of being influenced by events and experiences in the present as well as by our aspirations and goals for the future. An intermediate position has also been proposed. We might assume that early experiences shape personality but not rigidly or permanently. Later experiences may act to reinforce or modify early personality patterns.

historical determinism The view that personality is basically fixed in the early years of life and subject to little change thereafter.

Uniqueness or Universality?

Is human nature unique or universal? This is another issue that divides personality theorists. We may think of personality as so individual that each person's action, each utterance, has no counterpart or equivalent in any other person. This obviously makes the comparison of one person with another meaningless. Other positions allow for uniqueness but interpret this within overall patterns of behavior accepted as universal, at least within a given culture.

Equilibrium or Growth?

A fifth issue involves what we might call our ultimate and necessary life goals. Theorists differ on what constitutes our major motivation in life. Do we function like machines, like some sort of self-regulating mechanism, content as long as some internal equilibrium or balance is maintained? Do we act solely to satisfy physical needs, to obtain pleasure and avoid pain? Is our happiness totally dependent on keeping stress to a minimum? Some theorists believe that people are little more than tension-reducing, pleasure-seeking animals. Others consider us to be motivated primarily by the need to grow, to realize our full potential, and to reach for ever-higher levels of self-actualization and development.

Optimism or Pessimism?

One additional issue reflects a theorist's outlook on life. We may call it optimism versus pessimism. Are human beings basically good or evil, kind or cruel, compassionate or merciless? Here we are dealing with a question of morality, a value judgment, which supposedly has no place in the objective and dispassionate world of science. However, several theorists have dealt with the question and, as we shall see, it has spawned a vital body of research. Some theorists' views of the human personality are positive and hopeful, depicting us as humanitarian, altruistic, and socially conscious. Other theorists find few of these qualities in human beings, either individually or collectively.

Cultural Influences on Human Nature

We noted that cultural differences affect personality development and assessment. It should come as no surprise, then, to learn that cultural factors influence our image of human nature and the questions we may ask about it. Consider the concept of *karma*, which for centuries has shaped the outlook of the peoples of India and other countries that accept Hinduism or Buddhism. It may be seen as a fatalistic and deterministic view of human nature. The consequences of our present and past actions are believed to determine our destiny or fate, our happiness or unhappiness in the future. In other words, events don't occur because we make them happen but because they were destined to happen.

Thus, in this view, our fortune or misfortune, health or sickness, are preordained and independent of our own actions. This belief may lead to a passive, resigned personality type, accepting of whatever comes one's way and not motivated to take action to change. Contrast this with a view more typical of U.S. culture that emphasizes free choice and action, and the role of personal effort and initiative in engendering personal success or failure.

Or consider the impact of the emphasis on individualism in the United States and on collectivism in Asian countries such as China and Japan, as noted in some research studies described earlier in this chapter. In an individualistic society, the life view is on personal freedom, choice, and action. In a collectivist society, the focus is on group norms and values, group role expectations, and other cultural constraints on behavior. People in individualistic cultures have shown greater extraversion, self-esteem, happiness (or subjective well-being), optimism about their future, and a belief in their ability to control and direct it.

College students in the United States scored significantly higher than college students in Japan on measures of self-efficacy, that is, the feeling of being adequate, efficient, and competent in coping with life and in exerting control over life events (Morling, Kitayama, & Miyamoto, 2002). Other research found differences in subjective well-being between Asian-American students and European-American students at the same university in the United States. The European-American students attained their feeling of well-being by pursuing goals for the purpose of personal satisfaction. The Asian-American students seemed to "attain and maintain their well-being by achieving goals that they pursue to make important others [such as their parents] happy and [to] meet the expectations of others" (Oishi & Diener, 2001, p. 1680). Thus, the motivations and satisfactions of these students and their corresponding images of human nature differed with their cultural backgrounds. In addition, a comparison of Japanese and American college students revealed that the American students were far more likely to use positive terms to describe themselves. The Japanese students were more likely to use negative terms (Kanagawa, Cross, & Markus, 2001).

Consider the impact on behavior and personality of cultural differences in child-rearing practices. In the individualistic culture of the United States, parents tend to be noncoercive, democratic, and permissive in their child-rearing techniques. In collectivist cultures in predominantly Arab societies, parental practices tend to be more authoritarian, restrictive, and controlling. Studies of adolescents in several Arab countries showed that they felt a greater connection with their parents than did American adolescents. The researchers noted that Arab adolescents

> Follow their parents' directions in all areas of life, such as social behavior, interpersonal relationships, marriage, occupational preference, and political attitudes. . . . they do not feel that they suffer from their [parents'] authoritarian style and are even satisfied with this way of life. (Dwairy, Achoui, Abouserie, & Farah, 2006, p. 264)

The study concluded that these authoritarian parental practices did not adversely affect the mental health and emotional well-being of the Arab teenagers as they would in more liberal Western cultures. Clearly, these differences in child-rearing practices and their resulting values will help determine a person's image of human nature.

We have seen that the impact of cultural forces is significant and even applies to cultures that might appear similar and homogeneous. One might reasonably expect differences between Eastern cultures such as Japan and Western cultures such as the United States. But differences have also been reported between European cultures, such as Spain and the Netherlands. A comparison using a self-report inventory of people in these countries confirmed earlier findings. The Spanish people were more concerned with matters of honor and family-related values, such as family security, respect for parents, and recognition from others. In contrast, the Dutch people scored higher on individualistic values such as ambition, capability, and independence (Rodriguez Mosquera, Manstead, & Fischer, 2000).

Nordic cultures such as Norway, Sweden, and Denmark provide an example of yet another type of influence. The cultural concept of *Janteloven* enjoins people not to place their own interests above those of their community and to show humility in the presence of others. A comparison of college students in the United States and Norway found that the Americans rated themselves significantly higher than average on positive personality traits and lower than average on negative traits than the Norwegian students did. This tendency to self-enhancement among the U.S. students, which was not found to the same degree among the Norwegian students, appears to be culturally induced, determined by the values taught in the different countries (Silvera & Seger, 2004).

Self-enhancement (the belief that our skills and abilities are better than those of other people) is sometimes referred to as the "Lake Wobegon Effect," after the famous Garrison Keillor radio program *A Prairie Home Companion*. Lake Wobegon is the fictional rural Minnesota community where, as Keillor says, "all the women are strong, all the men are good looking, and all the children are above average." It is noteworthy that Lake Wobegon is inhabited by people whose ancestors immigrated from Norway, home of the concept of *Janteloven*.

Such basic values as these help determine our general image of human nature, that is, the lens through which we perceive, judge, and interact with other people in our culture. The significance of this discussion is to point out to you that there are many sources of influence on the growth and development of the human personality, and diverse ways of explaining its nature. Perhaps one or more of the explanations we describe in this book will be congenial to you, or perhaps they will clash with your views and your image of human nature. Few of us can approach this topic without preconceptions because it is, after all, the study of ourselves.

Chapter Summary

Wilhelm Wundt, who used the methods of the natural sciences to analyze conscious experience into its elemental parts, formally founded psychology in 1879. Early in the 20th century, John B. Watson developed the behavioral approach to psychology to protest against Wundt's focus on conscious experience. Watson argued that psychologists must study only overt behavior. Psychoanalysis, developed by Sigmund Freud, used clinical observation to probe the unconscious. The study of personality began in American psychology in the 1930s. Personality can be defined as an enduring, unique cluster of characteristics that may change in different situations. Differences in gender, ethnicity, and cultural background can influence personality development. Interest in cross-cultural psychology dates from the 1960s.

Techniques for assessing or measuring personality must meet two requirements: reliability (the consistency of responses on a test) and validity (the degree to which the test measures what it is intended to measure). The resulting assessment of personality can be influenced by the subject's gender and ethnic identity and by the test administrator's attitudes and beliefs.

Self-report inventories, in which people report on their own behavior and feelings in various situations, are objective in that scores are not influenced by personal or theoretical biases. Most self-report inventories can be computer-administered so they can be taken at almost any time and place. Projective techniques attempt to probe the unconscious by having people project their needs, fears, and values into their interpretation of ambiguous figures or situations. Projective techniques are subjective, low in reliability and validity, and usually poorly standardized.

Clinical interviews are used to assess personality, but the interpretation of interview results is subjective. In the behavioral assessment approach, an observer evaluates a subject's responses in specific situations. In thought and experience sampling, people record their thoughts, feelings, and experiences over a period of time.

People from collectivist societies, such as Asian countries, tend to score lower on factors such as self-enhancement and higher on pessimism, negative affectivity, and psychological distress than do people from more individualistic societies, such as the United States. Studies of the responses of Blacks and Whites on the MMPI revealed no significant differences as a function of race. Hispanics tend to obtain scores similar to those of Whites on the MMPI but not on projective techniques such as the Rorschach.

Translations of personality tests must take into account the nature of other cultures with regard to the kinds of questions that may be asked, the translated wording, and the manner in which the questions are to be answered.

Psychological research methods include the clinical, experimental, and correlational approaches. Such research requires objective observation, controlled and systematic conditions, and duplication and verifiability. Idiographic research involves the intensive study of one or a few subjects; nomothetic research involves statistical analysis of data obtained from a large sample of subjects. The clinical method relies on case studies, in which psychologists reconstruct patients' backgrounds and lives to find clues to their present emotional problems. The clinical approach does not satisfy the requirements of psychological research as well as the experimental and correlational methods do.

The experimental method is the most precise method of psychological research. Using this method, psychologists can determine the effect of a single variable or stimulus event on the subjects' behavior. The variable being studied (that is, the stimulus to which the subjects are exposed) is the independent variable; the subjects' responses or behavior is the dependent variable. Internet research offers a faster and less expensive alternative research methodology as well as access to a broader range of subjects. Online research has its limitations, but studies to date show that it produces results highly similar to those of laboratory research.

In the correlational method, psychologists study the relationship between two variables to determine how behavior on one variable changes as a function of the other. The correlation coefficient, the primary statistical measure of correlation, indicates the direction and intensity of the relationship.

A theory provides a framework for simplifying and describing data in a meaningful way. Personality theories must be testable, must clarify and explain the data of personality, and must be useful in understanding and predicting behavior. Formal theories are based on data from observation of large numbers and diverse kinds of people. These theories are objective and are repeatedly tested against reality. Some personality theories may be partially autobiographical, reflecting a theorist's life experiences. The first stage in theory construction may be intuitive; ideas based on intuition may later be modified by rational and empirical knowledge (the results of research and scientific study).

Personality theorists differ on basic questions about human nature: free will versus determinism, nature versus nurture, the importance of the past versus the present, uniqueness versus universality, equilibrium versus growth, and optimism versus pessimism. Cultural factors such as child-rearing practices can lead to differing images of human nature.

Review Questions

1. In what ways does our personality influence our eventual success in interpersonal relations, in our career, and in our general level of health and happiness?

2. Discuss various ways of defining personality.

3. What was the fundamental point of difference between the approaches of Wilhelm Wundt and John B. Watson?

4. When and where did the scientific study of personality begin? What role did Sigmund Freud play in the investigation of personality?

5. In what ways may gender and ethnic factors affect the study and assessment of personality?

6. Describe cross-cultural psychology and its impact on the study of personality.

7. Give examples of everyday situations that involve the assessment of personality. Recount your own experience of having your personality evaluated.

8. How do researchers determine the reliability of a psychological test?

9. What is the difference between predictive validity and content validity?

10. Distinguish between self-report techniques and projective techniques for assessing personality. What are the advantages and disadvantages of each approach?

11. Discuss the advantages of computerized test administration.

12. Give examples of the behavioral and the thought-sampling procedures for assessing personality.

13. Give examples of ways in which the personality assessment process can be influenced by the research participant's ethnic background.

14. What are the advantages and disadvantages of the case study approach?

15. What three requirements of scientific research are met by the experimental method?

16. What are the advantages and limitations of using the Internet for psychological research as compared to more traditional research conducted in a laboratory?

17. Give an example of personality research that uses the correlational method.

18. What is the relationship between data and theory?

19. Describe the differences between formal theories and personal theories.

20. How might cultural factors affect our image of human nature? Give examples.

21. We asked six questions in our discussion of human nature. Write down your thoughts on these issues. At the end of the book, you will be asked to reconsider these questions to see how your views might have changed.

Suggested Readings

Buchanan, R. D. (2002). On not "giving psychology away": The Minnesota Multiphasic Personality Inventory and public controversy over testing in the 1960s. *History of Psychology, 5,* 284–309. Describes the political and social issues involved in personality testing and the involvement of the U.S. Congress. Shows how public scrutiny led to the more appropriate use of tests and the preservation of client privacy.

Caspi, A., Roberts, B. W., & Shiner, R. L. (2005). Personality development: Stability and change. *Annual Review of Psychology, 56,* 453–484. An overview article that evaluates research on the structure of personality in childhood and adulthood, attempts to document the life stage at which personality change is most likely to occur, and reviews work on the relationship between personality and social relationships, status attainment, and health.

Chuah, S. C., Dragsow, F., & Brent, W. R. (2006). Personality assessment: Does the medium matter? No. *Journal of Research in Personality, 40,* 359–376. Compares the administration of personality tests to 728 participants under three conditions—traditional paper-and-pencil, proctored computer laboratory, and unproctored Internet—and reports statistical equivalence of paper-and-pencil and Internet measurements.

Dana, R. H. (2002). Mental health services for African Americans: A cultural/racial perspective. *Cultural Diversity and Ethnic Minority Psychology, 8,* 3–18. Addresses issues involved in the delivery of mental health services for African Americans, including cultural/racial identity, psychiatric diagnoses, and psychotherapy and other interventions.

Elms, A. C. (1994). *Uncovering lives: The uneasy alliance of biography and psychology.* New York: Oxford University Press. Contains insightful psychological portraits of writers, political leaders, and personality theorists, including Freud, Jung, Murray, Allport, and Skinner.

Ross, M. (1989). Relation of implicit theories to the construction of personal histories. *Psychological Review, 96,* 341–357. Suggests that people develop personal theories to provide a framework for understanding their own personality and use these theories as a basis for evaluating memories of past events. For example, they may recall incidents consistent with their theory and invent material to fill in gaps.

Tennen, H., Afflect, G., & Armeli, S. (2005). Personality and daily experience revisited. *Journal of Personality, 73*, 1–19. Reviews methods for recording daily personal experiences as a way of describing personality and predicting reactions to everyday life events. Relates personality in daily life to mental and physical health.

Triandis, H. C., & Suh, E. M. (2002). Cultural influences on personality. *Annual Review of Psychology, 53*, 133–160. Describes several dimensions of a culture, such as complexity, individualism, and collectivism that may account for variations in personality.

Viglione, D. J., & Hilsenroth, M. J. (2001). The Rorschach: Facts, fictions, and future. *Psychological Assessment, 13,* 452–471. Reviews research relating to reliability, validity, and utility of the Rorschach.

PART ONE

The Psychoanalytic Approach

The earliest approach to the formal study of personality was psychoanalysis, the creation of Sigmund Freud, who began his work in the closing years of the 19th century. So important and far-reaching were Freud's formulations that many of his ideas and his unique approach to psychotherapy remain influential into the 21st century. In addition, nearly every personality theory developed in the years since Freud's work owes a debt to his position—either building on it or opposing it.

Psychoanalysis as Freud conceived it emphasized unconscious forces, biologically based drives of sex and aggression, and unavoidable conflicts in early childhood. These were considered the rulers and shapers of our personality.

Freud's views had an impact not only on psychology but also on the general culture. He succeeded in redefining the human personality and revolutionizing our ways of thinking about human nature.

CHAPTER 1

Sigmund Freud: Psychoanalysis

Turn your eyes inward, look into your own depths, learn to first know yourself.

—SIGMUND FREUD

psychoanalysis
Sigmund Freud's theory of personality and system of therapy for treating mental disorders.

Personality theory has been influenced more by Sigmund Freud than by any other individual. His system of **psychoanalysis** was the first formal theory of personality and is still the best known. Freud's influence has been so profound that more than a century after his theory was proposed it remains the framework for the study of personality, despite its controversial nature. Not only did Freud's work affect thinking about personality in psychology and psychiatry, but it also made a tremendous impact on our view of human nature. Few ideas in the history of civilization have had such a broad and profound influence.

Many of the personality theories proposed after Freud are derivatives of or elaborations on his basic work. Others owe their impetus and direction in part to their opposition to Freud's psychoanalysis. It would be difficult to comprehend and assess the development of the field of personality without first understanding Freud's system.

The Life of Freud (1856–1939)

The Early Years

Freud was born on May 6, 1856, in Freiberg, Moravia (now Pribor, Czech Republic). In 1990, the town changed the name of its Stalin Square to Freud Square, and in 2006 the house in which Freud was born was restored and opened as a museum.

Freud's father was a relatively unsuccessful wool merchant. When his business failed in Moravia, the family moved to Leipzig, Germany, and later, when Freud was 4 years old, to Vienna, Austria. Freud remained in Vienna for nearly 80 years.

When Freud was born, his father was 40 years old and his mother (the elder Freud's third wife) only 20. The father was strict and authoritarian. As an adult, Freud recalled his childhood hostility, hatred, and rage toward his father. He wrote that he felt superior to his father as early as the age of 2.

Freud's mother was slender and attractive. Her behavior toward her first-born son was protective and loving. Freud felt a passionate, sexual attachment to her, a situation that set the stage for his later concept of the Oedipus complex. As we shall see, much of Freud's theory reflects his childhood experiences and can therefore be considered autobiographical in nature.

Freud's mother took pride in young Sigmund, convinced that he would become a great man. Among Freud's lifelong personality characteristics were a high degree of self-confidence, an intense ambition to succeed, and dreams of glory and fame. Reflecting the impact of his mother's continuing attention and support, Freud wrote: "A man who has been the indisputable favorite of his mother keeps for life the feeling of a conqueror, that confidence of success that often induces real success" (quoted in Jones, 1953, p. 5). There were eight children in the Freud family, two of them Freud's adult half-brothers with children of their own. Freud resented them all and became jealous and angry when competitors for his mother's affection were born.

From an early age, Freud exhibited a high level of intelligence, which his parents helped to foster. For example, his sisters were not allowed to practice the piano lest the noise disturb Freud's studies. He was given a room of his own, where he spent most of his time; he even took his meals there so as not to lose time from his studies. The room was the only one in the apartment to contain a prized oil lamp while the rest of the family used candles.

Freud entered high school a year earlier than was usual and was frequently at the head of his class. Fluent in German and Hebrew, he mastered Latin, Greek, French, and English in school and taught himself Italian and Spanish. From the age of 8, he enjoyed reading Shakespeare in English.

Freud had many interests, including military history, but when it came time to choose a career from among the few professions open to a Jew in Vienna, he settled on medicine. It was not that he wanted to be a physician, but rather that he believed that medical studies would lead to a career in scientific research, which might bring the fame he fervently desired. While completing work for his medical degree at the University of Vienna, Freud conducted physiological research on the spinal cord of fish and the testes of the eel, making respectable contributions to the field.

The Cocaine Episode

While in medical school, Freud also began to experiment with cocaine. (At that time, cocaine was not an illegal drug, and it was not yet known that cocaine could have an addictive effect on some, but not all, users.) He used the drug himself and insisted that his fiancée, sisters, and friends try it. He became highly enthusiastic about the substance, calling it a miracle drug and a magical substance that would cure many ills and be the means of securing the recognition he craved.

In 1884, he published an article about cocaine's beneficial effects. This article was later judged to be a contributor to the epidemic of cocaine use in Europe and the United States, which lasted into the 1920s. Freud was strongly criticized for his part in unleashing the cocaine plague. The matter brought him infamy rather than fame, and for the rest of his life he tried to eradicate his earlier endorsement of the drug, deleting all references to the substance from his own bibliography. However, according to letters published long after his death, he continued to use cocaine well into middle age (Freud, 1985).

The Sexual Basis of Neurosis

A professor discouraged Freud from pursuing his intended career in scientific research, pointing out that it would be many years before Freud could obtain a professorship and support himself financially in the university system of the day. Because Freud lacked an independent income, he believed he had no choice but to enter private practice. A further impetus toward private practice was his engagement to Martha Bernays, which lasted 4 years before they could afford to marry. Freud established practice as a clinical neurologist in 1881 and began to explore the personalities of those suffering from emotional disturbances.

He studied for several months in Paris with the psychiatrist Jean Martin Charcot, a pioneer in the use of hypnosis. Charcot also alerted Freud to the possible sexual basis of neurosis. Freud overheard Charcot comment that a particular patient's problem was sexual in origin. "In this sort of case," Charcot said, "it's always a question of the genitals—always, always, always" (Charcot quoted in Freud, 1914, p. 14). Freud noted that while Charcot was discussing this issue he "crossed his hands in his lap and jumped up and down several times. . . . for a moment I was almost paralyzed with astonishment" (Freud quoted in Prochnik, 2006, p. 135).

When Freud returned to Vienna, he was again reminded of the possible sexual origin of emotional problems. A colleague described a woman patient's anxiety, which the therapist believed stemmed from her husband's impotence. The husband had never had sexual relations with his wife in 18 years of marriage. "The sole prescription for such a malady," Freud's colleague said, "is familiar enough to us, but we cannot order it. It runs: *Penis normalis dosim repetatur!*" (quoted in Freud, 1914, p. 14). As a result of these incidents, and his own sexual conflicts, it can be suggested that Freud was certainly open to the possibility of a sexual basis for emotional disturbance.

Childhood Sexual Abuse: Fact or Fantasy?

By 1896, after several years in clinical practice, Freud was convinced that sexual conflicts were the primary cause of all neuroses. He claimed that the majority of his women patients reported traumatic sexual experiences from childhood. These events resembled seduction, with the seducer usually being an older male relative, typically the father. Today we call such experiences child abuse, and they often involve rape or incest. Freud believed that it was these early sexual traumas that caused neurotic behavior in adulthood.

About a year after he published this theory, Freud changed his mind. He decided that in most cases the childhood sexual abuse his patients mentioned had never really occurred. They had been telling him fantasies, Freud claimed. At first, this was a stunning blow, for it seemed that the foundation of his theory of neurosis had been undermined. How could childhood sexual traumas be the cause of neurotic behavior if they had never happened?

On reflection, Freud concluded that the fantasies his patients described were indeed quite real to them. They believed that the shocking sexual events had actually happened. And because the fantasies still focused on sex, sex remained the cause of adult neuroses. In 1898, he wrote that "the most immediate and, for practical purposes, the most significant causes of neurotic illness are to be found in factors arising from sexual life" (quoted in Breger, 2000, p. 117).

In 1984, nearly a century later, a psychoanalyst who briefly headed the Freud Archives charged that Freud lied and that his patients had truly been victims of childhood sexual abuse. Jeffrey Masson claimed that Freud called these experiences fantasies to make his ideas more palatable and acceptable to the public. Otherwise, who would believe that so many fathers and uncles were sexually abusing little girls? In other words, Masson said, Freud covered up the truth to make his theory of neurosis more acceptable (Masson, 1984).

The charges received much international publicity and were denounced by most Freud scholars on the grounds that Masson offered little persuasive evidence (see Gay, 1988; Krüll, 1986; Malcolm, 1984). It is important to note that Freud never claimed that all the childhood sexual abuses his patients reported were fantasies; what he did deny was that his patients' reports were always true. It was, Freud wrote, "hardly credible that perverted acts against children were so general" (Freud, 1954, pp. 215–216).

Today we know that childhood sexual abuse is far more common than once thought, which led contemporary scholars to suggest that Freud's original interpretation of the seduction experiences may have been correct. We do not know whether Freud deliberately suppressed the truth, as Masson claimed, or whether he genuinely believed that his patients were describing fantasies. It may well be that "more of Freud's patients were telling the truth about their childhood experiences than [Freud] was ultimately prepared to believe" (Crewsdon, 1988, p. 41).

A similar conclusion was reached by one of Freud's disciples in the 1930s, and Freud tried to suppress the publication of his ideas. It has also been suggested that Freud changed his position on the seduction theory because he realized that if sexual abuse was so widespread, then many fathers (including perhaps his own) would be considered suspect of perverse acts against their children (Krüll, 1986).

Freud's Sex Life

It is a paradox that Freud, who emphasized the importance of sex in emotional life, experienced so many personal sexual conflicts. His attitude toward sex was negative. He wrote about the dangers of sex, even for those who were not neurotic, and urged people to rise above what he called the common animal need for sex. The sex act was degrading, he wrote, because it contaminated mind and body. He apparently abandoned his own sex life at the age of 41, writing to a friend: "sexual excitation is of no more use to a person like me" (Freud, 1954, p. 227). He occasionally had been impotent during his marriage and had sometimes chosen to abstain from sex because he disliked condoms and *coitus interruptus,* the standard birth control methods of the day.

Freud blamed his wife, Martha, for the termination of his sex life, and for many years he had dreams involving his resentment toward her for forcing him to abandon sex. "He felt resentful because she became pregnant so easily, because she often became ill during her pregnancies, and because she refused to engage in any kind of sexual activity beyond [procreative acts]" (Elms, 1994, p. 45). Thus, Freud's periods of impotence may also have been related to his fear that Martha would become pregnant again.

Freud's personal frustrations and conflicts about sex surfaced in the form of neuroses; in the same way he believed sexual difficulties affected his patients. In his 40s, he experienced a severe neurotic episode, which he described as involving "odd states of mind not intelligible to consciousness—cloudy thoughts and veiled doubts, with barely here and there a ray of light....I still do not know what has been happening to me" (Freud, 1954, pp. 210–212). He was also troubled by a variety of physical symptoms, including migraine headaches, urinary problems, and a spastic colon. He worried about dying, feared for his heart, and became anxious about travel and open spaces.

Freud diagnosed his condition as anxiety neurosis and neurasthenia (a neurotic condition characterized by weakness, worry, and disturbances of digestion and circulation), and he traced both disturbances to an accumulation of sexual tension. In his writings, he proposed that neurasthenia in men resulted from masturbation, and anxiety neurosis arose from abnormal sexual practices such as *coitus interruptus* and abstinence. By so labeling his symptoms, "his personal life was thus deeply involved in this particular theory, since with its help he was trying to interpret and solve his own problems....Freud's theory of actual neurosis is thus a theory of his own neurotic symptoms" (Krüll, 1986, pp. 14, 20).

Despite Freud's personal conflicts about sex (or perhaps because of them), he was fascinated by beautiful women. A friend noted that "among [Freud's] students there were so many attractive women that it began to look like more than a matter of chance" (Roazen, 1993, p. 138).

For 3 years Freud psychoanalyzed himself through the study of his dreams. It was during this period that he performed his most creative work in developing his theory of personality. Through the exploration of his dreams, he realized, for the first time, how much hostility he felt toward his father. He recalled his childhood sexual longings for his mother and dreamed of a sex wish toward his eldest daughter. Thus, he formulated much of his theory around his own neurotic conflicts and childhood experiences, as filtered through his interpretations of his dreams. As he perceptively observed, "The most important patient for me was my own person" (Freud quoted in Gay, 1988, p. 96).

The Pinnacle of Success

Freud's theory, then, was formulated initially on an intuitive basis, drawn from his experiences and memories. He constructed it along more rational and empirical lines through his work with patients, examining their childhood experiences and memories through case studies and dream analysis. From this material, he fashioned a coherent picture of the development of the individual personality and its processes and functions.

As his work became known through published articles and books as well as papers presented at scientific meetings, Freud attracted a group of disciples who met with him weekly to learn about his new system. The topic of their first meeting was the psychology of cigar making. One writer referred to the group as a second-rate "collection of marginal neurotics" (Gardner, 1993, p. 51). Freud's daughter Anna described the early disciples a bit more charitably as

> the unconventional ones, the doubters, those who were dissatisfied with the limitations imposed on knowledge; also among them were the odd ones, the dreamers, and those who knew neurotic suffering from their own experience. (quoted in Coles, 1998, p. 144)

The disciples included Carl Jung and Alfred Adler, who later broke with Freud to develop their own theories. Freud considered them traitors to the cause, and he never forgave them for disputing his approach to psychoanalysis. At a family dinner, he complained about his followers' disloyalty. "The trouble with you, Sigi," said his aunt, "is that you just don't understand people" (quoted in Hilgard, 1987, p. 641).

In 1909, Freud received formal recognition from the American psychological community. He was invited to give a series of lectures at Clark University in Worcester, Massachusetts, and to receive an honorary doctoral degree. Although grateful for the honor, Freud did not like the United States, complaining of its informality, bad cooking, and scarcity of bathrooms. Although he had been troubled by gastrointestinal problems for many years prior to his visit to the U.S., nevertheless "he blamed the New World for ruining his digestion" (Prochnik, 2006, p. 35).

Freud's system of psychoanalysis was warmly welcomed in the United States. Two years after his visit, American followers founded the American Psychoanalytic Association and the New York Psychoanalytic Society. Over the next few years, psychoanalytic societies were established in Boston, Chicago, and Washington, D.C.

By 1920, only 11 years after his trip to America, more than 200 books had been published on psychoanalysis (Abma, 2004). Leading U.S. magazines such as *Ladies Home Journal*, *The New Republic*, and *Time* featured articles about Freud. Dr. Benjamin Spock's phenomenally successful baby and child care books that influenced the rearing of several generations of American children were based on Freudian teachings. Freud's work on dreams inspired a popular song that included the line: "Don't tell me what you dream'd last night—For I've been reading Freud" (quoted in Fancher, 2000, p. 1026). America may have made Freud sick, so he claimed, but it also helped bring him worldwide fame.

During the 1920s and 1930s, Freud reached the pinnacle of his success, but at the same time his health began to decline seriously. From 1923 until his death 16 years later, he underwent 33 operations for cancer of the mouth (he smoked 20 cigars daily). Portions of his palate and upper jaw were removed, and he experienced almost constant pain, for which he refused medication. He also received X-ray and radium treatments and had a vasectomy, which some physicians thought would halt the growth of the cancer.

When the Nazis came to power in Germany in 1933, they expressed their feelings about Freud by publicly burning his books, along with those of other so-called enemies of the state, such as the physicist Albert Einstein and the writer Ernest Hemingway. "What progress we are making. In the Middle Ages they would have burnt me; nowadays they are content with burning my books" (Freud quoted in Jones, 1957, p. 182).

In 1938, the Nazis occupied Austria, but despite the urgings of his friends, Freud refused to leave Vienna. Several times gangs of Nazis invaded his home. After his daughter Anna was arrested, Freud agreed to leave for London. Four of his sisters died in Nazi concentration camps.

Freud's health deteriorated dramatically, but he remained mentally alert and continued to work almost to the last day of his life. By late September 1939, he told his physician, Max Schur, "Now it's nothing but torture and makes no sense any more" (Schur, 1972, p. 529). The doctor had promised that he would not let Freud suffer needlessly. He administered three injections of morphine over the next 24 hours, each dose greater than necessary for sedation, and brought Freud's long years of pain to an end.

Instincts: The Propelling Forces of the Personality

instincts
In Freud's system, mental representations of internal stimuli, such as hunger, that drive a person to take certain actions.

Instincts are the basic elements of the personality, the motivating forces that drive behavior and determine its direction. Freud's German term for this concept is *Trieb*, which is best translated as a driving force or impulse (Bettelheim, 1984). Instincts are a form of energy—transformed physiological energy—that connects the body's needs with the mind's wishes.

The stimuli (hunger or thirst, for example) for instincts are internal. When a need such as hunger is aroused in the body, it generates a condition of physiological excitation or energy. The mind transforms this bodily energy into a wish. It is this wish—the mental representation of the physiological need—that is the instinct or driving force that motivates the person to behave in a way that satisfies the need. A hungry person, for example, will act to satisfy his or her need by looking for food. The instinct is not the bodily state; rather, it is the bodily need transformed into a mental state, a wish.

When the body is in a state of need, the person experiences a feeling of tension or pressure. The aim of an instinct is to satisfy the need and thereby reduce the tension. Freud's theory can be called a homeostatic approach insofar as it suggests that we are motivated to restore and maintain a condition of physiological equilibrium, or balance, to keep the body free of tension.

Freud believed that we always experience a certain amount of instinctual tension and that we must continually act to reduce it. It is not possible to escape the pressure of our physiological needs as we might escape some annoying stimulus in our external environment. This means that instincts are always influencing our behavior, in a cycle of need leading to reduction of need.

People may take different paths to satisfy their needs. For example, the sex drive may be satisfied by heterosexual behavior, homosexual behavior, or auto-sexual behavior, or the sex drive may be channeled into some other form of activity. Freud thought that psychic energy could be displaced to substitute objects, and this displacement was of primary importance in determining an individual's personality. Although the instincts are the exclusive source of energy for human behavior, the resulting energy can be invested in a variety of activities. This helps explain the diversity we see in human behavior. All the interests, preferences, and attitudes we display as adults were believed by Freud to be displacements of energy from the original objects that satisfied the instinctual needs.

Types of Instincts

life instincts
The drive for ensuring survival of the individual and the species by satisfying the needs for food, water, air, and sex.

Freud grouped the instincts into two categories: life instincts and death instincts. The **life instincts** serve the purpose of survival of the individual and the species by seeking to satisfy the needs for food, water, air, and sex. The life instincts are oriented toward growth and development. The psychic energy manifested by the life instincts is the **libido**. The libido can be attached to or invested in objects, a concept Freud called **cathexis**. If you like your roommate, for example, Freud would say that your libido is cathected to him or her.

libido
To Freud, the form of psychic energy, manifested by the life instincts, that drives a person toward pleasurable behaviors and thoughts.

The life instinct Freud considered most important for the personality is sex, which he defined in broad terms. He did not refer solely to the erotic but included almost all pleasurable behaviors and thoughts. He described his view as enlarging or extending the accepted concept of sexuality.

> That extension is of a twofold kind. In the first place, sexuality is divorced from its too close connection with the genitals and is regarded as a more comprehensive bodily function, having pleasure as its goal and only secondarily coming to serve the ends of reproduction. In the second place, the sexual impulses are regarded as including all of those merely affectionate and friendly impulses to which usage applies the exceedingly ambiguous word "love." (Freud, 1925, p. 38)

cathexis
An investment of psychic energy in an object or person.

Freud regarded sex as our primary motivation. Erotic wishes arise from the body's erogenous zones: the mouth, anus, and sex organs. He suggested that people are predominantly pleasure-seeking beings, and much of his personality theory revolves around the necessity of inhibiting or suppressing our sexual longings.

death instincts
The unconscious drive toward decay, destruction, and aggression.

In opposition to the life instincts, Freud postulated the destructive or **death instincts**. Drawing from biology, he stated the obvious fact that all living things decay and die, returning to their original inanimate state, and he proposed that people have an unconscious wish to die. One component of the death instincts is the **aggressive drive**, described as the wish to die turned against objects other than the self. The aggressive drive compels us to destroy, conquer, and kill. Freud came to consider aggression as compelling a part of human nature as sex.

aggressive drive
The compulsion to destroy, conquer, and kill.

Freud developed the notion of the death instincts late in life, as a reflection of his own experiences. He endured the physiological and psychological debilitations of age, his cancer worsened, and he witnessed the carnage of World War I. One of his daughters died at the age of 26, leaving two young children. All these events affected him deeply, and, as a result, death and aggression became major themes in his theory. In his later years, Freud dreaded his own death, and exhibited hostility, hatred, and aggressiveness toward colleagues and disciples who disputed his views and left his psychoanalytic circle.

The concept of the death instincts achieved only limited acceptance, even among Freud's most dedicated followers. One psychoanalyst wrote that the idea should be "relegated to the dustbin of history" (Sulloway, 1979, p. 394). Another suggested that if Freud were a genius, then the suggestion of the death instincts was an instance of a genius having a bad day (Eissler, 1971).

The Levels of Personality

Freud's original conception divided personality into three levels: the conscious, the preconscious, and the unconscious. The conscious, as Freud defined the term, corresponds to its ordinary everyday meaning. It includes all the sensations and experiences of which we are aware at any given moment. As you read these words, for example, you may be conscious of the feel of your pen, the sight of the page, the idea you are trying to grasp, and a dog barking in the distance.

Freud considered the conscious a limited aspect of personality because only a small portion of our thoughts, sensations, and memories exists in conscious awareness at any time. He likened the mind to an iceberg. The conscious is the portion above the surface of the water—merely the tip of the iceberg. More important, according to Freud, is the unconscious, that larger, invisible portion below the surface. This is the focus of psychoanalytic theory. Its vast, dark depths are the home of the instincts, those wishes and desires that direct our behavior. The unconscious contains the major driving power behind all behaviors and is the repository of forces we cannot see or control.

Between these two levels is the preconscious. This is the storehouse of memories, perceptions, and thoughts of which we are not consciously aware at the moment but that we can easily summon into consciousness. For example, if your mind strays from this page and you begin to think about a friend or about what you did last night, you would be summoning up material from your preconscious into your conscious. We often find our attention shifting back and forth from experiences of the moment to events and memories in the preconscious.

The Structure of Personality

The Id

Freud later revised this notion of three levels of personality and introduced three basic structures in the anatomy of the personality: the id, the ego, and the superego

Figure 1.1
Freud's levels and
structures of personality.
SOURCE: From *Psychology:
Themes and Variations,* 2nd
ed., by W. Weiten, p. 428,
Brooks/Cole Publishing Co.,
1992.

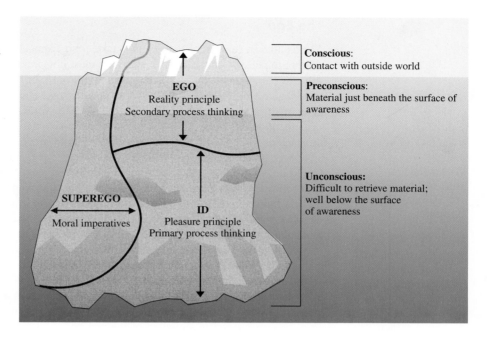

id
To Freud, the aspect of
personality allied with
the instincts; the source
of psychic energy, the
id operates according to
the pleasure principle.

pleasure principle
The principle by which
the id functions to avoid
pain and maximize
pleasure.

primary-process thought
Childlike thinking by
which the id attempts
to satisfy the instinctual
drives.

(see Figure 1.1). The **id** corresponds to Freud's earlier notion of the unconscious (although the ego and superego have unconscious aspects as well). The id is the reservoir for the instincts and libido (the psychic energy manifested by the instincts). The id is a powerful structure of the personality because it supplies all the energy for the other two components.

Because the id is the reservoir of the instincts, it is vitally and directly related to the satisfaction of bodily needs. As we noted earlier, tension is produced when the body is in a state of need, and the person acts to reduce this tension by satisfying the need. The id operates in accordance with what Freud called the **pleasure principle**; through its concern with tension reduction, the id functions to increase pleasure and avoid pain. The id strives for immediate satisfaction of its needs and does not tolerate delay or postponement of satisfaction for any reason. It knows only instant gratification; it drives us to want what we want when we want it, without regard for what anyone else wants. The id is a selfish, pleasure-seeking structure, primitive, amoral, insistent, and rash.

The id has no awareness of reality. We might compare the id to a newborn baby who cries and waves its fists when its needs are not met but who has no knowledge of how to bring about satisfaction. The hungry infant cannot find food on his or her own. The only ways the id can attempt to satisfy its needs are through reflex action and wish-fulfilling hallucinatory or fantasy experience, which Freud labeled **primary-process thought**.

The Ego

Most children learn that they cannot take food from other people unless they are willing to face the consequences, that they must postpone the pleasure obtained from relieving anal tensions until they get to a bathroom, or that they cannot indiscriminately give vent to sexual and aggressive longings. The growing child is taught to deal intelligently and rationally with the outside world and to develop the powers of perception, recognition, judgment, and memory—the powers adults use to satisfy their needs. Freud called these abilities **secondary-process thought**.

We can sum up these characteristics as reason or rationality, and they are contained in Freud's second structure of personality, the **ego**, which is the rational master of the personality. Its purpose is not to thwart the impulses of the id but to help the id obtain the tension reduction it craves. Because it is aware of reality, the ego decides when and how the id instincts can best be satisfied. It determines appropriate and socially acceptable times, places, and objects that will satisfy the id impulses.

The ego does not prevent id satisfaction. Rather, it tries to postpone, delay, or redirect it in terms of the demands of reality. It perceives and manipulates the environment in a practical and realistic manner and so is said to operate in accordance with the **reality principle**. (The reality principle stands in opposition to the pleasure principle, by which the id operates.) The ego thus exerts control over the id impulses. Freud compared the relationship of the ego and the id to that of a rider on a horse. The raw, brute power of the horse must be guided, checked, and reined in by the rider; otherwise the horse could bolt and run, throwing the rider to the ground.

The ego serves two masters—the id and reality—and is constantly mediating and striking compromises between their conflicting demands. Also, the ego is never independent of the id. It is always responsive to the id's demands and derives its power and energy from the id.

It is the ego, the rational master, which keeps you working at a job you may dislike, if the alternative is the inability to provide food and shelter for your family. It is the ego that forces you to get along with people you dislike because reality demands such behavior from you as an appropriate way of satisfying id demands. The controlling and postponing function of the ego must be exercised constantly. If not, the id impulses might come to dominate and overthrow the rational ego. Freud argued that we must protect ourselves from being controlled by the id and proposed various unconscious mechanisms with which to defend the ego.

So far, we have a picture of the personality in battle, trying to restrain the id while at the same time serving it, perceiving and manipulating reality to relieve the tensions of the id impulses. Driven by instinctual biological forces, which we continually try to guide, the personality walks a tightrope between the demands of the id and the demands of reality, both of which require constant vigilance.

The Superego

The id and the ego do not represent Freud's complete picture of human nature. There is a third set of forces—a powerful and largely unconscious set of dictates or beliefs—that we acquire in childhood: our ideas of right and wrong. In everyday

---

secondary-process thought
Mature thought processes needed to deal rationally with the external world.

ego
To Freud, the rational aspect of the personality, responsible for directing and controlling the instincts according to the reality principle.

reality principle
The principle by which the ego functions to provide appropriate constraints on the expression of the id instincts.

superego
To Freud, the moral aspect of personality; the internalization of parental and societal values and standards.

conscience
A component of the superego that contains behaviors for which the child has been punished.

ego-ideal
A component of the superego that contains the moral or ideal behaviors for which a person should strive.

language we call this internal morality a conscience. Freud called it the **superego**. The basis of this moral side of the personality is usually learned by the age of 5 or 6 and consists initially of the rules of conduct set down by our parents. Through praise, punishment, and example, children learn which behaviors their parents consider good or bad. Those behaviors for which children are punished form the **conscience**, one part of the superego. The second part of the superego is the **ego-ideal**, which consists of good, or correct, behaviors for which children have been praised.

In this way, children learn a set of rules that earn acceptance or rejection from their parents. In time, children internalize these teachings, and the rewards and punishments become self-administered. Parental control is replaced by self-control. We come to behave at least in partial conformity with these now largely unconscious moral guidelines. As a result of this internalization, we experience guilt or shame whenever we perform (or even think of performing) some action contrary to this moral code.

As the arbiter of morality, the superego is relentless, even cruel, in its quest for moral perfection. In terms of intensity, irrationality, and insistence on obedience, it is not unlike the id. Its purpose is not merely to postpone the pleasure-seeking demands of the id, as the ego does, but to inhibit them completely, particularly those demands concerned with sex and aggression. The superego strives neither for pleasure (as does the id) nor for attainment of realistic goals (as does the ego). It strives solely for moral perfection. The id presses for satisfaction, the ego tries to delay it, and the superego urges morality above all. Like the id, the superego admits no compromise with its demands.

The ego is caught in the middle, pressured by these insistent and opposing forces. Thus, the ego has a third master, the superego. To paraphrase Freud, the poor ego has a hard time of it, pressured on three sides, threatened by three dangers: the id, reality, and the superego. The inevitable result of this friction, when the ego is too severely strained, is the development of anxiety.

Anxiety: A Threat to the Ego

anxiety
To Freud, a feeling of fear and dread without an obvious cause: reality anxiety is a fear of tangible dangers; neurotic anxiety involves a conflict between id and ego; moral anxiety involves a conflict between id and superego.

We already have a general idea of what the word *anxiety* means and how we feel when we are anxious. We know that anxiety is not unlike fear, although we may not know what we are frightened of. Freud described **anxiety** as an objectless fear; often, we cannot point to its source, to a specific object that induced it.

Freud made anxiety an important part of his personality theory, asserting that it is fundamental to the development of neurotic and psychotic behavior. He suggested that the prototype of all anxiety is the birth trauma, a notion elaborated on by a disciple, Otto Rank.

The fetus in its mother's womb is in the most stable and secure of worlds, where every need is satisfied without delay. But at birth, the organism is thrust into a hostile environment. Suddenly, it is required to begin adapting to reality because its instinctual demands may not always be immediately met. The newborn's nervous system, immature and ill prepared, is bombarded with diverse sensory stimuli. Consequently, the infant engages in massive motor movements, heightened breathing, and increased heart rate. This birth trauma, with its tension and fear that the id instincts won't be satisfied, is our first experience with anxiety. From it is created the pattern of reactions and feelings that will occur whenever we are exposed to some threat in the future.

When we cannot cope with anxiety, when we are in danger of being overwhelmed by it, the anxiety is said to be traumatic. What Freud meant by this is that the person, regardless of age, is reduced to a state of helplessness like that experienced in infancy. In adult life, infantile helplessness is reenacted to some degree whenever the ego is threatened.

Reality Anxiety, Neurotic Anxiety, and Moral Anxiety

Freud proposed three types of anxiety: reality anxiety, neurotic anxiety, and moral anxiety. The first type of anxiety, the one from which the others are derived, is **reality anxiety** (or objective anxiety). This involves a fear of tangible dangers in the real world. Most of us justifiably fear fires, hurricanes, earthquakes, and similar disasters. We run from wild animals, speeding cars, and burning buildings. Reality anxiety serves the positive purpose of guiding our behavior to escape or protect ourselves from actual dangers. Our fear subsides when the threat is no longer present. These reality-based fears can be carried to extremes, however. The person who cannot leave home for fear of being hit by a car or who cannot light a match for fear of fire is carrying reality-based fears beyond the point of normality.

The other kinds of anxiety, neurotic anxiety and moral anxiety, are more consistently troublesome to our mental health. **Neurotic anxiety** has its basis in childhood, in a conflict between instinctual gratification and reality. Children are often punished for overtly expressing sexual or aggressive impulses. Therefore, the wish to gratify certain id impulses generates anxiety. This neurotic anxiety is an unconscious fear of being punished for impulsively displaying id-dominated behavior. Note that the fear is not of the instincts, but of what may happen as a result of gratifying the instincts. The conflict becomes one between the id and the ego, and its origin has some basis in reality.

Moral anxiety results from a conflict between the id and the superego. In essence, it is a fear of one's conscience. When you are motivated to express an instinctual impulse that is contrary to your moral code, your superego retaliates by causing you to feel shame or guilt. In everyday terms, you might describe yourself as conscience-stricken.

Moral anxiety is a function of how well developed the superego is. A person with a strong inhibiting conscience will experience greater conflict than a person with a less stringent set of moral guidelines. Like neurotic anxiety, moral anxiety has some basis in reality. Children are punished for violating their parents' moral codes, and adults are punished for violating society's moral code. The shame and guilt feelings in moral anxiety arise from within; it is our conscience that causes the fear and the anxiety. Freud believed that the superego exacts a terrible retribution for violation of its tenets.

Anxiety serves as a warning signal to the person that all is not as it should be within the personality. Anxiety induces tension in the organism and thus becomes a drive (much like the hunger or thirst drives) that the individual is motivated to satisfy. The tension must be reduced.

Anxiety alerts the individual that the ego is being threatened and that unless action is taken, the ego might be overthrown. How can the ego protect or defend itself? There are a number of options: running away from the threatening situation, inhibiting the impulsive need that is the source of the danger, or obeying the dictates of the conscience. If none of these rational techniques works, the person may resort to defense mechanisms—the non-rational strategies designed to defend the ego.

Defenses Against Anxiety

Anxiety is a signal that impending danger, a threat to the ego, must be counter-acted or avoided. The ego must reduce the conflict between the demands of the id and the strictures of society or the superego. According to Freud, this conflict is ever present because the instincts are always pressing for satisfaction, and the taboos of society are always working to limit such satisfaction. Freud believed that the defenses must, to some extent, always be in operation. All behaviors are motivated by instincts; similarly, all behaviors are defensive in the sense of defending against anxiety. The intensity of the battle within the personality may fluctuate, but it never ceases.

defense mechanisms Strategies the ego uses to defend itself against the anxiety provoked by conflicts of everyday life. Defense mechanisms involve denials or distortions of reality.

Freud postulated several **defense mechanisms** and noted that we rarely use just one; we typically defend ourselves against anxiety by using several at the same time (see Table 1.1). Also, some overlap exists among the mechanisms. Although defense mechanisms vary in their specifics, they share two characteristics: (1) they are denials or distortions of reality—necessary ones, but distortions nonetheless, and, (2) they operate unconsciously. We are unaware of them, which means that on the conscious level we hold distorted or unreal images of our world and ourselves.

Table 1.1 **Some Freudian defense mechanisms**

Repression: Involves unconscious denial of the existence of something that causes anxiety

Denial: Involves denying the existence of an external threat or traumatic event

Reaction Formation: Involves expressing an id impulse that is the opposite of the one truly driving the person

Projection: Involves attributing a disturbing impulse to someone else

Regression: Involves retreating to an earlier, less frustrating period of life and displaying the childish and dependent behaviors characteristic of that more secure time

Rationalization: Involves reinterpreting behavior to make it more acceptable and less threatening

Displacement: Involves shifting id impulses from a threatening or unavailable object to a substitute object that is available

Sublimation: Involves altering or displacing id impulses by diverting instinctual energy into socially acceptable behaviors

repression
A defense mechanism that involves unconscious denial of the existence of something that causes anxiety.

Repression. **Repression** is an involuntary removal of something from conscious awareness. It is an unconscious type of forgetting of the existence of something that brings us discomfort or pain and is the most fundamental and frequently used defense mechanism. Repression can operate on memories of situations or people, on our perception of the present (so that we may fail to see some obviously disturbing event), and even on the body's physiological functioning. For example, a man can so strongly repress the sex drive that he becomes impotent.

Once repression is operating, it is difficult to eliminate. Because we use repression to protect ourselves from danger, in order to remove it, we would have to know that the idea or memory is no longer dangerous. But how can we find out that the danger no longer exists unless we release the repression? The concept of repression is the basis of much of Freud's personality theory and is involved in all neurotic behavior.

denial
A defense mechanism that involves denying the existence of an external threat or traumatic event.

Denial. The defense mechanism of **denial** is related to repression and involves denying the existence of some external threat or traumatic event that has occurred. For example, a person with a terminal illness may deny the imminence of death. Parents of a child who has died may continue to deny the loss by keeping the child's room unchanged.

reaction formation
A defense mechanism that involves expressing an id impulse that is the opposite of the one that is truly driving the person.

Reaction Formation. One defense against a disturbing impulse is to actively express the opposite impulse. This is called **reaction formation**. A person who is strongly driven by threatening sexual impulses may repress those impulses and replace them with more socially acceptable behaviors. For example, a person threatened by sexual longings may reverse them and become a rabid crusader against pornography. Another person, disturbed by extreme aggressive impulses, may become overly solicitous and friendly. Thus, lust becomes virtue and hatred becomes love, in the unconscious mind of the person using this mechanism.

projection
A defense mechanism that involves attributing a disturbing impulse to someone else.

Projection. Another way of defending against disturbing impulses is to attribute them to someone else. This defense mechanism is called **projection**. Lustful, aggressive, and other unacceptable impulses are seen as being possessed by other people, not by oneself. The person says, in effect, "I don't hate him. He hates me." Or a mother may ascribe her sex drive to her adolescent daughter. The impulse is still manifested, but in a way that is less threatening to the individual.

regression
A defense mechanism that involves retreating to an earlier, less frustrating period of life and displaying the usually childish behaviors characteristic of that more secure time.

Regression. In **regression**, the person retreats or regresses to an earlier period of life that was more pleasant and free of frustration and anxiety. Regression usually involves a return to one of the psychosexual stages of childhood development. The individual returns to this more secure time of life by manifesting behaviors displayed at that time, such as childish and dependent behaviors.

rationalization
A defense mechanism that involves reinterpreting our behavior to make it more acceptable and less threatening to us.

Rationalization. **Rationalization** is a defense mechanism that involves reinterpreting our behavior to make it seem more rational and acceptable to us. We excuse or justify a threatening thought or action by persuading ourselves there is a rational explanation for it. The person who is fired from a job may rationalize by saying that the job wasn't a good one anyway. The loved one who turns you down now appears to have many faults. It is less threatening to blame someone or something else for our failures than to blame ourselves.

Displacement. If an object that satisfies an id impulse is not available, the person may shift the impulse to another object. This is known as **displacement**. For example, children who hate their parents or adults who hate their bosses, but are afraid to express their hostility for fear of being punished, may displace the aggression onto someone else. The child may hit a younger brother or sister, or the adult may shout at the dog. In these examples, the original object of the aggressive impulse has been replaced by an object that is not a threat. However, the substitute object will not reduce the tension as satisfactorily as the original object. If you are involved in a number of displacements, a reservoir of undischarged tension accumulates, and you will be driven to find new ways of reducing that tension.

Sublimation. Whereas displacement involves finding a substitute object to satisfy id impulses, **sublimation** involves altering the id impulses. The instinctual energy is diverted into other channels of expression, ones that society considers acceptable and admirable. Sexual energy, for example, can be diverted or sublimated into artistically creative behaviors. Freud believed that a variety of human activities, particularly those of an artistic nature, are manifestations of id impulses that have been redirected into socially acceptable outlets. As with displacement (of which sublimation is a form), sublimation is a compromise. As such, it does not bring total satisfaction but leads to a buildup of undischarged tension.

As we noted, Freud suggested that defense mechanisms are unconscious denials or distortions of reality. We are, in a sense, lying to ourselves when we use these defenses, but we are not aware of doing so. If we knew we were lying to ourselves, the defenses would not be so effective. If the defenses are working well, they keep threatening or disturbing material out of our conscious awareness. As a result, we may not know the truth about ourselves. We may have a distorted picture of our needs, fears, and desires.

Our rational cognitive processes, such as problem solving, decision making, and logical thinking, may then be based on an inaccurate self-image. To Freud, we are driven and controlled by internal and external forces of which we are unaware and over which we can exercise little rational control.

There are situations in which the truth about ourselves emerges, when the defenses break down and fail to protect us. This occurs in times of unusual stress or when undergoing psychoanalysis. When the defenses fail, we are stricken with overwhelming anxiety. We feel dismal, worthless, and depressed. Unless the defenses are restored or new ones form to take their place we are likely to develop neurotic or psychotic symptoms. Thus, defenses are necessary to our mental health. We could not survive long without them.

displacement
A defense mechanism that involves shifting id impulses from a threatening object or from one that is unavailable to an object that is available; for example, replacing hostility toward one's boss with hostility toward one's child.

sublimation
A defense mechanism that involves altering or displacing id impulses by diverting instinctual energy into socially acceptable behaviors.

Psychosexual Stages of Personality Development

psychosexual stages of development
To Freud, the oral, anal, phallic, and genital stages through which all children pass. In these stages, gratification of the id instincts depends on the stimulation of corresponding areas of the body.

Freud believed that all behaviors are defensive but that not everyone uses the same defenses in the same way. All of us are driven by the same id impulses, but there is not the same universality in the nature of the ego and superego. Although these structures of the personality perform the same functions for everyone, their content varies from one person to another. They differ because they are formed through experience, and no two people have precisely the same experiences, not even siblings reared in the same house. Thus, part of our personality is formed on the basis of the unique relationships we have as children with various people and objects. We develop a personal set of character attributes, a consistent pattern of behavior that defines each of us as an individual.

A person's unique character type develops in childhood largely from parent–child interactions. The child tries to maximize pleasure by satisfying the id demands, while parents, as representatives of society, try to impose the demands of reality and morality. So important did Freud consider childhood experiences that he said the adult personality was firmly shaped and crystallized by the fifth year of life. What persuaded him that these early years are crucial were his own childhood memories and the memories revealed by his adult patients. Invariably, as his patients lay on his psychoanalytic couch, they reached far back into childhood. Increasingly, Freud perceived that the adult neurosis had been formed in the early years of life.

Freud sensed strong sexual conflicts in the infant and young child, conflicts that seemed to revolve around specific regions of the body. He noted that each body region assumed a greater importance as the center of conflict at a different age. From these observations he derived the theory of the **psychosexual stages of development**; each stage is defined by an erogenous zone of the body (see Table 1.2). In each developmental stage a conflict exists that must be resolved before the infant or child can progress to the next stage.

Sometimes a person is reluctant or unable to move from one stage to the next because the conflict has not been resolved or because the needs have been so supremely satisfied by an indulgent parent that the child doesn't want to move on. In either case,

Table 1.2 **Freud's psychosexual stages of development**

Stages	Ages	Characteristics
Oral	Birth–1	Mouth is the primary erogenous zone; pleasure derived from sucking: id is dominant.
Anal	1–3	Toilet training (external reality) interferes with gratification received from defecation.
Phallic	4–5	Incestuous fantasies; Oedipus complex; anxiety; superego development.
Latency	5–Puberty	Period of sublimation of sex instinct.
Genital	Adolescence– Adulthood	Development of sex-role identity and adult social relationships.

fixation
A condition in which a portion of libido remains invested in one of the psychosexual stages because of excessive frustration or gratification.

the individual is said to be fixated at this stage of development. In **fixation**, a portion of libido or psychic energy remains invested in that developmental stage, leaving less energy for the following stages.

Central to the psychosexual theory is the infant's sex drive. Freud shocked his colleagues and the general public when he argued that babies are motivated by sexual impulses. Recall, however, that Freud did not define sex in a narrow way. He believed that the infant is driven to obtain a diffuse form of bodily pleasure deriving from the mouth, anus, and genitals, the erogenous zones that define the stages of development during the first 5 years of life.

The Oral Stage

The oral stage, the first stage of psychosexual development, lasts from birth until some time during the second year of life. During this period the infant's principal source of pleasure is the mouth. The infant derives pleasure from sucking, biting, and swallowing. Of course, the mouth is used for survival (for the ingestion of food and water), but Freud placed a greater emphasis on the erotic satisfactions derived from oral activities.

The infant is in a state of dependence on the mother or caregiver who becomes the primary object of the child's libido. In more familiar terms, we might say the

In the oral stage of psychosexual development, pleasure is derived from sucking, biting, and swallowing.

© Lucidio Studio Inc./CORBIS

infant is learning, in a primitive way, to love the mother. How the mother responds to the infant's demands, which at this time are solely id demands, determines the nature of the baby's small world. The infant learns from the mother to perceive the world as good or bad, satisfying or frustrating, safe or perilous.

There are two ways of behaving during this stage: oral incorporative behavior (taking in) and oral aggressive or oral sadistic behavior (biting or spitting out). The oral incorporative mode occurs first and involves the pleasurable stimulation of the mouth by other people and by food. Adults fixated at the oral incorporative stage are excessively concerned with oral activities, such as eating, drinking, smoking, and kissing. If, as infants, they were excessively gratified, their adult oral personality will be predisposed to unusual optimism and dependency. Because they were overindulged in infancy, they continue to depend on others to gratify their needs. As a consequence, they are overly gullible, swallow or believe anything they are told, and trust other people inordinately. Such people are labeled oral passive personality types.

The second oral behavior, oral aggressive or oral sadistic, occurs during the painful, frustrating eruption of teeth. As a result of this experience, infants come to view the mother with hatred as well as love. After all, she has been responsible for everything in the infant's environment, so she must also be responsible for the pain. Persons who become fixated at this level are prone to excessive pessimism, hostility, and aggressiveness. They are likely to be argumentative and sarcastic, making so-called biting remarks and displaying cruelty toward others. They tend to be envious of other people and try to exploit and manipulate them in an effort to dominate.

The oral stage concludes at the time of weaning, although some libido remains if fixation has occurred. Then the infant's focus shifts to the other end.

The Anal Stage

Society, in the form of parents, tends to defer to the infant's needs during the first year of life, adjusting to its demands and expecting relatively little adjustment in return. This situation changes dramatically around the age of 18 months, when a new demand, toilet training, is made of the child. Freud believed that the experience of toilet training during the anal stage had a significant effect on personality development. Defecation produces erotic pleasure for the child, but with the onset of toilet training, the child must learn to postpone or delay this pleasure. For the first time, gratification of an instinctual impulse is interfered with as parents attempt to regulate the time and place for defecation.

As any parent can attest, this is a time of conflict for all concerned. The child learns that he or she has (or is) a weapon that can be used against the parents. The child has control over something and can choose to comply or not with the parents' demands. If the toilet training is not going well—for example, if the child has difficulty learning or the parents are excessively demanding—the child may react in one of two ways. One way is to defecate when and where the parents disapprove, thus defying their attempts at regulation. If the child finds this a satisfactory technique for reducing frustration and uses it frequently, he or she may develop an anal aggressive personality. To Freud, this was the basis for many forms of hostile and sadistic behavior in adult life, including cruelty, destructiveness, and temper tantrums. Such a person is likely to be disorderly and to view other people as objects to be possessed.

A second way the child may react to the frustration of toilet training is to hold back or retain the feces. This produces a feeling of erotic pleasure (derived from a full lower intestine) and can be another successful technique for manipulating the parents. They may become concerned if the child goes several days without a bowel movement. Thus, the child discovers a new method for securing parental attention and affection. This behavior is the basis for the development of an anal retentive personality. Stubborn and stingy, such a person hoards or retains things because feelings of security depend on what is saved and possessed and on the order in which possessions and other aspects of life are maintained. The person is likely to be rigid, compulsively neat, obstinate, and overly conscientious.

The Phallic Stage

A new set of problems arises around the fourth to fifth year, when the focus of pleasure shifts from the anus to the genitals. Again the child faces a battle between an id impulse and the demands of society, as reflected in parental expectations.

Children at the phallic stage display considerable interest in exploring and manipulating the genitals, their own and those of their playmates. Pleasure is derived from the genital region not only through behaviors such as masturbation, but also through fantasies. The child becomes curious about birth and about why boys have penises and girls do not. The child may talk about wanting to marry the parent of the opposite sex.

The boy comes to resolve the Oedipus complex by identifying with his father.

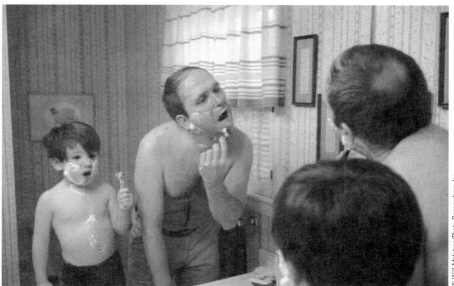

© Will McIntyre/Photo Researchers, Inc.

The phallic stage is the last of the pre-genital or childhood stages, and phallic conflicts are the most complex ones to resolve. They are difficult for many people to accept because they involve the notion of incest, a taboo in many cultures. Between incestuous desires and masturbation we can see the seeds of shock, anger, and suppression being sown in the parents of the typical 4-year-old. Reality and morality come to grips with the evil id once again.

The Oedipus complex in boys. The basic conflict of the phallic stage centers on the unconscious desire of the child for the parent of the opposite sex. Accompanying this is the unconscious desire to replace or destroy the parent of the same sex. Out of Freud's identification of this conflict came one of his best-known concepts: the **Oedipus complex**. Its name comes from the Greek myth described in the play *Oedipus Rex*, written by Sophocles in the fifth century B.C. In this story, young Oedipus kills his father and marries his mother, not knowing who they are.

The Oedipus complex operates differently for boys and girls; Freud developed the male part of the complex more fully. In the Oedipus complex, the mother becomes a love object for the young boy. Through fantasy and overt behavior, he displays his sexual longings for her. However, the boy sees the father as an obstacle in his path and regards him as a rival and a threat. He perceives that the father has a special relationship with the mother in which he, the boy, is not allowed to participate. As a result, he becomes jealous of and hostile toward the father. Freud drew his formulation of the Oedipus complex from his childhood experiences. He wrote, "I have found love of the mother and jealousy of the father in my own case, too" (Freud, 1954, p. 223).

Accompanying the boy's desire to replace his father is the fear that the father will retaliate and harm him. He interprets his fear of his father in genital terms, becoming fearful that his father will cut off the offending organ (the boy's penis), which is the source of the boy's pleasure and sexual longings. And so **castration anxiety**, as Freud called it, comes to play a role, as it may have done in Freud's childhood. "There are a number of indications that [Freud's father] enjoined little Sigmund not to play with his genitals, and even threatened him with castration if he did" (Krüll, 1986, p. 110).

Additional evidence to support this contention comes from Freud's later writings on masturbation, in which he saw such threats from fathers as common. Freud also reported that his adult dreams contained material relating to the fear of castration by his father.

Two other childhood events may have reinforced Freud's fear of castration. At around the age of 3, he and his nephew engaged in some rough sex play with his niece and discovered she did not have a penis. For a 3-year-old boy, this may have been sufficient evidence that penises can be cut off. In the opinion of one Freud biographer, "the threat of castration is particularly realistic to a Jewish boy, since it is easy to establish a connection between ritual circumcision and castration" (Krüll, 1986, p. 110). Freud confirmed this in his later writings.

So strong is the boy's fear of castration that he is forced to repress his sexual desire for his mother. To Freud, this was a way of resolving the Oedipal conflict. The

Oedipus complex
During the phallic stage (ages 4 to 5), the unconscious desire of a boy for his mother, accompanied by a desire to replace or destroy his father.

castration anxiety
A boy's fear during the Oedipal period that his penis will be cut off.

boy replaces the sexual longing for the mother with a more acceptable affection and develops a strong identification with the father. In so doing, the boy experiences a degree of vicarious sexual satisfaction. To enhance the identification, he attempts to become more like his father by adopting his mannerisms, behaviors, attitudes, and superego standards.

The Oedipus complex in girls. Freud was less clear about the female phallic conflict, which some of his followers termed the **Electra complex**. The name and notion were derived from another story by Sophocles in which Elektra persuades her brother to kill their mother, whom she hated.

Like the boy's, the girl's first object of love is the mother, because she is the primary source of food, affection, and security in infancy. During the phallic stage, however, the father becomes the girl's new love object. Why does this shift from mother to father take place? Freud said it was because of the girl's reaction to her discovery that boys have a penis and girls do not.

The girl blames her mother for her supposedly inferior condition and consequently comes to love her mother less. She may even hate the mother for what she imagines the mother did to her. She comes to envy her father and transfers her love to him because he possesses the highly valued sex organ. Freud wrote:

> girls feel deeply their lack of a sexual organ that is equal in value to the male one; they regard themselves on that account as inferior and this envy for the penis is the origin of a whole number of characteristic feminine reactions. (Freud, 1925, p. 212)

Thus, a girl develops **penis envy**, a counterpart to a boy's castration anxiety. She believes she has lost her penis; he fears he will lose his.

This female Oedipus complex, Freud suggested, can never be totally resolved, a situation he believed led to poorly developed superegos in women. Freud wrote that an adult woman's love for a man is always tinged with penis envy, for which she can partially compensate by having a male child. The girl comes to identify with the mother and repress her love for her father, but Freud was not specific about how this occurs.

The phallic personality. Phallic conflicts and their degree of resolution are of major importance in determining adult relations with and attitudes toward the opposite sex. Poorly resolved conflicts can cause lingering forms of castration anxiety and penis envy. The so-called phallic character or personality type evidences strong narcissism. Although continually acting to attract the opposite sex, these persons have difficulty establishing mature heterosexual relationships. They need continual recognition and appreciation of their attractive and unique qualities. As long as they receive such support they function well, but when it is lacking they feel inadequate and inferior.

Freud described the male phallic personality as brash, vain, and self-assured. Men with this personality try to assert or express their masculinity through activities such as repeated sexual conquests. The female phallic personality, motivated by penis envy, exaggerates her femininity and uses her talents and charms to overwhelm and conquer men.

Electra complex
During the phallic stage (ages 4 to 5), the unconscious desire of a girl for her father, accompanied by a desire to replace or destroy her mother.

penis envy
The envy the female feels toward the male because the male possesses a penis; this is accompanied by a sense of loss because the female does not have a penis.

The tense drama of the phallic stage is repressed in all of us. Its effects motivate us as adults at the unconscious level, and we recall little, if anything, of the conflict.

The Latency Period

The storms and stresses of the oral, anal, and phallic stages of psychosexual development are the amalgam out of which most of the adult personality is shaped. The three major structures of the personality—the id, ego, and superego—have been formed by approximately the age of 5, and the relationships among them are being solidified.

latency period
To Freud, the period from approximately age 5 to puberty, during which the sex instinct is dormant, sublimated in school activities, sports, and hobbies, and in developing friendships with members of the same sex.

Fortunately, because the child and parents certainly could use some rest, the next 5 or 6 years are quiet. The **latency period** is not a psychosexual stage of development. The sex instinct is dormant, temporarily sublimated in school activities, hobbies, and sports and in developing friendships with members of the same sex.

The Genital Stage

The genital stage, the final psychosexual stage of development, begins at puberty. The body is becoming physiologically mature, and if no major fixations have occurred at an earlier stage of development, the individual may be able to lead a normal life. Freud believed that the conflict during this period is less intense than in the other stages. The adolescent must conform to societal sanctions and taboos that exist concerning sexual expression, but conflict is minimized through sublimation. The sexual energy pressing for expression in the teenage years can be at least partially satisfied through the pursuit of socially acceptable substitutes and, later, through a committed adult relationship with a person of the opposite sex. The genital personality type is able to find satisfaction in love and work, the latter being an acceptable outlet for sublimation of the id impulses.

Freud emphasized the importance of the early childhood years in determining the adult personality. According to Freud, the first 5 years are the crucial ones. His personality theory pays less attention to later childhood and adolescence, and he was little concerned with personality development in adulthood. To Freud, what we are as adults—how we behave, think, and feel—is determined by the conflicts to which we are exposed and with which we must cope before many of us have even learned to read.

Questions About Human Nature

Freud did not present us with a flattering or optimistic image of human nature. Quite the opposite. He suggested that each person is a dark cellar of conflict in which a battle continually rages. Human beings are depicted in pessimistic terms, condemned to a struggle with our inner forces, a struggle we are almost always destined to lose. Doomed to anxiety, to the thwarting of at least some of our driving impulses, we experience continual tension and conflict. We are endlessly defending ourselves against the forces of the id, which stand ever alert to topple us.

In Freud's system, there is only one ultimate and necessary goal in life: to reduce tension. On the nature–nurture issue, Freud adopted a middle ground. The id, the most powerful part of the personality, is an inherited, physiologically based structure, as are the stages of psychosexual development. However, other parts of our personality are learned in early childhood, from parent–child interactions.

Although Freud recognized universality in human nature, in that we all pass through the same stages of psychosexual development and are motivated by the same id forces, he asserted that part of the personality is unique to each person. The ego and superego perform the same functions for everyone, but their content varies from one person to another because they are formed through personal experience. Also, different character types can develop during the psychosexual stages.

On the issue of free will versus determinism, Freud held a deterministic view: Virtually everything we do, think, and dream is predetermined by the life and death instincts, the inaccessible and invisible forces within us. Our adult personality is determined by interactions that occurred before we were 5, at a time when we had limited control. These experiences forever hold us in their grip.

Freud also argued, however, that people who underwent psychoanalysis could achieve the ability to exercise increased free will and take responsibility for their choices. "The more the individual is able to make conscious what had been unconscious, the more he or she can take charge of his or her own life" (Solnit, 1992, p. 66). Thus, Freud suggested that psychoanalysis had the potential to liberate people from the constraints of determinism.

Freud's overall picture of human nature, painted in these bleak hues, reflects his personal view of humanity, which darkened with age and declining health. His judgment of people in general was harsh. "I have found little that is 'good' about human beings on the whole. In my experience, most of them are trash" (Freud, 1963, pp. 61–62). We can see this stern judgment in his personality theory.

Assessment in Freud's Theory

Freud considered the unconscious to be the major motivating force in life; our childhood conflicts are repressed out of conscious awareness. The goal of Freud's system of psychoanalysis was to bring these repressed memories, fears, and thoughts back to the level of consciousness. How can the psychoanalyst evaluate or assess this invisible portion of the mind, this dark arena that is otherwise inaccessible to us? Over the course of his work with patients, Freud developed two methods of assessment: free association and dream analysis.

Free Association

free association
A technique in which the patient says whatever comes to mind. In other words, it is a kind of daydreaming out loud.

Freud's development of the technique of **free association** owes much to Josef Breuer, a Viennese physician who befriended Freud during Freud's early years in private practice. In treating a young woman who showed symptoms of hysteria, Breuer found that hypnotizing her enabled her to remember repressed events. Recalling the events—in a sense, reliving the experiences—brought relief of the disturbing symptoms.

catharsis
The expression of emotions that is expected to lead to the reduction of disturbing symptoms.

Freud used the technique with some success and called the process **catharsis**, from the Greek word for purification. After a while, however, Freud abandoned hypnosis, partly because he had difficulty hypnotizing some of his patients. Also, some patients revealed disturbing events during hypnosis but were unable to recall those events when questioned later.

Seeking a technique other than hypnosis for helping a patient recall repressed material, Freud asked the person to lie on a couch while he sat behind it, out of sight. (Freud may have chosen this arrangement because he disliked being stared at.) He encouraged the patient to relax and to concentrate on events in the past. The patient was to engage in a kind of daydreaming out loud, saying whatever came to mind. He or she was instructed to express spontaneously every idea and image exactly as it occurred, no matter how trivial, embarrassing, or painful the thought or memory might seem. The memories were not to be omitted, rearranged, or restructured.

Freud believed that there was nothing random about the information uncovered during free association and that it was not subject to a patient's conscious choice. The material revealed by patients in free association was predetermined, forced on them by the nature of their conflict.

He also found that sometimes the technique did not operate freely. Some experiences or memories were evidently too painful to talk about, and the patient would be reluctant to disclose them. Freud called these moments **resistances**. He believed they were significant because they indicate proximity to the source of the patient's problems. Resistance is a sign that the treatment is proceeding in the right direction and that the analyst should continue to probe in that area. Part of the psychoanalyst's task is to break down or overcome resistances so the patient can confront the repressed experience.

resistance
In free association, a blockage or refusal to disclose painful memories.

Dream Analysis

Freud believed that dreams represent, in symbolic form, repressed desires, fears, and conflicts. So strongly have these feelings been repressed that they can surface only in disguised fashion during sleep.

In his technique of **dream analysis**, Freud distinguished two aspects of dreams: the manifest content, which refers to the actual events in the dream, and the latent content, which is the hidden symbolic meaning of the dream's events. Over the years, Freud found consistent symbols in his patients' dreams, events that signified the same thing for nearly everyone (see Table 1.3). For example, steps, ladders, and staircases in a dream represented sexual intercourse. Candles, snakes, and tree trunks indicated the penis, and boxes, balconies, and doors signified the female body. Freud warned that despite this apparent universality of symbols, many symbols are specific to the person undergoing analysis and could have a different meaning for someone else.

dream analysis
A technique involving the interpretation of dreams to uncover unconscious conflicts. Dreams have a manifest content (the actual events in the dream) and a latent content (the symbolic meaning of the dream events).

Dreams reveal conflicts in a condensed, intensified form. Dream events rarely result from a single cause; any event in a dream can have many sources. Dreams may also have mundane origins. Physical stimuli, such as the temperature of the bedroom or contact with one's partner, can induce a dream, and dreams can also be triggered by internal stimuli, such as a fever or an upset stomach.

Table 1.3 **Dream symbols or events and their latent psychoanalytic meaning.**

Symbol	Interpretation
Smooth-fronted house	Male body
House with ledges, balconies	Female body
King and queen	Parents
Small animals	Children
Children	Genital organs
Playing with children	Masturbation
Baldness, tooth extraction	Castration
Elongated objects (e.g., tree trunks, umbrellas, neckties, snakes, candles)	Male genitals
Enclosed spaces (e.g., boxes, ovens, closets, caves, pockets)	Female genitals
Climbing stairs or ladders; driving cars; riding horses; crossing bridges	Sexual intercourse
Bathing	Birth
Beginning a journey	Dying
Being naked in a crowd	Desiring to be noticed
Flying	Desiring to be admired
Falling	Desiring to return to a state such as childhood where one is satisfied and protected

It is interesting that of the more than 40 of his own dreams Freud described in his book *The Interpretation of Dreams*, only a few had a sexual content, despite his conviction that dreams typically involve some infantile sexual wish. The dominant theme in Freud's reported dreams was ambition, a characteristic he denied having.

Both of these Freudian assessment techniques—free association and dream analysis—reveal to the psychoanalyst a great deal of repressed material, but all of it is in disguised or symbolic form. The therapist then must interpret or translate the material for the patient. Freud compared this procedure with the task of an archeologist reconstructing a community that has been destroyed and buried under the accumulation of centuries. Just as the archeologist attempts to reconstruct a building from broken fragments, so a psychoanalyst reconstructs an experience from buried, fragmented memories. Thus, the evaluation or assessment of a patient's personality, the uncovering of his or her unconscious conflicts, depends on the skill, training, and experience of the analyst.

Research on Freud's Theory

case study
A detailed history of an individual that contains data from a variety of sources.

Freud's major research method was the case study. We noted in the introduction that the case study method has several limitations. It does not rely on objective observation, the data are not gathered in systematic fashion, and the situation (the psychoanalytic session) is not amenable to duplication and verification. In addition, we cannot systematically vary the conditions of childhood in which patients are reared, nor can we replicate in the laboratory a person's home environment. Thus, clinical observations cannot be repeated, as they can in controlled psychological experiments.

A fundamental criticism of Freud's case studies involves the nature of his data. He did not keep verbatim records of the therapy sessions, and he warned analysts against taking notes during the sessions, believing it would distract their attention from their patients' words. Freud made notes several hours after seeing each patient. Describing his technique for recording his patients' comments, Freud said, "I write them down from memory in the evening after work is over" (quoted in Grubrich-Simitis, 1998, p. 20). Thus, it is possible that his data were incomplete, consisting only of what he later remembered.

It is also possible that his recollection was selective and that he recorded only the experiences that would support his theory, or that he interpreted those experiences in ways that would support his theory. Of course, Freud's notes may have been highly accurate, but we cannot be certain; we are unable to compare his case reports with what his patients said.

Even if Freud had kept a complete record of the therapy sessions, we cannot determine the validity of the patients' comments. Freud made few attempts to verify the accuracy of a patient's stories, which he might have done by questioning the patient's friends and relatives about the events described. Therefore, we must characterize the first step in Freud's research, the collection of data, as incomplete and inaccurate.

Some critics also suggest that Freud's patients did not actually reveal childhood sexual experiences because, in most cases, those experiences had never occurred. These writers argue that Freud inferred the stories of sexual seduction in childhood from his analysis of the patients' symptoms. For example, although Freud claimed that virtually all his women patients said they had been seduced by their fathers, his case notes do not show that any patient ever claimed that this had occurred (Kihlstrom, 1994).

Other critics agree that Freud was suggesting accounts of childhood seduction, without really hearing his patients say so, because he had already formed the hypothesis that such seductions were the true cause of adult neuroses. Still others charge that Freud may have used the power of suggestion to elicit or implant alleged memories of childhood seduction that had never taken place (McCullough, 2001). "Where patients did not of their own accord provide material which could be construed in sexual terms, Freud did not hesitate to point them in the 'right' direction" (Webster, 1995, p. 197).

Another criticism of Freud's research is that it is based on a small and unrepresentative sample of people, restricted to him and to those who sought psychoanalysis with him. Only a dozen or so cases have been detailed in Freud's writings, and most of these were of young, unmarried, upper-class women of good education. It is difficult to generalize from this limited sample to the population at large.

In addition, there may be discrepancies between Freud's notes on his therapy sessions and the case histories he published, which supposedly were based on these notes. Several investigators compared Freud's notes with the published case study of the Rat Man, one of his most famous patients. They found a lengthening of the period of analysis, an incorrect sequence of events disclosed by the patient, and unsubstantiated claims that the analysis resulted in a cure (Eagle, 1988; Mahoney, 1986). Thus, the published version of the case did not agree with the notes Freud made after his sessions with the patient. It is not possible to determine whether Freud deliberately made these changes to bolster his theory (or his ego) or whether they were the products of his unconscious. Nor do we know if such distortions characterize other Freudian case studies. It will remain a mystery because Freud destroyed most of his patient files not long after he compiled them.

Finally, it has been argued that none of Freud's handful of published case histories provides compelling supporting evidence for the theory. One of Freud's biographers concluded: "Some of the cases present such dubious evidence in favor of psychoanalytic theory that one may seriously wonder why Freud even bothered to publish them" (Sulloway, 1992, p. 160).

We see in later chapters that the criticisms leveled against Freud also apply to most of the later personality theorists who chose a neopsychoanalytic approach. They, too, used the case study as their primary research method and based their theories on their patients' reports. This does not mean that their work is devoid of merit; Freud and other analysts have offered a wealth of material about the human personality. If we accept their views as valid, however, we must do so on some basis other than experimental verification.

Although Freud was familiar with the experimental method, he had little confidence in it. An American psychologist once sent him information about experiments that had been conducted to validate Freudian concepts. Freud "threw the reprints across the table in a gesture of impatient rejection" and wrote to the psychologist that he did not "put much value on such confirmation" (Rosenzweig, 1985, pp. 171, 173). He believed there was no need for the kinds of experiments published in the psychology journals of the day because "they told him nothing more than he had already learned from his clinical encounters with patients" (Holzman, 1994, p. 190).

Freud insisted that his work was scientific, that he had amassed ample proof for his conclusions, and that only psychoanalysts who used his techniques were qualified to judge the scientific worth of his work. Freud wrote that psychoanalysis was based on "an incalculable number of observations and experiences, and only someone who has repeated those observations on himself and on others is in a position to arrive at a judgment of his own upon it" (Freud, 1940, p. 144). Difficulty arises because Freud's observations cannot be repeated. We do not know exactly what he did in collecting his data and in translating his observations into hypotheses and generalizations.

Scientific Validation of Freudian Concepts

In the years since Freud's death in 1939, many of his ideas have been submitted to experimental testing. In an exhaustive analysis of some 2,500 studies in psychology, psychiatry, anthropology, and related disciplines, Seymour Fisher and Roger Greenberg evaluated the scientific credibility of some of Freud's ideas. In this evaluation, case histories were not considered. Every effort was made to restrict the investigation to data thought to have a high degree of objectivity (Fisher & Greenberg, 1977, 1996).

The researchers found that some Freudian concepts—notably the id, ego, superego, death wish, libido, and anxiety—could not be tested by the experimental method. Concepts that could be so tested, and which evidence appeared to support, included the oral and anal character types, the basic concept of the Oedipal triangle, castration anxiety, and the notion that females resolve the Oedipal dilemma by having a child as compensation for the lack of a penis.

Concepts not supported by research evidence include those of dreams as disguised expressions of repressed wishes, resolution of the male Oedipus complex by identification with the father and acceptance of the father's superego standards out of fear, and the idea that women have inadequately developed superegos. In addition, researchers found no evidence to support the psychosexual stages of development or a relationship between Oedipal variables and sexual difficulties later in life.

The unconscious. The notion that unconscious forces can influence conscious thought and behavior is now well established. One personality researcher observed that "today there is agreement that much [psychological] functioning occurs without conscious choice and that some of our behavior actually occurs in opposition to what is consciously desired" (Pervin, 2003, p. 225). Psychologists also recognize that much of the information processing involved in cognitive activities is unconscious. Some even propose that the causal mechanisms underlying all behavior and thought may be unconscious (Bargh & Chartrand, 1999; Wegner & Wheatley, 1999).

> It now appears that the unconscious is "smarter" than first thought, capable of processing complex verbal and visual information and even anticipating (and planning for) future events.... No longer simply a repository for drives and impulses, the unconscious appears to play a role in problem solving, hypothesis testing, and creativity. (Bornstein & Masling, 1998, p. xx)

subliminal perception
Perception below the threshold of conscious awareness.

Much research on the nature of the unconscious involves **subliminal perception** (also called subliminal psychodynamic activation), in which stimuli are presented to research participants below their level of conscious awareness. (The word *subliminal* derives from *sub*, meaning below, and *limen*, meaning threshold.) Despite their inability to perceive the stimuli, the research participants' conscious processes and behavior are activated by the stimuli. In other words, people can be influenced by stimuli of which they are not consciously aware.

In one such study, research participants were shown a series of words and pictures for such a brief time that they could not consciously perceive them (Shevrin, 1977). Then they were asked to free-associate. What the research participants talked about reflected the stimuli they had been shown but had not actually been able to see. For example, when the stimulus was a picture of a bee, the associations included the words *sting* and *honey*. The research participants' thought processes were affected by the stimuli, even though they were unaware of having seen them. Many such studies using subliminal perception support the idea that cognitive activity is influenced by the unconscious (Westen, 1998).

A series of experiments on college students in the United States and in Germany showed that goals could be aroused, or activated, outside of conscious awareness. Also, behaviors to satisfy these goals were displayed, even though the research participants were not consciously aware of doing so. For example, the aroused goal of performing better on an experimental task led participants to actually perform better. In another instance, the unconsciously activated goal of being cooperative on an experimental task led to cooperative behaviors. The authors of the study concluded that "behavioral goals can become activated without any consciously made choice required" (Bargh, Gollwitzer, Lee-Chai, Barndollar, & Troetschel, 2001, p. 18).

A study of 124 adults in England found that those who scored high in anxiety sensitivity were far more likely to see anxiety-related words that were presented below the level of conscious awareness than were adults who scored low in anxiety sensitivity. The sensitivity of the first group made them more vigilant and thus more likely to perceive anxiety-related words, even though the words were presented so rapidly that the people did not consciously see them (Hunt, Keogh, & French, 2006).

Stimuli presented below conscious awareness can also influence behavior. When 39 college students in the United States were shown happy faces, below the level of conscious awareness, they consumed more of a beverage that was made available to them than did students who were exposed to images of angry faces. The happy-face group also indicated a greater willingness to pay for their drink and to want more of it than did the angry-face group. Although none of the students consciously saw the faces, the stimuli had registered in their unconscious and acted to influence their behavior (Winkielman, Berridge, & Wilbarger, 2005).

Other imaginative research has demonstrated that the unconscious can influence emotional as well as cognitive and behavioral processes. In one such study, the words *Mommy and I are one* were flashed for 4 milliseconds to research participants, along with a picture of a man and a woman joined together at their shoulders. Male schizophrenic patients exposed to this subliminally presented stimulus showed a greater improvement than did a control group not exposed to that message. Female schizophrenic patients showed no improvement when exposed to that message but did show improvement when presented with the subliminal message: *Daddy and I are one* (Silverman & Weinberger, 1985).

In other studies, the *Mommy and I are one* message was effective in helping a variety of research participants stop smoking and drinking, become more assertive, eat a more healthful diet, and reduce fears. Thus, a subliminally presented message of which the research participants have no conscious awareness has been shown to have therapeutic value (Weinberger & Silverman, 1990).

The ego. We noted that Freud viewed the ego's role as constantly mediating between reality and the insistent demands of the id. The ego is the rational part of the personality that must control and postpone the id's demands, balancing them with the circumstances of the real world. Psychoanalytic researchers have identified two components of the ego:

- ego control
- ego resiliency

Ego control, as you would expect from the name, is close to Freud's original conception. It refers to the amount of control we are able to exert over our impulses and feelings. The degree of ego-control ranges from under-controlled (in which we are unable to restrain any impulses and feelings) to over-controlled (in which we tightly inhibit the expression of our impulses). Both extremes are considered maladaptive.

Ego resiliency refers to our flexibility in modulating, adjusting, or changing our typical level of ego control to meet the daily changes in our environment. Persons with little ego resiliency are referred to as "ego brittle," meaning they are unable to alter their level of ego control to meet challenges or difficult life situations. Those high in ego resiliency are flexible and adaptable, able to tighten or loosen their degree of ego control as the situation warrants. Mothers between the ages of 21 and 27 who rated their mothering experiences as positive and satisfying were found to have increased, or remained high in, ego resiliency. Mothers who rated their mothering experiences as negative were found to have decreased ego resiliency. The researchers suggested that difficult life situations, setbacks and failures, or other negative experiences tend to lower ego resiliency (Paris & Helson, 2002).

Research has shown that children who score low on laboratory and observational measures of ego control are rated by their teachers as more aggressive and less compliant and orderly than children high on ego control. Children who score high on ego resiliency are rated by their teachers as better able to cope with stress, lower in anxiety, and less in need of reassurance than children low in ego resiliency.

High ego resiliency also correlated positively with general intelligence, good grades in school, and popularity with peers. Low ego control in boys and girls, and low ego resiliency in girls, was related positively to drug abuse in adolescence. Thus, important aspects of personality and behavior can be linked to ego control and ego resiliency (Block & Block, 1980; Shiner, 1998).

Ego control and ego resiliency were measured in a group of nearly 200 college students based on self-reports and descriptions from acquaintances and clinicians. Those low in ego control tended to be unpredictable, assertive, rebellious, moody, and self-indulgent. Those very high in ego control were described as bland, consistent, dependable, and calm. Students rated high in ego resilience were assertive, poised, socially skilled, and cheerful (Letzring, Block, & Funder, 2005).

A longitudinal study of 128 people that periodically assessed these personality characteristics from ages 3 to 23 found that both ego control and ego resiliency were generally stronger later in life than in childhood. Individual differences in ego control were seen at various ages, suggesting that one's degree of ego control could be identified early (Block & Block, 2006).

Another approach to defining ego control is in terms of three levels of development: pre-conformist, conformist, and post-conformist (Loevinger, 1976). The pre-conformist level is the most primitive, allowing the least control over impulse expression. The conformist level moderates impulse expression in terms of our awareness of the expectations of others and of the culture's rules of appropriate social conduct. At this stage of ego development we place a premium on being accepted by others. We are able to delay or redirect the manner, time, and place for expressing our impulses. The most mature stage of ego development is the post-conformist level. People at this level are highly conscientious and individualistic and rely more on personal goals and standards of appropriate conduct than on the standards of others.

A study of 248 identical and fraternal twins ages 16 to 70, separated at infancy and reared in different environments, used a self-report inventory to compare their levels of ego development. Although the research participants had been raised in different adoptive homes, the ego development of each pair of twins correlated significantly. The researchers concluded that their results indicated that ego development may be a heritable characteristic. Contrary to Freud's theory, the level of ego development among these research participants had been determined more by genetic factors than by child–parent interaction (Newman, Tellegen, & Bouchard, 1998).

Catharsis. To Freud, catharsis involved the physical expression of an emotion by recalling a traumatic event, which often led to relief of the disturbing symptom. In popular culture, the term *catharsis* has come to refer to expressing one's emotion as a way of reducing hostility and aggression. Self-help books urge us to give vent to anger by taking it out on some inanimate object—beating a pillow, breaking a dish, or hitting a punching bag. Does this work? Does acting out aggressively reduce negative emotions? The answer is no.

In one study of catharsis, two groups of college students were exposed to messages that either supported or disputed the notion that cathartic behavior is a good way of relieving anger. Next, some of the students were experimentally provoked to anger; an essay they had written was severely criticized. They were told that their paper was one of the worst essays ever written!

Students who were thus provoked and who had read the pro-catharsis message were significantly more prone to act out their aggression by hitting a punching bag. In a second experiment, those who received the pro-catharsis message not only hit the punching bag but also behaved aggressively toward the person who had annoyed them by criticizing their writing. They even displayed heightened aggression toward innocent people who had played no role in promoting their anger. Apparently, striking the punching bag had not been cathartic. It had not dissipated their anger but might even have increased it (Bushman, Baumeister, & Stack, 1999).

In another punching-bag study, male and female college students displayed more aggression toward the person who had angered them when they were instructed to think about that person while hitting the bag. Students who were told to think about how they could become physically fit while hitting the bag displayed significantly less aggression toward the person who angered them. Those who did not vent their anger by punching the bag displayed the fewest aggressive behaviors toward the person who had angered them. The experimenter suggested that these results reinforced the idea that venting anger does not reduce negative emotions (Bushman, 2002).

Displacement. Displacement involves shifting one's id impulses from a disturbing object that is not available to a substitute object or person. An analysis of 97 relevant studies supported the contention that displaced aggression is a viable and reliable phenomenon. The analysis also found that the more negative and stressful the setting or context in which displacement occurs, the greater the intensity of that displacement (Marcus-Newhall, Pedersen, Miller, & Carlson, 2000).

A study of 520 college students found that those in a group that was experimentally provoked to anger, and then left to spend 25 minutes focusing their attention on their angry thoughts and feelings, were far more likely to demonstrate displaced aggression than those whose experimental condition did not include the 25 minutes of brooding. The researchers concluded that dwelling on anger maintains the feeling and is likely to cause it to be expressed outwardly in aggressive behavior (Bushman, Bonacci, Pedersen, Vasquez, & Miller, 2005).

Repression. Experimental investigations of the Freudian defense mechanism of repression—the involuntary removal of some threatening idea or memory from conscious awareness—have provided supportive results, although some psychologists have questioned whether the work relates to repression precisely as Freud proposed it. In one study, research participants memorized two lists of words that were flashed on a screen (Glucksberg & King, 1967). Some words on the lists were conceptually similar; for example, *cats* and *dogs* are both animals. The research participants were given an electric shock with some words on the first list. No shocks were administered with the words on the second list. Then the research participants were tested on how well they remembered the words. The research participants forgot the words accompanied by the shock but recalled those not accompanied by the shock. They also repressed words on the second list that were conceptually similar to the words on the first list that had been accompanied by a shock. The researchers concluded that the threatening words had been pushed out of conscious awareness.

Research conducted in Australia identified research participants as "repressors" and "non-repressors based" on personality test scores that showed repressors to be low in anxiety and high in defensiveness. Repressors recalled fewer emotional experiences from childhood, particularly those involving fear and self-consciousness, than did non-repressors. In related research, repressors and non-repressors were compared on several experimental tasks. When they were shown pictures of neutral, non-threatening stimuli and pictures of embarrassing, threatening stimuli, the repressors avoided looking at the latter. When repressors were asked to free-associate to phrases with sexual or aggressive content (presumably threatening material), physiological measurements showed them to be highly emotionally aroused, yet their verbal responses gave no hint of anger or sexual arousal because they had repressed their emotional reactions. Non-repressors did not inhibit their emotional reactions, and this was evident in their verbal responses (Davis, 1987).

More recent studies conducted in Britain confirmed the Australian findings. Repressors were found to have significantly poorer recall of negative memories from childhood (Myers & Derakshan, 2004). In addition, repressors were shown to be far more likely to avoid romantic attachments than were non-repressors (Vetere & Myers, 2002).

Later research showed that repressors were significantly more likely than non-repressors to deny possessing personality traits they had identified as personally emotionally threatening (traits such as selfishness, laziness, rudeness, and dishonesty). Repressors also had fewer unpleasant or threatening emotional memories available for retrieval than did non-repressors because they had repressed them (Newman, Duff, & Baumeister, 1997; Newman & McKinney, 2002; Schimmack & Hartmann, 1997).

In another study, repressors and non-repressors were shown a disturbing film about animal mutation and lingering death from the effects of nuclear testing. When then asked to recall a personal experience that made them happy, repressors could recall more pleasant events and thoughts than could non-repressors. The researchers concluded that the repressors coped with the negative stimuli in the film by accessing positive memories. Thus, repressors did not experience to the same frequency and degree as non-repressors the distressing emotional states engendered by the film. The repressors were not merely pretending to be unaffected; they had repressed the experience successfully (Boden & Baumeister, 1997).

In research using physiological measures to differentiate repressors and non-repressors, the galvanic skin response (GSR) was taken to indicate the presence of stress, anxiety, and fear. When college students identified earlier as repressors or non-repressors were given a stressful speech assignment, repressors showed a significantly greater increase in GSR activity than non-repressors. The researchers concluded that repressors react automatically to threatening situations with increased levels of physiological stress (Barger, Kircher, & Croyle, 1997).

Studies have also found links between the repressive coping style and (1) high cholesterol level and (2) high cortisol level (cortisol is a stress hormone) (Brown, Tomarkin, Orth, Loosen, Kalin, & Davidson, 1996; Weinberger, 1995). Thus, repression may be effective in protecting us from anxiety, but its continued use may also be harmful to our physical health.

Repression was studied in two groups of children in the United States. Some of the children were healthy; others had cancer or other chronic debilitating illnesses. It was found that the sick children were more likely to be repressors and less likely to express anger than were the healthy children (Phipps & Steele, 2002).

In a group of 443 male and female college students, repressors were found to be less likely to smoke and drink than were non-repressors. Repressors in this study scored higher than non-repressors on the belief that excessive drinking would not lead to harmful consequences for them (Shirachi & Spirrison, 2006).

Other defense mechanisms. Researchers have suggested a hierarchy among the Freudian defense mechanisms in which the simpler ones are used earlier in life and the more complex ones emerge as we grow older. For example, studies show that denial (a simple, low-level defense mechanism) is used mostly by young children and less by adolescents. Identification, a more complex defense, is used considerably more by adolescents than by younger children (Brody, Rozek, & Muten, 1985; Cramer, 1987, 1990).

In research on students from grades 2, 5, 8, and 11, and first-year college classes, responses to the Thematic Apperception Test pictures showed clear age differences in defense mechanisms. The use of denial and projection decreased with age whereas identification increased with age (Porcerelli, Thomas, Hibbard, & Cogan, 1998). A longitudinal study of 150 students ages 11 to 18 found that the projection and identification defenses were used more often than denial, and that their use increased from early to late adolescence (Cramer, 2007).

Freud's contention that people with different forms of emotional disturbance tend to use different defenses has found moderate to strong research support. For example, people with obsessive-compulsive personalities are prone to use reaction formation as a defense, people with paranoid personalities are more likely to use projection, and people with passive-aggressive personalities are apt to rely on displacement (Busch, Shear, Cooper, Shapiro, & Leon, 1995; Sammallahti & Aalberg, 1995).

A longitudinal study of 90 research participants who were first tested in nursery school and later at age 23 found a link between preschool personality and the use of denial as young adults. As we noted earlier, denial tends to be used as a defense mechanism mostly by children and its use typically declines with age. In this study, however, the male research participants who at age 23 were still using denial had a number of psychological problems that had been identified when they were in nursery school. Their childhood personalities were characterized as high in emotional immaturity and unworthiness and low in personal competence and ego resiliency. For female research participants, no such clear relationship was found between childhood personality and the continued use of denial at age 23. The authors of the study suggested that boys might be more vulnerable to stress than girls (Cramer & Block, 1998).

Two studies conducted in Canada demonstrated that adolescent girls with anorexia nervosa (an eating disorder) and older women who had been victims of spouse abuse were far more likely to use denial as a coping mechanism than were girls or women who were not in these categories. The researchers suggested that by unconsciously denying their difficulties, the girls and women were attempting to minimize or distance themselves from the situations (Arokach, 2006; Couturier & Lock, 2006).

A study of 115 adult men found that those who tried to protect themselves from feelings of weakness by being more powerful and competitive and who avoided emotional expression tended to use more immature defense mechanisms. Those men who did not feel so great a need to be more powerful than others and who could express their emotions more freely used more mature defense mechanisms (Mahalik, Cournoyer, DeFrank, Cherry, & Napolitano, 1998).

Studies on the mechanism of projection—attributing one's negative traits and behaviors to someone else—have found that accusing another person of lying and cheating in a game increased the amount of blame placed on that person and reduced the amount of blame the research participant placed on himself or herself for showing the same negative behaviors (Rucker & Pratkanis, 2001).

Projection can also influence our judgments about our spouses or partners. A study of unemployed job seekers found that they projected their feelings of depression about the stresses of unemployment onto their partners when asked to make everyday judgments about them. Further, the more alike the partners were on a psychological measure of depression, the greater was the tendency for one to project that feeling when judging the other. The researchers noted: "Individuals seem more likely to assume that their spouses are like them when their spouses actually *are* like them" (Schul & Vinokur, 2000, p. 997). Thus, in this instance, the research participants were accurate in projecting their own characteristics onto their spouses or partners.

The notion of defense mechanisms was proposed and developed in a European setting from studies of White middle-class patients. Much of the ensuing research conducted on defense mechanisms was performed using research participants in the

United States. In an unusual study of Asians and Americans, a group of research participants in the United States was compared with a group of Asian Buddhists living in Thailand. A self-report inventory, the Instruments Life Style Index, was used to assess the use of defense mechanisms. The researchers found a strong similarity between people in the two cultures in their use of regression, reaction formation, projection, repression, denial, and compensation (Tori & Bilmes, 2002).

Dreams. Research on dreams has confirmed Freud's idea that dreams, in disguised or symbolic form, reflect emotional concerns. However, research does not appear to show that dreams represent a fulfillment of wishes or desires, as Freud proposed (Breger, Hunter, & Lane, 1971; Dement & Wolpert, 1958). Nevertheless, it does seem clear that dreams often are characterized by highly emotional content from the dreamers' lives. Large-scale surveys of German citizens during the period 1956–2000 showed that those old enough to have been affected directly by World War II (1939–1945) were still experiencing emotional war-related dreams more than 50 years after the war ended (Schredl & Piel, 2006). Studies of Kurdish and of Palestinian children who are exposed to physical dangers in their everyday lives show that they dream about threatening and traumatic situations far more than do children of these and of other cultures who are reared in more peaceful, non-threatening surroundings (Valli, Revonsuo, Palkas, & Punamaki, 2006).

A long-term study of 28 adults in Canada who kept diaries of their dreams showed a significant correlation between the nature of the dreams and self-report measures of psychological well-being. Those with lower levels of psychological well-being (and, thus, presumably, those who were less happy) reported more dreams of aggression toward others, negative emotions, and failure and misfortune. Those with higher levels of psychological well-being reported dreams of friendly interactions with others, positive emotions, and success and good fortune (Pesant & Zadra, 2006).

Other research confirmed that dreams reflect real-life experiences and that the emotional intensity of these experiences, as well as the person's mood, influences the stories and themes of the dreams (see, for example, Schredl, 2006; Schredl, Funkhouser, & Arn, 2006). Briefly, it may be that if you are having a bad day, you may have bad dreams that night.

Cultural differences in dreaming have been studied in several populations. A comparison of the dreams of college students in the United States and China revealed that the Chinese students reported more familiar people in their dreams and fewer aggressive situations than did the American students (Xian-Li & Guang-Xing, 2006).

A study of Caucasian and Asian-American college students showed that in childhood, the Caucasians were much more likely to tell their parents about their dreams. They were also more likely as they got older to describe their dreams to friends and to place a high value on their dreams. The Asian-American students were secretive about their dreams with their parents and with other people and were highly reluctant to talk about them (Fiske & Pillemer, 2006).

When Chinese college students were asked whether they dream in color or in black-and-white, those who had watched black-and-white television and films as children answered that they dreamed in black-and-white. Those who had greater exposure to color television and movies dreamed in color (Schwitzgebel, Huang, & Zhou, 2006).

The Oedipus complex. In an observational study to test the effects of the Oedipus complex, parents of boys and girls ages 3 to 6 years were asked to record affectionate behaviors and aggressive or hostile behaviors their children directed toward them. The results showed that acts of affection toward the parent of the opposite sex and displays of aggression toward the parent of the same sex occurred significantly more frequently than the reverse situation. These types of Oedipal behaviors were greatest around age 4 and began to decline by age 5 (Watson & Getz, 1990).

Dreams analyzed in research on the Oedipus complex supported Freud's theory in that significantly more men reported dreams reflecting castration anxiety, and significantly more women reported dreams reflecting castration wishes or penis envy (Hall & Van de Castle, 1965).

Freud proposed that penis envy in girls leads them to view the father as a love object, a desire later supplanted by the wish for a baby. In an experimental test of this proposal, college-age women research participants were exposed to subliminal messages containing pregnancy themes. Their later responses on an inkblot test were found to contain significantly more phallic imagery than the responses of women in the control group or of college-age men research participants exposed to the same stimuli. These results support Freud's belief that pregnancy has phallic significance for women (Jones, 1994).

A study conducted in Wales of 66 boys and girls ages 12 to 14 assessed their attitudes toward their parents. The results showed that children who were ambivalent toward their fathers (who viewed them with a mixture of both love and hatred) displayed a less secure attachment toward other people than did children who did not feel ambivalent about their fathers. The researchers noted that this finding supports Freud's insistence on the importance of the father in influencing the child's later relationships (Maio, Fincham, & Lycett, 2000).

Oral and anal personality types. An investigation of the oral personality type showed a strong relationship between the oral orientation, as identified by the Rorschach, and obesity (Masling, Rabie, & Blondheim, 1967). This supports Freud's contention that oral types are preoccupied with eating and drinking. Another study found oral personality types to be more conforming to the suggestions of an authority figure than anal personality types (Tribich & Messer, 1974). According to Freud, oral personalities are dependent and submissive and should be more conforming than anal personalities; anal types tend to be hostile and can be expected to resist conformity.

Freud also contended that women were more orally dependent than men were but later research found no such difference between the sexes (O'Neill & Bornstein, 1990). In general, then, research supports both the oral and anal personality types (Westen, 1998). There is little empirical evidence for the phallic personality type.

Aggression. Another aspect of Freudian theory put to experimental test is the idea that aggression is instinctive and universal. Freud was not alone in taking this position. Scientists who observe animals in their natural surroundings also posit an aggressive instinct in humans and in lower animals, although data from anthropology and psychology have challenged this view. Anthropologists have observed that people in some so-called primitive cultures do not exhibit aggressive behavior. Psychologists who argue against an aggressive instinct suggest that aggressive behavior may be caused by frustration.

Considerable research has demonstrated that although frustration can trigger aggression, it does not always do so. Aggressive responses to frustration can be modified by training. This idea supports the role of learning in aggression. The psychologist Albert Bandura (Chapter 13) has shown that we learn aggressive behavior the same way we learn many social behaviors, primarily by observing aggression in other people and imitating what we have seen.

Age and personality development. Freud proposed that personality was formed by about the age of 5 and was subject to little change thereafter. Studies of personality development over time indicate that the personality characteristics of preschool children changed dramatically, as shown by follow-up studies conducted over 6 to 7 years (Kagan, Kearsley, & Zelazo, 1978). Other studies suggest that the middle childhood years (ages 7 to 12) may be more important in establishing adult personality patterns than the early childhood years.

Noted child development psychologist Jerome Kagan reviewed the literature and concluded that personality appears to depend more on temperament and experiences in later childhood than on early parent–child interactions (Kagan, 1999). Although there is no denying that our first 5 years of life affect our personality, it is now obvious that personality continues to develop well beyond that time.

The Freudian slip. Now in our overview of research on Freudian concepts we come to the well-known Freudian slip. According to Freud, what appears to be ordinary forgetting or a casual lapse in speech is actually a reflection of unconscious motives or anxieties (Freud, 1901).

In research to test this phenomenon, two groups of male research participants were shown the same pairs of words flashed on a computer screen (Motley, 1987). When a buzzer sounded, they were asked to say the words aloud. One group of research participants had electrodes attached and was told that during the experiment they would receive a painful electric shock. This situation was an experimental way of engendering anxiety. In the second group of research participants, the experimenter was an attractive, sexily dressed woman. This group was given a test of sexual anxiety.

Research participants anxious about the electric shock made verbal slips such as *damn shock* when the words on the screen were *sham dock*. Research participants in the sexual anxiety condition revealed that anxiety in verbal slips such as *nude breasts* for *brood nests*. Those who scored high on the sexual anxiety test made the highest number of sex-related Freudian slips. Men in a control group exposed to the same words but to neither anxiety-arousing condition did not make verbal slips. Not all lapses in speech are Freudian slips, of course, but research indicates that at least some may be what Freud said they were—hidden anxieties revealing themselves in embarrassing ways.

Repressed memories of childhood sexual abuse. In the late 1980s, the issue of repressed memories resurfaced in sensational legal proceedings involving people who claimed they suddenly recalled incidents of abuse that had occurred years earlier. Women brought criminal charges against fathers, uncles, and family friends; men brought charges against priests, coaches, and teachers. Some accused persons were convicted and imprisoned on the basis of memories of incidents said to have taken place up to 20 years before.

How extensive is the repressed memory phenomenon in sexual abuse cases? The survey results vary. One study of 105 women (80 percent of whom were African Americans participating in court-ordered substance-abuse treatment programs) found that 54 percent reported a history of childhood sexual abuse. Only 19 percent of these women said they had forgotten the abuse for some period of time and recalled it at a later date (Loftus, Polonsky, & Fullilove, 1994). A survey of 330 male and female psychologists found that 24 percent reported childhood abuse, and 40 percent of those had forgotten the abuse for some period. There were no significant differences in this study between men and women in the incidence of these temporarily repressed memories (Feldman-Summers & Pope, 1994).

These and similar studies rely on retrospective reports—recalling the events up to 40 years after they allegedly occurred. But there is an obvious problem with retrospective research: How do we know the abuses actually happened? One researcher interviewed adult women (86 percent were categorized as low-income Blacks) who were documented victims of childhood abuse. The evidence for the abuse consisted of hospital emergency room records and forensic evidence collected at the time of admission (Williams, 1994). Thus, in this study, we can be certain that the reported incidents had occurred. Interviews with the adult women revealed that 38 percent did not recall the abuse, a figure close to the incidence of repressed memory among the psychologist research participants noted above but higher than the 19 percent reported by the women in the substance abuse treatment program. In the study of victims with documented childhood sexual abuse, the women most likely to have no memory of the event were those who were younger at the time of the abuse and had been molested by someone they knew.

A review of research on repressed memories of childhood sexual abuse concluded that there is ample evidence showing that such abuse can be forgotten for many years before being recalled (Delmonte, 2000). A study of 68 women who had either repressed memories of childhood abuse, recovered such memories, or had never forgotten the experiences found that those who reported recovered memories scored higher on measures of fantasy proneness and dissociation (a splitting off of mental processes into separate streams of awareness) (McNally, Clancy, Schacter, & Pitman, 2000). Such states could, of course, be a result of the childhood trauma.

Despite such impressive evidence to support the existence of repressed memories of childhood sexual abuse that actually occurred, it is important to note that research has also demonstrated how easily false memories can be implanted and recollections distorted, to the point where something that never occurred can be made conscious and appear genuine or threatening (Loftus & Ketcham, 1994; Ofshe & Watters, 1994).

In one study, fifteen 3- and 6-year-old children were interviewed 4 years after they had spent 5 minutes playing with a man while sitting across a table from him. The man never touched any of the children. During the follow-up interviews, the researchers created a climate of accusation by telling the children they would be questioned about an important event in their lives. "Are you afraid to tell?" they were asked. "You'll feel better once you've told" (Ceci & Bruck, 1993, p. 421). One-third of the children agreed with the interviewer's suggestion that, 4 years earlier, they had been hugged and kissed by the man. Two of the children agreed with the suggestion that they had been photographed in the bathroom; one agreed that the man had given her a bath.

A study involving 50 students at the University of Florence, Italy, showed that dream interpretation could be used to implant false memories. Half of the research participants were told by a persuasive psychologist who was a popular radio celebrity that their dreams were manifestations of repressed memories of traumatic childhood events. Examples of these incidents included being abandoned by their parents or being lost in an unfamiliar place. The other half of the subject population did not receive such interpretations of their dreams.

All research participants had been selected on the basis of questionnaire responses completed weeks earlier, when they had stated that no such traumatic events had occurred during their childhood. When questioned 10 to 15 days following the dream interpretations, the majority of the experimental research participants agreed that the traumatic experiences had really happened and that they had repressed the memories for years (Mazzoni, Lombardo, Malvagia, & Loftus, 1999).

Elizabeth Loftus, a pioneering researcher in the area, concluded that overall,

> there is little support for the notion that trauma is commonly banished out of awareness and later reliably recovered by processes beyond ordinary forgetting and remembering.... There can be no doubt that "memories" for factually fake as well as impossible, or at least highly improbable, horrific traumatic events were developed [or implanted], particularly among persons subjected to suggestive memory recovery procedures. (Loftus & Davis, 2006, pp. 6, 8)

However, it is important to keep in mind that childhood sexual abuse does occur. It is a haunting reality for many people and far more widespread than Sigmund Freud envisioned in the 19th century. The effects can be debilitating. Men and women who were sexually abused as children have strong tendencies toward anxiety, depression, self-destructiveness, low self-esteem, and suicide (see, for example, McNally, Perlman, Ristuccia, & Clancy, 2006; Pilkington & Lenaghan, 1998; Westen, 1998).

Extensions of Freudian Theory

Several of the theorists we discuss in the chapters to follow developed positions in opposition to Freud's. Other theorists remained faithful to some of Freud's basic assumptions but attempted to expand, extend, or elaborate on his views. The goal of the latter group, which included Freud's daughter Anna, was to counteract what were seen as weaknesses or omissions in the Freudian psychoanalytic system.

Ego Psychology: Anna Freud

Although Anna Freud (1895–1982) may have been an unplanned baby (she said she never would have been born had a safer contraceptive method been available to her parents), she became the only one of Sigmund Freud's six children to follow his path (Young-Bruehl, 1988). An unhappy child, Anna was jealous of the older sister favored by her mother and was ignored by her other siblings. She recalled "the experience of being...only a bore to them, and of feeling bored and left alone" (Appignanesi & Forrester, 1992, p. 273).

Anna was not ignored by her father. She became his favorite child and by the age of 14 was dutifully attending meetings of his psychoanalytic group, listening attentively to the case histories being presented and discussed. At 22, Anna began 4 years of psychoanalysis conducted by her father, who was later sharply criticized for analyzing his daughter. One historian called it "an impossible and incestuous treatment.... an Oedipal acting-in at both ends of the couch" (Mahoney, 1992, p. 307). But another explained: "No one else would presume to undertake the task, for Anna's analysis would inevitably call into question Freud's role as her father" (Donaldson, 1996, p. 167). To analyze one's child was a serious violation of Freud's rules for the practice of psychoanalysis; the situation with Anna was kept secret for many years. In her analysis, Anna reported violent dreams involving shooting, killing, and dying, as well as defending her father from his enemies.

Anna Freud joined the Vienna Psychoanalytic Society, presenting a paper entitled *Beating Fantasies and Daydreams*. Although she claimed to be describing the experiences of a patient, she was actually relating her own fantasies. She spoke of an incestuous love relationship between father and daughter, a physical beating, and sexual gratification through masturbation.

She devoted her life to the care of her father and to his system of psychoanalysis. Several years after he died she described a series of dreams she had about him.

> He is here again. All of these recent dreams have the same character: the main role is played not by my longing for him but rather his longing for me.... In the first dream of this kind, he openly said: "I have always longed for you so." (Anna Freud, quoted in Zaretsky, 2004, p. 263)

And while Anna was close to death, some 40 years after her father died, she would sit in a wheelchair wearing his old wool coat, which she had kept all those years (Webster, 1995).

Whereas the elder Freud had worked only with adults, attempting to reconstruct their childhood by eliciting their recollections and analyzing their fantasies and dreams, Anna worked only with children. She established a clinic and a center to train analysts in the building next door to her father's London home. In 1927 she published *Four Lectures on Child Analysis*. Sigmund Freud approved of her work: "Anna's views on child analysis are independent of mine; I share her views, but she has developed them out of her own independent experience" (Freud quoted in Viner, 1996, p. 9).

Anna Freud substantially revised orthodox psychoanalysis by expanding the role of the ego, arguing that the ego operates independently of the id. This was a major extension of the Freudian system, one that involved a fundamental and radical change.

She proposed further refinements in *The Ego and the Mechanisms of Defense*, published in 1936, in which she clarified the operation of the defense mechanisms. The book received widespread praise and is considered a basic work on ego psychology. The standard defense mechanisms we discussed earlier in this chapter owe their full development and articulation to Anna Freud. This is among her most significant contributions to psychoanalytic theory.

 LOG ON

Anna Freud

Offers a detailed biography of Anna Freud.

The Anna Freud Centre

A description of the Anna Freud Centre in London, which carries on her work with emotionally disturbed children and adolescents.

For direct links to these sites, log on to the student companion site for this book at http://www.academic.cengage.com/psychology/Schultz and choose Chapter 1.

Object Relations Theories: Heinz Kohut and Melanie Klein

We used the word *object* when we discussed Freud's concept of cathexis, which he defined as an investment of psychic energy in an object. By *object*, he meant any person or activity that can satisfy an instinct. Thus, we may invest psychic energy in people, such as our mothers, who are able to satisfy our basic needs. Freud suggested that the first instinct-gratifying object in an infant's life is the mother's breast. Later, the mother as a whole person becomes an object. As the child matures, other people also become such objects, as long as they satisfy the child's instinctual needs.

object relations theories Outgrowths of psychoanalytic theory that focus more on relationships with the objects (such as the mother) that satisfy instinctual needs, rather than on the needs themselves.

Object relations theories focus more on interpersonal relationships with such objects than they do on instinctual drives. Although drive satisfaction is important, it is secondary to the establishment of interrelationships. This primary emphasis on personal relations, over instinctual needs, tells us that unlike Freud, object relations theorists accept social and environmental factors as influences on personality.

They place particular emphasis on the mother–child relationship, suggesting that the core of personality is formed in infancy, at a younger age than Freud proposed.

Although they differ on specifics, object relations theorists tend to agree that the crucial issue in personality development is the child's growing ability to become increasingly independent of its primary object: the mother. These theorists also see as critical the emergence in the early years of a strong sense of self and the maturing of relations with objects other than the mother.

Although there is no single viewpoint or system that commands the allegiance of all object relations theorists, several approaches can claim a following. We consider briefly the work of Heinz Kohut and Melanie Klein.

Heinz Kohut (1913–1981). Kohut's emphasis is on the formation of the nuclear self, which he described as the foundation for becoming an independent person, capable of taking initiative and integrating ambitions and ideals. The nuclear self develops from the relationships that form between the infant and so-called *selfobjects* in the environment. These selfobjects are the people who play such a vital role in our lives that, as infants, we believe they are part of our selves.

Typically, the mother is the infant's primary selfobject. Kohut suggested that her role is to gratify not only the child's physical needs but also the psychological needs. To do this, the mother must act as a mirror to the child, reflecting back on the child a sense of uniqueness, importance, and greatness. By doing so, the mother confirms the child's sense of pride, which becomes part of the nuclear self. If the mother rejects her child, thus mirroring a sense of unimportance, then the child may develop shame or guilt. In this way, all aspects of the adult self (the positive and the negative) are formed by the child's initial relations with the primary selfobject.

Kohut was careful to point out the continuities between his work and that of Freud. He did not view his self psychology as a deviation from Freudian psychoanalysis but rather an expansion or extension of it (Siegel, 2001).

Melanie Klein (1882–1960). An unwanted child who felt rejected by her parents, Klein suffered periodic bouts of depression. She was estranged from her daughter, who later also became an analyst. The daughter accused Klein of interfering in her life and maintained that her brother, who died while mountain climbing, had actually committed suicide because of his poor relationship with their mother. Thus, Klein experienced difficulties both as a daughter and a mother. This may have been an influence on her formulation of a system of personality development that focused on the intense emotional relationship between infant and mother.

She emphasized the first 5 to 6 months of a child's life, in contrast to Freud's stress on the first 5 years. She assumed babies are born with active fantasy lives that harbor mental representations (images) of Freudian id instincts, which the images temporarily satisfy. For example, a hungry baby can imagine sucking at the mother's breast and so, for a time, assuage the hunger.

These fantasies experienced in infancy, which Klein called inner objects, are real and vivid because infants lack the ability to distinguish between real and fantasy worlds. As a result, infants come to believe that every frustration, every thwarting of an instinct, is a personal attack inflicted by a hostile world. Infants relate, initially, only to parts of objects, and the first such part-object for babies is the mother's breast. The breast either gratifies or fails to gratify an id instinct, and the infant comes to judge it as good or bad. The baby's world, as represented by this part-object, is thus seen as either satisfying or hostile. Gradually, as the world expands, infants relate to whole objects rather than part-objects, for example, to the mother as a person rather than solely a breast.

The infant derives pleasure from this whole person (the mother) and this increases self-confidence and the power to perceive and relate to other people. Thus, all other relationships develop out of the basic object relationship that began with the mother's breast. These experiences in infancy leave additional mental images that are stored and remain influential. The adult personality, then, is based on the relationship formed in the first few months of life.

It is important to remember that no matter how far the object relations theorists deviated from Freud's position by recognizing social and environmental influences, they remained Freudian in their basic approach. Their goal was to extend Freudian theory, not to replace it.

Reflections on Freud's Theory

Freud's system of psychoanalysis has had a phenomenal impact on theory and practice in psychology and psychiatry, on our image of human nature, and on our understanding of personality. His influence has also been felt in the general culture and his work has been featured in many popular books, magazines, and newspapers. One article called him an "inescapable force," exerting an impact even 65 years after his death (see Adler, 2006, p. 43).

Psychoanalysis contributed to the growing interest of American psychologists in the study of personality, beginning in the 1930s. In the 1940s and 1950s, the ideas of psychoanalysis influenced the emerging study of motivation in psychology. Contemporary psychology has absorbed many Freudian concepts, including the role of the unconscious, the importance of childhood experiences in shaping adult behavior, and the operation of the defense mechanisms. As we have seen, these and other ideas continue to generate a great deal of research.

We see further evidence of Freud's importance in the chapters about personality theorists who built on Freud's system or used it as a source of opposition for their ideas. Great ideas inspire not only by being considered valid, but also by being perceived as incorrect, thus stimulating the development of other viewpoints.

Freud's theory of personality remains more influential than his system of psychoanalytic therapy. Although research on Freud's ideas and experimental tests of his concepts continue to be plentiful, psychoanalysis as a therapeutic technique has declined in popularity. It is generally held to be ineffective for the diagnosis and treatment of many types of patients.

Growing numbers of people are seeking therapy for behavioral and emotional problems, but fewer are choosing the expensive, long-term approach Freud developed. Briefer courses of therapy, lasting from 1 to 15 sessions, have become the norm, along with the increasing use of psychotherapeutic drugs.

The trend away from orthodox psychoanalysis in the United States has also been reinforced by the managed-care approach to total health care. It is less costly for insurance companies to approve a treatment regimen that involves simply prescribing a drug rather than a course of psychoanalysis that might last several years. In addition, managed care demands empirical evidence of the effectiveness of therapeutic treatment before providing insurance reimbursement and the evidence for the effectiveness of psychotherapy is weak (see, for example, Bornstein, 2001, 2002; Mayes & Horwitz, 2005).

We have already noted the flaws in the case study approach, Freud's primary method of research. In addition to those issues, raised mainly by experimental psychologists, there are questions asked by other personality theorists. Some argue that Freud placed too great an emphasis on instinctual biological forces as determinants of personality. Others challenge Freud's focus on sex and aggression as major motivating forces and believe we are shaped more by social experiences than by sexual ones. Some theorists disagree with Freud's deterministic picture of human nature, suggesting that we have more free will than Freud acknowledged, and that we can choose to act and grow spontaneously, in at least partial control of our fate.

Another criticism focuses on Freud's emphasis on past behavior to the exclusion of our goals and aspirations. These theorists argue that we are also influenced by the future, by our hopes and plans, as much as or more than by our experiences before age 5. Still other personality theorists think Freud paid too much attention to the emotionally disturbed, to the exclusion of the psychologically healthy and emotionally mature. If we wish to develop a theory of human personality, why not study the best and the healthiest, the positive human qualities as well as the negative ones? Theorists also take exception to Freud's views on women, specifically to the concepts of penis envy, women's poorly developed superegos, and women's inferiority feelings about their bodies.

Ambiguous definitions of certain Freudian concepts have also been questioned. Critics point to confusion and contradiction in such terms as id, ego, and superego. Are they distinct physical structures in the brain? Are they fluid processes? In his later writings Freud addressed the difficulties of defining some of his concepts precisely, but the questions remain.

This book is a history of modern insights into personality. In our personal and social growth we are never free of our past, nor should we want to be. The past offers the foundation on which to build, as later personality theorists have built on Freud's work. If psychoanalysis has served no other purpose than to inspire others and provide a framework within which to develop new insights, then Freud's importance to the world of ideas is secure. Every structure depends on the soundness and integrity of its foundation. Sigmund Freud gave personality theorists a solid, challenging base on which to build.

Chapter Summary

Freud's theory is at least partly autobiographical in that he based some of his major concepts on his childhood experiences.

Instincts are mental representations of stimuli that originate within the body. Life instincts serve the purpose of survival and are manifested in a form of psychic energy called libido. Death instincts are an unconscious drive toward decay, destruction, and aggression.

The three structures of the personality are the id, ego, and superego. The id, the biological component of personality, is the storehouse of instincts and libido. It operates in accordance with the pleasure principle. The ego, the rational component of personality, operates in accordance with the reality principle. The superego, the moral side of personality, consists of the conscience (behaviors for which the child is punished) and the ego-ideal (behaviors for which the child is praised). The ego mediates among the demands of the id, the pressures of reality, and the dictates of the superego.

Anxiety develops when the ego is pressured too greatly. Reality anxiety is a fear of dangers in the real world. Neurotic anxiety is a conflict between instinctual gratification and reality. Moral anxiety is a conflict between the id and the superego.

Defense mechanisms operate unconsciously. They are distortions of reality that protect the ego from the threat of anxiety. Defense mechanisms include repression, reaction formation, projection, regression, rationalization, displacement, and sublimation.

Children pass through psychosexual stages of development defined by erogenous zones of the body. The oral stage involves two modes of behavior: oral incorporative and oral aggressive. The anal stage involves the first interference with the gratification of an instinctual impulse. The phallic stage involves the Oedipus complex, the child's unconscious sexual longings for the parent of the opposite sex, and feelings of rivalry and fear toward the parent of the same sex. Boys develop castration anxiety; girls develop penis envy. Boys resolve the Oedipus complex by identifying with their father, adopting their father's superego standards, and repressing their sexual longing for their mother. Girls are less successful in resolving the complex, which leaves them with poorly developed superegos. During the latency period, the sex instinct is sublimated in school activities, sports, and friendships with persons of the same sex. The genital stage, at puberty, marks the beginning of heterosexual relationships.

Freud's image of human nature is pessimistic. We are doomed to anxiety, to the thwarting of impulses, and to tension and conflict. The goal of life is to reduce tension. Much of human nature is inherited, but part is learned through parent–child interactions.

Two methods of personality assessment are free association and dream analysis. In free association, a patient spontaneously expresses ideas and images in random fashion. Sometimes resistances develop in which a patient resists talking about disturbing memories or experiences. Dreams have both a manifest content (the actual dream events) and a latent content (the symbolic meaning of those events).

Freud's research method was the case study, which does not rely on objective observation. It is not controlled and systematic, nor is it amenable to duplication and verification. Freud's data are not quantifiable, may be incomplete and inaccurate, and were based on a small and unrepresentative sample.

Some Freudian concepts have been supported by empirical research: the unconscious, repression, projection, displacement, verbal slips, characteristics of oral and anal personality types, the Oedipal triangle, castration anxiety, and the resolution of the Oedipal dilemma in women by bearing a child. Major portions of Freud's theory (the id, superego, death wish, libido, catharsis, and anxiety) have not been scientifically validated. Two components of the ego have been identified: ego control and ego resiliency. With regard to repressed memories of childhood sexual abuse, some may be real, whereas others may be implanted and distorted.

Freud's theory has been modified by Anna Freud, who elaborated on the role of the ego, and by object relations theorists such as Kohut and Klein, who focused on the mother–child relationship.

Personality theorists criticize Freud for placing too much emphasis on biological forces, sex, aggression, emotional disturbances, and childhood events. They also criticize his deterministic image of human nature, his negative views of women, and the ambiguous definitions of some of his concepts. However, there is no denying Freud's phenomenal impact on Western culture and on later personality theorists, who either elaborated upon or opposed his system.

Review Questions

1. In what ways did Freud's theory reflect his childhood experiences and his personal conflicts about sex?

2. How did Freud define instincts? How do instincts connect the body's needs with the mind's wishes?

3. Distinguish between the life instincts and the death instincts. How do they motivate behavior?

4. Define the id, the ego, and the superego. How are they interrelated?

5. What did Freud mean when he said that the ego is caught in the middle, pressured by three insistent and opposing forces?

6. What are the three types of anxiety Freud proposed? What is the purpose of anxiety? How do we defend ourselves against anxiety?

7. Describe how each of the following defense mechanisms protects us against anxiety: reaction formation, projection, and sublimation.

8. Describe the oral and anal stages of psychosexual development.

9. What activities characterize an adult fixated at the oral incorporative phase? At the anal retentive phase?

10. How do boys and girls resolve the conflicts of the phallic stage of psychosexual development?

11. In your opinion, how would boys and girls reared by a single mother resolve these conflicts?

12. What are Freud's views on the relative influences of heredity and environment? What is Freud's position on the issue of free will versus determinism?

13. What kind of information can be revealed by free association? What are resistances?

14. Describe two aspects or contents of dreams. Discuss research conducted to test Freud's ideas about dream contents.

15. Which of the propositions in Freud's theory have received empirical support?

16. What criticisms have been made of the case study method?

17. Describe examples of research conducted on the concepts of the Freudian slip, the ego, and catharsis.

18. How does research on subliminal perception support Freud's views on the unconscious?

19. What is the difference between ego control and ego resiliency? Describe some personality characteristics of people who score high in ego control.

20. In what ways do repressors differ from non-repressors? Which of the two repressive coping styles is associated with happier and healthier behavior?

21. At what ages are the defense mechanisms of denial, identification, and projection most likely to be used? Why?

22. Does the Freudian defense mechanism of repression explain all instances of repressed memories of childhood abuse? What other factors might account for such memories?

23. Describe some of the ways in which Anna Freud, Heinz Kohut, and Melanie Klein extended and modified traditional Freudian theory.

24. Discuss the current status and acceptance of psychoanalysis as a personality theory and as a method of psychotherapy.

Suggested Readings

Bronstein, C. (Ed.). (2001). *Kleinian theory: A contemporary perspective.* London: Routledge. Reviews the object relations approach of Melanie Klein, suggesting that it grew out of her belief in the accuracy of psychoanalysis and her personal sense of children's inner lives.

Bushman, B. J. (2002). Does venting anger feed or extinguish the flame? Catharsis, rumination, distraction, anger, and aggressive responding. *Personality and Social Psychology Bulletin, 28,* 724–731. Compares Freud's concept of catharsis with other approaches to dealing with anger.

Coles, R. (1993). *Anna Freud: The dream of psychoanalysis.* New York: Addison-Wesley. Describes Anna Freud's life, her work on defense mechanisms, and her hopes for the future of psychoanalysis.

Cramer, P. (2006). *Protecting the self: Defense mechanisms in action.* New York: Guilford Press. Evaluates the research on defense mechanisms, focusing on gender differences in the uses of denial, projection, and identification.

Ellenberger, H. F. (1970). *The discovery of the unconscious: The history and evolution of dynamic psychiatry.* New York: Basic Books. Traces the study of the unconscious from primitive times to Freudian psychoanalysis and its derivatives.

Krüll, M. (1986). *Freud and his father.* New York: Norton. Examines the lives of Sigmund Freud and his father and analyzes the influences of Freud's experiences as a son on the development of psychoanalysis.

Lerman, H. (1986). *A mote in Freud's eye: From psychoanalysis to the psychology of women.* New York: Springer-Verlag. Describes how Freud's negative bias toward women developed from his personal experiences and permeated his theory of psychoanalysis. Freud's proposed stages of psychosexual development as they apply to females have been largely disproved.

Maddox, B. (2007). *The importance of being Ernest.* Cambridge, MA: Da Capo Press. A biography of Ernest Jones, who was Freud's first biographer and who did more than any other follower at the time to promote the doctrine of psychoanalysis. Analyzes the impact of psychoanalysis on 20th-century intellectual and popular culture.

Roazen, P. (1975). *Freud and his followers.* New York: Alfred A. Knopf. A lively, well-written account of Freud's life and the men and women who became his disciples, some of whom broke away to form their own schools of thought.

Strozier, C. B. (2001). *Heinz Kohut: The making of a psychoanalyst.* New York: Farrar, Straus & Giroux. A well-researched biography of Kohut that provides insight into Kohut's thinking and an appreciation of his ideas as they apply to clinical work.

Sulloway, F. J. (1979). *Freud, biologist of the mind: Beyond the psychoanalytic legend.* New York: Basic Books. A biography that places Freud's work in the context of its times and disputes the legend that he was a lonely hero working in isolation.

Westen, D. (1998). The scientific legacy of Sigmund Freud: Toward a psychodynamically informed psychological science. *Psychological Bulletin, 124*, 333–371. Supports the relevance of Freudian psychodynamic theory for modern psychology in terms of its positions on unconscious processes, social forces in childhood, mental representations of the self, and aspects of the developmental stages.

PART TWO

The Neopsychoanalytic Approach

Several personality theorists, who initially were loyal to Freud and committed to his system of psychoanalysis, broke away because of their opposition to certain aspects of his approach. Carl Jung and Alfred Adler were associates of Freud's before they rebelled and offered their own views of personality. Karen Horney did not have a personal relationship with Freud but was an orthodox Freudian before seeking a different path. Henry Murray, the first American theorist we discuss, developed a view of personality that provides a unique interpretation of formal psychoanalytic concepts. The work of Erik Erikson, presented in Chapter 6, is also derived from Freudian psychoanalysis.

These neopsychoanalytic theorists differ from one another on a number of points but are grouped together here because of their shared opposition to two major points: Freud's emphasis on instincts as the primary motivators of human behavior and his deterministic view of personality. The neopsychoanalytic theorists present a more optimistic and flattering picture of human nature. Their work shows how quickly the field of personality diversified within a decade after it formally began.

CHAPTER 2

Carl Jung: Analytical Psychology

My life is a story of the self-realization of the unconscious. Everything in the unconscious seeks outward manifestation, and the personality too desires to evolve out of its unconscious conditions.

—CARL JUNG

analytical psychology
Jung's theory of
personality.

Sigmund Freud once designated Carl Jung as his spiritual heir, but Jung went on to develop a theory of personality that differed dramatically from orthodox psychoanalysis. Jung fashioned a new and elaborate explanation of human nature quite unlike any other, which he called **analytical psychology**.

The first point on which Jung came to disagree with Freud was the role of sexuality. Jung broadened Freud's definition of libido by redefining it as a more generalized psychic energy that includes sex but is not restricted to it.

The second major area of disagreement concerns the direction of the forces that influence personality. Whereas Freud viewed human beings as prisoners or victims of past events, Jung argued that we are shaped by our future as well as our past. We are affected not only by what happened to us as children, but also by what we aspire to do in the future.

The third significant point of difference revolves around the unconscious. Rather than minimizing the role of the unconscious, as did the other neopsychoanalytic dissenters we discuss, Jung placed an even greater emphasis on it than Freud did. He probed more deeply into the unconscious and added a new dimension: the inherited experiences of human and pre-human species. Although Freud had recognized this phylogenetic aspect of personality (the influence of inherited primal experiences), Jung made it the core of his system of personality. He combined ideas from history, mythology, anthropology, and religion to form his image of human nature.

The Life of Jung (1875–1961)

An Unhappy Childhood

Jung's difficult and unhappy childhood years were marked by black-frocked clergymen, deaths and funerals, neurotic parents in a failing marriage, religious doubts and conflicts, bizarre dreams and visions, and a wooden doll for a companion. Born in Switzerland into a family that included nine clergymen (eight uncles and his father), Jung was introduced at an early age to religion and the classics. He was close to his father but considered him weak and powerless. Although kind and tolerant, Jung's father experienced periods of moodiness and irritability and failed to be the strong authority figure his son needed.

Jung's mother was the more powerful parent, but her emotional instability led her to behave erratically. She could change in an instant from cheerful and happy to mumbling incoherently and gazing vacantly into space. As a boy, Jung came to view his mother as being two different people inhabiting the same body. Not surprisingly, this belief disturbed him. One biographer suggested that "the whole maternal side of the family appeared to be tainted with insanity" (Ellenberger, 1978, p. 149).

As a result of his mother's odd behavior, Jung became wary of women, a suspicion that took many years to dispel. In his autobiography, he described his mother as fat and unattractive, which may explain why he rejected Freud's notion that every boy has a sexual longing for his mother. Clearly, it did not reflect his experience.

To avoid his parents and their continuing marital problems, Jung spent many hours alone in the attic of his home, carving a doll out of wood, a figure in whom he could confide. He had one sibling, a sister, who was born when he was 9 years old and who had little influence on his development; her arrival did nothing to ease his loneliness.

Dreams and Fantasies

Distrustful of his mother and disappointed in his father, Jung felt cut off from the external world, the world of conscious reality. As an escape, he turned inward to his unconscious, to the world of dreams, visions, and fantasies, in which he felt more secure. This choice would guide Jung for the rest of his life. Whenever he was faced with a problem, he would seek a solution through his dreams and visions.

The essence of his personality theory was shaped in a similar way. When Jung was 3 years old, he dreamed he was in a cavern. In a later dream, he saw himself digging beneath the earth's surface, unearthing the bones of prehistoric animals. To Jung, such dreams represented the direction of his approach to the human personality. They prompted him to explore the unconscious mind, which lies beneath the surface of behavior. So strongly was he guided by these manifestations of his unconscious that he entitled his autobiography *Memories, Dreams, Reflections* (1961), and he believed his approach to personality resembled a subjective, personal confession. Thus, like Freud's work, Jung's personality theory was intensely autobiographical. In a lecture given at the age of 50, he acknowledged the influence of his life events on his theory.

As a child, Jung deliberately avoided other children, and they avoided him. A biographer wrote: "Carl usually played alone, for parents of the village children deliberately kept them away from the odd little boy whose parents were so peculiar" (Bair, 2003, p. 22). In describing his solitary childhood, Jung wrote, "The pattern of my relationship to the world was already prefigured; today as then I am a solitary" (Jung, 1961, pp. 41–42).

Jung's loneliness is reflected in his theory, which focuses on the inner growth of the individual rather than on relationships with other people. In contrast, Freud's theory is concerned more with interpersonal relationships, perhaps because Freud, unlike Jung, did not have such an isolated and introverted childhood.

The Study of Medicine

Jung disliked school and resented the time he had to devote to formal studies rather than to ideas that interested him. He preferred to read on his own, particularly about religious and philosophical issues. To his delight, he was forced to miss 6 months of school because he had suffered a series of fainting spells. He returned to school but his presence was disruptive. His teachers sent him home because his classmates were more interested in "waiting for Carl to faint than in doing their lessons" (Bair, 2003, p. 31). When Jung overheard his father say, "What will become of the boy if he cannot earn his living?" his illness suddenly disappeared, and he returned to school to work more diligently than before (Jung, 1961, p. 31). Jung later wrote that the experience taught him about neurotic behavior. He recognized that he had arranged the situation to suit himself, to keep him out of school, and that realization made him feel angry and ashamed.

Jung chose to study medicine at the University of Basel and decided, to the disappointment of his professors, to specialize in psychiatry, a field then held in low repute. He believed that psychiatry would give him the opportunity to pursue his interests in dreams, the supernatural, and the occult.

Beginning in 1900, Jung worked at a mental hospital in Zurich, under the direction of Eugen Bleuler, the psychiatrist who coined the term *schizophrenia*. When Jung married the second-richest heiress in all of Switzerland, he quit his job at the hospital, and spent his time riding around the countryside in his much-loved red Chrysler convertible. He also gave lectures at the University of Zurich and developed an independent clinical practice.

The Years with Freud

By the time he became associated with Sigmund Freud in 1907, Jung had already established a significant professional reputation. When Jung and Freud met for the first time, they were so congenial and had so much to share that they talked for 13 hours. Their friendship became a close one. "I formally adopted you as an eldest son," Freud wrote to Jung, "and anointed you as my successor and crown prince" (Freud & Jung, 1974, p. 218). Jung considered Freud a father figure. "Let me enjoy your friendship not as one between equals," he wrote to Freud, "but as that of father and son" (Freud & Jung, 1974, p. 122). Their relationship appeared to contain many of the elements of the Oedipus complex, with its inevitable wish of the son to destroy the father.

Also, their relationship may have been tainted, even doomed, by a sexual experience Jung had at the age of 18. A family friend, an older man who had been a father figure and confidant, made physical overtures to Jung, seeking a homosexual encounter. Repelled and disappointed, Jung broke off the relationship. Years later, when Freud, who was nearly 20 years older than Jung, attempted to designate Jung as son and heir, Jung may have felt Freud was, in a sense, forcing himself on Jung and changing the nature of their relationship. Because of Jung's earlier encounter with the older man, he may have been similarly disappointed in Freud and unable to sustain an emotionally close relationship with him.

For a time, however, the two men were close. Jung remained in Zurich, but he met with Freud periodically, continued a voluminous correspondence, and journeyed with Freud to the United States in 1909 to lecture at Clark University. Freud was grooming Jung to take over the presidency of the International Psychoanalytic Association. Concerned that psychoanalysis would be labeled a Jewish science (as it came to be called during the Nazi era), Freud wanted a non-Jew to assume titular leadership of the movement.

Contrary to Freud's hopes, Jung was not an uncritical disciple. Jung had his own ideas and unique view of the human personality, and when he began to express these notions, it became inevitable that they would part. They severed their relationship in 1913.

A Neurotic Episode

That same year, when Jung was 38 years old, he underwent a severe neurotic episode that lasted for 3 years. He believed he was in danger of losing contact with reality and was so distressed that he resigned his lectureship at the University of Zurich. At times he considered suicide; he "kept a revolver next to his bed in case he felt he had passed beyond the point of no return" (Noll, 1994, p. 207). Although he felt unable to continue with his scientific work, he persisted in treating his patients.

Freud had suffered a neurotic episode at approximately the same age and resolved it by analyzing his dreams, which formed a basis for his personality theory. Jung's situation offers a remarkable parallel. Jung overcame his disturbance by confronting his unconscious through the exploration of his dreams and fantasies. Although Jung's self-analysis was less systematic than Freud's, his approach was similar.

Out of Jung's confrontation with his unconscious he fashioned his approach to personality. He wrote, "The years when I was pursuing my inner images were the most important in my life—in them everything essential was decided" (Jung, 1961, p. 199). He concluded that the most crucial stage in personality development was not childhood, as Freud believed, but middle age, which was the time of Jung's own crisis.

Like Freud, Jung established his theory on an intuitive base, which derived from his personal experiences and dreams. It was then refined along more rational and empirical lines by data provided by his patients. Nearly two-thirds of them were middle-aged and suffering from the same difficulties Jung faced.

The rest of Jung's long life was personally and professionally fruitful, although some aspects of his behavior may be considered bizarre. He would greet the kitchen utensils every morning, saying "'greetings to you' to the frying pans or 'good morning to you' to the coffee pot" (Bair, 2003, p. 568). He also worried needlessly about money. He hid large amounts of cash inside books and then forgot the secret code he had devised to help him remember which books contained the money. He stuffed money in vases and jars and buried them in his garden and then forgot the elaborate system he had concocted to help him find them. After his death, family members recovered much of the money from his books but it is likely that the cash in his garden remains there today.

Jung and his wife adopted a cold, formal manner for dealing with their three daughters. There was limited physical contact, no hugging or kissing. "When they said hello or goodbye, they shook hands, if they touched at all" (Bair, 2003, p. 565).

Jung remained productive in research and writing for most of his 86 years. His books became popular, and his analytical psychology attracted increasing numbers of followers. His ideas spread to the English-speaking world, and particularly to the United States, primarily through the generous financial support of the Rockefellers, the McCormicks, and the Mellons, all prominent American families. A number of family members sought analysis with Jung and in return arranged for the translation and publication of his books. Otherwise, Jung's works might have remained little known, inaccessible to all but the German-speaking community (Noll, 1997).

Log On

Personality Theories: Carl Jung

A biography of Jung, an extensive discussion of his work, a list of readings, and links to other Web sites.

C. G. Jung Institute of Boston

The Web site for the C. G. Jung Institute of Boston, Massachusetts, noting current training and educational opportunities, programs available for the public, and links to other sites including those of Jungian analysts.

For direct links to these sites, log on to the student companion site for this book at http://www.academic.cengage.com/psychology/Schultz and choose Chapter 2.

Psychic Energy: Opposites, Equivalence, and Entropy

One of the first points on which Jung disputed Freud concerned the nature of libido. Jung did not agree that libido was primarily a sexual energy; he argued instead that libido was a broad, undifferentiated life energy. Interestingly, Jung, who minimized the importance of sex in his personality theory, maintained a vigorous, anxiety-free sex life and enjoyed a number of extramarital affairs. One of these relationships endured, with his wife's knowledge, for many years. He surrounded himself with adoring women patients and disciples who typically fell deeply in love with him. A biographer noted that this "happened with all of his female disciples sooner or later, as he often told them at the beginning of their treatment" (Noll, 1997, p. 253).

Contrast Jung's active sex life with Freud's troubled attitude toward sex and his cessation of sexual relations at the time he was fashioning a theory that focused on sex as the cause of neurotic behavior. "To Jung, who freely and frequently satisfied his sexual needs, sex played a minimal role in human motivation. To Freud, beset by frustrations and anxious about his thwarted desires, sex played the central role" (Schultz, 1990, p. 148).

libido
To Jung, a broader and more generalized form of psychic energy.

Jung used the term **libido** in two ways: first, as a diffuse and general life energy, and second, from a perspective similar to Freud's, as a narrower psychic energy that fuels the work of the personality, which he called the **psyche**. It is through psychic energy that psychological activities such as perceiving, thinking, feeling, and wishing are carried out.

psyche
Jung's term for personality.

When a person invests a great deal of psychic energy in a particular idea or feeling, that idea or feeling is said to have a high psychic value and can strongly influence the person's life. For example, if you are highly motivated to attain power, then you will devote most of your psychic energy to seeking power.

opposition principle
Jung's idea that conflict between opposing processes or tendencies is necessary to generate psychic energy.

Jung drew on ideas from physics to explain the functioning of psychic energy. He proposed three basic principles: opposites, equivalence, and entropy (Jung, 1928). The **principle of opposites** can be seen throughout Jung's system. He noted the existence of opposites or polarities in physical energy in the universe, such as heat versus cold, height versus depth, creation versus decay. So it is with psychic energy: Every wish or feeling has its opposite. This opposition or antithesis—this conflict between polarities—is the primary motivator of behavior and generator of energy. Indeed, the sharper the conflict between polarities, the greater the energy produced.

For his **principle of equivalence**, Jung applied to psychic events the physical principle of the conservation of energy. He stated that energy expended in bringing about some condition is not lost but rather is shifted to another part of the personality. Thus, if the psychic value in a particular area weakens or disappears, that energy is transferred elsewhere in the psyche. For example, if we lose interest in a person, a hobby, or a field of study, the psychic energy formerly invested in that area is shifted to a new one. The psychic energy used for conscious activities while we are awake is shifted to dreams when we are asleep.

The word *equivalence* implies that the new area to which energy has shifted must have an equal psychic value; that is, it should be equally desirable, compelling, or fascinating. Otherwise, the excess energy will flow into the unconscious. In whatever direction and manner energy flows, the principle of equivalence suggests that energy is continually redistributed within the personality.

In physics, the **principle of entropy** refers to the equalization of energy differences. For example, if a hot object and a cold object are placed in direct contact, heat will flow from the hotter object to the colder object until they are in equilibrium at the same temperature. In effect, an exchange of energy occurs, resulting in a kind of homeostatic balance between the objects.

Jung applied this law to psychic energy and proposed that there is a tendency toward a balance or equilibrium in the personality. If two desires or beliefs differ greatly in intensity or psychic value, energy will flow from the more strongly held to the weaker. Ideally, the personality has an equal distribution of psychic energy over all its aspects, but this ideal state is never achieved. If perfect balance or equilibrium were attained, then the personality would have no psychic energy because, as we noted earlier, the opposition principle requires conflict for psychic energy to be produced.

The Systems of Personality

In Jung's view, the total personality, or psyche, is composed of several distinct systems or structures that can influence one another. The major systems are the ego, the personal unconscious, and the collective unconscious.

The Ego

The **ego** is the center of consciousness, the part of the psyche concerned with perceiving, thinking, feeling, and remembering. It is our awareness of ourselves and is responsible for carrying out the normal activities of waking life. The ego acts in a selective way, admitting into conscious awareness only a portion of the stimuli to which we are exposed.

equivalence principle
The continuing redistribution of energy within a personality; if the energy expended on certain conditions or activities weakens or disappears, that energy is transferred elsewhere in the personality.

entropy principle
A tendency toward balance or equilibrium within the personality; the ideal is an equal distribution of psychic energy over all structures of the personality.

ego
To Jung, the conscious aspect of personality.

The Attitudes: Extraversion and Introversion

Much of our conscious perception of and reaction to our environment is determined by the opposing mental attitudes of **extraversion** and **introversion**. Jung believed that psychic energy could be channeled externally, toward the outside world, or internally, toward the self. Extraverts are open, sociable, and socially assertive, oriented toward other people and the external world. Introverts are withdrawn and often shy, and they tend to focus on themselves, on their own thoughts and feelings.

According to Jung, everyone has the capacity for both attitudes, but only one becomes dominant in the personality. The dominant attitude then tends to direct the person's behavior and consciousness. The non-dominant attitude remains influential, however, and becomes part of the personal unconscious, where it can affect behavior. For example, in certain situations an introverted person may display characteristics of extraversion, wish to be more outgoing, or be attracted to an extravert.

Psychological Functions

As Jung came to recognize that there were different kinds of extraverts and introverts, he proposed additional distinctions among people based on what he called the psychological functions. These functions refer to different and opposing ways of perceiving or apprehending both the external real world and our subjective inner world. Jung posited four functions of the psyche: sensing, intuiting, thinking, and feeling (Jung, 1927).

Sensing and intuiting are grouped together as non-rational functions; they do not use the processes of reason. These functions accept experiences and do not evaluate them. Sensing reproduces an experience through the senses the way a photograph copies an object. Intuiting does not arise directly from an external stimulus; for example, if we believe someone else is with us in a darkened room, our belief may be based on our intuition or a hunch rather than on actual sensory experience.

The second pair of opposing functions, thinking and feeling, are rational functions that involve making judgments and evaluations about our experiences. Although thinking and feeling are opposites, both are concerned with organizing and categorizing experiences. The thinking function involves a conscious judgment of whether an experience is true or false. The kind of evaluation made by the feeling function is expressed in terms of like or dislike, pleasantness or unpleasantness, stimulation or dullness.

Just as our psyche contains some of both the extraversion and introversion attitudes, so we have the capacity for all four psychological functions. Similarly, just as one attitude is dominant, so only one function is dominant. The others are submerged in the personal unconscious. Further, only one pair of functions is dominant—either the rational or the irrational—and within each pair only one function is dominant. A person cannot be ruled by both thinking and feeling or by both sensing and intuiting, because they are opposing functions.

Psychological Types

Jung proposed eight **psychological types**, based on the interactions of the two attitudes and four functions. (See Table 2.1.)

Table 2.1 Jung's psychological types

Extraverted thinking	Logical, objective, dogmatic
Extraverted feeling	Emotional, sensitive, sociable; more typical of women than men
Extraverted sensing	Outgoing, pleasure-seeking, adaptable
Extraverted intuiting	Creative, able to motivate others and to seize opportunities
Introverted thinking	More interested in ideas than in people
Introverted feeling	Reserved, undemonstrative, yet capable of deep emotion
Introverted sensing	Outwardly detached, expressing themselves in aesthetic pursuits
Introverted intuiting	Concerned with the unconscious more than everyday reality

The *extraverted thinking type* lives strictly in accordance with society's rules. These people tend to repress feelings and emotions, to be objective in all aspects of life, and to be dogmatic in thoughts and opinions. They may be perceived as rigid and cold. They tend to make good scientists because their focus is on learning about the external world and using logical rules to describe and understand it.

The *extraverted feeling type* tends to repress the thinking mode and to be highly emotional. These people conform to the traditional values and moral codes they have been taught. They are unusually sensitive to the opinions and expectations of others. They are emotionally responsive and make friends easily, and they tend to be sociable and effervescent. Jung believed this type was found more often among women than men.

Extraverts channel the libido externally, toward the outside world.

© Myrleen Ferguson Cate/PhotoEdit

The *extraverted sensing type* focuses on pleasure and happiness and on seeking new experiences. These people are strongly oriented toward the real world and are adaptable to different kinds of people and changing situations. Not given to introspection, they tend to be outgoing, with a high capacity for enjoying life.

The *extraverted intuiting type* finds success in business and politics because of a keen ability to exploit opportunities. These people are attracted by new ideas and tend to be creative. They are able to inspire others to accomplish and achieve. They also tend to be changeable, moving from one idea or venture to another, and to make decisions based more on hunches than on reflection. Their decisions, however, are likely to be correct.

The *introverted thinking type* does not get along well with others and has difficulty communicating ideas. These people focus on thought rather than on feelings and have poor practical judgment. Intensely concerned with privacy, they prefer to deal with abstractions and theories, and they focus on understanding themselves rather than other people. Others see them as stubborn, aloof, arrogant, and inconsiderate.

The *introverted feeling type* represses rational thought. These people are capable of deep emotion but avoid any outward expression of it. They seem mysterious and inaccessible and tend to be quiet, modest, and childish. They have little consideration for others' feelings and thoughts and appear withdrawn, cold, and self-assured.

The *introverted sensing type* appears passive, calm, and detached from the everyday world. These people look on most human activities with benevolence and amusement. They are aesthetically sensitive, expressing themselves in art or music, and tend to repress their intuition.

The *introverted intuiting type* focuses so intently on intuition that they have little contact with reality. These people are visionaries and daydreamers—aloof, unconcerned with practical matters, and poorly understood by others. Considered odd and eccentric, they have difficulty coping with everyday life and planning for the future.

The Personal Unconscious

personal unconscious
The reservoir of material that was once conscious but has been forgotten or suppressed.

The **personal unconscious** in Jung's system is similar to Freud's conception of the preconscious. It is a reservoir of material that was once conscious but has been forgotten or suppressed because it was trivial or disturbing. There is considerable two-way traffic between the ego and the personal unconscious. For example, our attention can wander readily from this printed page to a memory of something we did yesterday. All kinds of experiences are stored in the personal unconscious; it can be likened to a filing cabinet. Little mental effort is required to take something out, examine it for a while, and put it back, where it will remain until the next time we want it or are reminded of it.

complex
To Jung, a core or pattern of emotions, memories, perceptions, and wishes in the personal unconscious organized around a common theme, such as power or status.

Complexes

As we file more and more experiences in our personal unconscious, we begin to group them into what Jung called **complexes**. A complex is a core or pattern of emotions, memories, perceptions, and wishes organized around a common theme.

For example, we might say that a person has a complex about power or status, meaning that he or she is preoccupied with that theme to the point where it influences behavior. The person may try to become powerful by running for elective office, or to identify or affiliate with power by driving a motorcycle or a fast car. By directing thoughts and behavior in various ways, the complex determines how the person perceives the world.

Complexes may be conscious or unconscious. Those that are not under conscious control can intrude on and interfere with consciousness. The person with a complex is generally not aware of its influence, although other people may easily observe its effects.

Some complexes may be harmful, but others can be useful. For example, a perfection or achievement complex may lead a person to work hard at developing particular talents or skills. Jung believed that complexes originate not only from our childhood and adult experiences, but also from our ancestral experiences, the heritage of the species contained in the collective unconscious.

The Collective Unconscious

collective unconscious The deepest level of the psyche containing the accumulation of inherited experiences of human and pre-human species.

The deepest and least accessible level of the psyche, the **collective unconscious** is the most unusual and controversial aspect of Jung's system. Jung believed that just as each of us accumulates and files all of our personal experiences in the personal unconscious, so does humankind collectively, as a species, store the experiences of the human and pre-human species in the collective unconscious. This heritage is passed to each new generation.

Whatever experiences are universal—that is, are repeated relatively unchanged by each generation—become part of our personality. Our primitive past becomes the basis of the human psyche, directing and influencing present behavior. To Jung, the collective unconscious was the powerful and controlling repository of ancestral experiences. Thus, Jung linked each person's personality with the past, not only with childhood but also with the history of the species. We do not inherit these collective experiences directly. For example, we do not inherit a fear of snakes. Rather, we inherit the potential to fear snakes. We are predisposed to behave and feel the same ways people have always behaved and felt. Whether the predisposition becomes reality depends on the specific experiences each of us encounters in life.

Jung believed that certain basic experiences have characterized every generation throughout human history. People have always had a mother figure, for example, and have experienced birth and death. They have faced unknown terrors in the dark, worshipped power or some sort of godlike figure, and feared an evil being. The universality of these experiences over countless evolving generations leaves an imprint on each of us at birth and determines how we perceive and react to our world. Jung wrote, "The form of the world into which [a person] is born is already inborn in him, as a virtual image" (Jung, 1953, p. 188).

A baby is born predisposed to perceive the mother in a certain way. If the mother behaves the way mothers typically behave, in a nurturing and supportive manner, then the baby's predisposition will correspond with its reality.

Because the collective unconscious is such an unusual concept, it is important to note the reason Jung proposed it and the kind of evidence he gathered to support it. In his reading about ancient cultures, both mythical and real, Jung discovered what he believed to be common themes and symbols that appeared in diverse parts of the world. As far as he could determine, these ideas had not been transmitted or communicated orally or in writing from one culture to another.

In addition, Jung's patients, in their dreams and fantasies, recalled and described for him the same kinds of symbols he had discovered in ancient cultures. He could find no other explanation for these shared symbols and themes over such vast geographical and temporal distances than that they were transmitted by and carried in each person's unconscious mind.

Archetypes

archetypes
Images of universal experiences contained in the collective unconscious.

The ancient experiences contained in the collective unconscious are manifested by recurring themes or patterns Jung called **archetypes** (Jung, 1947). He also used the term *primordial images*. There are many such images of universal experiences, as many as there are common human experiences. By being repeated in the lives of succeeding generations, archetypes have become imprinted on our psyche and are expressed in our dreams and fantasies.

Among the archetypes Jung proposed are the hero, the mother, the child, God, death, power, and the wise old man. A few of these are developed more fully than others and influence the psyche more consistently. These major archetypes include the persona, the anima and animus, the shadow, and the self.

persona archetype
The public face or role a person presents to others.

The word *persona* refers to a mask that an actor wears to display various roles or faces to the audience. Jung used the term with basically the same meaning. The **persona archetype** is a mask, a public face we wear to present ourselves as someone different from who we really are. The persona is necessary, Jung believed, because we are forced to play many roles in life in order to succeed in school and on the job and to get along with a variety of people.

Although the persona can be helpful, it can also be harmful if we come to believe that it reflects our true nature. Instead of merely playing a role, we may become that role. As a result, other aspects of our personality will not be allowed to develop. Jung described the process this way: The ego may come to identify with the persona rather than with the person's true nature, resulting in a condition known as inflation of the persona. Whether the person plays a role or comes to believe that role, he or she is resorting to deception. In the first instance, the person is deceiving others; in the second instance, the person is deceiving himself or herself.

The anima and animus archetypes refer to Jung's recognition that humans are essentially bisexual. On the biological level, each sex secretes the hormones of the other sex as well as those of its own sex. On the psychological level, each sex manifests characteristics, temperaments, and attitudes of the other sex by virtue of centuries of living together. The psyche of the woman contains masculine aspects

In the fully developed personality, a person will express behaviors considered characteristic of the opposite sex.

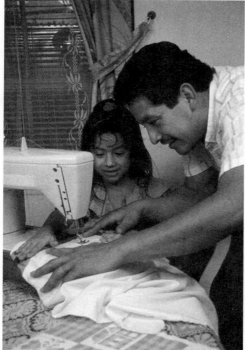

© Myrleen Ferguson Cate/PhotoEdit

anima archetype; animus archetype
Feminine aspects of the male psyche; masculine aspects of the female psyche.

(the **animus archetype**), and the psyche of the man contains feminine aspects (the **anima archetype**). (See Figure 2.1.)

These opposite sex characteristics aid in the adjustment and survival of the species because they enable a person of one sex to understand the nature of the other sex. The archetypes predispose us to like certain characteristics of the opposite sex; these characteristics guide our behavior with reference to the opposite sex.

Jung insisted that both the anima and the animus must be expressed. A man must exhibit his feminine as well as his masculine characteristics, and a woman must express her masculine characteristics along with her feminine ones. Otherwise,

Figure 2.1
The Yin-Yang symbol illustrates the complementary sides of our nature. The dark right side represents feminine aspects (the anima archetype) and the light left side represents masculine aspects (the animus archetype). The dot of the opposite color in each portion indicates the expression of the characteristics of the opposite archetype.

these vital aspects will remain dormant and undeveloped, leading to one-sidedness of the personality.

The most powerful archetype Jung proposed has the sinister and mysterious name of the **shadow**, which contains the basic, primitive animal instincts and therefore has the deepest roots of all the archetypes. Behaviors that society considers evil and immoral reside in the shadow, and this dark side of human nature must be tamed if people are to live in harmony. We must restrain, overcome, and defend against these primitive impulses. If we do not, society will likely punish us.

But we face a dilemma. Not only is the shadow the source of evil, it is also the source of vitality, spontaneity, creativity, and emotion. Therefore, if the shadow is totally suppressed, the psyche will be dull and lifeless. It is the ego's function to re-press the animal instincts enough so that we are considered civilized while allowing sufficient expression of the instincts to provide creativity and vigor.

If the shadow is fully suppressed, not only does the personality become flat, but the person also faces the possibility that the shadow will revolt. The animal instincts do not disappear when they are suppressed. Rather, they lie dormant, awaiting a crisis or a weakness in the ego so they can gain control. When that happens, the person becomes dominated by the unconscious.

The **self archetype** represents the unity, integration, and harmony of the total personality. To Jung, the striving toward that wholeness is the ultimate goal of life. This archetype involves bringing together and balancing all parts of the personality. We have already noted Jung's principle of opposites and the importance of polarities to the psyche. In the self archetype, conscious and unconscious processes become assimilated so that the self, which is the center of the personality, shifts from the ego to a point of equilibrium midway between the opposing forces of the conscious and the unconscious. As a result, material from the unconscious comes to have a greater influence on the personality.

The full realization of the self lies in the future. It is a goal—something to strive for but rarely achieved. The self serves as a motivating force, pulling us from ahead rather than pushing us from behind (as our past experiences do).

The self cannot begin to emerge until the other systems of the psyche have developed. This occurs around middle age, a crucial period of transition in Jung's system, as it was in his own life. The actualization of the self involves goals and plans for the future and an accurate perception of one's abilities. Because development of the self is impossible without self-knowledge, it is the most difficult process we face in life and requires persistence, perceptiveness, and wisdom.

shadow archetype
The dark side of the personality; the archetype that contains primitive animal instincts.

self archetype
To Jung, the archetype that represents the unity, integration, and harmony of the total personality.

The Development of the Personality

Jung proposed that personality is determined by what we hope to be as well as by what we have been. He criticized Freud for emphasizing only past events as shapers of personality, to the exclusion of the future. Jung believed we develop and grow regardless of age and are always moving toward a more complete level of self-realization (see Table 2.2)

Jung took a longer view of personality than Freud, who concentrated on the early years of life and foresaw little development after the age of 5. Jung did not

Table 2.2 **Jung's developmental stages**

Childhood	Ego development begins when the child distinguishes between self and others.
Puberty to young adulthood	Adolescents must adapt to the growing demands of reality. The focus is external, on education, career, and family. The conscious is dominant.
Middle age	A period of transition when the focus of the personality shifts from external to internal in an attempt to balance the unconscious with the conscious.

posit sequential stages of growth in as much detail as Freud but he wrote of specific periods in the overall developmental process (Jung, 1930).

Childhood to Young Adulthood

The ego begins to develop in early childhood, at first in a primitive way because the child has not yet formed a unique identity. What might be called the child's personality is, at this stage, little more than a reflection of the personalities of his or her parents. Obviously, then, parents exert a great influence on the formation of the child's personality. They can enhance or impede personality development by the way they behave toward the child.

Parents might try to force their own personalities on the child, desiring him or her to be an extension of them. Or they might expect their child to develop a personality different from their own as a way of seeking vicarious compensation for their deficiencies. The ego begins to form substantively only when children become able to distinguish between themselves and other people or objects in their world. In other words, consciousness forms when the child is able to say "I."

It is not until puberty that the psyche assumes a definite form and content. This period, which Jung called our psychic birth, is marked by difficulties and the need to adapt. Childhood fantasies must end as the adolescent confronts the demands of reality. From the teenage years through young adulthood, we are concerned with preparatory activities such as completing our education, beginning a career, getting married, and starting a family. Our focus during these years is external, our conscious is dominant, and, in general, our primary conscious attitude is that of extraversion. The aim of life is to achieve our goals and establish a secure, successful place for ourselves in the world. Thus, young adulthood should be an exciting and challenging time, filled with new horizons and accomplishments.

Middle Age

Jung believed that major personality changes occur between the ages of 35 and 40. This period of middle age was a time of personal crisis for Jung and many of his patients. By then, the adaptation problems of young adulthood have been resolved. The typical 40-year-old is established in a career, a marriage, and a community. Jung asked why, when success has been achieved, so many people that age are gripped by feelings of despair and worthlessness. His patients all told him essentially the same thing: They felt empty. Adventure, excitement, and zest had disappeared. Life had lost its meaning.

Middle age is a time of transition, when one's focus and interests change.

© Cheryl Maeder/Taxi/Getty Images

The more Jung analyzed this period, the more strongly he believed that such drastic personality changes were inevitable and universal. Middle age is a natural time of transition in which the personality is supposed to undergo necessary and beneficial changes. Ironically, the changes occur because middle-aged persons have been so successful in meeting life's demands. These people had invested a great deal of energy in the preparatory activities of the first half of life, but by age 40 that preparation was finished and those challenges had been met. Although they still possess considerable energy, the energy now has nowhere to go; it has to be rechanneled into different activities and interests.

Jung noted that in the first half of life we must focus on the objective world of reality—education, career, and family. In contrast, the second half of life must be devoted to the inner, subjective world that heretofore had been neglected. The attitude of the personality must shift from extraversion to introversion. The focus on consciousness must be tempered by an awareness of the unconscious. Our interests must shift from the physical and material to the spiritual, philosophical, and intuitive. A balance among all facets of the personality must replace the previous one-sidedness of the personality (that is, the focus on consciousness).

Thus, at middle age we must begin the process of realizing or actualizing the self. If we are successful in integrating the unconscious with the conscious, we are in a position to attain a new level of positive psychological health, a condition Jung called individuation.

Individuation

individuation
A condition of psychological health resulting from the integration of all conscious and unconscious facets of the personality.

Simply stated, **individuation** involves becoming an individual, fulfilling one's capacities, and developing one's self. The tendency toward individuation is innate and inevitable, but it will be helped or hindered by environmental forces, such as one's educational and economic opportunities and the nature of the parent–child relationship.

To strive for individuation, middle-aged persons must abandon the behaviors and values that guided the first half of life and confront their unconscious, bringing it into conscious awareness and accepting what it tells them to do. They must listen to their dreams and follow their fantasies, exercising creative imagination through writing, painting, or some other form of expression. They must let themselves be guided, not by the rational thinking that drove them before, but by the spontaneous flow of the unconscious. Only in that way can the true self be revealed.

Jung cautioned that admitting unconscious forces into conscious awareness does not mean being dominated by them. The unconscious forces must be assimilated and balanced with the conscious. At this time of life, no single aspect of personality should dominate. An emotionally healthy middle-aged person is no longer ruled by either consciousness or unconsciousness, by a specific attitude or function, or by any of the archetypes. All are brought into harmonious balance when individuation is achieved.

Of particular importance in the midlife process of individuation is the shift in the nature of the archetypes. The first change involves dethroning the persona. Although we must continue to play various social roles if we are to function in the real world and get along with different kinds of people, we must recognize that our public personality may not represent our true nature. Further, we must come to accept the genuine self that the persona has been covering.

Next, we become aware of the destructive forces of the shadow and acknowledge the dark side of our nature with its primitive impulses, such as selfishness. We do not submit to them or allow them to dominate us but simply accept their existence. In the first half of life, we use the persona to shield this dark side from ourselves, wanting people to see only our good qualities. But in concealing the forces of the shadow from others, we conceal them from ourselves. This must change as part of the process of learning to know ourselves. A greater awareness of both the destructive and the constructive aspects of the shadow will give the personality a deeper and fuller dimension, because the shadow's tendencies bring zest, spontaneity, and vitality to life.

Once again we see this central theme in Jung's individuation process—that we must bring each aspect of the personality into harmony with all other aspects. Awareness of only the good side of our nature produces a one-sided development of the personality. As with other opposing components of personality, both sides of this dimension must be expressed before we can achieve individuation.

We must also come to terms with our psychological bisexuality. A man must be able to express his anima archetype or traditionally feminine traits such as tenderness and a woman must come to express her animus or traditionally masculine traits such as assertiveness. Jung believed that this recognition of the characteristics of the other sex was the most difficult step in the individuation process because it represents the greatest change in our self-image. Accepting the emotional qualities of both sexes opens new sources of creativity and serves as the final release from parental influences.

Once the psyche's structures are individuated and acknowledged, the next developmental stage can occur. Jung referred to this as transcendence, an innate tendency toward unity or wholeness in the personality, uniting all the opposing aspects within the psyche. Environmental factors, such as an unsatisfactory marriage or frustrating work, can inhibit the process of transcendence and prevent the full achievement of the self.

Questions About Human Nature

Jung's image of human nature is quite different from Freud's. Jung did not hold such a deterministic view, but he did agree that personality may be partly determined by childhood experiences and by the archetypes. However, there is ample room in Jung's system for free will and spontaneity, the latter arising from the shadow archetype.

On the nature–nurture issue, Jung took a mixed position. The drive toward individuation and transcendence is innate, but it can be aided or thwarted by learning and experience. The ultimate and necessary goal of life is the realization of the self. Although it is rarely achieved, we are continually motivated to strive for it.

Jung disagreed with Freud on the importance of childhood experiences. Jung thought they were influential but did not completely shape our personality by age 5. We are affected more by our experiences in middle age and by our hopes and expectations for the future.

Each individual is unique, in Jung's view, but only during the first half of life. When some progress toward individuation is made in middle age, we develop what Jung designated as a universal kind of personality in which no single aspect is dominant. Thus, uniqueness disappears, and we can no longer be described as one or another particular psychological type.

Jung presented a more positive, hopeful image of human nature than Freud did, and his optimism is apparent in his view of personality development. We are motivated to grow and develop, to improve and extend our selves. Progress does not stop in childhood, as Freud had assumed, but continues throughout life; we always have the hope of becoming better. Jung argued that the human species also continues to improve. Present generations represent a significant advance over our primitive ancestors.

Despite his basic optimism, Jung expressed concern about a danger he saw facing Western culture. He referred to this danger as a sickness of dissociation. By placing too great an emphasis on materialism, reason, and empirical science, we are in danger of failing to appreciate the forces of the unconscious. He argued that we must not abandon our trust in the archetypes that form our heritage. Thus, Jung's hopefulness about human nature was a watchful, warning kind.

Assessment in Jung's Theory

Jung's techniques for assessing the functioning of the psyche drew on science and the supernatural, resulting in both an objective and a mystical approach. He investigated a variety of cultures and eras and recorded their symbols, myths, religions, and rituals.

He formed his personality theory on the basis of his patients' fantasies and dreams (as well as his own), and his explorations of ancient languages, alchemy, and astrology. Yet the work that first brought Jung to the attention of psychologists in the United States involved empirical and physiological assessments. His techniques were an unorthodox blend of opposites, which is not surprising for a theory based on a principle of opposition.

His sessions with patients were unusual, even chaotic. His patients did not lie on a couch. "I don't want to put the patient to bed," he remarked. Usually, Jung and the patient sat in comfortable chairs facing each other, although sometimes Jung faced a window so he could look out at the lake near his house. Occasionally, he took patients aboard his sailboat.

One patient recalled that

> [he] paced back and forth, gesturing as he talked, whether about a human problem, a dream, a personal reminiscence, an allegorical story, or a joke. Yet he could become quiet, serious, and extremely personal, sitting down almost too close for comfort and delivering a pointed interpretation of one's miserable personal problem so its bitter truth would really sink in. (quoted in Bair, 2003, p. 379)

Sometimes Jung could be rude. When one patient appeared at the appointed time, he said, "Oh no. I can't stand the sight of another one. Just go home and cure yourself today" (quoted in Brome, 1981, pp. 177, 185). When another patient began to talk about her mother, a topic Freud would have encouraged, Jung silenced her abruptly: "Don't waste your time" (Bair, 2003, p. 379).

Jung believed that his patients' fantasies were real to them and he accepted them at face value. When Marie-Louise von Franz (1915–1998), who later became a lifelong disciple, first met Jung, he told her about a patient who lived on the moon. She replied that surely Jung meant the patient *acted* as though she lived on the moon. Jung said no, the woman truly did live on the moon. Von Franz decided that "either [Jung] was crazy or I was" (quoted in obituary for Marie-Louise von Franz, *New York Times*, March 23, 1998).

Three basic techniques Jung used to evaluate personality were the word association test, symptom analysis, and dream analysis. A widely used self-report personality test, the Myers-Briggs Type Indicator, was developed to assess Jung's psychological types.

Word Association

word association test
A projective technique in which a person responds to a stimulus word with whatever word comes to mind.

The **word association test**, in which a subject responds to a stimulus word with whatever word comes immediately to mind, has become a standard laboratory and clinical tool in psychology. In the early 1900s, Jung used the technique with a list of 100 words he believed were capable of eliciting emotions (see Table 2.3). Jung measured the time it took for a patient to respond to each word. He also measured physiological reactions to determine the emotional effects of the stimulus words.

Jung used word association to uncover complexes in his patients. A variety of factors indicated the presence of a complex; these factors include physiological responses, delays in responding, making the same response to different words, slips

Table 2.3 **Normal and neurotic responses to Jung's word association test**

Stimulus word	Normal response	Neurotic response
Blue	Pretty	Color
Tree	Green	Nature
Bread	Good	To eat
Lamp	Bright	To burn
Rich	Beautiful	Money; I don't know
To sin	Much	This idea is totally alien to me; I do not acknowledge it
Needle	To prick	To sew
To swim	Healthy	Water

SOURCE: C. G. Jung. "The Association Method," 1909. In *The Collected Works of C.G. Jung,* Volume 2 (Princeton, NJ: Princeton University Press, 1973), pp. 442–444.

of the tongue, stammering, responding with more than one word, making up words, or failing to respond.

Symptom Analysis

symptom analysis
Similar to catharsis, the symptom analysis technique focuses on the symptoms reported by the patient and attempts to interpret the patient's free associations to those symptoms.

Symptom analysis focuses on the symptoms reported by the patient and is based on the person's free associations to those symptoms. It is similar to Freud's cathartic method. Between the patient's associations to the symptoms and the analyst's interpretation of them, the symptoms will often be relieved or disappear.

Dream Analysis

dream analysis
A technique involving the interpretation of dreams to uncover unconscious conflicts.

Jung agreed with Freud that dreams are the "royal road" into the unconscious. Jung's approach to **dream analysis** differed from Freud's in that Jung was concerned with more than the causes of dreams, and he believed that dreams were more than unconscious wishes. First, dreams are prospective; that is, they help us prepare for experiences and events we anticipate will occur. Second, dreams are compensatory; they help bring about a balance between opposites in the psyche by compensating for the overdevelopment of any one psychic structure.

Instead of interpreting each dream separately, as Freud did, Jung worked with a series of dreams reported by a patient over a period of time. In that way, Jung believed he could discover recurring themes, issues, and problems that persisted in the patient's unconscious.

Jung also used amplification to analyze dreams. In Freudian free association, the patient begins with one element in a dream and develops a chain of associations from it by reporting related memories and events. Jung focused on the original dream element and asked the patient to make repeated associations and responses to it until he detected a theme. He did not try to distinguish between manifest and latent dream content.

The Myers-Briggs Type Indicator

Myers-Briggs Type Indicator (MBTI)

An assessment test based on Jung's psychological types and the attitudes of introversion and extraversion.

An assessment instrument related to Jung's personality theory is the **Myers-Briggs Type Indicator (MBTI)**, developed in the 1920s by Katharine Cook Briggs and Isabel Briggs Myers (Briggs & Myers, 1943, 1976). Today, the MBTI is one of the most popular self-report inventories ever devised and is administered to approximately 2-1/2 million people annually. Of the leading corporations listed in the Fortune 100, 89 of them use the MBTI for employee hiring and promotion decisions. Thus, it is likely that you will be asked to take this test in order to get a job (see Table 2.4).

The test was developed in Washington, D.C. by Katharine Briggs, who doted on her teenage daughter Isabel. Katharine wrote a book-length manuscript about her remarkable daughter, calling her a genius, even "a little Shakespeare." When Isabel went away to college, mother and daughter corresponded almost every day. And then Isabel brought home a law student, Clarence Myers. "Katharine and Isabel were bold and imaginative and intuitive. Myers was practical and logical and detail-oriented" (Gladwell, 2004, p. 45). Katharine was so shocked by the personality differences between her daughter and her future son-in-law that she embarked on an intensive program of self-study in psychology to try to understand him.

In 1923 she read Jung's book, *Psychological Types*, and found what she was looking for, a way to categorize people and to explain the differences among them. And so, without research grant support, university affiliation, or graduate students to assist her, she developed, with Isabel's help, a test to measure those differences.

In 1975, Isabel Briggs Myers and Mary McCaulley established the Center for Applications of Psychological Type for MBTI training and research. In 1979, the Association for Psychological Type was founded. Two journals publish research

---

Table 2.4 Sample items from the Myers-Briggs Type Indicator

Which answer comes closer to telling how you usually feel or act?

1. When you go somewhere for the day, would you rather
   (a) plan what you will do and when, or
   (b) just go?
2. Do you tend to have
   (a) deep friendships with a very few people, or
   (b) broad friendships with many different people?
3. When you have a special job to do, do you like to
   (a) organize it carefully before you start, or
   (b) find out what is necessary as you go along?
4. When something new starts to be the fashion, are you usually
   (a) one of the first to try it, or
   (b) not much interested?
5. When the truth would not be polite, are you more likely to tell
   (a) a polite lie, or
   (b) the impolite truth?

SOURCE: Consulting Psychologists Press. Copyright © 1976, 1977 by Isabel Briggs Myers. Copyright 1943, 1944, 1957 by Katharine C. Briggs and Isabel Briggs Myers.

reports on applications of the test. The MBTI is considered the most visible practical outgrowth of Jung's work on the human personality.

Research on Jung's Theory

life-history reconstruction

Jung's type of case study that involves examining a person's past experiences to identify developmental patterns that may explain present neuroses.

Jung, like Freud, used the case study method, which Jung called **life-history reconstruction**. It involved an extensive recollection of a person's past experiences in which Jung sought to identify the developmental patterns he believed led to the present neurotic condition. The criticisms of Freud's data and research methods also apply to Jung's work. Jung's data did not rely on objective observation and were not gathered in a controlled and systematic fashion. Further, the situations in which they were obtained—the clinical interviews—were not amenable to duplication, verification, or quantification.

Like Freud, Jung did not keep verbatim records of his patients' comments, nor did he attempt to verify the accuracy of their reports. Jung's case studies involved (as did Freud's) a small and unrepresentative sample of people, making it difficult to generalize to the population at large.

Jung's analysis of the data was subjective and unreliable. We do not know how he analyzed his data because he never explained his procedures. It is obvious that the data were subjected to some of the most unusual interpretations of any personality theory. We noted earlier that Jung studied a variety of cultures and disciplines. It was on this basis, and that of his own dreams and fantasies, that he interpreted the information gathered from his patients.

His work has been criticized for drawing conclusions he may have slanted to fit his theory. It is also alleged that his visions, which he claimed to have experienced during his midlife confrontation with his unconscious, can be traced to material he had read (Noll, 1993, 1994).

As was the case with Freud's propositions, many of Jung's observations cannot be submitted to experimental test. Jung himself was indifferent to this criticism and commented that anyone who "wishes to know about the human mind will learn nothing, or almost nothing, from experimental psychology" (quoted in Ellenberger, 1970, p. 694).

Psychological Types

Despite Jung's negative view of experimental psychology, researchers have been able to submit aspects of Jungian theory to experimental test, with results that uphold some of Jung's propositions. Most of the supportive research uses the MBTI and focuses on the attitudes of introversion and extraversion. However, not all research supports the delineation of the psychological types (Cowan, 1989; DeVito, 1985; McCrae & Costa, 1989).

A study of college students found that their job interests were closely related to Jungian attitudes and psychological types (Stricker & Ross, 1962). Introverts showed strong interests in occupations that did not involve personal interaction, such as technical and scientific work. Extraverts were more interested in jobs that offered high levels of social interaction, such as sales and public relations.

Another study using the MBTI revealed that different psychological types are drawn to different professions (Hanewitz, 1978). The test was administered to a large sample of police officers, schoolteachers, and social work and dental school students. The teachers and social work students showed high levels of intuiting and feeling. Police officers and dental school students, who deal with people in a different way from teachers and social workers, scored high in extraversion and in sensing and thinking.

A study in which the MBTI was given to 130 female college students and 89 male college students found that those who scored high in intuiting were inclined toward more creative vocational interests. Those who scored high in sensing favored more conventional vocational interests (Apostal, 1991). And a study of 1,568 women admitted to the U.S. Naval Academy from 1988 to 1996 who took the MBTI found that the extraverted-sensing-thinking-judging types were the most likely to graduate. In contrast, the women most likely to drop out scored higher in feeling and perceiving (Murray & Johnson, 2001).

A 10-year research program on students at liberal arts colleges also found that those most likely to drop out before graduation scored high on the MBTI in perceiving (Barrineau, 2005).

Research on the MBTI scores of nearly 4,000 medical school students found that those who became primary care physicians had scored high in feeling and introversion. Those who became surgeons had been labeled extraverted and thinking types (Stilwell, Wallick, Thal, & Burleson, 2000). Among a sample of 97 college students who took the MBTI, extraverts scored higher than introverts in psychological well-being and general life satisfaction (Harrington & Loffredo, 2001).

Research on junior- and mid-level managers in India demonstrated that those who scored very high on the thinking function tended to be collaborative in their efforts to manage conflict. Those who scored high in feeling tended to avoid dealing with conflicts. The men in this study scored higher on thinking whereas the women scored higher on feeling (Mathew & Bhatewara, 2006). A study of managers in China, however, did not find any significant differences between men and women in scores on the MBTI (Huifang & Shuming, 2004). Other research has shown that people who score higher on intuiting and thinking tend to be more argumentative than those who score higher on sensing and feeling (Loffredo & Opt, 2006).

Jungian personality types appear to differ in cognitive or mental functioning. Researchers concluded that persons categorized as introverted thinking types have better memories for neutral or impersonal stimuli, such as numbers. Persons labeled extraverted feeling types have better memories for human stimuli with emotional overtones, such as facial expressions (Carlson & Levy, 1973). It was also found that brain wave activity, as measured by the EEG, differed for each of the psychological types, as assessed by the MBTI (Gram, Dunn, & Ellis, 2005).

Also, introverted thinking and extraverted feeling types differ in their ability to recall significant personal experiences (Carlson, 1980). When subjects were asked to recall their most vivid experiences involving such emotions as joy, anger, and shame, extraverted feeling types most often reported memories involving other people. Introverted thinking types more frequently recalled events that occurred when they were alone. In addition, extraverted feeling types recalled highly emotional

DILBERT © Scott Adams/Dist. By United Feature Syndicate, Inc. Reprinted by permission.

details, whereas introverted thinking types remembered more emotionally neutral and factual experiences.

Persons classified as introverts or extraverts on the MBTI were compared on the quality of their classroom discussion in undergraduate psychology courses (Carskadon, 1978). Extraverts contributed little to the discussion, but introverts made frequent, thoughtful contributions. Students high in intuiting on the MBTI made the best classroom contributions, whereas those high in sensing made the poorest contributions.

A study of 450 college students in Singapore showed that extraverts preferred to communicate with other people in person whereas introverts preferred online contacts. Those students who scored high on sensing, perceiving, intuiting, and judging also indicated a preference for face-to-face communication (Goby, 2006).

Research on the origins of introversion and extraversion points to both genetic and environmental influences. Studies of twins provide evidence of an inherited component to the two attitudes (Wilson, 1977). Significant differences have been found among the parents of introverts and extraverts. Parents of introverts were described as rejecting and cold; parents of extraverts were more accepting and loving (Siegelman, 1988).

Finally, and perhaps not surprisingly, a study of 200 Australians and Canadians found that the core, or fundamental, feature motivating people who scored high in extraversion was the social attention their behavior brought them (Ashton, Lee, & Paunonen, 2002).

Dreams

In research on dreams to study the occurrence of the archetypes, subjects were asked to recall their most recent dream, their most vivid dream, and their earliest dream (Cann & Donderi, 1986). For approximately 3 weeks, they were asked to record the dreams of the previous night as soon as they awakened each morning. Subjects were also given the MBTI and another personality test.

The results showed that introverts were more likely than extraverts to recall everyday dreams, those that bore no relation to archetypes. Intuiting types recalled more archetypal dreams than did sensing types. Persons who scored high in neuroticism recalled fewer archetypal dreams than those who scored low in neuroticism.

The researchers concluded that these findings agreed with predictions made on the basis of Jung's personality theory.

Individuation

An intensive investigation of men and women ages 37 to 55 who held senior executive positions found that they displayed behaviors that corroborate Jung's concept of individuation. The study involved interviews with the executives, their colleagues, and their family members as well as observations of their behavior on the job. They were also evaluated on the TAT, the MBTI, and the Adjective Check List.

The researcher concluded that the executives "looked within [themselves] for direction and energy, questioned their inherited values, relinquished outmoded aspects of their selves, revealed new dimensions of who they are, and allowed themselves to be more playful and spontaneous" (Lyons, 2002, p. 9). The executives also took actions according to their own wishes and desires instead of simply reacting to external demands and pressures. These behavioral and emotional characteristics correspond to Jung's description of the individuation process.

The Midlife Crisis in Women

We noted that the onset of middle age, around age 40, was a time of crisis for Jung and many of his patients. Jung, and others who have studied this so-called midlife crisis, initially viewed it as a phenomenon more likely to affect men than women. More recently, however, the idea that women undergo a similar crisis has been recognized. One national survey of 2,681 women in the United States found that they were in worse health than men, felt they had little or no control over their marriage, and had fewer opportunities to find employment (Barrett, 2005).

Studies of women by ethnicity and gender orientation found that lesbian women reported less emotional turmoil at midlife than did heterosexual women. Black women had more positive self-perceptions at middle age than did White women (Brown, Matthews, & Bromberger, 2005; Howell & Beth, 2004).

A survey of 88 women in their 50s, who had been studied periodically since their senior year in college, asked them to describe the most difficult period in their lives since graduation. A variety of ratings made of stability and adjustment (such as concern about impulses and potential and the search for an identity) revealed that the early 40s were the time of greatest conflict (Helson, 1992).

Other research demonstrated that many women in midlife undergo an intense period of self-evaluation, reviewing their lives and judging their relative success or failure. One study found that the midlife transition was less difficult for women who had actively pursued careers than for women who had focused solely on marriage and family. Many subjects in the latter group concluded that their marriage had been a partial or complete failure. Their regret over their choice led them to consider drastic changes. The career women felt significantly less need to make major changes at midlife (Levinson, 1996).

Research involving two samples of college-educated women confirmed these findings. Both subject groups graduated from college in the 1960s when the feminist movement was opening many new career paths. The women were studied initially as students and later when they were in their late 30s or early 40s. The majority of the women experienced a period of life reevaluation around age 40, as Jung had predicted. Approximately two-thirds made major life changes between the ages of 37 and 43 as a direct result of their self-evaluation. When asked at age 37 if they would opt again for the same life choices they had made when younger, 34 percent in the sample from an affluent private college and 61 percent in the sample from a large state university said they would not. If they could do it all over again, these women said they would pursue educational and career opportunities instead of family goals. Another sample of women studied at midlife also showed that two-thirds of them believed they had been less successful in life than their daughters who worked outside the home (Carr, 2004).

A sense of dissatisfaction at midlife motivated many women to change, but not all were able to return to school to enhance their skills or find a job that made full use of their abilities. Those women who were able to effect satisfactory life changes by age 43 reported significantly greater feelings of general well-being than those women who were unable to make such changes. The changed group experienced an increased sense of personal identity and an enlarged view of their own capabilities. Thus, regret about their earlier choices led to positive changes in midlife (Stewart & Ostrove, 1998; Stewart & Vandewater, 1999).

Another longitudinal study followed women for 20 years after they graduated from college in the late 1950s. The results showed that the personalities of the women at midlife, based on ratings by independent judges, could be divided into three levels or prototypes: conflicted, traditional, and individuated. The lowest level, the conflicted prototype, was characterized by personal conflicts, psychological problems, poor relationships with others, anxiety, hostility, and rigidity. The women at this level were considered to be psychologically immature.

The second level, the traditional prototype, was characterized by devotion to others, feelings of guilt, an emphasis on fulfilling duties and obligations at the expense of their own self-development and self-expression, and a concern for societal standards and with receiving the approval of others. They were also described as competent adults and good citizens who focused on marriage rather than career but lacking a high degree of psychological maturity and self-understanding.

The third level, the individuated prototype, appears to correspond to Jung's concept of individuation, the ideal outcome of the midlife personality crisis. Women at this level were described as high in autonomy, creativity, responsiveness and closeness to others, self-actualization, individual achievement orientation, empathy, tolerance, ego resilience, and intellectual and cultural sophistication (John, Pals, & Westenberg, 1998). Studies of women in the United States and in Australia confirmed that for some, middle age was a time of increasing personal growth, moving in new directions, ridding themselves of past problems, and experiencing the freedom to be themselves (Arnold, 2005; Leonard & Burns, 2006). In other words, they had reached a higher level of psychological maturity, a finding that supports Jung's view of individuation as the supreme state of psychological health and self-development.

Reflections on Jung's Theory

Jung's complex and unusual approach to the human personality has had considerable impact on a broad range of disciplines, notably psychiatry, cultural history, sociology, economics, political science, philosophy, and religion. Recognized by the intellectual community at large, Jung received honorary degrees from Harvard and Oxford universities and has been acknowledged as a powerful influence on the work of many scholars.

Jung made several important and lasting contributions to psychology. The word association test became a standard projective technique and inspired the development of the Rorschach inkblot test and so-called lie-detection techniques. The concepts of psychological complexes and of introverted versus extraverted personalities are widely accepted in psychology today. The personality scales that measure introversion and extraversion are standard diagnostic and selection devices. A great deal of research is being conducted on the introversion–extraversion personality dimensions.

In the following chapters, we see evidence of Jung's influence on the work of other theorists. Jung's notion of individuation, or self-actualization, anticipated the work of Abraham Maslow and other personality theorists. Jung was the first to emphasize the role of the future in determining behavior, an idea adopted by Alfred Adler. Portions of Henry Murray's theory can also be traced to Jung's ideas. Maslow, Erik Erikson, and Raymond Cattell embraced Jung's suggestion that middle age is a time of crucial personality change. The idea of a midlife crisis is now seen by many as a necessary stage of personality development and has been supported by considerable research.

Despite the significance of these formulations, the bulk of Jung's theory was not received enthusiastically by psychologists. One reason concerns the difficulty of understanding Jungian concepts. Sigmund Freud, Alfred Adler, and others wrote in a clear style that allows their books to be easily read and understood. Jung did not write for the general public. Reading his work can be frustrating, so beset are his books by inconsistencies and contradictions. Jung once said, "I can formulate my thoughts only as they break out of me. It is like a geyser. Those who come after me will have to put them in order" (quoted in Jaffé, 1971, p. 8). One Jungian scholar described one of Jung's major books as only partly intelligible. "The connection between one thought and the next is not clear and . . . there are many internal contradictions" (Noll, 1994, p. 109). This criticism can be applied to many of Jung's writings. They are difficult to comprehend and lack internal consistency and systematization.

Jung's embrace of the occult and the supernatural is probably the source of most of the criticism directed at his theory. Evidence from mythology and religion is not in favor in an era when reason and science are considered the most legitimate approaches to knowledge and understanding. Critics charge that Jung accepted as scientific evidence the mythical and mystical occurrences his patients reported.

Despite these problems, a surge of interest in Jung's work began in the late 1980s and continues today. Formal training in Jungian analysis is available in New York, Chicago, Boston, San Francisco, Los Angeles, and several other major cities in the

United States and Canada. There are also Jungian training institutes in a number of European countries. The Society of Analytical Psychology, founded in 1947, publishes the Jungian *Journal of Analytical Psychology*.

Chapter Summary

Parts of Jung's personality theory were influenced by his childhood experiences and his dreams and fantasies. Jung broadened Freud's definition of libido, redefining it as a more generalized dynamic force. Jung argued that personality is shaped by the future as well as the past, and he placed greater emphasis on the unconscious. Jung used the term libido in two ways: a diffuse, generalized life energy and a narrower energy that fuels the psyche. The amount of energy invested in an idea or feeling is called a value. Psychic energy operates in accordance with the principles of opposites, equivalence, and entropy. The principle of opposites states that every aspect of the psyche has its opposite and that this opposition generates psychic energy. The principle of equivalence states that energy is never lost to the personality but is shifted from one part to another. The principle of entropy states that there is a tendency toward equilibrium in the personality.

The ego is the center of consciousness and is concerned with perceiving, thinking, feeling, and remembering. Part of our conscious perception is determined by the attitudes of introversion and extraversion, in which libido is channeled internally or externally. The psychological functions include thinking, feeling, sensing, and intuiting. Thinking and feeling are rational functions; sensing and intuiting are nonrational. Only one attitude and function can be dominant. The eight psychological types are formed by combinations of the attitudes and functions.

The personal unconscious is a reservoir of material that was once conscious but has been forgotten or suppressed. Complexes, which may be conscious or unconscious, are patterns of emotions, memories, perceptions, and wishes centering on common themes. The collective unconscious is a storehouse of the experiences of humankind transmitted to each individual. Archetypes are recurring themes that express these experiences. The most powerful archetypes are the persona, anima, animus, shadow, and self.

Psychic birth occurs at puberty, when the psyche assumes a definite content. Preparatory activities mark the time from adolescence through young adulthood. In the period of middle age, when success has been achieved, the personality undergoes changes. Psychic energy must be rechanneled into the inner world of the unconscious, and the attitude must shift from extraversion to introversion. Individuation (the realization of one's capabilities) can occur only in middle age, when people must confront the unconscious and abandon the behaviors and values that guided the first half of life. Transcendence involves the unification of the personality.

Jung's image of human nature was more optimistic and less deterministic than Freud's view. Jung believed that part of personality is innate, and part is learned. The ultimate life goal is individuation. Childhood experiences are important, but personality is more affected by midlife experiences and hopes for the future. Personality is unique in the first half of life but not in the second.

Jung's methods of assessment include the investigation of symbols, myths, and rituals in ancient cultures; the word association test, used to uncover complexes; symptom analysis, in which patients free-associate to their symptoms; and dream analysis. The Myers-Briggs Type Indicator, an assessment instrument deriving from Jung's approach, is a highly popular employee selection technique and is also used for research on Jung's system.

Jung's case study method, called life-history reconstruction, did not rely on objective observation, was not systematic and controlled, and was not amenable to duplication and verification.

Research has supported Jung's ideas on attitudes, functions, and psychological types, but broader aspects of his theory have resisted attempts at scientific validation. His work has had considerable influence in several fields. Widely accepted Jungian ideas include the word association test, complexes, introversion–extraversion, self-actualization, and the midlife crisis.

Review Questions

1. In what ways was Jung's personality theory influenced by his childhood experiences and his dreams and fantasies?

2. Describe the principles of opposites, equivalence, and entropy. How do they relate to the concept of psychic energy?

3. What are the three major points of difference between Jung's theory of analytical psychology and Freud's theory of psychoanalysis?

4. How does the principle of opposites apply to the attitudes and functions?

5. Explain how the eight psychological types derive from the attitudes and functions.

6. Explain how introverts differ from extraverts.

7. Why are thinking and feeling considered to be rational functions while sensing and intuiting are said to be non-rational functions?

8. What is the relationship between the ego and the personal unconscious?

9. How does the personal unconscious differ from the collective unconscious?

10. What is a complex? How can a complex be helpful?

11. Distinguish between the persona archetype and the self archetype.

12. What are the similarities between Jung's concept of the shadow archetype and Freud's concept of the id?

13. What are the anima and animus archetypes? Did Jung suggest that they must be suppressed or expressed? Why?

14. Discuss Jung's ideas on the development of personality throughout the life span, especially the periods of adolescence and middle age.

15. What is individuation? How must our archetypes change if we are to achieve individuation?

16. How does Jung's image of human nature differ from Freud's?

17. What is the purpose of the word association test? What are the purposes of dreams?

18. Describe Jung's approach to his sessions with patients. How did his typical session differ from one of Freud's?

19. Discuss the MBTI research findings that show the occupational preferences of extraverts and introverts.

20. Describe the criticisms and the contributions of Jung's personality theory.

Suggested Readings

Bair, D. (2003). *Jung: A biography*. Boston: Little, Brown. A thoroughly researched biography that assesses Jung's complex personality and shows its impact on his theories. Notes the censorship Jung's heirs maintain over significant amounts of his correspondence, suggesting that the definitive biography has yet to be written.

Eisold, K. (2002). Jung, Jungians, and psychoanalysis. *Psychoanalytic Psychology, 19*, 501–524. Discusses the break between Freud and Jung and the consequent split between their followers, and how some Jungian concepts have been absorbed by mainstream psychoanalysis.

Ellenberger, H. F. (1970). *The discovery of the unconscious: The history and evolution of dynamic psychiatry*. New York: Basic Books. Traces the study of the unconscious from primitive times to Freudian psychoanalysis and its derivatives. See Chapter 9, "Carl Gustav Jung and Analytical Psychology."

Freud/Jung letters. (1974). Princeton, NJ: Princeton University Press. Contains some 360 letters, dating from 1906 to 1913, that show the development and dissolution of the friendship between Sigmund Freud and Carl Jung. Edited by William McGuire.

Iaccino, J. F. (1994). *Psychological reflections on cinematic terror: Jungian archetypes in horror films*. Westport, CT: Praeger. Uses Jungian archetypes to analyze recurrent themes in a wide range of significant horror movies, from classics to contemporary nightmare, alien, and vampire films.

Jung, C. G. (1961). *Memories, dreams, reflections*. New York: Vintage Books. Jung's recollections of his life, written at the age of 81.

Kerr, J. (1993). *A most dangerous method: The story of Jung, Freud, and Sabina Spielrein*. New York: Alfred A. Knopf. The story of a woman patient who became involved in a disastrous relationship with her analyst, Carl Jung.

Roazen, P. (1975). *Freud and his followers*. New York: Alfred A. Knopf. A lively, well-written account of Freud's life and the men and women who became his disciples. See Part 6, "The 'Crown Prince': Carl Gustav Jung."

Schultz, D. (1990). *Intimate friends, dangerous rivals: The turbulent relationship between Freud and Jung*. Los Angeles: Jeremy Tarcher. Describes the personal and professional collaboration between Freud and Jung and the parallels and differences in their childhoods, midlife crises, and relationships with women.

Tilander, A. (1991). Why did C. G. Jung write his autobiography? *Journal of Analytical Psychology, 36*, 111–124. Suggests that Jung chose to include in his autobiography those experiences that seemed to support his personality theory.

CHAPTER 3

Alfred Adler:
Individual Psychology

The goal of the human soul is conquest, perfection, security, superiority. Every child is faced with so many obstacles in life that no child ever grows up without striving for some form of significance.

—ALFRED ADLER

individual psychology
Adler's theory of
personality.

Alfred Adler fashioned an image of human nature that did not depict people as victimized by instincts and conflict and doomed by biological forces and childhood experiences. He called his approach **individual psychology** because it focused on the uniqueness of each person and denied the universality of biological motives and goals ascribed to us by Sigmund Freud.

In Adler's opinion, each individual is primarily a social being. Our personalities are shaped by our unique social environments and interactions, not by our efforts to satisfy biological needs. Although sex was of primary importance to Freud as a determining factor in personality, Adler minimized the role of sex in his system. To Adler, the conscious, not the unconscious, was at the core of personality. Rather than being driven by forces we cannot see and control, we are actively involved in creating our selves and directing our future.

With Adler and Freud, we see two vastly different theories created by two men brought up in the same city in the same era and educated as physicians at the same university. There was only a 14-year difference in their ages. And as with Freud, aspects of Adler's childhood may have influenced his way of looking at human nature.

The Life of Adler (1870–1937)

Childhood and Adolescence

Adler's early childhood was marked by illness, an awareness of death, and jealousy of his older brother. He suffered from rickets (a vitamin D deficiency characterized by softening of the bones), which kept him from playing with other children. At the age of 3, his younger brother died in the bed next to his. At 4, Adler himself was close to death from pneumonia. When he heard the doctor tell his father, "Your boy is lost," he decided to become a doctor (Orgler, 1963, p. 16).

Pampered by his mother because of his sickness, the young Adler was dethroned at the age of 2 by the arrival of another baby. Biographers have suggested that Adler's mother may then have rejected him, but he was clearly his father's favorite. Therefore, his childhood relations with his parents were different from Freud's. (Freud was closer to his mother than to his father.) As an adult, Adler discarded the Freudian concept of the Oedipus complex because it was so foreign to his childhood experiences.

Adler was jealous of his older brother, who was vigorous and healthy and could engage in the physical activities and sports in which Alfred could not take part. "I remember sitting on a bench, bandaged up on account of rickets, with my healthy elder brother sitting opposite me. He could run, jump, and move about quite effortlessly, while for me, movement of any sort was a strain and an effort" (Adler quoted in Bottome, 1939, pp. 30–31).

Adler felt inferior to this brother and to other neighborhood children, who all seemed healthier and more athletic. As a result, he resolved to work hard to overcome his feelings of inferiority and to compensate for his physical limitations. Despite his small stature, clumsiness, and unattractiveness, the legacies of his illness, he forced himself to join in games and sports. Gradually he won his victory and achieved a sense of self-esteem and social acceptance. He developed a fondness for the company of other people and retained this sociability all his life. In his personality theory, Adler emphasized the importance of the peer group and suggested that childhood relationships with siblings and with children outside the family were much more significant than Freud believed.

In school (the same school Freud had attended), Adler was initially unhappy and was only a mediocre student. Believing the boy unfit for anything else, a teacher advised Adler's father to apprentice him to a shoemaker, a prospect Adler found frightening. He was particularly bad in mathematics, but he persisted and eventually rose from being a failing student to the top of his class.

In many ways, the story of Adler's childhood reads like a tragedy, but it is also a textbook example of his personality theory, of overcoming childhood weakness and inferiority to shape his destiny. The theorist who would give the world the notion of inferiority feelings spoke from the depths of his own childhood. "Those who are familiar with my life work will clearly see the accord existing between the facts of my childhood and the views I expressed" (quoted in Bottome, 1939, p. 9).

Adulthood

Fulfilling his childhood ambition, Adler studied medicine at the University of Vienna but graduated with no better than a mediocre academic record. He entered private practice as an ophthalmologist but soon shifted to general medicine. He was interested in incurable diseases but became so distressed at his helplessness to prevent death, particularly in younger patients, that he chose to specialize in neurology and psychiatry.

Adler's 9-year association with Freud began in 1902, when Freud invited Adler and three others to meet once a week at Freud's home to discuss psychoanalysis. Although their relationship never became close, Freud initially thought highly of Adler and praised his skill as a physician who was able to gain the trust of his patients. It is important to remember that Adler was never a student or disciple of Freud's and was not psychoanalyzed by him. One of Freud's colleagues charged that Adler did not have the ability to probe the unconscious mind and psychoanalyze people. It is interesting to speculate on whether this supposed lack led Adler to base his personality theory on the more easily accessible consciousness and to minimize the role of the unconscious.

By 1910, although Adler was president of the Vienna Psychoanalytical Society and co-editor of its journal, he was also an increasingly vocal critic of Freudian theory. He soon severed all connection with psychoanalysis and went on to develop his own approach to personality. Freud reacted angrily to Adler's defection. He belittled Adler's physical stature (Adler was five inches shorter than Freud) and called Adler loathsome, abnormal, driven mad by ambition, filled with venom and meanness, paranoid, intensely jealous, and sadistic. He described Adler's theory as worthless (Fiebert, 1997; Gay, 1988; Wittels, 1924).

Adler showed similar hostility toward Freud, calling him a swindler and denouncing psychoanalysis as filth (Roazen, 1975). Adler became irate whenever he was introduced or referred to as a student of Freud's. In his later years Adler appeared as embittered toward defectors from his own approach as Freud had toward those, like Adler, who deviated from psychoanalysis. Adler was known to "flare suddenly into heated anger when he felt his authority challenged" (Hoffman, 1994, p. 148).

In 1912, Adler founded the Society for Individual Psychology. He served in the Austrian army during World War I (1914–1918) and later organized government sponsored child-counseling clinics in Vienna. In his clinics, Adler introduced group training and guidance procedures, forerunners of modern group therapy techniques. In 1926, he made the first of several visits to the United States, where he taught and gave popular lecture tours.

He moved to the United States in 1929, settling in New York City, where he continued his work to develop and promote his individual psychology. A biographer noted that Adler's "personal traits of geniality, optimism, and warmth coupled with an intensely ambitious drive . . . soon catapulted him to American prominence as a psychological expert" (Hoffman, 1994, p. 160).

Adler's books and lectures brought him recognition on a national scale, and he became America's first popular psychologist, a celebrity of the day. In 1937, while on an exhausting 56-lecture tour of Europe, Adler suffered a heart attack and died in Scotland.

 Log On

Classical Adlerian Psychology

The Alfred Adler Institute of San Francisco offers a comprehensive file of writings, videos, film clips, and recordings of everything you might want to know about Adler.

Personality Theories: Alfred Adler

An overview of Adler's life and work.

For direct links to these sites, log on to the student companion site for this book at http://www.academic.cengage.com/psychology/Schultz and choose Chapter 3.

Inferiority Feelings: The Source of Human Striving

inferiority feelings
The normal condition of all people; the source of all human striving.

compensation
A motivation to overcome inferiority, to strive for higher levels of development.

Adler believed that **inferiority feelings** are always present as a motivating force in behavior. "To be a human being means to feel oneself inferior," Adler wrote (1933/1939, p. 96). Because this condition is common to all of us, then, it is not a sign of weakness or abnormality.

Adler proposed that inferiority feelings are the source of all human striving. Individual growth results from **compensation**, from our attempts to overcome our real or imagined inferiorities. Throughout our lives, we are driven by the need to overcome this sense of inferiority and to strive for increasingly higher levels of development.

Many people with physical disabilities strive to compensate for their weaknesses.

The process begins in infancy. Infants are small and helpless and are totally dependent on adults. Adler believed that the infant is aware of his or her parents' greater power and strength and of the hopelessness of trying to resist or challenge that power. As a result, the infant develops feelings of inferiority relative to the larger, stronger people around him or her.

Although this initial experience of inferiority applies to everyone in infancy, it is not genetically determined. Rather, it is a function of the environment, which is the same for all infants—an environment of helplessness and dependency on adults. Thus, inferiority feelings are inescapable, but more important, they are necessary because they provide the motivation to strive and grow.

The Inferiority Complex

Suppose a child does not grow and develop. What happens when the child is unable to compensate for his or her feelings of inferiority? An inability to overcome inferiority feelings intensifies them, leading to the development of an **inferiority complex**. People with an inferiority complex have a poor opinion of themselves and feel helpless and unable to cope with the demands of life. Adler found such a complex in the childhood of many adults who came to him for treatment.

An inferiority complex can arise from three sources in childhood: organic inferiority, spoiling, and neglect. The investigation of organic inferiority, Adler's

inferiority complex
A condition that develops when a person is unable to compensate for normal inferiority feelings.

first major research effort, was carried out while he was still associated with Freud, who approved of the notion. Adler concluded that defective parts or organs of the body shape personality through the person's efforts to compensate for the defect or weakness, just as Adler had compensated for rickets, the physical inferiority of his childhood years. For instance, a child who is physically weak might focus on that weakness and work to develop superior athletic ability.

History records many examples of such compensation: In ancient times the Greek statesman Demosthenes overcame a stutter to become a great orator. The sickly Theodore Roosevelt, 26th president of the United States, became a model of physical fitness as an adult. Efforts to overcome organic inferiority can result in striking artistic, athletic, and social accomplishments, but if these efforts fail, they can lead to an inferiority complex.

Adler's work is another example of a conception of personality developed along intuitive lines, drawn from the theorist's personal experience, and later confirmed by data from patients. Adler's office in Vienna was near an amusement park, and his patients included circus performers and gymnasts. They possessed extraordinary physical skills that, in many cases, were developed as a result of hard work to overcome childhood disabilities.

Spoiling or pampering a child can also bring about an inferiority complex. Spoiled children are the center of attention in the home. Their every need or whim is satisfied, and little is denied them. Under the circumstances, these children naturally develop the idea that they are the most important persons in any situation and that other people should always defer to them. The first experience at school, where these children are no longer the focus of attention, comes as a shock for which they are unprepared. Spoiled children have little social feeling and are impatient with others. They have never learned to wait for what they want, nor have they learned to overcome difficulties or adjust to others' needs. When confronted with obstacles to gratification, spoiled children come to believe that they must have some personal deficiency that is thwarting them; hence, an inferiority complex develops.

It is easy to understand how neglected, unwanted, and rejected children can develop an inferiority complex. Their infancy and childhood are characterized by a lack of love and security because their parents are indifferent or hostile. As a result, these children develop feelings of worthlessness, or even anger, and view others with distrust.

The Superiority Complex

superiority complex
A condition that develops when a person overcompensates for normal inferiority feelings.

Whatever the source of the complex, a person may tend to overcompensate and so develop what Adler called a **superiority complex**. This involves an exaggerated opinion of one's abilities and accomplishments. Such a person may feel inwardly self-satisfied and superior and show no need to demonstrate his or her superiority with accomplishments. Or the person may feel such a need and work to become extremely successful. In both cases, persons with a superiority complex are given to boasting, vanity, self-centeredness, and a tendency to denigrate others.

Striving for Superiority, or Perfection

Inferiority feelings are the source of motivation and striving, but to what end? Are we motivated simply to be rid of inferiority feelings? Adler believed that we work for something more; however, his view of our ultimate goal in life changed over the years.

At first, he identified inferiority with a general feeling of weakness or of femininity, in recognition of the inferior standing of women in the society of his day. He spoke of compensation for this feeling as the masculine protest. The goal of the compensation was a will or a drive toward power in which aggression, a supposedly masculine characteristic, played a large part. Later he rejected the idea of equating inferiority feelings with femininity and developed a broader viewpoint in which we strive for superiority, or perfection.

striving for superiority
The urge toward perfection or completion that motivates each of us.

Adler described his notion of **striving for superiority** as the fundamental fact of life (Adler, 1930). Superiority is the ultimate goal toward which we strive. He did not mean superiority in the usual sense of the word, nor did the concept relate to the superiority complex. Striving for superiority is not an attempt to be better than everyone else, nor is it an arrogant or domineering tendency or an inflated opinion of our abilities and accomplishments. What Adler meant was a drive for perfection. The word *perfection* is derived from a Latin word meaning to complete or to finish. Thus, Adler suggested that we strive for superiority in an effort to perfect ourselves, to make ourselves complete or whole.

This innate goal, the drive toward wholeness or completion, is oriented toward the future. Whereas Freud proposed that human behavior is determined by the past (that is, by the instincts and by our childhood experiences), Adler saw human motivation in terms of expectations for the future. He argued that instincts and primal impulses were insufficient as explanatory principles. Only the ultimate goal of superiority or perfection could explain personality and behavior.

Fictional Finalism

Adler applied the term *finalism* to the idea that we have an ultimate goal, a final state of being, and a need to move toward it. The goals for which we strive, however, are potentialities, not actualities. In other words, we strive for ideals that exist in us subjectively. Adler believed that our goals are fictional or imagined ideals that cannot be tested against reality. We live our lives around ideals such as the belief that all people are created equal or that all people are basically good. Adler's life goal was to conquer death; his way of striving for that goal was to become a physician (Hoffman, 1994).

fictional finalism
The idea that there is an imagined or potential goal that guides our behavior.

These beliefs influence the ways we perceive and interact with other people. For example, if we believe that behaving a certain way will bring us rewards in a heaven or an afterlife, we will try to act according to that belief. Belief in the existence of an afterlife is not based on objective reality, but it is real to the person who holds that view.

Adler formalized this concept as **fictional finalism**, the notion that fictional ideas guide our behavior as we strive toward a complete or whole state of being. We direct the course of our lives by many such fictions, but the most pervasive one is the ideal of perfection. He suggested that the best formulation of this ideal developed by human beings so far is the concept of God. Adler preferred the terms "subjective final goal" or "guiding self-ideal" to describe this concept, but it continues to be known as "fictional finalism" (Watts & Holden, 1994).

There are two additional points about striving for superiority. First, it increases rather than reduces tension. Unlike Freud, Adler did not believe that our sole motivation was to reduce tension. Striving for perfection requires great expenditures of energy and effort, a condition quite different from equilibrium or a tension-free state. Second, the striving for superiority is manifested both by the individual and by society. Most of us are social beings. We strive for superiority or perfection not only as individuals but also as members of a group. We try to achieve the perfection of our culture. In Adler's view, individuals and society are interrelated and interdependent. People must function constructively with others for the good of all.

Thus, to Adler, human beings perpetually strive for the fictional, ideal goal of perfection. How in our daily lives do we try to attain this goal? Adler answered this question with his concept of the style of life.

The Style of Life

style of life
A unique character structure or pattern of personal behaviors and characteristics by which each of us strives for perfection. Basic styles of life include the dominant, getting, avoiding, and socially useful types.

The ultimate goal for each of us is superiority or perfection, but we try to attain that goal through many different behavior patterns. Each of us expresses the striving differently. We develop a unique pattern of characteristics, behaviors, and habits, which Adler called a distinctive character, or **style of life**.

To understand how the style of life develops, we return to the concepts of inferiority feelings and compensation. Infants are afflicted with inferiority feelings that motivate them to compensate for helplessness and dependency. In these attempts at compensation, children acquire a set of behaviors. For example, the sickly child may strive to increase physical prowess by running or lifting weights. These behaviors become part of the style of life, a pattern of behaviors designed to compensate for inferiority.

Everything we do is shaped and defined by our unique style of life. It determines which aspects of our environment we attend to or ignore and what attitudes we hold. The style of life is learned from social interactions that occur in the early years of life. Adler suggested that the style of life is so firmly crystallized by the age of 4 or 5 that it is difficult to change thereafter.

The style of life becomes the guiding framework for all later behaviors. As we noted, its nature depends on social interactions, especially the person's order of birth within the family and the nature of the parent–child relationship. Recall that one condition that can lead to an inferiority complex is neglect. Neglected children may feel inferior in coping with the demands of life and therefore may become distrustful and hostile toward others. As a result, their style of life may involve seeking revenge, resenting others' success, and taking whatever they feel is their due.

The Creative Power of the Self

You may have spotted an apparent inconsistency between Adler's notion of style of life and our earlier observation that his theory is less deterministic than Freud's. Adler said we are in control of our fate, not victims of it. But now we find that the style of life is determined by social relationships in the early years and subject to little change after that. This seems almost as deterministic as the Freudian view, which emphasized the importance of early childhood in the formation of the adult personality. However, Adler's theory is not as deterministic as it may seem at first. He resolved the dilemma by proposing a concept he described as the **creative power of the self**.

Adler believed that the individual creates the style of life. We create our *selves*, our *personality*, our *character*; these are all terms Adler used interchangeably with *style of life*. We are not passively shaped by childhood experiences. Those experiences themselves are not as important as our conscious attitude toward them. Adler argued that neither heredity nor environment provides a complete explanation for personality development. Instead, the way we interpret these influences forms the basis for the creative construction of our attitude toward life.

Adler argued for the existence of individual free will that allows each of us to create an appropriate style of life from the abilities and experiences given us by both our genetic endowment and our social environment. Although unclear on specifics, Adler insisted that our style of life is not determined for us; we are free to choose and create it ourselves. Once created, however, the style of life remains constant throughout life.

creative power of the self
The ability to create an appropriate style of life.

Dominant, Getting, Avoiding, and Socially Useful Styles

Adler described several universal problems and grouped them in three categories:

1. Problems involving our behavior toward others
2. Problems of occupation
3. Problems of love

He proposed four basic styles of life for dealing with these problems:

1. The dominant type
2. The getting type
3. The avoiding type
4. The socially useful type

The first type displays a dominant or ruling attitude with little social awareness. Such a person behaves without regard for others. The more extreme of this type attack others and become sadists, delinquents, or sociopaths. The less virulent become alcoholics, drug addicts, or suicides; they believe they hurt others by attacking themselves.

The getting type (to Adler, the most common human type) expects to receive satisfaction from other people and so becomes dependent on them.

The avoiding type makes no attempt to face life's problems. By avoiding difficulties, the person avoids any possibility of failure.

These three types are not prepared to cope with the problems of everyday life. They are unable to cooperate with other people and the clash between their style of life and the real world results in abnormal behavior, which is manifested in neuroses and psychoses. They lack what Adler came to call social interest.

The socially useful type cooperates with others and acts in accordance with their needs. Such persons cope with problems within a well-developed framework of social interest.

Adler was generally opposed to rigidly classifying or typing people in this way, stating that he proposed these four styles of life solely for teaching purposes. He cautioned therapists to avoid the mistake of assigning people to mutually exclusive categories.

Social Interest

social interest
Our innate potential to cooperate with other people to achieve personal and societal goals.

Adler believed that getting along with others is the first task we encounter in life. Our subsequent level of social adjustment, which is part of our style of life, influences our approach to all of life's problems. He proposed the concept of **social interest**, which he defined as the individual's innate potential to cooperate with other people to achieve personal and societal goals. Adler's term for this concept in the original German, *Gemeinschaftsgefuhl*, is best translated as "community feeling" (Stepansky, 1983, p. xiii). However, *social interest* has become the accepted term in English.

Although we are influenced more strongly by social than biological forces, in Adler's view, the potential for social interest is innate. In that limited sense, then, Adler's approach has a biological element. However, the extent to which our innate potential for social interest is realized depends on our early social experiences.

No one can avoid entirely other people or obligations toward them. From earliest times, people have congregated in families, tribes, and nations. Communities are indispensable to human beings for protection and survival. Thus, it has always been necessary for people to cooperate, to express their social interest. The individual must cooperate with and contribute to society to realize personal and communal goals.

The newborn is in a situation that requires cooperation, initially from the mother or primary caregiver, then from other family members and people at day care or school. Adler noted the importance of the mother as the first person with whom the baby comes in contact. Through her behavior toward the child, the mother can either foster social interest or thwart its development.

Adler believed the mother's role was vital in developing the child's social interest as well as other aspects of the personality. He wrote:

> This connection [between mother and child] is so intimate and far reaching that we are never able in later years to point to any characteristic as the effect of heredity. Every tendency which might be inherited has been adapted, trained, educated and made over again by the mother. Her skill or lack of skill will influence all the child's potentiality. (Adler quoted in Grey, 1998, p. 71)

The mother must teach the child cooperation, companionship, and courage. Only if children feel kinship with others can they act with courage in attempting to cope with life's demands. Children (and later, adults) who look upon others with suspicion and hostility will approach life with the same attitude. Those who have no feeling of social interest may become neurotics or even criminals. Adler noted that evils ranging from war to racial hatred to public drunkenness stemmed from a lack of community feeling.

It is interesting to note that early in his career, Adler suggested that people were driven by a lust for power and a need to dominate. He proposed this idea at the time he was struggling to establish his own point of view within the Freudian circle. After he broke with Freud and achieved recognition for his own work, he proposed that people are motivated more by social interest than by the needs for power and dominance.

When Adler was part of Freud's group, he was considered cantankerous and ambitious, quarreling over the priority of his ideas. But in later years, he mellowed and his system also changed, from emphasizing power and dominance as motivating forces to stressing the more benign force of social or community interest. (Here we see another example of how Adler's theory reflected his own life experiences.)

Birth Order

One of Adler's most enduring contributions is the idea that order of birth is a major social influence in childhood, one from which we create our style of life. Even though siblings have the same parents and live in the same house, they do not have identical social environments. Being older or younger than one's siblings and being exposed to differing parental attitudes create different childhood conditions that help determine personality. Adler liked to amaze lecture audiences and dinner guests by guessing a person's order of birth on the basis of his or her behavior. He wrote about four situations: the first-born child, the second-born child, the youngest child, and the only child.

The First-Born Child

At least for a while, first-born children are in a unique and enviable situation. Usually the parents are happy at the birth of the first child and devote considerable time and attention to the new baby. First-borns typically receive their parents' instant and undivided attention. As a result, first-borns have a happy, secure existence—until the second-born child appears.

Suddenly, no longer the focus of attention, no longer receiving constant love and care, first-borns are, in a sense, dethroned. The affection first-borns received during their reign must now be shared. They must often submit to the outrage of waiting until after the newborn's needs have been met, and they are admonished to be quiet so as not to disturb the new baby.

No one could expect first-borns to suffer this drastic displacement without putting up a fight. They will try to recapture their former position of power and privilege. The first-born's battle to regain supremacy in the family is lost from the beginning, however. Things will never be the same, no matter how hard the first-born tries.

For a time, first-borns may become stubborn, ill behaved, and destructive and may refuse to eat or go to bed. They are striking out in anger, but the parents will probably strike back, and their weapons are far more powerful. When first-borns are punished for their troublesome behavior, they may interpret the punishment as additional evidence of their fall and may come to hate the second child, who is, after all, the cause of the problem.

Adler believed all first-borns feel the shock of their changed status in the family, but those who have been excessively pampered feel a greater loss. Also, the extent of the loss depends on the first-born's age at the time the rival appears. In general, the older a first-born child is when the second child arrives, the less dethronement the first-born will experience. For example, an 8-year-old will be less upset by the birth of a sibling than will a 2-year-old.

Adler found that first-borns are often oriented toward the past, locked in nostalgia and pessimistic about the future. Having learned the advantages of power at one time, they remain concerned with it throughout life. They can exercise some power over younger siblings, but at the same time they are more subject to the power of their parents because more is expected of them.

There are advantages to being the first-born child, however. As the children age, the first-born often plays the role of teacher, tutor, leader, and disciplinarian, expected by parents to help care for younger siblings. These experiences often enable the first-born to mature intellectually to a higher degree than the younger children. One researcher described the situation as follows:

> Second-born children might ask older siblings about the meanings of words, about how some things work and why, about the whereabouts of candy or of a parent who is late in coming back home, and about countless other matters that older siblings must now explain. . . . In

One's order of birth within the family—being older or younger than one's siblings—creates different conditions of childhood that can affect personality.

© Brooklyn Productions/The Image Bank/Getty Images

this role of tutor, first-born children gain an intellectual advantage. By virtue of rehearsal, by virtue of having to articulate an explanation or offer the meaning of a word, firstborns gain more verbal fluency more quickly than the second-borns. (Zajonc, 2001, p. 491)

Adler believed that first-borns also take an unusual interest in maintaining order and authority. They become good organizers, conscientious and scrupulous about detail, authoritarian and conservative in attitude. Sigmund Freud was a first-born; Adler described him as a typical eldest son. First-borns may also grow up to feel insecure and hostile toward others. Adler believed that neurotics, perverts, and criminals were often first-borns.

The Second-Born Child

Second-born children, the ones who caused such upheaval in the lives of first-borns, are also in a unique situation. They never experience the powerful position once occupied by the first-borns. Even if another child is brought into the family, second-borns do not suffer the sense of dethronement felt by the first-borns. Furthermore, by this time the parents have usually changed their child-rearing attitudes and practices. A second baby is not the novelty the first was; parents may be less concerned and anxious about their own behavior and may take a more relaxed approach to the second child.

From the beginning, second-borns have a pacesetter in the older sibling. The second child always has the example of the older child's behavior as a model, a threat, or a source of competition. Adler was a second-born child who had a lifelong competitive relationship with his older brother (whose name was Sigmund). Even when Adler became a famous analyst, he still felt overshadowed by his brother.

Alfred [Adler] always felt eclipsed by his "model brother" and resented his favored status in the family. . . . Even in middle age, he would feel moved to comment wearily that wealthy businessman Sigmund, "a good industrious fellow [who] was always ahead of me—is still ahead of me!" (Hoffman, 1994, p. 11)

Competition with the first-born may serve to motivate the second-born, who may strive to catch up to and surpass the older sibling, a goal that spurs language and motor development in the second-born. Not having experienced power, second-borns are not as concerned with it. They are more optimistic about the future and are likely to be competitive and ambitious, as Adler was.

Other less beneficial outcomes may arise from the relationship between first-borns and second-borns. If, for example, the older sibling excels in sports or scholarship, the second-born may feel that he or she can never surpass the first-born and may give up trying. In this case, competitiveness would not become part of the second-born's style of life, and he or she may become an underachiever, performing below his or her abilities in many facets of life.

The Youngest Child

Youngest or last-born children never face the shock of dethronement by another child and often become the pet of the family, particularly if the siblings are more than a few years older. Driven by the need to surpass older siblings, youngest children often develop at a remarkably fast rate. Last-borns are often high achievers in whatever work they undertake as adults.

The opposite can occur, however, if the youngest children are excessively pampered and come to believe they needn't learn to do anything for themselves. As they grow older, such children may retain the helplessness and dependency of childhood. Unaccustomed to striving and struggling, used to being cared for, these people find it difficult to adjust to adulthood.

The Only Child

Only children never lose the position of primacy and power they hold in the family; they remain the focus and center of attention. Spending more time in the company of adults than a child with siblings, only children often mature early and manifest adult behaviors and attitudes.

Only children are likely to experience difficulties when they find that in areas of life outside the home, such as school, they are not the center of attention. Only children have learned neither to share nor to compete. If their abilities do not bring them sufficient recognition and attention, they are likely to feel keenly disappointed.

With his ideas about order of birth, Adler was not proposing firm rules of childhood development. A child will not automatically acquire a particular kind of character based solely on his or her position in the family. What Adler was suggesting was the likelihood that certain styles of life will develop as a function of order of birth combined with one's early social interactions. The creative self in constructing the style of life uses both influences.

Questions About Human Nature

Adler's system provides a hopeful, flattering picture of human nature that is the antithesis of Freud's dreary, pessimistic view. Certainly it is more satisfying to our sense of self-worth to consider ourselves capable of consciously shaping our development and destiny rather than being dominated by instinctual forces and childhood experiences over which we have no control.

Adler's image is an optimistic one, simply that people are not driven by unconscious forces. We possess the free will to shape the social forces that influence us and to use them creatively to construct a unique style of life. This uniqueness is another aspect of Adler's flattering picture; Freud's system offered a depressing universality and sameness in human nature.

Although, in Adler's view, some aspects of human nature are innate—for example, the potential for social interest and striving for perfection—it is experience that determines how these inherited tendencies will be realized. Childhood influences are important, particularly order of birth and interactions with our parents, but we are not victims of childhood events. Instead, we use them to create our style of life.

Adler saw each person as striving to achieve perfection, and he viewed humanity in similar terms; he was optimistic about social progress. He was attracted to socialism and was involved in school guidance clinics and prison reform, expressing his belief in the creative power of the individual.

Assessment in Adler's Theory

Like Freud, Adler developed his theory by analyzing his patients; that is, by evaluating their verbalizations and behavior during therapy sessions. Adler's approach was more relaxed and informal than Freud's. Whereas Freud's patients lay on a couch while he sat behind them, Adler and his patients sat in comfortable chairs facing each other. The sessions were more like chats between friends than like the formal relationships maintained by Freud.

Adler also liked to use humor in his therapy, sometimes teasing his patients in a lighthearted, friendly way. He had a storehouse of jokes appropriate for various neuroses and believed that making a joke would sometimes lead a patient to "see how ridiculous his sickness is." When an adolescent patient told Adler he felt guilty when he masturbated, Adler replied: "You mean to say you masturbate and feel guilty? That is too much. One would be enough: either masturbate or feel guilty. But both is too much" (Hoffman, 1994, pp. 209, 273).

Adler assessed the personalities of his patients by observing everything about them: the way they walked and sat, their manner of shaking hands, even their choice of which chair to sit in. He suggested that the way we use our bodies indicates something of our style of life. Even the position in which we sleep is revealing. For example, according to Adler, restless sleepers and those who sleep flat on their back want to seem more important than they are. Sleeping on one's stomach shows a stubborn and negative personality. Curling in the fetal position shows that the person is fearful of interacting with others. Sleeping with the arms outstretched reveals a need to be nurtured and supported.

Adler's primary methods of assessment, which he referred to as the entrance gates to mental life, are order of birth (discussed above), early recollections, and dream analysis. In addition, contemporary psychologists have developed psychological assessment tests based on Adler's concept of social interest. Adler's purpose in assessing personality was to discover the patient's style of life and to determine whether it was the most appropriate one for that person.

Early Recollections

According to Adler, our personality is created during the first 4 or 5 years of life. Our **early recollections**, our memories from that period, indicate the style of life that continues to characterize us as adults. Adler found that it made little difference whether his clients' early recollections were of real events or were fantasies. In either case, the primary interest of the person's life revolved around the remembered incidents and so, in Adler's view, early recollections are "the most satisfactory single indicators of lifestyle" (Manaster & Mays, 2004, p. 114).

Adler asked more than 100 physicians to describe their early memories. A majority of the recollections were concerned with illness or with a death in the family, which apparently led them to pursue a career in medicine, as was the case with Adler himself.

An early memory Adler recalled as an adult was that when he was 5 years old and had just started school, he was fearful because the path to school led through a

early recollections
A personality assessment technique in which our earliest memories, whether of real events or fantasies, are assumed to reveal the primary interest of our life.

cemetery (Adler, 1924/1963). He said he became terrified every time he walked to school, but he was also confused because other children seemed not to notice the cemetery. He was the only one who was afraid, and this experience heightened his sense of inferiority. One day, Adler decided to put an end to his fears. He ran through the cemetery a dozen times, until he felt he had overcome his feelings. Thereafter, he was able to attend school without being frightened whenever he passed the cemetery.

Thirty years later Adler met a former schoolmate and, in the course of their conversation, asked if the old cemetery was still there. The man expressed surprise and told Adler there had never been a cemetery near the school. Adler was shocked; his recollection had been so vivid! He sought out other classmates and questioned them about the cemetery. They all told him the same thing: There had been no cemetery. Adler finally accepted that his memory of the incident was faulty. Nonetheless, it symbolized the fear and inferiority, and his efforts to overcome them, which characterized his style of life. That early recollection thus revealed an important and influential aspect of his personality.

Although Adler believed that each early memory should be interpreted within the context of the patient's style of life, he found commonalities among them. He suggested that memories involving danger or punishment indicated a tendency toward hostility. Those concerning the birth of a sibling showed a continued sense of dethronement. Memories that focused on one parent showed a preference for that parent. Recollections of improper behavior warned against any attempt to repeat the behavior.

Adler believed that

[p]eople remember from early childhood (a) only images that confirm and support their current views of themselves in the world . . . and (b) only those memories that support their direction of striving for significance and security. [His] focus on selective memory and lifestyle emphasize what is *remembered*. In contrast, Freud's approach to interpreting early memories emphasizes what is *forgotten* through the mechanism of repression. (Kopp & Eckstein, 2004, p. 165)

Dream Analysis

Adler agreed with Freud about the value of dreams in understanding personality but disagreed on the way in which dreams should be interpreted. Adler did not believe that dreams fulfill wishes or reveal hidden conflicts. Rather, dreams involve our feelings about a current problem and what we intend to do about it.

One of Adler's own dreams illustrates this point. Before his first visit to the United States, Adler felt anxious and worried, concerned about how he and his theory of personality would be received. The night before he was scheduled to cross the Atlantic Ocean by ship, he dreamed that the ship, with him aboard, capsized and sank.

All of Adler's worldly possessions were on it and were destroyed by the raging waves. Hurled into the ocean, Adler was forced to swim for his life. Alone he thrashed and struggled through the choppy waters. But through the force of will and determination, he finally reached land in safety. (Hoffman, 1994, p. 151)

Table 3.1 **Dream events and their latent meanings**

Dream event	Adlerian interpretation
Being paralyzed	Facing insoluble problems
School exams	Being unprepared for situations
Wearing the wrong clothes	Being disturbed by one's faults
Sexual themes	Retreating from sex or inadequate information about sex
Rage	An angry or hostile style of life
Death	Unresolved issues about the dead person

SOURCE: Adapted from Grey, 1998, p. 93.

This dream revealed Adler's fear about what he would face in the United States and his intention to land safely—in other words, to achieve success for himself and for his theory of individual psychology.

In the fantasies of our dreams (both night dreams and daydreams), we believe we can surmount the most difficult obstacle or simplify the most complex problem. Thus, dreams are oriented toward the present and future, not toward conflicts from the past.

Dreams should never be interpreted without knowledge of the person and his or her situation. The dream is a manifestation of a person's style of life and so is unique to the individual. Adler did find common interpretations for some dreams, however. Many people reported dreams involving falling or flying. Freud interpreted such dreams in sexual terms.

According to Adler, a dream of falling indicates that the person's emotional view involves a demotion or loss, such as the fear of losing self-esteem or prestige. A flying dream indicates a sense of striving upward, an ambitious style of life in which the person desires to be above or better than others. Dreams that combine flying and falling involve a fear of being too ambitious and thus failing. A dream of being chased suggests a feeling of weakness in relation to other people. Dreaming one is naked indicates a fear of giving oneself away. Additional Adlerian dream interpretations are shown in Table 3.1.

Measures of Social Interest

Adler had no desire to use psychological tests to assess personality. He argued that tests create artificial situations that provide ambiguous results. Instead of relying on tests, Adler thought therapists should develop their intuition. He did, however, support tests of memory and intelligence; it was tests of personality he criticized.

Psychologists have developed tests to measure Adler's concepts of social interest and style of life. The Social Interest Scale (SIS) consists of pairs of adjectives (Crandall, 1981). Research participants choose the word in each pair that best describes an attribute they would like to possess. Words such as *helpful*, *sympathetic*, and *considerate* are thought to indicate one's degree of social interest. The Social Interest Index (SII) is a self-report inventory in which research participants judge the degree to which statements represent themselves or their personal characteristics (Greever, Tseng, & Friedland, 1973). The items, such as *I don't mind helping out friends*, were selected to reflect Adler's ideas and to indicate a person's ability to accept and cooperate with others.

Research has shown that people who score high on the SII, indicating a high degree of social interest, tend to be high in friendliness, empathy, cooperation with others, tolerance, and independence. They have also been found to be lower in anxiety, hostility, depression, and neuroticism (Leak, 2006a, 2006b).

The Basic Adlerian Scales for Interpersonal Success (BASIS-A), is a 65-item self-report inventory designed to assess lifestyle as well as degree of social interest. The five personality dimensions measured are social interest, going along, taking charge, wanting recognition, and being cautious (Peluso, Peluso, Buckner, Curlette, & Kern, 2004).

Research on Adler's Theory

Adler's primary research method was the case study. Unfortunately, little of Adler's data survived. He did not publish case histories except for two fragments: one written by a patient, the other written by a patient's physician. Adler did not know the patients involved, but he analyzed their personalities by examining their writings.

Adler's data and research method are subject to the same criticisms we discussed for Freud and Jung. His observations cannot be repeated and duplicated, nor were they conducted in a controlled and systematic fashion. Adler did not attempt to verify the accuracy of his patients' reports or explain the procedures he used to analyze the data, and he had no interest in applying the experimental method. A follower wrote: "Adler wanted his psychology to be a science, but it has not been a psychology easily verified by the scientific method" (Manaster, 2006, p. 6).

Although most of Adler's propositions have resisted attempts at scientific validation, several topics have been the subject of research. These include dreams, inferiority feelings, early recollections, pampering and neglect in childhood, social interest, and order of birth.

Dreams. Adler's belief that dreams help us solve current problems was investigated by exposing research participants to situations in which the failure to solve a puzzle was considered a threat to the personality. The research participants were then allowed to sleep. Some were permitted to dream; they were awakened only during non-rapid-eye-movement (NREM) sleep. Others were awakened during rapid-eye-movement (REM) sleep so that they could not dream. Research participants who dreamed recalled significantly more of the uncompleted puzzle than those who did not dream. The researchers concluded that dreaming enabled research participants to deal effectively with the current threatening situation—that is, the failure to solve the puzzle (Grieser, Greenberg, & Harrison, 1972).

In another study, the dreams of two groups of research participants were reported (Breger, Hunter, & Lane, 1971). One group consisted of college students who were anticipating a stressful psychotherapy session. The other group consisted of patients about to undergo major surgery. For both groups, the recalled dreams focused on their conscious worries, fears, and hopes. Both types of research participants dreamed about the current problems they were facing.

Inferiority feelings. Research on Adler's concept of inferiority feelings has found that adults who scored low on inferiority feelings tended to be more successful and self-confident and to be more persistent in trying to achieve their goals than adults who scored high on inferiority feelings. A study of American college students showed that those with moderate inferiority feelings had higher grade-point averages than those with low or high inferiority feelings (Strano & Petrocelli, 2005).

Early recollections. Classic research showed that early memories of people diagnosed as anxiety neurotics were concerned with fear; early memories of depressed persons centered on abandonment; and early memories of those with psychosomatic complaints involved illness (Jackson & Sechrest, 1962). Early memories of alcoholics contained threatening events, as well as situations in which they were controlled by external circumstances rather than by their own decisions. The early memories of a control group of nonalcoholics showed neither of these themes (Hafner, Fakouri, & Labrentz, 1982).

Early recollections of adult criminals dealt with disturbing or aggressive interactions with other people. They contained more unpleasant events than the early

Our earliest memories of childhood help reveal our lifestyle.

© Topham/The Image Works

recollections of a control group (Hankoff, 1987). The early memories of adolescent delinquents involved breaking rules, having difficulty forming social relationships, and being unable to cope with life on their own. They also perceived their parents as untrustworthy and as more likely to hurt than to help. These themes were not present in the early memories of a control group (Davidow & Bruhn, 1990).

Recollections of psychiatric patients considered dangerous to themselves and to others showed more aggressive early memories than did recollections of nondangerous psychiatric patients. The recollections of the dangerous patients revealed that they felt vulnerable and powerless and saw others as hostile and abusive (Tobey & Bruhn, 1992).

Research using objective scoring systems for early recollections has shown that these memories tend to be subjective re-creations rather than events that actually occurred, much like Adler's memory of the cemetery (Statton & Wilborn, 1991).

One study reported that when research participants were asked to make up early recollections that might have happened to someone else, the themes were similar to those revealed by their own recollections (Buchanan, Kern, & Bell-Dumas, 1991). This study also provided research support for Adler's contention that early recollections reveal one's current style of life and therefore can be used as a therapeutic device. (Table 3.2 summarizes possible themes of early recollections.)

Early recollections studied in adults in the United States and in Israel have been shown to predict career preferences. For example, the early memories of physicists, mathematicians, and psychologists included themes such as curiosity, independent thought, and skepticism about information from authority figures (Clark, 2005; Kasler & Nevo, 2005).

Neglect in childhood. Adler suggested that children who were neglected or rejected by their parents developed feelings of worthlessness. A study of 714 adults hospitalized for depression found that the patients rated their parents as having been hostile, detached, and rejecting (Crook, Raskin, & Eliot, 1981). Interviews with siblings,

Table 3.2 **Early recollections and style of life themes**

Recollection	Possible theme
First school memory	Attitudes toward achievement, mastery, and independence
First punishment memory	Attitude toward authority figures
First sibling memory	Evidence of sibling rivalry
First family memory	Functioning in social situations
Clearest memory of mother	Attitudes toward women
Clearest memory of father	Attitudes toward men
Memory of person you admire	Basis for role models
Happiest memory	Basis for how your strongest needs are best gratified

SOURCE: Adapted from A. R. Bruhn (1992a). The early memories procedure. *Journal of Personality Assessment*, 58(1), 1–15.

relatives, and friends of the patients confirmed that the parents had indeed behaved in hostile and neglectful ways.

In another study, parents of 8-year-old children completed a questionnaire to assess their child-rearing behaviors and their level of satisfaction with their children (Lefkowitz & Tesiny, 1984). Ten years later the children, then age 18, were given the depression scale of the Minnesota Multiphasic Personality Inventory (MMPI). Research participants whose test scores showed they were more depressed had been neglected in childhood by their parents. Those whose parents had not been indifferent or unloving scored lower on the depression scale.

Pampering in childhood. Adler noted that pampering in childhood could lead to a pampered style of life in which the person would demonstrate little or no social feelings for others. Research supports this idea and also suggests that pampering can lead to excessive narcissism, which involves a lack of responsibility or empathy for other people, an exaggerated sense of self-importance, and a tendency to exploit others. Studies have identified four types of pampering.

- Overindulgence, which involves the persistent parental gratification of a child's needs and desires, leading to feelings of entitlement as well as tyrannical and manipulative behavior
- Overpermissiveness, which involves allowing children to behave as they please with no consideration for the effects of their behavior on other people, leading to a disregard of social rules and the rights of others
- Overdomination, which involves exclusive parental decision-making, leading to a child's lack of self-confidence and a tendency to become dependent on others in adulthood
- Overprotection, which involves parental caution, excessively warning children of potential dangers in their environment, leading to generalized anxiety and a tendency to avoid or hide from social situations

Studies with college students found that children of overdomineering mothers were more likely to seek psychotherapy while in college. Students who rated their parents as both overindulgent and overprotective tended to be low in self-esteem. Students whose parents were considered to be both overindulgent and overdomineering scored high in narcissism (Capron, 2004).

Social interest. Research using the SIS showed that persons high in social interest reported less stress, depression, anxiety, and hostility than persons low in social interest. High social interest scorers scored higher on tests assessing cooperation with others, empathy, responsibility, and popularity (Crandall, 1984; Watkins, 1994; Watkins & St. John, 1994). Research with 105 college students found that those high in social interest scored high in spirituality and religiosity. However, their spirituality was of a positive, tolerant, and helping nature, not necessarily religious ethnocentrism or fundamentalism (Leak, 2006a). Another study of college students showed that those high in social interest were high in subjective well-being, agreeableness, self-identify, self-determination, and a strong sense of purpose in life (Leak & Leak, 2006).

A study of high-school adolescents in grades 9 to 12 found that those high in social interest scored significantly higher in overall life satisfaction, as well as satisfaction with friends and family, than did those who scored low in social interest (R. Gilman, 2001). Other research, conducted with male criminal offenders ranging in age from 18 to 40, showed that those who scored high in social interest were far less likely to commit additional crimes following their release from jail than were those who scored low in social interest (Daugherty, Murphy, & Paugh, 2001).

Studies with the SII showed that women who scored high in social interest were significantly higher in self-actualization, a characteristic of the healthy personality described by Abraham Maslow. Other research found that social interest was higher in women than in men and that it increased with age for both sexes (Greever, Tseng, & Friedland, 1973).

A study of 313 Latino men and women currently living in the United States found that research participants who were bicultural (well adjusted to living in both cultures) scored higher on social interest measures than research participants who were primarily acculturated to either the Latino lifestyle or the U.S. lifestyle alone (Miranda, Frevert, & Kern, 1998).

High social interest may also be good for your health. Social interest, with its related feelings of belonging, cooperation, and a sense of contributing to or receiving support from a social network has been positively associated with physical and mental well-being. For example, people who scored high in social interest tended to have stronger immune systems, fewer colds, lower blood pressure, and greater subjective well-being (Nikelly, 2005).

Birth order. Much research has been conducted on the effects of one's order of birth within the family. Obviously, being the first-born, second-born, last-born, or an only child influences personality in a variety of ways. Simply having older or younger siblings, regardless of one's own order of birth, can also affect personality. For example, studies of 18,876 people in England, Scotland, and Wales, and 3,432 people in the United States, found that the number of older brothers a man had could predict his sexual orientation. Boys who had older brothers were more sexually attracted to men than were boys who did not have older brothers. The more older brothers a man had, the greater was the attraction to the same sex. Having older sisters did not predict sexual orientation in women (Bogaert, 2003).

According to Adler, first-borns are concerned with power and authority. One way for first-borns to gain power and authority as adults is through achievement in their work. If Adler was correct, then first-borns should score high on measures of achievement, an idea that has received much research support. In many areas, from college attendance to high-level management, first-borns have been found to be overrepresented relative to their proportion of the population. More first-borns than later-borns become eminent, and they tend to attain greater intellectual achievement in academic settings and greater power and prestige in their careers (Breland, 1974; Schachter, 1963).

Studies conducted in the United States and in Poland found that first-borns scored higher in measures of intelligence, completed more years of formal education, and worked in more prestigious occupations than did later-borns (Herrera, Zajonc,

Wieczorkowska, & Cichomski, 2003). Research on adults in Sweden showed that first-borns scored higher than later-borns on tests of managerial or executive functioning. However, the first-borns in this study did not score higher than later-borns on intelligence tests (Holmgren, Molander, & Nilsson, 2006). A large-scale study of more than 240,000 male army recruits in Norway showed that older siblings scored higher on an IQ test than did younger siblings (Kristensen & Bjerkedal, 2007).

In general, then, evidence suggests that first-borns might be more intelligent than later-borns, although not all researchers agree (see, for example, Rodgers, 2001). The IQ scores of 400,000 European men were analyzed with respect to birth order (Belmont & Marolla, 1973). The results showed that first-borns had higher IQ scores than second-borns, second-borns had higher scores than third-borns, and so on. These findings were confirmed for men and women in several countries (Zajonc, Markus, & Markus, 1979). A possible explanation for the apparent higher intelligence of first-borns relates not to genetic differences but to the first-born's exclusive exposure to adults. Consequently, first-borns may have a more stimulating intellectual environment than later-borns.

Vocational preferences for first-borns were found to include teaching, medicine, science, and management (Bryant, 1987). First-borns' scores on an occupational interest inventory indicated a preference for socially oriented careers requiring good interpersonal skills (White, Campbell, Stewart, Davies, & Pilkington, 1997).

First-borns tend to be more dependent on other people and more suggestible. They are anxious in stressful situations and have a higher need for social relationships (Schachter, 1963, 1964). These findings could be predicted from Adler's theory. He noted that first-borns are made anxious when dethroned by a sibling, and they attempt to regain their position by eventually conforming to their parents' expectations. Accordingly, first-borns depend more than later-borns on the standards of others, including their parents, to guide their behavior and form the basis of their self-evaluations (Newman, Higgins, & Vookles, 1992).

Other research found that first-borns scored lower than later-borns on tests of depression and anxiety and higher on self-esteem (Gates, Lineberger, Crockett, & Hubbard, 1988). First-borns may also be more extraverted and conscientious than later-borns (Sulloway, 1995).

First-born girls were found to be more obedient and socially responsible than later-borns and tended to feel closer to their parents (Sutton-Smith & Rosenberg, 1970). Studies conducted in France, Croatia, Canada, and England showed that first-borns tended to be more closely supervised in childhood, were rated by their mothers as less fearful, reported more frightening childhood dreams, and scored higher in measures of dominance in college (Beck, Burnet, & Vosper, 2006; Begue & Roche, 2005; Kerestes, 2006; McCann, Stewin, & Short, 1990).

Less research has been conducted on second-born children. There appears to be no support for Adler's contention that they are more competitive and ambitious than their siblings. One study found second-borns to be lower in self-esteem than first-borns or last-borns, particularly if the age difference between them and the other siblings was approximately 2 years (Kidwell, 1982).

A study of 198 first-born and second-born siblings, conducted over a period of 3 years, found that the attitudes, personalities, and leisure activities of the second-born children were influenced more by their older siblings than by their parents (McHale, Updegraff, Helms-Erikson, & Crouter, 2001).

Adler predicted that last-born children, if excessively pampered, would have adjustment problems as adults. One frequently suggested reason for alcoholism is that some people cannot cope with the demands of everyday life. If so, then according to Adler's theory, more last-borns than early-borns would become alcoholics. This prediction has been supported by many studies dealing with alcoholism and order of birth. Also, binge drinking in college has been found to be significantly higher among last-borns than among first-borns (Laird & Shelton, 2006).

To Adler, only-born adults are overly concerned with being the center of attention, as they were in childhood. He also considered only-borns to be more selfish than children reared with siblings. Research has not consistently supported this contention. One study found that only-borns demonstrated more cooperative behaviors than first-borns or last-borns (Falbo, 1978). Another study found that only-borns were more self-centered and less popular than were children with siblings (Jiao, Ji, & Jing, 1986).

An analysis of 115 studies of only-borns reported higher levels of achievement and intelligence than, and comparable social and emotional adjustment with, people who have siblings (Falbo & Polit, 1986). Other research (Mellor, 1990) confirmed those results and found that only children had higher levels of initiative, aspiration, industriousness, and self-esteem.

It has also been suggested that only-borns earn better grades in school. The results of an analysis of several studies show that the number of siblings is a consistent predictor of educational success; "individuals with the fewest siblings do the best" (Downey, 2001, p. 497). Only-borns may have more opportunities and parental resources, enabling them to perform better than children with siblings.

Reflections on Adler's Theory

Adler's influence within psychology has been substantial. In later chapters we see examples of his ideas in the work of other personality theorists. These contributions make Adler's personality theory one of the most enduring. He was ahead of his time, and his cognitive and social emphases are more compatible with trends in psychology today than with the psychology of his own day. Abraham Maslow wrote: "Alfred Adler becomes more and more correct year by year. . . . As the facts come in, they give stronger and stronger support to his image of man" (Maslow, 1970a, p. 13).

Adler's emphasis on social forces in personality can be seen in the theory of Karen Horney. His focus on the whole person and the unity of personality is reflected in the work of Gordon Allport. The creative power of the individual in shaping his or her style of life, and the insistence that future goals are more important than past events, influenced the work of Abraham Maslow. A social-learning theorist, Julian Rotter, wrote that he "was and continues to be impressed by Adler's insights into human nature" (Rotter, 1982, pp. 1–2).

Adler's ideas also reached into Freudian psychoanalysis. It was Adler who proposed the aggressive drive more than 12 years before Freud included aggression with sex as primary motivating forces. The neo-Freudian ego psychologists, who focus more on conscious and rational processes and less on the unconscious, follow Adler's lead.

Adler disputed Freud's views on women, arguing that there was no biological basis, such as penis envy, for women's alleged sense of inferiority. Such a notion, Adler charged, was a myth invented by men to maintain their alleged sense of superiority. He acknowledged that women may feel inferior but believed that was attributable to social conditioning and sex-role stereotyping. He also believed in the idea of equality for the sexes and supported the women's emancipation movements of the day.

Specific Adlerian concepts of lasting importance to psychology include the early work on organic inferiority, which has influenced the study of psychosomatic disorders; the inferiority complex; compensation; and order of birth. Adler is also considered a forerunner of social psychology and group therapy.

Although his ideas have been widely accepted, Adler's public recognition declined after his death in 1937, and he has received relatively little subsequent praise or credit for his contributions. Many concepts have been borrowed from his theory without acknowledgment. A typical instance of this lack of recognition can be found in Sigmund Freud's obituary in the *Times* newspaper of London, which named Freud as the originator of the term *inferiority complex*. When Carl Jung died, the *New York Times* said *he* had coined the term. Neither newspaper mentioned Adler, the originator of the concept. However, Adler did receive one unique honor: a British composer named a string quartet for him.

As influential as Adler's work has been, it does have its critics. Freud charged that Adler's psychology was oversimplified and would therefore appeal to many people because it eliminated the complicated nature of the unconscious, had no difficult concepts, and ignored the problems of sex. Freud remarked that it could take 2 years or more to learn about his psychoanalysis, but "Adler's ideas and technique can be easily learned in two weeks, because with Adler there is so little to know" (quoted in Sterba, 1982, p. 156).

It is true that Adler's theory seems simpler than Freud's or Jung's, but that was Adler's intention. He wrote that it had taken him 40 years to make his psychology simple. One point that reinforces the charge of oversimplification is that his books are easy to read because he wrote for the general public and because some of them were compiled from his popular lectures. (Figure 3.1) A related charge is that Adler's concepts appear to rely heavily on commonsense observations from everyday life. A book reviewer in the *New York Times* noted: "Although [Adler] is one of the most eminent psychologists in the world, when he writes about psychology there is no other who can equal him in simplicity and non-technicality of language" (quoted in Hoffman, 1994, p. 276).

Critics allege that Adler was inconsistent and unsystematic in his thinking and that his theory contains gaps and unanswered questions. Are inferiority feelings the only problem we face in life? Do all people strive primarily for perfection? Can we become reconciled to a degree of inferiority and no longer attempt to compensate for it? These and other questions that have been posed cannot all be answered adequately by Adler's system; most theorists, however, leave us with unanswered questions.

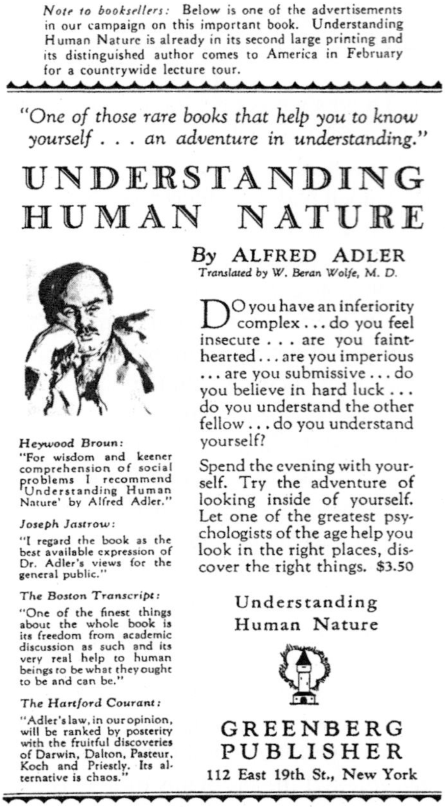

Figure 3.1
Adler's books achieved considerable popularity in the United States and spawned the genre of self-help books.
SOURCE: Edward Hoffman (1994). *The drive for self: Alfred Adler and the founding of individual psychology.* Reading, MA: Addison-Wesley.

Some psychologists dispute Adler's position on the issue of determinism versus free will. Early in his career, Adler did not oppose the notion of determinism. It was broadly accepted in science at the time, and it characterized Freud's psychoanalytic theory. Later, Adler felt the need to grant more autonomy to the self, and his final formulation rejected determinism. His concept of the creative self proposes that before the age of 5 we fashion a style of life using material provided by our heredity and our environment. However, it is not clear how a child is able to make such momentous decisions. We know that Adler favored free will and opposed the idea that we are victims of innate forces and childhood events. That position is clear, but the specifics of forming the style of life are not.

Adler's followers claim that individual psychology remains popular among psychologists, psychiatrists, social workers, and educators. *Individual Psychology: The Journal of Adlerian Theory, Research and Practice* is published quarterly by the North American Society of Adlerian Psychology. Other Adlerian journals are published in Germany, Italy, and France. Adlerian training institutes have been established in New York, Chicago, and other cities. Adlerian counseling techniques have been developed by Rudolph Dreikurs and others, and this work has influenced new generations of Adlerian clinicians in what Dreikurs calls family education centers. Dreikurs's work on child-rearing practices applies Adler's views to contemporary problems not only in child development, but also in the treatment of the family as a whole.

Chapter Summary

Adler's childhood was marked by intense efforts to compensate for his feelings of inferiority. His system of individual psychology differs from Freudian psychoanalysis in its focus on the uniqueness of the individual, on consciousness, and on social rather than biological forces. It minimizes the role of sex.

Inferiority feelings are the source of all human striving, which results from our attempts to compensate for these feelings. Inferiority feelings are universal and are determined by the infant's helplessness and dependency on adults. An inferiority complex (that is, an inability to solve life's problems) results from being unable to compensate for inferiority feelings. An inferiority complex can originate in childhood through organic inferiority, spoiling, or neglect. A superiority complex (an exaggerated opinion of one's abilities and accomplishments) results from overcompensation.

Our ultimate goal is superiority or perfection; that is, making the personality whole or complete. Fictional finalism refers to fictional ideas, such as perfection, that guide our behavior. Style of life refers to unique patterns of characteristics and behaviors by which we strive for perfection. The creative power of the self refers to our ability to create our selves from the materials provided by our heredity and environment. Four basic styles of life are the dominant or ruling type, the getting type, the avoiding type, and the socially useful type. Social interest is innate but the extent to which it is realized depends on early social experiences.

Order of birth is a major social influence in childhood from which one's style of life is created. First-borns are oriented toward the past, pessimistic about the future, and concerned with maintaining order and authority. Second-borns compete with first-borns and are apt to be ambitious. Last-borns, spurred by the need to surpass older siblings, may become high achievers. Only children may mature early but are apt to face a shock in school when they are no longer the center of attention.

Adler's image of human nature is more hopeful than is Freud's. In Adler's view, people are unique, and they possess free will and the ability to shape their own development. Although childhood experiences are important, we are not victims of them.

Adler's methods of assessment are order of birth, early recollections, and dream analysis. Research has provided support for Adler's views on the following: dreams, early memories, and childhood neglect and pampering; his belief that social interest is related to emotional well-being; the idea that first-borns are high achievers, dependent on others, suggestible, and anxious under stress; and the notion that last-borns are more likely to become alcoholics.

Adler's emphasis on cognitive and social factors in personality, the unity of personality, the creative power of the self, the importance of goals, and cognitive factors has influenced many personality theorists.

Review Questions

1. Explain how Adler's theory of personality is at least partly a reflection of his own childhood experiences.

2. On what points did Adler differ with Freud?

3. What is the difference between inferiority feelings and the inferiority complex? How does each develop?

4. How does the superiority complex differ from the idea of striving for superiority? How did Adler define superiority?

5. Describe the concept of fictional finalism. Explain how fictional finalism relates to the notion of striving for superiority.

6. How does the self develop? Do people play an active or a passive role in the development of the self?

7. What are the four basic styles of life, according to Adler?

8. What parental behaviors may foster a child's development of social interest? Which basic style of life is identified with social interest?

9. Describe the personality characteristics proposed by Adler that may develop in first-born, second-born, and youngest children as a result of their order of birth within the family.

10. According to Adler, what are the advantages and disadvantages of being an only child?

11. If it were possible to choose, which birth order position would you select for yourself in your family? Why?

12. Describe research on the personality of first-born and only-born children. Do the results support Adler's predictions?

13. How does Adler's image of human nature differ from Freud's?

14. Describe the approaches Adler used to assess the personalities of his patients.

15. What is the importance of early recollections in personality assessment? Give an example of how one of Adler's recollections revealed an aspect of his personality.

16. What is the purpose of dreams? Does contemporary research on sleep and dreaming support Adler's views?

17. How do people who score high in social interest differ from people who score low?

18. Discuss the criticisms and contributions of Adler's system within psychology today.

Suggested Readings

Adler, A. (1930). Individual psychology. In C. Murchison (Ed.). *Psychologies of 1930* (pp. 395–405). Worcester, MA: Clark University Press. Offers a clear exposition of the basic principles of Adler's individual psychology.

Ansbacher, H. L. (1990). Alfred Adler's influence on the three leading cofounders of humanistic psychology. *Journal of Humanistic Psychology, 30*(4), 45–53. Traces Adler's influence, in person and through his writings, on the development of humanistic psychology in the United States, most notably through his contact with Maslow and Rogers.

Ansbacher, R. R. (1997). Alfred Adler, the man, seen by a student and friend. *Individual Psychology, 53*, 270–274. Using Adler's technique of early recollections, the author evaluates her memories of Adler's lectures and therapy sessions in New York and Vienna.

Clark, A. J. (2005). An early recollection of Albert Einstein: Perspectives on its meaning and his life. *Journal of Individual Psychology, 61*, 126–136. Uses an Adlerian perspective to evaluate the first memory of the great physicist Albert Einstein within the historical context of his life.

Ellenberger, H. F. (1970). *The discovery of the unconscious: The history and evolution of dynamic psychiatry.* New York: Basic Books. Traces the study of the unconscious from primitive times to Freudian psychoanalysis and its derivatives. See Chapter 8, "Alfred Adler and Individual Psychology."

Fiebert, M. S. (1997). In and out of Freud's shadow: A chronology of Adler's relationship with Freud. *Individual Psychology, 53*, 241–269. Reviews the 7-year correspondence between Adler and Freud describing changes in their personal and professional relationships and their acrimonious breakup.

Grey, L. (1998). *Alfred Adler, the forgotten prophet: A vision for the 21st century.* Westport, CT: Praeger. A biography and an assessment of the continuing influence of Adler's ideas.

Hoffman, E. (1994). *The drive for self: Alfred Adler and the founding of individual psychology.* Reading, MA: Addison-Wesley. Discusses Adler's contributions to personality theory, psychoanalysis, and popular psychology. Recounts events in his life as the basis for familiar concepts such as inferiority complex, overcompensation, and lifestyle.

Kasler, J., & Nevo, O. (2005). Early recollections as predictors of study area choice. *Journal of Individual Psychology, 61*, 217–232. Research using Adler's concept of early memories to reveal career interests and preferences of pre-college young adults shows credibility for social, realistic, and artistic fields.

Rule, W., & Bishop, M. (2005). *Adlerian lifestyle counseling.* London: Routledge. Describes research on Adler's individual psychology and applications to behavioral, mental health, interpersonal, and goal-oriented counseling.

Sulloway, F. J. (1996). *Born to rebel: Birth order, family dynamics, and creative lives.* New York: Pantheon. Analyzes revolutions in social, scientific, and political thought, dating back to the 16th century, to demonstrate the influence of birth order on personality development. Suggests that birth-order effects transcend gender, social class, race, national origin, and time.

CHAPTER 4

Karen Horney: Neurotic Needs and Trends

The basic evil is invariably a lack of genuine warmth and affection.
—KAREN HORNEY

Karen Danielsen Horney was another defector from the orthodox Freudian point of view. Although never a disciple or colleague of Freud's, Horney was trained in the official psychoanalytic doctrine. But she did not remain long in the Freudian camp.

Horney began her divergence from Freud's position by disputing his psychological portrayal of women. An early feminist, she argued that psychoanalysis focused more on men's development than on women's. To counter Freud's contention that women are driven by penis envy, Horney said that men are envious of women for their ability to give birth. "I know just as many men with womb envy as women with penis envy," she said (quoted in Cherry & Cherry, 1973, p. 75).

She began her career by insisting that her work was an extension of Freud's. In a letter she wrote, "I do not want to found a new school but build on the foundations Freud has laid" (quoted in Quinn, 1987, p. 318). By the time Horney completed her theory, her criticisms of Freud were so broad that she *had* founded a new school. Hers was a new approach to psychoanalysis that had little in common with Freud's views.

Horney's theory was influenced by her gender and her personal experiences, as well as by social and cultural forces that differed greatly from those that had influenced Freud. Horney formulated her theory in the United States, a radically different culture from Freud's Vienna. By the 1930s and 1940s, major changes had occurred in popular attitudes about sex and the roles of men and women. These changes were taking place in Europe, too, but they were considerably more pronounced in the United States.

Horney found that her American patients were so unlike her previous German patients, both in their neuroses and in their normal personalities that she believed only the different social forces to which they had been exposed could account for the variation. Personality, she argued, cannot depend wholly on biological forces, as Freud proposed. If it did, we would not see such major differences from one culture to another.

Thus, Horney, like Alfred Adler, placed a greater emphasis than Freud did on social relationships as significant factors in personality formation. She argued that sex is not the governing factor in personality, as Freud had claimed, and she questioned his concepts of the Oedipus complex, the libido, and the three-part structure of personality. To Horney, people are motivated not by sexual or aggressive forces but by the needs for security and love. We shall see that this view reflected her personal experience.

The Life of Horney (1885–1952)

A Search for Love

Karen Danielsen was born in a village near Hamburg, Germany. She was the second-born child, and from an early age she envied her older brother, Berndt. He was attractive and charming, the adored first-born, but she was smarter and more vivacious. She confided to her diary, "It was always my pride that in school I was better than Berndt, that there were more amusing stories about me than about him" (Horney, 1980, p. 252). She also envied him because he was a boy, and girls were considered inferior. "I know that as a child I wanted for a long time to be a boy, that I envied Berndt because he could stand near a tree and pee" (Horney, 1980, p. 252).

A stronger influence was her father. At the time she was born, he was a 50-year-old ship's captain of Norwegian background. Her mother was 33 and of a vastly different temperament. Whereas the father was religious, domineering, imperious, morose, and silent, the mother was attractive, spirited, and freethinking. Horney's father spent long periods away at sea, but when he was home, the opposing natures of the parents led to frequent arguments. Karen's mother made no secret of her wish to see her husband dead. She told Karen that she had married not out of love but out of fear of becoming an old maid.

We can see roots of Horney's personality theory in her childhood experiences. For most of her childhood and adolescence, she doubted that her parents wanted her. She believed they loved Berndt more than they loved her. At age 16, Horney wrote in her diary, "Why is everything beautiful on earth given to me, only not the highest thing, not love! I have a heart so needing love" (Horney, 1980, p. 30). Although Horney desperately wanted her father's love and attention, he intimidated her. She recalled his frightening eyes and stern, demanding manner, and she felt belittled and rejected because he made disparaging comments about her appearance and intelligence.

As a way of retaining her mother's affection, she acted the part of the adoring daughter, and until the age of 8 was a model child, clinging and compliant. Despite her efforts, she did not believe she was getting sufficient love and security. Her self-sacrifice and good behavior were not working, so she changed tactics and became ambitious and rebellious. Horney decided that if she could not have love and security, she would take revenge for her feelings of unattractiveness and inadequacy. "If I couldn't be beautiful, I decided I would be smart" (Horney quoted in Rubins, 1978, p. 14).

As an adult she came to realize how much hostility she had developed as a child. Her personality theory describes how a lack of love in childhood fosters anxiety and hostility, thus providing another example of a theory developed initially in personal and intuitive terms. A biographer concluded, "In all her psychoanalytic writings— Karen Horney was struggling to make sense of herself and to obtain relief from her own difficulties" (Paris, 1994, p. xxii).

At 14, she developed an adolescent crush on a male teacher and filled her diary with paragraphs about him. She continued to have such infatuations, confused and unhappy as many adolescents are. At 17, she awakened to the reality of sex, and the following year, she met a man she described as her first real love, but the relationship lasted only 2 days. Another man came into her life, prompting 76 pages of soul-searching in her diary. Horney decided that being in love eliminated, at least temporarily, her anxiety and insecurity; it offered an escape (Sayers, 1991).

Although Horney's quest for love and security was often thwarted, her search for a career was straightforward and successful. She decided at the age of 12, after being treated kindly by a physician, that she would become a doctor. Despite the medical establishment's discrimination against women and her father's strong opposition, she worked hard in high school to prepare herself for medical studies. In

1906, she entered the University of Freiburg medical school, only 6 years after the first woman had, reluctantly, been admitted.

Marriage and Career

During her time at medical school, Horney met two men; she fell in love with one and married the other. Oskar Horney was studying for a Ph.D. in political science and after their marriage became a successful businessman. Karen Horney excelled in her medical studies and received her degree from the University of Berlin in 1913.

The early years of marriage were a time of personal distress. She gave birth to three daughters but felt overwhelming unhappiness and oppression. She complained of crying spells, stomach pains, chronic fatigue, compulsive behaviors, frigidity, and a longing for sleep, even death. The marriage ended in 1927, after 17 years.

During and after her marriage, Horney had a number of love affairs. A biographer wrote:

> When she did not have a lover, or a relationship was breaking down, she felt lost, lonely, desperate, and sometimes suicidal. When she was involved in a morbidly dependent relationship, she hated herself for her inability to break free. She attributed her desperate need for a man . . . to her unhappy childhood. (Paris, 1994, p. 140)

When she realized that these attachments were not helping to alleviate her depression and other emotional problems, she decided to undergo psychoanalysis.

Psychoanalysis and Compensation

The therapist Horney consulted, Karl Abraham (a loyal follower of Freud), attributed her problems to her attraction to forceful men, which he explained was a residue of her childhood Oedipal longings for her powerful father. "Her readiness to abandon herself to such patriarchal figures, said Abraham, was betrayed by her leaving her handbag [in Freud's view, a symbolic representation of the female genitals] in his office on her very first visit" (Sayers, 1991, p. 88). The analysis was not a success. She decided that Freudian psychoanalysis was of only minimal help to her, and she turned instead to self-analysis, a practice she continued throughout her life.

During her self-analysis, Horney was strongly influenced by Adler's notion of compensation for feelings of inferiority. She was particularly sensitive to Adler's remark that physical unattractiveness was a cause of inferiority feelings. She concluded that she "needed to feel superior because of her lack of beauty and sense of inferiority as a woman, which led her to masculine protest" by excelling in a male-dominated domain, such as medicine was at the time (Paris, 1994, p. 63). Apparently she believed that by studying medicine, and by promiscuous sexual behavior, she was acting more like a man.

Horney's search for love and security continued when she immigrated to the United States. During this period, her most intense love affair was with the analyst Erich Fromm. When it ended after 20 years, she was deeply hurt. Although Fromm was 15 years younger, she may have seen him as a father figure. One event that led to the breakdown of the relationship was that Horney persuaded Fromm to analyze her daughter Marianne. Fromm helped the woman understand her hostility toward her mother, giving Marianne the confidence to confront Horney for the first time in her life (McLaughlin, 1998).[1]

Horney's relentless search for love continued, and she chose younger and younger men, many of whom were analysts whose training she was supervising. Yet her attitude toward them could be detached. She told a friend about one young man, saying that she didn't know whether to marry him or get a cocker spaniel. She chose the dog (Paris, 1994).

From 1932 to 1952, Horney served on the faculty of psychoanalytic institutes in Chicago and New York. She was a founder of the Association for the Advancement of Psychoanalysis and the American Institute for Psychoanalysis. In 1941, she began the *American Journal of Psychoanalysis*. For many years she was a popular lecturer, writer, and therapist.

 LOG ON

Personality Theories: Karen Horney

Provides an overview of Horney's life and work.

For a direct link to this site, log on to the student companion site for this book at http://www.academic.cengage.com/psychology/Schultz and choose Chapter 4.

The Childhood Need for Safety

Horney agreed with Freud, in principle, about the importance of the early years of childhood in shaping the adult personality. However, they differed on the specifics of how personality is formed. Horney believed that social forces in childhood, not biological forces, influence personality development. There are neither universal developmental stages nor inevitable childhood conflicts. Instead, the social relationship between the child and his or her parents is the key factor.

safety need
A higher-level need for security and freedom from fear.

Horney thought childhood was dominated by the **safety need**, by which she meant the need for security and freedom from fear (Horney, 1937). Whether the infant experiences a feeling of security and an absence of fear is decisive in determining the normality of his or her personality development. A child's security depends entirely on how the parents treat the child. The major way parents weaken or prevent security is by displaying a lack of warmth and affection for the child. This was Horney's situation in childhood. Her parents had provided little warmth and affection; she behaved the same way with her three daughters. She believed children could withstand, without appreciable ill effect, much that is usually considered

---

[1] In 2006, in a commemoration of the 120th anniversary of Horney's birth, Marianne described her mother as a private person who "never was a good team player, never a family person" (Eckardt, 2006, p. 3).

The state of helplessness in infancy can lead to neurotic behavior.

© Charly Franklin/Photographer's Choice RR/Getty Images

traumatic—such as abrupt weaning, occasional beatings, or even premature sexual experiences—as long as they feel wanted and loved and are, therefore, secure.

Parents can act in various ways to undermine their child's security and thereby induce hostility. These parental behaviors include obvious preference for a sibling, unfair punishment, erratic behavior, promises not kept, ridicule, humiliation, and isolation of the child from peers. Horney suggested that children know whether their parents' love is genuine. False demonstrations and insincere expressions of affection do not easily fool children. The child may feel the need to repress the hostility engendered by the parents' undermining behaviors for reasons of helplessness, fear of the parents, need for genuine love, or guilt feelings.

Horney placed great emphasis on the infant's helplessness. Unlike Adler, however, she did not believe all infants necessarily feel helpless, but when these feelings do arise, they can lead to neurotic behavior. Children's sense of helplessness depends on their parents' behavior. If children are kept in an excessively dependent state, then their feelings of helplessness will be encouraged. The more helpless children feel, the less they dare to oppose or rebel against the parents. This means that the child will repress the resulting hostility, saying, in effect, "I have to repress my hostility because I need you."

Children can easily be made to feel fearful of their parents through punishment, physical abuse, or more subtle forms of intimidation. The more frightened children become, the more they will repress their hostility. In this instance, the child is saying, "I must repress my hostility because I am afraid of you."

Paradoxically, love can be another reason for repressing hostility toward parents. In this case, parents tell their children how much they love them and how greatly they are sacrificing for them, but the parents' warmth and affection are not honest. Children recognize that these verbalizations and behaviors are poor substitutes for genuine love and security, but they are all that is available. The child must repress his or her hostility for fear of losing even these unsatisfactory expressions of love.

Guilt is yet another reason why children repress hostility. They are often made to feel guilty about any hostility or rebelliousness. They may be made to feel unworthy, wicked, or sinful for expressing or even harboring resentments toward their parents. The more guilt the child feels, the more deeply repressed will be the hostility.

This repressed hostility, resulting from a variety of parental behaviors, undermines the childhood need for safety, and is manifested in the condition Horney called basic anxiety.

Basic Anxiety: The Foundation of Neurosis

basic anxiety
A pervasive feeling of loneliness and helplessness; the foundation of neurosis.

Horney defined **basic anxiety** as an "insidiously increasing, all-pervading feeling of being lonely and helpless in a hostile world" (Horney, 1937, p. 89). It is the foundation on which later neuroses develop, and it is inseparably tied to feelings of hostility. Regardless of how we express basic anxiety, the feeling is similar for all of us. In Horney's words, we feel "small, insignificant, helpless, deserted, endangered, in a world that is out to abuse, cheat, attack, humiliate, betray" (1937, p. 92). In childhood we try to protect ourselves against basic anxiety in four ways:

- Securing affection and love
- Being submissive
- Attaining power
- Withdrawing

By securing affection and love from other people, the person is saying, in effect, "If you love me, you will not hurt me." There are several ways by which we may gain affection, such as trying to do whatever the other person wants, trying to bribe others, or threatening others into providing the desired affection.

Being submissive as a means of self-protection involves complying with the wishes either of one particular person or of everyone in our social environment. Submissive persons avoid doing anything that might antagonize others. They dare not criticize or give offense. They must repress their personal desires and cannot defend against abuse for fear that such defensiveness will antagonize the abuser. Most people who act submissive believe they are unselfish and self-sacrificing. Such persons seem to be saying, "If I give in, I will not be hurt." This describes Horney's childhood behavior until the age of 8 or 9.

By attaining power over others, a person can compensate for helplessness and achieve security through success or through a sense of superiority. Such persons seem to believe that if they have power, no one will harm them. This could describe Horney's childhood once she decided to strive for academic success.

These three self-protective devices have something in common: by engaging in any of them the person is attempting to cope with basic anxiety by interacting with other people. The fourth way of protecting oneself against basic anxiety involves withdrawing from other people, not physically but psychologically. Such a person attempts to become independent of others, not relying on anyone else for the satisfaction of internal or external needs. For example, if someone amasses a houseful of material possessions, then he or she can rely on them to satisfy external needs. Unfortunately, that person may be too burdened by basic anxiety to enjoy the possessions. He or she must guard the possessions carefully because they are the person's only protection against anxiety.

The withdrawn person achieves independence with regard to internal or psychological needs by becoming aloof from others, no longer seeking them out to satisfy emotional needs. The process involves a blunting, or minimizing, of emotional needs. By renouncing these needs the withdrawn person guards against being hurt by other people.

The four self-protective mechanisms Horney proposed have a single goal: to defend against basic anxiety. They motivate the person to seek security and reassurance rather than happiness or pleasure. They are a defense against pain, not a pursuit of well-being.

Another characteristic of these self-protective mechanisms is their power and intensity. Horney believed they could be more compelling than sexual or other physiological needs. These mechanisms may reduce anxiety, but the cost to the individual is usually an impoverished personality.

Often, the neurotic will pursue the search for safety and security by using more than one of these mechanisms and the incompatibility among the four mechanisms can lay the groundwork for additional problems. For example, a person may be driven by the needs to attain power and gain affection. A person may want to submit to others while also desiring power over them. Such incompatibilities cannot be resolved and can lead to more severe conflicts.

Neurotic Needs and Trends

neurotic needs
Ten irrational defenses against anxiety that become a permanent part of personality and that affect behavior.

Horney believed that any of these self-protective mechanisms could become so permanent a part of the personality that it assumes the characteristics of a drive or need in determining the individual's behavior. She listed 10 such needs, which she termed **neurotic needs** because they are irrational solutions to one's problems. The 10 neurotic needs are as follows:

1. Affection and approval
2. A dominant partner
3. Power
4. Exploitation
5. Prestige
6. Admiration
7. Achievement or ambition
8. Self-sufficiency
9. Perfection
10. Narrow limits to life

The neurotic needs encompass the four ways of protecting ourselves against anxiety. Gaining affection is expressed in the neurotic need for affection and approval. Being submissive includes the neurotic need for a dominant partner. Attaining power relates to the

Table 4.1 Horney's neurotic needs and neurotic trends

Needs	Trends
Affection and approval A dominant partner	Movement toward other people (the compliant personality)
Power Exploitation Prestige Admiration Achievement	Movement against other people (the aggressive personality)
Self-sufficiency Perfection Narrow limits to life	Movement away from other people (the detached personality)

needs for power, exploitation, prestige, admiration, and achievement or ambition. With-drawing includes the needs for self-sufficiency, perfection, and narrow limits to life.

Horney noted that we all manifest these needs to some degree. For example, at one time or another, everyone seeks affection or pursues achievement. None of the needs is abnormal or neurotic in an everyday, transient sense. What makes them neurotic is the person's intensive and compulsive pursuit of their satisfaction as the only way to resolve basic anxiety. Satisfying these needs will not help us feel safe and secure but will aid only in our desire to escape the discomfort caused by our anxiety. Also, when we pursue gratification of these needs solely to cope with anxiety, we tend to focus on only one need and compulsively seek its satisfaction in all situations.

In her later writings, she reformulated the list of needs (Horney, 1945). From her work with patients, she concluded that the needs could be presented in three groups, each indicating a person's attitudes toward the self and others. She called these three categories of directional movement the **neurotic trends** (see Table 4.1).

Because the neurotic trends evolve from and elaborate on the self-protective mechanisms, we can see similarities with our earlier descriptions. The neurotic trends involve compulsive attitudes and behaviors; that is, neurotic persons are compelled to behave in accordance with at least one of the neurotic trends. They are also displayed indiscriminately, in any and all situations.

The neurotic trends are:

- Movement toward other people (the compliant personality),
- Movement against other people (the aggressive personality), and
- Movement away from other people (the detached personality).

neurotic trends
Three categories of behaviors and attitudes toward oneself and others that express a person's needs; Horney's revision of the concept of neurotic needs.

The Compliant Personality

compliant personality
Behaviors and attitudes associated with the neurotic trend of moving toward people, such as a need for affection and approval.

The **compliant personality** displays attitudes and behaviors that reflect a desire to move toward other people: an intense and continuous need for affection and approval, an urge to be loved, wanted, and protected. Compliant personalities display these needs toward everyone, although they usually have a need for one dominant person, such as a friend or spouse, who will take charge of their lives and offer protection and guidance.

Compliant personalities manipulate other people, particularly their partners, to achieve their goals. They often behave in ways others find attractive or endearing. For example, they may seem unusually considerate, appreciative, responsive, understanding, and sensitive to the needs of others. Compliant people are concerned with living up to others' ideals and expectations, and they act in ways others perceive as unselfish and generous.

In dealing with other people, compliant personalities are conciliatory and subordinate their personal desires to those of other people. They are willing to assume blame and to defer to others, never being assertive, critical, or demanding. They do whatever the situation requires, as they interpret it, to gain affection, approval, and love. Their attitude toward themselves is consistently one of helplessness and weakness. Horney suggested that compliant people are saying, "Look at me. I am so weak and helpless that you must protect and love me."

Consequently, they regard other people as superior, and even in situations in which they are notably competent, they see themselves as inferior. Because the security of compliant personalities depends on the attitudes and behavior of other people toward them, they become excessively dependent, needing constant approval and reassurance. Any sign of rejection, whether actual or imagined, is terrifying to them, leading to increased efforts to regain the affection of the person they believe has rejected them.

The source of these behaviors is the person's repressed hostility. Horney found that compliant persons have repressed profound feelings of defiance and vindictiveness. They have a desire to control, exploit, and manipulate others—the opposite of what their behaviors and attitudes express. Because their hostile impulses must be repressed, compliant personalities become subservient, always trying to please and asking nothing for themselves.

The Aggressive Personality

aggressive personality
Behaviors and attitudes associated with the neurotic trend of moving against people, such as a domineering and controlling manner.

Aggressive personalities move against other people. In their world, everyone is hostile; only the fittest and most cunning survive. Life is a jungle in which supremacy, strength, and ferocity are the paramount virtues. Although their motivation is the same as that of the compliant type, to alleviate basic anxiety, aggressive personalities never display fear of rejection. They act tough and domineering and have no regard for others. To achieve the control and superiority so vital to their lives, they must consistently perform at a high level. By excelling and receiving recognition, they find satisfaction in having their superiority affirmed by others.

Because aggressive personalities are driven to surpass others, they judge everyone in terms of the benefit they will receive from the relationship. They make no effort to appease others but will argue, criticize, demand, and do whatever is necessary to achieve and retain superiority and power.

They drive themselves hard to become the best; therefore, they may actually be highly successful in their careers, although the work itself will not provide intrinsic satisfaction. Like everything else in life, work is a means to an end, not an end in itself.

Aggressive personalities may appear confident of their abilities and uninhibited in asserting and defending themselves. However, like compliant personalities, aggressive personalities are driven by insecurity, anxiety, and hostility.

The Detached Personality

detached personality
Behaviors and attitudes associated with the neurotic trend of moving away from people, such as an intense need for privacy.

People described as **detached personalities** are driven to move away from other people and to maintain an emotional distance. They must not love, hate, or cooperate with others or become involved in any way. To achieve this total detachment, they strive to become self-sufficient. If they are to function as detached personalities, they must rely on their own resources, which must be well developed.

Detached personalities have an almost desperate desire for privacy. They need to spend as much time as possible alone, and it disturbs them to share even such an experience as listening to music. Their need for independence makes them sensitive to any attempt to influence, coerce, or obligate them. Detached personalities must avoid all constraints, including timetables and schedules, long-term commitments such as marriages or mortgages, and sometimes even the pressure of a belt or necktie.

They need to feel superior, but not in the same way aggressive personalities do. Because detached people cannot actively compete with other people for superiority—that would mean becoming involved with others—they believe their greatness should be recognized automatically, without struggle or effort on their part. One manifestation of this sense of superiority is the feeling that one is unique, that one is different and apart from everyone else.

Detached personalities suppress or deny all feelings toward other people, particularly feelings of love and hate. Intimacy would lead to conflict, and that must be avoided. Because of this constriction of their emotions, detached personalities place great stress on reason, logic, and intelligence.

You have probably noticed the similarity between the three personality types proposed by Horney and the styles of life in Adler's personality theory. Horney's compliant personality is similar to Adler's getting type, the aggressive personality is like the dominant or ruling type, and the detached personality is similar to the avoiding type. This is yet another example of how Adler's ideas influenced later explanations of personality.

Horney found that in the neurotic person, one of these three trends is dominant, and the other two are present to a lesser degree. For example, the person who is predominantly aggressive also has some need for compliance and detachment. The dominant neurotic trend is the one that determines the person's behaviors and attitudes toward others. This is the mode of acting and thinking that best serves to control basic anxiety and any deviation from it is threatening to the person. For this reason, the other two trends must actively be repressed, which can lead to additional problems. Any indication that a repressed trend is pushing for expression causes conflict within the individual.

conflict
To Horney, the basic incompatibility of the neurotic trends.

In Horney's system, **conflict** is defined as the basic incompatibility of the three neurotic trends; this conflict is the core of neurosis. All of us, whether neurotic or normal, suffer some conflict among these basically irreconcilable modes. The difference between the normal person and the neurotic person lies in the intensity of the conflict; it is much more intense in the neurotic. Neurotic people must battle to keep the non-dominant trends from being expressed. They are rigid and inflexible, meeting all situations with the behaviors and attitudes that characterize the dominant trend, regardless of their suitability.

In the person who is not neurotic, all three trends can be expressed as circumstances warrant. A person may sometimes be aggressive, sometimes compliant, and sometimes detached. The trends are not mutually exclusive and can be integrated harmoniously within the personality. The normal person is flexible in behaviors and attitudes and can adapt to changing situations.

The Idealized Self-Image

Horney argued that all of us, normal or neurotic, construct a picture of ourselves that may or may not be based on reality. Horney's own search for self was difficult. At age 21, she wrote in her diary:

> There's still such chaos in me. . . . Just like my face: a formless mass that only takes on shape through the expression of the moment. The searching for our selves is the most agonizing. (Horney, 1980, p. 174)

In normal persons, the self-image is built on a realistic appraisal of our abilities, potentials, weaknesses, goals, and relations with other people. This image supplies a sense of unity and integration to the personality and a framework within which to approach others and ourselves. If we are to realize our full potential, a state of self-realization, our self-image must clearly reflect our true self.

Neurotic persons, who experience conflict between incompatible modes of behavior, have personalities characterized by disunity and disharmony. They construct an **idealized self-image** for the same purpose as normal persons do: to unify the personality. But their attempt is doomed to failure because their self-image is not based on a realistic appraisal of personal strengths and weaknesses. Instead, it is based on an illusion, an unattainable ideal of absolute perfection.

idealized self-image For normal people, the self-image is an idealized picture of oneself built on a flexible, realistic assessment of one's abilities. For neurotics, the self-image is based on an inflexible, unrealistic self-appraisal.

tyranny of the shoulds An attempt to realize an unattainable idealized self-image by denying the true self and behaving in terms of what we think we should be doing.

To attempt to realize this unattainable ideal, neurotic people engage in what Horney called the **tyranny of the shoulds**. They tell themselves they should be the best or most perfect student, spouse, parent, lover, employee, friend, or child. Because they find their real self-image so undesirable, they believe they must act to live up to their illusory, idealized self-image, in which they see themselves in a highly positive light, for example, being virtuous, honest, generous, considerate, and courageous. In doing so, they deny their real selves and try to become what they think they should be or what they need to be to match their idealized self-image. However, their efforts are doomed to failure; they can never achieve their unrealistic self-image.

Although the neurotic or idealized self-image does not coincide with reality, it is real and accurate to the person who created it. Other people can easily see through this false picture, but the neurotic cannot. The neurotic person believes that the incomplete and misleading self-picture is real. The idealized self-image is a model of what the neurotic thinks he or she is, can be, or should be.

A realistic self-image, on the other hand, is flexible and dynamic, adapting as the individual develops and changes. It reflects strengths, growth, and self-awareness.

The realistic image is a goal, something to strive for, and as such it reflects and leads the person. By contrast, the neurotic self-image is static, inflexible, and unyielding. It is not a goal but a fixed idea, not an inducement to growth but a hindrance demanding rigid adherence to its proscriptions.

The neurotic's self-image is an unsatisfactory substitute for a reality-based sense of self-worth. The neurotic has little self-confidence because of insecurity and anxiety, and the idealized self-image does not allow for correction of those deficiencies. It provides only an illusory sense of worth and alienates the neurotic from the true self. Developed to reconcile incompatible modes of behavior, the idealized self-image becomes just one more element in that conflict. Far from resolving the problem, it adds to a growing sense of futility. The slightest crack in the neurotic's idealized self-picture threatens the false sense of superiority and security the whole edifice was constructed to provide, and little is needed to destroy it. Horney suggested that the neurotic self-image may be like a house filled with dynamite.

One way in which neurotics attempt to defend themselves against the inner conflicts caused by the discrepancy between idealized and real self-images is by **externalization**, projecting the conflicts onto the outside world. This process may temporarily alleviate the anxiety caused by the conflict but will do nothing to reduce the gap between the idealized self-image and reality.

Externalization involves the tendency to experience conflicts as though they were occurring outside of one. It also entails depicting external forces as the source of the conflicts. For example, neurotics who experience self-hatred because of the discrepancy between real and idealized selves may project that hatred onto other people or institutions and come to believe that the hatred is emanating from these external sources and not from themselves.

externalization
A way to defend against the conflict caused by the discrepancy between an idealized and a real self-image by projecting the conflict onto the outside world.

Feminine Psychology: Mommy Track or the Career Path?

feminine psychology
To Horney, a revision of psychoanalysis to encompass the psychological conflicts inherent in the traditional ideal of womanhood and women's roles.

Early in her career, Horney expressed her disagreement with Freud's views on women. She began work on her version of **feminine psychology** in 1922, the year she became the first woman to present a paper on the topic at an international psychoanalytic congress. That meeting, held in Berlin, was chaired by Sigmund Freud.

Horney was especially critical of Freud's notion of penis envy, which she believed was derived from inadequate evidence (that is, from Freud's clinical interviews with neurotic women). Freud offered descriptions and interpretations of this alleged phenomenon from a male point of view in a place and time when women were considered second-class citizens. He suggested that women were victims of their anatomy, forever envious, and resentful of men for possessing a penis. Freud also concluded that women had poorly developed superegos (a result of inadequately resolved Oedipal conflicts), and inferior body images, because women believed they were really castrated men.

womb envy
The envy a male feels toward a female because she can bear children and he cannot. Womb envy was Horney's response to Freud's concept of penis envy in females.

Womb Envy

Horney countered these ideas by arguing that men envied women because of their capacity for motherhood. Her position on this issue was based on the pleasure she had experienced in childbirth. She uncovered in her male patients what she called **womb envy**. "When one begins, as I did, to analyze men only after a fairly long

Horney disputed Freud's views on the accepted sex stereotypes of men and women.

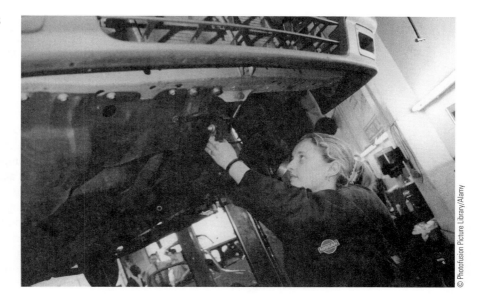

© Photofusion Picture Library/Alamy

experience of analyzing women, one receives a most surprising impression of the intensity of this envy of pregnancy, childbirth, and motherhood" (Horney, 1967, pp. 60–61).

Men have such a small part to play in the act of creating new life that they must sublimate their womb envy and overcompensate for it by seeking achievement in their work. Womb envy and the resentment that accompanies it are manifested unconsciously in behaviors designed to disparage and belittle women and to reinforce their inferior status. By denying women equal rights, minimizing their opportunities to contribute to society, and downgrading their efforts to achieve, men retain their so-called natural superiority. Underlying such typical male behavior is a sense of inferiority deriving from their womb envy.

Horney did not deny that many women believe themselves to be inferior to men. What she questioned was Freud's claim of a biological basis for these feelings. Although women may view themselves as inadequate compared to men, they do so for societal reasons, not because they were born female. If women feel unworthy, it is because they have been treated that way in male-dominated cultures. After generations of social, economic, and cultural discrimination, it is understandable that many women see themselves in this light.

The Flight from Womanhood

As a result of these feelings of inferiority, women may choose to deny their femininity and to wish, unconsciously, that they were men. Horney referred to this as the flight from womanhood, a condition that can lead to sexual inhibitions (Horney, 1926). Part of the sexual fear associated with this condition arises from childhood fantasies about the difference in size between the adult penis and the female child's vagina. The fantasies focus on vaginal injury and the pain of forcible penetration.

This produces a conflict between the unconscious desire to have a child and the fear of intercourse. If the conflict is sufficiently strong, it can lead to emotional disturbances that manifest themselves in relations with men. These women distrust and resent men and reject their sexual advances.

The Oedipus Complex

Horney also disagreed with Freud about the nature of the Oedipus complex. She did not deny the existence of conflicts between children and parents, but she did not believe they had a sexual origin. By removing sex from the Oedipus complex, she reinterpreted the situation as a conflict between dependence on one's parents and hostility toward them.

We discussed parental behaviors that undermine the satisfaction of the childhood need for safety and security and lead to the development of hostility. At the same time, the child remains dependent on the parents so that expressing hostility is unacceptable; it could further damage the child's security. The child is saying, in effect, "I have to repress my hostility because I need you."

As we noted, the hostile impulses remain and create basic anxiety. To Horney, "The resulting picture may look exactly like what Freud describes as the Oedipus complex: passionate clinging to one parent and jealousy toward the other" (Horney, 1939, p. 83). Thus, her explanation for Oedipal feelings lies in neurotic conflicts that evolve from parent–child interactions. These feelings are not based on sex or other biological forces, nor are they universal. They develop only when parents act to undermine their child's security.

Freud did not respond to Horney's challenge to his views on women, nor did he alter his concept of the Oedipus complex. In a veiled allusion to Horney's work, he wrote, "We shall not be very greatly surprised if a woman analyst, who has not been sufficiently convinced of the intensity of her own wish for a penis, also fails to attach proper importance to that factor in her patients" (Freud, 1940). Of Horney herself, Freud remarked, "She is able but malicious" (quoted in Blanton, 1971, p. 65). Horney was bitter about Freud's failure to recognize the legitimacy of her views.

Motherhood or Career?

As an early feminist, Horney adopted several positions that have a contemporary ring. In 1934, she wrote an essay describing the psychological conflicts in defining women's roles, contrasting the traditional ideal of womanhood with a more modern view (Horney, 1967). In the traditional scheme, promoted and endorsed by most men, the woman's role was to love, admire, and serve her man. Her identity was a reflection of her husband's. Horney suggested that women should seek their own identity, as she did, by developing their abilities and pursuing careers.

These traditional and modern roles create conflicts that many women to this day have difficulty resolving. Drawing on Horney's work, a later feminist wrote that

> modern women are caught between wanting to make themselves desirable to men and pursuing their own goals. The competing purposes elicit conflicting behaviors: seductive versus aggressive, deferential versus ambitious. Modern women are torn between love and work and are consequently dissatisfied in both. (Westkott, 1986, p. 14)

It remains as troublesome for 21st-century women to combine marriage, motherhood, and career as it was for Karen Horney in the 1930s. Her decision to develop her abilities and focus on her work brought her enormous satisfaction, but she continued throughout her life to search for security and love.

Cultural Influences on Feminine Psychology

Horney recognized the impact of social and cultural forces on the development of personality. She also recognized that different cultures and social groups view women's roles in different ways. Thus, there can be many different feminine psychologies. "The American woman is different from the German woman; both are different from certain Pueblo Indian women. The New York society woman is different from the farmer's wife in Idaho. . . . Specific cultural conditions engender specific qualities and faculties, in women as in men" (Horney, 1939, p. 119).

One example of the power of culture to shape women's lives and expectations can be found in traditional Chinese society. As far back as the first millennium B.C., women were considered subordinate to men. Society was governed by the belief that the universe contained two contrasting yet interacting elements, *yin* and *yang*. *Yang* represents the male element and contains all that is vital, positive, strong, and active. *Yin* represents the female element and contains all that is dark, weak, and passive. Over time, these elements came to form a hierarchy in which men were considered superior and women inferior.

This idea became part of the teaching of the Chinese philosopher Confucius (551–479 B.C.), whose work was the ruling ideology of China for centuries. Strict rules of conduct were established for women; they were expected to be submissive, obedient, respectful, chaste, and unselfish. The Chinese word for woman literally meant "inside person," denoting her status as restricted to the confines of the home.

> A respectable Chinese woman was not to be seen or heard. She was expected never to be freed from male domination, as her duty was to obey her father at home, her husband after marriage, and her eldest son when widowed. . . . Men were counseled against listening to women for fear that disaster would result. The exercise of willfulness and ambition, considered heroic in a man, was considered wicked and depraved in a woman. (Loo, 1998, p. 180)

If we contrast this attitude with the widely accepted views of a woman's place in contemporary American society, and in rapidly changing Chinese society as well, we can easily accept Horney's position that the feminine psyche is influenced, even determined, by cultural forces.

Questions About Human Nature

Horney's image of human nature is considerably more optimistic than Freud's. One reason for her optimism was her belief that biological forces do not condemn us to conflict, anxiety, neurosis, or universality in personality. To Horney, each person is unique. Neurotic behavior, when it occurs, results from social forces in childhood. Parent–child relationships will either satisfy or frustrate the child's need for safety.

If that need is frustrated, the outcome is neurotic behavior. Neuroses and conflicts can be avoided if children are raised with love, acceptance, and trust.

Each of us has the innate potential for self-realization, and this is our ultimate and necessary goal in life. Our intrinsic abilities and potential will blossom as inevitably and naturally as an acorn grows into an oak tree. The only thing that can obstruct our development is the thwarting in childhood of our need for safety and security.

Horney also believed that we have the capacity to consciously shape and change our personality. Because human nature is flexible, it is not formed into immutable shapes in childhood. Each of us possesses the capacity to grow. Therefore, adult experiences may be as important as those of childhood.

So confident was Horney of our capacity for self-growth that she emphasized self-analysis in her therapeutic work as well as in her own life. In her book entitled *Self-Analysis* (Horney, 1942), she noted our ability to help resolve our own problems. On the issue of free will versus determinism, then, Horney argued in favor of the former. We can all shape our lives and achieve self-realization.

Assessment in Horney's Theory

The methods Horney used to assess the functioning of the human personality were essentially those favored by Freud—free association and dream analysis—but with some modification. The most basic difference in technique between Horney and Freud was in the relationship between analyst and patient. Horney believed that Freud played too passive a role and was too distant and intellectual. She suggested that analysis should be an "exquisitely cooperative enterprise" between patient and therapist (Horney quoted in Cherry & Cherry, 1973, p. 84).

Although Horney kept a couch in her office, she did not use it with every patient. Adopting an attitude she called constructive friendliness, she approached the use of the couch as follows.

> This is something one needs to try through trial and error, asking if the patient operates better lying on the couch or sitting upright. It is particularly helpful to encourage a patient so he feels free to sit up, lie down, walk around, or whatever he wants. (Horney, 1987, p. 43)

With free association, Horney did not follow Freud's lead in trying to probe the unconscious mind. She believed that patients could easily distort or hide aspects of their inner lives or falsify feelings about events that they remembered. Instead, Horney focused on her patients' visible emotional reactions toward her, believing that these could explain her patients' attitudes toward other people. She pursued these attitudes through free association. She did not delve into presumed infantile sexual fantasies at the beginning of a course of analysis but inquired about the early years only after evaluating present attitudes, defenses, and conflicts.

Horney believed that each attitude or feeling resulted from a deeper, preexisting attitude, which in turn had resulted from a deeper one, and so on. Through free association, the analyst gradually uncovered the patient's early experiences and emotions, similar to peeling the layers of an onion.

Horney also believed that dream analysis could reveal a person's true self, and that dreams represented attempts to solve problems, in either a constructive or a neurotic way. Dreams can show us a set of attitudes that may differ from those of our self-image. She did not offer a list of universal dream symbols but insisted that each dream be explained within the context of the patient's conflict. Focusing on a dream's emotional content, she concluded that the "safest clue to the understanding of a dream is in the feelings of the patient as he has them in the dream" (Horney, 1987, p. 61).

A 35-item self-report inventory, the CAD, was devised to measure Horney's three neurotic trends, the *C*ompliant, *A*ggressive, and *D*etached personality types (Cohen, 1967). The Horney–Coolidge Type Indicator (HCTI), a 57-item self-report inventory, is another measure of Horney's three neurotic trends. Research with 198 college students confirmed the HCTI as a valid measure of the compliant, aggressive, and detached personality types (Coolidge, Moor, Yamazaki, Stewart, & Segal, 2001).

Other studies using college student responses on the HCTI found that men tended to score higher on the aggressive and detached scales whereas women scored higher in compliance. The research also showed a relationship between Horney's three neurotic types and various personality disorders. For example, aggression and detachment correlated highly with psychoticism; compliance was associated with neuroticism (Coolidge, Moor, Yamazaki, Stewart, & Segal, 2001; Shatz, 2004; for additional research support see Coolidge, Segal, Benight, & Danielian, 2004).

Research on Horney's Theory

Horney used the case study method. Therefore, her approach, data, and interpretations are subject to the same criticisms made of the work of Freud, Jung, and Adler. The weaknesses inherent in the case study method apply to her work no less than to theirs.

Horney was opposed to taking verbatim notes of her patients' recollections. "I don't see how anybody can employ a wholehearted receptivity and productivity of attention at the same time that he is anxiously scribbling everything down" (Horney, 1987, p. 30). As with Freud, Jung, and Adler, then, we do not have complete records of her analytic sessions and the data she collected during them. However, she tried to be rigorous and scientific in her clinical observations, formulating hypotheses, testing them in therapeutic situations, and maintaining that her data were tested the same way scientists in other fields test theirs.

Neurotic Trends

Researchers have studied Horney's three proposed neurotic trends, redefining them as follows: moving against people (ill-tempered), moving away from people (shy), and moving toward people (dependent) (Caspi, Elder, & Bem, 1987, 1988). The behavior of people belonging to each of these types in late childhood was compared with their behavior 30 years later to discover whatever continuities might exist.

Ill-tempered children, both boys and girls, tended to become ill-tempered adults, prone to divorce and downward occupational mobility. Gender differences were found in the shy and dependent types. Shy boys became aloof adults who experienced marital and job instability. On the other hand, shy girls manifested no such problems later in life. Dependent boys became agreeable, socially poised, warm, and giving adults with stable marriages and careers; the opposite was found for dependent girls (Caspi, Bem, & Elder, 1989).

A study dealing with the neurotic trends of moving against people (aggressive) and moving away from people (detached) compared measures from aggressive and detached children at ages 7 to 13 with their behavior 5 to 7 years later (Moskowitz & Schwartzman, 1989). Those high in aggressiveness were found to be low in school achievement and to have psychiatric problems. Those who were detached or withdrawn were found to have inaccurate and negative self-images. The researchers concluded that Horney's proposed personality types had predictive value for later behavior.

Research using the CAD inventory found that college students preparing for careers in helping professions such as nursing and social work scored higher in compliance than did students considering careers in business or science. The business students, on a more competitive career path, scored higher on aggression. Science students scored highest on the detached scale. These results appear to be consistent with Horney's descriptions of the three neurotic trends (Cohen, 1967; Rendon, 1987).

Feminine Psychology

Some research applies indirectly to Horney's ideas on feminine psychology. In our discussion of research on the Oedipus complex, we mentioned a study on dreams that provided support for the Freudian concept of penis envy (Hall & Van de Castle, 1965); this study fails to support Horney's questioning of the concept of penis envy. However, research that refutes Freud's notion that women have inadequately developed superegos and inferior body images can be taken to support Horney's views.

The Tyranny of the Shoulds

Research with 150 college students asked them to recall three things they did during the week prior to the study. They were also asked to indicate whether they did these things because they felt they should or ought to do them, or whether they really wanted to do them. Students who had done more things because they genuinely wanted to, rather than because they felt they should, scored significantly higher on general life satisfaction than those whose behavior was directed primarily by what they believed they ought to do (Berg, Janoff-Bulman, & Cotter, 2001).

Neurotic Competitiveness

neurotic competitiveness An indiscriminate need to win at all costs.

Horney spoke of **neurotic competitiveness** as a major aspect of contemporary culture. She defined it as an indiscriminate need to win at all costs. The feeling toward life of the person manifesting this need can be "compared to that of a jockey in a race, for whom only one thing matters—whether he is ahead of the others" (Horney, 1937, p. 189).

A self-report inventory, the Hypercompetitive Attitude Scale (HCA), was developed to test experimentally the concept of neurotic competitiveness (Ryckman, Thornton, & Butler, 1994). This 26-item scale contains such items as "Winning in competition makes me feel more powerful as a person." Research participants evaluate the items on a five-point continuum ranging from never true of me to always true of me.

Studies using the HCA and other measures of personality found that people who scored high on competitiveness were also high in narcissism, neuroticism, authoritarianism, dogmatism, and mistrust, and low in self-esteem and psychological health. Hypercompetitive men were also found to be hypermasculine or macho, believing that women were sex objects who deserved neither respect nor consideration. A comparison of college students in the United States and in the Netherlands found that the Americans scored higher in hypercompetitiveness, suggesting cultural differences in this aspect of their personality (Dru, 2003; Ryckman, Hammer, Kaczor, & Gold, 1990; Ryckman, Thornton, & Butler, 1994; Ryckman, Thornton, Gold, & Burckle, 2002). These findings support Horney's description of the neurotic competitive personality.

Reflections on Horney's Theory

Horney's contributions, although impressive, are not as well known or recognized within psychology as those of Freud, Jung, and Adler. However, her work drew a large public following, partly because of her personal qualities. A student recalled:

> There was about her an air of wholeness, of certainty, of total dedication and commitment, of a conviction that her ideas were valuable, that they were worth sharing with colleagues and students, because knowing them would make a difference to helping those in need. (Clemmens, 1987, p. 108)

These characteristics are evident in her books, which were written in a style readily understood by people who do not have professional analytical training. Her theory has a commonsense appeal and for many people it seems applicable to their own personality or to that of a relative or friend.

Horney's ideas may be more relevant to problems inherent in American culture than the ideas of Freud, Jung, or Adler. Many personality researchers see Horney's conception of the neurotic trends as a valuable way to categorize deviant behavior. Others accept Horney's emphasis on self-esteem, the need for safety and security, the role of basic anxiety, and the importance of the idealized self-image. Her work had a significant impact on the personality theories developed by Erik Erikson and Abraham Maslow. Maslow used her concept of the real self and self-realization; her notion of basic anxiety is similar to Erikson's concept of basic mistrust.

Although Horney was trained in orthodox Freudian theory and paid tribute to Freud for providing the foundation and tools for her work, her theory deviated from psychoanalysis in several ways. Not surprisingly, she received a great deal of criticism from those who continued to adhere to Freud's position. To the Freudians, Horney's denial of the importance of biological instincts and her reduced emphasis on sexuality and the unconscious were obvious weaknesses.

Horney's personality theory is not as completely or consistently developed as Freud's. It has been suggested that because Freud's model was constructed so elegantly and precisely, it would have been better for Horney to reject it and start anew rather than attempt to refashion it along different lines. Another criticism is that although Horney's theory notes the impact of social and cultural forces on personality, it makes little use of research data from sociology and anthropology to detail precisely how social forces shape personality. A related charge is that her observations and interpretations were too greatly influenced by middle-class American culture. In her defense, it must be said that all personality theorists are affected by the class, culture, and time in which they work.

Primarily due to the women's movement that began in the 1960s, Horney's books have enjoyed renewed interest. Her writings on feminine psychology and sexuality may constitute the most influential of her contributions, of value to scholars on the role of women in society well more than 50 years after Horney's death (see, for example, Gilman, 2001; Miletic, 2002). "Had she written nothing else," a biographer stated, "these papers would have earned Horney a place of importance in the history of psychoanalysis" (Quinn, 1987, p. 211). The work of the Karen Horney Clinic and the Karen Horney Psychoanalytic Institute (a training center for analysts), both in New York City, attests to the lasting impact of her work. A loyal, if small, group of disciples carries on her work, much of which is published in the *American Journal of Psychoanalysis.*

Chapter Summary

Karen Horney differed from Freud in her views on feminine psychology and her emphasis on social rather than biological forces as shapers of personality. Her childhood experiences helped shape her lifelong quest for love and security as well as her theory of personality.

The need for safety refers to security and freedom from fear. It depends on being loved and wanted as a child. When security is undermined, hostility is induced. The child may repress this hostility out of a sense of helplessness, fear of the parents, the need to receive parental affection, or guilt about expressing hostility. Repressing hostility leads to basic anxiety, defined as a feeling of being lonely and helpless in a hostile world.

Four ways to protect oneself against basic anxiety are by gaining affection, being submissive, attaining power, and withdrawing. Any of these protective devices may become a neurotic need or drive. Horney proposed 10 neurotic needs, which she later grouped as three neurotic trends: moving toward people (the compliant personality), moving against people (the aggressive personality), and moving away from people (the detached personality). Compliant types need affection and approval and will do what other people want. Aggressive types are hostile toward others and seek to achieve control and superiority. Detached types keep an emotional distance from others and have a deep need for privacy.

In the normal person, the idealized self-image is built on a realistic appraisal of one's abilities and goals. It helps the person achieve self-realization—the maximum development and use of one's potential. The idealized self-image in the neurotic person is based on an unrealistic, misleading appraisal of one's abilities.

Horney argued against Freud's contention that women have penis envy, poorly developed superegos, and inferior body images. She believed that men envy women because of their capacity for motherhood and, consequently, experience womb envy, which they sublimate through achievement. She rejected the sexual basis for the Oedipus complex, suggesting that it involved a conflict between dependence on and hostility toward parents.

Horney's image of human nature is more optimistic than is Freud's. Each person is unique and is not doomed to conflict. Although childhood influences are important, later experiences also shape personality. The ultimate goal of life is self-realization, an innate urge to grow, which can be helped or hindered by social forces. According to Horney, we can consciously shape and change our personalities.

Horney's methods of assessment were free association and dream analysis, and her research method was the case study. Some psychologists see value in her concepts of neurotic trends, the need for safety, the role of anxiety, and the idealized self-image. Research supports aspects of her theory, namely, the neurotic trends, feminine psychology, the tyranny of the shoulds, and neurotic competitiveness. The theory has been criticized for not being developed as fully as Freud's, for not using research data from sociology and anthropology, and for being heavily influenced by middle-class American culture.

Review Questions

1. How did Horney's childhood experiences influence her personality theory?

2. Describe the childhood need for safety and the kinds of parental behaviors necessary for a child's security.

3. What is basic anxiety and how does it originate?

4. Describe the four basic types of behavior people use in childhood to try to protect themselves from basic anxiety.

5. Discuss the three neurotic trends and the behaviors associated with each.

6. How do people labeled "compliant personalities" deal with other people?

7. In what ways do aggressive personalities differ from detached personalities? Which type is more likely to be successful in their career?

8. How are the neurotic trends related to the self-protective defenses against anxiety?

9. Explain the difference between normal persons and neurotic persons in terms of the neurotic trends.

10. How does the idealized self-image of the normal, realistic person differ from the idealized self-image of the neurotic person?

11. Contrast the tyranny of the shoulds and the process of externalization.

12. Horney rejected Freud's contention of a biological basis for female inferiority. How did she account for women's feelings of inadequacy?

13. What was Horney's interpretation of the Oedipus complex?

14. Discuss the impact of cultural forces on women's roles. Give examples.

15. In what ways does Horney's image of human nature differ from Freud's?

16. How did Horney's use of free association differ from Freud's?

17. Describe the results of research conducted on neurotic trends, on neurotic competitiveness, and on the tyranny of the shoulds.

18. What criticisms have been directed against Horney's theory of personality?

19. In your opinion, what is Horney's major contribution to the study of personality?

Suggested Readings

Berger, M. M. (Ed.). (1991, September). Special issue commemorating the 50th anniversary of the founding by Karen Horney, M.D. (1885–1952) of the Association for the Advancement of Psychoanalysis; the American Institute for Psychoanalysis; and the *American Journal of Psychoanalysis*. *American Journal of Psychoanalysis, 51*(3). Includes tributes to and personal recollections of Horney, along with an overview and evaluations of her work.

Eckardt, M. H. (2006). Karen Horney: A portrait: Celebrating the 120th anniversary of Karen Horney's birth. *American Journal of Psychoanalysis, 66*, 105–108. A biographical sketch by Horney's daughter Marianne.

Gilman, S. L. (2001). Karen Horney, M.D., 1885–1952. *American Journal of Psychiatry, 158*, 1205. Discusses Horney's life and work and assesses the impact of her ideas on the beginnings of feminist theory.

Horney, K. (1937). *The neurotic personality of our time.* New York: Norton. Describes the development of conflict and anxiety within the personality and relates neuroses to past experiences and to social and cultural forces.

Horney, K. (1980). *The adolescent diaries of Karen Horney.* New York: Basic Books. A compilation of diary entries Horney wrote between the ages of 13 and 25 showing intense emotion and intellectual honesty.

Horney, K. (1987). *Final lectures.* New York: Norton. Lectures Horney delivered during the last year of her life. Presents refinements of her views on psychoanalytic techniques such as free association and dream analysis.

Paris, B. J. (1994). *Karen Horney: A psychoanalyst's search for self-understanding.* New Haven, CT: Yale University Press. A study of Horney's life and work exploring the relationship between her struggle for self-understanding and the evolution of her ideas. Assesses her later contributions to psychology, psychoanalysis, and the study of gender and culture.

Patterson, R. H. (2006). The child within: Karen Horney on vacation. *American Journal of Psychoanalysis, 66*, 109–112. A memoir by Horney's youngest daughter, Renate.

Quinn, S. (1987). *A mind of her own: The life of Karen Horney.* New York: Summit Books. Discusses Horney's life, her work on feminine psychology, and her conflicts with the orthodox Freudian establishment.

Sayers, J. (1991). *Mothers of psychoanalysis: Helene Deutsch, Karen Horney, Anna Freud, Melanie Klein.* New York: Norton. Describes the post-Freudian modification of psychoanalytic theory from patriarchal to matriarchal. Shows how the experiences of these influential women psychoanalysts changed the focus from sex, repression, and castration anxiety to identification, projection, and separation anxiety.

CHAPTER 5

Henry Murray: Personology

For me, personality is [a] jungle without boundaries.

—HENRY MURRAY

Henry Murray designed an approach to personality that includes conscious and unconscious forces; the influence of the past, present, and future; and the impact of physiological and sociological factors. The influence of Freudian psychoanalysis can be seen in Murray's recognition of the effect on adult behavior of childhood experiences and in his notions of the id, ego, and superego. Although Freud's imprint is clear, Murray gave unique interpretations to these phenomena. His deviations from orthodox psychoanalysis are so extensive that his system must be classified with the neo-Freudians rather than with the Freudian loyalists.

Two distinctive features of Murray's system are a sophisticated approach to human needs and the data source on which he based his theory. His proposed list of needs is still widely used in personality research and assessment and in clinical treatment. His data, unlike those of theorists discussed in earlier chapters, come from so-called normal individuals (undergraduate male students at Harvard University) rather than from patients undergoing psychotherapy. Also, some of the data were derived from more empirically based laboratory procedures rather than from case histories.

Because of his long affiliation with a major university instead of relative isolation in a clinic or private practice, and because of his personal charisma, Murray gathered and trained a large number of psychologists, many of whom have since achieved prominence and carried on his teachings.

The Life of Murray (1893–1988)

Childhood Depression and Compensation

Henry Murray's childhood contained maternal rejection, elements of Adlerian compensation for a physical defect, and a supernormal sensitivity to the sufferings of others. Born into a wealthy family, Murray grew up in New York City, in a house on what is now the site of Rockefeller Center. His summers were spent on a Long Island beach. As a child, he accompanied his parents on four long trips to Europe. For the Adlerians among you, Murray reported that some of his earliest recollections focused on his privileged background (Triplet, 1993).

Another significant early memory is more intriguing. Murray called it "the marrow-of-my-being memory" (Murray, 1967, p. 299). At about age 4, he was looking at a picture of a sad woman sitting next to her equally sad son. This was the same kind of gloomy picture Murray later used in his Thematic Apperception Test. Murray's mother told him, "It is the prospect of death that has made them sad" (Murray, 1967, p. 299). Murray interpreted the memory as indicating the death of his emotional ties to his mother because she had abruptly weaned him when he was 2 months old, preferring, he believed, to lavish her affection on his siblings. He insisted that his mother's actions led to his lifelong depression, a condition that formed the core of his personality.

Murray referred to his depression as a source of "misery and melancholy" and he attempted to mask it in everyday behavior by adopting an ebullient, cheerful, and outgoing manner (Murray, 1967). This lack of a childhood attachment to his mother later led Murray to question Freud's Oedipus complex because it did not coincide with his own experiences. Another factor that made Murray sensitive to emotional problems and sufferings was his relationship with two emotionally disturbed aunts.

Murray was afflicted with crossed eyes, and at the age of 9, he underwent an operation that was performed in the dining room of his home. The condition was corrected, but a slip of the surgeon's blade left Murray with no stereoscopic vision. No matter how hard he tried, he was never able to succeed at games such as tennis or baseball because he could not focus both eyes on the ball. He remained unaware of his visual defect until he was in medical school, when a physician asked him if he had had trouble playing sports as a child.

Murray's physical ineptness and a speech impediment (a stutter) drove him to compensate for his limitations. When he tried to play football, he had to be quarterback, and when he was calling plays, he never stuttered. After being bested in a schoolyard fight, Murray took up boxing and won the local featherweight championship. He later agreed that "an Adlerian factor was at work" in these childhood efforts to compensate for his disabilities (Murray, 1967, p. 302).

Education

After attending Groton, a preparatory school, Murray enrolled at Harvard University. He studied history but earned mediocre grades because he preferred "the three Rs— Rum, Rowing, and Romanticism" (Robinson, 1992, p. 27). His career followed a devious route to the study of personality. He disliked the psychology course he took in college and dropped out after the second lecture. He did not attend another psychology course until years later, when he taught one himself.

In 1919, Murray graduated from Columbia University Medical School at the top of his class. He also earned an M.A. in biology from Columbia and taught physiology at Harvard. He served a 2-year internship in surgery at a New York hospital where he helped care for a future U.S. president, Franklin D. Roosevelt, who was suffering from polio. Following the internship, Murray spent 2 years at the Rockefeller Institute conducting biomedical research in embryology. He went abroad for further study and in 1927 received his Ph.D. in biochemistry from Cambridge University.

The Influence of Carl Jung

Murray's sensitivity and empathy toward others were reinforced during his internship, when he became interested in the psychological factors in his patients' lives. In 1923, he read Carl Jung's book *Psychological Types* and found it fascinating. "I found this book at the medical school bookstore on the way home one night, and I read it all night long and all the next day" (Murray quoted in Anderson, 1988, p. 147).

A few weeks after finishing the book, Murray was faced with a serious personal problem. He had fallen in love with Christiana Morgan, a beautiful, wealthy, depressive married woman who was also impressed by Jung's work. Murray did not want to leave his wife of 7 years—he claimed to abhor the idea of divorce—but neither did he want to give up his lover, whose spirited, artistic nature was the opposite of his wife's. Murray insisted he needed both women.

He lived with the conflict for 2 years until, at Christiana Morgan's suggestion, he went to Zurich to meet with Carl Jung. The two men spent a month together, and Jung was able to resolve Murray's difficulty by instruction and example. Jung was also having an affair with a younger woman, a relationship he maintained openly while living with his wife. Jung counseled Murray to do the same, and Murray did so for the next 40 years.

But first, the principal actors in this drama all found themselves in Zurich, with Jung in the role of director. He decreed that Christiana Morgan's husband should be analyzed by Toni Wolff, who was Jung's mistress. In addition, Jung spent many hours with Christiana, analyzing her bizarre dreams and visions. Murray's wife, Josephine, was reluctant to play her part. She spent 20 minutes listening to Jung insist that Murray needed to live with both his wife and his mistress and quickly decided that Jung was a dirty old man (Robinson, 1992). In time, however, both Murray's wife and Morgan's husband were persuaded to accept the affair.[1]

The experience with Jung and the resolution of Murray's marital dilemma turned Murray toward a career in psychology. He had sought help for a personal problem, and psychology had provided an answer (Anderson, 1988). Thus, Jung did more than resolve Murray's personal and career dilemmas; he made Murray aware of the breadth and impact of unconscious forces. Murray wrote, "The great floodgates of the wonder-world swung open. I had experienced the unconscious" (1940, p. 153).

Murray's attitude toward the man who helped him through his early crises changed dramatically over the years. His initial acceptance of Jung's views turned to scathing dismissal. Murray later said that Jung would "believe anything I told him that was along the lines that he liked, but he would overlook what did not fit his theories" (quoted in Anderson, 1988, p. 155).

The Harvard Psychological Clinic

In 1927, psychologist Morton Prince at the new Harvard Psychological Clinic, established specifically to study personality, offered Murray an appointment. A former student described the clinic as "wisteria on the outside, hysteria on the inside" (Smith, 1990, p. 537). As part of his training, Murray underwent orthodox Freudian psychoanalysis and reported that his analyst became bored by the phlegmatic nature of his childhood and his lack of complexes. Murray recalled that the analyst had little to say. The analyst's stomach rumbled, and his office was "depressing, the color of feces, [a] miserable room ... enough to send a patient into a morbid phase" (quoted in Anderson, 1988, p. 159).

In the 1930s, Murray and Morgan developed the Thematic Apperception Test (TAT), still one of the most widely used projective measures of personality (Morgan & Murray, 1935). For many years, it was thought that the TAT was primarily Murray's work, but in 1985, Murray revealed that Morgan had done most of the

---

[1] Christiana Morgan, who at age 63 was described as "attractive, sultry, and mysterious," drowned in 2 feet of water off an island in the Caribbean. By that time, Murray was reported to be "rather disgusted with her seemingly incurable alcoholism" and was already dating the woman he would marry after his first wife died (Schneidman, 2001, pp. 291, 294).

work to develop the test. Further, the original idea for the test had come from one of his women students (Bronstein, 1988, p. 64).

The TAT became a best-seller for Harvard University Press. Despite the magnitude of Morgan's contribution, her name was dropped from the publication, leaving Murray as sole author, an action taken with Murray's agreement (Douglas, 1993). This decision seems inexcusable, given her importance in the development of the test and in much of Murray's subsequent work. At age 94, long after Morgan's death, he acknowledged that she was "part of every paper he wrote and every lecture he gave, and that her very presence at the clinic raised the caliber of his thinking" (Douglas, 1993, p. 297).

In 1938, Murray published *Explorations in Personality: A Clinical and Experimental Study of Fifty Men of College Age*. This book assured his almost instant success as a leading personality theorist. Now considered a classic, it boosted the effort begun by Gordon Allport the year before to make the study of personality an academically respectable part of American psychology.

During World War II, Murray joined the U.S. Army and became director of assessment for the Office of Strategic Services (the OSS, a forerunner of the CIA), screening candidates for dangerous assignments. He maintained an interest in literature, especially the work of Herman Melville, and in 1951 published an analysis of the psychological meaning of Melville's novel *Moby-Dick*.

Murray remained at Harvard until his retirement in 1962, conducting research, refining his personality theory, and training new generations of psychologists. He received the American Psychological Foundation's Gold Medal Award and the American Psychological Association's Distinguished Scientific Contribution Award.

Although Murray lived to the age of 95, the debilitating effects of a stroke marred the last decade of his life. He came to view the sum of his career as a "series of failures and unfulfilled promises [and] could not escape the feeling that he had not quite made the grade" (Triplet, 1993, p. 386). At the end, as a biographer noted, Murray was

> certainly willing to be done with life, though never to the point of losing his sense of humor. "I am dead," he announced to his nurse. "No," she replied, pinching him gently on the cheek; "see, you're alive." "I'm the doctor," [he] snapped back, not without the hint of a smile—"I'm the doctor; you're the nurse; and I'm dead." Just days later, on Thursday, June 23, he had his way. (Robinson, 1992, p. 370)

Principles of Personology

personology
Murray's system of personality.

The first principle in Murray's **personology**, his term for the study of personality, is that personality is rooted in the brain. The individual's cerebral physiology guides and governs every aspect of the personality. A simple example of this is that certain drugs can alter the functioning of the brain, and so the personality. Everything on which personality depends exists in the brain, including feeling states, conscious and unconscious memories, beliefs, attitudes, fears, and values.

A second principle in Murray's system involves the idea of tension reduction. Murray agreed with Freud and other theorists that people act to reduce physiological and psychological tension, but this does not mean we strive for a tension-free state. It is the process of acting to reduce tension that is satisfying, according to Murray, rather than the attainment of a condition free of all tension.

Murray believed that a tension-free existence is itself a source of distress. We need excitement, activity, and movement, all of which involve increasing, not decreasing, tension. We generate tension in order to have the satisfaction of reducing it. Murray believed the ideal state of human nature involves always having a certain level of tension to reduce.

A third principle of Murray's personology is that an individual's personality continues to develop over time and is constructed of all the events that occur during the course of that person's life. Therefore, the study of a person's past is of great importance.

Murray's fourth principle involves the idea that personality changes and progresses; it is not fixed or static.

Fifth, Murray emphasized the uniqueness of each person while recognizing similarities among all people. As he saw it, an individual human being is like no other person, like some other people, and like every other person.

The Divisions of Personality

The Id

Murray divided personality into three parts, using the Freudian terms id, superego, and ego, but his concepts are not what Freud envisioned.

id
To Murray, the id contains the primitive, amoral, and lustful impulses described by Freud, but it also contains desirable impulses, such as empathy and love.

Like Freud, Murray suggested that the **id** is the repository of all innate impulsive tendencies. As such, it provides energy and direction to behavior and is concerned with motivation. The id contains the primitive, amoral, and lustful impulses Freud described. However, in Murray's personology system the id also encompasses innate impulses that society considers acceptable and desirable.

Here we see the influence of Jung's shadow archetype, which has both good and bad aspects. The id contains the tendencies to empathy, imitation, and identification; forms of love other than lustful ones; and the tendency to master one's environment.

The strength or intensity of the id varies among individuals. For example, one person may possess more intense appetites and emotions than another. Therefore, the problem of controlling and directing the id forces is not the same for all people because some of us have greater id energy with which we must cope.

The Superego

superego
To Murray, the superego is shaped not only by parents and authority figures, but also by the peer group and culture.

Murray defined the **superego** as the internalization of the culture's values and norms, by which rules we come to evaluate and judge our behavior and that of others. The substance of the superego is imposed on children at an early age by their parents and other authority figures.

Other factors may shape the superego, including one's peer group and the culture's literature and mythology. Thus, Murray deviated from Freud's ideas by allowing for influences beyond the parent–child interaction. According to Murray, the superego is not rigidly crystallized by age 5, as Freud believed, but continues to develop throughout life, reflecting the greater complexity and sophistication of our experiences as we grow older.

The superego is not in constant conflict with the id, as Freud proposed, because the id contains good forces as well as bad ones. Good forces do not have to be suppressed. The superego must try to thwart the socially unacceptable impulses, but it also functions to determine when, where, and how an acceptable need can be expressed and satisfied.

While the superego is developing, so is the **ego-ideal**, which provides us with long-range goals for which to strive. The ego-ideal represents what we could become at our best and is the sum of our ambitions and aspirations.

ego-ideal
A component of the superego that contains the moral or ideal behaviors for which a person should strive.

ego
To Murray, the conscious organizer of behavior; this is a broader conception than Freud's.

The Ego

The **ego** is the rational governor of the personality; it tries to modify or delay the id's unacceptable impulses. Murray extended Freud's formulation of the ego by proposing that the ego is the central organizer of behavior. It consciously reasons, decides, and wills the direction of behavior. Thus, the ego is more active in determining behavior than Freud believed. Not merely the servant of the id, the ego consciously plans courses of action. It functions not only to suppress id pleasure but also to foster pleasure by organizing and directing the expression of acceptable id impulses.

The ego is also the arbiter between the id and the superego and may favor one over the other. For example, if the ego favors the id, it may direct the personality toward a life of crime. The ego may also integrate these two aspects of the personality so that what we want to do (id) is in harmony with what society believes we should do (superego).

Opportunity exists in Murray's system for conflict to arise between the id and the superego. A strong ego can mediate effectively between the two, but a weak ego leaves the personality a battleground. Unlike Freud, however, Murray did not believe that this conflict was inevitable.

Needs: The Motivators of Behavior

Murray's most important contribution to theory and research in personality is his use of the concept of needs to explain the motivation and direction of behavior. He said that "motivation is the crux of the business and motivation always refers to something within the organism" (quoted in Robinson, 1992, p. 220).

A need involves a physicochemical force in the brain that organizes and directs intellectual and perceptual abilities. Needs may arise either from internal processes such as hunger or thirst, or from events in the environment. Needs arouse a level of tension; the organism tries to reduce this tension by acting to satisfy the needs. Thus, needs energize and direct behavior. They activate behavior in the appropriate direction to satisfy the needs.

Murray's research led him to formulate a list of 20 needs (Murray, 1938, pp. 144–145). Not every person has all of these needs. Over the course of your lifetime you may experience all these needs, or there may be some needs you never experience. Some needs support other needs, and some oppose other needs (see Table 5.1).

Table 5.1 Murray's list of needs

Abasement	To submit passively to external force. To accept injury, blame, criticism, and punishment. To become resigned to fate. To admit inferiority, error, wrongdoing, or defeat. To blame, belittle, or mutilate the self. To seek and enjoy pain, punishment, illness, and misfortune.
Achievement	To accomplish something difficult. To master, manipulate, or organize physical objects, human beings, or ideas. To overcome obstacles and attain a high standard. To rival and surpass others.
Affiliation	To draw near and enjoyably cooperate or reciprocate with an allied other who resembles one or who likes one. To adhere and remain loyal to a friend.
Aggression	To overcome opposition forcefully. To fight, attack, injure, or kill another. To maliciously belittle, censure, or ridicule another.
Autonomy	To get free, shake off restraint, or break out of confinement. To resist coercion and restriction. To be independent and free to act according to impulse. To defy conventions.
Counteraction	To master or make up for a failure by restriving. To obliterate a humiliation by resumed action. To overcome weaknesses and to repress fear. To search for obstacles and difficulties to overcome. To maintain self-respect and pride on a high level.
Defendance	To defend the self against assault, criticism, and blame. To conceal or justify a misdeed, failure, or humiliation.
Deference	To admire and support a superior other. To yield eagerly to the influence of an allied other. To conform to custom.
Dominance	To control one's environment. To influence or direct the behavior of others by suggestion, seduction, persuasion, or command. To get others to cooperate. To convince another of the rightness of one's opinion.
Exhibition	To make an impression. To be seen and heard. To excite, amaze, fascinate, entertain, shock, intrigue, amuse, or entice others.
Harmavoidance	To avoid pain, physical injury, illness, and death. To escape from a dangerous situation. To take precautionary measures.
Infavoidance	To avoid humiliation. To quit embarrassing situations or to avoid conditions that may lead to the scorn, derision, or indifference of others. To refrain from action because of the fear of failure.
Nurturance	To give sympathy to and gratify the needs of a helpless other, an infant or one who is weak, disabled, tired, inexperienced, infirm, humiliated, lonely, dejected, or mentally confused.
Order	To put things in order. To achieve cleanliness, arrangement, organization, balance, neatness, and precision.
Play	To act for fun, without further purpose.
Rejection	To exclude, abandon, expel, or remain indifferent to an inferior other. To snub or jilt another.
Sentience	To seek and enjoy sensuous impressions.
Sex	To form and further an erotic relationship. To have sexual intercourse.
Succorance	To be nursed, supported, sustained, surrounded, protected, loved, advised, guided, indulged, forgiven, or consoled. To remain close to a devoted protector.
Understanding	To be inclined to analyze events and to generalize. To discuss and argue and to emphasize reason and logic. To state one's opinions precisely. To show interest in abstract formulations in science, mathematics, and philosophy.

Types of Needs

primary needs
Survival and related needs arising from internal bodily processes.

secondary needs
Emotional and psychological needs, such as achievement and affiliation.

reactive needs
Needs that involve a response to a specific object.

proactive needs
Needs that arise spontaneously.

Primary and secondary needs. **Primary needs** (viscerogenic needs) arise from internal bodily states and include those needs required for survival (such as food, water, air, and harmavoidance), as well as such needs as sex and sentience. **Secondary needs** (psychogenic needs) arise indirectly from primary needs, in a way Murray did not make clear, but they have no specifiable origin within the body. They are called secondary not because they are less important but because they develop after the primary needs. Secondary needs are concerned with emotional satisfaction and include most of the needs on Murray's original list.

Reactive and proactive needs. **Reactive needs** involve a response to something specific in the environment and are aroused only when that object appears. For example, the harmavoidance need appears only when a threat is present. **Proactive needs** do not depend on the presence of a particular object. They are spontaneous needs that elicit appropriate behavior whenever they are aroused, independent of the environment. For example, hungry people look for food to satisfy their need; they do not wait for a stimulus, such as a television ad for a hamburger, before acting to find food. Reactive needs involve a response to a specific object; proactive needs arise spontaneously.

Characteristics of Needs

Needs differ in terms of the urgency with which they impel behavior, a characteristic Murray called a need's prepotency. For example, if the needs for air and water are not satisfied, they come to dominate behavior, taking precedence over all other needs.

The need for affection is expressed in cooperation, loyalty, and friendship.

© Stock4B/Getty Images

Some needs are complementary and can be satisfied by one behavior or a set of behaviors. Murray called this a fusion of needs. For instance, by working to acquire fame and wealth, we can satisfy the needs for achievement, dominance, and autonomy.

subsidiation
To Murray, a situation in which one need is activated to aid in the satisfaction of another need.

The concept of **subsidiation** refers to a situation in which one need is activated to aid in satisfying another need. For example, to satisfy the affiliation need by being in the company of other people, it may be necessary to act deferentially toward them, thus invoking the deference need. In this case, the deference need is subsidiary to the affiliation need.

press
The influence of the environment and past events on the current activation of a need.

Murray recognized that childhood events can affect the development of specific needs and, later in life, can activate those needs. He called this influence **press** because an environmental object or event presses or pressures the individual to act a certain way.

thema
A combination of press (the environment) and need (the personality) that brings order to our behavior.

Because of the possibility of interaction between need and press, Murray introduced the concept of **thema** (or unity thema). The thema combines personal factors (needs) with the environmental factors that pressure or compel our behavior (presses). The thema is formed through early childhood experiences and becomes a powerful force in determining personality. Largely unconscious, the thema relates needs and presses in a pattern that gives coherence, unity, order, and uniqueness to our behavior.

Personality Development in Childhood

Complexes

Drawing on Freud's work, Murray divided childhood into five stages, each characterized by a pleasurable condition that is inevitably terminated by society's demands. Each stage leaves its mark on our personality in the form of an unconscious **complex** that directs our later development.

complex
To Murray, a normal pattern of childhood development that influences the adult personality; childhood developmental stages include the claustral, oral, anal, urethral, and genital complexes.

According to Murray, everyone experiences these five complexes because everyone passes through the same developmental stages. There is nothing abnormal about them except when they are manifested in the extreme, a condition that leaves the person fixated at that stage. The personality is then unable to develop spontaneity and flexibility, a situation that interferes with the formation of the ego and superego. The stages of childhood and their corresponding complexes are shown in Table 5.2.

Table 5.2 **The childhood stages and complexes in Murray's personology**

Stage	Complex
The secure existence within the womb	Claustral complexes
The sensuous enjoyment of sucking nourishment while being held	Oral complexes
The pleasure resulting from defecation	Anal complexes
The pleasure accompanying urination	Urethral complex
Genital pleasures	Genital or castration complex

Stages of Development

The claustral stage. The fetus in the womb is secure, serene, and dependent, conditions we may all occasionally wish to reinstate. The *simple claustral complex* is experienced as a desire to be in small, warm, dark places that are safe and secluded. For example, one might long to remain under the blankets instead of getting out of bed in the morning. People with this complex tend to be dependent on others, passive, and oriented toward safe, familiar behaviors that worked in the past. The *insupport* form of the claustral complex centers on feelings of insecurity and helplessness that cause the person to fear open spaces, falling, drowning, fires, earthquakes, or simply any situation involving novelty and change. The *anti-claustral* or *egression* form of the claustral complex is based on a need to escape from restraining womblike conditions. It includes a fear of suffocation and confinement and manifests itself in a preference for open spaces, fresh air, travel, movement, change, and novelty.

The oral stage. The *oral succorance complex* features a combination of mouth activities, passive tendencies, and the need to be supported and protected. Behavioral manifestations include sucking, kissing, eating, drinking, and a hunger for affection, sympathy, protection, and love. The *oral aggression complex* combines oral and aggressive behaviors, including biting, spitting, shouting, and verbal aggression such as sarcasm. Behaviors characteristic of the *oral rejection complex* include vomiting, being picky about food, eating little, fearing oral contamination (such as from kissing), desiring seclusion, and avoiding dependence on others.

The anal stage. In the *anal rejection complex*, there is a preoccupation with defecation, anal humor, and feces-like material such as dirt, mud, plaster, and clay. Aggression is often part of this complex and is shown in dropping and throwing things, firing guns, and setting off explosives. Persons with this complex may be dirty and disorganized. The *anal retention complex* is manifested in accumulating, saving, and collecting things, and in cleanliness, neatness, and orderliness.

The urethral stage. Unique to Murray's system, the *urethral complex* is associated with excessive ambition, a distorted sense of self-esteem, exhibitionism, bedwetting, sexual cravings, and self-love. It is sometimes called the Icarus complex, after the mythical Greek figure that flew so close to the sun that the wax holding his wings melted. Like Icarus, persons with this complex aim too high, and their dreams are shattered by failure.

The genital or castration stage. Murray disagreed with Freud's contention that fear of castration is the core of anxiety in adult males. He interpreted the *castration complex* in narrower and more literal fashion as a boy's fantasy that his penis might be cut off. Murray believed such a fear grows out of childhood masturbation and the parental punishment that may have accompanied it.

Questions About Human Nature

Although Murray's personality theory is similar to Freud's in several ways, his image of human nature is quite different. Even the ultimate and necessary goal in life—which, like Freud's, is the reduction of tension—is considered from a different perspective. According to Murray, our goal is not a tension-free state but rather the satisfaction derived from acting to reduce the tension.

On the free will versus determinism issue, Murray argued that personality is determined by our needs and by the environment. He accorded us some free will in our capacity to change and to grow. Each person is unique, but there are also similarities in the personalities of all of us.

Murray believed we are shaped by our inherited attributes and by our environment; each is of roughly equal influence. We cannot understand the human personality unless we accept the impact of the physiological forces and the stimuli in our physical, social, and cultural environments.

Murray's view of human nature was optimistic. He criticized a psychology that projected a negative and demeaning image of human beings. He argued that, with our vast powers of creativity, imagination, and reason, we are capable of solving any problem we face. Also, our orientation is largely toward the future. Although Murray recognized the imprint of childhood experiences on current behavior, he did not envision people as captives of the past. The childhood complexes unconsciously affect our development, but personality is also determined by present events and by aspirations for the future.

We have the ability to grow and develop, and such growth is a natural part of being human. We can change through our rational and creative abilities and can reshape our society as well.

Assessment in Murray's Theory

Murray's techniques for assessing personality differ from those of Freud and the other neopsychoanalytic theorists. Because Murray was not working with emotionally disturbed persons, he did not use such standard psychoanalytic techniques as free association and dream analysis.

For his intensive evaluation of the normal personality, Murray used a variety of techniques to collect data from 51 male undergraduate students at Harvard University. The research participants were interviewed and given projective tests, objective tests, and questionnaires covering childhood memories, family relations, sexual development, sensory-motor learning, ethical standards, goals, social interactions, and mechanical and artistic abilities. This assessment program was so comprehensive that it took Murray's staff of 28 investigators 6 months to complete. We discuss these data in the section on research in Murray's theory.

The OSS Assessment Program

During the World War II years (1941–1945), Murray directed an assessment program for the Office of Strategic Services (OSS), a forerunner of the CIA. His goal was to select people to serve as spies and saboteurs, operating behind enemy lines in hazardous situations. Potential candidates for OSS positions were interviewed and given the Rorschach and the TAT projective tests and questionnaires covering a variety of topics. In addition, candidates participated in situational tests, which were stressful situations that simulated experiences they could expect to encounter on the job. Their behavior in these tests was closely observed (OSS Assessment Staff, 1948).

One such test required the candidate to build a bridge across a stream in a fixed period of time. No plans were provided, but the person was assigned a group of workers to assist him. In this way the candidate's ingenuity, ability to improvise, and leadership skills could be assessed in a realistic setting. To determine the candidate's reaction to frustration, the assistants included some stooges—people instructed to do everything possible to prevent the building of the bridge. Many candidates became enraged, and some were even reduced to tears, when faced with the lack of cooperation and the mounting frustration at being unable to complete the task.

This pioneering attempt at employee selection through large-scale personality assessment has evolved into the successful assessment-center approach widely used in business today to select promising leaders and executives. The OSS program provides a striking example of the practical application of assessment techniques originally intended purely for research.

The Thematic Apperception Test

The assessment technique most often associated with Murray is the Thematic Apperception Test. The TAT consists of a set of ambiguous pictures depicting simple scenes. The person taking the test is asked to compose a story that describes the people and objects in the picture, including what might have led up to the situation and what the people are thinking and feeling.

Murray derived the TAT, which is a projective technique, from Freud's defense mechanism of projection. In projection, a person attributes or projects disturbing impulses onto someone else. In the TAT, the person projects those feelings onto the characters in the pictures and thereby reveals his or her troubling thoughts to the researcher or therapist (see Figure 5.1). Thus, the TAT is a device for assessing unconscious thoughts, feelings, and fears.

Interpreting the responses to the TAT pictures is a subjective process, as Murray admitted in an interview. He referred to the TAT as

> a kind of booby trap which may catch more embryo psychologists than patients. The patient reveals parts of himself when he composes a story to explain the picture. Then the psychologist may reveal parts of himself when he composes a formulation to explain the patient's story. (quoted in Hall, 1968, p. 61)

In the hands of a trained clinician, the TAT can reveal considerable useful information. Because of its subjectivity, however, the information obtained should be used to supplement data from more objective methods rather than as the sole means of diagnosis. Yet despite the TAT's lack of standardized procedures for administering, scoring, and interpreting it, as well as its low criterion-related validity, the test continues to be used frequently for research, therapy, and assessment (see Kaplan & Saccuzzo, 2005).

Figure 5.1 The Thematic Apperception Test

A typical picture contained in the Thematic Apperception Test (TAT). In describing a TAT picture, people may reveal their own feelings, needs, and values.

Typical Responses to TAT Card:

1. This is the picture of a woman who all of her life has been a very suspicious, conniving person. She's looking in the mirror and she sees reflected behind her an image of what she will be as an old woman—still a suspicious, conniving sort of person. She can't stand the thought that that's what her life will eventually lead her to and she smashes the mirror and runs out of the house screaming and goes out of her mind and lives in an institution for the rest of her life.

2. This woman has always emphasized beauty in her life. As a little girl she was praised for being pretty and as a young woman was able to attract lots of men with her beauty. While secretly feeling anxious and unworthy much of the time, her outer beauty helped to disguise these feelings from the world and, sometimes, from herself. Now that she is getting on in years and her children are leaving home, she is worried about the future. She looks in the mirror and imagines herself as an old hag—the worst possible person she could become, ugly and nasty—and wonders what the future holds for her. It is a difficult and depressing time for her. (Pervin, 1984, p. 110)

SOURCE: Reprinted by permission of the publishers from Henry A. Murray, *Thematic Apperception Test*, Cambridge, Mass: Harvard University Press, Copyright © 1943 by the President and Fellows of Harvard College, © 1971 by Henry A. Murray.

Research on Murray's Theory

Murray's original research program involved the intensive study of the personalities of 51 male undergraduate students undertaken by a staff of psychiatrists, psychologists, and anthropologists. Thus, specialists with different training observed each subject using various techniques, in much the same way a complex medical diagnosis is prepared. Each observer presented his or her diagnosis to the Diagnostic Council, a committee of the five most experienced staff members. The council met with each subject for 45 minutes and rated the subject on several variables. As the data accumulated, the council reassessed its ratings, reviewed the information, and arrived at a final determination.

So much information was collected on each person's life that the data had to be divided into time segments; these were called proceedings and serials. The basic behavior segment, the **proceeding**, was defined as the period of time required for the occurrence and completion of a pattern of behavior—from beginning to end. A proceeding involves a real or fantasized interaction between the person and other people or objects in the environment. An imaginary interaction is called an internal proceeding; a real interaction is called an external proceeding.

proceeding
A basic segment of behavior; a time period in which an important behavior pattern occurs from beginning to end.

Proceedings are linked in time and function. For example, on Monday a man may meet a woman (an external proceeding) and ask her for a Saturday night date. He may daydream about her throughout the week (internal proceedings) and may have his hair styled or wash his car (external proceedings) in preparation for the date. Each of these actions is a proceeding. Taken together, because they relate to the same function or purpose, they are called a **serial**.

serial
A succession of proceedings related to the same function or purpose.

Considerable research has been conducted on several of the needs Murray proposed, notably the affiliation and achievement needs.

The Need for Affiliation

The need for affiliation is strong in many people, particularly in stressful situations. In a classic experiment, research participants who knew they were going to receive an electric shock in an experiment were much more likely to prefer waiting in the company of others than were research participants who were not facing the stress of a potential electric shock (Schachter, 1959). Apparently, the presence of other people helped allay the anxiety associated with the stress of the anticipated shock. Another study found that people who had experienced severe effects of a thunderstorm, such as property damage, were much more likely to seek the company of others than were those who had experienced no such harmful effects of the storm (Strumpfer, 1970).

A study of 212 children and 212 parents in Israel showed that when they faced the possibility of a wartime rocket attack, their tendency to affiliate with other people rose significantly. The affiliation need during this stressful period was apparent with both children and adults (Rofe, 2006).

A group of college students kept a daily log of their stressful experiences and social interactions for 2 weeks. The results showed that the students were much more likely to want to affiliate with others after stressful events than after non-stressful periods (Cohen & Wills, 1985).

A study of 176 people in Sweden who were alcoholics showed that those who demonstrated a higher likelihood of affiliating with a support group were far more likely to abstain from drinking than were those who did not have the tendency to affiliate (Bodin & Romelsjo, 2006).

Additional research has found that people who score high in the affiliation need are unpopular, apt to avoid interpersonal conflicts, and likely to be unsuccessful as business managers. These tendencies may be due to their high level of anxiety about whether other people will like them. They may act in an overly assertive manner to avoid any possible rejection (McClelland, 1985; McClelland & Boyatzis, 1982).

What impact does the Internet age have on the need for affiliation? Can this need be satisfied by virtual interactions or does such satisfaction require the presence of other people? Research on 687 teenagers in the Netherlands found that those with a higher affiliation need preferred to communicate through the Internet rather than in person. The virtual social setting allowed them to be more honest, open, and intimate with others than they thought they could be in a face-to-face situation (Peter & Valkenburg, 2006). This suggests that for people with a strong need for affiliation, Internet contacts can be more satisfying and less threatening than actual contacts.

The Need for Achievement

need for achievement
The need to achieve, overcome obstacles, excel, and live up to a high standard.

The **need for achievement**, which Murray defined as the need to overcome obstacles, to excel, and to live up to a high standard, has been studied extensively by David McClelland (1917–1998), using the Thematic Apperception Test.

In the initial research, McClelland and his associates asked groups of male college students to write brief stories about the TAT pictures (McClelland, Atkinson, Clark, & Lowell, 1953). To vary the experimental conditions, the researchers gave different test-taking instructions to different groups, urging a high achievement need in one condition and a low achievement need in the other. The results showed that the stories written under the high-achievement condition contained significantly more references to attaining standards of excellence, desiring to achieve, and performing well. For example, one picture showed a young man sitting at a desk with an open book in front of him. Stories from high-need-achievement research participants involved working hard, striving for excellence, and doing one's best. Stories from low-need-achievement research participants dealt with sedentary activities such as daydreaming, thinking, and recalling past events. Later analyses have confirmed the validity of the TAT as a way of measuring the need for achievement (see, for example, Spangler, 1992; Tuerlinckx, DeBoeck, & Lens, 2002).

A great deal of research has been conducted on the differences between people who measure high in the need for achievement and people who measure low. Research participants testing high in the need for achievement were found more often in middle and upper socioeconomic classes than in lower socioeconomic groups. They demonstrated a better memory for uncompleted tasks and were more likely to volunteer to serve as research participants for psychological research. They were more resistant to social pressures and less conforming than were research participants testing low in need achievement. Young people high in the need to achieve were more likely to attend college, earn higher grades, and be involved in college and community activities. High-need-achievement people were also more likely to cheat on examinations in certain situations. They got along better with other people and enjoyed greater physical health (McClelland, 1985; Piedmont, 1988).

Do people high in achievement motivation perform better in every situation? No. Only when high-need-achievers are challenged to excel will they do so. From these findings, McClelland predicted that people with a high need to achieve will seek life and career situations that allow them to satisfy this need. They will set personal achievement standards and work hard to meet them (McClelland, Koestner, & Weinberger, 1989).

People high in the need for achievement more frequently hold high-status jobs. They work harder, have a greater expectation of success, and report more job satisfaction than do people low in the need for achievement. High-need-achievers choose jobs that provide personal responsibility, in which success depends primarily on their own efforts, and they are dissatisfied with jobs in which success depends on other people or on factors beyond their control (Reuman, Alwin, & Veroff, 1984).

Because high-need-achievement people prefer jobs with considerable responsibility, McClelland suggested that they prefer to be entrepreneurs, to operate their own business and be their own boss. This kind of work situation provides optimal challenge and authority. In a follow-up study of male college students 14 years after their achievement-motivation scores had first been measured, it was found that 83 percent of those who had become successful entrepreneurs had scored high in the need to achieve. Only 21 percent of those who had become successful in non-entrepreneurial jobs had scored high in the need to achieve. Research in several countries supports the finding that high-need-achievement people are more attracted to entrepreneurial jobs (McClelland, 1965a, 1987).

These early workplace studies were conducted only with male research participants. To determine whether women entrepreneurs were also high in achievement motivation, psychologists studied 60 female business owners in Australia. Approximately 82 percent of these entrepreneurial women showed moderate to high levels of the need to achieve, a finding similar to McClelland's research with entrepreneurial men (Langan-Fox & Roth, 1995).

High-need-achievers even prefer different kinds of vacations. A study of American tourists showed that those scoring high in the need to achieve preferred adventure tourism with travel to remote or exotic places and challenging activities such as white-water rafting, mountain climbing, or scuba diving. People high in the need for affiliation, in contrast, seemed to prefer cultural tourism involving museums, concerts, and tours of famous writers' houses (Tran & Ralston, 2006).

Cultural factors can influence a person's need for achievement. A cross-cultural study compared need achievement among 372 male and female high school and college students living in Hong Kong. Some of the students were from England (children of British parents working in Hong Kong); other students were native Chinese. The British students focused on individual achievement in competitive situations, that is, what they could accomplish for themselves. The Chinese students, with the stronger sense of collectivism fostered by their culture, focused more on affiliative achievement (family and group achievement) rather than acting to satisfy personal goals (Salili, 1994). An analysis of later research provides support for these cultural differences between European-American and Asian subject samples. Studies show the first group to focus more on individualistic striving for personal goals and the second group more on group, community, and family goals (Church & Lonner, 1998).

The need for achievement is affected by child-rearing practices. Early research identified the parental behaviors likely to produce a high need for achievement in boys. These include setting realistic and challenging standards of performance at an age when such standards can be reached, not being overprotective or indulgent, not interfering with the child's efforts to achieve, and demonstrating genuine pleasure in the child's achievements (Winterbottom, 1958).

Studies of adolescent emigrants to the United States from Vietnam showed that family and cultural values emphasizing education resulted in high levels of achievement motivation (Nguyen, 2006). Research with U.S.-born Latino teenagers found that parental involvement was positively related to the need to achieve. The more the parents stressed the value of education, the higher the measured achievement motivation among their children (Ibanez, Kuperminc, Jurkovic, & Perilla, 2004).

In a longitudinal study, 89 men and women in their early 40s responded to stimulus pictures similar to those of the TAT. Their responses were coded for the presence or absence of TAT imagery. What makes this research unique is that their mothers had been interviewed many years earlier when the subjects were 5 years old and questioned extensively about their child-rearing practices. Thus, it was possible to compare differences in maternal behavior with the need-achievement levels of the children when they became adults. The results showed that parental pressure to achieve during the first 2 years of life led to higher levels of need achievement in adulthood, whereas pressure to achieve during later childhood years was not related to a high need achievement in adulthood. McClelland concluded from this research that parental behaviors during the first 2 years of life were crucial to the formation of a high level of need achievement in adulthood (McClelland & Franz, 1992).

Although need achievement apparently is established in childhood, the possibility exists that it could be enhanced or suppressed, strengthened or weakened, by expectations of caregivers in day-care centers or teachers in schools. If these adults do not expect a high level of performance and set challenging standards, the way parents of high-need-achievement children were found to do, then they may be depriving children of an incentive to continue to achieve at a high level.

Some evidence suggests that this may operate with members of some minority groups. For example, when 392 White college students were asked to provide feedback on poorly written essays prepared, they were told, by Black or by White fellow students, the feedback was consistently less critical of Black writers than of White writers. Indeed, the comments were lenient and supportive of the work of the Black students whereas the comments offered to the White students were often harsh. Such inflated praise and gentle criticism in this example could deprive Black students of the high expectations and challenges provided to White students. That, in turn, could reduce the amount of effort and striving needed to maintain high achievement and result in lowered performance (Harber, 1998).

Gender is another factor that has an impact on the need to achieve. Studies of children and adolescents suggest that some girls and young women experience conflict between the need to do their best and achieve at a high level versus the need to appear feminine, empathic, and caring. These research participants feared that achieving at too high a level would lead to unpopularity, especially with boys. A study of gifted third- to sixth-grade girls revealed several concerns they saw as barriers to achieving at a level appropriate to their abilities (Eccles, Barber, & Jozefowicz, 1999, p. 179):

- Concern about hurting other people's feelings by winning
- Concern about being seen as a show-off by expressing pride in one's achievements
- Concern about reacting negatively to situations in which one is not successful
- Concern about physical appearance and standards of beauty
- Concern about being seen as too aggressive in classroom situations

Another area of investigation deals with the distinction between the achievement need as an *approach* motive and that need as an *avoidance* motive. The question is whether behavior in achievement settings such as school or place of employment is directed primarily toward attaining success or toward avoiding failure. In other words, are we driven to win, or are we motivated instead to avoid losing? Perhaps it is some combination of the two and depends on the situation.

Studies of college students in the United States found that pursuing avoidance goals over the course of a semester led to a decline in self-esteem and in feelings of competence and control, as well as reduced vitality and overall life satisfaction. The researchers suggested that satisfying the achievement need by striving for success rather than acting to avoid failure is vital to subjective well-being (Elliot & Church, 1997; Elliot & Sheldon, 1997). A study of 93 German university students found that success-motivated students performed significantly better and persisted more in achievement-related tasks than did students whose motivation was to avoid failure (Puca & Schmalt, 2001).

Other research has shown that simply recalling a previous episode of achievement was associated with a variety of positive emotions including surprise, happiness, and excitement (Zurbriggen & Sturman, 2002). A study of college students in Israel demonstrated that those high in need achievement tended to be more extraverted and conscientious than those low in need achievement (Roccas, Sagiu, Schwartz, & Knafo, 2002).

Finally, research suggests two types of goals in achievement motivation, *mastery* and *performance*, or two ways of satisfying the need to achieve. Mastery involves developing competence through the acquisition of knowledge and skills to satisfy oneself. Performance goals involve acquiring competence with a view toward performing better than other people (Barron & Harackiewicz, 2001).

Research conducted in the Netherlands involving more than 600 college students found that the majority (two-thirds) preferred the mastery instead of the performance goal attainment approach, which was associated with greater subjective well-being, more positive emotional states, and higher levels of perfectionism. In other words, it seemed preferable to these students to be motivated to achieve for self-satisfaction rather than to show that they could do better than other people (Van Yperen, 2006).

Reflections on Murray's Theory

Murray has exerted an impressive and lasting influence on the study of personality. Of particular importance is his list of needs, which is of continuing value for research, clinical diagnosis, and employee selection, and his techniques for assessing personality. Overall, these innovations, and the personal impact he made on at least two generations of personology researchers at Harvard, have had a more lasting effect than the details of his theory.

Murray's theory is not without its critics. One problem in evaluating his position is that only some portions of it have been published. His ingenuity and full range of thought were not widely revealed. Those who worked with him and had access to his broad speculations, which he offered in almost casual conversation, felt Murray's influence most keenly. Although students and colleagues have pursued some of these ideas, others have been lost to view.

Research has been conducted on some of Murray's ideas, particularly the achievement and affiliation needs, and the assessment techniques, but only limited portions of his theory have been put to experimental test. Of course, as we have seen in previous chapters, this criticism is not unique to Murray.

Murray's research method in the study of Harvard undergraduates has also been questioned. The Diagnostic Council may have been laudably democratic, but it was hardly scientific; to reach a scientific conclusion by majority rule is not the most objective procedure. In addition, some concepts, such as proceedings and serials, are defined too vaguely. What constitutes an important pattern of behavior? What happens to those judged insignificant? How long is a proceeding? These questions have not been answered satisfactorily.

Murray's classification of needs may be overly complex and a great deal of overlap exists among the needs. It is unclear how the needs relate to other aspects of personality and how the needs develop within an individual. However, the list of needs has had considerable impact on the construction of psychological tests. Further, the concept of need and the importance Murray placed on motivation in his system have influenced the modern study of personality.

Chapter Summary

Murray's childhood was characterized by maternal rejection, Adlerian compensation, and depression. The major principle of Murray's work is the dependence of psychological processes on physiological processes. Altering the level of need-induced tension is vital to the personality. We generate tension to have the satisfaction of reducing it.

Three basic divisions of personality are the id, superego, and ego. The id contains primitive, amoral impulses as well as tendencies to empathy, imitation, and identification. The superego is shaped by parents, peer groups, and cultural factors. The ego consciously decides and wills the direction of behavior.

Needs are physiologically based hypothetical constructs that arise from internal processes or environmental events. Needs arouse a tension level that must be reduced; thus, they energize and direct behavior. Needs may be primary (viscerogenic), arising from internal bodily processes, or secondary (psychogenic), concerned with mental and emotional satisfaction. Proactive needs are spontaneous and do not depend on environmental objects; reactive needs involve a response to a specific environmental object. A need's prepotency is its urgency or insistence. The fusion of needs refers to needs that can be satisfied by one behavior or set of behaviors. Subsidiation involves a situation in which one need is activated to aid in the satisfaction of another need.

Press refers to the pressure, caused by environmental objects or childhood events, to behave in a certain way. Thema is an amalgamation of personal factors (needs) and environmental factors (presses).

Complexes are patterns formed in the five childhood stages of development that unconsciously direct adult development. The claustral complex involves the secure existence within the womb. The oral complex involves the sensuous enjoyment of sucking nourishment. The anal complex involves the pleasure resulting from defecation. The urethral complex involves the pleasure accompanying urination. The castration complex involves genital pleasure and the fantasy that the penis might be cut off.

According to Murray, the ultimate goal in life is to reduce tension. Although we have some free will, much of personality is determined by needs and by the environment. Each person is unique yet shares similarities, which are determined by inherited and environmental forces, with other people. Murray held an optimistic view of human nature, which is oriented toward the future and grants us the ability to grow and develop.

Murray and Morgan developed the TAT, based on the Freudian concept of projection. Considerable research has been conducted on Murray's proposed needs for affiliation and for achievement. Those found to be high in the achievement need are typically middle-class, have a better memory for uncompleted tasks, are more active in college and community activities, and are more resistant to social pressures. People high in need achievement are more likely to attend college and do well, to take high-status jobs with a great deal of personal responsibility, and to expect to be successful. They often succeed as entrepreneurs or managers. Parental behaviors likely to produce a high need for achievement in children include setting realistically high performance standards, not overprotecting or indulging, not interfering with the child's efforts to achieve, and showing pleasure in the child's achievements. Parental authoritarianism tends to lower a child's need for achievement. Gender and cultural factors can influence the need for achievement. Both mastery goals and performance goals can satisfy the achievement need. In summary, Murray's importance lies in his list of needs and his techniques for assessing personality.

Review Questions

1. Explain how Murray's childhood provided a good background for him to become a personality theorist.

2. How did Jung influence Murray's personal life and theory of personality?

3. What is the relationship between physiological processes and psychological processes?

4. Describe the role of tension in the development of personality. Is our ultimate goal a life free of tension? Why or why not?

5. How do Murray's views of the id, ego, and superego differ from Freud's conception of these structures of personality?

6. What factors and influences shape the superego? Explain Murray's view of the relationship between the superego and the id.

7. From what sources do needs arise?

8. Describe ways of classifying needs, and give examples for each category.

9. Define the concepts of subsidiation, thema, and press.

10. What are the five childhood stages of personality development and the complexes associated with each stage?

11. Describe the behavior of a person suffering from the egression form of the claustral complex,

the anal rejection complex, and the urethral complex.

12. How does Murray's image of human nature differ from Freud's?

13. How is the Thematic Apperception Test used to assess personality?

14. What criticisms can be made of projective techniques for personality assessment?

15. Distinguish between proceedings and serials, and between internal and external proceedings.

16. What type of data did Murray collect in his study of Harvard undergraduate students?

17. Is Murray's view of human nature optimistic or pessimistic? Why?

18. Describe the differences between high and low achievers in terms of college and career performance.

19. How may gender and culture affect the need for achievement?

20. What parental behaviors can influence the development of a child's need for achievement?

21. Explain the difference between performance goals and mastery goals in achievement motivation. Which would you say is the more desirable? Why?

Suggested Readings

Anderson, J. W. (1988). Henry A. Murray's early career: A psychobiographical exploration. *Journal of Personality, 56*(1), 139–171. An analysis of Murray's life through his early 30s, examining his decision to become a psychologist, his involvement with psychoanalysis, and the impact of his personal and academic experiences on his work.

Douglas, C. (1993). *Translate this darkness: The life of Christiana Morgan.* New York: Simon & Schuster. A biography of the codeveloper of the Thematic Apperception Test, describing her career and her personal relationship with Murray.

McClelland, D. C. (1961). *The achieving society.* New York: Free Press. A classic work that applies psycho-

logical methods to the evaluation of economic, historical, and social forces that explain the rise and fall of civilizations.

McClelland, D. C., & Winter, D. G. (1969). *Motivating economic achievement.* New York: Free Press. Describes psychological training programs to increase achievement motivation among business leaders in order to accelerate a nation's economic development.

Murray, H. A. (1938). *Explorations in personality.* New York: Oxford University Press. Murray's classic work on personology that includes the evaluation of a typical subject by the Diagnostic Council, the list of human needs, and the advantages of projective techniques for personality assessment. The 70th anniversary edition, published in 2007 with a foreword by Northwestern University professor Dan McAdams, provides a contemporary evaluation of Murray's achievements.

Murray, H. A. (1967). Autobiography. In E. G. Boring & G. Lindzey (Eds.), *A history of psychology in autobiography* (Vol. 5, pp. 283–310). New York: Appleton-Century-Crofts. Murray's reflections on his life and work.

Murray, H. A. (1981). *Endeavors in psychology: Selections from the personology of Henry A. Murray.* New York: Harper & Row. A collection of Murray's writings on personality theory, creativity, and the Thematic Apperception Test. Edited by Edwin S. Schneidman.

Robinson, F. G. (1992). *Love's story told: A life of Henry A. Murray.* Cambridge, MA: Harvard University Press. A biography that relates some of the more sensational aspects of Murray's marriage and love affairs.

Schneidman, E. S. (2001). My visit with Christiana Morgan. *History of Psychology, 4,* 289–296. An interview with Morgan describing her life and work and her influence on Murray's ideas.

Smith, M. B. (1990). Henry A. Murray (1893–1988): Humanistic psychologist. *Journal of Humanistic Psychology, 30*(1), 6–13. A biographical sketch relating Murray's work to the humanistic psychology movement.

Triplet, R. G. (1992). Henry A. Murray: The making of a psychologist? *American Psychologist, 47,* 299–307. Assesses the impact of Murray's work at the Harvard Psychological Clinic and recounts personal and academic disputes between the clinic and the college's psychology department.

PART THREE

The Life-Span Approach

Most personality theorists devote some attention to the way personality develops over time. Some describe stages in the development of specific aspects of personality; others posit general patterns of growth. Theorists also differ regarding the time period during which they believe personality continues to develop. For example, Sigmund Freud proposed that personality evolves through a sequence of steps until the age of 5; Henry Murray took a similar position. Carl Jung argued that middle age was the most important time of change for the personality.

The life-span approach, represented here by the work of Erik Erikson, focuses on the development of the personality over the entire course of life. Erikson's theory attempts to explain human behavior and growth through eight stages, from birth to death. Erikson believed that all aspects of personality could be explained in terms of turning points, or crises, we must meet and resolve at each developmental stage.

CHAPTER 6

Erik Erikson: Identity Theory

The personality is engaged with the hazards of existence continuously, even as the body's metabolism copes with decay.

—Erik Erikson

The work of Erik Erikson has had a profound influence on psychoanalysis and on our general culture. Erikson's books sold hundreds of thousands of copies, and his likeness appeared on the covers of *Newsweek* and the *New York Times Magazine*, an unusual sign of recognition for a personality theorist. His book on the origins of militant nonviolence, *Gandhi's Truth*, was awarded a Pulitzer Prize. And he achieved this prominence without ever earning a university degree.

Trained in the Freudian tradition by Sigmund Freud's daughter Anna, Erikson developed an approach to personality that broadened the scope of Freud's work while maintaining much of its core. Although Erikson offered significant innovations, his ties to the Freudian position were strong. "Psychoanalysis is always the starting point," he said (quoted in Keniston, 1983, p. 29). For all of his professional life, Erikson "publicly defined himself as a loyal Freudian, even as he departed substantially from orthodox psychoanalytic theory" (Anderson & Friedman, 1997, p. 1063).

Erikson extended Freud's theory in three ways. First, he elaborated on Freud's stages of development. Whereas Freud emphasized childhood and proposed that personality is shaped by approximately age 5, Erikson suggested that personality continues to develop in a succession of eight stages over the entire life span.

Erikson's second departure from Freudian theory was to place greater emphasis on the ego than on the id. In Erikson's view, the ego is an independent part of the personality; it is not dependent on or subservient to the id.

Third, Erikson recognized the impact on personality of cultural and historical forces. He argued that we are not governed entirely by innate biological factors at work in childhood. Although they are important, they do not provide the complete explanation for personality.

Because of his elaboration of these basic Freudian themes, Erikson could have been grouped with the neopsychoanalytic theorists in this book. But we have chosen instead to emphasize the unique aspect of his theory—the life-span, or developmental, approach, which centers on the search for an ego identity.

The Life of Erikson (1902–1994)

Personal Identity Crises

It is not surprising that the theorist who gave us the concept of the identity crisis experienced several such crises of his own. Erikson was born in Frankfurt, Germany. His Danish mother, who was from a wealthy Jewish family, had married several years earlier but her husband disappeared within hours of the wedding. She became pregnant by another man, whose name she never revealed, and was sent by her family to Germany to give birth, in order to avoid the social disgrace of a child out of wedlock. She remained in Germany after the baby was born and married Dr. Theodore Homburger, the infant's pediatrician. Erik did not know for some years that Dr. Homburger was not his biological father, and claimed that he grew up unsure of his name and psychological identity. He retained the surname Homburger until age 37 when he became a United States citizen and took the name Erik Homburger Erikson.

Another crisis of identity occurred when Erik started school. Despite his Danish parentage he considered himself German, but his German classmates rejected him because his mother and stepfather were Jewish. His Jewish peers rejected him because he was tall and blond and had Nordic facial features.

In school, Erikson earned mediocre grades. He showed some talent for art, however, and after graduating from high school he used that ability to try to establish his identity. He dropped out of conventional society and traveled through Germany and Italy, reading, recording his thoughts in a notebook, and observing life around him. He described himself as morbidly sensitive and neurotic, even close to psychotic. Many years later one of his daughters wrote:

> My father suffered terribly from the sense that his real father had abandoned him and had never cared to know him. . . . he struggled with a depressive tendency all his life. His childhood experience of abandonment and rejection had left him plagued with self-doubt. . . . he felt deeply insecure and unsure of his footing. He craved constant support, guidance, and reassurance from others. (Bloland, 2005, pp. 52, 71)

Erikson studied at two art schools and even had his work exhibited at a gallery in Munich, but each time he left formal training to resume his wandering, his search for an identity. Later, discussing his proposed concept of the identity crisis, Erikson wrote, "No doubt, my best friends will insist that I needed to name this crisis and to see it in everybody else in order to really come to terms with it in myself" (Erikson, 1975, pp. 25–26).

As with many of the personality theorists described in this textbook, we can find a correspondence between Erikson's life experiences, particularly in childhood and adolescence, and the personality theory he developed as an adult. A biographer noted that what Erikson "saw and felt happening to himself (as with Freud's examination of his own dreams, memories, fantasies) became the 'research' that enabled a flow of ideas, articles, books" (Friedman, 1999, p. 16).

Child Development Studies

At the age of 25, Erikson received an offer to teach at a small school in Vienna established for the children of Sigmund Freud's patients and friends. Freud was attracting patients from all over the world. Being wealthy, they settled in Vienna with their families for the duration of their psychoanalysis. Erikson later confessed that he was drawn to Freud in part because of his search for a father. It was then that Erikson's professional career began and that he felt he had finally found an identity.

He trained in psychoanalysis and was analyzed by Anna Freud. The analytic sessions were held almost daily for 3 years; the fee was $7 per month. Anna Freud's interest was the psychoanalysis of children. Her influence, plus Erikson's own teaching experiences, made him aware of the importance of social influences on personality and led him to focus on child development. After he completed his program of study, he became a member of the Vienna Psychoanalytic Institute.

In 1929, when attending a masked ball in Vienna, Erikson met Joan Serson, a Canadian-born artist and dancer who had been analyzed by one of Freud's disciples. They fell in love, but when she became pregnant, Erikson refused to marry her. He explained that he was afraid to make a permanent commitment and he believed that his mother and stepfather would disapprove of a daughter-in-law who was not Jewish. Only the intercession of friends persuaded him that if he did not marry Joan, he would be repeating the behavior pattern of the man who had fathered him and condemning his child to the stigma of illegitimacy, which Erikson himself had felt so keenly.

When he did decide to marry Joan, he did so three times, in separate Jewish, Protestant, and civil ceremonies. Joan abandoned her career interests to become Erikson's lifelong intellectual partner and editor. She provided a stable social and emotional foundation for his life and helped him develop his approach to personality. Erikson's half-sister commented that "He would have been nothing without Joan" (quoted in Friedman, 1999, p. 86). Erikson agreed.

In 1933, recognizing the growing Nazi menace, the Eriksons immigrated to Denmark and then to the United States, settling in Boston. Erikson established a private psychoanalytic practice specializing in the treatment of children. He became affiliated with Henry Murray's Harvard clinic, serving on the Diagnostic Council. He also joined a guidance center for emotionally disturbed delinquents and served on the staff of Massachusetts General Hospital.

Erikson began graduate work at Harvard, intending to obtain a Ph.D. in psychology, but he failed his first course and decided that a formal academic program was unsatisfying. In 1936, he was invited to the Institute of Human Relations at Yale University, where he taught in the medical school and continued his psychoanalytic work with children. Erikson and a Yale anthropologist collaborated on a study of the child-rearing practices of South Dakota's Sioux Indians. This research reinforced his belief in the influence of culture on childhood. Erikson continued to expand on his ideas at the Institute of Human Development of the University of California at Berkeley. Unlike many psychoanalysts, Erikson wanted his clinical experience to be as broad as possible, so he sought patients from diverse cultures and saw those he considered normal as well as those who were emotionally disturbed.

Identity Confusion

In his observations of American Indian peoples in South Dakota and in California, Erikson noted certain psychological symptoms that could not be explained by orthodox Freudian theory. The symptoms appeared to be related to a sense of alienation from cultural traditions and resulted in the lack of a clear self-image or self-identity. This phenomenon, which Erikson initially called identity confusion, was similar to the condition he had observed among emotionally disturbed veterans after World War II. Erikson suggested that those men were not suffering from repressed conflicts but rather from confusion brought about by traumatic war experiences and by being temporarily uprooted from their culture. He had described the veterans' situation as a confusion of identity about whom and what they were.

In 1950, Erikson joined the Austen Riggs Center in Stockbridge, Massachusetts, which was a treatment facility for emotionally disturbed adolescents. Ten years later he returned to Harvard to teach a graduate seminar and a popular undergraduate course on the human life cycle, retiring in 1970. At the age of 84 Erikson published a book about old age.

Nevertheless, toward the end of a lifetime of accomplishments, honors, and accolades, he felt, according to his daughter, disappointed with what he had achieved.

"It was still a source of shame to this celebrated man that he had been an illegitimate child" (Bloland, 2005, p. 51).

 LOG ON

Personality Theories: Erik Erikson

A discussion of Erikson's life and work.

Key Theorists/Theories in Psychology: Erik Erikson

Multimedia material on Erikson's life, research, and theories including evaluations of his ideas and information on his personal identity crisis.

For direct links to these sites, log on to the student companion site for this book at http://www.academic.cengage.com/psychology/Schultz and choose Chapter 6.

Psychosocial Stages of Personality Development

psychosocial stages of development
To Erikson, eight successive stages encompassing the life span. At each stage, we must cope with a crisis in either an adaptive or a maladaptive way.

epigenetic principle of maturation
The idea that human development is governed by a sequence of stages that depend on genetic or hereditary factors.

crisis
To Erikson, the turning point faced at each developmental stage.

Erikson divided the growth of the personality into eight **psychosocial stages**. The first four are similar to Freud's oral, anal, phallic, and latency stages. The major difference between their theories is that Erikson emphasized psychosocial correlates, whereas Freud focused on biological factors.

Erikson suggested that the developmental process was governed by what he called the **epigenetic principle of maturation**. By this he meant that inherited forces are the determining characteristics of the developmental stages. The prefix *epi* means "upon"; thus, development depends upon genetic factors. The social and environmental forces to which we are exposed influence the ways in which the genetically predetermined stages of development are realized. In this way, personality development is affected by both biological and social factors, or by both personal and situational variables.

In Erikson's theory, human development involves a series of personal conflicts. The potential for these conflicts exists at birth as innate predispositions; these will become prominent at different stages when our environment demands certain adaptations. Each confrontation with our environment is called a **crisis**. The crisis involves a shift in perspective, requiring us to refocus our instinctual energy in accordance with the needs of each stage of the life cycle.

Each developmental stage has its particular crisis or turning point that necessitates some change in our behavior and personality. We may respond to the crisis in one of two ways: a maladaptive (negative) way or an adaptive (positive) way. Only when we have resolved each conflict can the personality continue its normal developmental sequence and acquire the strength to confront the next stage's crisis. If the conflict at any stage remains unresolved, we are less likely to be able to adapt to later problems. A successful outcome is still possible, but it will be more difficult to achieve.

However, Erikson believed that the ego must incorporate maladaptive as well as adaptive ways of coping. For example, in infancy, the first stage of psychosocial development, we can respond to the crisis of helplessness and dependency by developing a sense of trust or a sense of mistrust. Trust, the more adaptive, desirable way of coping, is obviously the healthier psychological attitude. Yet each of us must also develop some degree of mistrust as a form of protection. If we are totally trusting and gullible, we will be vulnerable to other people's attempts to deceive, mislead, or manipulate us. Ideally, at every stage of development the ego will consist primarily of the positive or adaptive attitude but will be balanced by some portion of the negative attitude. Only then can the crisis be considered satisfactorily resolved.

basic strengths
To Erikson, motivating characteristics and beliefs that derive from the satisfactory resolution of the crisis at each developmental stage.

Erikson also proposed that each of the eight psychosocial stages provides an opportunity to develop our **basic strengths**. These strengths, or virtues, emerge once the crisis has been resolved satisfactorily. He suggested that basic strengths are interdependent; any one strength cannot develop until the strength associated with the previous stage has been confirmed (see Table 6.1).

Trust versus Mistrust

The oral-sensory stage of psychosocial development, paralleling Freud's oral stage of psychosexual development, occurs during our first year of life, the time of our greatest helplessness. The infant is totally dependent on the mother or primary caregiver for survival, security, and affection. During this stage the mouth is of vital importance. Erikson wrote that the infant "lives through, and loves with, [the] mouth" (1959, p. 57). However, the relationship between the infant and his or her world is not exclusively biological. It is also social. The baby's interaction with the mother determines whether an attitude of trust or mistrust for future dealings with the environment will be incorporated into his or her personality.

If the mother responds appropriately to the baby's physical needs and provides ample affection, love, and security, then the infant will develop a sense of trust, an attitude that will characterize the growing child's view of himself or herself and of others. In this way, we learn to expect "consistency, continuity, and sameness" from other people and situations in our environment (Erikson, 1950, p. 247). Erikson said

Table 6.1 Erikson's stages of psychosocial development and basic strengths

Stage	Ages	Adaptive vs. maladaptive ways of coping	Basic strength
Oral-sensory	Birth–1	Trust vs. mistrust	Hope
Muscular-anal	1–3	Autonomy vs. doubt, shame	Will
Locomotor-genital	3–5	Initiative vs. guilt	Purpose
Latency	6–11	Industriousness vs. inferiority	Competence
Adolescence	12–18	Identity cohesion vs. role confusion	Fidelity
Young adulthood	18–35	Intimacy vs. isolation	Love
Adulthood	35–55	Generativity vs. stagnation	Care
Maturity—old age	55+years	Ego integrity vs. despair	Wisdom

that this expectation provides the beginning of our ego identity and he recalled that he had formed such a bond of trust with his mother.

On the other hand, if the mother is rejecting, inattentive, or inconsistent in her behavior, the infant develops an attitude of mistrust and will become suspicious, fearful, and anxious. According to Erikson, mistrust can also occur if the mother does not display an exclusive focus on the child. Erikson argued that a new mother who resumes a job outside the home and leaves her infant in the care of relatives or in a day care center risks promoting mistrust in the child.

Although the pattern of trust or mistrust as a dimension of personality is set in infancy, the problem may reappear at a later developmental stage. For example, an ideal infant–mother relationship produces a high level of trust, but this secure sense of trust can be destroyed if the mother dies or leaves home. If that occurs, mistrust may overtake the personality. Childhood mistrust can be altered later in life through the companionship of a loving and patient teacher or friend.

The basic strength of *hope* is associated with the successful resolution of the crisis during the oral-sensory stage. Erikson described this strength as the belief that our desires will be satisfied. Hope involves a persistent feeling of confidence, a feeling we will maintain despite temporary setbacks or reverses.

Autonomy versus Doubt and Shame

During the muscular-anal stage at the second and third years of life, corresponding to Freud's anal stage, children rapidly develop a variety of physical and mental abilities and are able to do many things for themselves. They learn to communicate more effectively and to walk, climb, push, pull, and hold on to an object or let it go. Children take pride in these skills and usually want to do as much as possible for themselves.

Of all these abilities, Erikson believed the most important involved holding on and letting go. He considered these to be prototypes for reacting to later conflicts in behaviors and attitudes. For example, holding on can be displayed in a loving way or in a hostile way. Letting go can become a venting of destructive rage or a relaxed passivity.

The important point is that during this stage, for the first time, children are able to exercise some degree of choice, to experience the power of their autonomous will. Although still dependent on their parents, they begin to see themselves as persons or forces in their own right and they want to exercise their newfound strengths. The key question becomes how much will society, in the form of parents, allow children to express themselves and do all they are capable of doing?

The major crisis between parent and child at this stage typically involves toilet training, seen as the first instance when society attempts to regulate an instinctual need. The child is taught to hold on and let go only at appropriate times and places. Parents may permit the child to proceed with toilet training at his or her own pace or may become annoyed. In that case, parents may deny the child's free will by forcing the training, showing impatience and anger when the child does not behave correctly. When parents thus thwart and frustrate their child's attempt to exercise his or her independence, the child develops feelings of self-doubt and a sense of shame in dealing with others. Although the anal region is the focus of this stage because of the toilet training crisis, you can see that the expression of the conflict is more psychosocial than biological.

The basic strength that develops from autonomy is *will*, which involves a determination to exercise freedom of choice and self-restraint in the face of society's demands.

Initiative versus Guilt

The locomotor-genital stage, which occurs between ages 3 and 5, is similar to the phallic stage in Freud's system. Motor and mental abilities are continuing to develop, and children can accomplish more on their own. They express a strong desire to take the initiative in many activities. Initiative may also develop in the form of fantasies, manifested in the desire to possess the parent of the opposite sex and in rivalry with the parent of the same sex. How will the parents react to these self-initiated activities and fantasies? If they punish the child and otherwise inhibit these displays of initiative, the child will develop persistent guilt feelings that will affect self-directed activities throughout his or her life.

In the Oedipal relationship, the child inevitably fails, but if the parents guide this situation with love and understanding, then the child will acquire an awareness of what is permissible behavior and what is not. The child's initiative can be channeled toward realistic and socially sanctioned goals in preparation for the development of adult responsibility and morality. In Freudian terms, we would call this the superego.

Children take pride in developing new skills and abilities.

© Alan Oddie/PhotoEdit

The basic strength called *purpose* arises from initiative. Purpose involves the courage to envision and pursue goals.

Industriousness versus Inferiority

Erikson's latency stage of psychosocial development, which occurs from ages 6 to 11, corresponds to Freud's latency period. The child begins school and is exposed to new social influences. Ideally, both at home and at school, the child learns good work and study habits (what Erikson referred to as industriousness) primarily as a means of attaining praise and obtaining the satisfaction derived from the successful completion of a task.

The child's growing powers of deductive reasoning and the ability to play by rules lead to the deliberate refinement of the skills displayed in building things. Here Erikson's ideas reflect the sex stereotypes of the period in which he proposed his theory. In his view, boys will build tree houses and model airplanes; girls will cook and sew. However, whatever the activities associated with this age, the children are making serious attempts to complete a task by applying concentrated attention, diligence, and persistence. In Erikson's words, "The basic skills of technology are developed as the child becomes ready to handle the utensils, the tools, and the weapons used by the big people" (1959, p. 83).

Again, the attitudes and behaviors of parents and teachers largely determine how well children perceive themselves to be developing and using their skills. If children are scolded, ridiculed, or rejected, they are likely to develop feelings of inferiority and inadequacy. On the other hand, praise and reinforcement foster feelings of competence and encourage continued striving.

The basic strength that emerges from industriousness during the latency stage is *competence*. It involves the exertion of skill and intelligence in pursuing and completing tasks.

The outcome of the crisis at each of these four childhood stages depends on other people. The resolution is a function more of what is done to the child than of what the child can do for himself or herself. Although children experience increasing independence from birth to age 11, psychosocial development remains mostly under the influence of parents and teachers, typically the most significant people in our life at this time.

In the last four stages of psychosocial development, we have increasing control over our environment. We consciously and deliberately choose our friends, colleges, careers, spouses, and leisure activities. However, these deliberate choices are obviously affected by the personality characteristics that have developed during the stages from birth to adolescence. Whether our ego at that point shows primarily trust, autonomy, initiative, and industriousness, or mistrust, doubt, guilt, and inferiority, will determine the course of our life.

Identity Cohesion versus Role Confusion: The Identity Crisis

ego identity
The self-image formed during adolescence that integrates our ideas of what we are and what we want to be.

Adolescence, between ages 12 and 18, is the stage at which we must meet and resolve the crisis of our basic **ego identity**. This is when we form our self-image, the integration of our ideas about ourselves and about what others think of us. If this process is resolved satisfactorily, the result is a consistent and congruent picture.

Shaping an identity and accepting it are difficult tasks, often filled with anxiety. Adolescents experiment with different roles and ideologies, trying to determine the most compatible fit. Erikson suggested that adolescence was a hiatus between childhood and adulthood, a necessary psychological moratorium to give the person time and energy to play different roles and live with different self-images.

People who emerge from this stage with a strong sense of self-identity are equipped to face adulthood with certainty and confidence. Those who fail to achieve a cohesive identity—who experience an **identity crisis**—will exhibit a confusion of roles. They do not seem to know who or what they are, where they belong, or where they want to go. They may withdraw from the normal life sequence (education, job, marriage) as Erikson did for a time or seek a negative identity in crime or drugs. Even a negative identity, as society defines it, is preferable to no identity, although it is not as satisfactory as a positive identity.

Erikson noted the potentially strong impact of peer groups on the development of ego identity in adolescence. He noted that excessive association with fanatical groups and cults or obsessive identification with icons of popular culture could restrict the developing ego.

The basic strength that should develop during adolescence is *fidelity*, which emerges from a cohesive ego identity. Fidelity encompasses sincerity, genuineness, and a sense of duty in our relationships with other people.

identity crisis
The failure to achieve ego identity during adolescence.

Intimacy versus Isolation

Erikson considered young adulthood to be a longer stage than the previous ones, extending from the end of adolescence to about age 35. During this period we establish our independence from parents and quasi-parental institutions, such as

Adolescents who experience an identity crisis do not seem to know where they belong or what they want to become.

© Russell Blake/Alamy

college, and begin to function more autonomously as mature, responsible adults. We undertake some form of productive work and establish intimate relationships—close friendships and sexual unions. In Erikson's view, intimacy was not restricted to sexual relationships but also encompassed feelings of caring and commitment. These emotions could be displayed openly, without resorting to self-protective or defensive mechanisms and without fear of losing our sense of self-identity. We can merge our identity with someone else's without submerging or losing it in the process.

People who are unable to establish such intimacies in young adulthood will develop feelings of isolation. They avoid social contacts and reject other people, and may even become aggressive toward them. They prefer to be alone because they fear intimacy as a threat to their ego identity.

The basic strength that emerges from the intimacy of the young adult years is *love*, which Erikson considered to be the greatest human virtue. He described it as a mutual devotion in a shared identity, the fusing of oneself with another person.

Generativity versus Stagnation

Adulthood—approximately ages 35 to 55—is a stage of maturity in which we need to be actively involved in teaching and guiding the next generation. This need extends beyond our immediate family. In Erikson's view, our concern becomes broader and more long-range, involving future generations and the kind of society in which they will live. One need not be a parent to display generativity, nor does having children automatically satisfy this urge.

Erikson believed that all institutions—whether business, government, social service, or academic—provide opportunities for us to express generativity. Thus, in whatever organizations or activities we are involved, we can usually find a way to become a mentor, teacher, or guide to younger people for the betterment of society at large.

When middle-aged people cannot or will not seek an outlet for generativity, they may become overwhelmed by "stagnation, boredom, and interpersonal impoverishment" (Erikson, 1968, p. 138). Erikson's depiction of these emotional difficulties in middle age is similar to Jung's description of the midlife crisis. These people may regress to a stage of pseudo-intimacy, indulging themselves in childlike ways. And they may become physical or psychological invalids because of their absorption with their own needs and comforts.

Care is the basic strength that emerges from generativity in adulthood. Erikson defined care as a broad concern for others and believed it was manifested in the need to teach, not only to help others but also to fulfill one's identity.

Ego Integrity versus Despair

During the final stage of psychosocial development, maturity and old age, we are confronted with a choice between ego integrity and despair. These attitudes govern the way we evaluate the whole of our life. At this time, our major endeavors are at or nearing completion. We examine and reflect on our life, taking its final measure. If we look back with a sense of fulfillment and satisfaction, believing we have adequately coped with life's victories and failures, then we are said to possess ego integrity. Simply stated, ego integrity involves accepting one's place and one's past.

On the other hand, if we review our life with a sense of frustration, angry about missed opportunities and regretful of mistakes that cannot be rectified, then we will feel despair. We will become disgusted with ourselves, contemptuous of others, and bitter over what might have been.

At the age of 84, Erikson published a book reporting the results of a long-term study of 29 people in their 80s on whom life-history data had been collected since 1928. The title, *Vital Involvement in Old Age*, indicates Erikson's prescription for achieving ego integrity (Erikson, Erikson, & Kivnick, 1986). Older people must do more than reflect on the past. They must remain active, vital participants in life, seeking challenge and stimulation from their environment. They must involve themselves in such activities as grandparenting, returning to school, and developing new skills and interests.

The basic strength associated with this final developmental stage is *wisdom*. Deriving from ego integrity, wisdom is expressed in a detached concern with the whole of life. It is conveyed to succeeding generations in an integration of experience best described by the word *heritage*.

Basic Weaknesses

basic weaknesses
Motivating characteristics that derive from the unsatisfactory resolution of developmental crises.

maldevelopment
A condition that occurs when the ego consists solely of a single way of coping with conflict.

Similar to the way basic strengths arise at each stage of psychosocial development, so may **basic weaknesses**. We noted earlier that the adaptive and maladaptive ways of coping with the crisis at each stage are incorporated in the ego identity in a kind of creative balance. Although the ego should consist primarily of the adaptive attitude, it will also contain a share of the negative attitude.

In an unbalanced development, the ego consists solely of one attitude, either the adaptive or the maladaptive one. Erikson labeled this condition **maldevelopment**. When only the positive, adaptive, tendency is present in the ego, the condition is said to be "maladaptive." When only the negative tendency is present, the condition is called "malignant." Maladaptions can lead to neuroses; malignancies can lead to psychoses.

Erikson expected that both conditions could be corrected through psychotherapy. Maladaptions, which are the less severe disturbances, can also be relieved through a process of re-adaptation, aided by environmental changes, supportive social relationships, or successful adaptation at a later developmental stage. Table 6.2 lists the maldevelopmental characteristics for each of the eight stages.

Questions About Human Nature

A personality theorist who delineates basic human strengths would be thought to possess an optimistic view of human nature. Erikson believed that although not everyone is successful in attaining hope, purpose, wisdom, and the other virtues, we all have the potential to do so. Nothing in our nature prevents it. Nor must we

Table 6.2 **Erikson's maldevelopmental tendencies**

Stage	Way of coping	Maldevelopment
Oral-sensory	Trust	Sensory maladjustment
	Mistrust	Withdrawal
Muscular-anal	Autonomy	Shameless willfulness
	Doubt, shame	Compulsion
Locomotor-genital	Initiative	Ruthlessness
	Guilt	Inhibition
Latency	Industriousness	Narrow virtuosity
	Inferiority	Inertia
Adolescence	Identity cohesion	Fanaticism
	Role confusion	Repudiation
Young adulthood	Intimacy	Promiscuity
	Isolation	Exclusivity
Adulthood	Generativity	Overextension
	Stagnation	Rejectivity
Maturity and old age	Ego integrity	Presumption
	Despair	Disdain

SOURCE: Adapted from *Vital Involvement in Old Age*, by Erik H. Erikson, Joan M. Erikson, and Helen Q. Kivnick by permission of W. W. Norton & Company, Inc. Copyright ©1986 by Joan M. Erikson, Erik H. Erikson, and Helen Kivnick.

inevitably suffer conflict, anxiety, and neurosis because of instinctual biological forces.

Erikson's theory allows for optimism because each stage of psychosocial growth, although centered on a crisis, offers the possibility of a positive outcome. We are capable of resolving each situation in a way that is adaptive and strengthening. Even if we fail at one stage and develop a maladaptive response or a basic weakness, there remains hope for change at a later stage.

We have the potential to direct consciously our growth throughout our lives. We are not exclusively products of childhood experiences. Although we have little control during the first four developmental stages, we gain increasing independence and the ability to choose ways of responding to crises and to society's demands. Childhood influences are important, but events at later stages can counteract unfortunate early experiences.

Erikson's theory is only partially deterministic. During the first four stages, the experiences to which we are exposed through parents, teachers, peer groups, and various opportunities are largely beyond our control. We have more chance to exercise free will during the last four stages, although the attitudes and strengths we have formed during the earlier stages will affect our choices.

In general, Erikson believed that personality is affected more by learning and experience than by heredity. Psychosocial experiences, not instinctual biological forces, are the greater determinant. Our ultimate, overriding goal is to develop a positive ego identity that incorporates all the basic strengths.

Assessment in Erikson's Theory

Erikson agreed with certain of Freud's theoretical formulations but deviated from Freudian thinking in his methods of assessing personality. Erikson questioned the usefulness and even the safety of some Freudian techniques, beginning with the psychoanalytic couch. To Erikson, asking patients to lie on a couch could lead to sadistic exploitation. It could create an illusion of objectivity, foster an overemphasis on unconscious material, and engender excessive impersonality and aloofness on the part of the therapist. To promote a more personal relationship between therapist and patient and to ensure that they viewed each other as equals, Erikson preferred that patients and therapists face each other and be seated in comfortable chairs.

In dealing with his patients, Erikson relied less on formal assessment techniques than did Freud. Erikson occasionally used free association but rarely attempted to analyze dreams, a technique he called wasteful and harmful. He believed that assessment techniques should be selected and modified to fit the unique requirements of the individual patient.

In developing his personality theory, Erikson used data obtained primarily from play therapy, anthropological studies, and psychohistorical analysis. For work with emotionally disturbed children and in research on normal children and adolescents, Erikson chose play therapy. He provided a variety of toys and observed how children interacted with them. The form and intensity of play revealed aspects of personality that might not be manifested verbally because of a child's limited powers of verbal expression.

We mentioned earlier Erikson's anthropological studies of American Indian peoples. Living among these groups to observe them, Erikson recorded their behavior and interviewed them at length, particularly with regard to child-rearing practices.

Psychohistorical Analysis

psychohistorical analysis The application of Erikson's life-span theory, along with psychoanalytic principles, to the study of historical figures.

Erikson's most unusual assessment technique is **psychohistorical analysis**. These analyses are essentially biographical studies. Erikson used the framework of his life-span theory of personality to describe the crises and the ways of coping of significant political, religious, and literary figures, such as Gandhi, Martin Luther, and George Bernard Shaw. Erikson's psychohistories typically focus on a significant crisis, an episode that represents a major life theme uniting past, present, and future activities. Using what he called "disciplined subjectivity," Erikson adopted the subject's viewpoint as his own to assess life events through that person's eyes.

Psychological Tests

Although Erikson did not use psychological tests for personality assessment, several instruments have been based on his formulations. The Ego-Identity Scale is designed to measure the development of ego identity during adolescence (Dignan, 1965). The Ego Identity Process Questionnaire, also for adolescents, contains 32 items to measure the dimensions of exploration and commitment (Balistreri, Busch-Rossnagel, & Geisinger, 1995). The Loyola Generativity Scale (see Table 6.3) is a

Table 6.3 **Examples of items from a scale to measure generativity**

Do these apply to any middle-aged people you know?

1. I try to pass along to others the knowledge I have gained through my experiences.
2. I do not believe that other people need me.
3. I believe I have made a difference in the lives of other people.
4. Other people say I am a productive person.
5. I believe I have done nothing that will survive after I die.
6. People come to me for advice.
7. I believe that society cannot be responsible for providing sustenance and shelter for all homeless people.
8. I have important skills that I try to teach others.
9. I do not like to do volunteer work for charities.
10. Throughout my life I have made and kept many commitments to people, groups, and activities.

SOURCE: Adapted from D.P. McAdams & E. de St. Aubin (1992). A theory of generativity and its assessment through self-report, behavioral acts, and narrative themes in autobiography. *Journal of Personality and Social Psychology, 62*, 1003–1015.

20-item self-report inventory to measure the level of generativity or stagnation in adulthood (McAdams & de St. Aubin, 1992).

Research on Erikson's Theory

Erikson's primary research method was the case study. By now you are familiar with the weaknesses of this method—the difficulty of duplicating and verifying case material—but you also know that much useful information can be obtained through this technique. Erikson argued that case histories yield many insights into personality development and can help resolve a patient's problems.

Play Constructions

play constructions
A personality assessment technique for children in which structures assembled from dolls, blocks, and other toys are analyzed.

Erikson used play therapy to conduct research on his theory, focusing on what he called **play constructions**. In one study, 300 boys and girls, ages 10 to 12, were asked to construct a scene from an imaginary movie using dolls, toy animals, automobiles, and wooden blocks. The girls tended to build static, peaceful scenes that contained low, enclosed structures. Intruders (animal figures or male figures, never female figures) tried to force their way into the interiors. By contrast, the boys focused on exteriors, action, and height. Their creations tended to be action-oriented, with tall towering structures and cars and people in motion (see Figure 6.1).

Trained as an orthodox Freudian, Erikson interpreted these play constructions along psychoanalytic lines. He wrote:

Sexual differences in the organization of a play space seem to parallel the morphology of genital differentiation itself: in the male, an external organ, erectable and intrusive in character . . . in the female, internal organs, with vestibular access, leading to a statically expectant ova. (Erikson, 1968, p. 271)

Figure 6.1
Play constructions created by boys (top) and girls (bottom).
SOURCE: Redrawn from *Childhood and Society*, 2nd ed., by Erik H. Erikson, by permission of W. W. Norton & Company, Inc. Copyright 1950, © 1963 by W. W. Norton & Company, Inc. Copyright renewed 1978, 1991 by Erik H. Erikson.

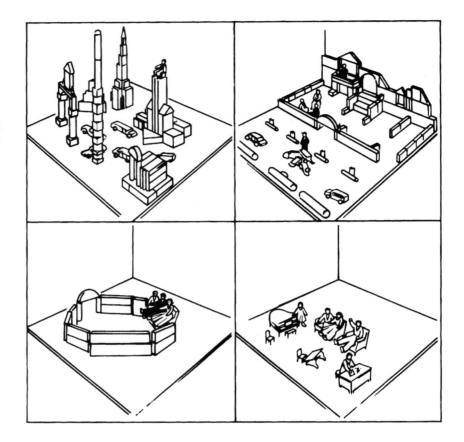

In other words, based on the determining effect of biological differences, girls would build low enclosures in which people are walled in, and boys would build towers.

Erikson has been criticized for this view, which suggests that women are victims of their anatomy and that their personalities are determined by the absence of a penis. Erikson admitted that differences in play constructions could also result from differences in society's sex-role training, in which girls are less oriented toward action, aggression, and achievement than boys are.

One replication of this study used younger children, boys and girls between the ages of 2 and 5 (Caplan, 1979). The results failed to support Erikson's findings. No significant sex differences were reported in the building of towers and enclosures. This raises the possibility that sex-role training was more complete in Erikson's 10- to 12-year-olds. Perhaps the younger children in this later study had not yet been sufficiently indoctrinated in the behavior society expected of them.

More than 50 years after Erikson's research on play constructions, traditional gender stereotyping with regard to toys and play behaviors persists. Most children still prefer gender-based toys. Boys typically play with trucks, soldiers, and guns. Girls typically play with dolls, jewelry, and toy kitchen implements.

These patterns of toy preferences have been found to exist as early as age 2 and are taught and encouraged by the parents. It is the parents who purchase most of their children's toys (though often at the child's urging). Parents praise children for playing with the appropriate gender-typed toy and discourage them from playing with toys intended for the other sex. The message is learned quickly. One psychologist observed a boy who "had been playing with a race car and its driver when the driver's helmet fell off revealing long blond hair. The driver was a woman. The boy dropped the race car like it was a hot potato" (Martin, 1999, p. 49).

Studies show that fathers treat boys and girls in a more stereotypical way than mothers do. Thus, it is primarily the fathers who teach and reinforce gender-based play. They also instruct their sons and daughters in other gender-typed behaviors and attitudes. Fathers tend to reward passive, compliant behaviors in girls and assertive, aggressive behaviors in boys (Quiery, 1998).

Trust and Security

Erikson emphasized the importance of developing an early sense of trust if we are to achieve feelings of security and well-being later in life. This position has received strong research support (see, for example, Jacobson & Wille, 1986; Londerville & Main, 1981; Sroufe, Fox, & Pancake, 1983).

Studies of infants aged 12 to 18 months showed that those who had a strong emotional bond with their mother (therefore presumed to be high in trust) functioned, when observed 3 years later, at a higher social and emotional level than infants whose attachment to their mother was less secure. Children with a well-developed sense of trust were also more curious, sociable, and popular. They were more likely to be leaders at games and showed greater sensitivity to the needs and feelings of others. Those low in trust were more withdrawn socially and emotionally, reluctant to play with other children, less curious, and less forceful in pursuing goals.

A study of 50 survivors of the Holocaust who were interviewed some 30 to 40 years after the end of World War II (1945) showed that they had dealt successfully with all of Erikson's proposed psychosocial stages except the first: trust versus mistrust. Their view of other people included significantly more mistrust than trust (Suedfeld, Soriano, McMurtry, Paterson, Weiszbeck, & Krell, 2005). However, the fact that they were able to cope with the later developmental crises confirms Erikson's notion that positive events at later stages can counteract or overcome negative early experiences.

The Psychosocial Stages

Other research has been concerned with the psychosocial developmental stages. Children aged 4, 8, and 11 were asked to make up stories based on several test pictures (Ciaccio, 1971). The stories were analyzed to determine which psychosocial stage they reflected. The results supported the themes proposed in Erikson's theory. For example, the stories of the 4-year-olds concerned autonomy (the stage just completed). Similarly, the stories of the older children reflected their developmental stages.

Psychohistorical analysis of the diaries, letters, and novels of Vera Brittain, a British feminist and writer, from age 21 into middle age, showed an initial concern with ego identity. This changed over time to a concern with intimacy and then generativity (Peterson & Stewart, 1990). These changes are in line with Erikson's developmental theory.

A study using the Inventory of Psychosocial Development, a test designed to assess adaptive and maladaptive development in Erikson's first six stages, found a significant relationship between happiness and adaptive development at each stage (Constantinople, 1969). Another study showed a high correlation between maladaptive development in the first six stages and a sense of alienation and uprootedness (Reimanis, 1974). These findings offer support for Erikson's work as does a study of 920 adults ages 18 to 25 in Canada. That research found that the period of emerging adulthood was a time of increased psychological well-being (Galambos, Barker, & Krahn, 2006).

Research that supports Erikson's stages also used the Inventory of Psychosocial Development. Over a 22-year period the test was administered to a total of 474 college students. The results showed increasingly positive resolution of the crises of the psychosocial stages through their middle forties. As Erikson predicted, a favorable outcome at one stage was dependent on the successful resolution of the crisis at an earlier stage (Whitbourne, Elliot, Zuschlag, & Waterman, 1992).

Psychologists tested Erikson's belief that positive outcomes in resolving the identity crisis are related to positive outcomes at prior developmental stages (Waterman, Buebel, & Waterman, 1970). Adolescents who developed trust, autonomy, initiative, and industriousness (adaptive ways of coping) in the first four stages of psychosocial development displayed a high level of identity cohesion rather than role confusion. Adolescents who had not resolved their identity crisis and who experienced role confusion had not developed adaptive ways of coping in the earlier stages.

Three groups of men in Canada (ages 19–25, 35–55, and 65–87) were asked to take self-report measures of identity, self-worth, and psychological distress. The results confirmed Erikson's theory. The younger men experienced the highest levels of distress while the older men had the lowest rates of distress. This is in line with Erikson's view that "the older the individual, the better one is able to cope with life's challenges due to exposure and resolution of earlier psychological dilemmas" (Beaumont & Zukanovic, 2005, p. 77).

When 50 adults in Britain ages 62 to 89 were asked to recall memories from earlier times the results supported the psychosocial developmental stages. Memories of their first decade of life focused on issues of trust, autonomy, initiative, and industry. Memories of their second decade (ages 11 to 20) dealt with identity issues while memories from young adulthood centered on intimacy. Thus, recollections of each succeeding period centered on those situations Erikson foresaw as crucial to development (Conway & Holmes, 2004).

Adolescent Development

An extensive research program on the adolescent stage of development identified five psychosocial types, or statuses, for that period (Marcia, 1966, 1980). These are identity achievement, moratorium, foreclosure, identity diffusion, and alienated achievement.

Identity achievement describes adolescents who are committed to occupational and ideological choices. A study of 74 college students found a positive correlation between achieved identity status and objective measures of commitment (Streitmatter, 1993). These students had developed a strong ego identity. They were stable, concerned with realistic goals, and able to cope with changing environmental demands. They performed better on difficult tasks than adolescents experiencing role confusion. These stable adolescents majored in more difficult areas in college, attracted to courses in engineering and the physical sciences (Marcia & Friedman, 1970).

A study of 502 high school students found that the identity achievement status correlated highly with self-esteem and positive forms of coping. It represented the most psychologically and socially mature identity status (Markstron & Marshall, 2007).

There is also evidence that adolescents who engaged in serious contemplation about what they wanted to do with their lives, and so were more likely to achieve an identity, had parents who provided direction and control in a loving and caring way, in contrast to parents who were either too permissive or too authoritarian (Berzonsky, 2004).

Moratorium, the second adolescent status, describes people who are still undergoing their identity crisis. Their occupational and ideological commitments are vague. They hold ambivalent views toward authority figures, alternately rebelling and needing guidance from them. Their behavior ranges from indecisive to active and creative (Blustein, Devenis, & Kidney, 1989; Podd, Marcia, & Rubin, 1968). They also tend to daydream, to believe in supernatural phenomena, and to enjoy behaving childishly (Bilsker & Marcia, 1991).

Foreclosure describes adolescents who have not experienced an identity crisis but who are firmly committed to an occupation and an ideology. However, these commitments often have been determined for them by their parents and do not result from the adolescents' deliberate choice. These teens tend to be rigid and authoritarian and have difficulty coping with change (Marcia, 1967). However, a study of 23 male and 37 female college students showed that those in the foreclosure status tended to be achievement-oriented and to focus their energy toward external rather than internal goals (Stephen, Fraser, & Marcia, 1992).

The *identity diffusion* status characterizes people who have no occupational or ideological commitments in adolescence and who may not have experienced an identity crisis. Their chosen lifestyle may actively reject commitments and in the extreme may result in aimless drifting. These adolescents have distant relationships with their parents, whom they see as indifferent and rejecting (Waterman, 1982).

Several studies of adolescents in Greece, Belgium, and the United States in the identity diffusion status showed that they ranked lower in psychological adjustment and subjective well-being and higher in unstable self-image and interpersonal relationships. They were also more likely to engage in impulsive and self-destructive behavior, to show an excessive need for attention, and to have grandiose fantasies (Crawford, Cohen, Johnson, Sheed, & Brook, 2004; Luyckx, Goossens, Soenens, Beyers, & Vansteenkiste, 2005; Vleioras & Bosma, 2005).

The fifth status, *alienated achievement*, describes adolescents who have experienced an identity crisis, have no occupational goal, and cling to beliefs that are critical of the social and economic system. Their commitment to this rationale precludes any career that would entangle them in the very system they oppose. As students they tend to be cerebral, philosophical, and cynical (Marcia & Friedman, 1970; Orlofsky, Marcia, & Lesser, 1973).

Four of these statuses, in the following order (identity diffusion, foreclosure, moratorium, and identity achievement), represent increasingly successful resolutions of the identity problem. Erikson predicted that people who are close to achieving or who have achieved an integrated ego identity will have greater ego strength than those who are farther from resolving their identity dilemma. That prediction was supported by research on college men (Bourne, 1978a, 1978b).

A study of more than 500 high school students found that those who were more heavily involved in extracurricular and volunteer activities were higher in the ego strength of fidelity than were those not so involved (Markstrom, Li, Blackshire, & Wilfong, 2005).

In other research, sex differences were found in the resolution of the identity crisis. Men in one study showed a tendency toward separation and detachment from other people; women showed a tendency toward connection and attachment to others (Mellor, 1989). Other studies support and extend that finding, showing that male identity focuses on individual competence and knowledge whereas female identity is more centered on relating to others. In other words, when women establish an identity, they depend heavily on social relationships. Men focus more on self and individual skills and abilities (Curry, 1998).

You may recall your own adolescence as a turbulent and stressful period. Three key elements for this developmental stage have been identified as follows.

- Conflict with parents, characterized by a forceful resistance to adult authority,
- Mood disruption, characterized by a volatile emotional life, mood swings, and episodes of depression, and
- Risky behaviors, characterized by reckless, rule-breaking, and antisocial behavior that may harm themselves and others.

A study in which 155 adolescents kept diaries of their daily interactions over a 2-week period showed that 31 percent of their interactions involved conflicts with other people. The teenage subjects reported that conflicts with their parents were more important to them, and more emotionally intense, than were conflicts with their peers (Jensen-Campbell & Graziano, 2000).

Studies tracking individuals from childhood to adolescence found that many of those who experienced depression and other emotional problems during the teen years had also suffered some form of psychological distress as children. This suggests that difficulties reported in adolescence do not necessarily arise because of adolescence (Steinberg & Morris, 2001).

Studies have found that a stressful adolescence is far more likely to occur among White middle-class teenagers than among Mexican-American or Asian-American teenagers. However, the more acculturated minority-group members become, the more likely it is that their adolescents will experience the typical signs and symptoms of the majority population (Arnett, 1999).

Virtual Identity

Computer games and Internet sites may afford adolescents a unique, high-tech opportunity to do precisely what Erikson said was so necessary at that developmental stage: to try different roles to see which offers the best fit. And when surfing the Web, one can do so anonymously. This is exemplified in the role-playing game called *Dungeons and Dragons*, which allowed young people to take on fictional personas to act out complex fantasies.

The word *dungeon* is now used in specialized computer vocabulary to denote a virtual place. Virtual places shared by a number of computer users simultaneously are known as multi-user dungeons or MUDs. MUDs allow a player to interact with others and also to build a personal virtual world whose imaginary characters interact with others. Participants can play roles as like or unlike their real selves as they choose without revealing their real identity. "You can be whoever you want to be," one writer noted. "You can completely redefine yourself if you want" (Turkle, 1995, p. 184). That is precisely what Erikson urged us to do during adolescence, to experiment with different identities.

A study of 217 MUD players ("MUDders") in Germany, whose average age was 25, found that interpersonal attraction among the players increased the longer they played, as did the intensity of their social identification with the virtual community (Utz, 2003). The degree of identification with their virtual world was thought to be as intense and satisfying as identifying with the real world.

Of course this can lead to the danger that a person could become so absorbed in a virtual identity that it comes to replace the true developing self. But that can also happen in the real world by adopting a different persona. The point is that for some adolescents the Internet offers a secure way of trying to establish an identity.

Gender and Ego Identity

Erikson believed that social and historical factors affect the formation of ego identity, which in turn affects the nature of the personality. The women's movement of the 1960s and 1970s provided a real-world laboratory in which to test the effects of social forces. Specifically, psychologists asked whether women then at the adolescent stage of psychosocial development, the time of striving for an ego identity, were more influenced by the women's movement than women who were older at that time. It was assumed that the identity of the older women already had been formed.

Two studies answered yes. Both chose women who had graduated from one of three colleges during the 1940s to mid-1960s. Data were gathered from interviews, questionnaires, and self-report personality tests. Women attending college when the women's movement began were found to have greater aspirations. They valued their independence more than did the older women and eventually attained higher levels of education, job status, and income. They were more assertive and self-confident in middle age than were women who had passed through the adolescent stage before the advent of the women's movement (Duncan & Agronick, 1995; Helson, Stewart, & Ostrove, 1995).

One legacy of the women's movement is that more adolescent women today include a career orientation as part of their ego identity. This viewpoint has been found to affect dating behavior as well as age at the time of marriage (Matula, Huston, Grotevant, & Zamutt, 1992). Questionnaire studies of several hundred women college students revealed that those who are career oriented tend to marry later in life. They date less while in college and are more wary of committed relationships. The same study found the opposite situation for men. Questionnaire results for 56 college men revealed that the stronger their career identity, the more committed they were to a dating relationship. Indeed, they were unlikely to become involved in a dating relationship until they felt a definite commitment to an occupation.

Additional longitudinal research studied women who graduated from college in the 1960s and the men they married. It focused on changes in their emotional life over time, specifically,

- Changes in positive emotionality (PEM), defined as an active, happy involvement in one's work and social environments, and
- Negative emotionality (NEM), characterized by feelings of stress, anxiety, anger, and other negative emotions.

Measures of these two factors, taken at various ages from late 20s to middle 50s, showed that in young adulthood women tended to score higher on NEM than did their spouses and to score higher on PEM in late middle age. These findings were interpreted by the investigators to indicate that women showed greater feelings of social power, accomplishment, and breadth of interest, along with reduced stress and alienation, once the period of child rearing ended. Thus, social factors were seen to influence the affective dimension of ego identity (Helson & Klohnen, 1998).

Erikson defined identity consolidation as the process of dealing successfully with the social realities of adult life. This involves making adjustments to the changing demands of our social world. He believed that identity consolidation usually occurs during the 20s, as people assume adult responsibilities of marriage, family, and career. A study of women college graduates evaluated at ages 21 and 27 found that those who ranked high in ego resiliency and had found an identity in marriage were higher in identity consolidation than those who did not meet these criteria (Pals, 1999).

A study of 112 women ages 22 to 60 found a positive relationship between their readiness and willingness to change and changes in their identity commitment at different developmental stages. Looking ahead and contemplating life changes was positively linked to the likelihood of exploring a different identity later in life (Anthis & LaVoie, 2006).

The Identity Crisis

Some research has focused on the timing of the identity crisis. Erikson suggested that it began around age 12 and was resolved, one way or another, by approximately age 18. However, for some people the identity crisis may not occur until later. In one study, up to 30 percent of the research participants were still searching for an identity as late as age 24 (Archer, 1982).

Also, college may delay the resolution of the identity crisis and prolong the period during which young adults experiment with different roles and ideologies (Cote & Levine, 1988). When college students were compared with people of the same age who held full-time jobs, it was found that employed persons had achieved ego identity at an earlier age than students had. The students remained longer in the moratorium status (Adams & Fitch, 1982). Additional research suggests that the construction of a person's identity may even be a continuing process that occurs over the entire life span (McAdams, 2001).

Generativity

Research on the adulthood stage of psychosocial development has shown that generativity in middle age is positively correlated with power and with intimacy motivation (McAdams, Ruetzel, & Foley, 1986). Thus, as Erikson's theory predicts, generativity evokes the needs to feel close to others and to feel strong in relation to them. Another study associated generativity with nurturance (Van de Water & McAdams, 1989). All these are necessary characteristics for teaching and mentoring the next generation.

Generativity in middle age appears to be significantly related to having experienced warm, affectionate parenting in childhood (Franz, McClelland, & Weinberger, 1991). Research supports the importance of both mother and father to a child's emotional well-being. Middle-aged adults who scored high in generativity tended to believe in the goodness and worth of human life and to feel happier and more satisfied with their own life than did people who scored low in generativity (McAdams & de St. Aubin, 1992; Van de Water & McAdams, 1989).

Other studies corroborated and extended these findings. People high in generativity also scored higher on extraversion, conscientiousness, and openness to new experiences than people low in generativity (Peterson, Smirles, & Wentworth, 1997). Those high in generativity were more likely to be involved in meaningful, satisfying social relationships, to feel strongly attached to their community, and to be more emotionally stable than those low in generativity (McAdams, Hart, & Maruna, 1998). Those high in generativity were also more likely to have successful marriages, greater achievements at work, and more close friendships. In addition they displayed more altruistic behavior than those who scored low on measures of generativity (Westermeyer, 2004). A study of adult subjects in Belgium showed that those high in generativity were also high in measures of extraversion, agreeableness, openness to new experiences, and conscientiousness (Van Hiel, Mervielde, & DeFruyt, 2006).

Two longitudinal studies of college-educated women tested and observed at intervals from ages 31 to 48 found that those who were high in generativity at midlife scored significantly higher in emotional well being than those low in generativity (Vandewater, Ostrove, & Stewart, 1997). Another longitudinal study of college-educated women found that those who valued social recognition and achievement had more fully developed identities in their 40s, and were significantly higher in generativity, than were those who did not value social recognition and achievement (Helson & Srivastava, 2001).

Additional research on college-educated women in their 40s found that, as Erikson predicted, generativity was higher during that stage of life than it was when the women were in their 20s. However, this study also reported, contrary to Erikson's view, that the level of generativity remained at the same level in these women well into their 60s (Zucker, Ostrove, & Stewart, 2002).

In a related study, college-educated women who scored high in generativity at age 43 maintained that level 10 years later. They also demonstrated a higher level of care-giving to their aging parents and reported a higher level of care for their spouses and children than did women scoring low in generativity at age 43 (Peterson, 2002).

When a group of 70 men and women were asked to describe the major themes of their life, persons who had previously scored high on the Loyola Generativity Scale revealed different issues from persons who had scored low. Common themes of the high scorers included some event of good fortune in their early life, sensitivity to the suffering of others, a stable personal belief system, and clear goals for themselves and for society. Low scorers did not record any of these themes (McAdams, Diamond, de St. Aubin, & Mansfield, 1997).

A group of middle-aged adults were asked to write accounts of personally meaningful episodes from their past, including events that were high points, low points, and turning points. Those who scored high in generativity were far more likely to describe scenes in which a negative life experience was transformed into a positive redemptive experience. Those who scored low in generativity tended to describe the opposite, in which a positive life experience was transformed into a negative life event. Those high in generativity also scored significantly higher on measures of life satisfaction and self-esteem than did those low in generativity (McAdams, Reynolds, Lewis, Patten, & Bowman, 2001). Thus, we may conclude that, as Erikson's theory suggests, generativity offers many benefits in the midlife years.

Maturity

Erikson believed that people in the maturity and old age stage of psychosocial development spend time recalling and examining their life, accepting or regretting past choices. A study using 49 psychologists as research participants found that most of their memories were of college and early adult years, the period involving the greatest number of critical decisions that affected the course of their life (Mackavey, Malley, & Stewart, 1991). Other research found that elderly subjects who scored high in ego integrity devoted time to reviewing their life to resolve troubling issues and come to a better understanding of their circumstances. In general, persons scoring low in ego integrity reported that they did not engage in such self-examination Taft & Nehrke, 1990). A study of 259 adults ages 60–65 found that, as Erikson predicted, acknowledging regrets and missed opportunities related directly to life satisfaction and physical health for both men and women (Torges, Stewart, & Miner-Rubino, 2005).

A comparison of the younger and older stages of the life span in a sample of 108 adults (ages 17–82) found that older people were far more concerned with generativity and ego integrity, and less concerned with ego identity, than were younger people. These findings support Erikson's views. The results also found a significant positive correlation between age and subjective well-being; in general, older people were happier than younger people (Sheldon & Kasser, 2001). A study of 184 men and women in Australia ages 55 to 93 showed that continued involvement in family and community activities led to continued feelings of generativity well into old age (Warburton, McLaughlin, & Pinsker, 2006).

In another study, younger adults (ages 25–35) were compared with older adults (ages 60–85). The research showed no significant differences between the groups in reported frequency of life reflections. However, the reasons for reflecting on life events did differ. Younger people engaged in reflection to gain self-insight and find solutions to current problems. Older people reflected on their past to evaluate their lives and achieve a sense of ego integrity (Staudinger, 2001a, 2001b).

Gender differences in aging may make it more difficult for women than for men to engage in a dispassionate process of reflection, or taking stock of life, such as Erikson described. This was demonstrated in research involving 259 adults in their 60s. Men reported much higher levels of identity certainty, confidence, and power than women did (Miner-Rubino, Winter, & Stewart, 2004). The so-called double standard in society considers aging as more negative for women and sees women as "old" at an earlier age than men. For example, whereas a 50-year-old male actor may still be offered thoughtful, mature, and powerful movie roles, a 50-year-old female actor may be stereotyped as a widow or grandmother, if she is offered movie roles at all.

In addition, women tend to live longer than men, so they are more likely to have to deal with issues of illness and incapacity, bereavement, loss of social support, and reduced income. This may contribute to the observation that women's retrospective reviews of their lives are often less positive than those of men and more likely to lead to the condition Erikson noted as despair in later years, rather than ego integrity (Rainey, 1998).

Ethnic Identity

One aspect of ego development not considered by Erikson is the impact of ethnic identity. Research on this topic consistently shows the importance of racial or ethnic identity to members of minority groups; denying one's racial identity can be highly stressful (see, for example, Franklin-Jackson & Carter, 2007). A large-scale study of 582 White and ethnic minority men and women, including adolescents and adults, found that Whites scored significantly lower on measures of racial and ethnic identity than did members of any of the minority groups studied (Gaines et al., 1997). A study of more than 6,000 students (ages 14–18) showed that African-Americans were far more likely to choose friends on the basis of ethnic identity than were Whites or Asian-Americans (Hamm, 2000).

Research involving nearly 300 Black adolescents showed clear, consistent, and strong relationships between racial identity and psychological health. Those who scored high on racial identity were also high in subjective well-being, life satisfaction, and self-esteem (Constantine, Alleyne, Wallace, & Franklin-Jackson, 2006;

Pillay, 2005). A study of more than 3,000 Black, Asian, and biracial teens found that self-esteem was highest among Blacks and lowest among Asians. The self-esteem of the biracial adolescents was significantly lower than for Blacks and significantly higher than for Asians (Bracey, Bamaca, & Umana-Taylor, 2004). Thus, racial identity appeared to be a stronger and more important factor for self-esteem among Black adolescents than among biracial or Asian adolescents.

Group esteem (that is, how people feel about being members of their racial or ethnic group) has been shown to increase in African-American and Latino-American teenagers during the period of early and middle adolescence. Group esteem among White students remained stable; it measured high at both the beginning and the end of the period studied (French, Seidman, Allen, & Aber, 2006).

Among Black women adolescents, ethnic identity was found to be the most significant factor in defining their sense of self (Aries & Moorehead, 1989). Other research showed that adolescents of both sexes considered ethnic identity the most important factor in developing a strong ego identity (Helms, 1990). Low ethnic identity in Black college students was related to low self-esteem and to anxiety and inferiority feelings (Parkham & Helms, 1985a, 1985b).

Other research found that Black adolescents who scored high in ethnic identity expressed less positive attitudes toward drugs and more positive attitudes toward school, which were related to more positive behaviors at school. Those who scored high on a measure of anti-White attitudes were far more likely to use drugs, have negative attitudes toward school, and exhibit negative behaviors at school (Resnicow, Soler, Braithwaite, Ben Selassie, & Smith, 1999).

A survey of 248 Black college students found that those who favored a strong Black Nationalist identity, focusing on the uniqueness of the Black experience, had significantly lower grade-point averages than those who held a less extreme position. Black students who scored high on a questionnaire about assimilating into main-stream society earned lower grades than those who took a more moderate position (Sellers, Chavous, & Cooke, 1998). Research with 474 Black college students found that those high in ethnic identity were more likely to enroll in Black studies courses and to interact socially with other Black students. Those who emphasized the similarities between Blacks and other racial and ethnic groups rather than the uniqueness of the Black identity were more likely to interact socially with Whites. Students who attended Black colleges were far more likely to emphasize the uniqueness of the Black experience than were Black students who attended primarily White colleges (Sellers, Rowley, Chavous, Shelton, & Smith, 1997).

In addition, students who experienced more racism reported higher levels of stress and lower levels of psychological functioning than did those who experienced little or no racism (Bynum, Burton, & Best, 2007).

A study of Black women and Hispanic women found that identity confusion (a conflict in identity between one's minority culture and the majority culture) may lead to eating disorders. Identification with a North American model of beauty that emphasizes extreme thinness created in some women a tendency to exhibit disorders such as anorexia. The researchers suggested that this condition resulted from an attempt to emulate the appearance standards of the ideal woman of the majority White culture (Harris & Kuba, 1997).

Studies of Asian-American and Hispanic-American adolescents confirm that ethnicity is a central concern in forming an ego identity. A strong ethnic identity was associated with high self-esteem and with better peer and family relations (Phinney & Chavira, 1992). A study of 1062 Hispanic-American adolescents found that those who attended predominantly White schools reported significantly higher levels of ethnic identity than those who attended more ethnically balanced schools (Umana-Taylor, 2004).

Asian-American young people with a high ethnic identity showed a stronger resistance to drinking alcoholic beverages or smoking marijuana than did Asian-American youth with a high degree of assimilation into the majority culture (Suinn, 1999).

One model of ethnic identity for African-American adolescents is the Revised Racial Identity Model proposed by William Cross. He also published the 64-item Cross Racial Identity Scale to measure the developmental stages of the model. Research has shown the scale to be a valid test of ethnic identity (Vandiver, Cross, Worrell, & Fhagen-Smith, 2002). Cross's model posits the following four stages in the development of a psychologically healthy Black identity (Cokley, 2002):

1. Pre-encounter
2. Encounter
3. Immersion–emersion
4. Internalization

The *pre-encounter stage* includes three identity clusters. The pre-encounter assimilation identity contains little racial awareness or racial identity. The pre-encounter miseducation identity internalizes negative stereotypes about being Black. The pre-encounter self-hatred identity involves holding highly negative views about Blacks, resulting in anti-Black and self-hating attitudes.

In the *encounter stage* the person is subjected to racism or discrimination, which causes a shift in the adolescent's worldview. The *immersion–emersion stage* proposes two identities. The immersion–emersion intense Black involvement identity celebrates everything Black as good and desirable. The immersion–emersion anti-White identity views everything White as evil and wrong.

The *internalization stage* also consists of two identities. One is Black Nationalism, which adheres to a pro-Black Afrocentric perspective, whereas the multiculturalist inclusive identity embraces not only a Black identity but also other types of ethnic, racial, and gender identity.

A study of 130 Black men, average age 20, showed that those in the pre-encounter stage of their ethnic identity reported significantly less self-esteem, greater psychological distress, and lower psychological well-being than those in the internalization stage (Pierre & Mahalik, 2005). And a study of Black college students found that as racial identity proceeded from the earliest through the more mature stages of this model, the level of defense mechanisms changed from the least sophisticated and immature defenses to more mature ones. This is what could be predicted as a person's racial identity becomes more fully developed (Nghe & Mahalik, 2001).

The importance of this kind of minority ego identity development model lies in the recognition of ethnic identity as a vital component of ego identity and in the suggestion that ethnic identity develops over a series of stages, similar to the concept of the psychosocial stages. As we noted, Erikson did not deal directly with the concept of ethnic identity, but this model adheres to the developmental pattern he proposed.

Gender Preference Identity

Another aspect of ego identity not considered directly by Erikson, is gender preference identity, which may have an impact on overall ego identity and may vary as a function of ethnic identity. For example, a study of 863 White, Black, and Hispanic children, average age 11, found that the Black and Hispanic children reported far more pressure for gender conformity than did the White children (Corby, Hodges, & Perry, 2007).

Researchers have proposed that homosexual or gay identity develops over a series of stages, similar to the way Erikson and others explained the development of ego or ethnic identity. One model lists four stages in the development of gender preference identity (Frable, 1997).

1. Sensitization. This stage, which occurs prior to adolescence, refers to one's initial perception of being different from peers of the same sex.
2. Identity confusion. This adolescent stage is marked by the confusing, perhaps frightening, realization that one's feelings and thoughts could be characterized as homosexual.
3. Identity assumption. During this stage the person comes to believe that he or she is homosexual and begins to accept the beginnings of a gay identity.
4. Commitment. In this stage the person fully accepts the gay identity as a way of life.

Studies have shown that people who score high on gay identity self-report inventories also score high on measures of mental and emotional well-being and express no desire to alter their identity or to conceal it from other people (Frable, 1997). A study of 825 homosexual and bisexual men found no differences in self-esteem, emotional well-being, and general level of adjustment between those who believed they were stigmatized socially because of their gender preference and those who did not feel so stigmatized. However, men who kept their gender preference less visible in their social behaviors scored higher in self-esteem and well-being than men who were more openly gay in their social behaviors (Frable, Wortman, & Joseph, 1997).

Those who have conflicts over their gender preference have been found to experience negative psychological effects. These include low self-esteem, stress, the use of neurotic defenses, depression, anxiety, and substance abuse as well as feelings of failure, guilt, and pessimism (Liu, Rochlen, & Mohr, 2005).

A study of 366 male inmates in a medium-security prison found that those whose personality style included a strong need for personal relationships had less gender role conflict. "This need for others may override their homophobia or fear of appearing feminine" in a culture such as prison, which typically dictates a wariness of forming close relationships with other inmates. Those who personalities showed less need for personal contact had greater gender role conflict about homosexual tendencies (Schwartz, Buboltz, Seemann, & Flye, 2004, p. 63).

Reflections on Erikson's Theory

Erikson's substantial contributions to psychology include the recognition of personality development throughout the life span, the concept of the identity crisis in adolescence, and the incorporation in his theory of the impact of cultural, social, and historical forces. However, his system does not lack critics. Some point to ambiguous terms and concepts, conclusions drawn in the absence of supporting data, and an overall lack of precision (Rosenthal, Gurney, & Moore, 1981; Waterman, 1982). Erikson agreed that these charges were valid and blamed them on his artistic temperament and lack of formal training in science. He wrote, "I came to psychology from art, which may explain, if not justify, the fact that at times the reader will find me painting contexts and backgrounds where he would rather have me point to facts and concepts" (Erikson, 1950, p. 13).

A more specific criticism relates to the incomplete description of the developmental stage of maturity, which Erikson attempted to correct in his 1986 book (Erikson, Erikson, & Kivnick, 1986). Also, some psychologists question whether personality development after age 55 is likely to be as positive as Erikson suggested with his concept of ego integrity. For many people, this stage of life is characterized by pain, loss, and depression, even for people who develop the basic strength of wisdom.

Erikson's position on sex differences, as revealed in his interpretation of the play-constructions research, has also come under attack. What he saw as biologically based differences in personality for boys and girls, emerging from the presence or absence of a penis, could as well be cultural differences or the result of sex-role training. Erikson later admitted these possibilities.

Erikson's developmental stages may not be applicable to women. When social psychologist Carol Tavris read Erikson's description of his so-called stages of *man*, she wrote, "It was worrying. I wasn't having any of my crises in the right order. . . . My identity was shaky, although I was no longer a teenager, and I hadn't married when I was supposed to, which was putting my intimacy and generativity crises on hold" (Tavris, 1992, p. 37).

Some critics charge that Erikson's personality theory does not apply to people in reduced economic circumstances who cannot afford a moratorium in adolescence to explore different roles and develop an ego identity. This stage may be a luxury available only to those with the means to attend college or take time out to travel (Slugoski & Ginsburg, 1989).

Erikson showed little interest in responding to his critics. He recognized that there are many ways of describing personality development and that no single view was adequate. His influence grew through his books and the work of succeeding generations of psychologists, psychiatrists, teachers, and counselors who found in his ideas useful ways to describe personality development from infancy through old age. His ideas have been recognized in both professional and popular circles. *Time* magazine called him the "most influential living psychoanalyst" (March 17, 1975), and *Psychology Today* described him as "an authentic intellectual hero" (Hall, 1983, p. 22). His concepts are useful in education, social work, vocational and marriage counseling, and clinical practice with children and adolescents. The Erikson Institute for Early Childhood Education was established at Chicago's Loyola University.

The field of life-span developmental psychology, which has seen a massive increase in research and theory in recent years, owes much of its spark to Erikson's approach, as does the current interest in developmental problems of middle and old age.

In addition, Erikson's method of play therapy has become a standard diagnostic and therapeutic tool for work with emotionally disturbed and abused children. Youngsters who cannot verbalize the details of a physical or sexual attack can express their feelings through play, using dolls to represent themselves and their abusers.

Chapter Summary

Erikson suffered several personal identity crises and developed a personality theory in which the search for identity plays a major role. He built on Freud's theory by elaborating on the developmental stages, emphasizing the ego over the id, and recognizing the impact on personality of culture, society, and history. The growth of personality is divided into eight stages. A conflict at each stage confronts the person with adaptive and maladaptive ways of coping. Development is governed by the epigenetic principle; each stage depends on genetic forces but the environment helps determine whether they are realized.

The oral-sensory stage (birth to age 1) can result in trust or mistrust. The muscular-anal stage (ages 1 to 3) leads to an autonomous will or to self-doubt. The locomotor-genital stage (3 to 5) develops initiative or guilt. The latency stage (6 to 11) results in industriousness or inferiority. Adolescence (12 to 18) is the stage in which the ego identity is formed (the time of the identity crisis), leading to identity cohesion or role confusion. Young adulthood (18 to 35) results in intimacy or isolation. Adulthood (35 to 55) leads to generativity or stagnation. Maturity (over 55) is expressed in ego integrity or despair.

Each stage allows for the development of basic strengths that emerge from the adaptive ways of coping with the conflicts. The basic strengths are hope, will, purpose, competence, fidelity, love, care, and wisdom. Maldevelopment can occur if the ego consists solely of either the adaptive or the maladaptive tendency.

Erikson presented a flattering, optimistic image of human nature. We have the ability to achieve basic strengths, to resolve each conflict in a positive way, and to consciously direct our growth. We are not victims of biological forces or childhood experiences and are influenced more by learning and social interactions than by heredity.

Erikson's assessment methods were play therapy, anthropological studies, and psychohistorical analysis. His research relied on case studies. There is considerable research support for the first six stages of psychosocial development and for the concept of ego identity. However, the identity crisis may occur later than Erikson believed, and attending college may delay resolution of the crisis. Other research confirms the importance of developing a sense of trust early in life, and the benefits of generativity in middle age. Among minority-group members, the formation of ethnic identity in adolescence may affect the development of ego identity and influence subsequent behavior. The Cross Racial Identity Model describes four stages in the development of a psychologically healthy adolescent Black identity. Gender preference identity may also affect characteristics of ego identity. People who have conflicts about their gender preference appear to be less psychologically healthy than people who experience no such conflicts.

Criticisms of Erikson's theory focus on ambiguous terminology, incomplete descriptions of the psychosocial stages, and poorly supported claims of male–female personality differences based on biological factors.

Review Questions

1. Describe the kinds of identity crises Erikson experienced in childhood and adolescence. Note how they were reflected in his theory.

2. In what ways is Erikson's theory similar to and different from Freud's theory?

3. What did Erikson mean by the concept of identity confusion? What evidence did he find for it among Native Americans?

4. How does Erikson's epigenetic principle of maturation account for the effects of genetic and social factors on personality?

5. Describe the role of conflict in the stages of psychosocial development.

6. Describe the four childhood stages of psychosocial development. Discuss the effects of various parental behaviors on the possible outcomes of each stage.

7. Contrast identity cohesion and role confusion as adaptive versus maladaptive ways of coping during adolescence.

8. What is the major difference between the first four developmental stages and the last four developmental stages?

9. What factors affect the development of ego identity? Why do some people fail to achieve an identity at this stage?

10. How can the conflicts of the adult stages of psychosocial development be resolved in positive ways?

11. What are the two ways of adapting to maturity and old age? How can a person achieve the positive way of adapting?

12. Describe the basic strengths at each stage of psychosocial development.

13. Distinguish between the two types of maldevelopment. How can these conditions be corrected?

14. How does Erikson's image of human nature differ from Freud's?

15. What methods of assessment did Erikson use in developing his theory?

16. Based on the results of his play-constructions research, what did Erikson conclude about sex differences in personality? On what grounds can we criticize these conclusions?

17. Describe research findings on the development of ego identity in adolescence and on generativity in middle age.

18. Discuss how the ethnic identity of ethnic-minority adolescents can affect the formation of ego identity as well as subsequent attitudes and behavior.

19. How can online role-playing games help adolescents establish an ego identity?

20. In what ways do people high in generativity differ from people low in generativity?

21. Describe the proposed stages for the development of gender preference identity.

Suggested Readings

Bloland, S. E. (2005). *In the shadow of fame*. New York: Viking. A memoir by Erikson's daughter.

Erikson, E. H. (1950). *Childhood and society*. New York: Norton. A collection of essays on child-rearing practices, family life, and social and cultural structures showing their relationship to personality development. This book was an instant success with scholars and the general public.

Erikson, E. H. (1968). *Identity: Youth and crisis*. New York: Norton. Erikson's classic work on the identity crisis and ways of coping with its conflicts.

Erikson, E. H. (1987). *A way of looking at things: Selected papers from 1930 to 1980*. New York: Norton. A collection of Erikson's writings on children's play constructions, adult dreams, cross-cultural research, and development over the life cycle. Edited by Stephen Schlein.

Erikson, E. H., Erikson, J. M., & Kivnick, H. Q. (1986). *Vital involvement in old age*. New York: Norton. A sensitive psychosocial analysis of the need for stimulation and challenge in old age and a personal perspective on Erikson as he approached the age of 90.

Evans, R. I. (1967). *Dialogue with Erik Erikson*. New York: Harper & Row. Conversations with Erikson about his life and work.

Friedman, L. J. (1999). *Identity's architect: A biography of Erik H. Erikson*. New York: Simon & Schuster. A sympathetic treatment showing how Erikson's ideas on the identity crisis and the stages of the life cycle grew out of his own experiences.

Hopkins, J. R. (1995). Erik Homburger Erikson (1902–1994). *American Psychologist, 50*, 796–797; Wallerstein, R. S. (1995). Erik Erikson (1902–1994). *International Journal of Psycho-Analysis, 76*, 173–175. Obituaries and tributes to Erikson.

Josselson, R. (1996). *Revising herself: The story of women's identity from college to midlife*. New York: Oxford University Press. In an outgrowth of Erikson's theory, this longitudinal account compiled from interviews traces the cultural changes in women's roles and identities in the last third of the 20th century.

McAdams, D. P. (2001). The psychology of life stories. *Review of General Psychology, 5*, 100–122. Explores the idea that identity is a life story; we construct changing self-narratives over the life span to give meaning and purpose to our existence.

Snarey, J. (1993). *How fathers care for the next generation: A four-decade study*. Cambridge, MA: Harvard University Press. Reports and analyzes a 30-year study of fatherhood and generativity conducted within the framework of Erikson's psychosocial theory of development.

PART FOUR

The Trait Approach: The Genetics of Personality

A trait is a distinguishing personal characteristic or quality. In our daily lives, we frequently use the trait approach to describe the personality of people we know. We tend to select outstanding characteristics or features to summarize what a person is like. We may say, "Alyssa is very self-assured," or "Kito is so competitive," or "Mohammed is really smart."

Grouping people by traits is easy and has a commonsense appeal, which may explain why the trait approach to personality has been popular for so long. Trait classifications date from the time of the Greek physician Hippocrates (460–377 B.C.), more than 2,000 years before the theories described in this book. Hippocrates distinguished four types of people: happy, unhappy, temperamental, and apathetic. The causes of these different types were internal bodily fluids, or "humors." He believed that these personality traits were constitutionally based, determined by biological functioning rather than by experience or learning.

In the 1940s, American physician William Sheldon (1899–1977) offered another constitutionally based personality typology, based on body build (see Figure 7.1). He proposed three body types, each associated with a different temperament (Sheldon, 1942). Like the approach taken by Hippocrates, Sheldon's work considers personality traits or characteristics to be largely fixed, that is, constant and unvarying regardless of the situations in which we find ourselves.

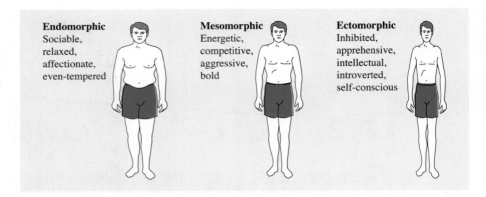

Figure 7.1
The body types and personality characteristics proposed by Sheldon. The theory has not been supported by research.

Endomorphic
Sociable, relaxed, affectionate, even-tempered

Mesomorphic
Energetic, competitive, aggressive, bold

Ectomorphic
Inhibited, apprehensive, intellectual, introverted, self-conscious

Some personality psychologists criticized the notion that personality consists of distinct traits. They argued instead that if individual traits are sufficient to explain personality, then people will behave consistently in all situations. This idea is not supported by research or by our own experiences in dealing with other people. As we all know, human behavior tends to vary with the situation.

Participants in that debate sometimes overlooked the fact that later trait theorists, notably Gordon Allport and Raymond Cattell, never implied a cross-situational consistency in human behavior. Indeed, both theorists took into account the effect on behavior of specific events and of environmental and social influences. Theirs was an interactionist approach, recognizing that behavior is a function of the interaction between both personal and situational variables.

The trait approach to personality remains vital. The field begun by Allport and Cattell several decades ago is central to the study of personality today. These theorists differed from most of the others we have discussed in one important respect. Their insights are not based on the psychotherapeutic approach using case studies or interviews with emotionally disturbed patients on a couch or in a clinic. Instead, they studied personality by observing emotionally healthy persons in an academic laboratory setting. Beyond that similarity, and the fact that their goal was to identify personality traits, Allport and Cattell each approached their study differently. (Allport may also be considered within the humanistic framework because he focused on the total human being and the innate potential for growth and self-realization.)

Allport and Cattell agreed on the importance of genetic factors in the formation of traits. A growing body of research evidence supports the notion that personality traits are influenced by inherited biological factors. In other words, there appears to be a significant genetic component to personality. After describing the theories of Allport and Cattell we discuss the work of Hans Eysenck, the five-factor model, and the temperament theory.

CHAPTER 7

Gordon Allport: Motivation and Personality

As the individual matures, the bond with the past is broken.

—GORDON ALLPORT

During a career that spanned more than four decades, Gordon Allport became one of the most stimulating and provocative psychologists to study personality. Along with Henry Murray, Allport made personality an academically respectable topic. Psychoanalysis and the personality theories that derived from it were not considered part of mainstream scientific psychology. The systematic, formal study of personality was not recognized by the psychology establishment until the 1930s.

In 1937, Allport published *Personality: A Psychological Interpretation*. The book was an immediate success and became a landmark in the study of personality. Thus, Allport served two purposes: He helped bring personality into the mainstream and he formulated a theory of personality development in which traits play a prominent role.

Allport disputed Sigmund Freud's psychoanalysis on several points. First, Allport did not accept the notion that unconscious forces dominate the personality of normal, mature adults. He suggested that emotionally healthy people function in rational and conscious terms, aware and in control of many of the forces that motivate them. According to Allport, the unconscious is important only in neurotic or disturbed behavior.

Second, with regard to historical determinism—the importance of the past in determining the present—Allport said that we are not prisoners of childhood conflicts and past experiences, as Freud believed. Rather, we are guided more by the present and by our view of the future. Allport wrote that people are "busy leading their lives into the future, whereas psychology, for the most part, is busy tracing them into the past" (Allport, 1955, p. 51).

Third, Allport opposed collecting data from emotionally disturbed persons. Whereas Freud saw a continuum between normal and abnormal personalities, Allport saw a clear distinction. To Allport, the abnormal personality functioned at an infantile level. The only proper way to study personality was to collect data from emotionally healthy adults. Other populations—such as neurotics, children, and animals—should not be compared with normal adults. No functional similarity in personality existed between child and adult, abnormal and normal, or animal and human.

Another distinguishing feature of Allport's theory is his emphasis on the uniqueness of personality as defined by each person's traits. Allport opposed the traditional scientific emphasis on forming general constructs or laws to be applied universally. He argued that personality is not general or universal but is particular and specific to the individual.

The Life of Allport (1897–1967)

Isolation and Identity

Born in Montezuma, Indiana, Allport was the youngest of four sons. His mother was a teacher and his father was a salesman who decided to become a doctor. They were in such dire financial circumstances while the elder Allport attended medical school in Baltimore that he smuggled drugs from Canada into the United States and sold them to support the family. When the law came knocking on the front door, he skipped out the back and escaped over a fence. He took the family to Indiana and opened a private practice. Allport believed that his own birth there was his father's first case.

The piety and devout religious beliefs and practices of Allport's mother dominated the household. No smoking, drinking, dancing, or card playing were permitted, nor could a family member wear bright colors, distinctive clothing, or jewelry of any kind. Allport wrote that his mother was "on the severe side with a strong sense of right and wrong and quite strict in her moral ideals" (quoted in Nicholson, 2003, p. 17).

Too young to be a playmate to his older brothers, Allport was isolated from children outside the family as well. He recalled, "I fashioned my own circle of activities. It was a select circle, for I never fitted the general boy assembly" (Allport, 1967, p. 4). He later wrote, "I suffered agonies on the playground. I never really got on with my brothers. They didn't like me and they weren't kind and I couldn't possibly compete with them. They were all a little more masculine in type than I was" (quoted in Nicholson, 2003, p. 25). He described himself as skillful with words but not at sports or games and as someone who worked hard to be the center of attention of the few friends he did have.

In Allport's personality theory, one of the major propositions is that psychologically healthy adults are unaffected by childhood events. Perhaps reflecting this belief, Allport revealed little information about his childhood years. What he did tell, however, demonstrates a parallel between his own early experiences and the theory he later developed.

Arising from his childhood conditions of isolation and rejection, Allport developed inferiority feelings for which he attempted to compensate by striving to excel. He wrote about the identity quest that resulted from his inferiority feelings with respect to his brothers and other children. As Allport grew older, he began to identify with his oldest brother, Floyd, perhaps envious of his brother's accomplishments.

Well into adulthood, Gordon Allport continued to feel inferior compared to Floyd, whose achievements he tried to emulate. He followed Floyd to Harvard University and earned a Ph.D. in psychology, as Floyd had done. Floyd became a noted social psychologist, and even when Gordon was becoming well known himself in the field, the feelings of being in his brother's shadow persisted. At the age of 31, Gordon wrote that he had "published several articles of no great importance and [was] not to be confused with my more eminent brother" (quoted in Nicholson, 2003, pp. 168–169).

The attempt to emulate Floyd may have threatened Gordon's sense of identity. To assert his individuality, Gordon Allport may have been motivated to refute his identification with Floyd by declaring in his personality theory that his adult motives and interests were independent of his childhood feelings. He later formalized this idea as the concept of functional autonomy.

College Years

Although Allport ranked second in his high school graduating class of 100, he admitted to being uninspired about what to do next. At the end of the summer of 1915, he applied to Harvard and was accepted. He wrote, "Overnight my world was remade." Allport's college years were a great adventure for him as he discovered new frontiers of intellect and culture. But shocked by low grades on his first exams, he doubled his efforts and finished the year with straight A's. Allport's interest in social ethics and social service, acquired from his parents, was reinforced at Harvard. He did volunteer work for a boy's club, a group of factory workers, and a contingent of foreign students. He also worked as a probation officer. He found these activities satisfying because he genuinely liked to help people. "It gave me a feeling of competence, to offset a generalized inferiority feeling." He believed this kind of service reflected his search for an identity (Allport, 1967, pp. 5–7).

He took undergraduate courses in psychology but at that time did not intend to pursue a career in the field. He graduated in 1919 with a bachelor's degree, on the same day Floyd received his Ph.D. After graduation, Gordon spent a year on the faculty of Robert College in Istanbul, Turkey, and later accepted the fellowship Harvard offered for graduate study in psychology. His biographer noted, "The thought of becoming a psychologist and perhaps becoming more like his successful brother appealed to Allport" (Nicholson, 2003, p. 67).

The Meeting with Freud

On his return trip to the United States, Allport stopped in Vienna, Austria, to see one of his brothers. While there, he sent a note to Sigmund Freud and received an invitation to visit the great man. When Allport entered Freud's office, he found Freud waiting patiently, expecting the young American to explain the purpose of his visit. The awkward period of silence lengthened until an uncomfortable Allport blurted out an account of an incident he had witnessed on the streetcar ride to Freud's office. He told of watching a small boy who had an obvious fear of dirt. Everything seemed dirty to the child. He even changed his seat, telling his mother not to let a dirty man sit beside him.

Freud studied the prim, proper, carefully groomed young man and asked, "Was that little boy you?" By asking this question, Freud was expressing his belief that the story Allport told betrayed his own unconscious fears and conflicts. Allport appeared to Freud to be "neat, meticulous, orderly and punctual—possessing many of the characteristics [he] associated . . . with the compulsive personality" (Pervin, 1984, p. 267). Henry Murray later commented that "Freud just hit [Allport] right on the head, right on the nose" (quoted in J. W. Anderson, 1990, p. 326).

Allport was shaken by Freud's question. For the rest of his life, Allport denied that he was the super-clean, proper little boy in the story but the incident clearly left a deep impression on him. Years later he wrote, "My single encounter with Freud was traumatic" (Allport, 1967, p. 22). He suspected that psychoanalysis probed the unconscious too deeply, as Freud tried to do with him. Psychology, Allport decided, should pay more attention to conscious or visible motivations. This was the path he chose for his study of personality.

The Study of Traits

Allport completed his Ph.D. at Harvard in 1922, after two years of graduate study. His dissertation, "An Experimental Study of the Traits of Personality," foreshadowed his lifelong work and was the first research conducted on personality traits in the United States. Awarded a traveling fellowship, Allport spent 2 years studying with noted psychologists in Germany and England. He returned to Harvard as an instructor, offering a course on the psychological and social aspects of personality, probably the first formal American college course on the subject. He spent nearly four decades at Harvard, conducting research on personality and social psychology and instructing several generations of students.

Considered an elder statesman in the field, Allport received many awards, including the American Psychological Foundation's Gold Medal, the American Psychological Association's Distinguished Scientific Contribution Award, and the presidencies of the American Psychological Association and the Society for the Psychological Study of Social Issues.

 ## Log On

Personality Theories: Gordon Allport

A brief biography of Allport and a lengthy overview of his theory.

For a direct link to this site, log on to the student companion site for this book at http://www.academic.cengage.com/psychology/Schultz and choose Chapter 7.

The Nature of Personality

In his book *Pattern and Growth in Personality*, Allport reviewed some 50 definitions of personality before offering his own. "Personality is the dynamic organization within the individual of those psychophysical systems that determine . . . characteristic behavior and thought" (Allport, 1961, p. 28).

By *dynamic organization*, Allport means that although personality is constantly changing and growing, the growth is organized, not random. *Psychophysical* means that personality is composed of mind and body functioning together as a unit; personality is neither all mental nor all biological. By *determine*, Allport means that all facets of personality activate or direct specific behaviors and thoughts. The phrase *characteristic behavior and thought* means that everything we think and do is characteristic, or typical, of us. Thus, each person is unique.

Heredity and Environment

To support his emphasis on the uniqueness of the individual personality, Allport stated that we reflect both our heredity and our environment. Heredity provides the personality with raw materials (such as physique, intelligence, and temperament) that may be shaped, expanded, or limited by the conditions of our environment. In this way, Allport invokes both personal and situational variables to denote the importance of both genetics and learning. However, our genetic background is responsible for the major portion of our uniqueness. An infinite number of possible genetic combinations exist, and, except for identical twins, the chance that someone else's genetic endowment will be duplicated in any one of us is too small to consider.

Our genetic endowment interacts with our social environment, and no two people, not even siblings reared in the same house, have precisely the same environment. The inevitable result is a unique personality. Therefore, Allport concluded that to study personality, psychology must deal with the individual case and not with average findings among groups.

Two Distinct Personalities

Allport considered personality to be discrete, or discontinuous. Not only is each person distinct from all others, but each adult is also divorced from his or her past. He found no continuum of personality between childhood and adulthood. Primitive biological urges and reflexes drive infant behavior, whereas adult functioning is more psychological in nature. In a sense there are two personalities: one for childhood and one for adulthood. The adult personality is not constrained by childhood experiences.

Thus, we have Allport's unique view of the nature of personality. He emphasized the conscious rather than the unconscious, the present and future rather than the past. He recognized the uniqueness of personality rather than proposing generalities or similarities for large groups of people. And he chose to study the normal rather than the abnormal personality.

Personality Traits

traits
To Allport, distinguishing characteristics that guide behavior. Traits are measured on a continuum and are subject to social, environmental, and cultural influences.

Allport considered personality **traits** to be predispositions to respond, in the same or a similar manner, to different kinds of stimuli. In other words, traits are consistent and enduring ways of reacting to our environment. He summarized the characteristics of traits as follows (Allport, 1937):

1. Personality traits are real and exist within each of us. They are not theoretical constructs or labels made up to account for behavior.
2. Traits determine or cause behavior. They do not arise only in response to certain stimuli. They motivate us to seek appropriate stimuli, and they interact with the environment to produce behavior.
3. Traits can be demonstrated empirically. By observing behavior over time, we can infer the existence of traits in the consistency of a person's responses to the same or similar stimuli.
4. Traits are interrelated; they may overlap, even though they represent different characteristics. For example, aggressiveness and hostility are distinct but related traits and are frequently observed to occur together in a person's behavior.
5. Traits vary with the situation. For example, a person may display the trait of neatness in one situation and the trait of disorderliness in another situation.

Initially, Allport proposed two types of traits: individual and common. *Individual traits* are unique to a person and define his or her character. *Common traits* are shared by a number of people, such as the members of a culture. It follows that people in different cultures will have different common traits. Common traits are also likely to change over time as social standards and values change. This demonstrates that common traits are subject to social, environmental, and cultural influences.

Personal Dispositions

personal dispositions
Traits that are peculiar to an individual, as opposed to traits shared by a number of people.

Because Allport realized that some confusion could result from calling both of these phenomena *traits*, he later revised his terminology. He relabeled common traits as **traits** and individual traits as **personal dispositions**. Our personal dispositions do not all have the same intensity or significance. They may be cardinal traits, central traits, or secondary traits.

A **cardinal trait** is so pervasive and influential that it touches almost every aspect of a person's life. Allport described it as a ruling passion, a powerful force that dominates behavior. He offered the examples of sadism and chauvinism. Not everyone has a ruling passion, and those who do may not display it in every situation.

cardinal traits
The most pervasive and powerful human traits.

Everyone has a few **central traits**, some 5 to 10 themes that best describe our behavior. Allport's examples are aggressiveness, self-pity, and cynicism. These are the kinds of characteristics we would mention when discussing a friend's personality or writing a letter of recommendation.

central traits
The handful of outstanding traits that describe a person's behavior.

The least influential individual traits are the **secondary traits**, which appear much less consistently than cardinal and central traits. Secondary traits may be so inconspicuous or weak that only a close friend would notice evidence of them. They may include, for example, a minor preference for a particular type of music or for a certain food.

secondary traits
The least important traits, which a person may display inconspicuously and inconsistently.

Habits and Attitudes

As Allport developed his system, he argued that traits and personal dispositions are distinct from other characteristics, such as habits and attitudes. He agreed, however, that habits and attitudes are also capable of initiating and guiding behavior.

habits
Specific, inflexible responses to specific stimuli; several habits may combine to form a trait.

You have only to consider your own **habits** to see how they influence the way you behave. Habits have a more limited impact than traits and personal dispositions because they are relatively inflexible and involve a specific response to a specific stimulus. Traits and personal dispositions are broader because they arise from the integration of several habits that share some adaptive function. In this way, habits may combine to form a single trait.

Children learning to brush their teeth or wash their hands before eating illustrate Allport's point. After a while these behaviors become automatic, or habitual. Taken together, these habits are directed toward the same purpose and form the trait we label *cleanliness*.

attitudes
To Allport, attitudes are similar to traits. However, attitudes have specific objects of reference and involve either positive or negative evaluations.

It is more difficult to explain the difference between traits and **attitudes**. Consider patriotism: Is it a trait fostered by the traditions of a culture, or is it an attitude toward one's nation? Authoritarianism and extraversion could also be labeled both traits and attitudes. Allport did not resolve the question except to note that both categories would be appropriate.

However, it is possible to distinguish between traits and attitudes in two general ways. First, attitudes have some specific object of reference. A person has an attitude toward something, for example, toward red-haired people, a musical group, or a brand of athletic shoe. A trait or personal disposition is not specifically directed toward a single object or category of objects. A person with the personal disposition of shyness will interact with most other people in the same way, regardless of their hair or shoes. Therefore, traits are broader in scope than attitudes.

Second, attitudes are positive or negative, for something or against it. They lead a person to like or hate, to accept or reject, to approach or avoid an object. Unlike a trait or personal disposition, an attitude involves a judgment or evaluation.

Motivation: The Functional Autonomy of Motives

Allport believed that the central problem for any personality theory is how it treats the concept of motivation. Allport emphasized the influence of a person's present situation not only in his personality theory but also in his view of motivation. It is the individual's current state that is important, not what happened in the past during toilet training, schooling, or some other childhood crisis. Whatever happened in the past is exactly that: *past*. It is no longer active and does not explain adult behavior unless it exists as a current motivating force.

Cognitive processes—that is, our conscious plans and intentions—are a vital aspect of our personality. Allport criticized approaches such as Freud's that focused on unconscious, irrational forces at the expense of the conscious and rational. Deliberate intentions are an essential part of our personality. What we want and what we strive for are the keys to understanding our behavior. Thus, Allport attempted to explain the present in terms of the future rather than in terms of the past.

functional autonomy of motives
The idea that motives in the normal, mature adult are independent of the childhood experiences in which they originally appeared.

Allport's concept of **functional autonomy** proposes that the motives of mature, emotionally healthy adults are not functionally connected to the prior experiences in which they initially appeared. Forces that motivated us early in life become autonomous, or independent, of their original circumstances. Similarly, when we mature, we become independent of our parents. Although we remain related to them, we are no longer functionally dependent on them and they should no longer control or guide our life. Allport offered the example of a tree. It is obvious that the tree's development can be traced to its seed. Yet when the tree is fully grown, the seed is no longer required as a source of nourishment. The tree is now self-determining, no longer functionally related to its seed.

Consider new college graduates embarking on a career in business and motivated to work hard to achieve financial success. Eventually their investment of time and energy pays off, and they amass enough money to be able to retire by age 50. Yet they continue to work just as hard as they did when first hired. Such behavior can no longer be for the same goal—the goal of financial security has been reached and surpassed. The motivation to work hard, once a means to a specific end (for money), has now become an end in itself. The motive has become independent of its original source.

We are all familiar with similar instances: the skilled craftsperson who insists on doing a meticulous job even when the extra effort brings in no additional monetary reward, or the miser who chooses a life of poverty while hoarding vast wealth. The behavior that once satisfied a specific motive now serves only itself. The original motive has been transformed into something autonomous. Therefore, adult motives cannot be understood by exploring a person's childhood. The only way to understand them is to investigate why people behave as they do today.

Perseverative Functional Autonomy

perseverative functional autonomy
The level of functional autonomy that relates to low-level and routine behaviors.

Allport proposed two levels of functional autonomy: perseverative functional autonomy and propriate functional autonomy. **Perseverative functional autonomy**, the more elementary level, is concerned with such behaviors as addictions and repetitive physical actions such as habitual ways of performing some everyday task. The behaviors continue or persevere on their own without any external reward. The actions once served a purpose but no longer do so and are at too low a level to be considered an integral part of personality.

Allport cited both animal and human examples as evidence for perseverative functional autonomy. When a rat that has been trained to run a maze for food is given more than enough food, it may still run the maze, but obviously for some purpose other than the food. At the human level, consider our preference for routine, familiar behaviors we maintain even in the absence of external reinforcement.

Propriate Functional Autonomy

propriate functional autonomy
The level of functional autonomy that relates to our values, self-image, and lifestyle.

proprium
Allport's term for the ego or self.

Propriate functional autonomy is more important than perseverative functional autonomy and is essential to understanding adult motivation. The word *propriate* derives from **proprium**, Allport's term for the ego or self. Propriate motives are unique to the individual. The ego determines which motives will be maintained and which will be discarded. We retain motives that enhance our self-esteem or self-image. Thus, a direct relationship exists between our interests and our abilities: We enjoy doing what we do well.

The original motivation for learning a skill such as playing the piano may have nothing to do with our interests. For example, in childhood we may be forced to take piano lessons and to practice. As we become proficient, we may become more committed to playing the piano. The original motive (fear of parental displeasure) has disappeared, and the continued behavior of playing the piano becomes necessary to our self-image.

Our propriate functioning is an organizing process that maintains our sense of self. It determines how we perceive the world, what we remember from our experiences, and how our thoughts are directed. These perceptual and cognitive processes are selective. They choose from the mass of stimuli in our environment only those that are relevant to our interests and values. This organizing process is governed by the following three principles:

- Organizing the energy level
- Mastery and competence
- Propriate patterning

The first principle, *organizing the energy level*, explains how we acquire new motives. These motives arise from necessity, to help consume excess energy that we might otherwise express in destructive and harmful ways. For example, when people retire from their jobs, they have extra time and energy that, ideally, they should direct toward new interests and activities.

Mastery and competence, the second principle, refers to the level at which we choose to satisfy motives. It is not enough for us to achieve at an adequate level. Healthy, mature adults are motivated to perform better and more efficiently, to master new skills, and to increase their degree of competence. The third principle, *propriate patterning*, describes a striving for consistency and integration of the personality. We organize our perceptual and cognitive processes around the self, keeping what enhances our self-image and rejecting the rest. Thus, our propriate motives are dependent on the structure or pattern of the self.

Allport noted that not all behaviors and motives could be explained by the principles of functional autonomy. Some behaviors—such as reflexes, fixations, neuroses, and behaviors arising from biological drives—are not under the control of functionally autonomous motives.

Personality Development in Childhood: The Unique Self

As we noted, Allport chose the term *proprium* for the self or ego. He rejected the words *self* and *ego* because of the diversity of meanings ascribed to them by other theorists. We can best understand the word *proprium* by considering it in the sense of the adjective *appropriate*. The proprium includes those aspects of personality that are distinctive and thus appropriate to our emotional life. These aspects are unique to each of us and unite our attitudes, perceptions, and intentions.

Stages of Development

Allport described the nature and development of the proprium over seven stages from infancy through adolescence (see Table 7.1).

Before the proprium begins to emerge, the infant experiences no self-consciousness, no awareness of self. There is not yet a separation of "me" from everything else. Infants receive sensory impressions from the external environment and react to them automatically and reflexively, with no ego to mediate between stimulus and response. Allport described infants as pleasure seeking, destructive, selfish, impatient, and dependent. He called them "unsocialized horrors." Our genetic inheritance, which is the basis of our eventual personality, does exist in infancy, but there is little of what could be called a "personality." The infant simply is driven by reflexes to reduce tension and maximize pleasure.

The first three stages in the development of the proprium span the years from birth to about age 4. The bodily self develops when infants begin to be aware of what Allport referred to as a "bodily me." For example, infants begin to distinguish between their own fingers and the object they are grasping. Next, the self-identity stage is marked by a sense of continuity of one's identity. Children realize that they remain the same people, despite changes in their bodies and their abilities. Self-identity is

Table 7.1 **The development of the proprium**

Stage	Development
1. *Bodily self*	Stages 1–3 emerge during the first three years. In this stage, infants become aware of their own existence and distinguish their own bodies from objects in the environment.
2. *Self-identity*	Children realize that their identity remains intact despite the many changes that are taking place.
3. *Self-esteem*	Children learn to take pride in their accomplishments.
4. *Extension of self*	Stages 4 and 5 emerge during the fourth through sixth year. In this stage, children come to recognize the objects and people that are part of their own world.
5. *Self-image*	Children develop actual and idealized images of themselves and their behavior and become aware of satisfying (or failing to satisfy) parental expectations.
6. *Self as a rational coper*	Stage 6 develops during ages 6–12. Children begin to apply reason and logic to the solution of everyday problems.
7. *Propriate striving*	Stage 7 develops during adolescence. Young people begin to formulate long-range goals and plans.
Adulthood	Normal, mature adults are functionally autonomous, independent of childhood motives. They function rationally in the present and consciously create their own lifestyles.

enhanced when children learn their name and see themselves as distinct from other people. Self-esteem develops when they discover that they can accomplish things on their own. They are motivated to build, explore, and manipulate objects, behaviors that sometimes can be destructive. If parents frustrate their child's need to explore at this stage, then the emerging sense of self-esteem can be thwarted, replaced by feelings of humiliation and anger.

The extension-of-self stage involves the growing awareness of objects and people in the environment and the identification of them as belonging to the child. Children speak of "my house," "my parents," and "my school." A self-image develops next, incorporating how children see and would like to see themselves. These actual and ideal self-images develop from interaction with the parents, who make the child aware of their expectations and of the extent to which the child is satisfying or failing to satisfy those expectations. The self-extension and self-image stages typically occur between the ages of 4 and 6.

The self as a rational coper stage occurs between ages 6 and 12, when children realize that reason and logic can be applied to solving everyday problems. The propriate striving stage follows, when adolescents begin to formulate plans and goals for the future. Until they do so, their sense of self (their proprium) will remain incomplete.

Parent–Child Interactions

Our social interaction with our parents is vitally important throughout the stages of the development of the proprium. Of particular significance is the infant-mother bond as a source of affection and security. If the mother or primary caregiver provides sufficient

Children develop actual and idealized self-images, reflecting how they actually see and would like to see themselves.

affection and security, the proprium will develop gradually and steadily, and the child will achieve positive psychological growth. Childhood motives will be free to be transformed into the autonomous propriate strivings of adulthood. A pattern of personal dispositions will form and the result will be a mature, emotionally healthy adult.

If childhood needs are frustrated, however, the self will not mature properly. The child becomes insecure, aggressive, demanding, jealous, and self-centered. Psychological growth is stunted. The result is a neurotic adult who functions at the level of childhood drives. Adult motives do not become functionally autonomous but remain tied to their original conditions. Traits and personal dispositions do not develop and the personality remains undifferentiated, as it was in infancy.

The Healthy Adult Personality

In Allport's view, the healthy personality changes from being a biologically dominated organism in infancy to a mature psychological organism in adulthood. Our motivations become separated from childhood and are oriented toward the future. As we noted, if our childhood needs for affection and security have been met, the

Normal, mature adults are functionally autonomous, independent of childhood motives. They function rationally in the present and consciously create their own lifestyles.

© Suzanne Arms/The Image Works

proprium will develop satisfactorily. The adult personality grows out of childhood but is no longer dominated or determined by childhood drives. Allport did not explain whether the neurotic adult could counteract or overcome unfortunate childhood experiences; he was more interested in positive psychological growth. He described six criteria for the normal, mature, emotionally healthy, adult personality:

1. The mature adult extends his or her sense of self to people and to activities beyond the self.
2. The mature adult relates warmly to other people, exhibiting intimacy, compassion, and tolerance.
3. The mature adult's self-acceptance helps him or her achieve emotional security.
4. The mature adult holds a realistic perception of life, develops personal skills, and makes a commitment to some type of work.
5. The mature adult has a sense of humor and self-objectification (an understanding of or insight into the self).
6. The mature adult subscribes to a unifying philosophy of life, which is responsible for directing the personality toward future goals.

By meeting these six criteria, adults can be described as emotionally healthy and functionally autonomous, independent of childhood motives. As a result, they cope with the present and plan for the future without being victimized by the experiences of their early years.

Questions About Human Nature

Allport's conception of functional autonomy and personality development holds that emotionally healthy adults are not tied to or driven by childhood conflicts. Thus, his theory presents an optimistic view of adults in conscious control of their lives, rationally attending to current situations, planning for the future, and actively fashioning an identity. Always in the process of becoming, we creatively design and implement an appropriate style of life, influenced more by events of the present and plans for the future than by our past.

Allport took a moderate stance on the question of free will versus determinism. He granted free choice in our deliberations about our future, but he also recognized that some behaviors are determined by traits and personal dispositions. Once these behaviors are formed, they are difficult to change. On the nature–nurture issue, he believed that both heredity and environment influence personality. Our genetic background explains a significant portion of personality, supplying our basic physique, temperament, and level of intelligence. These raw materials are shaped by learning and experience. Allport believed in each person's uniqueness. Although common traits show some universality in behavior, individual traits or personal dispositions describe our nature more precisely.

To Allport, the ultimate and necessary goal of life is not to reduce tension, as Freud proposed, but rather to increase tension, impelling us to seek new sensations and challenges. When we have met one challenge, we are motivated to seek another. The reward is the process of achieving rather than the specific achievement, striving for the goal rather than reaching it. We require goals to motivate us and to maintain an optimal level of tension in the personality.

Allport's optimistic image of human nature was reflected in his personal liberal stance and his interest in social reform. The humanistic attitude expressed in his work was mirrored in his own personality. His colleagues and students recall that he genuinely cared about people and that these feelings were reciprocated.

Assessment in Allport's Theory

Allport wrote more about personality assessment techniques than most other theorists did. In his popular book *Pattern and Growth in Personality* (1961), he noted that, despite the existence of many approaches to assessment, there was no single best technique. Personality is so complex that to evaluate it we must employ many legitimate techniques. He listed 11 major methods:

- Constitutional and physiological diagnosis
- Cultural setting, membership, and role
- Personal documents and case studies
- Self-appraisal
- Conduct analysis
- Ratings
- Tests and scales
- Projective techniques
- Depth analysis

- Expressive behavior
- Synoptic procedures (combining information from several sources in a synopsis)

Allport relied heavily on the personal-document technique and the Study of Values. He also observed expressive behavior, which we discuss in the section on research.

The Personal-Document Technique

personal-document technique
A method of personality assessment that involves the study of a person's written or spoken records.

The **personal-document technique** involves examining diaries, autobiographies, letters, literary compositions, and other samples of a person's written or spoken records to determine the number and kinds of personality traits. Allport's most famous case is an analysis of a collection of more than 300 letters written over a 12-year period by a middle-aged woman identified as Jenny (Allport, 1965, 1966). It was later revealed that Jenny was the mother of Allport's college roommate and had written the letters to Allport and his wife (Winter, 1993a).

A similar analysis can be performed with third-person material, such as case histories and biographies. In Allport's technique, a group of judges would read the autobiographical or biographical material and record the traits they found in it. Given a reasonable degree of agreement among the judges, the assessments can be grouped into a relatively small number of categories. In the research with Jenny's letters, 36 judges listed nearly 200 traits. Because many terms were synonymous, Allport was able to reduce them to eight categories.

One of Allport's students performed a computer analysis on the letters to find categories of words that might indicate the existence of a particular trait (Paige, 1966). For example, words expressing anger, rage, hostility, and aggression were coded as constituting the trait of aggression. This approach is more sophisticated and quantitative than Allport's original analysis of the letters because it involves fewer subjective judgments. The computer analysis yielded eight prominent traits in Jenny's personality similar to the categories Allport identified. Because of that consistency, Allport concluded that his subjective approach to personality assessment provided information on traits that was valid and comparable to the more objective computer analysis.

The Study of Values

Allport and two colleagues developed an objective self-report assessment test called the Study of Values (Allport, Vernon, & Lindzey, 1960). They proposed that our personal values are the basis of our unifying philosophy of life, which is one of the six criteria for a mature, healthy personality. Our values are personality traits and represent strongly held interests and motivations. Allport believed that everyone possesses some degree of each type of value but one or two will be dominant in the personality. The categories of values are as follows.

1. *Theoretical values* are concerned with the discovery of truth and are characterized by an empirical, intellectual, and rational approach to life.
2. *Economic values* are concerned with the useful and practical.

3. *Aesthetic values* relate to artistic experiences and to form, harmony, and grace.
4. *Social values* reflect human relationships, altruism, and philanthropy.
5. *Political values* deal with personal power, influence, and prestige in all endeavors, not just in political activities.
6. *Religious values* are concerned with the mystical and with understanding the universe as a whole.

 LOG ON

Allport's Study of Values

Try it for yourself. See how you score on a brief test adapted from the Study of Values.

For a direct link to this site, log on to the student companion site for this book at http://www.academic.cengage.com/psychology/Schultz and choose Chapter 7.

Research on Allport's Theory

Allport criticized psychologists who insisted that experimental and correlational methods were the only legitimate research approaches to the study of personality. He argued that not every aspect of personality could be tested in these ways. Therefore, psychologists should be more open and eclectic in their research methodology. He also opposed applying methods used with emotionally disturbed persons (such as case studies and projective techniques) to the study of emotionally healthy persons. Because case studies focus on the past, Allport considered them to be of no value for understanding normal adults because their personality is divorced from childhood influences.

Projective techniques, such as the Thematic Apperception Test and the Rorschach inkblot test, may present a distorted picture of the normal personality because they deal with unconscious forces that have little effect on the normal adult personality. Allport suggested that more reliable information could be obtained by simply asking people to describe themselves, a method that reveals their dominant traits.

Allport favored the idiographic approach—the study of the individual case—as indicated by his use of personal documents. However, he did use nomothetic methods when he believed them to be appropriate. Psychological tests such as the Study of Values employ the nomothetic approach.

expressive behavior
Spontaneous and seemingly purposeless behavior, usually displayed without our conscious awareness.

coping behavior
Consciously planned behavior determined by the needs of a given situation and designed for a specific purpose, usually to bring about a change in one's environment.

Expressive Behavior

Allport conducted considerable research on what he called **expressive behavior**, described as behavior that expresses our personality traits. He also identified **coping behavior**, which is oriented toward a specific purpose and is consciously planned and carried out. Coping behavior is determined by needs inspired by the situation and ordinarily is directed toward bringing about some change in our environment.

Expressive behavior is spontaneous and reflects basic aspects of the personality. In contrast to coping behavior, expressive behavior is difficult to change, has no specific purpose, and is usually displayed without our awareness. Allport offered the example of public speaking. The speaker communicates with the audience on two levels. The formal, planned level (coping behavior) includes the lecture's content. The informal, unplanned level (expressive behavior) consists of the speaker's movements, gestures, and vocal inflections. The speaker may be nervous, talk rapidly, pace, or fidget with an earring. These spontaneous behaviors express elements of his or her personality.

In his landmark study of expressive behavior, Allport gave subjects a variety of tasks to perform and then judged the consistency of their expressive movements over the different situations (Allport & Vernon, 1933). He found a high level of consistency in voice, handwriting, posture, and gestures. From these behaviors, he deduced the existence of such traits as introversion and extraversion.

Research on expressive behavior has become more popular today than it was in Allport's time. There has been considerable theoretical and experimental work describing both facial and vocal expressive behavior (see Russell, Bachorowski, & Fernandez-Dols, 2003). This research has shown that personality can be assessed from audiotapes, films, and videotapes. Facial expressions, vocal inflections, and idiosyncratic gestures and mannerisms reveal personality traits to a trained observer. The expressive behaviors linked to specific traits have even been assessed from still photographs (Allport & Cantril, 1934; Berry, 1990; DePaulo, 1993; Riggio & Friedman, 1986; Riggio, Lippa, & Salinas, 1990).

An analysis of the yearbook photographs of women college graduates found that those who exhibited positive emotional expressions at approximately age 21 scored higher on self-report inventories of feelings of subjective well-being when tested at ages 27, 43, and 52. They also reported better marriages and scored higher in affiliation, competence, and achievement orientation than did those who displayed less positive emotions in their yearbook pictures at age 21 (Harker & Keltner, 2001).

Researchers have accumulated an impressive body of evidence to show that some people can form reliable impressions of a stranger's personality based solely on facial appearance and expression (Berry & Wero, 1993). For example, studies have shown that observers accurately assess personality factors such as anxiety from watching a film of the person as brief as 30 seconds (Ambody & Rosenthal, 1992). In another study, observers formed impressions of strangers by looking at their photographs. The assessments were found to be just as accurate as ratings made by classmates who had known the subjects for several weeks (Berry, 1990). These and similar studies provide strong support for Allport's proposition that expressive behavior reflects personality traits.

A long-term research program conducted by Paul Ekman identified facial expressions of seven emotions that can be objectively and consistently distinguished from one another. These emotions are anger, contempt, disgust, fear, sadness, surprise, and happiness (Ekman, Matsumoto, & Friesen, 1997). Ekman, director of the Human Interaction Laboratory at the University of California at San Francisco, and his colleagues, have developed a coding system based on their analysis of 43 facial muscles. The system provides 3,000 different configurations useful in reading the emotional expressions in a person's face. This Facial Action Coding System (FACS) is currently being used in the United States by police departments, as well as the CIA and the FBI, to detect lying by criminal suspects and by terrorists. According to the FACS, tiny movements of their facial muscles will betray them (Kaufman, 2002).

Other research has shown that some basic aspects of personality are revealed by facial expressions. For example, neuroticism reveals itself in looks of anger, contempt, and fear. Agreeableness shows in laughter and other expressions of friendly social interaction. Extraversion appears in smiles, laughter, and other expressions of enjoyment and amusement. Conscientiousness is marked by expressions of embarrassment including a tightly controlled smile, an averted gaze, and head movements down and away from the observer (Keltner, 1997).

Sometimes our personal experiences can influence our ability to recognize emotions in the facial expressions of other people. For example, a study of 8- to 10-year-old children who had been physically abused showed that they could more readily identify facial displays of anger in pictures of female adults than could a control group of children who had not been abused (Pollak & Sinha, 2002).

Type A behavior, the pattern suggested to be associated with the potential for heart disease, has been distinguished from Type B behavior by expressions of disgust, glaring, grimacing, and scowling (Chesney, Ekman, Friesen, Black, & Hecker, 1997). A study of depressed patients in Switzerland found that facial expressions distinguished those who later attempted suicide from those who did not (Heller & Haynal, 1997). Research on college students in Japan found that those who scored high on a test of anxiety exhibited different facial expressions, particularly around the mouth and the left side of the face, than did those who scored low on anxiety (Nakamura, 2002). These results confirm Allport's ideas.

A study of 76 adults demonstrated that emotional state may influence the ability to read the facial expressions of other people. Those diagnosed with major depression needed to see facial expressions of greater intensity in order to identify correctly happiness on the faces of the pictures they were shown. In contrast, to correctly identify sadness they required less intense facial expressions (Joormann & Gotlib, 2006).

What about the universality of facial expressions? Do the same expressions reveal the same personality factors from one culture to another? The evidence is not consistent. Studies of American and Chinese infants and adults found that some basic emotions were revealed by identical facial expressions in both cultures and in both age groups (Albright et al., 1997; Camras, Oster, Campos, Miyake, & Bradshaw, 1997). However, a study comparing facial expressions of American, Chinese, and Japanese infants reached a different conclusion. Chinese infants showed consistently less variety in facial expressive behavior than American and Japanese infants. American infants differed significantly in facial expressions of emotions from Chinese infants but not so much from Japanese infants (Camras, 1998).

Additional research involving 163 3-year-old girls found that Caucasian-American children smiled more than mainland Chinese or Chinese-American children. The degree of maternal strictness and the number of other children and adults in the home also influenced the intensity of facial expression in those cultures.

The depth to which the girls' faces expressed their emotions was found to vary as a function of both cultural and family characteristics (Camras, Bakeman, Chen, Norris, & Cain, 2006).

If we can accurately interpret the facial expressions of others, can computer recognition be far behind? Apparently not. A computer program has been developed that monitors video images of faces at the rate of 30 frames per second. The computer achieved a high degree of accuracy in recognizing basic emotions including happiness, sadness, fear, disgust, anger, and surprise (Susskind, Littlewort, Bartlett, Movellan, & Anderson, 2007).

And if computers can recognize the emotions expressed in the human face, can they also be used to transmit emotional states? In research involving 158 adolescents in the Netherlands, average age 16, emoticons were used to study the online transmission of personal feelings. (An emoticon—emote + icon—is a shorthand method of conveying feelings; it is widely used in e-mail, chat rooms, and instant messaging.) In simulated chat rooms the teenagers were found to use more emoticons in their communication in a social context than in a task- or job-oriented context. They used more positive icons, such as those representing smiles, in positive situations and more negative icons, such as those representing sadness, in negative situations; the way people do in face-to-face contact. Thus, the researchers concluded that people express emotions in computer-mediated communication in a similar way as in face-to-face situations (Derks, Bos, & Von Grumbkow, 2007).

Reflections on Allport's Theory

Although considerable research has been conducted on expressive behavior, Allport's theory as a whole has stimulated little research to test its propositions. His idiographic research approach ran counter to the main current of thought in contemporary psychology, which accepted nomothetic research instead (the study of large subject groups through sophisticated statistical analysis). Allport's focus on emotionally healthy adults was also at variance with the then prevalent position in clinical psychology, which dealt with the neurotic and psychotic.

It is difficult to translate Allport's concepts into specific terms and operations suitable for study by the experimental method. For example, how do we observe functional autonomy or propriate striving in the laboratory? How can we manipulate them to test their effects or the impact of other variables on them?

Criticisms have been leveled against the concept of functional autonomy. Allport did not make clear how an original motive is transformed into an autonomous one. For example, once a person is financially secure, by what process is the motive to work hard for financial gain altered to become a motive to work hard for the sake of the task itself? If the mechanism of transformation is not explained, how can we predict which childhood motives will become autonomous in adulthood?

Allport's emphasis on the uniqueness of personality has been challenged because his position focuses so exclusively on the individual that it is impossible to generalize from one person to another. Many psychologists find it difficult to accept Allport's proposed discontinuity between child and adult, animal and human, normal and abnormal. They point out that research on the behavior of children, animals, and emotionally disturbed subjects has yielded considerable knowledge about the functioning of the normal, emotionally healthy adult.

Despite these criticisms, Allport's theory has been well received in the academic community. His approach to personality development, his emphasis on uniqueness, and his focus on the importance of goals are reflected in the work of the humanistic psychologists Carl Rogers and Abraham Maslow. Interest in Allport's work has been revived recently as part of the current focus on personality traits, which is providing empirical support for some of his ideas. His books are written in a readable style and his concepts have a commonsense appeal. The emphasis on conscious, rational determinants of behavior provides an alternative to the psychoanalytic position that sees people irrationally and unconsciously driven by uncontrollable forces. Allport's view that people are shaped more by future expectations than by past events is congenial with a hopeful and humanistic philosophy. His most enduring contributions to psychology are making the study of personality academically respectable and emphasizing the role of genetic factors within a trait approach to personality.

Chapter Summary

Gordon Allport focused on the conscious instead of the unconscious. He believed that personality is guided more by the present and future than by the past. He studied normal rather than emotionally disturbed persons. Personality is defined as the dynamic organization within the individual of those psychophysical systems that determine characteristic behavior and thought. It is a product of heredity and environment and divorced from childhood experiences.

Traits are consistent, enduring predispositions to respond in the same or a similar way to different stimuli. Individual traits (personal dispositions) are unique to the person; common traits are shared by many people. Habits are narrower than traits, are relatively inflexible, and involve a specific response to a specific stimulus. Attitudes have specific objects of reference and are for or against something. Cardinal traits are powerful and pervasive; central traits are less pervasive. Secondary traits are displayed less conspicuously and less consistently than other types of traits.

Functional autonomy means that a motive in the normal adult is not functionally related to the past experiences in which it originally appeared. Two levels of functional autonomy are perseverative (behaviors such as addictions and repeated physical movements) and propriate (interests, values, attitudes, intentions, lifestyle, and self-image related to the core of personality). Three principles of propriate functional autonomy are organizing the energy level, mastery and competence, and propriate patterning.

The proprium (self or ego) develops from infancy to adolescence in seven stages: bodily self, self-identity, self-esteem, extension of self, self-image, self as a rational coper, and propriate striving. An infant is controlled by drives and reflexes and has little personality. The mature, healthy adult personality is characterized by an extension of self to other people and activities, a warm relating to others, emotional security, a realistic perception, the development of skills, a commitment to work, self-objectification, and a unifying philosophy of life.

Allport presented an optimistic image of human nature and emphasized the uniqueness of the individual. We are not driven by childhood events. In conscious control of our lives, we creatively design a lifestyle and grow through an inherent need for autonomy, individuality, and selfhood. Our ultimate goal is for increases in tension that impel us to seek new sensations and challenges.

The personal-document approach to personality assessment involves the examination of diaries, letters, and other personal records to uncover personality traits. The Study of Values is a psychological test to assess six types of values. Research on expressive behavior reveals a consistency in expressive facial movements and relates them to a variety of emotions and personality patterns. Some research suggests a consistency of facial expressions from one culture to another and that computer programs can recognize facial expressions and can be used to communicate emotions to others.

Allport's theory has been criticized on the grounds that it is difficult to test empirically such concepts as functional autonomy. Allport's focus on the uniqueness of personality and on the discontinuity between childhood and adult personalities has also been questioned.

Review Questions

1. What were the dominant themes, issues, and problems in Allport's childhood and adolescence?

2. How did Allport's visit to Freud influence his approach to understanding personality?

3. In what ways does Allport's personality theory differ from Freud's?

4. Explain Allport's definition of personality. In Allport's system, how do heredity and environment influence personality?

5. Describe four characteristics of traits. How do traits differ from attitudes?

6. How do cardinal traits, central traits, and secondary traits differ from one another? Which type exerts the most powerful influence on the personality?

7. According to Allport, what is the relationship between personality and motivation?

8. What is propriate functional autonomy? Describe three principles that govern propriate functional autonomy.

9. What is the role of cognitive processes in personality development?

10. What is the relationship between adult motives and childhood experiences?

11. According to Allport, what are the first three stages of human development? Describe briefly the changes that occur at each stage.

12. Define the concept of proprium.

13. What parental behaviors are necessary for a child to achieve positive psychological growth?

14. How does Allport's theory account for emotional disturbances in adulthood?

15. What are the characteristics of the mature, healthy adult personality?

16. Describe Allport's proposed ultimate and necessary goal of life. How do we achieve it?

17. Describe the research findings on how expressive behavior can reveal aspects of our personality.

18. Is there a universality of facial expressions over all cultures or do they vary from one culture to another?

Suggested Readings

Allport, G. W. (1937). *Personality: A psychological interpretation*. New York: Holt. Allport's classic book that established the study of personality as an integral part of scientific academic psychology and defined the focus of personality psychology as the unique individual.

Allport, G. W. (1955). *Becoming: Basic considerations for a psychology of personality*. New Haven, CT: Yale University Press. Outlines Allport's approach to personality, emphasizing the human capacity for growth and development.

Allport, G. W. (1967). Autobiography. In E. G. Boring & G. Lindzey (Eds.), *A history of psychology in autobiography* (Vol. 5, pp. 1–25). New York: Appleton-Century-Crofts. Allport's account of his life and career.

Elms, A. C. (1994). *Uncovering lives: The uneasy alliance of biography and psychology*. New York: Oxford University Press. Chapter 5, "Allport meets Freud and the clean little boy" (pp. 71–84), discusses his 1920 encounter with Sigmund Freud.

Evans, R. I. (1971). *Gordon Allport: The man and his ideas*. New York: Dutton. Interviews with Allport about his life and work.

Harker, L., & Keltner, D. (2001). Expressions of positive emotion in women's college yearbook pictures and their relationship to personality and life outcomes across adulthood. *Journal of Personality and Social Psychology, 80*, 112–124. Explores the idea that positive emotions shown in facial expressions correlate with personality dimensions and with favorable outcomes in marriage and personal well-being.

Rosenzweig, S., & Fisher, S. L. (1997). "Idiographic" vis–à–vis "idiodynamic" in the historical perspective of personality theory: Remembering Gordon Allport, 1897–1997. *Journal of the History of the Behavioral Sciences, 33*, 405–419. Reappraises Allport's focus on the uniqueness of personality and suggests that his spiritual and religious views may have affected his image of human nature.

CHAPTER 8

Raymond Cattell, Hans Eysenck, and Other Trait Theorists

Personality is that which permits a prediction of what a person will do in a given situation.
—RAYMOND CATTELL

Cattell's goal in his study of personality was to predict how a person will behave in response to a given stimulus situation. Cattell made no reference to changing or modifying behavior from undesirable to desirable or from abnormal to normal, which had been the approach of some other personality theorists. These more clinically oriented theorists based their work on case studies of patients who sought a psychologist's services because they were unhappy or emotionally disturbed and wanted to change. In contrast, Cattell's subjects were so-called normal people. His aim was to study their personality, not to treat it. He believed it was impossible, or at least unwise, to attempt to change a personality before understanding fully what was to be modified.

Cattell's theory of personality, then, did not originate in a clinical setting. His approach is rigorously scientific, relying on observations of behavior and masses of data. In Cattell's research, it was not unusual for more than 50 kinds of measurements to be obtained from a single subject. "His theory of personality [was] rivaled by no other in its comprehensiveness and adherence to evidence derived from empirical research" (Horn, 2001, p. 72).

factor analysis
A statistical technique based on correlations between several measures, which may be explained in terms of underlying factors.

The hallmark of Cattell's approach was his treatment of the data. He submitted them to the statistical procedure called **factor analysis**, which involves assessing the relationship between each possible pair of measurements taken from a group of subjects to determine common factors. For example, scores on two different psychological tests or on two subscales of the same test would be analyzed to determine their correlation. If the two measures showed a high correlation, Cattell concluded that they measured similar or related aspects of personality. If the guilt-proneness and introversion subscales of a personality test, let us say, yielded a high correlation coefficient, we could infer that both subscales provided information on the same personality factor. Thus, two sets of data about a person are combined to form a single dimension, or factor, that describes the information provided by both sets of data.

Cattell referred to these factors as *traits*, which he defined as the mental elements of the personality. Only when we know someone's traits can we predict how that person will behave in a given situation. Thus, to understand someone fully, we must be able to describe in precise terms the entire pattern of traits that define that person as an individual.

The Life of Cattell (1905–1998)

Cattell was born in Staffordshire, England, where he had a happy childhood. His parents were exacting about the standards of performance they expected from their children but permissive about how the children spent their time. Cattell and his brothers and friends spent much time outdoors, sailing, swimming, exploring caves, and fighting mock battles. He recalled that they "occasionally drowned or fell over cliffs." When Cattell was 9, England entered World War I. A mansion near his home was converted to a hospital and he remembered seeing trainloads of wounded soldiers returning from the battlefields of France. He wrote that this experience made him unusually serious for a young boy and aware of the "brevity of life and the need to accomplish while one might." His intense dedication to work may have originated from these experiences. He also felt highly competitive with an older brother and wrote of the problems of maintaining his own freedom of development while confronted with this brother who could not be "overcome" (Cattell, 1974a, pp. 62–63).

At age 16, Cattell enrolled at the University of London to study physics and chemistry, graduating with honors in 3 years. His time in London intensified his interest in social problems, but he realized that training in the physical sciences did not equip him to deal with social ills. He decided that the best solution was to master the study of the human mind. This was a courageous decision to make in 1924 because the field of psychology in England offered few professional opportunities and only six academic professorships. It was regarded as a discipline for eccentrics. Against the advice of friends, Cattell began graduate studies at the University of London, working with the eminent psychologist-statistician Charles E. Spearman, who had developed the technique of factor analysis.

Awarded his Ph.D. in 1929, Cattell found that his friends were right. There were few jobs for psychologists. He did some lecturing at Exeter University, wrote a book about the English countryside, and established a psychology clinic for the schools in the city of Leicester, all while pursuing his own research interests. Whereas Spearman had used factor analysis to measure mental abilities, Cattell resolved to apply the method to the structure of personality.

During this period, Cattell developed chronic digestive disorders resulting from overwork, a deficient diet, and being forced to live in a cold basement apartment. His wife left him due to his poor economic prospects and total absorption in his work. However, Cattell did claim some positive benefits to that time of hardship. The experience forced him to focus on practical problems rather than theoretical or experimental issues, which he might have done given more secure and comfortable circumstances. "Those years made me as canny and distrustful as a squirrel who has known a long winter. It bred asceticism, and impatience with irrelevance, to the point of ruthlessness" (Cattell, 1974b, p. 90).

Eight years after he earned his doctoral degree, Cattell finally received an opportunity to work full-time in his chosen field. The prominent American psychologist Edward L. Thorndike invited Cattell to spend a year at Thorndike's laboratory at Columbia University in New York. The following year, Cattell accepted a professorship at Clark University in Worcester, Massachusetts, and in 1941 moved to Harvard, where, he said, the "sap of creativity" rose (Cattell, 1974a, p. 71). His colleagues included Henry Murray, Gordon Allport, and William Sheldon, who was developing his theory of personality and body type. Cattell married a mathematician who shared his research interests, and at the age of 40 settled at the University of Illinois as a research professor. He published more than 500 articles, as well as 43 books, a monumental accomplishment that reflects his dedication and perseverance.

> For the next twenty years, my life was that of a humming dynamo—smooth but powerful. I was generally the last out of the parking lot at midnight. There is a story that I arrived at the laboratory one day to find, to my amazement, not a soul there. I phoned [home] and was told, "We are just sitting down to Thanksgiving dinner." All days were the same to me. (Cattell, 1993, p. 105)

In his 70s, Cattell joined the graduate faculty of the University of Hawaii, where he permitted himself the luxury of swimming in the ocean every day. It was said that he worked "as hard as an assistant professor up for tenure and not sure that it will be granted" (Johnson, 1980, p. 300). He died in Honolulu at the age of 92.

In 1997, Cattell received the Gold Medal Award for Life Achievement in Psychological Science from the American Psychological Association. The citation noted,

> In a remarkable 70-year career, Raymond B. Cattell has made prodigious, landmark contributions to psychology, including factor analytic mappings of the domains of personality, motivation, and abilities. . . . Cattell stands without peer in his creation of a unified theory of individual differences in integrating intellectual, temperamental, and dynamic domains of personality. (Gold Medal Award, 1997, p. 797)

 ## Log On

Key Theorists/Theories in Psychology: Raymond Cattell

Information on Cattell's life and theory, including a 1984 interview with him. Also provides an evaluation of his work.

Raymond B. Cattell: A Memorial

A memorial site dedicated to Cattell by his family. Contains a biography, photographs, awards, eulogies, and obituaries.

For direct links to these sites, log on to the student companion site for this book at http://www.academic.cengage.com/psychology/Schultz and choose Chapter 8.

Cattell's Approach to Personality Traits

traits
To Cattell, reaction tendencies, derived by the method of factor analysis, that are relatively permanent parts of the personality.

Cattell defined **traits** as relatively permanent reaction tendencies that are the basic structural units of the personality. He classified traits in several ways (see Table 8.1).

Common Traits and Unique Traits

common traits
Traits possessed in some degree by all persons.

Cattell distinguished between common traits and unique traits. A **common trait** is one that is possessed by everyone to some degree. Intelligence, extraversion, and gregariousness are examples of common traits. Everyone has these traits, but some people have them to a greater extent than others. Cattell's reason for suggesting that common traits are universal is that all people have a similar hereditary potential and are subject to similar social pressures, at least within the same culture.

unique traits
Traits possessed by one or a few persons.

People differ, as we said, in that they possess different amounts or degrees of these common traits. They also differ because of their **unique traits**, those aspects of personality shared by few other people. Unique traits are particularly apparent in our interests and attitudes. For example, one person may have a consuming interest in genealogy, whereas another may be passionately interested in Civil War battles or baseball or Chinese martial arts.

Table 8.1 **Ways of classifying traits**

Common traits	Everyone shares common traits to some degree; for example, everyone has some measure of intelligence or of extraversion.
Unique traits	Each of us has unique traits that distinguish us as individuals; for example, a liking for politics or an interest in baseball.
Ability traits	Our skills and abilities determine how well we can work toward our goals.
Temperament traits	Our emotions and feelings (whether we are assertive, fretful, or easygoing, for example) help determine how we react to the people and situations in our environment.
Dynamic traits	The forces that underlie our motivations and drive our behavior.
Surface traits	Characteristics composed of any number of source traits, or behavioral elements; they may be unstable and impermanent, weakening or strengthening in response to different situations.
Source traits	Single, stable, permanent elements of our behavior.
Constitutional traits	Source traits that have biological origins, such as the behaviors that result from drinking too much alcohol.
Environmental-mold traits	Source traits that have environmental origins, such as the behaviors that result from the influence of our friends, work environment, or neighborhood.

ability traits
Traits that describe our skills and how efficiently we will be able to work toward our goals.

temperament traits
Traits that describe our general behavioral style in responding to our environment.

dynamic traits
Traits that describe our motivations and interests.

surface traits
Traits that show a correlation but do not constitute a factor because they are not determined by a single source.

Ability, Temperament, and Dynamic Traits

A second way to classify traits is to divide them into ability traits, temperament traits, and dynamic traits. **Ability traits** determine how efficiently we will be able to work toward a goal. Intelligence is an ability trait; our level of intelligence will affect the ways in which we strive for our goals. **Temperament traits** describe the general style and emotional tone of our behavior, for example, how assertive, easygoing, or irritable we are. These traits affect the ways we act and react to situations. **Dynamic traits** are the driving forces of behavior. They define our motivations, interests, and ambitions.

Surface Traits and Source Traits

A third class of traits is surface traits versus source traits according to their stability and permanence. **Surface traits** are personality characteristics that correlate with one another but do not constitute a factor because they are not determined by a single source. For example, several behavioral elements such as anxiety, indecision, and irrational fear combine to form the surface trait labeled neuroticism. Thus, neuroticism does not derive from a single source. Because surface traits are composed of several elements, they are less stable and permanent and therefore less important in describing personality.

source traits
Stable, permanent traits that are the basic factors of personality, derived by the method of factor analysis.

Of greater importance are **source traits**, which are unitary personality factors that are much more stable and permanent. Each source trait gives rise to some aspect of behavior. Source traits are those individual factors derived from factor analysis that combine to account for surface traits.

Constitutional Traits and Environmental-Mold Traits

constitutional traits
Source traits that depend on our physiological characteristics.

Source traits are classified by their origin as either constitutional traits or environmental-mold traits. **Constitutional traits** originate in biological conditions but are not necessarily innate. For example, alcohol intake can lead to behaviors such as carelessness, talkativeness, and slurred speech. Factor analysis would indicate that these characteristics are source traits.

environmental-mold traits
Source traits that are learned from social and environmental interactions.

Environmental-mold traits derive from influences in our social and physical environments. These traits are learned characteristics and behaviors that impose a pattern on the personality. The behavior of a person reared in an impoverished inner-city neighborhood is molded differently from the behavior of a person reared in upper-class luxury. A career military officer shows a different pattern of behavior from a jazz musician. Thus, we see that Cattell recognized the interaction between personal and situational variables.

Source Traits: The Basic Factors of Personality

After more than two decades of intensive factor-analytic research, Cattell identified 16 source traits as the basic factors of personality (Cattell, 1965). These factors are best known in the form in which they are most often used, in an objective personality test called the Sixteen Personality Factor (16 PF) Questionnaire (see Table 8.2).

Cattell presented the traits in bipolar form, and, as you can see, the personality characteristics associated with these traits are expressed in words we are likely to use in everyday conversation when describing our friends and ourselves. No doubt you can tell at a glance whether you score high, low, or somewhere in between on these basic personality factors. Cattell later identified additional factors he designated *temperament traits* because they relate to the general style and emotional tone of behavior. He gave as examples excitability, zest, self-discipline, politeness, and self-assurance (Cattell, 1973; Cattell & Kline, 1977).

It is important to remember that in Cattell's system, source traits are the basic elements of personality just as atoms are the basic units of the physical world. He argued that psychologists cannot understand or generate laws about personality without describing precisely the nature of these elements.

Dynamic Traits: The Motivating Forces

Cattell described dynamic traits as the traits concerned with motivation, which is an important issue in many personality theories. Cattell believed that a personality theory that failed to consider the impact of dynamic, or motivating, forces is incomplete, like trying to describe an engine but failing to mention the type of fuel on which it runs.

Table 8.2 Cattell's source traits (factors) of personality

Factor	Low scorers	High scorers
A	Reserved, aloof, detached	Outgoing, warmhearted, easygoing
B	Low in intelligence	High in intelligence
C	Low ego strength, easily upset, less emotionally stable	High ego strength, calm, emotionally stable
E	Submissive, obedient, docile, unsure, meek	Dominant, assertive, forceful
F	Serious, sober, depressed, worrying	Happy-go-lucky, enthusiastic, cheerful
G	Expedient, low in superego	Conscientious, high in superego
H	Timid, shy, aloof, restrained	Bold, adventurous
I	Tough-minded, self-reliant, demanding	Tender-minded, sensitive, dependent
L	Trusting, understanding, accepting	Suspicious, jealous, withdrawn
M	Practical, down-to-earth, concerned with detail	Imaginative, absentminded
N	Forthright, naïve, unpretentious	Shrewd, worldly, insightful
O	Self-assured, secure, complacent	Apprehensive, insecure, self-reproaching
Q_1	Conservative, holds traditional values, dislikes change	Radical, liberal, experimenting, embraces change
Q_2	Group-dependent, prefers to join and follow others	Self-sufficient, resourceful, independent
Q_3	Uncontrolled, lax, impulsive	Controlled, compulsive, exacting
Q_4	Relaxed, tranquil, composed	Tense, driven, fretful

Ergs and Sentiments

ergs
Permanent constitutional source traits that provide energy for goal-directed behavior. Ergs are the basic innate units of motivation.

Cattell proposed two kinds of dynamic, motivating traits: ergs and sentiments. The word *erg* derives from the Greek word *ergon*, which means work or energy. Cattell used **erg** to denote the concept of instinct or drive. Ergs are the innate energy source or driving force for all behaviors, the basic units of motivation that direct us toward specific goals.

Cattell's factor-analytic research identified 11 ergs. These are:

- anger
- appeal
- curiosity
- disgust
- gregariousness
- hunger
- protection
- security
- self-assertion
- self-submission
- sex

sentiments
To Cattell, environmental-mold source traits that motivate behavior.

Whereas an erg is a constitutional source trait, a **sentiment** is an environmental-mold source trait because it derives from external social and physical influences. A sentiment is a pattern of learned attitudes that focuses on an important aspect of life, such as a person's community, spouse, occupation, religion, or hobby. Both ergs and sentiments motivate behavior, but there is a vital difference between them. Because an erg is a constitutional trait, it is a permanent structure of the personality. It may strengthen or weaken but it cannot disappear. A sentiment, because it results from learning, can be unlearned and can disappear so that it is no longer important to a person's life. (Cattell later called these learned traits SEMS, which stands for Socially Shaped Ergic Manifolds, which may be reason enough for us to continue to call them sentiments.)

Attitudes

attitudes
To Cattell, attitudes are our interests in and emotions and behaviors toward some person, object, or event. This is a broader definition than typically used in psychology.

Cattell defined **attitudes** as our interests in and our emotions and behaviors toward some person, object, or event. As Cattell applied the term, it does not refer exclusively to an opinion for or against something, which is a commonplace usage of the word *attitude*. Cattell's definition is broader, encompassing all our emotions and actions toward an object or situation.

Subsidiation

subsidiation
To Cattell, the relationships among ergs, sentiments, and attitudes, in which some elements are subordinate to others.

Our dynamic traits—the ergs and sentiments—are related to our attitudes through the concept of **subsidiation**, which means that within the personality some elements *subsidiate*, or are subordinate to, other elements. Attitudes are subsidiary to sentiments; sentiments are subsidiary to ergs. Cattell expressed these relationships in a diagram he called the **dynamic lattice** (Figure 8.1). Our motivating forces, the ergs, are listed at the right. Sentiments are indicated in the circles at the center of the diagram. Note that each sentiment is subsidiary to one or more ergs. The attitudes, at the left, show the person's feelings and behaviors toward an object.

dynamic lattice
The representation in a chart or diagram of the relationships among ergs, sentiments, and attitudes.

The Self-Sentiment

self-sentiment
The self-concept, which is the organizer of our attitudes and motivations.

Each person's pattern of sentiments is organized by a master sentiment called the **self-sentiment**. This is our self-concept, reflected in virtually all of our attitudes and behaviors. The self-sentiment provides stability, coherence, and organization to the source traits and is linked to the expression of the ergs and sentiments. It is among the last of the sentiments to reach a full level of development. The self-sentiment contributes to the satisfaction of the dynamic traits and therefore controls all of the structures in the personality.

The Influences of Heredity and Environment

Cattell showed great interest in the relative influences of heredity and environment in shaping personality. He investigated the importance of hereditary and environmental factors by statistically comparing similarities found between twins reared in

Figure 8.1
Fragment of a dynamic lattice showing attitude subsidiation, sentiment structure, and ergic goals.
SOURCE: R. B. Cattell, *Personality: A Systematic Theoretical and Factual Study* (New York: McGraw-Hill, 1950), p. 158. Copyright 1950 by Raymond B. Cattell. Reprinted by permission.

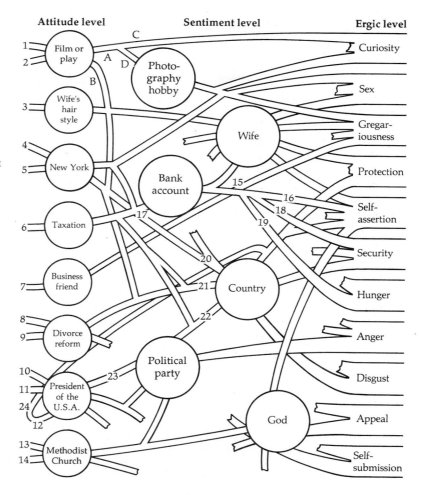

the same family, twins reared apart, non-twin siblings reared in the same family, and non-twin siblings reared apart. Thus, he was able to estimate the extent to which differences in traits could be attributed to genetic or to environmental influences.

The results of his analyses showed that for some traits, heredity plays a major role. For example, Cattell's data suggest that 80 percent of intelligence (Factor B) and 80 percent of timidity-versus-boldness (Factor H) can be accounted for by genetic factors. Cattell concluded that overall, one-third of our personality is genetically based, and two-thirds is determined by social and environmental influences.

Stages of Personality Development

Cattell proposed six stages in the development of personality covering the entire life span (Table 8.3). The period of infancy, from birth to age 6, is the major formative period for personality. The child is influenced by parents and siblings and by the

Table 8.3 Cattell's stages of personality development

Stage	Age	Development
Infancy	Birth–6	Weaning; toilet training; formation of ego, superego, and social attitudes
Childhood	6–14	Independence from parents and identification with peers
Adolescence	14–23	Conflicts about independence, self-assertion, and sex
Maturity	23–50	Satisfaction with career, marriage, and family
Late maturity	50–65	Personality changes in response to physical and social circumstances
Old age	65+	Adjustment to loss of friends, career, and status

experiences of weaning and toilet training. Social attitudes develop along with the ego and the superego, feelings of security or insecurity, attitudes toward authority, and a possible tendency to neuroticism. Cattell was not a follower of Freud's, but he incorporated in his theory several Freudian ideas, namely, that the early years of life are crucial in personality formation, and that oral and anal conflicts can affect personality.

Between ages 6 and 14, the childhood stage of personality formation, there are few psychological problems. This stage marks the beginning of a trend toward independence from parents and an increasing identification with peers. The childhood stage is followed by a more troublesome and stressful stage, adolescence, from 14 to 23. Emotional disorders and delinquency may be evident as young people experience conflicts centered on the drives for independence, self-assertion, and sex.

Adolescence can be a stressful stage of development.

© Richard Hutchings/CORBIS

In late maturity, after one's children have left home, there is often a reexamination of the values of one's life.

The fourth phase of development, maturity, lasts from approximately age 23 to age 50. It is generally a productive, satisfying time in terms of career, marriage, and family situations. The personality becomes less flexible, compared with earlier stages, and thus emotional stability increases. Cattell found little change in interests and attitudes during this period.

Late maturity, ages 50 to 65, involves personality developments in response to physical, social, and psychological changes. Health, vigor, and physical attractiveness may decline and the end of life may be in view. During this phase people reexamine their values and search for a new self. You will recognize here the similarity with Carl Jung's view of the midlife period. The final stage, old age, involves adjustments to different kinds of losses—the death of spouses, relatives, and friends; a career lost to retirement; loss of status in a culture that worships youth; and a pervasive sense of loneliness and insecurity.

Questions About Human Nature

Cattell's definition of personality gives us clues about his view of human nature. He wrote, "Personality is that which permits a prediction of what a person will do in a given situation" (Cattell, 1950, p. 2). For behavior to be considered predictable, it must be lawful and orderly. Prediction would be difficult without regularity and consistency in the personality. For example, one spouse can usually predict with considerable accuracy what the other spouse will do in a given situation because that person's past behavior has been consistent and orderly. Therefore, Cattell's view of human nature admits little spontaneity because that would make predictability more difficult. On the free will versus determinism issue, then, Cattell falls more on the side of determinism.

He did not propose any ultimate or necessary goal that dominates behavior, no drive for self-actualization to pull us, no psychosexual conflicts to push us. Although he noted the impact of early life events, we do not get the impression from his writings that he believed childhood forces determined the personality permanently.

Cattell accepted the influence of both nature and nurture. For example, constitutional traits and ergs are innate, whereas environmental-mold traits are learned. On the uniqueness-universality issue, Cattell took a moderate position, noting the existence of common traits, which apply to everyone in a culture, and unique traits, which describe the individual.

Cattell's personal view of human nature is clearer. In his younger years he was optimistic about our ability to solve social problems. He predicted we would gain greater awareness of and control over our environment. He expected to see the level of intelligence rise, along with the development of "a more gracious community life of creatively occupied citizens" (Cattell, 1974b, p. 88). Reality did not live up to his expectations, and eventually he came to believe that human nature and society had regressed.

Assessment in Cattell's Theory

Cattell's objective measurements of personality used three primary assessment techniques, which he called L-data (life records), Q-data (questionnaires), and T-data (tests).

L-data
Life-record ratings of behaviors observed in real-life situations, such as the classroom or office.

Life records (L-data). The **L-data** technique involves observers' ratings of specific behaviors exhibited by people in real-life settings such as a classroom or office. For example, observers might record frequency of absence from work, grades at school, conscientiousness in performing job duties, emotional stability on the soccer field, or sociability in the office. The important point about L-data is that they involve overt behaviors that can be seen by an observer and occur in a naturalistic setting rather than in the artificial situation of a psychology laboratory.

Q-data
Self-report questionnaire ratings of our characteristics, attitudes, and interests.

Questionnaires (Q-data). The **Q-data** technique relies on questionnaires. Whereas L-data calls for observers to rate the research subjects, Q-data requires subjects to rate themselves. Cattell recognized the limitations of Q-data. First, some research participants may have only superficial self-awareness, so their answers will not reflect the true nature of their personality. Second, even if research participants do know themselves well, they may not want researchers to know them. Therefore, they may deliberately falsify their responses. Because of these problems, Cattell warned that Q-data must not automatically be assumed to be accurate.

T-data
Data derived from personality tests that are resistant to faking.

Personality tests (T-data). The **T-data** technique involves the use of what Cattell called "objective" tests, in which a person responds without knowing what aspect of behavior is being evaluated. These tests circumvent the Q-data's shortcomings by making it difficult for a subject to know precisely what a test is measuring. If you cannot guess what the experimenter is trying to find out, then you cannot distort your responses to conceal your traits. For example, if you were shown an inkblot, you probably would not be able to predict whether the researcher's interpretation of your response revealed that you were conservative, relaxed, adventurous, or apprehensive.

Cattell considered such tests as the Rorschach, the Thematic Apperception Test, and the word association test to be *objective* because they are resistant to faking. However, it is important to note that to most psychologists, this use of the word *objective* is misleading; such tests are usually called *subjective* because of the biases that affect scoring and interpretation.

The 16 PF (Personality Factor) Test

Cattell developed several tests to assess personality. The most notable is the 16 PF, which is based on the 16 major source traits. The test is intended for use with people 16 years of age and older and yields scores on each of the 16 scales. The responses are scored objectively; computerized scoring and interpretation are available. The 16 PF is widely used to assess personality for research, clinical diagnosis, and predicting occupational success. It has been translated into some 40 languages.

Consider the sample 16 PF Test profile for a hypothetical airline pilot (see Figure 8.2). By reading the high and low points of the plot of test scores, we can see that this person is emotionally stable, conscientious, adventurous, tough-minded, practical, self-assured, controlled, and relaxed. The pilot is not tense, apprehensive, or timid.

Figure 8.2
16 PF profile of a hypothetical airline pilot.
SOURCE: Based on Cattell, Eber, and Tatsuoka, 1970.

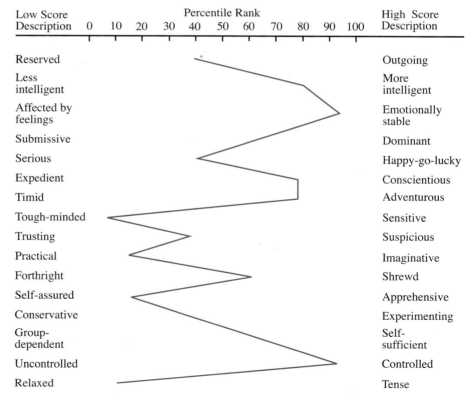

Low Score Description	Percentile Rank	High Score Description
	0 10 20 30 40 50 60 70 80 90 100	
Reserved		Outgoing
Less intelligent		More intelligent
Affected by feelings		Emotionally stable
Submissive		Dominant
Serious		Happy-go-lucky
Expedient		Conscientious
Timid		Adventurous
Tough-minded		Sensitive
Trusting		Suspicious
Practical		Imaginative
Forthright		Shrewd
Self-assured		Apprehensive
Conservative		Experimenting
Group-dependent		Self-sufficient
Uncontrolled		Controlled
Relaxed		Tense

Cattell developed several variations of the 16 PF Test. Scales have been prepared to measure specific aspects of personality—such as anxiety, depression, and neuroticism—and for special purposes such as marriage counseling and performance evaluation of business executives. There are also versions of the test for use with children and with adolescents.

Research on Cattell's Theory

In discussing research methods, Cattell listed three ways to study personality: bivariate, clinical, and multivariate approaches. The *bivariate,* or two-variable, approach is the standard laboratory experimental method. The psychologist manipulates the independent variable to determine its effect on the research participants' behavior (the dependent variable). This approach has also been called *univariate* because only one variable is studied at a time. Cattell agreed that bivariate research is scientific, rigorous, and quantitative but argued that it dealt with only limited aspects of personality. In reality, personality is affected by many interacting variables. Also, in the typical artificial laboratory situation, significant emotional experiences cannot be manipulated and duplicated. Thus, for Cattell, the bivariate approach was too restrictive to reveal much about personality traits.

The *clinical* approach, which includes case studies, dream analysis, free association, and similar techniques, is highly subjective, as we noted in the chapters on the psychoanalytic theorists. These methods do not yield verifiable and quantifiable data. Cattell wrote, "The clinician has his heart in the right place, but perhaps we may say that he remains a little fuzzy in his head" (1959, p. 45).

Cattell chose to study personality through the multivariate approach, which yields highly specific data. It involves the sophisticated statistical procedure of factor analysis. Cattell favored two forms of factor analysis: the R technique and the P technique. The R technique involves collecting large amounts of data from a group of people. Correlations among all the scores are made to determine personality factors or traits. The P technique involves collecting a large amount of data from a single subject over a long period.

Let us consider a few of the hundreds of factor-analytic studies Cattell and his associates conducted. We noted that he was interested in the relative effects on personality of heredity and environment. From a factor analysis of 16 PF data from 3,000 male subjects ages 12 to 18, Cattell concluded that three source traits were determined primarily by heredity (Cattell, 1982). These source traits are Factor F (serious versus happy-go-lucky), Factor I (tough-minded versus tender-minded or sensitive), and Factor Q3 (uncontrolled versus controlled). Three other traits were found to be determined primarily by environmental influences: Factor E (submissive versus dominant), Factor G (expedient versus conscientious), and Factor Q4 (relaxed versus tense).

Cattell also used the 16 PF Test to define the relationship between personality traits and marital stability (Cattell & Nesselroade, 1967). The research participants were married couples identified as having either a stable or an unstable marriage. The criterion for stability was whether a couple had taken steps toward dissolving the marriage. Factor analysis showed that marital stability could be predicted from the test scores. Partners in stable marriages had similar personality traits whereas partners in unstable marriages showed highly different personality traits.

Reflections on Cattell's Theory

Despite Cattell's legitimate claim that factor analysis is an objective, precise technique, critics note that the opportunity exists for subjectivity to affect the outcome. At several stages in the research process, decisions are required that may be influenced by personal preferences. In the initial step of data collection, the researcher must decide which tests to use and what aspects of behavior to measure. He or she then determines which factor-analytic technique to apply and what level of statistical significance will be accepted as appropriate. Once the factors, or traits, have been identified, the researcher labels them. If these names are ambiguous in any way, they may not accurately express the nature of the factors. This criticism does not suggest inherent weaknesses in Cattell's theory but that there is potential for subjective error in the factor-analytic approach. Perhaps it is this very subjectivity that accounts for the difficulty other researchers have in replicating Cattell's findings and confirming his 16 basic source traits.

Cattell organized a huge amount of research, accumulating monumental quantities of experimental data in an area frequently characterized by case histories, intuitions, and speculations. However, the sheer quantity of Cattell's work and the complexity of the factor-analytic method are among the reasons for a general lack of acceptance of his theory.

He understood his failure to persuade other psychologists of the wisdom of his views and defended his approach as the only one of value for studying personality. At the age of 85, he reiterated this point, criticizing contemporary psychologists for failing to master and apply factor analysis and lamenting that his work remained isolated from the mainstream of personality theorizing. He remained convinced that one day his work would allow for the prediction of human behavior with the same degree of accuracy with which astronomers predict the movements of planets (Cattell, 1974a, 1974b, 1990, 1993).

Cattell's publications may be described as widely respected but seldom read, at least in the United States. Sales of his 1970 undergraduate textbook, *The Scientific Analysis of Personality,* were higher in England, Germany, Australia, and Japan. European psychologists tend to rate his theory and research as being of greater relevance to the study of personality than American psychologists do.

Whatever the eventual outcome for Cattell's specific proposals, it is clear that the trait approach to personality and the investigation of genetic influences continue to fascinate contemporary researchers.

Behavioral Genetics

behavioral genetics
The study of the relationship between genetic or hereditary factors and personality traits.

We have mentioned the growing evidence to support the idea that some traits are influenced by hereditary factors. The area of study focusing on the connection between genetics and personality is often called **behavioral genetics.** Regardless of the method used to evaluate or investigate personality, a significant genetic component must be considered. Allport and Cattell were among the first to suggest that inherited factors shape personality and rank in importance with environmental factors. Let us consider other researchers who have pursued this causal connection between genetic inheritance and personality.

Hans Eysenck (1916–1997)

Hans Eysenck was born in Berlin, Germany, and emigrated to England in 1934, after Adolf Hitler came to power in Germany. Eysenck planned to study physics at the University of London but was told that he lacked the requisite academic background. Discouraged, he asked university officials if there was any other science in which he could major. Eysenck recalled, "I was told there was always psychology. 'What on earth is that?' I inquired in my ignorance. 'You'll like it,' they said. And so I enrolled in a subject whose scientific status was perhaps a little more questionable than my advisers realized" (Eysenck, 1980, p. 156). More than 40 years later, the highly successful and productive Eysenck was asked if he had ever regretted his career choice. Often, he noted, but admitted that he was resigned to it.

Over the course of a long, productive career, Eysenck published 79 books, including some for the general public, and 1,097 journal articles. At the time of his death, he was the world's most frequently cited psychologist (Farley, 2000). He developed several personality assessment devices including the Eysenck Personality Inventory, the Eysenck Personality Profiler, the Maudsley Medical Questionnaire, and the Maudsley Personality Inventory. His work has been pivotal in supporting the role of inheritance in the description of personality.

The Dimensions of Personality

Eysenck spent most of his career at the University of London's Maudsley Hospital and Institute of Psychiatry, conducting research on the measurement of personality. He agreed with Cattell that personality is composed of traits, or factors, derived by the factor-analytic method. Nevertheless, Eysenck has been a critic of factor analysis and of Cattell's research because of the potential subjectivity in the technique and the difficulty in replicating Cattell's findings. Although Eysenck used factor analysis to uncover personality traits, he supplemented the method with personality tests and experimental studies that considered a wide range of variables.

Eysenck and his wife, Sybil (Ph.D., University of London), together developed many of the questionnaires used in their research. The Eysenck Personality Inventory (Eysenck & Eysenck, 1963) required 12 years of joint research and 20 factor analyses. Hans Eysenck wrote, "Although published in our joint names, [it] is largely a monument to her skill, patience, and endurance" (Eysenck, 1980, p. 172). Few scientists in any discipline have been so straightforward in acknowledging the research contributions of their spouses.

The result of their efforts is a personality theory based on three dimensions, defined as combinations of traits or factors. We might think of the dimensions as *superfactors* (Eysenck, 1990a, 1990b; Eysenck & Eysenck, 1985). The three personality dimensions are as follows.

E—Extraversion versus introversion
N—Neuroticism versus emotional stability
P—Psychoticism versus impulse control (or superego functioning)

Table 8.4 **Traits of Eysenck's personality dimensions**

Extraversion/introversion	Neuroticism/emotional stability	Psychoticism/impulse control
Sociable	Anxious	Aggressive
Lively	Depressed	Cold
Active	Guilt feelings	Egocentric
Assertive	Low self-esteem	Impersonal
Sensation seeking	Tense	Impulsive
Carefree	Irrational	Antisocial
Dominant	Shy	Creative
Venturesome	Moody	Tough-minded

Eysenck noted that the dimensions of extraversion and neuroticism have been recognized as basic elements of personality since the time of the ancient Greek philosophers. He also suggested that formulations of the same dimensions could be found on nearly every personality assessment device ever developed (Eysenck, 1997).

Consider the list of personality traits associated with Eysenck's three personality dimensions (see Table 8.4). You can see clearly, for example, that people who score high on the traits of the E dimension would be classified as extraverts whereas people who score low would be classified as introverts.

Research has shown that the traits and dimensions Eysenck proposed tend to remain stable throughout the life span from childhood through adulthood, despite the different social and environmental experiences each of us has. Our situations may change but the dimensions remain consistent. For instance, the introverted child tends to remain introverted as an adult.

Eysenck also conducted considerable research on intelligence. Although he did not list intelligence as a personality dimension, he considered it an important influence on personality. He noted that a person with an IQ of 120 is likely to have a more complex and multidimensional personality than is a person with an IQ of 80. He presented evidence to suggest that some 80 percent of our intelligence is inherited, leaving only 20 percent as the product of social and environmental forces (Eysenck & Eysenck, 1985).

 Log On

Personality Theories: Hans Eysenck

A discussion of Eysenck's life and work along with other trait and temperament theories covered in this chapter, including those of Sheldon, Cattell, Buss and Plomin, and the five-factor theory.

For a direct link to this site, log on to the student companion site for this book at http://www.academic.cengage.com/psychology/Schultz and choose Chapter 8.

Extraversion

Based on your own experience, you can probably describe most extraverts and introverts with accuracy. Extraverts are oriented toward the outside world, prefer the company of other people, and tend to be sociable, impulsive, adventurous, assertive, and dominant. In addition, people who score high on extraversion on the Eysenck Personality Inventory have been found to experience more pleasant emotions than those who score low on extraversion (Lucas & Fujita, 2000). Introverts are reported to be the opposite on these characteristics.

Eysenck was interested in how extraverts and introverts might differ biologically and genetically. He found that extraverts have a lower base level of cortical arousal than introverts do. Because the cortical arousal levels for extraverts are low, they need, and actively seek, excitement and stimulation. In contrast, introverts shy away from excitement and stimulation because their cortical arousal levels are already high (Eysenck, 1990b).

As a result, introverts react more strongly than extraverts to sensory stimulation. Studies have shown that introverts exhibit greater sensitivity to low-level stimuli and have lower pain thresholds than extraverts. Other research supports differential responses to sensory stimulation but reports less convincing evidence that such differences can be attributed to variations in cortical arousal levels (Bullock & Gilliland, 1993; Stelmack, 1997). Nevertheless, as Eysenck predicted, these differences are genetically based.

Neuroticism

Consider the traits associated with the neuroticism dimension. As you can see from Table 8.4, neurotics are characterized as anxious, depressed, tense, irrational, and moody. They may have low self-esteem and be prone to guilt feelings. Eysenck suggested that neuroticism is largely inherited, a product of genetics rather than learning or experience. It is expressed in biological and behavioral characteristics that differ from those of people at the emotional stability end of the neuroticism dimension.

Research on 1,130 subjects ages 16–70 conducted in the United States over a 2-year period showed that increasing satisfaction gained from work and social relationships was associated with a lower level of neuroticism and a higher level of extraversion (Scollon & Diener, 2006). Studies in Australia found that people who scored high in neuroticism on the Eysenck Personality Inventory outperformed those who scored low when their work environment was fast-paced and stressful. In other words, this research showed that neurotics seemed to function best in busy situations where they were forced to work harder (Smillie, Yeo, Furnham, & Jackson, 2006).

A study in England showed that people high in neuroticism scored lower on verbal abilities than did people low in neuroticism (Chamorro-Premuzic, Furnham, & Petrides, 2006). And research on more than 4,000 people in Sweden found that those who scored high in neuroticism in middle age were much more likely to show cognitive impairments when tested again 25 years later (Crowe, Andel, Pedersen, Fratiglioni, & Gatz, 2006).

People high in neuroticism seem to have greater activity in the brain areas that control the sympathetic branch of the autonomic nervous system. This is the body's alarm system, which responds to stressful or dangerous events by increasing breathing rate, heart rate, blood flow to the muscles, and release of adrenaline. Eysenck argued that in neurotics, the sympathetic nervous system overreacts even to mild stressors, resulting in chronic hypersensitivity. This condition leads to heightened emotionality in response to almost any difficult situation. Indeed, neurotics react emotionally to events other people consider insignificant. According to Eysenck, these differences in biological reactivity on the neuroticism dimension are innate. People are genetically predisposed either toward neuroticism or toward emotional stability.

Psychoticism

People who score high in psychoticism are aggressive, antisocial, tough-minded, cold, and egocentric. Also, they have been found to be cruel, hostile, and insensitive to the needs and feelings of others. In addition, they are reported to have greater problems with alcohol and drug abuse than people who score low in psychoticism (Sher, Bartholow, & Wood, 2000).

Paradoxically, people who score high in psychoticism can also be highly creative. The research evidence tends to suggest a large genetic component. However, it has also been found that those who scored high in psychoticism had more authoritarian and controlling parents than those who scored low, thus supporting the influence of the childhood environment (Heaven & Ciarrochi, 2006).

Men as a group generally score higher than women do on the psychoticism dimension, but a study of 660 adolescents in Australia found that both boys and girls who were high in psychoticism scored lower on emotional well-being (Ciarrochi & Heaven, 2007). Nevertheless, the findings led Eysenck to suggest that psychoticism may be related to male hormones. He also speculated that people who score high on all three dimensions may be apt to display criminal behavior but cited only modest empirical support for this idea (Eysenck & Gudjonsson, 1989). Research conducted in China has demonstrated a significant positive correlation between criminal behavior and high scores on the psychoticism and neuroticism dimensions (Huo-Liang, 2006).

In Eysenck's view, society needs the diversity provided by people characterized by all aspects of these three personality dimensions. An ideal society affords each person the opportunity to make the best use of his or her traits and abilities. However, some people will adapt to the social environment better than others will. The person high in psychoticism, for example, typified by hostile and aggressive behaviors, may become emotionally disturbed, or exhibit criminal tendencies, or channel the aggressive traits into a socially acceptable enterprise such as coaching college football.

The Primary Role of Heredity

To Eysenck, traits and dimensions are determined primarily by heredity, although the research evidence shows a stronger genetic component for extraversion and neuroticism than for psychoticism. Eysenck did not rule out environmental and situational influences on personality, such as family interactions in childhood, but he believed their effects on personality were limited (Eysenck, 1990a).

His research design involved comparisons of identical (monozygotic) and fraternal (dizygotic) twins. The studies showed that identical twins are more alike in their personalities than are fraternal twins, even when the identical twins were reared by different parents in different environments during childhood. Studies of adopted children demonstrate that their personalities bear a greater similarity to the personalities of their biological parents than of their adoptive parents, even when the children had no contact with their biological parents. This is additional support for Eysenck's idea that personality owes more to our genetic inheritance than to our environment.

Cross-cultural research demonstrates that Eysenck's three personality dimensions have been found consistently in more than 35 nations including the United States, England, Australia, Japan, China, Nigeria, and Sweden (see, for example, Bouchard, 1985; Eaves, Eysenck, & Martin, 1989; Floderus-Myrhed, Pedersen, & Rasmuson, 1980; Martin & Jardine, 1986; Tellegen et al., 1988). The confirmation of the same three personality dimensions in diverse cultures is further evidence for the primacy of inherited factors in the shaping of personality.

Robert McCrae and Paul Costa: The Five-Factor Model

Using the factor-analytic method, the personality traits Cattell and Eysenck derived varies in number. This does not suggest an inherent weakness in the method but instead reflects the way each theorist chose to measure personality. Some personality researchers have expressed dissatisfaction with both theories, suggesting that Eysenck has too few dimensions and Cattell has too many factors. More contemporary work has typically yielded five broad personality factors.

Working at the Gerontology Research Center of the National Institutes of Health in Baltimore, Maryland, Robert McCrae (1949–) and Paul Costa (1942–) embarked on an extensive research program that identified five so-called robust or Big Five factors (McCrae & Costa, 1985b, 1987). These factors are neuroticism, extraversion, openness, agreeableness, and conscientiousness.

The factors were confirmed through a variety of assessment techniques including self-ratings, objective tests, and observers' reports. The researchers then developed a personality test, the NEO Personality Inventory, using an acronym derived from the initials of the first three factors. A shorter version has been developed for research use on the Internet (Buchanan, Johnson, & Goldberg, 2005). The consistent finding of the same factors from different assessment procedures suggests that these factors can be relied on as distinguishing aspects of personality. The five factors and their characteristic traits are listed in Table 8.5.

Other researchers, following the lead provided by McCrae and Costa, developed adjective checklists that have proven to be quicker measures of the five factors. Research subjects typically respond to the lists by selecting the words that best describe themselves. One such list uses 100 adjectives to measure the five factors; another uses only 40. A different approach to measuring the Big Five factors and their personality traits uses a structured interview consisting of 120 items to which research participants respond orally (Trull et al., 1998).

Table 8.5 **McCrae and Costa's Big Five personality factors**

Factor	Description
Neuroticism	Worried, insecure, nervous, highly strung
Extraversion	Sociable, talkative, fun-loving, affectionate
Openness	Original, independent, creative, daring
Agreeableness	Good-natured, softhearted, trusting, courteous
Conscientiousness	Careful, reliable, hardworking, organized

It is important to note that even though other tests have been proposed as ways to measure the Big Five factors, the NEO remains the most frequently used technique. However, research has shown that the results of the NEO, like most personality tests, can be distorted by the deliberate behavior of subjects who want to create the impression of positive psychological adjustment.

You can see a similarity between the extraversion and neuroticism factors of McCrae and Costa and the extraversion and neuroticism dimensions proposed by Eysenck. Further, agreeableness and conscientiousness in the McCrae–Costa model may represent the low end of Eysenck's psychoticism dimension (impulse control). Openness shows a high positive correlation with intelligence. Similarly, agreeableness correlates with Adler's concept of social interest, which we discussed in Chapter 3.

Studies of twins have found that four of the five factors show a stronger hereditary component: neuroticism, extraversion, openness, and conscientiousness. Agreeableness was found to have a stronger environmental component (Bergeman et al., 1993; Pedersen, Plomin, McClearn, & Friberg, 1998).

Cross-Cultural Consistency

The five factors have been consistently observed in Eastern as well as Western cultures, a finding that also supports a genetic component. McCrae and Costa noted that the Big Five factors and their traits appear to represent a "common human structure of personality" that transcends cultural differences (McCrae & Costa, 1997, p. 515). These five factors and their traits have been found in more than 50 diverse nations including Britain, Germany, Portugal, the Czech Republic, Turkey, Israel, China, Korea, Japan, France, the Philippines, Russia, India, Denmark, Italy, Lebanon, and Canada, and among both native-born and Hispanic residents of the United States.

Although the same factors are common to many cultures, major differences have been recognized in their relative importance and social desirability. For example, Australians consider extraversion and agreeableness to be more desirable to have than the other three factors. By contrast, Japanese consider conscientiousness to be more important than all other factors. In other words, in Japanese society it is more important for a person to be conscientious than to be extraverted, agreeable, open, or even emotionally stable.

In Hong Kong and in India, agreeableness was found to be the most important factor. In Singapore, emotional stability was more important, whereas in Venezuela, the primary characteristic to praise is extraversion. No single factor was found to be more significant than others in Chile, Finland, Germany, the Netherlands, Norway, Turkey, and the United States. Overall, Europeans and Americans tended to score higher in extraversion and openness to experience and lower in agreeableness than did Asians and Africans (Allik & McCrae, 2004; McCrae & Terracciano, 2005).

Stability of the Factors

The factors have been detected in children as well as adults. Longitudinal research studying the same people over a 6-year period demonstrated a high level of stability for all five traits (Costa & McCrae, 1988). Persons high in agreeableness as children were likely to remain so as adults. A study in Finland of approximately 15,000 twins, ages 18 to 59, found a high degree of stability for both men and women on extraversion and neuroticism over that 40-year age span (Viken, Rose, Kaprio, & Koskenvuo, 1994). A study of 121 American men and women over 19 years, from late adolescence into adulthood, found modest but statistically significant stability for the extraversion and neuroticism factors (Carmichael & McGue, 1994). A comparison of more than 2,000 American and 789 Belgian adolescents over a 4-year period showed that the factors of extraversion, agreeableness, and conscientiousness remained stable, whereas openness to experience increased for both males and females (McCrae et al., 2002).

More than 3,000 men and women college graduates were tested for extraversion when they were students and again 20 years later. The researchers found a significant positive correlation between the test scores at the two ages, suggesting that those who were extraverted in college remained so at midlife. The study also showed that those who scored high in extraversion were, as expected, more sociable and outgoing than were those who scored low. The high scorers were also more likely than the low scorers to seek social support when faced with stressful situations in midlife (Von Dras & Siegler, 1997).

Another large-scale study comparing measures taken 40 years apart from almost 800 adults in the United States found that the factors of extraversion and conscientiousness remained the most stable over the duration of the research period (Hampson & Goldberg, 2006). Changes in personality over a shorter time period, from adolescence to adulthood, as studied in the Czech Republic and in Russia, showed that neuroticism, extraversion, and openness to experience declined during those years, whereas agreeableness and conscientiousness rose (McCrae et al., 2004a, 2004b). Research on 865 adults in Germany in their 40s and 60s showed that neuroticism declined from the earlier decade to the later one (Allemand, Zimprich, & Hertzog, 2007).

In another study, preschool teachers were asked to predict what their students, then ages 3 to 6 years, would be like in 20 years' time. Their expectations, based on observations of the children's behavior, corresponded with the students' scores on the Big Five personality factors. These results suggest that the teachers assumed that preschool behavior would be closely related to adult behavior (Graziano, Jensen-Campbell, & Sullivan-Logan, 1998).

This raises the question whether such expectations lead teachers and parents to reinforce certain behaviors to strengthen genetically based personality characteristics. Would caregivers treat extraverted children differently from introverted children, for example, thus strengthening each group's differential inherited behavioral tendencies?

Emotional Correlates

In a number of studies, extraversion was positively related to emotional well-being (see, for example, Heller, Watson, & Hies, 2004; Lischetzke & Eid, 2006). Neuroticism has been negatively related to emotional well-being. Researchers have concluded that people high in extraversion and low in neuroticism were genetically predisposed to emotional stability (Costa & McCrae, 1984; Watson, Clark, McIntyre, & Hamaker, 1992). A study of 100 men and women college students found that those high in extraversion were able to cope with everyday life stress better than those scoring low in extraversion did. Extraverts were also more likely to seek social support to help them deal with stress (Amirkhan, Risinger, & Swickert, 1995).

This agrees with the finding reported earlier that extraverts at midlife were more likely to seek social support in coping with stressful life events. It has also been found that the depression facet of neuroticism and the positive emotions/cheerfulness facet of extraversion are the most consistent predictors of general life satisfaction and emotional well-being (Schimmack, Oishi, Furr, & Funder, 2004).

Studies of college students in the United States found that those who scored high in extraversion enjoyed higher status and prominence among their peers than those who scored low in extraversion (Anderson, John, Keltner, & Kring, 2001). Those high in extraversion rated social situations as positive only if the situation was pleasant, indicating the importance of positive emotions in the factor of extraversion (Lucas & Diener, 2001).

Other research with college students found that over a 4-year period, extraverts were likely to experience a greater number of positive events, such as a good grade, a pay raise, or marriage. Students scoring high in neuroticism were more predisposed to negative events such as illness, weight gain, traffic tickets, or rejection by graduate school (Magnus, Diener, Fujita, & Pavot, 1993). Research on more than 1,000 adults in the United States, ages 25 to 74, found that everyday life stressors had significantly higher negative emotional effects for the people who scored high in neuroticism (Mroczek & Almeida, 2004).

A study in Sweden of 320 pairs of identical and fraternal twins reared together and apart confirmed the relationship for women between personality variables and desirable life events. Women who scored high on extraversion and openness to experience were significantly more likely to experience positive life events. Women who scored high on neuroticism were significantly more likely to experience negative life events (Saudino, Pedersen, Lichtenstein, McClearn, & Plomin, 1997).

In another study, persons high in agreeableness and conscientiousness showed greater emotional well-being than persons low in these traits (McCrae & Costa, 1991). Other researchers found that people high in neuroticism were prone to depression, anxiety, and self-blame (Jorm, 1987; Parkes, 1986). More physical illness and psychological distress has been associated with high scores on the neuroticism factor (DeRaad, 2000; Larsen & Kasimatis, 1991; Ormel & Wohlfarth, 1991). A study of 174 male and female patients with chronic renal insufficiency (a kidney disorder), conducted over a 4-year period, found that those who scored higher on neuroticism on the NEO had a mortality rate 37.5 percent higher than those who scored lower on neuroticism (Christensen et al., 2002).

A group of 48 healthy adult males were asked to keep detailed diaries of their problems and moods over an 8-day period. The results showed that men who scored high in neuroticism reported having more frequent daily problems and finding them to be more distressing than did men who scored low in neuroticism (Suls, Green, & Hillis, 1998). Other research demonstrated that adults who scored low in neuroticism and high in extraversion and conscientiousness were also high in subjective vitality, which the investigators described in terms of energy, enthusiasm, and spirit (Ryan & Frederick, 1997).

Behavioral Correlates

People high in openness tend to have a wide range of intellectual interests and to seek challenges. They are more likely to change jobs, try different careers, and expect more varied life experiences than people scoring low in openness (McCrae & Costa, 1985a, 1985b).

Not surprisingly, people high in conscientiousness tend to be reliable, responsible, punctual, efficient, and dependable, and usually earn better grades in school than people low in conscientiousness (Back, Schmukle, & Egloff, 2006; Chowdhury & Amin, 2006; Wagerman & Funder, 2007). A study of more than 300 British university students found that those high in conscientiousness were more organized, self-disciplined, and achievement oriented in terms of planning for future goals (Conner & Abraham, 2001). In research conducted in the workplace, it was found that people who scored high in conscientiousness were more likely than low scorers to set high goals and strive to achieve them, to initiate desirable work behaviors, and to receive high performance ratings. The conscientiousness factor was also shown to be a valid predictor of job performance for professional, police, managerial, sales, and skilled labor jobs (Barrick & Mount, 1996; Barrick, Mount, & Strauss, 1993; Stewart, Carson, & Cardy, 1996).

A study of 256 5th- to 8th-grade students showed that those high in conscientiousness were more likely to be accepted by their peers, to have more and better quality friendships, and to be less likely to be the target of aggression than were students who scored low in conscientiousness (Jensen-Campbell & Malcolm, 2007).

Research also indicates that high scorers on conscientiousness are likely to be healthier and to live longer. A study of 343 adult smokers showed that those who were more conscientious were less likely to smoke at home than were those low in conscientiousness. This suggests that the conscientious smokers were more aware of the health risks of smoking indoors (both to themselves and to others living with them) and acted to reduce those risks (Hampson, Andrews, Barckley, Lichtenstein, & Lee, 2000).

Research on 358 adolescents and young adults who had been diagnosed with diabetes showed that those who scored higher in conscientiousness sought more information about managing their condition and were more diligent about self-care than were those lower in conscientiousness (Skinner, Hampson, Fife-Schau, 2002). A study of 366 British university students revealed that those who were more conscientious were far less likely to display hypochondriacal complaints (that is, to believe, and fear, that they were sick) than those low in conscientiousness (Ferguson, 2000). And a telephone survey of 509 American adults showed that those who scored higher in conscientiousness took greater responsibility for engaging in healthy behaviors than did those who were lower in conscientiousness (Tucker, Elliott, & Klein, 2006).

Longitudinal studies, some investigating the same people for nearly 70 years, showed that children who were high scorers on conscientiousness turned out to be physically healthier and to live longer than children who were low scorers (Booth-Kewley & Vickers, 1994; Friedman et al., 1993, 1995; Marshall, Wortman, Vickers, Kusulas, & Hervig, 1994).

In other work, research participants high in the agreeableness factor were found to be cooperative, helpful, altruistic, honest, and selfless (Digman, 1990; John, 1990). A 25-year study of 194 residents of Finland found that those who were high in agreeableness at age 8 earned better grades in school and exhibited fewer behavior problems than those low in agreeableness at age 8. As adults 25 years later, the high agreeable types reported less alcoholism and lower levels of depression, had lower arrest records, and showed greater career stability than those low in agreeableness (Laursen, Pulkkinen, & Adams, 2002). A study of 835 adults showed that those who scored low on conscientiousness and agreeableness were far more likely to be heavy users of alcohol or illegal drugs than were those who scored high on these factors (Walton & Roberts, 2004).

Research on 1,620 people diagnosed with attention-deficit/hyperactivity disorder found that symptoms such as hyperactivity, impulsivity, inattention, and cognitive and behavioral disorganization were significantly lower in subjects who scored higher in agreeableness than in those who scored low (Nigg et al., 2002).

An 18-month study of 132 university students in Germany from the beginning of their first year of college found significant effects of three of the Big Five personality factors on their social relationships. Students scoring high in extraversion made more friends during the 18-month period and were more likely to fall in love than students low in extraversion. Those high in agreeableness experienced less conflict with acquaintances of the opposite sex, and those high in conscientiousness were more likely to maintain contact with parents and siblings. The factor of openness showed no significant effect on social relationships (Asendorpf & Wilpers, 1998).

A study of 690 heterosexual couples in the Netherlands showed that low scores on neuroticism and high scores on extraversion for both partners was related to marital happiness (Barelds, 2005). Research on newlywed couples in the United States showed that self-ratings of agreeableness and conscientiousness increased significantly and self-ratings in neuroticism decreased significantly over the first 2 years of the marriage. Ratings of each person made by his or her spouse were different, however. These showed significant decreases in conscientiousness, agreeableness, extraversion, and openness over the 2-year period (Watson & Humrichouse, 2006). In other words, the adults believed they were becoming better people during the 2 years they had been married but their spouses did not agree.

When 672 college students in the United States were asked to rate the importance they placed on a variety of life goals—for example, marriage, fun-filled activities, and the serious pursuit of a career—it was found that those who desired higher economic, social, and political status scored high in extraversion and low in agreeableness (Roberts & Robins, 2000).

The evidence is clear from studies of a wide range of emotions and behaviors that the five-factor model of personality has a high predictive value. Most research uses the five factors as self-contained entities and not the individual traits of which they are composed (see Table 8.5). Research comparing the predictive value of the five factors and of the traits found that higher level factors and lower level traits have high predictive validities but that validities of the traits were higher than those of the factors (Paunonen, 1998; Paunonen & Ashton, 2001).

Factor analyses of 14 studies of children, college students, and adults in the United States, Germany, and Hong Kong, including children in the United States of Asian ancestry, suggests the existence of two higher-order factors drawn from the five factor model. Factor A incorporates agreeableness, conscientiousness, and emotional stability and includes a constellation of traits that are considered socially desirable in many cultures. Factor B includes extraversion and an independent factor designated as "intellect." Extraversion in this case refers not only to sociability but also to an active, zestful, and venturesome attitude toward life. Intellect refers not to the standard conception of intelligence but rather to creative and divergent thinking and openness to new ideas (Digman, 1997).

Not all psychologists accept McCrae and Costa's factors. Some researchers have proposed more than five personality dimensions. Others argue that no list of factors can fully describe the complex human personality. And still others agree that there may, indeed, be five major factors but disagree on what they are. Nevertheless, McCrae and Costa's findings have been replicated and continue to inspire considerable research. They provided an intriguing and well-supported approach to personality and to our understanding of the relative importance of heredity and environment.

Arnold Buss and Robert Plomin: The Temperament Theory

We noted that Cattell classified some personality factors as temperament traits, those traits that describe the general style and emotional level of our behavior. Beginning in the 1970s, Arnold Buss (1924–) of the University of Texas at Austin and Robert Plomin (1948–) of Pennsylvania State University identified three temperaments that they believe are the basic building blocks of personality. These are Emotionality, Activity, and Sociability. Buss and Plomin suggest that each person's personality is composed of different amounts of each temperament. The temperaments combine to form personality patterns or so-called supertraits, such as introversion or extraversion (Buss & Plomin, 1984, 1986).

Buss and Plomin developed two tests to assess personality: the Emotionality, Activity, Sociability Survey for Adults (EAS), and the Emotionality, Activity, Sociability Infant Temperament Survey (EASI) for children. For the latter test, the questionnaire is filled out by the parent or primary caregiver (Buss & Plomin, 1975, 1986). Based on extensive research with identical and fraternal twins, Buss and Plomin concluded that temperaments are primarily inherited, part of the genetic package with which we are equipped at birth. These findings have been replicated and supported by considerable independent research. Some research findings also suggest the existence of a strong relationship between the temperamental dispositions and the Big Five personality factors.

Because the three inherited temperaments are broad, they account for the range of individual differences in behavior that permits each of us to be unique. In addition, the temperaments persist throughout the life span, indicating the relatively minor impact of learning from environmental and social interactions.

However, Buss and Plomin recognize environmental influences. What we inherit is not a specific amount of a temperament but a range of response potential. One person will inherit more than another. What determines how much or how little of our potential for a given temperament we realize? Our social environment is the key. One researcher wrote, "We inherit dispositions, not destinies" (Rose, 1995, p. 648). Whether our genetic predispositions are realized depends on experience, particularly in childhood. Thus, Buss and Plomin do consider the impact of external stimulus or situational variables as well as of internal genetic variables. But they suggest limits on how greatly environment can modify temperament. If events force us to deviate from an innate temperamental tendency and to behave contrary to our nature for too long a period of time, the result will be conflict and stress.

Emotionality

The Emotionality temperament refers to our level of arousal or excitability. It consists of three components: distress, fearfulness, and anger. When we describe people as emotional, we mean they are easily upset and given to outbursts. At one extreme of the Emotionality continuum are people who appear unemotional in that nothing seems to disturb them. At the other extreme are people who are sensitive to the slightest provocation. Both extreme responses are maladaptive because they prevent a person from reacting to a given situation in an appropriate manner. An optimal degree of Emotionality arouses a person to respond quickly, appropriately, and alertly.

In Buss and Plomin's view, Emotionality refers to negative or unpleasant emotions such as distress, fearfulness, and anger, rather than to pleasant feelings such as happiness or love. This view agrees with our common usage of the word emotional. In general, we do not call people "emotional" when they appear well balanced and content. We usually reserve the term for those who are easily upset or agitated. The Emotionality components of distress, fearfulness, and anger have been observed in animal species as well as humans. Emotionality is relatively stable in childhood and continues into the adult years.

Activity

Buss and Plomin define the Activity temperament in terms of physical energy and vigor. We all know people who are more energetic and active than others and who display their energy in many different situations. They walk and talk fast and find it hard to sit still, fidgeting with their fingers or tapping their toes. Research with twins revealed an inherited component to Activity. It was found to be moderately stable through childhood and adulthood.

Sociability

The Sociability temperament refers to the degree of preference for contact and interaction with other people. Highly sociable persons prefer group activities and the company of others. Persons who are not sociable choose solitary activities and tend to avoid other people. Research suggests that Sociability is a persistent trait from infancy. Approximately 10 percent of the population has a high degree of Sociability at birth and 10 percent has a low degree of Sociability (Kagan, 1984).

Research on social inhibition shows that 15 to 20 percent of infants exhibit behaviors we may call "inhibited" when confronted with unfamiliar people (Kagan, Snidman, & Arcus, 1992). This social inhibition phenomenon may be related to a low level of the Sociability temperament. The temperament has been found to remain stable during childhood and to persist in adulthood.

Sociability is an adaptive characteristic. We must interact with other people to satisfy many of our needs and to obtain positive reinforcement. Many work and leisure activities are better accomplished socially than individually. The empirical evidence supporting the three temperaments is strongest for Sociability.

Twin Studies and Other Research

Much of the research on temperaments stems directly from the work of Buss and Plomin, whereas other studies focus more generally on the notion of inherited dispositions. We note the results of a few representative studies, most of which use the twin-comparison approach.

The inherited nature of temperaments has been demonstrated by research comparing identical and fraternal twins.

© Esbin-Anderson/The Image Works

Identical twins, ages 42 to 57, were found to be more alike than fraternal twins on empathy, the ability to experience vicariously the feelings of others (Matthews, Batson, Horn, & Rosenman, 1981). If empathy is inherited, then there may be a genetic basis for altruistic, or helping, behavior. Additional support for this proposition was found in a study of twins in England (Rushton, Fulker, Neale, Blizard, & Eysenck, 1984).

The results of twin studies on sociability support Buss and Plomin's position that this temperament is inherited. Identical twins during their first 12 months were found to be much more alike than fraternal twins on behaviors such as smiling at other people or displaying a fear of strangers (Freedman, 1974). When twins were compared on these behaviors at 18 and 24 months of age, researchers found the same differences in sociability between identical and fraternal twins (Matheny, 1983). Comparisons of twins between ages 6 and 10 showed that identical twins were much more similar than fraternal twins in their desire to affiliate with other people and on ratings of friendliness and shyness (Scarr, 1968).

A study involving two sets of parental ratings, taken 10 years apart, of adopted and non-adopted children measured extraversion, socialization, and stability. The results revealed that on average the children tended to change in the direction of the personalities of their biological parents (Loehlin, Horn, & Willerman, 1990). This evidence suggests that hereditary rather than environmental influences play the primary role in shaping personality.

In another study, children who at age 3 were described as restless were found at age 18 to be impulsive, aggressive, danger seeking, and alienated from others. Those who at age 3 were more inhibited scored significantly lower at age 18 on measures of impulsiveness (Caspi & Silva, 1994). These results support other findings suggesting that temperaments that define us as children are stable and persistent throughout life and thus are characteristic of us in adulthood.

In other work, 133 subjects were rated periodically from infancy to early adulthood in an attempt to establish a temperament labeled *difficult*. Infants thought to possess this temperament were described as hard to manage. Any new activity "became the occasion for noisy outbursts of crying. Sleeping and feeding schedules were irregular, and the children had many expressions of intense negative mood" (Thomas, 1986, p. 50). A high correlation was found between this temperament and the later development of behavior disorders (Thomas, Chess, & Korn, 1982).

Infants' temperaments can affect how their parents treat them. Mothers and fathers are typically considered to be environmental and social influences, yet there is obviously a genetic component to the relationship. One study compared irritable and non-irritable babies ranging in age from 1 to 6 months. Mothers of non-irritable babies treated their infants more positively than mothers of irritable babies did. The mothers in the first group were more responsive, stimulating, and soothing in their behavior and initiated significantly more frequent visual and physical contact (van den Boom & Hoeksma, 1994).

Some twin studies on general personality attributes suggest that at least 50 percent of an individual's total personality is inherited. Supporting research was based on 850 pairs of twins in the United States (Loehlin & Nichols, 1976), 573 pairs of twins in England (Rushton et al., 1984), and data collected by researchers in Sweden on 13,000 pairs of twins (Floderus-Myrhed, Pedersen, & Rasmuson, 1980). A study of 300 pairs of twins in Germany suggests that at least 40 percent of the total personality is inherited. Also, the major share of the dimension of extraversion appeared to be inherited (Borkenau, Riemann, Angleitner, & Spinath, 2001).

It is important to remember that although these results support the influence of genetic factors on personality, the evidence for the heritability of Buss and Plomin's specific Emotionality, Activity, and Sociability temperaments is even stronger than for these general personality attributes.

These studies also indicate the role of the environment in shaping personality. Buss and Plomin, who do not dispute environmental or situational influences, recognize this point. In one study, researchers reported a significant relationship between shyness in adopted children and the sociability of their adoptive mothers (Daniels & Plomin, 1985). Because the adopted children and adoptive mothers share no genetic background, the researchers concluded that the research participants' similarity on Sociability was attributable to environmental influences.

Environmental factors affect the personality of siblings in different ways because experiences are different for each child. For example, parents treat sons differently from daughters and first-borns differently from later-borns. Brothers and sisters provide another set of social experiences. A dominant and assertive first-born may influence younger siblings in such a way that they develop passive, noncompetitive personalities.

Whatever the relative influence of heredity and environment on the personality, strong evidence exists that temperaments remain stable from birth into adulthood and that the strength of that stability increases dramatically after age 3. Plomin also presented evidence to suggest that genetic factors influence our perception of stressful life events such as retirement or the death of a child or spouse. Thus, inherited temperaments exert pervasive, long-lasting influences on our behavior.

Reflections on the Trait Approach

The theories presented in this chapter, together with their supporting research, indicate that inheritance may account for as much as 50 percent of personality (Brody, 1997; Buss, 1988; Stelmack, 1997). The evidence is greatest for the factors of extraversion, neuroticism, and psychoticism, but virtually every other dimension investigated by personality researchers displays a strong biological component. In many cases, a shared family environment has only a minor influence. Some researchers hold a more uncompromising view, arguing that twins, whether reared together or apart, will be alike in all facets of their personality regardless of family situation, suggesting that the genetic effect far outweighs the environmental effect.

This area of research has practical and theoretical implications for personality psychologists, who in the past tended to concentrate on the family and social interactions in early childhood. Findings from behavioral genetics may require a restructuring of research efforts in the future if we are to account fully for the development of personality. However, caution is necessary. We must not conclude prematurely that family and other environmental factors can be discounted as shapers of personality. Plomin noted,

It is good for the field of personality that it has moved away from simple-minded environmentalism. The danger now, however, is that the rush from environmentalism will carom too far—to a view that personality is almost completely biologically determined. (Plomin, Chipeur, & Loehlin, 1990, pp. 225–226)

The various components of personality remain products of both our genetic makeup and the experiences of our life. The task for psychologists remains to determine the relative importance of each.

Chapter Summary

According to Cattell, factors, or traits, are the basic structural units of personality. We all possess the common traits to some degree; unique traits typify one or a few persons. Ability traits determine how efficiently we work toward a goal. Temperament traits define emotional style of behavior. Dynamic traits are concerned with motivation.

Surface traits are personality characteristics that correlate with one another but do not constitute a factor because they are not determined by a single source. The 16 source traits Cattell identified are single factors, and each is the sole source of some aspect of behavior. Source traits may be constitutional traits, which originate in internal bodily conditions, or environmental-mold traits, which derive from environmental influences.

Dynamic traits include ergs (the energy source for all behavior) and sentiments (learned patterns of attitudes). Ergs and sentiments are manifested in attitudes, which are a person's interests in some area, object, or other person. The self-sentiment is a person's self-concept and provides stability and organization to the source traits. Cattell's research suggests that one-third of personality is genetically determined; the rest is determined by environmental influences. Thus, Cattell holds a deterministic view of personality. He does not suggest any ultimate life goals. Childhood influences are important in personality development, as are heredity and environment.

Cattell's three major assessment techniques are L-data (ratings made by observers), Q-data (self-ratings made through questionnaires, personality inventories, and attitude scales), and T-data (data from tests that are resistant to faking). Cattell developed the 16 PF and the Clinical Analysis Questionnaire. He used two forms of factor analysis: the R technique, which gathers large amounts of data from groups of research participants, and the P technique, which collects a large amount of data from a single subject over time. Cattell's work is highly technical, and the amount of supporting data is massive. Factor analysis has been criticized for its potential subjectivity.

Research on behavioral genetics shows a significant influence of genetic factors on personality. Eysenck demonstrated a genetic influence on the personality dimensions of extraversion, neuroticism, and psychoticism. McCrae and Costa proposed five biologically based factors: neuroticism, extraversion, openness, agreeableness, and conscientiousness. The factors are stable over the lifetime and appear in many cultures. The factors are valid predictors of emotions and behaviors. Buss and Plomin documented the innate potential for three temperaments: Emotionality, Activity, and Sociability. Twin studies on personality attributes suggest that as much as 50 percent of personality is inherited.

Review Questions

1. In what ways does Cattell's concept of personality traits differ from Allport's view of traits?

2. How does Cattell use factor analysis to identify traits?

3. Describe three ways to categorize traits.

4. Define surface traits and source traits. Give examples of each.

5. Distinguish between ergs, sentiments, and attitudes.

6. What is the difference between source traits and environmental-mold traits?

7. According to Cattell's research, which source traits are determined primarily by heredity?

8. What did Cattell mean by the concept of *subsidiation?*

9. What is the self-sentiment? What is its role in personality?

10. What Freudian ideas did Cattell incorporate in his stages of personality development?

11. Identify the three types of data collected by Cattell. Give an example of each.

12. Describe Cattell's position on free will versus determinism.

13. Describe the three personality types proposed by Eysenck. Does Eysenck suggest that personality traits are determined largely by genetic factors or by environmental factors?

14. In what ways do people who score high in extraversion on Eysenck's personality test differ from people who score low?

15. Describe the behavior of people who score high in psychoticism on Eysenck's personality test.

16. How does Eysenck's research on identical and fraternal twins and on adopted children support his conclusion about the role of genetic factors in personality?

17. Describe McCrae and Costa's five factors of personality. What is the role of heredity and of environment in each of these factors?

18. In what ways do people who score high on extraversion and on conscientiousness differ from people who score low on these factors?

19. What are the emotional and behavioral correlates of high scores on neuroticism?

20. Describe the three temperaments proposed by Buss and Plomin.

21. How do the results of twin studies support Buss and Plomin's temperament theory?

Suggested Readings

Buss, A. H. (1989). Personality as traits. *American Psychologist, 44,* 1378–1388. Discusses the trait approach and notes that the goal of trait research is to understand people as combinations of traits.

Cattell, R. B. (1974). Autobiography. In G. Lindzey (Ed.), *A history of psychology in autobiography* (Vol. 6, pp. 59–100). Englewood Cliffs, NJ: Prentice-Hall; Travels in psychological hyperspace. In T. S. Krawiec (Ed.), *The psychologists* (Vol. 2, pp. 85–133). New York: Oxford University Press. Two essays by Cattell about his life and work.

Cattell, R. B. (1993). Planning basic clinical research. In E. C. Walker (Ed.), *The history of clinical psychology in autobiography* (Vol. 2, pp. 101–111). Pacific Grove, CA: Brooks/Cole. Cattell's evaluation of his work, which concludes that his approach to the measurement of personality was the only correct one to pursue.

Eysenck, H. J. (1976). H. J. Eysenck. In R. I. Evans (Ed.), *The making of psychology: Discussions with creative contributors* (pp. 255–265). New York: Alfred A. Knopf. Interviews with Eysenck about his work, his criticisms of psychoanalysis, and his views on the genetic basis of intelligence.

Eysenck, H. J. (1990). Genetic and environmental contributions to individual differences: The three major dimensions of personality. *Journal of Personality, 58,* 245–261. Describes the relative impact of heredity and environment on Eysenck's proposed dimensions of personality (extraversion, neuroticism, and psychoticism) and emphasizes the importance of behavioral genetics.

Eysenck, H. J. (1997). *Rebel with a cause: The autobiography of Hans Eysenck.* London: Transaction Publishers. Eysenck's reflections on his life and work. Notes the continuing impact of his ideas about personality dimensions and suggests the relative importance of heredity versus environment in his own personality.

Farley, F. (2000). Hans J. Eysenck (1916–1997). *American Psychologist, 55,* 674–675. A memorial note describing Eysenck's contributions to psychology.

Hampson, S., & Goldberg, L. (2006). A first large cohort study of personality trait stability over the 40 years between elementary school and midlife. *Journal of Personality and Social Psychology, 91,* 763–779. Describes methodology for investigating the Big Five factors across the life span.

Horn, J. (2001). Raymond Bernard Cattell (1905–1998). *American Psychologist, 56,* 71–72. A memorial note describing Cattell's contributions to psychology.

McCrae, R. R., Costa, P. T., Ostendorf, F., Angleitner, A., Avia, M. D., Sanz, J., Sanchez-Bernardos, M. L., Kusdil, M. E., Woodfield, R., Saunders, P. T., & Smith, P. T. (2000). Nature over nurture: Temperament, personality, and life span development. *Journal of Personality and Social Psychology, 78,* 173–186. Discusses large-scale cross-cultural research on the heritability of the five factors as an explanation for the entire range of personality traits.

Nettle, D. (2006). The evolution of personality variation in humans and other animals. *American Psychologist, 61,* 622–631. Reviews research and theory on the Big Five personality factors within the framework of evolutionary psychology and suggests that inherited variations can be documented in most species.

Plomin, R. (1990). *Nature and nurture: An introduction to human behavioral genetics.* Pacific Grove, CA: Brooks/Cole. Reviews research methods and empirical findings in behavioral genetics and explains how heredity affects behavior.

Triandis, H. C., & Suh, E. M. (2002). Cultural influences on personality. *Annual Review of Psychology, 53,* 133–160. The section "Dimensions of Personality" explores the transcultural nature of the personality traits proposed by McCrae and Costa.

Wright, L. (1997). *Twins and what they tell us about who we are.* New York: Wiley. Describes research and theories about twins and the relative effects on personality of genetic determinism versus environmental conditions. Suggests that theorists on both sides of the issue have used twin studies to bolster their positions.

PART FIVE

The Humanistic Approach

Humanism is a system of thought in which human interests and values are of primary importance. The humanistic approach to personality is part of the humanistic movement in psychology that flourished in the 1960s and 1970s and continues to influence psychology today. The goal of the proponents of this movement was to alter psychology's methods and subject matter. Humanistic psychologists objected to psychoanalysis and to behaviorism, then the two major forces in American psychology, arguing that these systems presented too limited and demeaning an image of human nature.

Humanistic psychologists criticized Freud and others following the psychoanalytic tradition for studying only the emotionally disturbed side of human nature. They questioned how we could ever hope to learn about positive human characteristics and qualities if we focused only on neuroses and psychoses. Instead, humanistic psychologists studied our strengths and virtues and explored human behavior at its best, not worst.

The humanistic psychologists thought that the behavioral psychologists were narrow and sterile in their outlook because they disavowed conscious and unconscious forces to focus exclusively on the objective observation of overt behavior. But a psychology based on conditioned responses to stimuli depicts human beings as little more than mechanized robots, reacting to events in predetermined ways. The humanistic psychologists objected to this view, arguing that people are not big white rats or slow computers. Human behavior is too complex to be explained solely by the behaviorists' methods.

The term *humanistic psychology* was first used by Gordon Allport in 1930. Allport and Henry Murray are considered forerunners of the humanistic approach to personality, represented in this section by the works of Abraham Maslow and Carl Rogers. Their theories emphasize human strengths and aspirations, conscious free will, and the fulfillment of our potential. They present a flattering and optimistic image of human nature and describe people as active, creative beings concerned with growth and self-actualization.

CHAPTER 9

Abraham Maslow: Needs-Hierarchy Theory

What humans can be, they must be. They must be true to their own nature.
—ABRAHAM MASLOW

Abraham Maslow is considered the founder and spiritual leader of the humanistic psychology movement. He was strongly critical of behaviorism and of psychoanalysis, particularly Sigmund Freud's approach to personality. According to Maslow, when psychologists study only abnormal, emotionally disturbed examples of humanity, they ignore positive human qualities such as happiness, contentment, and peace of mind. A frequently quoted statement sums up Maslow's position: "The study of crippled, stunted, immature, and unhealthy specimens can yield only a cripple psychology" (Maslow, 1970b, p. 180).

We underestimate human nature, Maslow charged, when we fail to examine the best examples of humanity, society's most creative, healthy, and mature people. Thus, Maslow determined that his approach to personality would assess the best representatives of the human species. When you want to determine how fast humans can run, you study not the average runner but the fastest runner you can find. Only in this way is it possible to determine the full range of human potential.

Maslow's personality theory does not derive from case histories of clinical patients but from research on creative, independent, self-sufficient, fulfilled adults. Maslow concluded that each person is born with the same instinctive needs that enable us to grow, develop, and fulfill our potentials.

The Life of Maslow (1908–1970)

Inferiority Feelings and Compensation

The oldest of seven children, Maslow was born in 1908 in Brooklyn, New York. His parents were immigrants with little education and few prospects for rising above their marginal economic circumstances. At the age of 14, Maslow's father had walked and hitchhiked from Russia across Western Europe, so great was his ambition to reach the United States. The elder Maslow instilled in his son this intense drive to succeed.

Maslow's childhood was difficult. He told an interviewer, "with my childhood, it's a wonder I'm not psychotic" (quoted in Hall, 1968, p. 37). In a statement uncovered in his unpublished papers, years after his death, Maslow had written, "My family was a miserable family and my mother was a horrible creature" (quoted in Hoffman, 1996, p. 2). Isolated and unhappy, he grew up without close friends or loving parents. His father was aloof and periodically abandoned his unhappy marriage. Maslow said that his father "loved whiskey and women and fighting" (quoted in Wilson, 1972, p. 131). Eventually Maslow reconciled with his father but as a child and adolescent felt only hostility toward him.

Maslow's relationship with his mother was worse. A biographer reported that Maslow "grew to maturity with an unrelieved hatred toward [her] and he never achieved the slightest reconciliation" (Hoffman, 1988, p. 7). She was superstitious and would quickly punish Maslow for the slightest wrongdoing. She announced that God would retaliate for his misbehavior. Unaffectionate and rejecting of him, she openly favored the younger siblings. When Maslow brought home two stray kittens, his mother killed them, bashing their heads against a wall. Maslow never forgave her treatment of him, and when she died, he refused to attend her funeral.

The experience affected not only his emotional life but also his work in psychology. "The whole thrust of my life-philosophy, and all my research and theorizing . . . has its roots in a hatred for and revulsion against everything she stood for" (quoted in Hoffman, 1988, p. 9).

As a child, Maslow believed he was different from others. Embarrassed about his scrawny physique and large nose, he remembered his teenage years as marked by a huge inferiority complex. "I was all alone in the world," Maslow told an interviewer. "I felt peculiar. This was really in my blood, a very profound feeling that somehow I was wrong. Never any feelings that I was superior. Just one big aching inferiority complex" (quoted in Milton, 2002, p. 42).

Elsewhere he had written, "I tried to compensate for what I felt was a great [physical] lack by forcing my development in the direction of athletic achievements" (quoted in Hoffman, 1988, p. 13). Thus, the man who would later become interested in Alfred Adler's work was in many ways a living example of Adler's concept of compensation for inferiority feelings.

When Maslow's early attempts at compensation to achieve recognition and acceptance as an athlete did not succeed, he turned to books. The library became the playground of his childhood and adolescence, and reading and education marked the road out of the ghetto of poverty and loneliness. Maslow's early memories are significant because they indicate the style of life—the life of scholarship—he would fashion for himself. He recalled going to the neighborhood library early in the morning and waiting on the steps until the doors opened. He typically arrived at school an hour before classes began, and his teacher would let him sit in an empty classroom, reading the books she had loaned him. Although his grades remained mediocre, they were sufficient to gain him acceptance at City College of New York. He failed a course during his first semester and by the end of his freshman year was on academic probation, but with persistence his grades improved. He began the study of law, at his father's request, but decided after two weeks that he did not like it. What he really wanted to do was study *everything*.

From Monkeys to Self-Actualization

Maslow's desire for learning was matched by a passion for his cousin Bertha. He soon left home, first for Cornell University and then for the University of Wisconsin, where she joined him. He was 20 and she was 19 when they married. The union provided Maslow with a feeling of belonging and a sense of direction. He later said that life had little meaning until he married Bertha and began his studies at Wisconsin. Earlier, at Cornell, he had enrolled in a psychology course and pronounced that he found it "awful and bloodless." It had "nothing to do with people, so I shuddered and turned away from it" (quoted in Hoffman, 1988, p. 26). At Wisconsin, however, he found the behavioral psychology of John B. Watson, leader of the revolution to make psychology a science of behavior. Like many people in the early 1930s, Maslow became enraptured, believing that behaviorism could solve all the world's problems. His training in experimental psychology included work on dominance and sexual behavior in primates. So obviously it was a giant step from this type of research in the behaviorist framework to the ideas of humanistic psychology—from monkeys to self-actualization.

Several influences brought about this profound shift in his thinking. He read the works of Freud, the Gestalt psychologists, and the philosophers Alfred North Whitehead and Henri Bergson. He was deeply affected by the onset of World War II and by the birth of his first child. About the baby he said, "I was stunned by the mystery and by the sense of not really being in control. I felt small and weak and feeble before all this. I'd say anyone who had a baby couldn't be a behaviorist" (quoted in Hall, 1968, p. 56).

Maslow received his Ph.D. from the University of Wisconsin in 1934 and returned to New York, first for a postdoctoral fellowship under E. L. Thorndike at Columbia University, and later to teach at Brooklyn College, where he remained until 1951. Maslow took several intelligence and scholastic aptitude tests, scoring an IQ of 195, which Thorndike described as within the genius range. At first Maslow was surprised, but soon he accepted the revelation and thereafter considered it a triumph and frequently managed to work the information into social conversations.

Teaching in New York in the late 1930s and early 1940s, Maslow had the opportunity to meet the wave of emigrant intellectuals fleeing Nazi Germany, including Karen Horney and Alfred Adler. Maslow "talked about Adler all the time and was tremendously excited by his theories" recalled Bertha Maslow (quoted in Hoffman, 1988, p. 304). He also met the Gestalt psychologist Max Wertheimer and the American anthropologist Ruth Benedict. His admiration for Wertheimer and Benedict kindled his ideas about self-actualization.

In 1941, Maslow witnessed a parade shortly after Japan's surprise attack on the American naval base at Pearl Harbor in Hawaii, precipitating the onset of U.S. involvement in World War II. The experience changed his life. He resolved to devote himself to developing a psychology that would deal with the highest human ideals. He would work to improve the human personality and to demonstrate that people are capable of displaying better behaviors than prejudice, hatred, and aggression.

From 1951 to 1969, Maslow taught at Brandeis University in Massachusetts. A foundation grant enabled him to move to California to work on his philosophy of politics, economics, and ethics based on a humanistic psychology. He became an immensely popular figure in psychology and among the general public. He received many awards and honors and was elected president of the American Psychological Association in 1967.

At the peak of his fame, Maslow developed a variety of ailments including stomach disorders, insomnia, depression, and heart disease. In the face of these growing physical limitations, he pushed himself to work even harder to accomplish his goal of humanizing psychology. "I find myself getting narrow," he said in a 1968 interview. "I've given up plays and poetry and making new friends. . . . I love my work so much, and am so absorbed with it, that everything else starts to look smaller and smaller" (quoted in Frick, 2000, p. 135).

Maslow died in 1970 of a massive heart attack, which he suffered while jogging around his swimming pool, an exercise that had been recommended by his cardiologist.

↖ Log On

Personality theories: Abraham Maslow

An overview of Maslow's life and theory, including an evaluation of Maslow's research techniques.

Key Theorists/Theories in Psychology: Abraham Maslow

Links to almost everything you might ever want to know about Maslow and his work. Includes his original (1943) article on motivation and personality, and discusses the applications of his theories to education and to employee motivation.

For direct links to these sites, log on to the student companion site for this book at http://www.academic.cengage.com/psychology/Schultz and choose Chapter 9.

Personality Development: The Hierarchy of Needs

hierarchy of needs
An arrangement of innate needs, from strongest to weakest, that activates and directs behavior.

instinctoid needs
Maslow's term for the innate needs in his needs-hierarchy theory.

Maslow proposed a **hierarchy of five innate needs** that activate and direct human behavior (Maslow, 1968, 1970b). They are the physiological, safety, belongingness and love, esteem, and self-actualization needs (see Figure 9.1). Maslow described these needs as **instinctoid**, by which he meant that they have a hereditary component. However, these needs can be affected or overridden by learning, social expectations, and fear of disapproval. Although we come equipped with these needs at birth, the behaviors we use to satisfy them are learned and therefore subject to variation from one person to another.

The needs are arranged in order from strongest to weakest. Lower needs must be at least partially satisfied before higher needs become influential. For example, hungry people feel no urge to satisfy the higher need for esteem. They are preoccupied

Figure 9.1
Maslow's hierarchy of needs

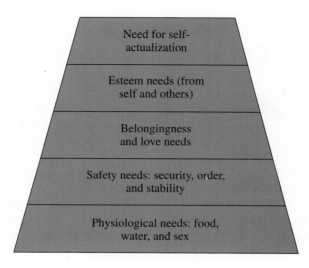

Need for self-actualization

Esteem needs (from self and others)

Belongingness and love needs

Safety needs: security, order, and stability

Physiological needs: food, water, and sex

with satisfying the physiological need for food, not with obtaining approval and esteem from other people. It is only when people have adequate food and shelter and when the rest of the lower needs are satisfied that they are motivated by needs that rank higher in the hierarchy.

Thus, we are not driven by all the needs at the same time. In general, only one need will dominate our personality. Which one it will be depends on which of the others have been satisfied. People who are successful in their careers are no longer driven by, or even aware of, their physiological and safety needs. These needs have been amply taken care of. Successful people are more likely to be motivated by the needs for esteem or self-actualization. However, Maslow suggested that the order of the needs can be changed. If an economic recession causes some people to lose their jobs, the safety and physiological needs may reassume priority. Being able to pay the mortgage becomes more prized than popularity with colleagues or an award from a civic organization.

Characteristics of Needs

Maslow described several characteristics of needs.

- The lower the need is in the hierarchy, the greater are its strength, potency, and priority. The higher needs are weaker needs.
- Higher needs appear later in life. Physiological and safety needs arise in infancy. Belongingness and esteem needs arise in adolescence. The need for self-actualization does not arise until midlife.
- Because higher needs are less necessary for actual survival, their gratification can be postponed. Failure to satisfy a higher need does not produce a crisis. Failure to satisfy a lower need does produce a crisis. For this reason, Maslow called lower needs **deficit, or deficiency, needs**; failure to satisfy them produces a deficit or lack in the individual.
- Although higher needs are less necessary for survival, they contribute to survival and growth. Satisfaction of higher needs leads to improved health and longevity. For this reason, Maslow called higher needs **growth, or being, needs**.
- Satisfaction of higher needs is also beneficial psychologically. Satisfaction of higher needs leads to contentment, happiness, and fulfillment.
- Gratification of higher needs requires better external circumstances (social, economic, and political) than does gratification of lower needs. For example, pursuing self-actualization requires greater freedom of expression and opportunity than pursuing safety needs.
- A need does not have to be satisfied fully before the next need in the hierarchy becomes important. Maslow proposed a declining percentage of satisfaction for each need. Offering a hypothetical example, he described a person who satisfied, in turn, 85 percent of the physiological needs, 70 percent of the safety needs, 50 percent of the belongingness and love needs, 40 percent of the esteem needs, and 10 percent of the self-actualization need.

deficit (deficiency) needs The lower needs; failure to satisfy them produces a deficiency in the body.

growth (being) needs The higher needs; although growth needs are less necessary than deficit needs for survival, they involve the realization and fulfillment of human potential.

Physiological Needs

If you have ever been swimming and had to struggle for air while under water, or if you have gone too long without eating, you may have realized how trivial the needs for love or esteem or anything else can be when your body is experiencing a physiological deficiency. As we noted, a starving person craves only food. But once that need is satisfied, the person is no longer driven by it. The need ceases to direct or control behavior.

This describes the situation for most people in an affluent, industrialized culture. It is rare for middle-class Americans to be concerned with satisfying their survival needs. Physiological needs have a greater personal impact as motivating forces in cultures where basic survival remains an everyday concern. Because a need that has been gratified no longer serves to motivate behavior, the physiological needs play a minimal role for most of us.

Safety Needs

Maslow believed that the needs for safety and security typically are important drives for infants and neurotic adults. Emotionally healthy adults have usually satisfied their safety needs, a condition that requires stability, security, and freedom from fear and anxiety. For infants and children, the safety needs can be seen clearly in their behavior because youngsters react visibly and immediately to any threat to their security. Adults have learned ways to inhibit their reactions to dangerous situations.

When the basic needs for food and shelter are unsatisfied, the higher needs, such as esteem and self-actualization, are of less importance.

© Michael Newman/PhotoEdit

Another visible indication of children's safety needs is their preference for a structure or routine, for an orderly and predictable world. Too much freedom and permissiveness leads to an absence of structure and order. This situation is likely to produce anxiety and insecurity in children because it threatens their security. Some measure of freedom must be granted to children, but only within the limits of their capacity to cope. This freedom must be offered with guidance because children are not yet capable of directing their own behavior and realizing the consequences.

Neurotic and insecure adults also need structure and order because their safety needs still dominate their personality. Neurotics compulsively avoid new experiences. They arrange their world to make it predictable, budgeting their time and organizing their possessions. Pencils must be kept in a certain drawer, and shirts hung in the closet facing the same direction.

Maslow pointed out that although most normal adults have satisfied the safety needs, those needs may still have an impact on behavior. Many of us choose the predictable over the unknown; we prefer order to chaos. That is why we save for the future, buy insurance, and opt to remain in a secure job rather than risk a new venture. However, the safety needs are not as overwhelming a driving force for normal adults as they are for children or neurotics.

Belongingness and Love Needs

Once our physiological and safety needs have been reasonably well satisfied, we attend to the needs for belongingness and love. These needs can be expressed through a close relationship with a friend, lover, or mate, or through social relationships formed within a group.

The need to belong has grown more difficult to satisfy in our increasingly mobile society. Few of us live in the neighborhood where we grew up and keep friends from our early schooldays. We change schools, jobs, and communities too frequently to put down roots, to develop a secure sense of belonging. Many of us attempt to satisfy the need to belong in other ways, such as joining a church, club, or Internet chat room, enrolling in a class, or volunteering for a service organization.

The need to give and receive love can be satisfied in an intimate relationship with another person. Maslow did not equate love with sex, which is a physiological need, but he recognized that sex is one way of expressing the love need. He suggested that the failure to satisfy the need for love is a fundamental cause of emotional maladjustment.

Esteem Needs

Once we feel loved and have a sense of belonging, we may find ourselves driven by two forms of the need for esteem. We require esteem and respect from ourselves, in the form of feelings of self-worth, and from other people, in the form of status, recognition, or social success. Satisfaction of the need for self-esteem allows us to feel confident of our strength, worth, and adequacy, which will help us become more competent and productive in all aspects of our life. When we lack self-esteem, we feel inferior, helpless, and discouraged with little confidence in our ability to cope.

The Self-Actualization Need

self-actualization
The fullest development of the self.

The highest need in Maslow's hierarchy, **self-actualization**, depends on the maximum realization and fulfillment of our potentials, talents, and abilities. Although a person may satisfy all the other needs in the hierarchy, if that person is not self-actualizing, he or she will be restless, frustrated, and discontent. Maslow wrote, "A musician must make music, an artist must paint, a poet must write . . . to be ultimately at peace" (1970b, p. 46).

The self-actualizing process may take many forms, but each person, regardless of occupation or interests, is capable of maximizing personal abilities and reaching the fullest personality development. Self-actualization is not limited to creative and intellectual superstars such as musicians, artists, and astrophysicists. What is important is to fulfill one's own potentials at the highest level possible, whatever one's chosen endeavor. Maslow put it this way, "A first-rate soup is more creative than a second-rate painting . . . cooking or parenthood or making a home could be creative, while poetry need not be" (1987, p. 159).

The following conditions are necessary in order for us to satisfy the self-actualization need:

- We must be free of constraints imposed by society and by ourselves.
- We must not be distracted by the lower-order needs.
- We must be secure in our self-image and in our relationships with other people; we must be able to love and be loved in return.
- We must have a realistic knowledge of our strengths and weaknesses, virtues and vices.

Belongingness and love needs can be satisfied through a relationship with a friend.

© Kathrin Miller/The Image Bank/Getty Images

Although the hierarchy of needs Maslow proposed applies to most of us, there can be exceptions. Some people dedicate their lives to an ideal and willingly sacrifice everything for their cause. People have been known to fast until death in the service of their beliefs, thus denying their physiological and safety needs. Religious figures may abandon worldly goods to fulfill a vow of poverty, thus satisfying the self-actualization need while frustrating the lower-order needs. Artists throughout history have imperiled health and security for the sake of their work. A more common reversal in the hierarchy occurs when people place a greater importance on esteem than on love, believing that the belongingness and love needs can be satisfied only if they first feel self-confident.

Cognitive Needs

cognitive needs
Innate needs to know
and to understand.

Maslow also proposed a second set of innate needs, the **cognitive needs**—to know and to understand, which exist outside the hierarchy we have described. The need to know is stronger than the need to understand. Thus, the need to know must be at least partially satisfied before the need to understand can emerge. Several points of evidence support the existence of cognitive needs (Maslow, 1970b).

- Laboratory studies show that animals explore and manipulate their environment for no apparent reason other than curiosity, that is, a desire to know and to understand.
- Historical evidence shows that people often have sought knowledge at the risk of their lives, thus placing the needs to know and to understand above the safety needs.
- Studies suggest that emotionally healthy adults are attracted to mysterious and unexplained events and are motivated to improve their knowledge about them.
- Emotionally healthy adults in Maslow's own clinical practice complained of boredom and a lack of zest and excitement in life. He described them as "intelligent people leading stupid lives in stupid jobs" and found that they improved when they took steps to fulfill the needs to know and to understand by becoming involved in more challenging activities.

The needs to know and to understand appear in late infancy and early childhood and are expressed by children as a natural curiosity. Because the needs are innate, they do not have to be taught, but the actions of parents and teachers can serve to inhibit a child's spontaneous curiosity. Failure to satisfy the cognitive needs is harmful and hampers the full development and functioning of the personality.

The hierarchy of these two needs overlaps the original five-need hierarchy. Knowing and understanding—essentially, finding meaning in our environment—are basic to interacting with that environment in an emotionally healthy, mature way to satisfy physiological, safety, love, esteem, and self-actualization needs. It is impossible to become self-actualizing if we fail to meet the needs to know and to understand.

The Study of Self-Actualizers

metamotivation
The motivation of self-actualizers, which involves maximizing personal potential rather than striving for a particular goal object.

According to Maslow's theory, self-actualizing persons differ from others in terms of their basic motivation. Maslow proposed a distinct type of motivation for self-actualizers called **metamotivation** (sometimes called B-motivation or Being). The prefix *meta-* means after or beyond. Metamotivation, then, indicates that it goes beyond psychology's traditional idea of motivation.

Metamotivation

Metamotivation implies a condition in which motivation as we know it plays no role. Self-actualizing persons are not motivated to strive for a particular goal. Instead, they are said to be developing from within. Maslow described the motivation of people who are not self-actualizers as a condition of D-motivation or Deficiency. D-motivation involves striving for something specific to make up for something that is lacking within us. For example, failure to eat produces a deficiency in the body that we feel as discomfort. This feeling motivates us to take some action to reduce the resulting tension. Thus, a specific physiological need (hunger) that requires a specific goal object (food) produces a motivation to act to attain something we lack (we search for food). Maslow's writings about the development of B-motivation and D-motivation are incomplete, but apparently D-motivation applies not only to physiological needs, as in the example above, but also to the needs for safety, belongingness and love, and esteem (Maslow, 1971).

In contrast, self-actualizing persons are concerned with fulfilling their potential and with knowing and understanding their environment. In their state of metamotivation, they are not seeking to reduce tension, satisfy a deficiency, or strive for a specific object. Their goal is to enrich their lives by acting to increase tension to experience a variety of stimulating and challenging events. Because their lower-order deficiency needs have been met, self-actualizers function at a level beyond striving for specific goal objects to satisfy a deficit. Thus, they are in a state of "being," spontaneously, naturally, and joyfully expressing their full humanity.

metaneeds
States of growth or being toward which self-actualizers evolve.

metapathology
A thwarting of self-development related to failure to satisfy the metaneeds.

Having explained that self-actualizers are thus, in a sense, unmotivated, Maslow proposed a list of **metaneeds** toward which self-actualizers evolve (see Table 9.1). Metaneeds are states of being—such as goodness, uniqueness, and perfection—rather than specific goal objects. Failure to satisfy metaneeds is harmful and produces a kind of **metapathology**, which thwarts the full development of the personality. Metapathology prevents self-actualizers from expressing, using, and fulfilling their potential. They may come to feel helpless and depressed, unable to pinpoint a source for these feelings or identify a goal that might alleviate the distress.

Characteristics of Self-Actualizers

Maslow's research on emotionally healthy people formed the basis of his personality theory (Maslow, 1970b, 1971). He did not find many examples of self-actualizers; he estimated that they constitute 1 percent or less of the population. However, he concluded that they share certain characteristics (see Table 9.2).

Table 9.1 Maslow's metaneeds and metapathologies

Metaneeds	Metapathologies
Truth	Mistrust, cynicism, skepticism
Goodness	Hatred, repulsion, disgust, reliance only upon self and for self
Beauty	Vulgarity, restlessness, loss of taste, bleakness
Unity, wholeness	Disintegration
Dichotomy-transcendence	Black/white thinking, either/or thinking, simplistic view of life
Aliveness, process	Deadness, robotizing, feeling oneself to be totally determined, loss of emotion and zest in life, experiential emptiness
Uniqueness	Loss of feeling of self and individuality, feeling oneself to be interchangeable or anonymous
Perfection	Hopelessness, nothing to work for
Necessity	Chaos, unpredictability
Completion, finality	Incompleteness, hopelessness, cessation of striving and coping
Justice	Anger, cynicism, mistrust, lawlessness, total selfishness
Order	Insecurity, wariness, loss of safety and predictability, necessity for being on guard
Simplicity	Overcomplexity, confusion, bewilderment, loss of orientation
Richness, totality, comprehensiveness	Depression, uneasiness, loss of interest in the world
Effortlessness	Fatigue, strain, clumsiness, awkwardness, stiffness
Playfulness	Grimness, depression, paranoid humorlessness, loss of zest in life, cheerlessness
Self-sufficiency	Responsibility given to others
Meaningfulness	Meaninglessness, despair, senselessness of life

SOURCE: Adapted from *The Farther Reaches of Human Nature*, by A. H. Maslow. Copyright © 1971 by Bertha G. Maslow.

Table 9.2 Characteristics of self-actualizing people

Clear perception of reality
Acceptance of self, others, and nature
Spontaneity, simplicity, and naturalness
Dedication to a cause
Independence and need for privacy
Freshness of appreciation
Peak experiences
Social interest
Deep interpersonal relationships
Tolerance and acceptance of others
Creativeness and originality
Resistance to social pressures

- *An efficient perception of reality.* Self-actualizers perceive their world, including other people, clearly and objectively, unbiased by prejudgments or preconceptions.
- *An acceptance of themselves, others, and nature.* Self-actualizers accept their strengths and weaknesses. They do not try to distort or falsify their self-image and they do not feel guilty about their failings. They also accept the weaknesses of other people and of society in general.
- *A spontaneity, simplicity, and naturalness.* The behavior of self-actualizers is open, direct, and natural. They rarely hide their feelings or emotions or play a role to satisfy society, although they may do so to avoid hurting other people. Self-actualizers are individualistic in their ideas and ideals but not necessarily unconventional in their behavior. They feel secure enough to be themselves without being overly assertive.
- *A focus on problems outside themselves.* Self-actualizers have a sense of mission, a commitment, to which they devote their energy. This dedication to a cause or vocation is a requirement for self-actualization. Self-actualizers find pleasure and excitement in their hard work. Through their intense dedication, self-actualizers are able to satisfy the metaneeds. A writer or scientist may search for truth, an artist for beauty, an attorney for justice. Self-actualizers do not undertake their tasks for money, fame, or power but rather to satisfy the metaneeds. Their commitment challenges and develops their abilities and helps define their sense of self.
- *A sense of detachment and the need for privacy.* Self-actualizers can experience isolation without harmful effects and seem to need solitude more than persons who are not self-actualizing. Self-actualizers depend on themselves, not on others, for their satisfactions. This independence may make them seem aloof or unfriendly, but that is not their intent. They are simply more autonomous than most people and do not crave social support.
- *A freshness of appreciation.* Self-actualizers have the ability to perceive and experience their environment with freshness, wonder, and awe. An experience may grow stale for someone who is not self-actualizing, but self-actualizers will enjoy each recurrence as though it was the first. Whether it is a sunset, a painting, or a symphony, a baseball game or a birthday gift—all of these experiences can be viewed with delight. Self-actualizers appreciate what they have and take little for granted.
- *Mystical or peak experiences.* Self-actualizers know moments of intense ecstasy, not unlike deep religious experiences, that can occur with virtually any activity. Maslow called these events **peak experiences**, during which the self is transcended and the person feels supremely powerful, confident, and decisive. Maslow wrote that a peak experience involves

peak experience
A moment of intense ecstasy, similar to a religious or mystical experience, during which the self is transcended.

a feeling of great ecstasy and wonder and awe, the loss of placing in time and space with, finally, the conviction that something extremely important and valuable had happened, so that the subject is . . . transformed and strengthened" (Maslow, 1970b, p. 164).

Maslow noted differences among self-actualizers in the quantity and quality of their peak experiences. So-called *peakers* have more peak experiences than *non-peakers*, and the experiences of peakers tend to be more mystical and religious. Indeed, peakers may be described as more saintly and poetical than non-peakers. Non-peakers are more practical and more concerned with worldly affairs. Peakers have been identified among diverse occupational groups including artists, writers, scientists, business leaders, educators, and politicians. Maslow noted that it was possible for a person who is not self-actualizing occasionally to have a peak experience.

- *Social interest.* Maslow adopted Alfred Adler's concept of social interest to indicate the sympathy and empathy self-actualizing persons have for all humanity. Although often irritated by the behavior of other people, self-actualizers feel a kinship with and an understanding of others as well as a desire to help them.
- *Profound interpersonal relations.* Although their circle of friends is not large, self-actualizers have deep, lasting friendships. They tend to select as friends those with personal qualities similar to their own, just as we all choose as friends the people we find compatible. Self-actualizers often attract admirers or disciples. These relationships are usually one-sided; the admirer asks more of the self-actualizer than the self-actualizer is able or willing to give.
- *A democratic character structure.* Self-actualizers are tolerant and accepting of the personality and behavior of others. They display no racial, religious, or social prejudice. They are willing to listen to and learn from anyone capable of teaching them and are rarely condescending.
- *Creativeness.* Self-actualizing people are highly creative and exhibit inventiveness and originality in their work and other facets of life. They are flexible, spontaneous, and willing to make mistakes and learn from them. They are open and humble, in the way children are before society teaches them to be embarrassed or shy about possibly doing something foolish.
- *Resistance to enculturation.* Self-actualizers are autonomous, independent, and self-sufficient. They feel free to resist social and cultural pressures to think or behave in a certain way. They do not openly rebel against cultural norms or social codes, but they are governed by their own nature rather than the strictures of society.

This is quite an amazing set of attributes. According to Maslow's research, self-actualizers seem almost perfect. But they do have human flaws and imperfections. On occasion they can be rude, even ruthless, and they experience doubts, conflicts, and tension. Nevertheless, such incidents are rare and less intense than for the person who is not self-actualizing.

Failure to Become Self-Actualizing

If the need for self-actualization is innate and therefore does not have to be taught and learned, then why isn't everyone self-actualizing? Why has less than 1 percent of the population reached this state of being? One reason is that the higher the need in Maslow's proposed hierarchy, the weaker it is. As the highest need, self-actualization is the least potent. Thus, it can easily be inhibited. For example, hostile

Among the self-actualizers Maslow studied by analyzing biographies and other written records were the noted physicist Albert Einstein, and Harriet Tubman, a leader of the antislavery movement at the time of the American Civil War.

or rejecting parents make it difficult for a person to satisfy love and esteem needs. In this case, the self-actualization need may not emerge. At a lower level, poor economic conditions can make it difficult to satisfy physiological and safety needs, so self-actualization assumes less importance.

Inadequate education and improper child-rearing practices can thwart the drive for self-actualization in adulthood. Maslow cited the typical sex-role training for boys, who are taught to inhibit such qualities as tenderness and sentimentality. Thus, this aspect of their nature is not encouraged to fully develop.

If children are overprotected and not permitted to try new behaviors, explore new ideas, or practice new skills, then they are likely to be inhibited as adults, unable to express themselves fully in activities vital to self-actualization. The opposite behavior—excessive parental permissiveness—can also be harmful. Too much freedom in childhood can lead to anxiety and insecurity, thus undermining the safety needs. To Maslow, the ideal situation in childhood is a balance of permissiveness and regulation.

Sufficient love in childhood is a prerequisite for self-actualization, as well as satisfaction of physiological and safety needs within the first two years of life. If children feel secure and confident in the early years, they will remain so as adults. This position is similar to Erik Erikson's emphasis on the development of trust in early childhood and to Karen Horney's ideas on the childhood need for security.

Jonah complex
The fear that maximizing our potential will lead to a situation with which we will be unable to cope.

Without adequate parental love, security, and esteem in childhood, it is difficult to strive for self-actualization in adulthood.

Another reason for the failure to self-actualize is what Maslow called the **Jonah complex**. This idea is based on the biblical tale of Jonah, described by Maslow as "called by God to prophesy, but [Jonah] was afraid of the task. He tried to run away from it. But no matter where Jonah ran, he could find no hiding place. Finally, he understood that he had to accept his fate" (quoted in Hoffman, 1996, p. 50).

Thus, the Jonah complex refers to our doubts about our own abilities. We may fear that taking action to maximize our potential will lead to new situations with which we may be unable to cope. Simultaneously, we are afraid of and thrilled by the possibilities but too often the fear takes precedence.

Self-actualization requires courage. Even when the lower needs have been satisfied, we cannot simply sit back and wait to be swept along some flower-strewn path to ecstasy and fulfillment. The self-actualizing process takes effort, discipline, and self-control. Thus, for many people, it may seem easier and safer to accept life as it is rather than seek new challenges. Self-actualizers will constantly test themselves by abandoning secure routines and familiar behaviors and attitudes.

 LOG ON

Association for Humanistic Psychology

The Web site for the Association for Humanistic Psychology includes access to their online bookstore, a list of college programs in humanistic studies, a history of the humanistic psychology movement, and links to related sites.

APA: Humanistic Psychology

The Web site for the Humanistic Psychology Division of the American Psychological Association provides the history and goals of the division as well as access to its journal, programs of study, student awards, and more.

For direct links to these sites, log on to the student companion site for this book at http://www.academic.cengage.com/psychology/Schultz and choose Chapter 9.

Questions About Human Nature

Maslow's view of personality is humanistic and optimistic. He focused on psychological health rather than illness, growth rather than stagnation, virtues and potentials rather than weaknesses and limitations. He had a strong sense of confidence in our ability to shape our lives and our society.

Maslow believed that we are capable of shaping our free will even in the face of negative biological and constitutional factors. He wrote,

> the reality of biological injustice and unfairness: that some babies are born healthy and others unhealthy, some smart and others stupid, and some beautiful and others ugly. . . . It

is not something we can do anything about. It is determined. It is a limitation on free will. [Yet, everyone has] a great deal of leeway for free will, responsibility, and becoming an active agent rather than a pawn in life. There is a lot of leeway for helping myself rather than giving up and sinking, for doing the best that I can rather than whining. . . . What I do with my genetic endowment and my body is definitely more important than merely the given of my biological inheritance. (quoted in Hoffman, 1996, pp. 64–65)

We have the free will to choose how best to satisfy our needs and actualize our potential. We can either create an actualizing self or refrain from pursuing that supreme state of achievement. Thus, we are responsible for the level of personality development we reach.

Although the needs in Maslow's hierarchies are innate, the behaviors by which we satisfy them are learned. Therefore, personality is determined by the interaction of heredity and environment, of personal and situational variables. Although not explicit in his writings, Maslow seemed to favor the uniqueness of personality. Our motivations and needs are universal, but the ways in which the needs are satisfied will vary from person to person because these ways of behaving are learned. Even among self-actualizers, although they share certain qualities, their behaviors are not identical.

Maslow recognized the importance of early childhood experiences in fostering or inhibiting adult development, but he did not believe that we are victims of these experiences. We have more potential than we may realize to manage our life and our society and would be happier and more productive if we would learn to do so. Self-actualization as the ultimate and necessary goal reflects Maslow's belief that, given the proper conditions, we are capable of reaching the highest level of human functioning.

He argued that human nature is basically good, decent, and kind, but he did not deny the existence of evil. He believed some people were evil beyond reclamation and wrote in his journal that "nothing will work ultimately [with them] but shooting" (Maslow, 1979, p. 631). He suggested that wickedness was not an inherited trait but rather the result of an inappropriate environment. Maslow's compassion for humanity is clear in his writings, and his optimism is expressed in the belief that each of us is capable of fulfilling our vast human potential.

Assessment in Maslow's Theory

Maslow's work on self-actualization did not begin as a formal program of personality assessment and research. He started his investigation out of curiosity about two people who impressed him, the anthropologist Ruth Benedict and the Gestalt psychologist Max Wertheimer. Maslow admired them greatly and wanted to understand what made them so different from the other people he knew. After observing them carefully he concluded that they shared certain qualities that set them apart from the average individual.

Maslow then attempted to assess these characteristics in other people. His first research subjects were college students, but he found only 1 out of 3,000 he could describe as self-actualizing. He decided that the characteristics for the self-actualizing personality, those qualities he had identified in Benedict and Wertheimer, were not developed in young people. His next step was to study middle-aged and older persons. However, even among this group Maslow found less than 1 percent of the population capable of meeting his criteria for self-actualization.

The self-actualizers he finally identified included several dozen persons he designated as sure or probable cases, partial cases, or potential cases. Some were Maslow's contemporaries. Others were historical figures such as Thomas Jefferson, Albert Einstein, George Washington Carver, Harriet Tubman, and Eleanor Roosevelt. Maslow used a variety of techniques to assess their personalities. For historical figures, he worked with biographical material, analyzing written records for similarities in personal characteristics. For the living subjects he relied on interviews, free association, and projective tests. He found that many of these people were self-conscious when questioned, so often he was forced to study them indirectly, although he did not explain precisely how this was done.

The Personal Orientation Inventory

The Personal Orientation Inventory (POI), a self-report questionnaire consisting of 150 pairs of statements, was developed by psychologist Everett Shostrom to measure self-actualization (Shostrom, 1964, 1974). People taking the test must indicate which of each pair is more applicable to them (see Table 9.3).

The POI is scored for two major scales and 10 subscales. The major scales are time competence, which measures the degree to which we live in the present, and inner directedness, which assesses how much we depend on ourselves rather than on others for judgments and values.

Table 9.3 Sample items from the Personal Orientation Inventory. Respondents select the item in each pair that is more descriptive of them.

I do what others expect of me.
I feel free to not do what others expect of me.

I must justify my actions in the pursuit of my own interests.
I need not justify my actions in the pursuit of my own interests.

I live by the rules and standards of society.
I do not always need to live by the rules and standards of society.

Reasons are needed to justify my feelings.
Reasons are not needed to justify my feelings.

I only feel free to express warm feelings to my friends.
I feel free to express both warm and hostile feelings to my friends.

I will continue to grow only by setting my sights on a high-level, socially approved goal.
I will continue to grow best by being myself.

People should always control their anger.
People should express honestly felt anger.

SOURCE: From "An Inventory for the Measurement of Self-Actualization" by E. L. Shostrom, 1964, *Educational and Psychological Measurement, 24*, pp. 207–218.

Research on Maslow's Theory

Maslow did not use case studies or the experimental or correlational methods in his research. Critics have charged that Maslow's methods for studying his self-actualizers were not rigorous or controlled. Maslow agreed; he knew his investigations failed to adhere to the requirements of scientific research. He wrote, "By ordinary standards of laboratory research, this simply was not research at all" (1971, p. 42). But he believed that because self-actualization could not be studied by accepted scientific procedures, the alternative was to wait until appropriate techniques were developed or not to study the issue at all.

Maslow was too impatient to postpone his research, too committed to the conviction that he could help humanity. He wrote that he did not have enough time to perform careful experiments. "They take too long in view of the years I have left and the extent of what I want to do" (1979, p. 694). He referred to his program as consisting of pilot studies only. Convinced that the results were valid, he expected other researchers to eventually confirm his theory. Maslow also suggested that to support and justify his conclusions, which he knew were correct, he somehow needed to collect less data than did other theorists.

Correlational Studies

The POI has been widely used for correlational research in which POI scores are correlated with other measures of behavior and personality. Scores indicating higher self-actualization have been positively related to several factors: emotional health, creativity, well-being following therapy, academic achievement, autonomy, and racial tolerance. Other studies report negative correlations between high self-actualization scores and alcoholism, institutionalization for mental disturbances, neuroticism, depression, and hypochondriasis. These results are in the expected directions based on Maslow's description of self-actualizers. POI research on women, ages 19 to 55, confirmed Maslow's view that self-actualization occurs gradually over the life span.

It is important to remember that this research involves correlational studies and that there is no valid independent measure of self-actualization with which to correlate the POI scores. It does not necessarily follow that the POI is actually measuring self-actualization, even though it correlates well with variables believed to be associated with self-actualization.

The Hierarchy of Needs

In support of Maslow's theory, a study of men and women college students found that satisfaction of the needs for safety, belongingness, and esteem was negatively related to neuroticism and depression (Williams & Page, 1989). This research, using a test designed to measure the three needs, also showed that esteem needs were stronger than belongingness needs. The subjects expressed less concern with safety needs, as expected among people of college age.

A study using the Need Satisfaction Inventory, a self-report questionnaire designed to measure how well a person satisfies Maslow's needs, correlated test scores of college students with their scores on the Eysenck Personality Inventory. Again, the results showed that those who were higher in need satisfaction were lower in neuroticism (Lester, 1990).

An elaborate test of the hierarchy using a sample representative of the general population supported the order of the five needs (Graham & Balloun, 1973). The study also demonstrated that the amount of concern people expressed about each need increased from the lowest to the highest need. Physiological needs, presumably well satisfied in these subjects, were of little concern to them. The self-actualization need was of the greatest interest, presumably because it was not so well satisfied.

The Belongingness Need

Maslow's proposed need for belongingness can only be satisfied through association with, and, more important, acceptance by other people. Some psychologists consider the need to belong to be as powerful a drive as the physiological needs for food and water. In one study, 91 college students who were led to believe they were interacting with others in an Internet chat room were then excluded and rejected by these other perceived participants. No one responded to their messages; no one replied to their comments and questions. All the other participants seemed to be engaged in convivial online conversation. But the participants in the study had been made social isolates.

Following that experience, the research participants were asked to read a diary, allegedly written by a college student. They were then instructed to write down as many of the activities mentioned in the diary as they could remember. Those students whose need to belong had been thwarted by the online experience recalled significantly more social events from the diary than did students whose need to belong had been satisfied in the simulated chat room. The researchers concluded that failure to satisfy the need to belong can influence a cognitive activity such as memory and affect the type of events a person will recall (Gardner, Pickett, & Brewer, 2000).

In another study, 43 college students were led to believe that they had been excluded or rejected by members of an Internet chat room. The students reported lower levels of self-esteem, control, and belongingness than students who had not been told they had been ostracized (Smith & Williams, 2004). These negative feelings developed within 8 minutes of being informed of their exclusion.

Self-Esteem

Research supports Maslow's position that people high in self-esteem have greater self-worth and self-confidence. They also feel more competent and productive than do people low in self-esteem. People high in self-esteem function better in many situations. In a study of college students seeking jobs, those with high self-esteem received more job offers and were rated more favorably by recruiters than were students with low self-esteem (Ellis & Taylor, 1983). Another study found that people with high self-esteem coped more effectively with the difficulties of job loss than did those with low self-esteem (Shamir, 1986). In addition, people high in self-esteem were found to perceive themselves to be significantly higher in intellectual skills, agreeableness, and morality, and to be more extraverted, than those who measured low in self-esteem (Campbell, Rudich, & Sedikides, 2002).

Research with young adults in the United States and in Canada showed that those who measured high in self-esteem were much more likely to participate in school sports and to have lower levels of anxiety and defensive behaviors (Bowker, 2006; Pyszczynski, Greenberg, Solomon, Arndt, & Schimel, 2004).

Two large-scale research programs studied nearly 6,000 male and female subjects, ages 5 to 26, over an 11-year period in the United States and in New Zealand. The results showed that low self-esteem was related to anxiety, depression, smoking addiction, school dropout rates, criminal convictions, financial problems, and difficulties at work (see Donnellan, Trzesniewski, Robins, Moffitt, & Caspi, 2005; Trzesniewski, Donnellan, Moffitt, Robins, Poulton, & Caspi, 2006).

A study of 1,362 adolescents in Canada in the 7th, 9th, and 11th grades of school found that more than one-third reported that their perceived physical appearance (how attractive they thought they were) determined their level of self-esteem. The results also showed that teenagers who were more concerned with their appearance reported lower self-esteem than those who were less concerned about how they looked. No differences were found between boys and girls on these variables (Seidah & Bouffard, 2007).

Research has also shown that people who measured low in self-esteem and who had been led to believe they had been deliberately excluded from a laboratory group by the other members reported a significantly greater feeling of rejection than did people high in self-esteem (Nezlek, Kowalski, Leary, Blevins, & Holgate, 1997). A longitudinal study of 642 college students found that those rated low in self-esteem experienced significantly more social problems of adjustment and getting along with other people than those high in self-esteem (Crocker & Luhtanen, 2003).

Even the accuracy of memory can be affected by self-esteem. In a study using college students, the research participants were given feedback about their personality, some of which was favorable and flattering, and some of which was unfavorable and unflattering. Those with high self-esteem recalled the favorable feedback far more accurately than did those with low self-esteem. Conversely, research participants low in self-esteem recalled the unfavorable feedback better than did those with high self-esteem (Story, 1998).

Studies on other aspects of self-esteem have shown that research subjects with an unstable sense of self-esteem do not possess as strong a sense of self as do those whose self-esteem remains stable over most or all situations (Kernis, Paradise, Whitaker, Wheatman, & Goldman, 2000). Large-scale studies involving more than 400,000 research participants found that self-esteem levels were high in childhood, dropped during adolescence, and rose in adulthood. They then began to decline in middle age and old age, eventually reaching levels as low as during adolescence (Robins, Trzesniewski, Tracy, Gosling, & Potter, 2002; Trzesniewski, Donnellan, & Robins, 2003).

Other research has demonstrated that Black teenagers report higher self-esteem than White teenagers. High self-esteem has also been shown to correlate with delinquency rates among a sample of Mexican-American teenage boys (Caldwell, Beutler, Ross, & Silver, 2006; Swenson & Prelow, 2005).

Although the benefits of high self-esteem appear obvious, failure to achieve self-esteem goals, such as high grades in school or success on the job, can lead to increased anger, shame, sadness, and feelings of worthlessness among high self-esteem subjects

(Crocker & Park, 2004). Thus, one's level of self-esteem can have enduring effects; people with low self-esteem may think and act in self-defeating ways that "diminish their quality of life" (Swann, Chang-Schneider, & McClarty, 2007, p. 92).

Self-Determination Theory

A contemporary outgrowth of the spirit, or essence, of Maslow's self-actualization theory is the self-determination theory, which suggests that people have an innate tendency to express their interests, exercise and develop their capabilities and potentials, and overcome challenges (Ryan & Deci, 2000). Self-determination is facilitated by a person's focus on *intrinsic motivation*, such as engaging in an activity because of the interest and challenge of the activity itself. (*Extrinsic motivation* involves engaging in some activity only for the sake of external rewards such as praise, a promotion, or a higher grade.) You can see a basic similarity between the notions of intrinsic motivation and self-determination, and Maslow's description of self-actualization. Both are concerned with fulfilling or realizing one's talents and abilities for the goal of inner satisfaction rather than some external reward.

Self-determination theory specifies three basic needs; only through the satisfaction of these needs can a person reach a state of well-being.

1. Competence—the need to feel that one can master difficult tasks
2. Autonomy—the freedom to base one's course of action on one's own interests, needs, and values
3. Relatedness—the need to feel a close connection with other people

Studies have shown that the satisfaction of these needs, and the corresponding focus on intrinsic motivation, is positively associated with high self-esteem and self-actualization (Ryan & Deci, 2000).

Reflections on Maslow's Theory

Criticisms of Maslow's theory center on his research methods and lack of experimentally generated supporting data. The sample from which the data were derived, fewer than half of whom were interviewed, is too small for generalization to the population at large. The ways Maslow amassed information about his self-actualizing subjects are inconsistent and vague. He did not describe how he interpreted test results or analyzed biographical materials, nor did he indicate how free associations and interview responses led him to identify those particular persons as self-actualizing. However, as we noted with other theorists, weakness in scientific methodology is not unique.

For his subjects Maslow selected people he admired, according to his criteria for self-actualization. These criteria were not specified at the time, and he later admitted that self-actualization was difficult to describe accurately. His list of characteristics of self-actualizers derives solely from his clinical interpretations of the data and may easily have been influenced by his personal philosophy and moral values. Thus, the descriptions may actually reflect Maslow's own ideal of the worthy and emotionally healthy individual.

Other criticisms have been directed at Maslow's definitions of various concepts such as metaneeds, metapathology, peak experiences, and self-actualization. His use of these terms could be inconsistent and ambiguous. Critics also have asked on what basis self-actualization is presumed to be innate. Why could it not be learned behavior, the result of some unique combination of childhood experiences? Maslow's defense against these charges was that although his theory was not widely supported by laboratory research, it was successful in social, clinical, and personal terms. He wrote, "It has fitted very well with the personal experience of most people, and has often given them a structured theory that has helped them to make better sense of their inner lives" (Maslow, 1970b, p. xii).

Partly because of Maslow's optimism and compassion, his theory, and the humanistic approach to psychology in general, became popular in the 1960s and 1970s. The trappings of a formal school of thought were then set in place. Journals and organizations relating to humanistic psychology were founded, and a division of humanistic psychology was created within the American Psychological Association. Today, the concerns of humanistic psychologists are experiencing a rebirth in the positive psychology movement. More than one leader of that movement credits humanistic psychology as a forerunner of positive psychology (see, for example, Diener, Oishi, & Lucas, 2003). Thus, Maslow's legacy has endured for more than 40 years, from one century to the next.

As a pioneer of humanistic psychology, Maslow attracted admirers and disciples among students and professionals who had become disenchanted with behaviorist and psychoanalytic approaches to personality and to psychology. Few theories have had such a broad impact beyond the discipline. Teachers and counselors, business and government leaders, health care professionals, and many people trying to cope with everyday hassles have found Maslow's views compatible with their needs and useful in solving problems. Maslow issued a call to make psychology responsive to the problems of modern society. He argued forcefully that the survival of civilization depends on our ability to develop our full potential and to become self-actualizing.

Chapter Summary

Maslow argued that each person is born with instinctoid needs that lead to growth, development, and actualization. The hierarchy of needs includes physiological needs (for food, water, air, sleep, and sex) and the needs for safety, belongingness and love, esteem, and self-actualization. The lower needs must be satisfied before the higher needs emerge. The lower the need, the greater its strength. Lower needs are called deficit needs because failure to satisfy them produces a deficit in the body. Higher needs (growth or being needs) are less necessary for survival but enhance physical and emotional well-being. Safety needs (for security, stability, order, and freedom from fear and anxiety) are most important in infants and neurotic adults. Belongingness and love needs can be satisfied through association with a group or affectionate relations with one person or with people in general. Esteem needs include self-esteem and esteem from others. Self-actualization involves the realization of one's potential and requires a realistic knowledge of one's strengths and weaknesses. The needs to know and to understand form a hierarchy of cognitive needs that emerges in late infancy and early childhood.

Motivation in self-actualizers (metamotivation) serves not to make up for deficits or reduce tension but to enrich life and increase tension. Metaneeds are states of growth toward which self-actualizers move. Frustration of metaneeds produces metapathology, a formless illness for which no specific cause can be identified. Self-actualizers constitute less than one percent of the population. They share the following characteristics: efficient perception of reality; acceptance of themselves and others; spontaneity and simplicity; focus on problems rather than self in which metaneeds are satisfied through commitment to work; privacy and independence; freshness of appreciation; peak experiences; social interest; intense interpersonal relationships; creativeness; democratic character structure; and resistance to enculturation. Not everyone becomes self-actualizing because self-actualization is the weakest need in the hierarchy and easily interfered with. Too much freedom or lack of security in childhood inhibits self-actualization. Also, some people fear realizing their highest potential, what Maslow termed the Jonah complex.

Maslow's image of human nature is optimistic, emphasizing free will, conscious choice, uniqueness, the ability to overcome childhood experiences, and innate goodness. Personality is influenced both by heredity and by environment. Our ultimate goal is self-actualization.

Maslow used interviews, free association, projective techniques, and biographical material to assess personality. The Personal Orientation Inventory is a self-report test to measure self-actualization. Some research supports the characteristics of self-actualizers, the relationship between self-esteem and self-competence and self-liking, the order of the needs in the hierarchy, and the greater concern with higher than lower needs. People high in self-esteem feel better about themselves, work harder at tasks, and see themselves as more intelligent, agreeable, and moral than people low in self-esteem. Self-esteem levels are reported to be high in childhood and low in adolescence, rising in adulthood and falling in middle age and old age. A contemporary outgrowth of Maslow's work is self-determination theory, which posits three needs: competence, autonomy, and relatedness.

Maslow has been criticized for using too small a sample as the basis for his theory and for not making explicit his criteria for selecting self-actualizing research participants. His theory has had a broad impact in education, counseling, health care, and business and government. It has proven to be a stimulus for the positive psychology movement, which focuses on subjective well-being.

Review Questions

1. What criticisms did the humanistic psychologists make of behaviorism and psychoanalysis?

2. In what ways was Maslow's childhood an example of Adler's theory of personality?

3. Describe the hierarchy of needs Maslow proposed.

4. What are the differences between the higher needs and the lower needs?

5. Distinguish between deficiency needs and growth needs. Which type was Maslow concerned with?

6. Describe Maslow's characteristics of needs.

7. Discuss the differences between the safety needs and the belongingness and love needs.

8. What conditions are necessary in order to satisfy the self-actualization need?

9. At what age do we develop the needs to know and to understand? Which of these needs is the stronger?

10. Define metaneeds and metapathology.

11. Discuss the motivation and the characteristics of self-actualizing people.

12. What are peak experiences? Are they necessary for self-actualization?

13. Why do so few people satisfy the need for self-actualization?

14. What child-rearing practices can thwart the drive for self-actualization?

15. How does Maslow's image of human nature differ from Freud's?

16. What does correlational research reveal about the relationship between self-actualization and certain personality characteristics?

17. How does self-esteem affect memory? How does it affect feelings of rejection?

18. How do people who are high in self-esteem differ from people who are low in self-esteem?

19. Describe the nature of self-determination theory. Identify the three needs proposed by the theory.

20. On what grounds has Maslow's work on self-actualization been criticized? How did he respond to his critics?

Suggested Readings

Crocker, J., & Park, L. (2004). The costly pursuit of self-esteem. *Psychological Bulletin, 130*, 392–414. Reviews the research literature on the self-esteem need, as proposed by Maslow, and suggests that how people strive for self-esteem is more important than whether it is high or low because short-term emotional benefits can often be outweighed by long-term costs.

Frick, W. B. (2000). Remembering Maslow: Reflections on a 1968 interview. *Journal of Humanistic Psychology, 40*, 128–147. Excerpts from an interview with Maslow and comments on his problems with his work as well as the likely impact of the concept of self-actualization and humanistic psychology.

Hall, M. H. (1968, July). A conversation with Abraham H. Maslow. *Psychology Today*, pp. 35–37, 54–57. An interview with Maslow about the scope of his work.

Hoffman, E. (1988). *The right to be human: A biography of Abraham Maslow*. Los Angeles: Jeremy Tarcher. A biography based on published and unpublished material describing Maslow's difficult childhood, tracing his career from his early work with primates to his involvement with the human potential movement.

Maslow, A. H. (1968). *Toward a psychology of being* (2nd ed.). New York: Van Nostrand Reinhold. States Maslow's view that humans can be loving, noble, and creative and are capable of pursuing the highest values and aspirations. Also acknowledges the importance of Freud's concept of the unconscious.

Maslow, A. H. (1970). *Motivation and personality* (2nd ed.). New York: Harper & Row. Presents Maslow's theory of motivation and personality, emphasizing psychological health and self-actualization. A third edition (Harper & Row, 1987), revised and edited by Robert Frager and James Fadiman, includes material on Maslow's life, the historical significance of his work, and applications of self-actualization to management, medicine, and education.

Maslow, A. H. (1996). *The unpublished papers of Abraham Maslow*. Edited by E. Hoffman. Thousand Oaks, CA: Sage. Includes previously unpublished essays, articles, and papers with annotations and a biographical sketch.

Milton, J. (2002). *The road to Malpsychia: Humanistic psychology and our discontents*. San Francisco: Encounter Books. A cultural and social history of the humanistic psychology movement including an assessment of the contributions of Abraham Maslow.

Mittelman, W. (1991). Maslow's study of self-actualization: A reinterpretation. *Journal of Humanistic Psychology, 31*, 114–135. Suggests that Maslow's self-actualizing subjects were distinguished not by an ability to actualize their potential but by their degree of openness, that is, being receptive and responsive to information from one's self and the environment, and not ignoring difficulties and problems.

Robins, R. W., Trzesniewski, K. H., Tracy, J. L., Gosling, S. D., & Potter, J. (2002). Global self-esteem across the life span. *Psychology and Aging, 17*, 423–434. Examines Maslow's proposed self-esteem need among more than 300,000 people of diverse nationalities, aged 9–90, from data collected through Internet questionnaires.

CHAPTER 10

Carl Rogers:
Self-Actualization Theory

The organism has one basic tendency and striving—to actualize, maintain, and enhance the experiencing organism.

—CARL ROGERS

Carl Rogers originated a popular approach to psychotherapy known initially as non-directive or client-centered therapy and later as person-centered therapy. This form of psychotherapy has generated an enormous amount of research and is widely applied in the treatment of emotional disturbances. Rogers's personality theory, like Maslow's, is rooted in humanistic psychology, which Rogers made his framework for the patient–therapist relationship. Rogers developed his theory not from experimental laboratory research but from his experiences working with clients. Thus, his formulations on the structure and dynamics of personality derive from his therapeutic approach. Rogers's view of the therapeutic situation tells much about his view of human nature.

Consider the phrase *person-centered therapy*. It suggests that the ability to change and improve personality is centered within the person. In other words, it is the person and not the therapist who directs such change. The therapist's role is to assist or facilitate the change.

Rogers believed that we are rational beings ruled by a conscious perception of our selves and our experiential world. Rogers did not ascribe much importance to unconscious forces or other Freudian explanations. He also rejected the notion that past events exert a controlling influence on present behavior. Although he recognized that childhood experiences affect the way we perceive our environment, and ourselves, Rogers insisted that current feelings and emotions have a greater impact on personality. Because of this emphasis on the conscious and the present, Rogers suggested that personality could only be understood from our own viewpoint, based on our subjective experiences. Rogers dealt with reality as consciously perceived by each of us, and he noted that this perception did not always coincide with objective reality.

Rogers proposed a single, innate, overriding motivation: the inborn tendency to actualize, to develop our abilities and potentials, from the strictly biological to the most sophisticated psychological aspects of our being. This ultimate goal is to actualize the self, to become what Rogers called a *fully functioning person*. His approach to therapy and theory, and the optimistic and humanistic picture he painted, received enthusiastic acceptance in psychology, education, and family-life research.

The Life of Rogers (1902–1987)

A Reliance on His Own Experience

The fourth child in a family of six, Rogers was born in 1902 in Oak Park, Illinois, a suburb of Chicago. His parents held strict religious views and emphasized moral behavior, the suppression of displays of emotion, and the virtue of hard work. Their fundamentalist teachings gripped Rogers like a vise, as he described it, throughout his childhood and adolescence. These beliefs forced him to live by someone else's view of the world rather than his own. He soon made them a target for revolt.

His parents promoted their influence in subtle and loving ways, as Rogers later did in his nondirective approach to counseling. It was understood by all the children that they did not "dance, play cards, attend movies, smoke, drink, or show any sexual interest" (Rogers, 1967, p. 344). Rogers had little social life outside his family. Because he came to believe that his parents showed favoritism toward an older brother, there was considerable competitiveness between them. Rogers described himself as shy, solitary, dreamy, and often lost in fantasy. A biographer noted that Rogers grew up with "bitter memories of being the inevitable butt of his brother's jokes, even as he was starved of joy by his mother" (Milton, 2002, p. 128).

In a bid to escape this loneliness, he read incessantly, any book he could find, even the dictionary and encyclopedia. His solitude led him to depend on his own resources and experiences, his personal view of the world. This characteristic remained with him throughout his life and became the foundation of his personality theory. In later years, he realized how strongly his loneliness had influenced his theory as well as his own personality.

> As I look back, I realize that my interest in interviewing and in therapy certainly grew out of my early loneliness. Here was a socially approved way of getting really close to individuals and thus filling some of the hunger I had undoubtedly felt. (Rogers, 1980, p. 34)

When Rogers was 12, the family moved to a farm 30 miles from Chicago. Rural life awakened his interest in science. First, he became fascinated by a species of moth he discovered in the woods. He observed, captured, and bred them over many months. Second, he became interested in farming, which his father pursued with modern, scientific methods. Rogers read about farming and agricultural experiments and came to appreciate the value of the scientific approach with its use of control groups, isolation of a variable for study, and statistical analysis of data. It was an unusual undertaking for an adolescent. At the same time, his emotional life was in turmoil, the nature of which he never fully explained. He wrote, "My fantasies during this period were definitely bizarre, and probably would be classified as schizoid by a diagnostician, but fortunately, I never came in contact with a psychologist" (Rogers, 1980, p. 30).

He chose to study agriculture at the University of Wisconsin, the college his parents, two older brothers, and a sister had attended. But following his sophomore year, he abandoned the scientific study of agriculture to prepare for the ministry. In his junior year at Wisconsin, Rogers was selected to attend an international Christian student conference in Beijing, China. During his 6 months of travel, he wrote to his parents that his philosophy of life was changing. His religious views had swung from fundamentalist to liberal.

Freeing himself of his parents' ways grieved them, but the shift brought Rogers emotional and intellectual independence. He realized, he later wrote, that he could "think my own thoughts, come to my own conclusions, and take the stands I believed in" (Rogers, 1967, p. 351). This liberation, and the confidence and direction it gave him, reinforced Rogers's opinion that all human beings must learn to rely on their own experiences, ideas, and beliefs. But for Rogers, reaching this conclusion was a difficult process, and he paid a high emotional price. After being hospitalized for 5 weeks for ulcers, which may have been induced by stress, he remained at the family farm for a year to recuperate before returning to college.

A Unique Approach to Counseling

In 1924, Rogers graduated from the University of Wisconsin, married a childhood friend, and enrolled at Union Theological Seminary in New York. Still intending to become a clergyman, he nevertheless transferred after two years to Teachers College of Columbia University, across the street, to study clinical and educational psychology. He received his Ph.D. in 1931 and joined the staff of the Child Study Department of the Society for the Prevention of Cruelty to Children in Rochester, New York. His job involved diagnosing and treating delinquent and underprivileged children.

In 1940, he moved from a clinical to an academic setting with an appointment as professor of psychology at Ohio State University. There, Rogers began to formulate his views on counseling for emotionally disturbed persons. He also worked to bring clinical psychology into the mainstream of contemporary psychological thought. He spent the years 1945 to 1957 at the University of Chicago, teaching and developing the Counseling Center. Once when he was unable to help a severely disturbed client, he became so upset that he fell ill himself, suffering what was then called a nervous breakdown. His self-confidence was shattered. He wrote that he felt "deeply certain of my complete inadequacy as a therapist, my worthlessness as a person, and my lack of any future in the field of psychology" (Rogers, 1967, p. 367).

He quickly made the decision to leave Chicago. He and his wife set out for their cabin in upstate New York where Rogers remained secluded for the next 6 months. When he felt well enough to return to the university, he also began therapy, becoming aware of just how deep his feelings of insecurity were. He said he believed that "no one could ever love *me*, even though they might like what I did" (quoted in Milton, 2002, p. 131). Rogers's therapy was apparently successful; he emerged with a newfound ability to give and receive love and to form deep emotional relationships with other people, including his clients.

Rogers taught at the University of Wisconsin from 1957 to 1963. During these years, he published many articles and books that brought his personality theory and person-centered therapy to a wide audience. His clinical experience while in academia was mostly with college students in the counseling centers. Thus, the kind of person he treated during that time—young, intelligent, highly verbal, and, in general, facing adjustment problems rather than severe emotional disorders—was vastly different from the kind of person treated by the Freudians or by clinical psychologists in private practice.

In 1964, Rogers became a resident fellow at the Western Behavioral Sciences Institute in California, working to apply his person-centered philosophy to international problems such as the reduction of tension between Protestants and Catholics in Northern Ireland, and Jews and Arabs in the Middle East. He served as president of the American Psychological Association in 1946 and received that organization's Distinguished Scientific Contribution Award and Distinguished Professional Contribution Award.

 Log On

Psychology History: Carl Rogers

A brief biography of Rogers, an overview of his theory, an example of his form of therapy, a timeline, and a bibliography.

Personality Theories: Carl Rogers

A biography of Rogers and a detailed discussion of the major aspects of his personality theory and his person-centered therapy.

For direct links to these sites, log on to the student companion site for this book at http://www.academic.cengage.com/psychology/Schultz and choose Chapter 10.

The Self and the Tendency toward Actualization

During his trip to China, Rogers came to recognize the importance of an autonomous self as a factor in his own development. His early research reinforced the importance of the self in the formation of the personality. In the 1930s, he developed a method for determining whether a child's behavior was healthy and constructive or unhealthy and destructive. He investigated the child's background and had the child rated on factors he believed would influence behavior. These factors included the family environment, health, intellectual development, economic circumstances, cultural influences, social interactions, and level of education. All of these factors are external, that is, part of the child's environment. Rogers also investigated a potential internal influence, the child's self-understanding or self-insight. Rogers described self-insight as an acceptance of self and reality, and a sense of responsibility for the self.

Approximately a decade later, William Kell, one of Rogers's students, adopted this evaluative approach in an attempt to predict the behavior of delinquent children. Rogers suggested that the factors of family environment and social interactions would correlate most strongly with delinquent behavior, but he was wrong. The factor that most accurately predicted later behavior was self-insight.

Surprised to learn that family environment did not relate highly to later delinquent behavior, Rogers wrote, "I was simply not prepared to accept this finding, and the study was put on the shelf" (1987, p. 119). As we noted earlier, scientists sometimes reject data that do not agree with their views and expectations. Two years later, Helen McNeil replicated the study using a different group of research participants. She obtained similar results. One's level of self-insight was the single most important predictor of behavior.

This time, faced with an accumulation of data, Rogers accepted the findings and, on reflection, came to appreciate their significance. If one's attitude toward the self were more important in predicting behavior than the external factors widely thought to be so influential in childhood, then counselors and social workers were emphasizing the wrong things in trying to treat delinquent children and adolescents! Counselors traditionally focus on external factors such as a poor family environment and alter the circumstances by removing children from a threatening home situation and placing them in foster care. Instead, they should be trying to modify the children's self-insight. That realization was important to Rogers personally.

> This experience helped me decide to focus my career on the development of a psychotherapy that would bring about greater awareness of self-understanding, self-direction, and personal responsibility, rather than focusing on changes in the social environment. It led me to place greater emphasis on the study of the self and how it changes. (Rogers, 1987, p. 119)

Thus, the self became the core of Rogers's theory of personality, as it had become the core of his own life.

Rogers believed people are motivated by an innate tendency to actualize, maintain, and enhance the self. This drive toward self-actualization is part of a larger **actualization tendency**, which encompasses all physiological and psychological needs. By attending to basic requirements—such as the needs for food, water, and safety—the actualization tendency serves to maintain the organism, providing for sustenance and survival.

actualization tendency
The basic human motivation to actualize, maintain, and enhance the self.

The actualization tendency begins in the womb, facilitating human growth by providing for the differentiation of the physical organs and the development of physiological functioning. It is responsible for maturation—the genetically determined development of the body's parts and processes—ranging from the growth of the fetus to the appearance of the secondary sex characteristics at puberty. These changes, programmed into our genetic makeup, are all brought to fruition by the actualization tendency.

Even though such changes are genetically determined, progress toward full human development is neither automatic nor effortless. To Rogers, the process involved struggle and pain. For example, when children take their first steps they may fall and hurt themselves. Although it would be less painful to remain in the crawling stage, most children persist. They may fall again and cry, but they persevere despite the pain because the tendency to actualize is stronger than the urge to regress simply because the growth process is difficult.

organismic valuing process
The process by which we judge experiences in terms of their value for fostering or hindering our actualization and growth.

The governing process throughout the life span, as Rogers envisioned it, is the **organismic valuing process**. Through this process we evaluate all life experiences by how well they serve the actualization tendency. Experiences that we perceive as promoting actualization are evaluated as good and desirable; we assign them a positive value. Experiences perceived as hindering actualization are undesirable and thus earn a negative value. These perceptions influence behavior because we prefer to avoid undesirable experiences and repeat desirable experiences.

The Experiential World

In developing his theory, Rogers weighed the impact of the experiential world in which we operate daily. This provides a frame of reference or context that influences our growth. We are exposed to countless sources of stimulation, some trivial and some important, some threatening and others rewarding. He wanted to know how we perceive and react to this multifaceted world of experience.

He answered the question by saying that the reality of our environment depends on our perception of it, which may not always coincide with reality. We may react to an experience far differently from the way our best friend does. You may judge the behavior of your roommate in a dramatically different way than does someone decades older. Our perceptions change with time and circumstances. Your own opinion of what you consider to be acceptable collegiate behavior will be different by the time you are 70.

The notion that perception is subjective is an old one and not unique to Rogers. This idea, called *phenomenology*, argues that the only reality of which we can be sure is our own subjective world of experience, our inner perception of reality. The phenomenological approach within philosophy refers to an unbiased description of our conscious perception of the world, just as it occurs, without any attempt on our part at interpretation or analysis. In Rogers's view, the most important point about our world of experience is that it is private and thus can only be known completely to each of us.

As the actualization tendency in infancy leads us to grow and develop, our experiential world broadens. Infants are exposed to more and more sources of stimulation and respond to them as they are subjectively perceived. Our experiences become the only basis for our judgments and behaviors. Rogers wrote, "Experience is, for me, the highest authority. The touchstone of validity is my own experience" (1961, p. 23). Higher levels of development sharpen our experiential world and ultimately lead to the formation of the self.

The Development of the Self in Childhood

As infants gradually develop a more complex experiential field from widening social encounters, one part of their experience becomes differentiated from the rest. This separate part, defined by the words *I*, *me*, and *myself*, is the self or self-concept. The formation of the self-concept involves distinguishing what is directly and immediately a part of the self from the people, objects, and events that are external to the self. The self-concept is also our image of what we are, what we should be, and what we would like to be.

Ideally, the self is a consistent pattern, an organized whole. All aspects of the self strive for consistency. For example, people who are disturbed about having aggressive feelings and choose to deny them dare not express any obvious aggressive behaviors. To do so would mean taking responsibility for actions that are inconsistent with their self-concept, because they believe they should not be aggressive.

Positive Regard

positive regard
Acceptance, love, and approval from others.

As the self emerges, infants develop a need for what Rogers called **positive regard**. This need is probably learned, although Rogers said the source was not important. The need for positive regard is universal and persistent. It includes acceptance, love, and approval from other people, most notably from the mother during infancy.

Infants find it satisfying to receive positive regard and frustrating not to receive it or to have it withdrawn. Because positive regard is crucial to personality development, infant behavior is guided by the amount of affection and love bestowed. If the mother does not offer positive regard, then the infant's innate tendency toward actualization and development of the self-concept will be hampered. Infants perceive parental disapproval of their behavior as disapproval of their newly developing self. If this occurs frequently, infants will cease to strive for actualization and development. Instead, they will act in ways that will bring positive regard from others, even if these actions are inconsistent with their self-concept.

unconditional positive regard
Approval granted regardless of a person's behavior. In Rogers's person-centered therapy, the therapist offers the client unconditional positive regard.

Even though infants may receive sufficient acceptance, love, and approval, some specific behaviors may bring punishment. However, if positive regard for the infant persists despite the infant's undesirable behaviors, the condition is called **unconditional positive regard**. By this, Rogers meant that the mother's love for the child is granted freely and fully; it is not conditional or dependent on the child's behavior.

Ideally, a parent provides unconditional positive regard.

© James Doberman/Iconica/Getty Images

An important aspect of the need for positive regard is its reciprocal nature. When people perceive themselves to be satisfying someone else's need for positive regard, they in turn experience satisfaction of that need themselves. Therefore, it is rewarding to satisfy someone else's need for positive regard. Because of the importance of satisfying the need for positive regard, particularly in infancy, we become sensitive to the attitudes and behaviors of other people. By interpreting the feedback we receive from them (either approval or disapproval), we refine our self-concept. Thus, in forming the self-concept we internalize the attitudes of other people.

positive self-regard
The condition under which we grant ourselves acceptance and approval.

In time, positive regard will come more from within us than from other people, a condition Rogers called **positive self-regard**. Positive self-regard becomes as strong as our need for positive regard from others, and it may be satisfied in the same way. For example, children who are rewarded with affection, approval, and love when they are happy will come to generate positive self-regard whenever they behave in a happy way. Thus, in a sense, we learn to reward ourselves. Positive self-regard, like positive regard, is reciprocal. When people receive positive regard and develop positive self-regard, in turn they may provide positive regard to others.

Conditions of Worth

conditions of worth
To Rogers, a belief that we are worthy of approval only when we express desirable behaviors and attitudes and refrain from expressing those that bring disapproval from others; similar to the Freudian superego.

Conditions of worth evolve from this developmental sequence of positive regard leading to positive self-regard. Positive self-regard is Rogers's version of the Freudian superego, and it derives from **conditional positive regard**. We noted that *unconditional* positive regard involves the parents' love and acceptance of the infant without conditions, independent of the child's behavior. *Conditional* positive regard is the opposite. Parents may not react to everything their infant does with positive regard. Some behaviors annoy, frighten, or bore them and for those behaviors they may not provide affection or approval. Thus, infants learn that parental affection has a price; it depends on behaving appropriately. They come to understand that sometimes they are prized, and sometimes they are not.

conditional positive regard
Approval, love, or acceptance granted only when a person expresses desirable behaviors and attitudes.

If a parent expresses annoyance every time the infant drops an object out of the crib, the child learns to disapprove of himself or herself for behaving that way. External standards of judgment become internal and personal. In a sense, then, children come to punish themselves as their parents did. Children develop self-regard only in situations that have brought parental approval, and in time the self-concept, thus formed, comes to function as a parental surrogate. These are conditions of worth. Children believe they are worthy only under certain conditions, the ones that brought parental positive regard and then personal positive self-regard. Having internalized their parents' norms and standards, they view themselves as worthy or unworthy, good or bad, according to the terms their parents defined.

Children thus learn to avoid behaviors that otherwise might be personally satisfying. Therefore, they no longer function freely. Because they feel the need to evaluate their behaviors and attitudes so carefully, and refrain from taking certain actions, children are prevented from fully developing or actualizing the self. They inhibit their development by living within the confines of their conditions of worth.

Incongruence

Not only do children learn, ideally, to inhibit unacceptable behaviors, but they also may come to deny or distort unacceptable ways of perceiving their experiential world. By holding an inaccurate perception of certain experiences, they risk becoming estranged from their true self. We come to evaluate experiences, and accept or reject them, not in terms of how they contribute to the overall actualization tendency through the organismic valuing process, but in terms of whether they bring positive regard from others. This leads to **incongruence** between the self-concept and the experiential world, the environment as we perceive it.

incongruence
A discrepancy between a person's self-concept and aspects of his or her experience.

Experiences that are incongruent or incompatible with our self-concept become threatening and are manifested as anxiety. For example, if our self-concept includes the belief that we love all humanity, once we meet someone toward whom we feel hatred, we are likely to develop anxiety. Hating is not congruent with our image of us as loving persons. To maintain our self-concept, we must deny the hatred. We defend ourselves against the anxiety that accompanies the threat by distorting it, thus closing off a portion of our experiential field. The result is a rigidity of some of our perceptions.

Our level of psychological adjustment and emotional health is a function of the congruence or compatibility between our self-concept and our experiences. Psychologically healthy people are able to perceive themselves, other people, and events in their world much as they really are. Psychologically healthy people are open to new experiences because nothing threatens their self-concept. They have no need to deny or distort their perceptions because as children they received unconditional positive regard and did not have to internalize any conditions of worth. They feel worthy under all conditions and situations and are able to use all their experiences. They can develop and actualize all facets of the self, proceeding toward the goal of becoming a fully functioning person and leading what Rogers called "the good life."

Characteristics of Fully Functioning Persons

fully functioning person
Rogers's term for self-actualization, for developing all facets of the self.

To Rogers, the **fully functioning person** is the desired result of psychological development and social evolution (Rogers, 1961). He described several characteristics of **fully functioning (self-actualizing) persons** (see Table 10.1).

Fully functioning persons are aware of all experience. No experience is distorted or denied; all of it filters through to the self. There is no defensiveness because there is nothing to defend against, nothing to threaten the self-concept. Fully functioning persons are open to positive feelings such as courage and tenderness, and to negative feelings such as fear and pain. They are more emotional in the sense that they accept a wider range of positive and negative emotions and feel them more intensely.

Fully functioning persons live fully and richly in every moment. All experiences are potentially fresh and new. Experiences cannot be predicted or anticipated but are participated in fully rather than merely observed.

Fully functioning persons trust in their own organism. By this phrase Rogers meant that fully functioning persons trust their own reactions rather than being guided by the opinions of others, by a social code, or by their intellectual judgments. Behaving in a way that feels right is a good guide to behaving in a way that is satisfying. Rogers did not suggest that fully functioning persons ignore information from their own intellect or from other people. Rather, he meant that all data are accepted as congruent with the fully functioning person's self-concept. Nothing is threatening; all information can be perceived, evaluated, and weighed accurately. Thus, the decision about how to behave in a particular situation results

Table 10.1 Characteristics of fully functioning people

Awareness of all experience; open to positive as well as negative feelings
Freshness of appreciation for all experiences
Trust in one's own behavior and feelings
Freedom of choice, without inhibitions
Creativity and spontaneity
Continual need to grow, to strive to maximize one's potential

from a consideration of all experiential data. Fully functioning persons are unaware of making such considerations, however, because of the congruence between their self-concept and experience, so their decisions appear to be more intuitive and emotional than intellectual.

Fully functioning persons feel free to make choices without constraints or inhibitions. This brings a sense of power because they know their future depends on their own actions and not by present circumstances, past events, or other people. They do not feel compelled, either by themselves or by others, to behave in only one way.

Fully functioning persons are creative and live constructively and adaptively as environmental conditions change. Allied with creativity is spontaneity. Fully functioning persons are flexible and seek new experiences and challenges. They do not require predictability, security, or freedom from tension.

Fully functioning persons may face difficulties. The condition involves continually testing, growing, striving, and using all of one's potential, a way of life that brings complexity and challenge. Rogers did not describe fully functioning persons as happy, blissful, or contented, although at times they may be. More appropriately their personality may be described as enriching, exciting, and meaningful.

Rogers used the word *actualizing*, not *actualized*, to characterize the fully functioning person. The latter term implies a finished or static personality, which was not Rogers's intent. Self-development is always in progress. Rogers wrote that being fully functioning is "a direction, not a destination" (Rogers, 1961, p. 186). If striving and growing cease, then the person loses spontaneity, flexibility, and openness. Rogers's emphasis on change and growth is neatly captured in the word *becoming* in the title of his book, *On Becoming a Person* (Rogers, 1961).

Fully functioning people feel a sense of freedom and have the ability to live richly and creatively in every moment.

© Paul Barton/CORBIS

Questions About Human Nature

On the issue of free will versus determinism, Rogers's position is clear. Fully functioning persons have free choice in creating their selves. In other words, no aspect of personality is predetermined for them. On the nature–nurture issue, Rogers gave prominence to the role of the environment. Although the actualization tendency is innate, the actualizing process itself is influenced more by social than by biological forces. Childhood experiences have some impact on personality development, but experiences later in life have a greater influence. Our present feelings are more vital to our personality than the events of our childhood.

Rogers recognized a universal quality in personality when he noted that fully functioning persons share certain qualities. However, we may infer from his writings that there is opportunity for uniqueness in the ways these characteristics are expressed. The ultimate and necessary goal of life is to become a fully functioning person.

A personality theorist who credits people with the ability, motivation, and responsibility to understand and improve themselves obviously views people in an optimistic and positive light. Rogers believed we have a basically healthy nature and an innate tendency to grow and fulfill our potential. Rogers never lost this optimism. In an interview at the age of 85, he said, "in working with individuals and working with groups my positive view of human nature is continually reinforced" (Rogers, 1987, p. 118).

In Rogers's opinion, we are not doomed to conflict with our selves or with our society. We are not ruled by instinctive biological forces or controlled by events of the first 5 years of life. Our outlook is progressive rather than regressive, toward growth rather than stagnation. We experience our world openly, not defensively, and we seek challenge and stimulation instead of the security of the familiar. Emotional disturbances may occur, but these are uncommon. Through Rogers's person-centered therapy, people are able to overcome difficulties by using their inner resources, the innate drive for actualization.

> I am quite aware that out of defensiveness and inner fear individuals can and do behave in ways which are incredibly cruel, horribly destructive, immature, regressive, antisocial, hurtful. Yet one of the most refreshing and invigorating parts of my experience is to work with such individuals and to discover the strongly positive directional tendencies which exist in them, as in all of us. (Rogers, 1961, p. 27)

The urge to become a fully functioning person benefits society as well. As more people in a given culture become self-actualizing, the improvement of society will naturally follow.

Assessment in Rogers's Theory

To Rogers, the only way to assess personality is in terms of the person's subjective experiences, the events in the person's life as he or she perceives them and accepts them as real. Rogers maintained that his clients had the ability to examine the roots of their problems and to redirect the personality growth that had been impeded by some incongruence between their self-concept and their experiences.

Person-Centered Therapy

person-centered therapy
Rogers's approach to therapy in which the client (not the "patient") is assumed to be responsible for changing his or her personality.

In the technique of **person-centered therapy**, Rogers explored the client's feelings and attitudes toward the self and toward other people. He listened without preconceptions, trying to understand the client's experiential world. Although Rogers considered person-centered therapy the only worthwhile approach to personality assessment, he noted that it was not infallible. By focusing on subjective experiences, the therapist learns only about those events the client consciously expresses. Experiences that are not in conscious awareness remain hidden. The danger in trying to infer too much about these non-conscious experiences is that the inferences the therapist draws may represent the therapist's own projections more than the client's actual experiences. Also, what the therapist learns about a client depends on the client's ability to communicate. Because all forms of communication are imperfect, the therapist necessarily will see the client's world of experience imperfectly.

Within these limits, Rogers argued that person-centered therapy provides a clearer view of a person's experiential world than other forms of assessment and therapy. One advantage Rogers claimed for his approach is that it does not rely on a predetermined theoretical structure (such as Freudian psychoanalysis) into which the therapist must fit the patient's problem. The only predetermined belief of the person-centered therapist is the client's inherent value and worth. Clients are accepted as they are. The therapist gives them unconditional positive regard and offers no judgments about their behavior or advice on how to behave. Everything centers on the client, including the responsibility for changing behavior and reevaluating relationships.

Rogers opposed assessment techniques such as free association, dream analysis, and case histories. He believed they made clients dependent on the therapist, who then assumed an aura of expertise and authority. These techniques removed personal responsibility from the clients by giving them the impression that the therapist knew all about them. Clients could conclude that the therapist would solve their problems and all they needed to do was sit back and follow the expert's instructions.

Encounter Groups

Rogers demonstrated that person-centered therapy could help individuals who were out of touch with their feelings and closed to life's experiences. Through the therapeutic process, people could develop or regain flexibility, spontaneity, and openness. With missionary zeal, Rogers wanted to bring this state of enhanced psychological health and functioning to greater numbers of people, so he developed a group technique in which people could learn more about themselves and how they related to, or encountered one another. He called his approach the **encounter group** (Rogers, 1970). During the 1960s and 1970s, millions of people in the United States took part in encounter-group situations.

encounter groups
A group therapy technique in which people learn about their feelings and about how they relate to (or encounter) one another.

Group size ranges from 8 to 15 people. They typically meet 20 to 60 hours over several sessions. They begin with no formal structure or agenda. The group facilitator is not a leader in the usual sense. He or she establishes an atmosphere in which group members can express themselves and focus on how others perceive them. The facilitator's job is to make it easier for members to achieve self-insight and become more fully functioning. Some people report feeling better and more aware of their true nature once they have participated in an encounter group. Rogers believed that most (though not all) participants would become more fully functioning.

Not all psychologists agree. A meta-analysis of 63 studies on encounter groups revealed that their efficacy was comparable to traditional psychotherapies (Faith, Wong, & Carpenter, 1995). The analysis also showed that larger groups that met more frequently produced more favorable outcomes than smaller groups that met less frequently. Encounter groups are no longer as popular as when Rogers himself was promoting them, but they are still conducted by some of his followers as a way of inducing people to enhance their potentials.

Psychological Tests

Rogers did not use psychological tests to assess personality, nor did he develop any tests. However, other psychologists have devised tests to measure aspects of the experiential world. The Experience Inventory (Coan, 1972), a self-report questionnaire, attempts to assess openness or receptivity to experience, a characteristic of the fully functioning person. The Experiencing Scale (Gendlin & Tomlinson, 1967) measures our level of self-trust. Persons being assessed by this test do not respond directly. They may talk about whatever they choose, and their tape-recorded comments are later rated for degree of self-trust; for example, how much they claim their feelings are an important source of information on which to base behavior, or how much they deny that personal feelings influence their decisions.

The Experiencing Scale has been used with person-centered therapy. For example, one study reported that people who made the greatest improvement during therapy revealed an increase in self-trust from before therapy to after therapy. Those who showed little improvement during therapy showed a small or no increase in self-trust over the period. Those with less severe emotional disorders showed greater self-trust than those with more severe disorders (Klein, Malthieu, Gendlin, & Kiesler, 1969).

Research on Rogers's Theory

Rogers believed that person-centered interviews, which rely on clients' self-reports, were of greater value than experimental methods. In his view, the more orthodox scientific approaches yielded less information on the nature of personality than did his clinical approach. He said, "I never learned anything from research. Most of my research has been to confirm what I already felt to be true" (quoted in Bergin & Strupp, 1972, p. 314). Although Rogers did not use laboratory methods to collect data about personality, he did use them to attempt to verify and confirm his clinical observations. He was enthusiastic about research on the nature of the therapy sessions, an idea resisted by many clinicians who see it as a violation of privacy.

What Rogers did was to introduce what was then a radical procedure. He recorded and filmed therapy sessions to enable researchers to study the client–therapist interaction. Before Rogers's innovation, the only data available from therapy sessions were the therapist's after-the-fact reconstructions. In addition to distortions of memory with the passage of time, a written record misses the client's emotional state and body language. Sometimes a facial expression or tone of voice reveals more than words. With recorded therapy sessions, everything became available for study. Rogers referred to it as a microscope with which to examine the "molecules of personality change" (Rogers, 1974, p. 120). He always obtained the client's permission to record the sessions and he found that the presence of the equipment did not impede the course of therapy.

Evaluating Person-Centered Therapy

Q-sort technique
A self-report technique for assessing aspects of the self-concept.

Rogers and his associates also studied how the self-concept changes during a course of therapy. Using qualitative and quantitative techniques in the scientific tradition (despite Rogers's claim of not being a scientist), they analyzed the therapy sessions. By applying rating scales and content analyses of a client's verbalizations, they investigated changes in the self-concept. Much of the research used the **Q-sort technique**, a procedure developed by William Stephenson (Stephenson, 1953). In this technique, clients sort a large number of statements about the self-concept into categories that range from most descriptive to least descriptive. Thus, the Q sort is a way of empirically defining the client's self-image.

Typical Q-sort statements include the following.

- I enjoy being alone.
- I feel helpless.
- I am emotionally mature.

The Q sort can be used in several ways. For example, after sorting the statements in terms of the perceived self, clients can be asked to sort the same statements in terms of an ideal self, that is, the person they would most like to be. Applying the correlational method, Rogers used Q-sort responses to determine how closely a client's self-image or perceived self corresponded to the ideal self. He also noted how greatly the self-concept changed from the period before therapy to the period following therapy. For one client, identified as "Mrs. Oak," the data yielded an initial correlation coefficient of +.36 between perceived self and ideal self. A year after therapy, the correlation coefficient had increased to +.79, indicating to Rogers that Mrs. Oak's perceived self had become much more congruent with her ideal or desired self (Rogers, 1954). He concluded that this dramatic change reflected an increase in emotional health.

Mrs. Oak chose different Q-sort phrases to describe herself before and after therapy. Prior to her sessions with Rogers, she saw her self-image as dependent and passive. She also felt rejected by other people. After the course of therapy, Mrs. Oak believed she was more like the self she really wanted to be. She felt more secure, less fearful, and better able to relate to other people (see Table 10.2).

A study by Rogers's associates measured the discrepancy between perceived self and ideal self in 25 clients (Butler & Haigh, 1954). The researchers found that the discrepancy decreased over time during and following therapy. Before therapy,

Table 10.2 Mrs. Oak's Q-sort statements of perceived self before and after therapy

Self before therapy	Self 12 months after therapy
I usually feel driven.	I express my emotions freely.
I am responsible for my troubles.	I feel emotionally mature.
I am really self-centered.	I am self-reliant.
I am disorganized.	I understand myself.
I feel insecure within myself.	I feel adequate.
I have to protect myself with excuses, with rationalizing.	I have a warm emotional relationship with others.

SOURCE: From "The Case of Mrs. Oak: A Research Analysis" by C. R. Rogers. In *Psychotherapy and Personality Change* by C. R. Rogers and R. F. Dymond, 1954, Chicago: University of Chicago Press.

the average correlation coefficient between perceived self and ideal self was $-.01$. After therapy it was $+.31$.

Research using the Q sort provides impressive evidence for the effectiveness of person-centered therapy but offers little information about the validity of Rogers's personality theory. Other studies have tested some of his concepts. For example, a study of three generations of women and of 110 men and women college students demonstrated that the use of conditional positive regard by parents successfully brought about the behaviors they desired in their children. Providing love and affection when the children behaved appropriately and withholding love and affection when they did not, was effective. However, self-reports from children whose parents used conditional regard showed poor coping skills, fluctuating levels of self-esteem, low self-worth, feelings that their parents disapproved of them, and resentment toward their parents. No such negative consequences were reported by children whose parents did not use conditional regard (Assor, Roth, & Deci, 2004).

There is some evidence to support Rogers's concept of the organismic valuing process. Studies have also suggested that positive self-regard may not be as prevalent in a collectivist culture such as Japan as it is in a more individualistic culture such as the United States (Heine, Lehman, Markus, & Kitayama, 1999; Joseph & Linley, 2005; Sheldon, Arndt, & Houser-Marko, 2003).

Openness to Experience

College students completed the Q-sort list to test Rogers's proposition that fully functioning persons are open to all experiences, whereas psychologically unhealthy persons erect defenses to protect themselves against experiences that threaten their self-image (Chodorkoff, 1954). A separate Q-sort description of each subject was prepared by clinicians who based their reports on a variety of data including responses to the Thematic Apperception Test and the Rorschach inkblot test. Based on these clinical measurements, the students were divided into good- and poor-adjustment groups.

Measures of perceptual defense against material perceived to be threatening were obtained from the subjects' reactions to neutral words such as *table* and to allegedly threatening words such as *penis*. The results showed that all subjects were slower to perceive threatening words than neutral words, but this response was more marked in the defensive subjects of the poorly adjusted group. Significantly less perceptual defense was shown by people in the good-adjustment group, presumed to be psychologically healthier. With regard to agreement between the students' self-descriptions and the clinicians' descriptions, researchers found that the closer the two sets of Q-sort statements, the better adjusted that person was found to be.

Acceptance of Self

A study of 56 mothers explored the relationship between their self-acceptance and the extent to which they accepted their children as they were rather than as they desired them to be (Medinnus & Curtis, 1963). This early research was based on Rogers's idea that people who accept their own nature realistically (whose perceived and ideal selves are congruent) are more likely to accept others as they really are. The results revealed significant differences between self-accepting mothers and those who were not self-accepting. Self-accepting mothers were more accepting of their children's nature. Also, the child's degree of self-acceptance depended to some extent on the mother's degree of self-acceptance.

Other classic studies support Rogers's belief that parental behavior affects a child's self-image. Parents who accept their children unconditionally and display democratic child-rearing practices were found to have children with higher self-esteem and greater emotional security than parents who failed to accept their children and who displayed authoritarian behavior (Baldwin, 1949). Parents of children with high self-esteem displayed their affection and used reward rather than punishment to guide their child's behavior. Parents of children with low self-esteem were more aloof, less loving, and more likely to use punishment (Coopersmith, 1967). Adolescents whose parents provided unconditional positive regard and allowed them to express themselves without restraint developed greater creative potential than did adolescents whose parents did not provide those situations (Harrington, Block, & Block, 1987).

In another study, adolescents who received unconditional positive regard from their parents were found to be confident and hopeful about their ability to receive support from others in the future. They also engaged in more behaviors that were consistent with their perception of their interests and talents. Teens who received conditional positive regard from their parents lacked such confidence and hope. They took more actions that were inconsistent with their true selves in an effort to obtain support and approval from their parents (Harter, Marold, Whitesell, & Cobbs, 1996).

Emotional Adjustment

Several studies provide support for Rogers's suggestion that incongruence between perceived self and ideal self indicates poor emotional adjustment. Researchers have concluded that the greater the discrepancy, the higher the anxiety, insecurity, self-doubt, depression, social incompetence, and other psychological disorders. Also, high inconsistency between perceived and ideal self correlates with low levels of self-actualization and self-esteem (Achenbach & Zigler, 1963; Gough, Fioravanti, & Lazzari, 1983; Mahoney & Hartnett, 1973; Moretti & Higgins, 1990; Straumann, Vookles, Berenstein, Chaiken, & Higgins, 1991). Persons with a great discrepancy between perceived and ideal selves were rated by others as awkward, confused, and unfriendly (Gough, Lazzari, & Fioravanti, 1978).

Rogers believed that failure to realize our innate actualization tendency can lead to maladjustment. To test this idea, one researcher studied the inherited temperaments proposed by Buss and Plomin (Emotionality, Activity, and Sociability, or EAS) in male and female college students (Ford, 1991). Using the EASI Temperament Survey to assess behavior, the college students' parents were asked to recall their children's temperaments when very young. These temperament profiles were compared with the college students' current self-perceptions on the three temperaments. The results supported Rogers's views. The greater the discrepancy in temperament between childhood potential and adult realization, the greater was the level of maladjustment.

Reflections on Rogers's Theory

Critics have faulted Rogers for failing to explain more precisely his proposed innate potential for actualization. Is it wholly physiological or does it have a psychological component? Are individual differences possible? Rogers did not answer these and related questions. He described the actualization tendency as a kind of genetic blueprint for the organism's development but did not clarify how the mechanism operates.

Rogers insisted that the only way to explore personality is through person-centered therapy to examine a person's subjective experiences. Rogers did this by listening to a client's self-reports. Critics charge that he ignored those factors of which the client was not consciously aware but which could influence behavior. People may distort reports of their subjective experiences, repressing some events and elaborating on or inventing others, to conceal their true nature and present an idealized self-image.

Rogers's person-centered psychotherapy quickly became popular. Its rapid acceptance was fostered in part by social circumstances in the United States at the end of World War II (1945). Veterans returning from service overseas needed help readjusting to civilian life. The result was a demand for psychologists and for a counseling technique they could master and put into practice quickly. Training in traditional psychoanalysis required a medical degree and a lengthy period of specialization. However, "person-centered psychotherapy," wrote one analyst, "was simple, informal, and brief, and it required little training" (DeCarvalho, 1999, p. 142).

Rogers's therapy has found broad application not only as a treatment for emotional disturbances but also as a means of enhancing the self-image. In the business world, it has been used as a training method for managers. In the helping professions it is used to train clinical psychologists, social workers, and counselors. In addition, psychotherapists of many different orientations have accepted some of Rogers's core concepts in their therapeutic work with clients. Thus, the person-centered approach remains influential in counseling and psychotherapy (see Kirschenbaum & Jourdan, 2005; Patterson & Joseph, 2007). More than 200 training centers, mostly in Europe, promote Rogers's form of therapy. In addition, several dozen journals are devoted to research and application of Rogers's ideas.

His personality theory, although less influential than his psychotherapy, has also received wide recognition, particularly for its emphasis on the self-concept. However, Rogers did not believe he had influenced academic or scientific psychology. Nonetheless, his theory and therapy have stimulated research on the nature of psychotherapy, the client–therapist interaction, and the self-concept. His ideas have had a significant impact on psychology's theoretical and empirical definitions of the self.

Rogers's background was a unique combination of clinic, lecture hall, and laboratory. He drew on his considerable experience with emotionally disturbed clients and on the intellectual stimulation of colleagues and students. He attracted large numbers of followers who continue to test his ideas in the clinic and in the laboratory.

Chapter Summary

Rogers's person-centered theory proposes that we are conscious, rational beings not controlled by unconscious forces or past experiences. Personality can only be understood by a phenomenological approach, that is, from an individual's own viewpoint based on his or her subjective experiences (one's experiential field). Our goal is self-actualization, an innate tendency to growth and development. The organismic valuing process evaluates life experiences in terms of how well they serve the actualizing tendency. Experiences that promote actualization will be sought; experiences that hinder it will be avoided.

Positive regard is a need for acceptance, love, and approval from others, particularly from the mother, during infancy. In unconditional positive regard, the mother's love and approval are granted freely and are not conditional on the child's behavior. When love and approval are conditional, a state of conditional positive regard exists. Once we internalize the attitudes of others, positive regard comes from ourselves (positive self-regard). Conditions of worth (similar to the Freudian superego) involve seeing ourselves as worthy only under conditions acceptable to our parents. We avoid behaviors and perceptions that oppose our parents' conditions of worth. Incongruence develops between the self-concept and behaviors that threaten the self-image. We defend against anxiety by denying threatening aspects of the experiential field.

The fully functioning person represents the peak of psychological development. Characteristics of the fully functioning person are an awareness of all experiences, no conditions to defend against, the ability to live fully in each moment, trust in one's self, a sense of freedom and personal power, creativity, and spontaneity. Rogers's optimistic image of human nature encompassed a belief in free will, the prominence of environment over heredity, and some universality in personality. Individuals and societies can grow unhampered by past events.

Personality can be assessed in terms of subjective experiences as revealed in self-reports. In this person-centered approach, the therapist gives the client unconditional positive regard. Rogers opposed free association and dream analysis because they make the client dependent on the therapist. By recording therapy sessions, Rogers enabled researchers to investigate the nature of the client–therapist interaction.

The Q-sort technique, in which clients sort statements about their self-concept into categories ranging from most to least descriptive, is a way of quantifying the self-image. Q-sort research has revealed a greater correspondence between perceived self and ideal self after therapy. The better adjusted a person is, the greater the agreement between self-descriptions and descriptions made by others. Discrepancies between perceived self and ideal self indicate poor psychological adjustment. Rogers's work has been criticized for failing to define precisely the nature of self-actualization, for ignoring the impact of unconscious forces, and for accepting the possible distortion of a client's subjective experiences in self-reports.

Review Questions

1. What aspect of Rogers's childhood led to his interest in interviewing and in therapy?

2. How did Carl Rogers's clinical experience differ from Sigmund Freud's?

3. Describe the research on delinquent children that influenced Rogers's view of the role of the self in personality.

4. How does the need to actualize promote biological and psychological growth?

5. What is the organismic valuing process? How does it influence behavior?

6. What is phenomenology and how does it relate to Rogers's theory of personality?

7. What is the experiential field? How does our experiential field change with age?

8. Distinguish between positive regard and positive self-regard.

9. What parental behaviors affect a child's development of positive self-regard?

10. Compare Rogers's concept of conditions of worth with Freud's concept of the superego.

11. Describe Rogers's concept of incongruence. How is incongruence related to anxiety?

12. Describe the roles of (a) the intellect, (b) positive and negative feelings, and (c) spontaneity in becoming a fully functioning person.

13. Describe the characteristics of the fully functioning person. Can we say that a fully functioning person is self-actualized?

14. How does Rogers's image of human nature differ from that of Freud? Would you describe Rogers as an optimist or a pessimist in his view of human nature?

15. How does the clinical interview in Rogers's system differ from the psychoanalytic clinical interview?

16. What did Rogers call his approach? Why?

17. How does the Q-sort technique measure a person's self-image?

18. What has Q-sort research shown about the self-concept before and after therapy?

19. What do studies show to be the results of parental use of conditional positive regard?

20. Describe ways in which parents' behavior can affect the behavior of their children, according to Rogers.

21. What was Rogers's position on the importance of childhood experiences and adult experiences in personality development?

22. Discuss several criticisms of Rogers's personality theory. Why was his person-centered therapy accepted so quickly?

Suggested Readings

DeCarvalho, R. J. (1999). Otto Rank, the Rankian circle in Philadelphia, and the origins of Carl Rogers' person-centered psychotherapy. *History of Psychology, 2,* 132–148. Traces the roots of Rogers's style of therapy to the psychiatric social work of the 1930s and the ideas of Otto Rank, a disciple of Freud, and emphasizes the significance of the relationship between client and therapist.

Evans, R. I. (1975). *Carl Rogers: The man and his ideas.* New York: Dutton. Interviews with Rogers on the evolution of the self, techniques of person-centered therapy, and applications of his theory to education. Contrasts his humanistic views with B. F. Skinner's behaviorist views.

Kirschenbaum, H. (1979). *On becoming Carl Rogers.* New York: Delacorte Press. A biography of Rogers and his contributions to humanistic psychology.

Kirschenbaum, H., & Jourdan, A. (2005). The current status of Carl Rogers and the person-centered approach. *Psychotherapy: Theory, Research, Practice, Training, 42,* 37–51. Describes the continuing influence on clinical psychology, psychotherapy, and counseling of Rogers's work in the United States and internationally.

Milton, J. (2002). *The road to Malpsychia: Humanistic psychology and our discontents.* San Francisco: Encounter Books. A cultural and social history of the humanistic psychology movement including an assessment of the contributions of Carl Rogers.

Patterson, T., & Joseph, S. (2007). Person-centered personality theory. *Journal of Humanistic Psychology, 47,* 117–139. Discusses support for Rogers's approach to therapy from recent work in positive psychology and self-determination theory.

Rogers, C. R. (1961). *On becoming a person: A therapist's view of psychotherapy.* Boston: Houghton Mifflin. Rogers's views on psychotherapy, especially problems in communication and interpersonal relations; discusses the effects of enhanced personal growth on personal and family life.

Rogers, C. R. (1967). Autobiography. In E. G. Boring & G. Lindzey (Eds.), *A history of psychology in autobiography* (Vol. 5, pp. 341–384). New York: Appleton-Century-Crofts. Rogers's assessment of his work and the influence of his early experiences.

Rogers, C. R. (1974). In retrospect: Forty-six years. *American Psychologist, 29,* 115–123. Rogers evaluates the impact of his work on the fields of counseling, psychotherapy, education, leadership, and international relations and on the empirical investigation of subjective phenomena.

Rogers, C. R. (1980). *A way of being.* Boston: Houghton Mifflin. Describes the work of Rogers's later years on individual and group psychotherapy, the helping professions, scientific progress, and personal growth.

Rogers, C. R. (1989). *The Carl Rogers reader.* Boston: Houghton Mifflin. A selection of Rogers's writings over 60 years, edited by Howard Kirschenbaum and Valerie Henderson, including personal recollections, case studies, and essays on personality change, psychotherapy, education, marriage, aging, international relations, and world peace.

PART SIX

The Cognitive Approach

If you look up the word *cognition* in a dictionary, you will find that it means the act or process of knowing. The cognitive approach to personality focuses on the ways in which people come to know their environment and themselves, how they perceive, evaluate, learn, think, make decisions, and solve problems. This is a truly *psychological* approach to personality because it focuses exclusively on conscious mental activities.

It may appear that this concentration on the mind or mental processes neglects ideas dealt with by other theorists. For example, in the cognitive approach, we do not find needs, drives, or emotions as separate activities of the personality. Instead, they are aspects of personality under the control of the cognitive processes.

Contemporary psychoanalysts acknowledge the importance of cognitive processes. So, too, did Erik Erikson, who granted greater autonomy to the ego and to cognitive functioning. The humanistic psychologists Abraham Maslow and Carl Rogers dealt with perceptions, how we evaluate and mentally process our experiences. Henry Murray and Gordon Allport wrote about human reasoning, and Alfred Adler proposed a creative self, which results from our perception or interpretation of experience. Social-learning theorists also invoke cognitive processes. The difference between these approaches and George Kelly's cognitive theory of personality is that Kelly attempted to describe *all* aspects of personality, including its emotional components, in terms of cognitive processes.

CHAPTER 11

George Kelly:
Personal Construct Theory

It occurred to me that what seemed true of myself was probably no less true of others. If I initiated my actions, so did they.

—GEORGE KELLY

The Cognitive Movement in Psychology

personal construct theory
Kelly's description of personality in terms of cognitive processes. We are capable of interpreting behaviors and events and of using this understanding to guide our behavior and to predict the behavior of other people.

Kelly's **personal construct theory** of personality differs greatly from other approaches discussed in this book. Kelly warned us we would not find in his system such familiar concepts as the unconscious, the ego, needs, drives, stimuli and responses, and reinforcement—not even motivation and emotion. The obvious question is how can we understand the human personality without considering these ideas, especially motivation and emotion?

Kelly's answer was that each person creates a set of cognitive constructs about the environment. By that he meant that we interpret and organize the events and social relationships of our lives in a system or pattern. On the basis of this pattern, we make predictions about ourselves and about other people and events, and we use these predictions to formulate our responses and guide our actions. Therefore, to understand personality, we must first understand our patterns, the ways we organize or construct our world. According to Kelly, our interpretation of events is more important than the events themselves.

Like Maslow, Kelly was opposed to the behavioral and the psychoanalytic approaches to the study of personality. He viewed them both as denying the human ability to take charge of our lives, to make our own decisions, and to pursue our chosen course of action. He argued that behaviorism viewed people as merely passive responders to events in their environment, and that psychoanalysis viewed people as passive responders to their unconscious forces. In contrast, "for Kelly, [people] are forms of motion and we propel ourselves. No one or no thing does it to us" (Fransella & Neimeyer, 2003, p. 25).

The personality theory Kelly offered derived from his experience as a clinician. For several reasons, he interpreted his clinical experience differently from Freud and other theorists who treated patients. The model of human nature Kelly developed from his clinical work is unusual. He concluded that people function in the same way scientists do.

Scientists construct theories and hypotheses and test them against reality by performing experiments in the laboratory. If the results of their experiments support the theory, it is retained. If the data do not support the theory, it must be rejected or modified and retested.

As we have seen, this is how psychologists who study personality typically proceed. Yet Kelly noted that psychologists do not attribute to their subjects the same intellectual and rational abilities they ascribe to themselves. It is as if psychologists have two theories about human nature, one that applies to scientists and their way of looking at the world, and another that applies to everybody else. The logical assumption, then, is that psychologists view their subjects as incapable of rational functioning, as being motivated by all sorts of conflicting drives or as victims of rampant unconscious forces. Thus, human beings are believed to function largely on an emotional level, unlikely to use their cognitive processes to learn, think, evaluate experiences, or solve problems. Surely this is quite unlike the way psychologists function.

Are psychologists really superior beings? Kelly said they are no different from the people they study. What works for one works for the other; what explains one explains the other. Both are concerned with predicting and controlling the events in their lives, and both are capable of doing so rationally. Like scientists, all of us construct theories, which Kelly called *personal constructs*, by which we try to predict and control the events in our lives. He proposed that the way to understand someone's personality is to examine his or her personal constructs.

How does Kelly's cognitive theory fit with the cognitive movement that began around 1960 and now dominates mainstream experimental psychology? Despite the similarity in terminology, the cognitive movement has not embraced Kelly's work because the theory is not consistent with the movement's subject matter and methods.

Kelly's approach is that of the clinician dealing with the conscious constructs by which people arrange their lives. In contrast, cognitive psychologists are interested in both cognitive variables and overt behavior, which they study primarily in an experimental, not a clinical, setting. Also, cognitive psychologists do not limit their focus to personality. They study overt behavior and learning in social situations. They believe that cognitive processes such as learning influence a person's response to a given stimulus situation.

Although cognitive psychology took hold some time after Kelly proposed his explanation of personality, his theory had little influence on it. At best, Kelly's theory could be considered a precursor to contemporary cognitive psychology. The two approaches share the term *cognitive*, with its implied interest in conscious activities, but little else. Kelly's recognition of the importance of cognitive processes is noteworthy, but we must place it in perspective. It is not part of mainstream American psychology as defined by experimental psychologists, but that does not detract from its usefulness for studying personality.

The Life of Kelly (1905–1967)

Kelly was born on a farm in Kansas. An only child, he received a great deal of attention and affection from his parents, who were fundamentalist in their religious beliefs and committed to helping the less fortunate. They opposed frivolous entertainment such as dancing and card playing. When Kelly was 4 years old, the family traveled by covered wagon to Colorado to try farming there but soon returned to Kansas. Kelly's early education was erratic and conducted as much by his parents as by schoolteachers. At 13, he went to high school in Wichita and seldom lived at home after that. In 1926, he earned a bachelor's degree in physics and mathematics from Park College in Parkville, Missouri. But his interests had shifted from science to social problems. Kelly's future was uncertain.

He worked briefly as an engineer, and then took a teaching job at a labor college in Minneapolis. Next, he became an instructor in speech for the American Banking Association and also taught citizenship courses to immigrants. He then enrolled in graduate school and received a master's degree in educational sociology from the University of Kansas in Lawrence. Accepting a job offer from a junior college in Iowa, Kelly taught various courses and coached the drama program. His career certainly showed no inclination toward psychology. In college, he had not been impressed by coursework in the field.

> In the first course in psychology, I sat in the back row of a very large class, tilted my chair against the wall, made myself as comfortable as possible, and kept one ear cocked for anything interesting that might turn up. One day the professor, a very nice person who seemed to be trying hard to convince himself that psychology was something to be taken seriously, turned to the blackboard and wrote an "S," an arrow, and an "R." Thereupon I straightened up in my chair and listened, thinking to myself that now, after two or three weeks of preliminaries, we might be getting to the meat of the matter. (Kelly, 1969, p. 46)

Kelly paid attention for several more class meetings and then gave up. He did not comprehend what the arrow connecting the stimulus (S) and the response (R) stood for. He never did figure it out. The traditional behaviorist, experimental approach to psychology had failed to spark his interest. He also explored psychoanalysis. He wrote, "I don't remember which one of Freud's books I was trying to read, but I do remember the mounting feeling of incredulity that anyone could write such nonsense, much less publish it" (1969, p. 47).

Kelly's professional training took a different turn in 1929 when he was awarded a fellowship at the University of Edinburgh, Scotland. During his year there, he earned a Bachelor of Education degree and developed an interest in psychology. He returned to the United States for doctoral studies at the State University of Iowa and received his Ph.D. in 1931.

An Intellectual Approach to Counseling

Kelly began his academic career at Fort Hays Kansas State College in the midst of the economic depression of the 1930s. There was little opportunity to conduct research in physiological psychology, the specialty in which he had trained, so he switched to clinical psychology for which there was a need. He developed a clinical psychology service for the local public school system and for the students at his college. He established traveling clinics, going from school to school, which gave him the opportunity to deal with a variety of problems and to try different approaches to treatment.

Kelly was not committed to any particular therapeutic technique or to a specific theory about the nature of personality. He felt free to use traditional methods of assessment and treatment as well as those of his own design. His clinical experiences strongly influenced the nature of his personal construct theory. The people he treated were not severely disturbed psychotics in mental hospitals or neurotics with troublesome emotional problems. His patients were students who had been referred by their teachers for counseling.

Thus, unlike the emotionally maladjusted patients in a psychiatric ward or a psychoanalyst's office, Kelly's clients were much more capable of discussing their concerns rationally, of expressing their problems in intellectual terms, the level of functioning expected in an academic setting. In the classroom, we are taught to analyze, to think and process information logically. This intellectual attitude carried over from the classroom to the counseling situation. Had circumstances placed Kelly during his formative professional years at work with schizophrenics in a mental institution, his theory might not have depended so heavily on cognitive information-processing abilities.

World War II interrupted Kelly's academic career. He joined the U.S. Navy and served as a psychologist in the Bureau of Medicine and Surgery in Washington, D.C. When the war ended in 1945, he taught for a year at the University of Maryland before joining the faculty of Ohio State University. There he spent 19 years teaching, refining his personality theory, and conducting research. Kelly also lectured at universities throughout the world about how his personal construct theory of personality could be used to resolve international tensions. In 1965, he accepted an appointment to an endowed chair at Brandeis University but died shortly thereafter.

Kelly was a major force in the development of the clinical psychology profession during its rapid growth following World War II. He held several honored positions in the field, including the presidencies of the Clinical and Consulting divisions of the American Psychological Association and the American Board of Examiners in Professional Psychology.

 Log On

Personal Construct Psychology: George Kelly

A brief biography of Kelly's life, a bibliography of his works, and links to related sources.

Personality Theories: George Kelly

Information on Kelly's life and an extensive discussion of his theory and unique approach to therapy.

For direct links to these sites, log on to the student companion site for this book at http://www.academic.cengage.com/psychology/Schultz and choose Chapter 11.

Personal Construct Theory

Kelly suggested that people perceive and organize their world of experiences the same way scientists do, by formulating hypotheses about the environment and testing them against the reality of daily life. In other words, we observe the events of our life—the facts or data of our experience—and interpret them in our own way. This personal interpreting, explaining, or *construing* of experience is our unique view of events. It is the pattern within which we place them. Kelly said that we look at the world through "transparent patterns that fit over the realities of which the world is composed" (Kelly, 1955, pp. 8–9).

We might compare these patterns to sunglasses that add a particular tint or coloring to everything we see. One person's glasses may have a bluish tint whereas another's may have a greenish tint. Several people can look at the same scene and perceive it differently, depending on the tint of the lenses that frame their point of view. So it is with the hypotheses or patterns we construct to make sense of our world. This special view, the unique pattern created by each individual, is what Kelly called our *construct system*.

construct
An intellectual hypothesis that we devise and use to interpret or explain life events. Constructs are bipolar, or dichotomous, such as tall versus short or honest versus dishonest.

A **construct** is a person's unique way of looking at life, an intellectual hypothesis devised to explain or interpret events. We behave in accordance with the expectation that our constructs will predict and explain the reality of our world. Like scientists, we constantly test these hypotheses. We base our behavior on our constructs, and we evaluate the effects.

Consider a student who is in danger of failing an introductory psychology course and is trying to persuade the professor to give a passing grade. After observing the professor for most of the semester, the student concludes that the professor behaves in a superior and authoritarian manner in class and has an inflated sense of personal importance. From this observation, the student forms the hypothesis, or construct, that acting to reinforce the professor's exaggerated self-image will bring a favorable response.

The student tests this idea against reality. The student reads an article the professor has written and praises it to the professor. If the professor feels flattered and gives the student a good grade, then the student's construct has been confirmed. It has been found to be useful and can be applied the next time the student takes a course with that professor or with any professor who behaves similarly. However, if the student receives a failing grade, then the construct was found to be inappropriate. A new one will be required for dealing with that professor.

Over the course of life, we develop many constructs, one for almost every type of person or situation we encounter. We expand our inventory of constructs as we meet new people and face new situations. Further, we may alter or discard constructs periodically as situations change. Revising our constructs is a necessary and continuous process; we must always have an alternative construct to apply to a situation. If our constructs were inflexible and incapable of being revised (which is what would happen if personality was totally determined by childhood influences), then we would not be able to cope with new situations. Kelly called this adaptability **constructive alternativism** to express the view that we are not controlled by our constructs but we are free to revise or replace them with other alternatives.

constructive alternativism
The idea that we are free to revise or replace our constructs with alternatives as needed.

Ways of Anticipating Life Events

Kelly's personal construct theory is presented in a scientific format, organized into a fundamental postulate and 11 corollaries (see Table 11.1). The fundamental postulate states that *our psychological processes are directed by the ways in which we anticipate events.*

By using the word *processes*, Kelly was not suggesting some kind of internal mental energy. Rather, he believed that personality was a flowing, moving process. Our psychological processes are directed by our constructs, by the way each of us construes our world. Another key word in the fundamental postulate is *anticipate*. Kelly's notion of constructs is anticipatory. We use constructs to predict the future so that we have some idea of the consequences of our actions, of what is likely to occur if we behave in a certain way.

Table 11.1 Corollaries of personal construct theory

Construction	Because repeated events are similar, we can predict or anticipate how we will experience such an event in the future.
Individuality	People perceive events in different ways.
Organization	We arrange our constructs in patterns, according to our view of their similarities and differences.
Dichotomy	Constructs are bipolar; for example, if we have an opinion about honesty, that idea must also include the concept of dishonesty.
Choice	We choose the alternative for each construct that works best for us, the one that allows us to predict the outcome of anticipated events.
Range	Our constructs may apply to many situations or people, or they may be limited to a single person or situation.
Experience	We continually test our constructs against life's experiences to make sure they remain useful.
Modulation	We may modify our constructs as a function of new experiences.
Fragmentation	We may sometimes have contradictory or inconsistent subordinate constructs within our overall construct system.
Commonality	Although our individual constructs are unique to us, people in compatible groups or cultures may hold similar constructs.
Sociality	We try to understand how other people think and predict what they will do, and we modify our behavior accordingly.

The Construction Corollary

Similarities among repeated events. Kelly believed no life event or experience could be reproduced exactly as it occurred the first time. An event can be repeated, but it will not be experienced in precisely the same way. For example, if you watch a movie today that you first saw last month, your experience of it will be different the second time. Your mood may not be the same, and during the elapsed month you were exposed to events that affected your attitudes and emotions. Maybe you read something unpleasant about an actor in the film. Or you may feel more content because your grades are improving.

However, although such repeated events are not experienced identically, recurrent features or themes will emerge. Some aspects of a situation will be similar to those experienced earlier. It is on the basis of these similarities that we predict or establish anticipations about how we will deal with that type of event in the future. Our predictions rest on the idea that future events, though they are not duplicates of past events, will nevertheless be similar. For example, some scenes in the movie probably affect you the same way every time. If you liked the car chase scenes the first time, you will probably like them again. You base your behavior on your anticipation of liking the chases, so that explains why you choose to watch the film again. Themes of the past reappear in the future, and we formulate our constructs on the basis of these recurring themes.

The Individuality Corollary

Individual differences in interpreting events. With this corollary, Kelly introduced the notion of individual differences. He pointed out that people differ from one another in how they perceive or interpret an event, and because people construe events differently, they thus form different constructs. Our constructs do not so much reflect the objective reality of an event as they constitute the unique interpretation each of us places on it.

The Organization Corollary

Relationships among constructs. We organize our individual constructs into a pattern according to our view of their interrelationships, that is, their similarities and differences. People who hold similar constructs may still differ from one another if they organize those constructs in different patterns.

Typically, we organize our constructs into a hierarchy, with some constructs subordinate to others. A construct can include one or more subordinate constructs. For example, the construct *good* may include among its subordinates the constructs *intelligent* and *moral*. Thus, if we meet someone who fits our idea of a good person, we anticipate that he or she will also have the attributes of intelligence and high moral standards.

The relationships among constructs are usually more enduring than the specific constructs themselves, but they, too, are open to change. A person who feels insulted by someone who appears more intelligent may switch the construct *intelligent* from a subordinate place under the construct *good* to a place under the construct *bad*. The only valid test for a construct system is its predictive efficiency. If the organization of our constructs no longer provides a useful way to predict events, we will modify it.

The Dichotomy Corollary

Two mutually exclusive alternatives. All constructs are bipolar or dichotomous. This is necessary if we are to anticipate future events correctly. Just as we note similarities among people or events, we must also account for dissimilarities. For example, it is not enough to have a construct about a friend that describes the personal characteristic of *honesty*. We must also consider the opposite, *dishonesty*, to explain how the honest person differs from someone who is not honest. If we did not make this distinction—if we assumed that all people are honest—then forming a construct about honesty would not help us anticipate or predict anything about people we might meet in the future. A person can be expected to be honest only in contrast to someone who is expected to be dishonest. The appropriate personal construct in this example, then, is *honest versus dishonest*. Our constructs must always be framed in terms of a pair of mutually exclusive alternatives.

The Choice Corollary

Freedom of choice. The notion that people have freedom of choice is found throughout Kelly's writings. According to the dichotomy corollary described above, each construct has two opposing poles. For every situation we must choose the alternative that works best for us, the one that allows us to anticipate or predict the outcome of future events.

Kelly suggested that we have some latitude in deciding between the alternatives, and he described it as a choice between security and adventure. Suppose you must decide which of two courses to take next semester. One is easy because it is not much different from a course you've already taken and is taught by a professor known to give high grades for little work. There is virtually no risk involved in choosing that course, but there may not be much reward either. You know the professor is dull, and you have already studied much of the course material. However, it is the secure choice, because you can make a highly accurate prediction about the consequences of deciding to take it.

The other course is more of a gamble. The professor is new and rumored to be tough, and you don't know much about the subject. It would expose you to a field of study you've been curious about. In this case, you cannot make an accurate prediction about the outcome of your choice. This more adventurous alternative means more risk, but the potential reward and satisfaction are greater.

You must choose between the low-risk, minimal-reward secure option and the high-risk, high-reward adventurous option. The first has a high predictive efficiency, the second a lower predictive efficiency. Kelly believed we face such choices throughout life, choices between defining or extending our personal construct system. The secure choice, which is similar to past choices, further defines our construct system by repeating experiences and events. The more adventurous choice extends our construct system by encompassing new experiences and events.

People differ from one another in the ways they perceive and interpret the same event.

© Jeff Greenberg/Photo Researchers, Inc.

The popular tendency to opt for the secure, low-risk alternative may explain why some people persist in behaving in an unrewarding way. For example, why does someone act aggressively toward other people even when continually rebuffed? Kelly's answer was that the person is making the low-risk choice because he or she has come to know what to expect from others in response to aggressive behavior. The hostile person does not know how people will react to friendliness because he or she has rarely tried it. The potential rewards may be greater for friendly behavior but so is the uncertainty for this person.

Remember that our choices are made in terms of how well they allow us to anticipate or predict events, not necessarily in terms of what is best for us. And it is Kelly's contention that each of us, in the best scientific tradition, desires to predict the future with the highest possible degree of certainty.

The Range Corollary

range of convenience
The spectrum of events to which a construct can be applied. Some constructs are relevant to a limited number of people or situations; other constructs are broader.

The range of convenience. Few personal constructs are appropriate or relevant for all situations. Consider the construct *tall versus short*, which obviously has a limited **range of convenience** or applicability. It can be useful with respect to buildings, trees, or basketball players, but it is of no value in describing a pizza or the weather.

Some constructs can be applied to many situations or people, whereas others are more limited, perhaps appropriate for one person or situation. The range of convenience or relevance for a construct is a matter of personal choice. For example, we may believe that the construct *loyal versus disloyal* applies to everyone we meet or only to our family members or to our pet dog. According to Kelly, if we are to understand personality fully, it is just as important to know what is excluded from a construct's range of convenience as it is to know what is included.

The Experience Corollary

Exposure to new experiences. We have said that each construct is a hypothesis generated on the basis of past experience to predict or anticipate future events. Each construct is then tested against reality by determining how well it predicted a given event. Most of us are exposed to new experiences daily, so the process of testing the fit of a construct to see how well it predicted the event is ongoing. If a construct is not a valid predictor of the outcome of the situation, then it must be reformulated or replaced. Thus, we evaluate and reinterpret our constructs as our environment changes. Constructs that worked for us at age 16 may be useless, or even harmful, at age 40. In the intervening years, our experiences will have led us to revise our construct system. If you never have any new experiences, then your construct system would never have to change. But for most of us, life involves meeting new people and coping with new challenges. Therefore, we must re-construe our experiences and constructs accordingly.

permeability
The idea that constructs can be revised and extended in light of new experiences.

The Modulation Corollary

Adapting to new experiences. Constructs differ in their **permeability**. To permeate means to penetrate or pass through something. A permeable construct is one that allows new elements to penetrate or be admitted to the range of convenience. Such a construct is open to new events and experiences and is capable of being revised or extended by them.

How much our construct system can be modulated, or adjusted, as a function of new experience and learning depends on the permeability of the individual constructs. An impermeable or rigid construct is not capable of being changed, no matter what our experiences tell us. For example, if a bigoted person applies the construct *high intelligence versus low intelligence* in a fixed or impermeable way to people of a certain ethnic minority group, believing that all members of this group have low intelligence, then new experiences will not penetrate or alter this belief. The prejudiced person will not modify that construct, no matter how many highly intelligent people of that ethnic group he or she meets. The construct is a barrier to learning and to new ideas because it is incapable of being changed or revised.

The Fragmentation Corollary

Competition among constructs. Kelly believed that within our construct system some individual constructs might be incompatible, even though they coexist within the overall pattern. Recall that our construct system may change as we evaluate new experiences. However, new constructs do not necessarily derive from old ones. A new construct may be compatible or consistent with an old one in a given situation, but if the situation changes, then these constructs can become inconsistent.

People may accept one another as friends in one situation, such as playing a board game, but may act as adversaries in another situation, such as a political debate.

© Benelux/zefa/Corbis

Consider the following situation. A man meets a woman in a psychology class and decides that he is attracted to her. She is also a psychology major, and her interests seem similar to his. She fits the *friend* alternative of the construct *friend versus enemy*. Thus, she is someone to be liked and respected. He sees her the next day at a political rally and is disappointed to find her loudly expressing conservative views that are the opposite of his own liberal opinions. Now she also fits the opposite alternative of the construct. In that situation she has become the *enemy*.

This inconsistency in the man's construct about this woman is at a subordinate level in his overall construct system. In one situation she is a friend, and in another situation she is an enemy. However, his broader construct, that liberals are friends and conservatives are enemies, remains undisturbed. According to Kelly, this is the process by which we tolerate subordinate inconsistencies without damaging our overall construct system.

The Commonality Corollary

Similarities among people in interpreting events. Because people differ in the ways they construe events, each person develops unique constructs. However, people also show similarities in their ways of construing events. Kelly suggested that if several people construe an experience similarly, we can conclude that their cognitive processes are similar. Consider a group of people with the same cultural norms and ideals. Their anticipations and expectations of one another will have much in common and they will construe many of their experiences in the same way. People from the same culture may show a resemblance in their behaviors and characteristics even though they are exposed to different life events.

The Sociality Corollary

Interpersonal relationships. We noted above that people in the same culture tend to construe events similarly. Although this accounts for some commonalities among people, it does not in itself bring about positive social relationships. It is not enough for one person to construe or interpret experiences in the same way as another person. The first person must also construe the other person's constructs. In other words, we must understand how another person thinks if we are to anticipate how that person will predict events.

Construing another person's constructs is something we do routinely. Think about driving a car. We stake our lives on being able to anticipate what the other drivers on the road will do; we anticipate that they will stop at a red light and move ahead at a green light. It is only when we can predict with some certainty what drivers of SUVs, friends, bosses, or teachers will do that we can adjust our behaviors to theirs. And while we are adapting to them, they are doing the same to us.

Each person assumes a role with respect to others. We play one role with a partner, another with a child, another with our supervisor at work. Each role is a behavior pattern that evolves from understanding how the other person construes events. In a sense, then, we fit ourselves into the other person's constructs.

Log On

The Psychology of Personal Constructs

Official Web site of the Personal Construct Psychology Information Center, Hamburg, Germany. Includes considerable English-language information on Kelly's personal construct psychology as well as links to related sites.

Personal Construct Theory and Practice

Check out the free Internet journal called *Personal Construct Theory and Practice*.

For direct links to these sites, log on to the student companion site for this book at http://www.academic.cengage.com/psychology/Schultz and choose Chapter 11.

Questions About Human Nature

Kelly's personality theory presents an optimistic, even flattering, image of human nature (Kelly, 1969). Kelly treated people as rational beings capable of forming a framework of constructs through which to view the world. He believed we are the authors, not the victims, of our destiny. His view endows us with free will, the ability to choose the direction our life will take, and we are able to change when necessary by revising old constructs and forming new ones. We are not committed to a path laid down in childhood or adolescence. Our direction is clearly toward the future because we formulate constructs to predict or anticipate events.

Thus, Kelly did not accept historical determinism. He did not consider past events to be the determinants of present behavior. We are not prisoners of toilet training, early sex experiences, or parental rejection, nor are we bound by biological instincts or unconscious forces. We need no push from internal drives or needs because we are motivated by the fact of being alive. Kelly saw no reason to invoke any other explanation.

Although Kelly did not discuss the role of heredity in personality, he noted that we are not totally determined by environmental influences. We live by constructs based on our interpretation of events. Therefore, it is the operation of our rational mental processes and not the specific events that influence the formation of personality. Kelly did not posit an ultimate and necessary life goal, but we may infer that our goal is to establish a construct system that enables us to predict events. On the question of uniqueness versus universality, Kelly took a moderate position. The commonality corollary states that people in the same culture develop similar constructs, whereas the individuality corollary emphasizes the uniqueness of many of our constructs and therefore of the self.

Assessment in Kelly's Theory

The Interview

Kelly's primary assessment technique was the interview. He wrote, "If you don't know what is going on in a person's mind, ask him; he may tell you!" (1958, p. 330). Adopting what he called a "credulous attitude," Kelly accepted the client's words at face value, believing this was the best way to determine the person's constructs. He also recognized that a person might deliberately lie or distort the reported version of events. However, what the client said must be respected, even if not fully believed.

Self-Characterization Sketches

self-characterization sketch
A technique designed to assess a person's construct system; that is, how a person perceives himself or herself in relation to other people.

Another technique used to assess a construct system is to have the person write a **self-characterization sketch**. Kelly's instructions to the client were as follows. "I want you to write a character sketch of [client's name] just as if he were the principal character in a play. Write it as it might be written by a friend who knew him very intimately and very sympathetically, perhaps better than anyone ever really could know him" (1955, p. 323). Kelly found this technique useful for learning how clients perceive themselves in relation to other people.

The Role Construct Repertory Test

Kelly devised the Role Construct Repertory (REP) Test to uncover the constructs we apply to the important people in our lives. The client is asked to list by name the people who have played a significant role in his or her life such as mother, father, spouse, closest friend, and the most intelligent or interesting person he or she knows (see Table 11.2). The names are sorted, three at a time, and clients are asked to select from each group of three the two people who are most alike, noting how they differ from the third. For example, the client may be given the names of most threatening person, successful person, and attractive person and must describe how any two of them are similar in some aspect of behavior or character and how they differ from the other.

This information is presented in a diagram called a repertory grid (see Figure 11.1). For each row the client judges the three people indicated by the circles and formulates a construct about them, such as *happy versus sad*. The client writes a word or phrase that describes two of them in the column labeled *Emergent Pole* (in our example, the word *happy*). The client writes the opposite word (*sad*) to describe the third person in the group in the column labeled *Implicit Pole*. The client places a check mark in the squares of anyone else in the grid who shares the *Emergent Pole* characteristics, in this case, anyone significant in the client's life who could be described as happy.

The assumption underlying the REP Test is that people construe events in dichotomies, according to the dichotomy corollary, in terms of like versus unlike or similar versus dissimilar. By forcing clients to make repeated judgments about their social relationships, Kelly believed he could uncover their anticipations and expectations. The dichotomies or alternatives by which we guide our life will show the pattern of our personal constructs.

Table 11.2 Role title list from the Role Construct Repertory Test

1. A teacher you liked.
2. A teacher you disliked.
3. Your wife/husband or present boyfriend/girlfriend.
4. An employer, supervisor, or officer under whom you worked or served and whom you found hard to get along with.
5. An employer, supervisor, or officer under whom you worked or served and whom you liked.
6. Your mother or the person who has played the part of a mother in your life.
7. Your father or the person who has played the part of a father in your life.
8. Your brother nearest your age or the person who has been most like a brother.
9. Your sister nearest your age or the person who has been most like a sister.
10. A person with whom you have worked who was easy to get along with.
11. A person with whom you have worked who was hard to understand.
12. A neighbor with whom you get along well.
13. A neighbor whom you find hard to understand.
14. A boy you got along well with when you were in high school.
15. A girl you got along well with when you were in high school.
16. A boy you did not like when you were in high school.
17. A girl you did not like when you were in high school.
18. A person of your own sex whom you would enjoy having as a companion on a trip.
19. A person of your own sex whom you would dislike having as a companion on a trip.
20. A person with whom you have been closely associated recently who appears to dislike you.
21. The person whom you would most like to be of help to or whom you feel most sorry for.
22. The most intelligent person whom you know personally.
23. The most successful person whom you know personally.
24. The most interesting person whom you know personally.

SOURCE: Reprinted from *The Psychology of Personal Constructs,* by George A. Kelly. Copyright © 1991 by Routledge, Chapman & Hall, Inc. Reprinted by permission.

Interpretation of the REP Test depends on the skill and training of the psychologist who administers it. Kelly did not intend the test to be a standardized, objective self-report inventory. He designed it as a way to assess constructs as a necessary stage in psychotherapy, to induce clients to reveal the constructs by which they organize their world. However, computer programs have since been developed to analyze individual repertory grids.

Fixed Role Therapy

fixed role therapy
A psychotherapeutic technique in which the client acts out constructs appropriate for a fictitious person. This shows the client how the new constructs can be more effective than the old ones he or she has been using.

After assessing a client's system of personal constructs, Kelly attempted to bring about a change in undesirable or ineffective constructs. He promoted a form of psychotherapy he called **fixed role therapy**. To help clients formulate new constructs and discard old ones, he asked them to write a self-characterization sketch describing them as the lead character in a play.

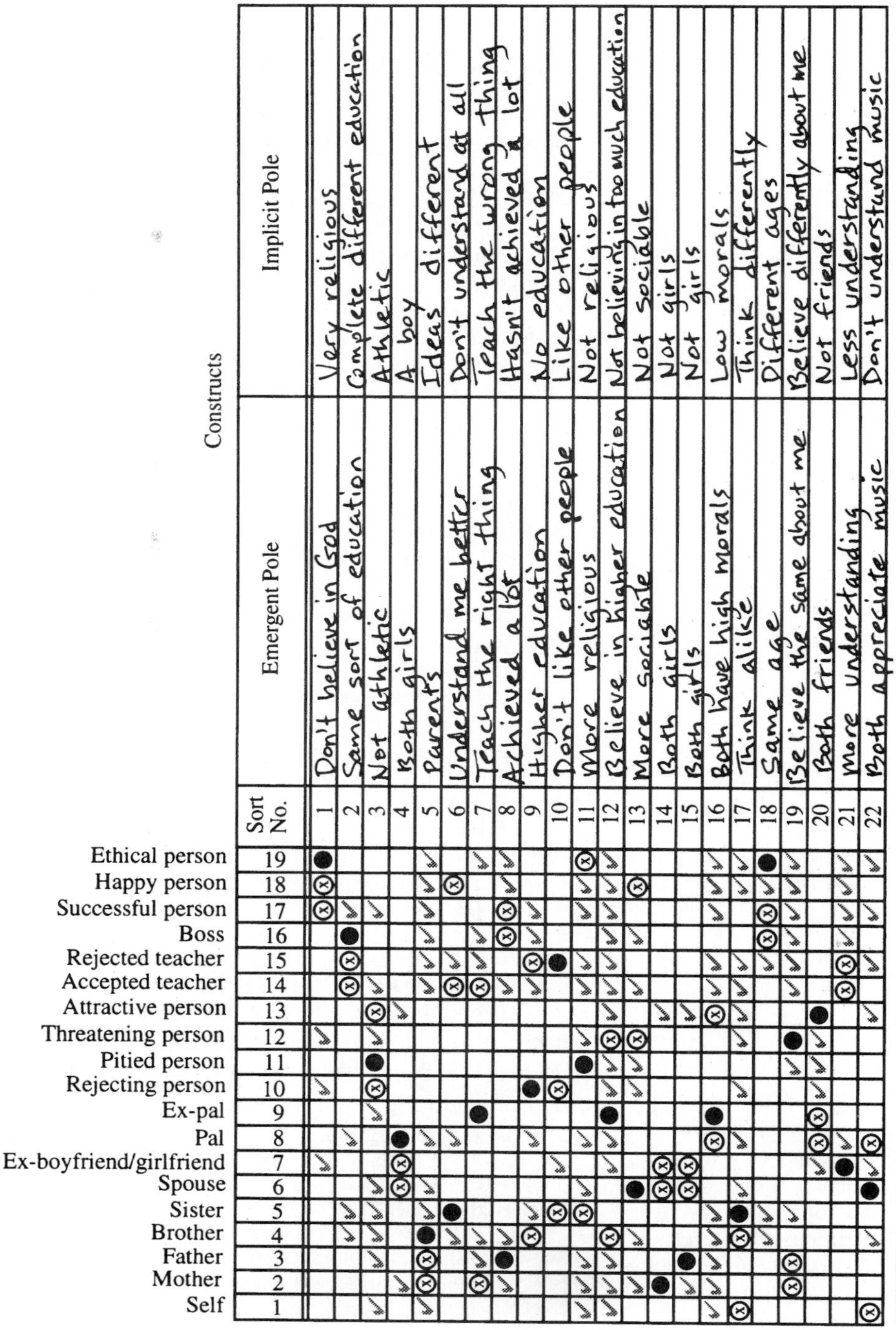

Figure 11.1
A grid for the Role Construct Repertory Test.

SOURCE: Reprinted from *The Psychology of Personal Constructs*, by George A. Kelly. Copyright © 1991 by Routledge, Chapman & Hall, Inc. Reprinted by permission.

In fixed role therapy, the therapist prepares a fixed role sketch containing constructs that differ from the client's negative self-perceptions as revealed in the self-characterization sketch. The client is told that the fixed role sketch is about a fictitious character and is asked to act out that character in the therapist's office and later in everyday life. Through this role-playing the client is expected to project personal needs and values onto the fictitious character. The therapist expects the client to discover that the new constructs in the fixed role sketch work better in anticipating events than do the old constructs by which the client was living. Once the client realizes this, he or she can incorporate the new constructs into the overall construct system and function in a more satisfying and effective way.

Kelly developed fixed role therapy from observing a friend who began to live the role he was playing in a college dramatic production. The friend was so strongly influenced by the part that his behavior offstage gradually became more and more like the character. The goal of fixed role therapy, then, is to first play a role and then come to live it.

Consider the following example. Based on interviews with a male client, his written self-characterization sketch, and his REP Test results, the therapist concluded that the client was overly concerned with finding a female companion. His efforts were having a negative impact on his other social relationships. The client had difficulty being open and assertive because in his construct system assertiveness and extraversion were negative personality characteristics. Yet in dealing with other people, he was convinced that his opinions were the correct ones and that everybody else was wrong. At work, he felt isolated, believing he belonged to a higher social class than his colleagues.

The therapist's fixed role sketch for this client made no mention of the client's desire to have an intimate relationship with a woman. Instead, taking as a framework the client's skill at tennis, the therapist encouraged the client, through the fictitious character, to be more curious about and tolerant of different kinds of people and their views (Winter, 1992, pp. 270–271).

> Roy Taylor's philosophy of life very much reflects his approach to his favorite sport, tennis: it's not whether a player wins or loses that's important but whether they've played the game to the best of their ability. Whether at work or at play, he believes that if a job is worth doing it's worth doing well, and he brings to everything that he does a certain passion and conviction, which cannot fail to earn your respect. Although you might perhaps think that this would make him appear a little too serious and intense, once you get to know him you soon realize that his main concern is to live life to the full and that this includes having fun as well as working hard. Life doesn't always run smoothly for him, of course, but when he has a disappointment he always seems able to learn something from it, and to look to the future rather than brooding on his present or past misfortunes.
>
> One of his greatest strengths at tennis is his ability to anticipate the moves of the other players, be they his opponents or doubles partners. In other areas of his life, he also always tries to see the world through the eyes of the people with whom he comes into contact, perhaps because he has mixed with people from so many different walks of life. His lively curiosity in what makes other people tick is usually reciprocated and leads him, almost before he knows it, into some very rewarding relationships. He also, of course, has his fair share of disagreements with others, but when this happens he always

makes an effort to understand the other person's point of view, even though he might not accept it. Because of this, he has a reputation both for commitment to those causes that are close to his heart and tolerance of the right of others to hold different opinions.

The therapist reviewed the fixed role sketch with the client and asked whether the character seemed like someone that the client might want to know. The client agreed to try behaving like the character in the sketch while in the therapist's office. He was asked to try acting, thinking, and talking like the character for the next two weeks. Behavioral changes instilled by fixed role therapy are reported to last far beyond the two-week role-playing period. However, positive case reports on treatment outcomes for individual clients must be balanced by the fact that there has been little controlled research on the technique's effectiveness.

Research on Kelly's Theory

Studies using the REP Test have shown that a person's constructs remain stable over time. One group of subjects took the test twice, using the names of different people as role figures each time. Although the role models changed, the constructs that were important to the subjects remained the same. However, research has shown that the validity of the REP Test depends heavily on the skill of the psychologist interpreting the results.

One REP Test study investigated the complexity of a person's construct system. The results showed that the pattern becomes increasingly differentiated and integrated over the life span and can process more information as it is able to function in more abstract terms (Crockett, 1982). Another study suggested that forming friendships depends on a similarity of personal constructs. A group of students took the REP Test during their first week at college and again 6 months later. The data showed that the similarity in constructs or attitudes among friends did not develop during the 6-month period but had existed before the relationships were formed. The researchers concluded that we seek as friends those people whose constructs are already similar to ours (Duck & Spencer, 1972). Also, for married subjects, spouses whose constructs were more alike reported greater happiness with their marriage than did couples whose constructs were more unlike (Neimeyer, 1984).

Other research showed a correspondence between one's personal characteristics and the ways of construing other people. Among a group of student nurses, those identified as highly anxious tended to use *anxious versus non-anxious* as a construct for evaluating others. Those who were judged by peers as friendly tended to view others in terms of a *friendly versus unfriendly* construct (Sechrest, 1968).

The REP Test has been used to study schizophrenics, neurotics, depressives, and persons with organic brain damage. Compared with normal subjects, schizophrenics were found to be unstable and inconsistent in construing other people. However, their construing of objects was stable and consistent, suggesting that their thought disorders applied only to social situations. Their thought processes were also characterized by paranoid delusions and irrational links between constructs (see, for example, Bannister, Fransella, & Agnew, 1971; Bannister & Salmon, 1966; Winter, 1992).

A study using a modified version of the REP Test compared the personal construct systems of repeat patients in psychiatric hospitals with persons hospitalized for the first time. The repeat patients construed their social network as small, limited to a few people on whom they believed they could depend. First-time patients construed their social network as significantly larger (Smith, Stefan, Kovaleski, & Johnson, 1991). REP Test research with juvenile and adult offenders revealed that delinquents tended to identify with action-oriented television heroes rather than with real adults. Newly released prisoners showed poor self-esteem and lowered aspirations for the future. Rapists felt inadequate, immature, and preoccupied with personal failure (Needs, 1988).

Researchers have applied the REP Test in market research to assess the criteria consumers use to evaluate products. Industrial-organizational psychologists have used the REP Test for vocational counseling, employee selection, job performance evaluation, and evaluation of training programs.

Cognitive Complexity and Cognitive Simplicity

An outgrowth of Kelly's work on personal constructs relates to cognitive styles, that is, differences in how we perceive or construe the persons, objects, and situations in our environment. Research on cognitive styles was derived from the REP Test and focuses on the concept of **cognitive complexity**.

cognitive complexity
A cognitive style or way of construing the environment characterized by the ability to perceive differences among people.

A person's degree of cognitive complexity can be determined from the pattern of Xs on the repertory grid. A highly differentiated pattern of Xs indicates cognitive complexity, defined as the ability to discriminate in the process of applying personal constructs to other people. People high in cognitive complexity are able to see variety among people and can easily place a person in many categories.

cognitive simplicity
A cognitive style or way of construing the environment characterized by a relative inability to perceive differences among people.

The other extreme, **cognitive simplicity**, applies when the pattern of Xs on the repertory grid is the same or highly similar for each construct. This indicates that the person is less capable of perceiving differences when judging other people. Persons high in cognitive simplicity are likely to place others in only one or two categories, unable to see much variety.

Research has confirmed personality differences in terms of cognitive style. People high in cognitive complexity are better able to make predictions about other people's behavior. They more readily recognize differences between themselves and others, are more empathic, and deal better with inconsistent information in construing others than do people high in cognitive simplicity (Crockett, 1982). Studies of politicians in the United States and England found that conservatives were high in cognitive simplicity, whereas moderates and liberals displayed higher levels of cognitive complexity (Tetlock, 1983, 1984).

In Kelly's theory, cognitive complexity is the more desirable and useful cognitive style. Our goal in developing a construct system is to reduce uncertainty by being able to predict or anticipate what people will do. This gives us a guide for our own behavior. People with a more complex cognitive style will be more successful at this task than will people with a simpler cognitive style. Therefore, cognitive style is an important dimension of personality.

Studies show that cognitive complexity increases with age; adults generally possess greater cognitive complexity than children. However, age is not a complete explanation for cognitive complexity; many adults still possess cognitive simplicity. Much depends on the level of complexity of our childhood experiences. Adults high in cognitive complexity typically had more diverse experiences in childhood. Their parents were less authoritarian and more likely to grant autonomy than parents of adults high in cognitive simplicity (Sechrest & Jackson, 1961).

A study of first-year college students in Canada found that those who scored higher in cognitive complexity adjusted better to the stresses of college life than did those lower in cognitive complexity (Pancer, Hunsberger, Pratt, & Alisat, 2000).

A study of 40 couples found that although the women scored significantly higher in cognitive complexity than the men did, there was a high correlation in cognitive complexity between men and women who were partners. The researcher suggested that these partners may have chosen each other because of their similar pre-existing levels of cognitive complexity, or else they developed this similarity as a result of living together. Either way, these partners tended to construe their worlds in a similar manner (Adams-Webber, 2001).

Comparisons were made of monocultural Anglo-American and bicultural Chinese-American college students. The Chinese-American students had been born in China and lived at least 5 years in the United States. The results showed that the bicultural students scored higher in cognitive complexity than the monocultural students (Benet-Martinez, Lee, & Leu, 2006).

Reflections on Kelly's Theory

Kelly developed a unique personality theory that did not derive from or build on other theories. It emerged from his interpretation, his own construct system, of data provided by his clinical practice. It is a personal view, and its originality parallels its message, that we are capable of developing the framework for our life.

Kelly's system has been criticized on several points. It focuses on intellectual and rational aspects of human functioning to the exclusion of emotional aspects. Kelly's image of a person rationally constructing the present and future, forming and testing hypotheses, and making predictions as the basis for behavior does not coincide with the everyday experiences of clinical psychologists who see more extreme examples of human behavior. To them, Kelly's rational being seems to be an ideal that exists in the abstract but not in reality. Although Kelly did not deal explicitly with emotions, he recognized them as personal constructs, similar in their formation to other constructs.

We noted that Sigmund Freud's view of personality derived from his exposure to neurotic, middle-class Viennese patients, who presented him with a distorted, unrepresentative sample of human nature. Other theorists have been similarly criticized. Kelly's viewpoint was also unrepresentative, limited largely to Midwestern young adults in the process of defining a construct system that would help them cope with college life.

Kelly's theory, like many others, leaves unanswered questions. Each of us is able to construe events in a unique way, but why does one person construe an event in one way while another person construes the same event in a different way? What process or mechanism accounts for the difference? A person makes choices about defining or extending the construct system. What determines whether to opt for security or for adventure, for the safer or the riskier alternative?

Personal construct theory continues to enjoy a large and growing base of support, although this is much broader in Europe, Canada, and Australia than in the United States. In the mid-1980s, the Centre for Personal Construct Psychology was established in England to train clinicians in Kelly's psychotherapeutic techniques and to promote applications of the theory. The *International Journal of Personal Construct Psychology* and the *Journal of Constructivist Psychology* began publication in the late 1980s, and in 1990 the first volume of the series *Advances in Personal Construct Psychology* appeared. References to Kelly's work have appeared in almost half of the volumes of the *Annual Review of Psychology* over a 40-year period from 1955 to 2005.

Kelly's work is not as popular in the United States for several reasons. First, many psychologists see it as too different from prevailing ideas. Personality psychologists typically think in terms of the familiar concepts of motivation and emotion, unconscious forces, drives, and needs, which form no part of Kelly's system. Second, Kelly published few books, articles, or case studies, devoting most of his time to clinical work and to training graduate students. The writing style of his two major books is scholarly, not intended for the public or for the therapist seeking explanations of human passions and emotions, loves and hatreds, fears and dreams. Such was not the style of the man or his theory.

Kelly recognized the limitations of his program and made no pretense of setting forth a finished theory. Just as an individual's constructs change in light of new experiences, so Kelly expected the personal construct theory to change with further research and application. His contributions have been recognized with honors from the profession and from former students. His theory is one of the most unusual to appear in a century of theorizing about the nature of the human personality. Adherents continue to apply it to problems in clinical psychology, industrial psychology, anthropology, criminology, and urban planning as a way of modifying and predicting behavior in many walks of life (Walker & Winter, 2007).

Chapter Summary

Kelly viewed people as similar to scientists who construct hypotheses and test them against reality. A personal construct is a way of looking at events. Kelly's fundamental postulate states that psychological processes are directed by the ways we anticipate events and construe our world. The theory includes 11 corollaries. Kelly presented an optimistic image of human nature that depicts us as rational beings with free will, capable of directing our destiny. We are not bound by constructs developed at one stage of life or by past experiences, unconscious conflicts, and biological instincts. Our goal is to define a set of constructs that enables us to predict events.

Kelly assessed personality by accepting a person's words at face value, by having the person write a self-characterization sketch, and by the Role Construct Repertory (REP) Test. The REP Test uncovers dichotomies important in a person's life, revealing the pattern of personal constructs. Fixed role therapy involves having a client act out the constructs of an imaginary person to demonstrate how to implement new constructs that will be more effective than old ones. REP Test research has shown that constructs are stable over time. The validity of the test depends on the skill of the psychologist interpreting it. The test has been used for market research, performance appraisal, and vocational counseling.

People high in cognitive complexity are better able to predict the behavior of others. They more readily recognize differences between themselves and others. They are more empathic, deal better with inconsistent information in construing others, and experienced greater complexity in childhood than did people high in cognitive simplicity.

Kelly's work has been criticized for omitting familiar concepts such as motivation and emotion, for focusing on the rational aspects of human functioning to the exclusion of emotional aspects, and for relying on an unrepresentative sample of subjects.

Review Questions

1. What did Kelly mean when he suggested that we all function like scientists in trying to predict and control the events in our lives?

2. How does Kelly's approach to personality differ from the other approaches we have discussed?

3. What is the relationship between Kelly's cognitive theory and modern cognitive psychology?

4. How might Kelly's theory have been influenced by the kinds of clients he treated?

5. What is Kelly's definition of the term *construct*? Why must constructs be dichotomous?

6. Why did Kelly believe that we must always be revising our constructs?

7. What factors influence the ways we anticipate those events that are similar to past events?

8. How do we choose between the two alternatives offered by a construct?

9. How does our anticipation of events, and of how other people will behave, influence our personality?

10. Explain how the individuality corollary differs from the organization corollary.

11. What is a construct's range of convenience?

12. In your construct system, what is the range of convenience for the construct *cheerful versus sad*?

13. What mechanism did Kelly propose to account for changes in a construct's range of convenience?

14. How is it possible to hold incompatible or inconsistent constructs?

15. Why is it important to construe the constructs of other people in our daily lives?

16. What is Kelly's position on the issue of free will versus determinism?

17. What is a self-characterization sketch? How is it used in therapy?

18. Describe how the Role Construct Repertory Test works with clients.

19. What is fixed role therapy? How does it relate to role-playing?

20. How do people high in cognitive complexity differ from people high in cognitive simplicity?

21. Discuss some of the criticisms that have been made of Kelly's approach to personality.

Suggested Readings

Epting, F. R. (1984). *Personal construct counseling and psychotherapy.* New York: Wiley. The first major textbook on the principles of Kelly's personality theory and their clinical applications.

Fransella, F. (1995). *George Kelly.* London: Sage. Describes Kelly's life and the development and applications of personal construct theory. Reviews the concept of constructive alternativism using Kelly's own personality as an example.

Fransella, F. (Ed.). (2003). *International handbook of personal construct psychology.* New York: Wiley. A comprehensive reference sourcebook on Kelly's theory and the application of his ideas to forensic psychology, psychotherapy and counseling, cross-cultural issues, nursing, law enforcement, artificial intelligence, and sports psychology.

Jancowicz, A. D. (1987). Whatever became of George Kelly? Applications and implications. *American Psychologist,* *42,* 481–487. Published on the 20th anniversary of Kelly's death, this article reviews and assesses the impact of Kelly's work.

Kelly, G. A. (1969). *Clinical psychology and personality: The selected papers of George Kelly.* New York: Wiley. Selections from Kelly's writings, edited by Brendan Maher. See Chapter 2, "The Autobiography of a Theory," for Kelly's description of the impact of his personal experiences on the development of his theory.

Thompson, G. G. (1968). George Alexander Kelly: 1905–1967. *Journal of General Psychology, 79,* 19–24. Reviews and assesses Kelly's life and work.

Winter, D. A. (1992). *Personal construct psychology in clinical practice: Theory, research and applications.* London: Routledge. Reviews 35 years of clinical work with personal construct theory and compares it with diagnosis and treatment using other major approaches.

PART SEVEN

The Behavioral Approach

At the beginning of this text we briefly considered the work of John B. Watson, the founder of behaviorism. His behaviorist psychology focused on overt behavior, on how people respond to external stimuli. This natural-science approach to psychology, based on careful experimental research and the precise quantification of stimulus and response variables, became immensely popular in the 1920s and remained a dominant force in psychology for more than 60 years.

Watson's behaviorism had no place for conscious or unconscious forces because they could not be seen, manipulated, or measured. Watson believed that whatever might be happening inside an organism—a person or an animal—between the presentation of the stimulus and the elicitation of the response had no value, meaning, or use for science. Why? Because scientists could not perform experiments on such internal conditions. In the behavioral approach, therefore, we find no reference to anxiety, drives, motives, needs, or defense mechanisms—the kinds of internal processes invoked by most other personality theorists. To behaviorists, personality is merely an accumulation of learned responses to stimuli, sets of overt behaviors, or habit systems. Personality refers only to what can be objectively observed and manipulated.

The behavioral approach to personality is represented here by the work of B. F. Skinner, whose ideas follow the Watsonian tradition. Skinner rejected as irrelevant any alleged internal forces or processes. His sole concern was with overt behavior and the external stimuli that shape it. Skinner attempted to understand what we call "personality" through laboratory research with rats and pigeons rather than clinical work with patients. His ideas have proved immensely useful in the clinical setting, however, through the application of behavior modification techniques.

CHAPTER 12

B. F. Skinner:
Reinforcement Theory

It is the environment which must be changed.
—B. F. SKINNER

Rats, Pigeons, and an Empty Organism

Skinner did not offer a personality theory that can easily be contrasted and compared with others discussed in this textbook. In fact, he did not offer a personality theory at all, nor does his research deal specifically with personality. His work attempted to account for *all* behavior, not just personality, in factual, descriptive terms. Skinner argued that psychologists must restrict their investigations to facts, to what they can see, manipulate, and measure in the laboratory. That means an exclusive emphasis on the overt responses a subject makes and nothing more. Skinner's contention was that psychology is the science of behavior, of what an organism does. His study of behavior is the antithesis of the psychoanalytic, trait, life-span, cognitive, and humanistic approaches, differing not only in subject matter but in methodology and aims.

In explaining personality, most other theorists look inside the person for clues. The causes, motives, and drives—the forces that direct our development and behavior—originate within each of us. In contrast, Skinner made no reference to internal, subjective states to account for behavior. Unconscious influences, defense mechanisms, traits, and other driving forces cannot be seen, he argued, and therefore have no place in a scientific psychology. They have no more value for science than the old theological concept of the soul. Skinner did not deny the existence of internal forces, only their usefulness for science. Skinner applied similar reasoning to physiological processes, which are not overtly observable and so have no relevance for science. He said, "The inside of the organism is irrelevant either as the site of physiological processes or as the locus of mentalistic activities" (quoted in Evans, 1968, p. 22). He saw no need to look inside the organism for some form of inner activity. To Skinner, human beings are "empty organisms," by which he meant that there is nothing inside us that can explain behavior in scientific terms.

Another way Skinner differed from other theorists is in his choice of experimental subject. Some personality theorists focus on emotionally disturbed persons, others on normal or average individuals. At least one based his theory on the best and brightest people. Although Skinner's ideas about behavior have been applied to people, the research for his behavioral approach used rats and pigeons. What can we learn from pigeons about the human personality? Remember that Skinner's interest was in behavioral responses to stimuli, not in childhood experiences or adult feelings. Responding to stimuli is something animals do well, sometimes better than people do. Skinner admitted that human behavior is more complex than animal behavior but suggested that the differences are in degree, not in kind. He believed that the fundamental processes are similar. And because a science must proceed from simple to complex, the more elemental processes should be studied first. Thus, he chose animal behavior because it is simpler than human behavior.

Skinner's work has had wide practical applications. Therapeutic techniques derived from his research are used in clinical settings to treat a variety of disorders including psychoses, mental retardation, and autism. His behavior modification techniques are also used in schools, businesses, correctional institutions, and hospitals.

The Life of Skinner (1904–1990)

B. F. Skinner was born in Susquehanna, Pennsylvania, the elder of two sons; his brother died at the age of 16. His parents were hardworking people who instilled in their children clear rules of proper behavior. "I was taught to fear God, the police, and what people will think" (Skinner, 1967, p. 407). His mother never deviated from her strict standards. Her method of control was to say "tut tut." Skinner's grandmother made certain that he understood the punishments of Hell by pointing out the red-hot coals in the parlor stove. Skinner's father contributed to his son's moral education by teaching him the fate that befell criminals. He showed Skinner the county jail and took him to a lecture about life in a notorious New York state prison.

Skinner's autobiography contains many references to the impact of these childhood warnings on his adult behavior. He wrote of visiting a cathedral as an adult and taking care to avoid stepping on the gravestones set in the floor; as a child he had been instructed that such behavior wasn't proper. Such events made it clear to Skinner that his adult behaviors were determined by the rewards and punishments (the "reinforcements") he had received as a child. Thus, his system of psychology and his view of people as "complex system[s] behaving in lawful ways" reflected his own early life experiences (Skinner, 1971, p. 202).

Prophetic of his view of people as machines that operate predictably were the many hours he spent constructing mechanical devices such as wagons, seesaws, carousels, slingshots, model airplanes, and a steam cannon that shot potato and carrot plugs over neighboring houses. Skinner also worked on a perpetual-motion machine, which perpetually failed. His interest in animal behavior also derived from childhood. He made pets of turtles, snakes, toads, lizards, and chipmunks. A flock of performing pigeons at a county fair fascinated him. The pigeons raced onstage, pulled a fire engine up to a burning building, and shoved a ladder against it. One trained pigeon wearing a firefighter's red hat climbed to an upper-story window to rescue a stranded pigeon. Skinner later would train pigeons to play Ping-Pong and to guide a missile to its target.

Finding an Identity

Skinner majored in English at Hamilton College in upstate New York and after graduation expected to become a novelist. Encouraged by favorable comment on his work from the eminent poet Robert Frost, Skinner built a study in the attic of his parents' home in Scranton, Pennsylvania, and sat down to write. The results were disastrous. He read, listened to the radio, played the piano, and built ship models while waiting for inspiration. He considered seeing a psychiatrist, but his father argued that it would be a waste of money. Skinner was 22 years old and a failure at the only thing he wanted to do.

He later referred to that time as his dark year, what Erikson would call an identity crisis. Skinner's occupational identity as a writer, which he carefully constructed during his college years and which Robert Frost reinforced, had collapsed and took with it his sense of self-worth. He left Scranton for New York City's Greenwich Village but found he could not write there either. Worse, in his view, was that several women spurned his proclaimed love for them, leaving him so upset that he branded one woman's initial on his arm, where it remained for years (Skinner, 1983).

Just when Skinner believed he had lost all hope, he discovered a new identity that suited him, and to which he would cling for the rest of his life. He decided that since writing had failed him (rather than the other way around), he would study human behavior by the methods of science rather than the methods of fiction. He read books by Ivan Pavlov and John B. Watson, and chose to become a behaviorist. Thus, his self-image and identity became secure.

Skinner entered Harvard University in 1928 to study psychology. He had never taken a course in the field but earned his Ph.D. in three years. His choice of behaviorism led him to reject the feelings and emotions he had tried to draw on as a writer. One historian of psychology noted:

> [There are] essential differences between a career devoted to writing poetry and fiction and one devoted to promoting the cause of behaviorism. The former requires commitment to such intra-psychic processes as inspiration, intuition, free association, the stream of consciousness, and the participation of the unconscious, as well as considering fantasies and feelings important parts of one's being. The latter denies it all—makes fantasies and feelings, indeed the entire intra-psychic domain, recede into a background of (to use Skinner's favorite term) "pre-scientific" notions, while attention is focused on observable behavior and the operations necessary to record, predict, and control it effectively. (Mindess, 1988, p. 105)

Psychic processes appear in Skinner's work only as objects of derision.

With postdoctoral fellowships, Skinner stayed at Harvard until 1936. He then taught at the University of Minnesota and Indiana University, returning to Harvard in 1947. In his 40s, Skinner experienced a period of depression, which he resolved by returning to his failed identity as a writer. Skinner projected his emotional and intellectual discontent onto the protagonist of a novel, *Walden Two*, letting the character vent his personal and professional frustrations (Skinner, 1948). The book, which is still in print, has sold more than 2 million copies. It describes a society in which all aspects of life are controlled by positive reinforcement, which is the basic principle of Skinner's system of psychology.

Well into his 80s, Skinner continued to work with enthusiasm and dedication. He regulated his habits, recording his daily work output and the average time spent per published word (2 minutes). Thus, he became a living example of his definition of humans as complex systems behaving in lawful ways. He once commented to a friend that he was cited in the psychology literature more frequently than Freud was. When asked if that had been his goal, Skinner said, "I thought I might make it" (quoted in Bjork, 1993, p. 214).

Log On

The B. F. Skinner Foundation

The Web site for the B. F. Skinner Foundation contains a biography written by one of Skinner's daughters, discussions of operant behavior, lectures, photographs, and a DVD of Skinner reading *Walden Two*.

Personality Theories: B. F. Skinner

A brief biography and a more extensive discussion of the major aspects of Skinner's work.

Key Theorists/Theories in Psychology: B. F. Skinner

An enormous amount of information about Skinner's life and work including Sniffy, the virtual rat, an interactive program with which you can perform online experiments without the odors of a real-world rat laboratory.

For direct links to these sites, log on to the student companion site for this book at http://www.academic.cengage.com/psychology/Schultz and choose Chapter 12.

Reinforcement: The Basis of Behavior

Skinner's approach to behavior, simple in concept, is based on thousands of hours of well-controlled research. His fundamental idea is that behavior can be controlled by its consequences, that is, by what follows the behavior. Skinner believed that an animal or a human could be trained to perform virtually any act and that the type of reinforcement that followed the behavior would be responsible for determining it. Thus, whoever controls the reinforcers has the power to control human behavior, in the same way an experimenter can control the behavior of a laboratory rat.

Respondent Behavior

respondent behavior
Responses made to or elicited by specific environmental stimuli.

Skinner distinguished between two kinds of behavior: respondent behavior and operant behavior. **Respondent behavior** involves a response made to or elicited by a specific stimulus. A reflexive behavior such as a knee jerk is an example of respondent behavior. A stimulus is applied (a tap on the knee) and the response occurs (the leg jerks). This behavior is unlearned. It occurs automatically and involuntarily. We do not have to be trained or conditioned to make the appropriate response.

At a higher level is respondent behavior that is learned. This learning, called *conditioning*, involves the substitution of one stimulus for another. The concept originated in the work of the Russian physiologist Ivan Pavlov in the early 1900s. Later, Pavlov's ideas on conditioning were adopted by John B. Watson as the basic research method for behaviorism.

Working with dogs, Pavlov discovered that they would salivate to neutral stimuli such as the sound of their keeper's footsteps. Previously, the salivation response had been elicited by only one stimulus, the sight of food. Intrigued by this observation, Pavlov studied the phenomenon systematically. He sounded a bell shortly before feeding a dog. At first, the dog salivated only in response to the food and not to the bell because the bell had no meaning. However, after a number of pairings of the bell followed by the food, the dog began to salivate at the sound of the bell. Thus, the dog had been conditioned, or trained, to respond to the bell. The dog's response shifted from the food to what previously had been a neutral stimulus.

This classic experiment by Pavlov demonstrated the importance of **reinforcement**. The dogs would not learn to respond to the bell unless they were rewarded for doing so. In this example, the reward was food. Pavlov then formulated a fundamental law of learning: A conditioned response cannot be established in the absence of reinforcement. The act of reinforcing a response strengthens it and increases the likelihood that the response will be repeated.

However, an established conditioned response will not be maintained in the absence of reinforcement. Consider a dog conditioned to respond to the sound of a bell. Every time the bell rings, the dog salivates. Then the experimenter stops presenting food after sounding the bell. The dog hears the bell and nothing happens—no more food, no more reinforcement or reward. With successive ringing of the bell, the dog's salivary response decreases in frequency and intensity until no response occurs at all. This process is called **extinction**. The response has been wiped out or extinguished because reinforcers or rewards for it were no longer provided. A great deal of research has demonstrated that the greater the reinforcement given during training, the more resistant the conditioned response will be to extinction (see, for example, Shull & Grimes, 2006). Eventually, however, extinction will occur.

reinforcement
The act of strengthening a response by adding a reward, thus increasing the likelihood that the response will be repeated.

extinction
The process of eliminating a behavior by withholding reinforcement.

Animals can be conditioned by reinforcing them with food when they exhibit desired behaviors.

© Spencer Grant/PhotoEdit

Operant Behavior

operant behavior
Behavior emitted spontaneously or voluntarily that operates on the environment to change it.

Respondent behavior depends on reinforcement and is related directly to a physical stimulus. Every response is elicited by a specific stimulus. To Skinner, respondent behavior was less important than **operant behavior**. We are conditioned to respond directly to many stimuli in our environment, but not all behavior can be accounted for in this way. Much human behavior appears to be spontaneous and cannot be traced directly to a specific stimulus. Such behavior is emitted rather than elicited by a stimulus. It involves acting in a way that appears to be voluntary rather than reacting involuntarily to a stimulus to which we have been conditioned.

The nature and frequency of operant behavior will be determined or modified by the reinforcement that follows the behavior. Respondent behavior has no effect on the environment. In Pavlov's experiment, the dog's salivary response to the ringing bell did nothing to change the bell or the reinforcer (the food) that followed. In contrast, operant behavior operates on the environment and, as a result, changes it.

Operant Conditioning and the Skinner Box

operant conditioning
The procedure by which a change in the consequences of a response will affect the rate at which the response occurs.

To illustrate the **operant-conditioning** process, let us follow the progress of a rat in Skinner's operant-conditioning apparatus, also known as the Skinner box (see Figure 12.1). When a food-deprived rat is placed in the box, its behavior at first is spontaneous and random. The rat is active, sniffing, poking, and exploring its environment. These behaviors are emitted, not elicited; in other words, the rat is not responding to any specific stimulus in its environment.

At some time during this activity, the rat will depress a lever or bar located on one wall of the Skinner box, causing a food pellet to drop into a trough. The rat's behavior (pressing the lever) has operated on the environment and, as a result, has changed it. How? The environment now includes a food pellet. The food is a reinforcer for the behavior of depressing the bar. The rat begins to press the bar more often. What happens? It receives more food—more reinforcement—and so presses

Figure 12.1
A simple operant-conditioning apparatus

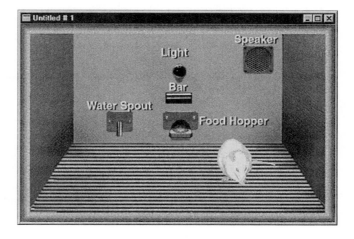

the bar even more frequently. The rat's behavior is now under the control of the reinforcers. Its actions in the box are less random and spontaneous because it is spending most of its time pressing the bar, and eating.

If we put the rat back in the box the next day, we can predict its behavior and we can control its bar-pressing actions by presenting or withholding the reinforcers or by presenting them at a different rate. Withholding the food extinguishes operant behavior in the same way that it extinguishes respondent behavior. If the unreinforced behavior no longer works, in that it no longer brings a reward, after a while it will stop. Thus, the person who controls the reinforcers controls the subjects' behavior.

Skinner believed that most human and animal behavior is learned through operant conditioning. Consider how babies learn. An infant initially displays random, spontaneous behaviors, only some of which are reinforced (rewarded with food or hugs or toys, for example) by parents, siblings, or caregivers. As the infant grows, the positively reinforced behaviors, those of which the parents approve, will persist, whereas those of which the parents disapprove will be extinguished or discontinued. The concept is the same with the rat in the Skinner box. Behaviors that work (pressing the bar to obtain food) are displayed frequently, and behaviors that do not work are not repeated. Thus, the organism's behavior operates on the environment. And in turn, the environment, in the form of reinforcement, operates on the organism's behavior.

You can see how powerful reinforcement can be in determining and controlling behavior. Skinner wrote, "Operant conditioning shapes behavior as a sculptor shapes a lump of clay" (1953, p. 91). If that lump of clay, that organism, needs the reinforcer badly enough, there is virtually no limit to how its behavior can be shaped—by an experimenter with a food pellet, a puppy owner with a dog biscuit, a mother with a smile, a boss with a pat on the back, or a government with a promise.

From infancy on, we display many behaviors, and those that are reinforced will strengthen and form patterns. This is how Skinner conceived of personality, as a pattern or collection of operant behaviors. What other psychologists called neurotic or abnormal behavior was nothing more mysterious to Skinner than the continued performance of undesirable behaviors that somehow have been reinforced.

Having demonstrated how behavior could be modified by continuous reinforcement—that is, by presenting a reinforcer after every response—Skinner decided to consider how behavior would change if he varied the rate at which it was reinforced.

 LOG ON

Operant Conditioning

Offers training in the principles of operant conditioning plus exercises and test questions to assess your progress (answers are provided).

For a direct link to this site, log on to the student companion site for this book at http://www.academic.cengage.com/psychology/Schultz and choose Chapter 12.

Schedules of Reinforcement

Skinner pointed out that in everyday life outside the psychology laboratory, our behavior is rarely reinforced every time it occurs. A baby is not picked up and cuddled every time he or she cries. Baseball superstars do not hit a home run every time at bat. The bagger in the supermarket does not receive a tip for each bag packed. And your favorite singing group doesn't win a Grammy for every album it records. You can think of many more examples of behaviors that persist even though they are reinforced only occasionally.

After observing that his rats continued to press the bar at a fairly constant rate even when they were not being reinforced for each response, Skinner decided to investigate different **reinforcement schedules** to determine their effectiveness in controlling behavior. Among the rates of reinforcement he tested are the following.

reinforcement schedules
Patterns or rates of providing or withholding reinforcers.

- Fixed interval
- Fixed ratio
- Variable interval
- Variable ratio

A *fixed-interval schedule of reinforcement* means that the reinforcer is presented following the first response that occurs after a fixed time interval has elapsed. That interval might be 1 minute, 3 minutes, or any other fixed period of time. The timing of the reinforcement has nothing to do with the number of responses. Whether the rat responds 3 times or 20 times a minute during the fixed time interval, the reinforcer still arrives only after the passage of a given time period and the emission of the correct response.

Many situations operate in accordance with the fixed-interval reinforcement schedule. If your professor gives a midterm and a final examination, he or she is using a fixed-interval schedule. A job in which your salary is paid once a week or once a month operates on the fixed-interval schedule. You are not paid according to the number of items you produce or the number of sales you make (the number of responses) but by the number of hours, days, or weeks that elapse.

Skinner's research showed that the shorter the interval between presentations of the reinforcer, the greater the frequency of response. The response rate declined as the interval between reinforcements lengthened. How frequently reinforcers appeared also affected how quickly the response could be extinguished. The response stopped sooner if the rat had been reinforced continuously and the reinforcement was then stopped than if the rat had been reinforced intermittently.

In the *fixed-ratio schedule of reinforcement*, reinforcers are given only after the organism has made a specified number of responses. For example, the experimenter could reinforce after every 10th or 20th response. In this schedule, unlike the fixed-interval schedule, the presentation of reinforcers depends on how often the subject responds. The rat will not receive a food pellet until it emits the required number of responses. This reinforcement schedule brings about a faster rate of responding than does the fixed-interval schedule.

The higher response rate for the fixed-ratio reinforcement schedule also applies to humans. In a job in which your pay is determined on a piece-rate basis, how

A parent's smile of approval can reinforce a child's behavior.

much you earn depends on how much you produce. The more items you produce, the higher your pay. Your reward is based directly on your response rate. The same is true for a salesperson working on commission. Income depends on the number of products sold; the more sold, the more earned. In contrast, a salesperson on a weekly salary earns the same amount each week regardless of the number of items sold.

But everyday life doesn't always permit a fixed-interval or fixed-ratio reinforcement schedule. Sometimes reinforcers are presented on a variable basis. In the *variable-interval schedule of reinforcement*, the reinforcer might appear after 2 hours in the first instance, after 1 ½ hours the next time, and after 2 hours and 15 minutes the third time. A person who spends the day fishing might be rewarded, if at all, on a variable-interval basis. The reinforcement schedule is determined by the random appearance of fish nibbling at the bait.

A *variable-ratio schedule of reinforcement* is based on an average number of responses between reinforcers, but there is great variability around that average. Skinner found that the variable-ratio schedule is effective in bringing about high and stable response rates, as the people who operate gambling casinos can happily attest. Slot machines, roulette wheels, horse races, and the state lottery games pay on a variable-ratio reinforcement schedule, an extremely effective means of controlling behavior. Variable reinforcement schedules result in enduring response behaviors that tend to resist extinction. Most everyday learning occurs as a result of variable-interval or variable-ratio reinforcement schedules.

Skinner's research on reinforcement schedules provides an effective technique for controlling, modifying, and shaping behavior. If you are in charge of rats, salespeople, or assembly-line workers, or are trying to train your pet or your child, these operant-conditioning techniques can bring about the behaviors you desire.

Successive Approximation: The Shaping of Behavior

In Skinner's original operant-conditioning experiment, the operant behavior (pressing the lever) is a simple behavior that a laboratory rat would be expected to display eventually in the course of exploring its environment. Thus, the chance is high that such a behavior will occur, assuming the experimenter has sufficient patience. It is obvious, however, that animals and humans demonstrate many more complex operant behaviors that have a much lower probability of occurrence in the normal course of events. How are these complex behaviors learned? How can an experimenter or a parent reinforce and condition a pigeon or a child to perform behaviors that are not likely to occur spontaneously?

successive approximation
An explanation for the acquisition of complex behavior. Behavior such as learning to speak will be reinforced only as it comes to approximate or approach the final desired behavior.

Skinner answered these questions with the method of **successive approximation**, or *shaping* (Skinner, 1953). He trained a pigeon in a very short time to peck at a specific spot in its cage. The probability that the pigeon on its own would peck at that exact spot was low. At first, the pigeon was reinforced with food when it merely turned toward the designated spot. Then reinforcement was withheld until the pigeon made some movement, however slight, toward the spot. Next, reinforcement was given only for movements that brought the pigeon closer to the spot. After that, the pigeon was reinforced only when it thrust its head toward the spot. Finally, the pigeon was reinforced only when its beak touched the spot. Although this sounds like a time-consuming process, Skinner conditioned pigeons in less than 3 minutes.

The experimental procedure itself explains the term *successive approximation*. The organism is reinforced as its behavior comes in successive, or consecutive, stages to approximate the final behavior desired. Skinner suggested that this is how children learn the complex behavior of speaking. Infants spontaneously emit meaningless sounds, which parents reinforce by smiling, laughing, and talking. After a while, parents reinforce this babbling in different ways, providing stronger reinforcers for sounds that approximate words. As the process continues, parental reinforcement becomes more restricted, given only for appropriate usage and pronunciation. Thus, the complex behavior of acquiring language skills is shaped by providing differential reinforcement in stages.

Skinner once shaped the behavior of a noted psychoanalyst, Erich Fromm, whose comments during a lecture annoyed him.

> Fromm proved to have something to say about almost everything, but with little enlightenment. When he began to argue that people were not pigeons, I decided that something had to be done. On a scrap of paper I wrote [to a colleague] "Watch Fromm's left hand. I am going to shape a chopping motion" . . . [Fromm] gesticulated a great deal as he talked, and whenever his left hand came up, I looked straight at him. If he brought the hand down, I nodded and smiled. Within five minutes he was chopping the air so vigorously that his wristwatch kept slipping out over his hand. (Skinner, 1983, pp. 150–151)

Parents teach their children acceptable behaviors by reinforcing those activities that approximate the final desired behaviors.

© Brand X Pictures/Jupiterimages

Superstitious Behavior

We know that life is not always as orderly or well controlled as events in the psychology laboratory. Sometimes we are reinforced accidentally after we have displayed some behavior. As a result, that behavior, which did not lead to or cause the reinforcement, may be repeated in a similar situation.

Consider an example from football. An offensive lineman for the Tampa Bay (FL) Buccaneers was having a terrible season early in his career. He asked his roommate to switch beds so that he could sleep closer to the bathroom. Immediately thereafter, his playing improved. For the rest of his career, he insisted on the bed nearest the bathroom door in every motel in which the team stayed. And the NFL kicker who hugged the goal posts before each game? He had done it once before making a successful kick, so because it had worked then, he continued the practice. He told a reporter that he wanted the goal posts to know he loved them and to implore them to stay still when he kicked.

Skinner called this phenomenon **superstitious behavior** and demonstrated it in the laboratory. A hungry pigeon was placed in the operant-conditioning apparatus

superstitious behavior Persistent behavior that has a coincidental and not a functional relationship to the reinforcement received.

and reinforced every 15 seconds on a fixed-interval schedule. It is likely that the pigeon would be doing something, displaying some behavior or activity, when the reinforcing food pellet was presented. It might be turning, raising its head, strutting, hopping, or standing still. Whatever behavior was being emitted at the moment of reward would be reinforced.

Skinner found that a single reinforcement was powerful enough to lead the pigeon to repeat the accidentally reinforced behavior more frequently for a while, which increased the probability that another food pellet would appear while the same behavior was being shown. And with short intervals between reinforcers, superstitious behaviors are learned quickly. Like the football players in the examples above, the superstitious behaviors offered by the pigeon have no functional relationship to the reinforcers. The connection is unintentional. In humans, such behaviors may persist throughout life and require only occasional reinforcement to sustain them.

A study of 77 big-league baseball players in the United States and Japan found that 74 percent of the players admitted engaging in superstitious behavior. In general, however, American players were more superstitious than Japanese players, suggesting that cultural differences may influence the extent of these actions (Burger & Lynn, 2005).

The Self-Control of Behavior

self-control
The ability to exert control over the variables that determine our behavior.

According to Skinner, behavior is controlled and modified by variables that are external to the organism. There is nothing inside us—no process, drive, or other internal activity—that determines behavior. However, although these external stimuli and reinforcers are responsible for shaping and controlling behavior, we have the ability to use what Skinner called **self-control**, which he described as acting to alter the impact of external events. Skinner did not mean acting under the control of some mysterious "self." He suggested that to some extent we can control the external variables that determine our behavior.

Skinner proposed several self-control techniques. In *stimulus avoidance*, for example, if the music from your roommate's stereo annoys you and interferes with your studying, you could leave the room and go to the library, removing yourself from an external variable that affects your behavior. By avoiding a person or situation that makes you angry, you reduce the control that person or situation has over your behavior. Similarly, alcoholics can act to avoid a stimulus that controls their behavior by not allowing liquor to be kept in their home.

Through the technique of *self-administered satiation*, we exert control to cure ourselves of bad habits by overdoing the behavior. Smokers who want to quit can chain-smoke for a period of time, inhaling until they become so disgusted, uncomfortable, or ill that they quit. This technique has been successful in formal therapeutic programs designed to eliminate smoking. The *aversive stimulation* technique of self-control involves unpleasant or repugnant consequences. Obese people who want to lose weight declare their intention to their friends. If they do not keep their resolution, they face the unpleasant consequences of personal failure, embarrassment, and criticism. In *self-reinforcement*, we reward ourselves for displaying good or desirable behaviors. A teenager who agrees to strive for a certain grade point average or to care for a younger brother or sister might reward himself or herself by buying concert tickets or new clothes.

To Skinner, then, the crucial point is that external variables shape and control behavior. But sometimes, through our own actions, we can modify the effects of these external forces.

A large-scale study of 606 college students in the United States found that those who scored high on a measure of self-control had better grades, higher psychological adjustment scores, and greater self-acceptance and self-esteem. They also showed better interpersonal skills and family relationships, as well as lower levels of anger compared to those who scored low on self-control (Tangney, Baumeister, & Boone, 2004). Research involving 670 African-American children (average age 11.2 years) found that those whose parents were more nurturing and involved in their upbringing had higher levels of self-control than those whose parents were less nurturing and involved (Wills et al., 2007).

Applications of Operant Conditioning

behavior modification
A form of therapy that applies the principles of reinforcement to bring about desired behavioral changes.

Psychologists have applied Skinner's operant conditioning techniques to modify human behavior in clinical, business, and educational settings. **Behavior modification** has been successful with children and adults, with the mentally healthy and the mentally disturbed, and with individual as well as group behaviors.

Token Economy Programs

token economy
A behavior modification technique in which tokens, which can be exchanged for valued objects or privileges, are awarded for desirable behaviors.

The classic application is the **token economy**. In the pioneering study, a ward of more than 40 psychotic female patients in a state mental institution was treated as a giant Skinner box (Ayllon & Azrin, 1968). The patients could no longer be helped by conventional treatments. They had been institutionalized for a long time and were unable to care for themselves.

In this setting, the patients were offered opportunities to work at jobs, usually performed by paid hospital attendants, for which they would receive tokens. The tokens functioned like money, hence the term *token economy*. Like people outside the institution, the patients could buy goods and privileges to improve the quality of life. With a certain number of tokens, they could purchase candy, cigarettes, lipstick, gloves, and newspapers. By paying with tokens, they could attend a movie on the ward, walk around the hospital grounds, or upgrade to a better room. The most expensive privileges, requiring 100 tokens, were an escorted trip into town and a private meeting with a social worker. A private meeting with a psychologist was worth only 20 tokens.

What kinds of behaviors did the patients have to emit to be reinforced and receive tokens? If they bathed at the time designated, brushed their teeth, made their bed, combed their hair, and dressed properly, they earned a token for each activity. They would be paid up to 10 tokens for each work period in the hospital kitchen or laundry or for helping to clean the ward, run errands, or take other patients for walks. The tasks may seem simple to us, but before the token economy program began, these patients were considered helpless and aimless.

The conditioning worked dramatically. Not only did the patients groom themselves and clean their surroundings, but they also busied themselves at a variety of tasks. They interacted socially with one another and with the staff and assumed some responsibility for patient care. Their self-esteem improved markedly, and they became less dependent.

A note of caution about these impressive results: Token economies have been found to be effective only within the setting in which they are implemented. In general, the modified behaviors do not carry over to life outside the institution. Reinforcement must be continued if the desired behavior changes are to persist. When tokens are no longer provided, reinforced behaviors usually revert to their original state (Kazdin & Bootzin, 1972; Repucci & Saunders, 1974). However, if caregivers are trained to reward desirable behaviors with reinforcers such as smiles, praise, hugs, and other signs of affection, then behaviors conditioned in the institutional token-economy situation are more likely to be continued in the home setting (Kazdin, 1989).

This token-economy approach to changing behavior has also worked online, as shown in a study of heavy smokers. Over a 4-week period the smokers made video recordings of themselves at home twice a day. They also used a Web camera to provide a carbon monoxide sample, which was sent electronically to the smoking clinic. The subjects could earn vouchers by reducing their carbon monoxide level over a 4-day period and by maintaining a level consistent with that of a non-smoker. The vouchers could be exchanged for various items purchased over the Internet.

The technique proved effective. Subjects showed significant decreases in carbon monoxide levels and sustained abstinence throughout the period of the study. However, it is not known whether this change in behavior was maintained after the study was over and the behavior was no longer being reinforced (Dallery, Glenn, & Raiff, 2007).

 Log On

Classroom Interventions for Children with Attention Deficit Disorder

A detailed description of a token economy intervention in a classroom setting for children with attention deficit disorder.

For a direct link to this site, log on to the student companion site for this book at http://www.academic.cengage.com/psychology/Schultz and choose Chapter 12.

Behavior Modification Programs

Operant-conditioning techniques have been applied to problems in business and industry. Behavior modification programs at major manufacturers, financial institutions, and government agencies have been shown to reduce absenteeism, lateness, and abuse of sick-leave privileges, and to lead to improvements in job performance and safety. The techniques can also be used to teach low-level job skills. Reinforcers used in business include pay, job security, recognition from supervisors, perks and status within the company, and the opportunity for personal growth. No attempt is made to deal with any alleged anxieties, repressed traumas, or unconscious motivating forces. The focus is on changing overt behavior, defining the nature of the appropriate reinforcers, and determining their optimal rate of presentation to modify behavior.

Punishment and Negative Reinforcement

punishment
The application of an aversive stimulus following a response in an effort to decrease the likelihood that the response will recur.

Most operant-conditioning applications involve positive reinforcement rather than **punishment**. The token-economy patients were not punished for failing to behave appropriately. Instead, they were reinforced when their behavior changed in positive ways. Skinner said that punishment was ineffective in changing behavior from undesirable to desirable or from abnormal to normal. Positive reinforcement administered for desirable behaviors is much more effective than punishment.

> What's wrong with punishments is that they work immediately, but give no long-term results. The responses to punishment are either the urge to escape, to counterattack, or a stubborn apathy. These are the bad effects you get in prisons or schools, or wherever punishments are used. (Skinner quoted in Goleman, 1987)

negative reinforcement
The strengthening of a response by the removal of an aversive stimulus.

Negative reinforcement is not the same as punishment. A negative reinforcer is an aversive or noxious stimulus, the removal of which is rewarding. In the laboratory or classroom, an operant-conditioning situation can be established in which the unpleasant stimulus (such as a loud noise or an electric shock) will continue until the subject emits the desired response. As with positive reinforcement, the environment changes as a consequence of the behavior; in this case, the noxious stimulus will disappear.

We can see examples of negative reinforcement in everyday situations. A person may stop smoking to avoid the aversive stimulus of a nagging spouse or colleague. The aversive stimulus (the nagging) should cease when the desirable behavior (not lighting a cigarette in the home or office) is displayed. Skinner opposed using noxious stimuli to modify behavior, noting that the consequences were not as predictable as with positive reinforcement. Also, negative reinforcement does not always work whereas positive reinforcement is more consistently effective.

Questions About Human Nature

Skinner's position is clear on the nature–nurture issue. People are primarily products of learning, shaped more by external variables than genetic factors. We may infer that childhood experiences are more important in Skinner's view than are later experiences because our basic behaviors are formed in childhood. This does not mean that behavior cannot change in adulthood. What is learned in childhood can be modified, and new behavior patterns can be acquired at any age. The success of behavior modification programs verifies that assertion. Skinner's belief that behavior is shaped by learning also leads us to conclude that each person is unique. Because we are shaped by experience—and we all have different experiences, particularly in childhood—no two people will behave in precisely the same way.

Skinner did not address the issue of an ultimate and necessary goal. He made no reference to overcoming inferiority, reducing anxiety, or striving for self-actualization. Such motives assume internal, subjective states, which Skinner did

Reinforcement Theory

B.F. Skinner – Beyond Freedom and Dignity

Behaviorism or operant conditioning

How do different personalities react to Reinforcement theory

Research first

not accept. Any indication of a life goal in Skinner's work seems to be societal, not individual. In his novel *Walden Two* and in other writings, he discussed his notion of the ideal human society. He stated that individual behavior must be directed toward the type of society that has the greatest chance of survival.

On the issue of free will versus determinism, people function like machines, in lawful, orderly, predetermined ways. Skinner rejected all suggestions of an inner being or autonomous self that determines a course of action or chooses to act freely and spontaneously.

From Skinner's scholarly writings to his popular novel about a Utopian society based on operant conditioning his message is the same: Behavior is controlled by reinforcers. In a sense, this means that it is pointless to blame or punish people for their actions. A dictator who orders the mass killing of thousands of people, or a serial killer who murders a dozen, can no more be held responsible for their actions than can a driverless car that plunges down a hill. Both operate in lawful, predictable ways, controlled by external variables.

Are we left with a pessimistic conception of people as helpless and passive robots, unable to play an active role in determining their behavior? That is not Skinner's complete view. Despite his belief that behavior is controlled by external stimuli and reinforcers, we are certainly not victims. Although controlled by our environment, we are responsible for designing that environment. Our buildings, cities, consumer goods, factories, and government institutions are the result of human fabrication. So, too, are our social systems, languages, customs, and recreations. We constantly change our environment, often to our advantage. When we do so, we are acting as both controller and controlled. We design the controlling culture, and we are products of that culture. "We may not be free agents," he wrote, "but we can do something about our lives, if we would only rearrange the controls that influence our behavior. . . . I am not trying to change people. All I want to do is change the world in which they live" (quoted in Bjork, 1993, pp. 16, 233).

The world may impose limits on our freedom to bring about change. In making changes, we will be guided and sometimes restricted by situations that provided positive reinforcement for us in the past. In acting to change our environment, we will seek greater opportunities for positive reinforcement and in the process modify our own behavior. Skinner left us with a paradox, an image of person-as-machine capable of altering the environmental conditions that guide the machine's behavior.

Assessment in Skinner's Theory

Skinner did not use the typical assessment techniques favored by other theorists. There was no place in his work for free association, dream analysis, or projective techniques. Because he was not dealing directly with personality, he really had no interest in assessing it. He did, however, assess behavior. In the application of his behavior modification techniques, it is necessary first to assess specific behaviors, both desirable and undesirable. Also to be assessed are the environmental factors that serve as reinforcers and that can be manipulated to alter behavior. No behavior can be modified appropriately without such prior assessment. Skinner's approach

functional analysis
An approach to the study of behavior that involves assessing the frequency of a behavior, the situation in which it occurs, and the reinforcers associated with it.

to assessing behavior is called **functional analysis** and it involves three aspects of behavior.

1. The frequency of the behavior
2. The situation in which the behavior occurs
3. The reinforcement associated with the behavior

Unless these factors have been evaluated, it is not possible to plan and implement a behavior modification program.

Consider a functional analysis for cigarette smokers who want to break the smoking habit. The smokers are asked to keep an accurate record of the number of cigarettes they smoke each day and the situations in which the cigarettes are smoked. Does smoking occur in a particular place or at a certain time? In the presence of others or alone? After meals or while driving? And what are the reinforcers? Most smokers smoke more frequently in the presence of certain stimuli. Identifying these stimuli is necessary because modifying them should lead to a change in the smoking behavior.

Direct Observation of Behavior

Three approaches to assessing behavior are direct observation, self-reports, and physiological measurements. Many behaviors can be assessed through direct observation. Usually, two or more people conduct the observation to assure accuracy and reliability. For example, in a classic report of a behavior modification situation, a woman sought treatment for her 4-year-old son whose behavior was considered unruly (Hawkins, Peterson, Schweid, & Bijou, 1966). Two psychologists observed the mother and child in their home to evaluate the nature and frequency of the child's undesirable behaviors, when and where they occurred, and the reinforcers the child received for the behaviors.

Nine undesirable behaviors were identified, including kicking, throwing things, biting, and pushing a sibling. The psychologists observed that the mother reinforced the child by giving him toys or food when he behaved badly. Her intention was to get him to stop misbehaving. Instead, she was rewarding him and thus reinforcing the misbehavior. The direct observation assessment lasted 16 hours, but without it the psychologists would not have known exactly which undesirable behaviors to try to eliminate or what reinforcers the child expected.

With a comprehensive direct-observation program, it is possible to plan a course of behavior modification. In this case, the psychologists instructed the mother to use attention and approval as reinforcers when the child behaved in positive ways and never to reward him when he displayed one of the nine observed undesirable behaviors. The frequency of the undesirable behaviors, as determined in the direct observation assessment, provided a baseline against which to compare behavior during and after treatment.

Self-Reports of Behavior

Another approach to assessing behavior is the self-report technique carried out through interviews and questionnaires. The person observes his or her own behavior and reports on it. For example, a questionnaire may assess the extent of a person's fear in situations such as driving a car, going to the dentist, or speaking in public. Questionnaires for assessing behavior are similar in format to self-report inventories that assess personality. The difference lies in the way they are interpreted, as described by the **sign-versus-sample approach**.

In the sign approach, which is used to assess *personality*, the psychologist infers the existence of character types, traits, or unconscious conflicts from the individual's responses. For example, if a person indicates that he or she is afraid of being in an elevator, this fear can be interpreted as a sign, or an indirect symptom, of some underlying motive or conflict. In the sample approach, which is used to assess *behavior*, questionnaire responses are interpreted as directly indicative of a sample of behavior. No attempt is made to draw inferences or conclusions about the person's character or personality traits. The behavior itself and the stimulus associated with it are the important things. There is no concern with subjective motives, childhood experiences, or other mental processes.

sign-versus-sample approach
In the sign approach to assessing *personality*, character types, traits, or unconscious conflicts are inferred from questionnaires and other self-report inventories. In the sample approach to assessing *behavior*, test responses are interpreted as directly indicative of present behavior, not of traits, motives, or childhood experiences.

Physiological Measurements of Behavior

Physiological assessments of behavior include heart rate, muscle tension, and brain waves. By recording such measurements, it is possible to evaluate the physiological effects of various stimuli. The measures can also be used to confirm the accuracy of information obtained by other assessment methods. For example, a person who is too embarrassed to reveal in an interview or on a questionnaire a fear of being in an elevator might exhibit a change in heart rate or muscle tension when asked in general about elevators.

Whatever assessment technique is chosen to assess behavior in different stimulus situations, the focus remains on what people do, not on what might have motivated them to do it. The ultimate goal is to modify behavior, not to change personality.

Research on Skinner's Theory

You can see that Skinner's assessment methods differ radically from those used by other theorists we have discussed. His research methods also diverged from mainstream experimental psychology. The usual procedure is to study large groups of animal or human subjects and to statistically compare their average responses. In contrast, Skinner preferred the intensive study of a single subject. He argued that data on the average performance of groups is of little value in dealing with a particular case. A science that deals with averages provides little information to help in understanding the unique individual.

Skinner believed that valid and replicable results could be obtained without statistical analysis, as long as sufficient data were collected from a single subject under well-controlled experimental conditions. The use of large groups of subjects forced the experimenter to deal with average behavior. The resulting data could not reflect individual response behavior and individual differences in behavior. Thus, Skinner favored the idiographic rather than the nomothetic approach.

reversal experimental design

A research technique that involves establishing a baseline, applying an experimental treatment, and withdrawing the experimental treatment to determine whether the behavior returns to its baseline value or whether some other factor is responsible for the observed behavior change.

Skinner's single-subject experiments follow the **reversal experimental design**, which proceeds in four stages.

- The first stage involves establishing a *baseline*. The subject's behavior (the dependent variable) is observed to determine the normal rate of response before beginning the experimental treatment.
- The second stage is the *conditioning*, or experimental, stage, when the independent variable is introduced. If this variable affects behavior, it will produce a notable change from the subject's baseline response rate.
- The third stage, called *reversal*, determines whether some factor other than the independent variable is responsible for the observed behavior change. During this stage, the independent variable is no longer applied. If the behavior returns to its baseline rate, then the researcher can conclude that the independent variable was responsible for the difference observed during the conditioning stage. If the behavior does not return to the baseline rate, then some factor other than the independent variable affected the behavior.
- The baseline, conditioning, and reversal stages are sufficient for most laboratory experiments. When the procedure is applied to behavior modification, a *reconditioning* stage is added. The independent variable is reintroduced, assuming it had been effective in changing behavior. Without the fourth stage, subjects in behavior modification programs would remain in reversal with behavior at their baseline level, unchanged by a treatment shown to be effective. It would be unethical not to restore the effective treatment.

Skinner and his followers conducted thousands of operant-conditioning experiments on topics such as reinforcement schedules, language acquisition, behavior shaping, superstitious behavior, and behavior modification. The results have been highly supportive of Skinner's ideas.

Reflections on Skinner's Theory

Skinner's approach has been criticized on several points. Those who oppose determinism find much to dislike in Skinner's views. The humanistic psychologists, who believe that people are more complex than machines or rats or pigeons, object to Skinner's image of human nature. They argue that the exclusive emphasis on overt behavior ignores uniquely human qualities such as conscious free will. There has been criticism of the type of subject and the simplicity of the situations in Skinner's experiments. He made assertions and predictions about human behavior and society—about social, economic, religious, and cultural issues—with considerable confidence. But can we extrapolate from a pigeon pecking at a disc to a person functioning in the real world? The gap seems too vast to permit broad generalizations. Many aspects of human behavior cannot be reduced meaningfully to the level at which Skinner conducted his research.

Skinner's belief that all behaviors are learned was challenged by two former students. More than 6,000 animals of 38 species were conditioned to perform various behaviors for television commercials and tourist attractions. The animals included pigs, raccoons, chickens, hamsters, porpoises, whales, and cows. The animals

instinctive drift
The substitution of
instinctive behaviors for
behaviors that had been
reinforced.

displayed a tendency toward **instinctive drift** by substituting instinctive behaviors for the behaviors that had been reinforced, even when the instinctive behaviors interfered with receiving food.

In one example, pigs and raccoons were conditioned to pick up a coin, carry it some distance, and deposit it in a toy bank (a piggy bank, of course). When the animals had deposited a certain number of coins, they were given food as a reinforcer. They learned the desired behaviors quickly,

> but after having performed the sequence nicely for some time, they began to engage in undesirable behaviors, at least from the viewpoint of the trainers. Pigs would stop on their way [to the bank], bury the coin in the sand, and take it out with their snout; raccoons would spend a lot of time handling the coin, with their well-known washing-like movements. This was at first amusing, but eventually it became time-consuming and would make the whole show appear very imperfect to the spectator. Commercially, it was a disaster. (Richelle, 1993, p. 68)

What had happened was that instinctive behavior—such as the pigs' rooting in the dirt and the raccoons' rubbing their paws as if washing their hands—came to take precedence over the learned behavior, even though it meant a delay in receiving the reinforcement (the food). The trainers published an article on the phenomenon and with Skinner's encouragement called it "The Misbehavior of Organisms" (Breland & Breland, 1961). This was a parody of the title of Skinner's groundbreaking book, *The Behavior of Organisms* (1938).

Skinner ignored most of the criticism his work received. He told an interviewer about one critic's book review, "I read a bit of it and saw that he missed the point. . . . There are better things to do with my time than clear up their misunderstandings" (quoted in Rice, 1968). When asked how he dealt with being misunderstood so frequently, he said, "I find that I need to be understood only three or four times a year" (quoted in Blackman, 1995, p. 126).

Skinner was a potent force in 20th-century American psychology. He shaped the field perhaps more than any other individual. The *Journal of the Experimental Analysis of Behavior*, begun in 1958, publishes research on the behavior of individual subjects. In 1968, the *Journal of Applied Behavior Analysis* was established as an outlet for work on behavior modification techniques.

The American Psychological Foundation awarded Skinner its Gold Medal, and the American Psychological Association gave him the Distinguished Scientific Contribution Award (1958). The citation reads: "Few American psychologists have had so profound an impact on the development of psychology and on promising younger psychologists." Skinner's first book on behaviorism, *The Behavior of Organisms: An Experimental Analysis* (Skinner, 1938), was described as one of the few books to truly change the nature of the field (Thompson, 1988). Skinner also received the U.S. National Medal of Science and appeared on the cover of *Time*, headlined as the world's most famous American psychologist. His controversial 1971 book, *Beyond Freedom and Dignity*, became a best-seller and made him a celebrity.

> Skinner was, for a short period, the hottest item on national and big-city talk shows. . . . Within a month, millions of Americans had read or heard about B. F. Skinner and

Beyond Freedom and Dignity. He was "completely swamped" by mail, telephone calls, and visits. . . . Strangers often asked to shake his hand in restaurants. He had, as one writer noted, "acquired the celebrity of a movie or TV star." (Bjork, 1993, p. 192)

Although Skinner's radical behaviorist position continues to be applied in laboratory, clinical, and organizational settings, its dominance has been challenged by the cognitive movement in psychology, which began in the 1960s. Skinner conceded that his form of psychology lost ground to the cognitive approach. Other psychologists agreed, noting that Skinnerian behaviorism had "fallen from favor among the majority of active workers in the field [and was] often referred to in the past tense" (Baars, 1986, pp. viii, 1). Despite the inroads of cognitive psychology, however, Skinner's position remains influential in many areas, from classrooms to assembly lines, from Skinner boxes to mental institutions. Skinner believed that with operant conditioning he offered a technique to improve human nature and the societies people design.

Chapter Summary

Skinner denied the existence of an entity called personality and did not seek causes of behavior within the organism. Mental and physiological processes are not overtly observable, so they have no relevance for science. The causes of behavior are external to the organism. Behavior can be controlled by its consequences, by the reinforcer that follows the behavior. Respondent behavior involves a response elicited by specific environmental stimuli. Conditioning (respondent behavior that is learned) involves substituting one stimulus for another. Pavlov demonstrated the importance of reinforcement. Conditioning will not occur without reinforcement. Operant behavior is emitted and is determined and modified by the reinforcer that follows it. Operant behavior cannot be traced to a specific stimulus; it operates on the environment and changes it. Personality is simply a pattern of operant behaviors.

Reinforcement schedules include fixed interval, fixed ratio, variable interval, and variable ratio. Shaping (successive approximation) involves reinforcing the organism only as its behavior comes to approximate the behavior desired. Superstitious behavior results when reinforcement is presented on a fixed- or variable-interval schedule. Whatever behavior is occurring at the moment of reinforcement will come to be displayed more frequently. Self-control of behavior refers to altering or avoiding certain external stimuli and reinforcers. Other self-control techniques are satiation, aversive stimulation, and self-reinforcement for displaying desirable behaviors.

Behavior modification applies operant-conditioning techniques to real-world problems. Desirable behaviors are positively reinforced; undesirable behaviors are ignored. The token-economy approach rewards desirable behaviors with tokens that can be used to acquire objects of value. Behavior modification deals only with overt behavior and uses positive reinforcement, not punishment. Negative reinforcement involves removing an aversive or noxious stimulus. It is less effective than positive reinforcement.

Skinner's image of human nature emphasizes determinism, uniqueness, the importance of the environment, and the design of a society that maximizes the opportunity for survival. Although people are controlled by the environment, they can exert control by designing that environment properly.

Skinner assessed behavior (not personality) using functional analyses to determine the frequency of the behavior, the situation in which the behavior occurred, and the reinforcers associated with the behavior. Three ways to assess behavior are direct observation, self-report, and physiological measures. Skinner's research was idiographic, focusing on the intensive study of a single subject. His reversal experimental design consists of baseline, conditioning, reversal, and reconditioning stages.

Skinner's system has considerable empirical support but has been criticized for its deterministic view, the simplicity of the experimental situations, the lack of interest in behavior other than response rate, and the failure to consider human qualities that set us apart from rats and pigeons. Skinner's techniques for the modification of behavior using operant conditioning remain popular, but his behavioristic position has been overtaken by the cognitive movement within psychology.

Review Questions

1. How does Skinner's approach to personality differ from other approaches we have discussed?

2. How did Skinner justify the use of rats and pigeons instead of humans as subjects in the study of behavior?

3. How did Skinner's childhood experiences influence his later approach to studying behavior?

4. Distinguish between operant behavior and respondent behavior. Give an example of each.

5. Describe Pavlov's classical-conditioning experiment with dogs. How did Pavlov extinguish conditioned responses?

6. What is the role of reinforcement in modifying behavior?

7. Distinguish between positive reinforcement, negative reinforcement, and punishment.

8. In Skinner's view, why is positive reinforcement more effective than punishment in changing behavior?

9. Explain the difference between the fixed-interval and variable-interval schedules of reinforcement.

10. Which reinforcement schedule applies to the person who sells computer software on commission? Which schedule applies to the child who is allowed to have an ice-cream cone for good behavior only occasionally?

11. Explain how a complex behavior such as learning to speak is acquired through successive approximation.

12. Describe how you would use the method of successive approximation to train a dog to walk in a circle.

13. How does the notion of reinforcement account for the acquisition of superstitious behaviors?

14. Explain the use of self-administered satiation in getting rid of bad habits.

15. What are the techniques for the self-control of behavior?

16. Describe the token-economy approach to behavior modification. Give an example.

17. Why did Skinner prefer to study the individual case rather than groups of subjects?

18. Describe the stages in a typical Skinnerian experiment with a human subject.

19. What was Skinner's position on the nature–nurture issue? On free will versus determinism?

20. What techniques do Skinner's followers use to assess human behavior?

21. Discuss the impact of cognitive psychology on Skinnerian behaviorism.

Suggested Readings

Elms, A. C. (1981). Skinner's dark year and Walden Two. *American Psychologist, 36,* 470–479. Suggests that Skinner experienced an identity crisis in his youth and that writing his novel was a form of therapy.

Nye, R. D. (1992). *The legacy of B. F. Skinner: Concepts and perspectives, controversies and misunderstandings.* Pacific Grove, CA: Brooks/Cole. Presents Skinner's basic concepts and their relevance for everyday situations. Examines controversies and misunderstandings surrounding Skinner's views and compares his system with those of Freud and Rogers.

O'Donohue, W., & Ferguson, K. E. (2001). *The psychology of B. F. Skinner.* Thousand Oaks, CA: Sage. Discusses the controversies surrounding Skinner's work on behaviorism, cognition, verbal behavior, and applied behavior analysis. Includes his ideas for improving society as a whole.

Skinner, B. F. (1948). *Walden Two.* New York: Macmillan. Skinner's novel about human values and conduct in a Utopian society based on behaviorist principles.

Skinner, B. F. (1976). *Particulars of my life;* (1979). *The shaping of a behaviorist;* (1983). *A matter of consequences.* New York: Alfred A. Knopf. Skinner's three-volume autobiography.

Skinner, B. F. (1987). *Upon further reflection.* Englewood Cliffs, NJ: Prentice-Hall. Essays on cognitive psychology, verbal behavior, education, and self-management in old age.

Skinner, B. F. (1987). Whatever happened to psychology as the science of behavior? *American Psychologist, 42,* 780–786. Charges that humanistic psychology, psychotherapy, and cognitive psychology are obstacles in the path of psychology's acceptance of his program for the experimental analysis of behavior.

PART EIGHT

The Social-Learning Approach

The social-learning approach to personality, represented in this section by the work of Albert Bandura, is an outgrowth of Skinner's behaviorist approach. Like Skinner, Bandura focuses on overt behavior rather than on needs, traits, drives, or defense mechanisms. Unlike Skinner, Bandura allows for internal cognitive variables that mediate between stimulus and response. Cognitive variables have no place in Skinner's system.

Bandura has investigated cognitive variables with a high degree of experimental sophistication and rigor, drawing inferences from careful observations of behavior in the laboratory. He observed the behavior of human subjects in social settings, whereas Skinner dealt with animal subjects in individual settings. Bandura agrees with Skinner that behavior is learned and that reinforcement is vital to learning, but he differs from Skinner in his interpretation of the nature of reinforcement.

Bandura and Skinner both attempted to understand personality through laboratory rather than clinical work, but their principles have been applied in the clinical setting through behavior modification techniques. Because Bandura uses cognitive variables, his work reflects and reinforces the cognitive movement in psychology. His approach has also been called *cognitive-behavioral* in recognition of this emphasis.

CHAPTER 13

Albert Bandura:
Modeling Theory

Virtually every phenomenon that occurs by direct experience can occur vicariously as well—by observing other people and the consequences for them.

—ALBERT BANDURA

Bandura agrees with Skinner that behavior is learned, but with that point their similarity ends. Bandura criticized Skinner's emphasis on individual animal subjects rather than on human subjects interacting with one another. Bandura's approach is a social-learning theory that investigates behavior as it is formed and modified in a social context. He argues that we cannot expect data from experiments that involve no social interaction to be relevant to the everyday world, because few people truly function in social isolation.

observational learning
Learning new responses by observing the behavior of other people.

Although Bandura, like Skinner, recognizes that much learning takes place as a result of reinforcement, he also stresses that virtually all forms of behavior can be learned without directly experiencing any reinforcement. Bandura's approach is also called **observational learning**, indicating the importance in the learning process of observing other people's behavior. Rather than experiencing reinforcement ourselves for each of our actions, we learn through **vicarious reinforcement** by observing the behavior of other people and the consequences of that behavior. This focus on learning by observation or example, rather than always by direct reinforcement, is a distinctive feature of Bandura's theory.

vicarious reinforcement
Learning or strengthening a behavior by observing the behavior of others, and the consequences of that behavior, rather than experiencing the reinforcement or consequences directly.

Another feature of Bandura's observational-learning approach is its treatment of internal cognitive or thought processes. Unlike Skinner, Bandura believes that cognitive processes can influence observational learning. We do not automatically imitate the behaviors we see other people displaying. Rather, we make a deliberate, conscious decision to behave in the same way. To learn through example and vicarious reinforcement we must be capable of anticipating and appreciating the consequences of the behaviors we observe. We can regulate and guide our behavior by visualizing or imagining those consequences, even though we have not experienced them ourselves. No direct link exists between stimulus and response or between behavior and reinforcer, as Skinner proposed. Instead, our cognitive processes mediate between the two.

Bandura presents a less extreme form of behaviorism than Skinner. He emphasizes the observation of others as a means of learning, and he considers learning to be mediated by cognitive processes. His theory is based on rigorous laboratory research with normal people in social interaction rather than a rat in a cage or a neurotic person on a couch.

The Life of Bandura (1925–)

Bandura was born in the province of Alberta, Canada, in a town so small that his high school had only two teachers and 20 students. His parents were immigrants from Poland who emphasized the value of education. "You have a choice," his mother had told him when he was young. "You can work in the field and get drunk in the beer parlor, or you might get an education" (quoted in Foster, 2007, p. 3).

During the summer following his graduation from high school, he took a construction job in the wilderness of the Yukon Territory, filling holes in the Alaska Highway. It was a fascinating experience for a bright, inquisitive young person.

> Finding himself in the midst of a curious collection of characters, most of whom had fled creditors, alimony, and probation officers, Bandura quickly developed a keen

appreciation for the psychopathology of everyday life, which seemed to blossom in the austere tundra. (Distinguished Scientific Contribution Award, 1981, p. 28)

He attended the University of British Columbia in Vancouver as an undergraduate and took a course in psychology, only out of expediency. The carpool in which he commuted to the campus included engineering and pre-med students, all of whom had early-morning classes. Psychology was offered in that time period, so Bandura enrolled in the course. He found the material fascinating. He pursued his studies in the field, earning his Ph.D. in 1952 from the University of Iowa. After a year at the Wichita, Kansas, Guidance Center, he joined the faculty of Stanford University and has compiled an extensive record of publications. In 1973, he was elected president of the American Psychological Association. In 1980 he received its Distinguished Scientific Contribution Award and in 2006 was presented with the American Psychological Foundation's Gold Medal Award for Life Achievement.

Bandura's sense of humor has often been directed at himself. When asked whether he walked to his office or drove his car, he said, "Both, sometimes in the same day." Having driven to work, he would be so absorbed in his ideas that he would absentmindedly walk home, leaving his car in the university parking lot.

 ## Log On

Key Theorists/Theories in Psychology: Albert Bandura

Material on Bandura's life, research, and theories plus access to some of his publications, including overheads and other images.

Albert Bandura Biographical Sketch

A discussion of Bandura's life (with personal photographs) and his personality research.

For direct links to these sites, log on to the student companion site for this book at http://www.academic.cengage.com/psychology/Schultz and choose Chapter 13.

Modeling: The Basis of Observational Learning

Bandura's basic idea is that learning can occur through observation or example rather than solely by direct reinforcement. Bandura does not deny the importance of direct reinforcement as a way to influence behavior, but he challenges the notion that behavior can be learned or changed only through direct reinforcement. He argues that operant conditioning, in which trial-and-error behavior continues until the person happens upon the correct response, is an inefficient and potentially dangerous way to learn skills such as swimming or driving. A person could drown or crash before finding the correct sequence of behaviors that brings positive reinforcement. To Bandura, most human behavior is learned through example, either intentionally or accidentally. We learn by observing other people and patterning our behavior after theirs.

Courtesy of Dr. Albert Bandura, Stanford University

In the Bobo doll studies, children exhibited aggressive behavior after observing an aggressive model.

Bobo Doll Studies

modeling
A behavior modification technique that involves observing the behavior of others (the models) and participating with them in performing the desired behavior.

Through **modeling**, by observing the behavior of a model and repeating the behavior ourselves, it is possible to acquire responses that we have never performed or displayed previously and to strengthen or weaken existing responses. Bandura's now-classic demonstration of modeling involves the Bobo doll, an inflatable plastic figure 3 to 4 feet tall (Bandura, Ross, & Ross, 1963).

The subjects in the initial studies were preschool children who watched an adult hit and kick Bobo. While attacking the doll, the adult model shouted, "Sock him in the nose!" and "Throw him in the air!" When the children were left alone with the doll, they modeled their behavior after the example they had just witnessed. Their behavior was compared with that of a control group of children who had not seen the model attack the Bobo doll. The experimental group was found to be twice as aggressive as the control group.

The intensity of the aggressive behavior remained the same in the experimental subjects whether the model was seen live, on television, or as a cartoon character. The effect of the model in all three media was to elicit aggressive behavior, actions that were not displayed with the same strength by children who had not observed the models.

Other Modeling Studies

In additional research on the impact of modeling on learning, Bandura compared the behavior of parents of two groups of children (Bandura & Walters, 1963). One group consisted of highly aggressive children, the other of more inhibited children. According to Bandura's theory, the children's behavior should reflect their parents' behavior. The research showed that the parents of the inhibited children were inhibited, and the parents of the aggressive children were aggressive.

Verbal modeling can induce certain behaviors, as long as the activities involved are fully and adequately explained. Verbal modeling is often used to provide instructions, a technique applicable to teaching such skills as driving a car. Verbal instructions are usually supplemented by behavioral demonstrations, such as when a driving instructor serves as a model performing the behaviors involved in driving.

Disinhibition

disinhibition
The weakening of inhibitions or constraints by observing the behavior of a model.

Research has shown that behaviors a person usually suppresses or inhibits may be performed more readily under the influence of a model (Bandura, 1973, 1986). This phenomenon, called **disinhibition**, refers to the weakening of an inhibition or restraint through exposure to a model. For example, people in a crowd may start a riot, breaking windows and shouting, exhibiting physical and verbal behaviors they would never perform when alone. They are more likely to discard their inhibitions against aggressive behavior if they see other people doing so.

The disinhibition phenomenon can influence sexual behavior. In an experiment that demonstrated how sexual responses could be disinhibited by models, a group of male undergraduate college students was shown a film that contained erotic pictures of nude males and females (Walters, Bowen, & Parke, 1963). The students were told that a spot of light would move over the film, indicating the eye movements of a previous subject, to show what parts of the pictures that subject looked at. These alleged eye movements of the previous subject represented the model. For half the subjects, the spot of light concentrated on breasts and genitals. For the other half, the light stayed in the background, as though the model had avoided looking at the naked bodies.

After watching the film, the students were shown stills from the movie while their eye movements were recorded. Those subjects whose model was considered uninhibited (who had looked directly at the erotic parts of the bodies) behaved similarly. Those whose model had avoided looking at the nudes spent significantly more time examining the background of the pictures. The researchers concluded that modeling affected the subjects' perceptual responses to the stimuli. In other words, modeling determined not only what the subjects did but also what they looked at and perceived.

The Effects of Society's Models

On the basis of extensive research, Bandura concluded that much behavior—good and bad, normal and abnormal—is learned by imitating the behavior of other people. From infancy on, we develop responses to the models society offers us. Beginning with parents as models, we learn their language and become socialized by the culture's customs and acceptable behaviors. People who deviate from cultural norms have learned their behavior the same way as everyone else. The difference is that deviant persons have followed models the rest of society considers undesirable.

Bandura is an outspoken critic of the type of society that provides the wrong models for its children, particularly the examples of violent behavior that are standard fare on television and in movies and video games. His research clearly shows the effect of models on behavior. If what we see is what we become, then the distance between watching an aggressive animated character and committing a violent act ourselves is not very great.

Among the many behaviors children acquire through modeling are non-rational fears. A child who sees that his or her parents are fearful during thunderstorms or are nervous around strangers will easily adopt these anxieties and carry them into adulthood with little awareness of their origin. Of course, positive behaviors such as strength, courage, and optimism will also be learned from parents and other models. In Skinner's system, reinforcers control behavior; for Bandura, it is the models who control behavior.

Characteristics of the Modeling Situation

Bandura and his associates (Bandura, 1977, 1986) investigated three factors found to influence modeling: the characteristics of the models, the characteristics of the observers, and the reward consequences associated with the behaviors.

Characteristics of the models. The characteristics of the models affect our tendency to imitate them. In real life, we may be more influenced by someone who appears to be similar to us than by someone who differs from us in obvious and significant ways. In the laboratory, Bandura found that although children imitated the behavior of a child model in the same room, a child in a film, and a filmed cartoon character, the extent of the modeling decreased as the similarity between the model and the subject decreased. The children showed greater imitation of a live model than an animated character, but even in the latter instance the modeled behavior was significantly greater than that of the control group that observed no models.

Other characteristics of the model that affect imitation are age and sex. We are more likely to model our behavior after a person of the same sex than a person of the opposite sex. Also, we are more likely to be influenced by models our own age. Peers who appear to have successfully solved the problems we are facing are highly influential models.

Status and prestige are also important factors. It was found that pedestrians were much more likely to cross a street against a red light if they saw a well-dressed person crossing than if they saw a poorly dressed person crossing. Television commercials make effective use of high-status, high-prestige models with athletes or celebrities who claim to use a particular product. The expectation is that consumers will imitate their behavior and buy the advertised product.

The type of behavior the model performs affects the extent of imitation. Highly complex behaviors are not imitated as quickly and readily as simpler behaviors. Hostile and aggressive behaviors tend to be strongly imitated, especially by children.

Children tend to imitate the behavior of an adult model of the same sex who is considered high in status.

© Tony Freeman/PhotoEdit

Characteristics of the observers. The attributes of the observers also determine the effectiveness of observational learning. People who are low in self-confidence and self-esteem are much more likely to imitate a model's behavior than are people high in self-confidence and self-esteem. A person who has been reinforced for imitating a behavior—for example, a child rewarded for behaving like an older sibling—is more susceptible to the influence of models.

The reward consequences associated with the behaviors. The reward consequences linked to a particular behavior can affect the extent of the modeling and even override the impact of the models' and observers' characteristics. A high-status model may lead us to imitate a certain behavior, but if the rewards are not meaningful to us, we will discontinue the behavior and be less likely to be influenced by that model in the future.

Seeing a model being rewarded or punished for displaying a particular behavior affects imitation. In a Bobo doll study, some of the children watched as the model who hit the Bobo doll was given praise and a soda and candy. Another group of children saw the model receive verbal and physical punishment for the same aggressive behavior. The children who observed the punishment displayed significantly less aggression toward the Bobo doll than did the children who saw the model being reinforced (Bandura, 1965).

The Processes of Observational Learning

Bandura analyzed the nature of observational learning and found it to be governed by four related mechanisms: attentional processes, retention processes, production processes, and incentive and motivational processes (see Table 13.1).

Attentional Processes

Observational learning or modeling will not occur unless the subject pays attention to the model. Merely exposing the subject to the model does not guarantee that the subject will be attentive to the relevant cues and stimulus events or even perceive the situation accurately. The subject must perceive the model accurately enough to acquire the information necessary to imitate the model's behavior.

Several variables influence attentional processes. In the real world, as in the laboratory, we are more attentive and responsive to some people and situations than to others. Thus, the more closely we pay attention to a model's behavior, the more likely we are to imitate it.

We have mentioned such characteristics as age, status, sex, and the degree of similarity between model and subject. These factors help determine how closely a subject attends to the model. It has also been found that celebrity models, experts, and those who appear confident and attractive command greater attention and imitation than models who lack these attributes. Some of the most effective models in American culture today appear on television. Viewers often focus on them even in the absence of reinforcement.

Table 13.1 Observational learning processes

Attentional processes	Developing our cognitive processes and perceptual skills so that we can pay sufficient attention to a model, and perceiving the model accurately enough, to imitate displayed behavior. Example: Staying awake during driver's education class.
Retention processes	Retaining or remembering the model's behavior so that we can imitate or repeat it at a later time; for this, we use our cognitive processes to encode or form mental images and verbal descriptions of the model's behavior. Example: Taking notes on the lecture material or the video of a person driving a car.
Production processes	Translating the mental images or verbal symbolic representations of the model's behavior into our own overt behavior by physically producing the responses and receiving feedback on the accuracy of our continued practice. Example: Getting in a car with an instructor to practice shifting gears and dodging the traffic cones in the school parking lot.
Incentive and motivational processes	Perceiving that the model's behavior leads to a reward and thus expecting that our learning—and successful performance—of the same behavior will lead to similar consequences. Example: Expecting that when we have mastered driving skills, we will pass the state test and receive a driver's license.

Attention to modeled behavior varies as a function of the observers' cognitive and perceptual skills and the value of the behavior being modeled. The more highly developed are our cognitive abilities and the more knowledge we have about the behavior being modeled, the more carefully we will attend to the model and perceive the behavior. When observers watch a model doing something they expect to do themselves, they pay greater attention than when the modeled behavior has no personal relevance. Observers also pay closer attention to modeled behavior that produces positive or negative consequences rather than neutral outcomes.

Retention Processes

We must be able to remember significant aspects of the model's behavior in order to repeat it later. To retain what has been attended to, we must encode it and represent it symbolically. These internal retention processes of symbolic representation and image formation are cognitive processes. Thus, Bandura recognizes the importance of cognitive processes in developing and modifying behavior. Recall, for comparison, that Skinner's focus was exclusively on overt behavior.

We retain information about a model's behavior in two ways: through an imaginal internal representational system or through a verbal system. In the imaginal system, we form vivid, easily retrievable images while we are observing the model. This common phenomenon accounts for your being able to summon up a picture of the person you dated last week or the place you visited last summer. In observational learning, we form a mental picture of the model's behavior and use it as a basis for imitation at some future time.

The verbal representational system operates similarly and involves a verbal coding of some behavior we have observed. For example, during observation we might describe to ourselves what the model is doing. These descriptions or codes can be rehearsed silently, without overtly displaying the behavior. For example, we might talk ourselves through the steps in a complicated skill, mentally rehearsing the sequence of behaviors we will perform later. When we wish to perform the action, the verbal code will provide hints, reminders, and cues. Together, these images and verbal symbols offer the means by which we store observed situations and rehearse them for later performance.

Production Processes

Translating imaginal and verbal symbolic representations into overt behavior requires the production processes, described more simply as practice. Although we may have attended to, retained, and rehearsed symbolic representations of a model's behavior, we still may not be able to perform the behavior correctly. This is most likely to occur with highly skilled actions that require the mastery of many component behaviors.

Consider learning to drive a car. We learn fundamental motions from a lecture and from watching a model drive. We may consider the symbolic representations of the model's behavior many times, but at first our translation of these symbols into actual driving behavior will be clumsy. We may apply the brakes too soon or too late or overcorrect the steering. Our observations may not have been sufficient to ensure immediate and skilled performance of the actions. Practice of the proper physical movements, and feedback on their accuracy, is needed to produce the smooth performance of the behavior.

Incentive and Motivational Processes

No matter how well we attend to and retain behaviors we observe or how much ability we have to perform them, we will not do so without the incentive or motivation processes. When incentives are available, observation is more quickly translated into action. Incentives also influence the attentional and retention processes. We may not pay as much attention without an incentive to do so, and when less attention is paid, there is less to retain.

Our incentive to learn is influenced by our anticipation of the reinforcement or punishment for doing so. Seeing that a model's behavior produces a reward or avoids a punishment can be a strong incentive for us to pay attention to, remember, and perform a behavior correctly. The reinforcement is experienced vicariously during our observation of the model, after which we expect our performance of the same behavior to lead to the consequences we saw.

Bandura pointed out that although reinforcement can facilitate learning, reinforcement is not required for learning to occur. Many factors other than the reward consequences of the behavior determine what we attend to, retain, and rehearse. For example, loud sounds, bright lights, and exciting videos may capture our interest even though we may not have received any reinforcement for paying attention to them. Bandura's research showed that children watching a model on television imitate the model's behavior regardless of whether they have been promised a reward. Therefore, reinforcement can assist in modeling but is not vital to it. When reinforcement occurs, it can be given by another person, experienced vicariously, or administered by oneself.

Self-Reinforcement and Self-Efficacy

In Bandura's approach to personality, the self is not some psychic agent that determines or causes behavior. Rather, the self is a set of cognitive processes and structures concerned with thought and perception. Two important aspects of the self are self-reinforcement and self-efficacy.

Self-Reinforcement

self-reinforcement
Administering rewards or punishments to oneself for meeting, exceeding, or falling short of one's own expectations or standards.

Self-reinforcement is as important as reinforcement administered by others, particularly for older children and adults. We set personal standards of behavior and achievement. We reward ourselves for meeting or exceeding these expectations and standards and we punish ourselves for our failures. Self-administered reinforcement can be tangible such as a new pair of gym shoes or a car, or it can be emotional such as pride or satisfaction from a job well done. Self-administered punishment can be expressed in shame, guilt, or depression about not behaving the way we wanted to.

Self-reinforcement appears conceptually similar to what other theorists call *conscience* or *superego*, but Bandura denies that it is the same.

A continuing process of self-reinforcement regulates much of our behavior. It requires internal standards of performance, subjective criteria or reference points against which we evaluate our behavior. Our past behavior may become a reference point for evaluating present behavior and an incentive for better performance in the future. When we reach a certain level of achievement, it may no longer challenge, motivate, or satisfy us, so we raise the standard and require more of ourselves. Failure to achieve may result in lowering the standard to a more realistic level.

People who set unrealistic performance standards—who observed and learned behavioral expectations from unusually talented and successful models—may continue to try to meet those excessively high expectations despite repeated failures. Emotionally, they may punish themselves with feelings of worthlessness and depression. These self-produced feelings can lead to self-destructive behaviors such as alcohol and drug abuse or a retreat into a fantasy world.

We learn our initial set of internal standards from the behavior of models, typically our parents and teachers. Once we adopt a given style of behavior, we begin a lifelong process of comparing our behavior with theirs.

Self-Efficacy, or "Believing You Can"

self-efficacy
Our feeling of adequacy, efficiency, and competence in coping with life.

How well we meet our behavioral standards determines our **self-efficacy**. In Bandura's system, self-efficacy refers to feelings of adequacy, efficiency, and competence in coping with life. Meeting and maintaining our performance standards enhances self-efficacy; failure to meet and maintain them reduces it.

Another way Bandura described self-efficacy was in terms of our perception of the control we have over our life.

> People strive to exercise control over events that affect their lives. By exerting influence in spheres over which they can command some control, they are better able to realize desired futures and to forestall undesired ones. The striving for control over life circumstances permeates almost everything people do because it can secure them innumerable personal and social benefits. The ability to affect outcomes makes them predictable. Predictability fosters adaptive preparedness. Inability to exert influence over things that adversely affect one's life breeds apprehension, apathy, or despair. (Bandura, 1995, p. 1)

People low in self-efficacy feel helpless, unable to exercise control over life events. They believe any effort they make is futile. When they encounter obstacles, they quickly give up if their initial attempt to deal with a problem is ineffective. People who are extremely low in self-efficacy will not even attempt to cope because they are convinced that nothing they do will make a difference. Why, they ask, should they even try? Low self-efficacy can destroy motivation, lower aspirations, interfere with cognitive abilities, and adversely affect physical health.

People high in self-efficacy believe they can deal effectively with events and situations. Because they expect to succeed in overcoming obstacles, they persevere at tasks and often perform at a high level. These people have greater confidence in their abilities than do persons low in self-efficacy, and they express little self-doubt. They view difficulties as challenges instead of threats and actively seek novel situations. High self-efficacy reduces fear of failure, raises aspirations, and improves problem solving and analytical thinking abilities.

One researcher defined self-efficacy quite simply and effectively as the "power of believing you can," and added that "believing that you can accomplish what you want to accomplish is one of the most important ingredients . . . in the recipe for success" (Maddux, 2002, p. 277). Thus, believing that you have the ability to be successful becomes a powerful asset as you strive for achievement.

Sources of information about self-efficacy. Our judgment about our self-efficacy is based on four sources of information: performance attainment, vicarious experiences, verbal persuasion, and physiological and emotional arousal.

The most influential source of efficacy judgments is *performance attainment*. Previous success experiences provide direct indications of our level of mastery and competence. Prior achievements demonstrate our capabilities and strengthen our feelings of self-efficacy. Prior failures, particularly repeated failures in childhood, lower self-efficacy.

An important indicator of performance attainment is receiving feedback on one's progress or one's performance on a task, such as a work assignment or a college examination. One study of 97 college students performing complicated puzzles found that those who received positive feedback on their performance reported higher levels of perceived competence at that task than did those who received negative feedback (Elliot, Faler, McGregor, Campbell, Sedikides, & Harackiewicz, 2000).

A study of 49 older adults showed that those who completed a 6-month training program in the Chinese art of Tai Chi reported significant increases in self-efficacy as compared to those who did not undertake the training (Li, McAuley, Harmer, Duncan, & Chaumeton, 2001). Similar results were obtained in a study of 125 women college students who completed a 16-hour physical self-defense training course. These students showed significantly higher levels of self-efficacy in a variety of areas including physical competence, general coping skills, and interpersonal assertiveness. A control group that had not taken the self-defense course showed no change in self-efficacy (Weitlauf, Cervone, Smith, & Wright, 2001). Thus, put simply, the more we achieve, the more we believe we can achieve, and the more competent and in control we feel.

Short-term failures in adulthood can lower self-efficacy. In one study, 60 college students were given a cognitive task. Ratings of item difficulty and feedback indicated that they performed either very well or very poorly. Self-report measures of their self-efficacy expectations for future tasks showed that people who believed they had performed well on the cognitive task had high self-efficacy expectations for their future performance. Those who thought they had performed poorly had a low expectation about their future performance (Sanna & Pusecker, 1994).

Vicarious experiences—seeing other people perform successfully—strengthen self-efficacy, particularly if the people we observe are similar in abilities. In effect, we are saying, "If they can do it, so can I." In contrast, seeing others fail can lower self-efficacy: "If they can't do it, neither can I." Therefore, effective models are vital in influencing our feelings of adequacy and competence. These models also show us appropriate strategies for dealing with difficult situations.

Verbal persuasion, which means reminding people that they possess the ability to achieve whatever they want to achieve, can enhance self-efficacy. This may be the most common of the four informational sources and one frequently offered by parents, teachers, spouses, coaches, friends, and therapists who say, in effect, "You can do it." To be effective, verbal persuasion must be realistic. It is probably not the best advice to encourage someone 5 feet tall to play professional basketball when other sports, such as martial arts, might be more appropriate.

A fourth source of information about self-efficacy is *physiological and emotional arousal*. How fearful or calm do we feel in a stressful situation? We often use this type of information as a basis for judging our ability to cope. We are more likely to believe we will master a problem successfully if we are not agitated, tense, or bothered by headaches. The more composed we feel, the greater our self-efficacy. Whereas the higher our level of physiological and emotional arousal, the lower our self-efficacy. The more fear, anxiety, or tension we experience in a given situation, the less we feel able to cope.

Bandura concluded that certain conditions increase self-efficacy:

1. Exposing people to success experiences by arranging reachable goals increases performance attainment.
2. Exposing people to appropriate models who perform successfully enhances vicarious success experiences.
3. Providing verbal persuasion encourages people to believe they have the ability to perform successfully.
4. Strengthening physiological arousal through proper diet, stress reduction, and exercise programs increases strength, stamina, and the ability to cope.

In his research, Bandura applied these conditions to enhance self-efficacy in a variety of situations. He has helped subjects learn to play musical instruments, relate better to persons of the opposite sex, master computer skills, give up cigarette smoking, and conquer phobias and physical pain.

 LOG ON

Information on Self-Efficacy

A wealth of information about self-efficacy including the latest research findings, books, articles, and tests to measure your own level of self-efficacy.

Test for Self-Efficacy

A 10-item scale to measure self-efficacy developed by psychologists at the Free University of Berlin, Germany. It has been used with thousands of subjects and is available in 29 languages.

For direct links to these sites, log on to the student companion site for this book at http://www.academic.cengage.com/psychology/Schultz and choose Chapter 13.

Developmental Stages of Modeling and Self-Efficacy

Childhood

In infancy, modeling is limited to immediate imitation. Infants have not yet developed the cognitive capacities (the imaginal and verbal representational systems) needed to imitate a model's behavior at some time after observing it. In infancy, it is necessary for the modeled behavior to be repeated several times after the infant's initial attempt to duplicate it. Also, the modeled behavior must be within the infant's range of sensorimotor development. By about age 2, children have developed sufficient attentional, retention, and production processes to begin imitating behavior some time after the observation rather than immediately.

The behaviors we find reinforcing, and thus choose to imitate, will change with age. Younger children are reinforced primarily by physical stimuli such as food, affection, or punishment. Older children associate positive physical reinforcers with signs of approval from significant models and unpleasant reinforcers with signs of disapproval. Eventually these rewards or punishments become self-administered.

Self-efficacy also develops gradually. Infants begin to develop self-efficacy as they attempt to exercise greater influence over their physical and social environments. They learn about the consequences of their own abilities such as their physical prowess, social skills, and language competence. These abilities are in almost constant use acting on the environment, primarily through their effects on parents. Ideally, parents are responsive to their growing child's activities and attempts to communicate, and will provide stimulating surroundings that permit the child the freedom to grow and explore.

These early efficacy-building experiences are centered on the parents. Parental behaviors that lead to high self-efficacy in children differ for boys and girls. Studies have shown that high self-efficacy men had, when they were children, warm relationships with their fathers. Mothers were more demanding than fathers, expecting higher levels of performance and achievement. In contrast, high self-efficacy women experienced, as children, pressure from their fathers for high achievement (Schneewind, 1995).

The significance of parental influence diminishes as the child's world expands and admits additional models such as siblings, peers, and other adults. Like Adler, Bandura considered birth order within the family to be important. He argued that first-born children and only children have different bases for judging their own abilities than do later-born children. Also, siblings of the same sex are likely to be more competitive than are siblings of the opposite sex, a factor also related to the development of self-efficacy. Among playmates, children who are the most experienced and successful at tasks and games serve as high-efficacy models for other children. Peers provide comparative reference points for appraising one's own level of achievement.

Teachers influence self-efficacy judgments through their impact on the development of cognitive abilities and problem-solving skills, which are vital to efficient adult functioning. Children often rate their own competence in terms of their teachers' evaluations of them. In Bandura's view, schools that use ability groupings undermine self-efficacy and self-confidence in students who are assigned to the lower groups. Competitive practices such as grading on a curve also doom poor achievers to average or low grades.

Adolescence

The transitional experiences of adolescence involve coping with new demands and pressures, from a growing awareness of sex to the choice of college and career. Adolescents must establish new competencies and appraisals of their abilities. Bandura noted that the success of this stage typically depends on the level of self-efficacy established during the childhood years.

Adulthood

Bandura divided adulthood into two periods: young adulthood and the middle years. Young adulthood involves adjustments such as marriage, parenthood, and career advancement. High self-efficacy is necessary for successful outcomes of these experiences. People low in self-efficacy will not be able to deal adequately with these situations and are likely to fail to adjust.

Studies show that women who feel high in self-efficacy about their parenting skills are likely to promote self-efficacy in their children. Women who believe they are good parents are less subject to despondency and emotional strain in their role as parent than are women low in self-efficacy (Olioff & Aboud, 1991; Teti & Gelfand, 1991). High self-efficacy mothers who worked outside the home experienced significantly less physical and emotional strain from work–family conflicts than did women low in self-efficacy (Bandura, 1995).

The middle years of adulthood are also stressful as people reevaluate their careers and their family and social lives. As we confront our limitations and redefine our goals, we must reassess our skills and find new opportunities for enhancing our self-efficacy.

Old Age

Self-efficacy reassessments in old age are difficult. Declining mental and physical abilities, retirement from active work, and withdrawal from social life may force a new round of self-appraisal. A lowering of self-efficacy can further affect physical and mental functioning in a kind of self-fulfilling prophecy. For example, reduced self-confidence about sexual performance can lead to a reduction in sexual activity. Lower physical efficacy can lead to fatigue and a curtailing of physical activities. If we no longer believe we can do something we used to enjoy and do well, then we may not even try. To Bandura, self-efficacy is the crucial factor in determining success or failure throughout the entire life span.

Behavior Modification

Bandura's goal in developing his social-cognitive theory was to modify or change those learned behaviors that society considers undesirable or abnormal. Like Skinner's approach to therapy, Bandura's focuses on external aspects, those inappropriate or destructive behaviors, in the belief that they are learned, just as all behaviors are learned. Bandura does not attempt to deal with underlying unconscious conflicts. It is the behavior or symptom, rather than any presumed internal neurosis that is the target of the social-learning approach.

Fears and Phobias

If modeling is the way we learn our behaviors originally, then it should also be an effective way to relearn or change behavior. Bandura applied modeling techniques to eliminate fears and other intense emotional reactions. In one early study, children who were afraid of dogs observed a child of the same age playing with a dog (Bandura, Grusec, & Menlove, 1967). While the subjects watched from a safe distance, the model made progressively bolder movements toward the dog. The model petted the dog through the bars of a playpen, then went inside the pen and played with the dog. The observers' fear of dogs was considerably reduced as a result of this observational-learning situation.

In the classic study of snake phobia, Bandura and his associates eliminated an intense fear of snakes in adult subjects (Bandura, Blanchard, & Ritter, 1969). The subjects watched a film in which children, adolescents, and adults made progressively closer contact with a snake. At first, the filmed models handled plastic snakes, then touched live snakes, and finally let a large snake crawl over their body. The phobic subjects were allowed to stop the film whenever the scenes became too threatening. Gradually, their fear of snakes was overcome.

A technique called *guided participation* involves watching a live model and then participating with the model. For example, to treat a snake phobia, subjects watch through an observation window while a live model handles a snake. The subjects enter the room with the model and observe the handling of the snake at close range. Wearing gloves, subjects are coaxed into touching the middle of the snake while the model holds the head and tail. Subjects eventually come to touch the snake without gloves.

Modeling has been shown to be effective even in the absence of an observable model. In *covert modeling*, subjects are instructed to imagine a model coping with a feared or threatening situation; they do not actually see a model. Covert modeling has been used to treat snake phobias and social inhibitions.

You may not think that a fear of snakes is so terrible, but overcoming this fear has brought about significant changes in many people's lives, even for those who never encounter snakes. In addition to bolstering self-esteem and self-efficacy, eliminating a snake phobia can alter personal and work habits. One subject after modeling therapy was able to wear a necklace for the first time; previously she had not been able to do so because necklaces reminded her of snakes. A realtor treated successfully for snake phobia was able to increase his income because he no longer feared visiting properties in rural areas. Many other phobics treated by modeling therapy were freed from nightmares about snakes.

Phobias restrict our daily life. For example, many people who fear spiders react with rapid heartbeat, shortness of breath, and vomiting even from seeing a picture of a spider. Phobics doubt their self-efficacy in these fear-provoking situations and have little confidence in their ability to deal with the source of the phobia. To relieve people of these fears expands their environment and increases their self-efficacy.

Modeling therapy, particularly using film and video techniques, offers several practical advantages. Complex behaviors can be seen as a whole. Extraneous behaviors can be edited out so that the subject's time is spent viewing only relevant behaviors. Films can be repeated with many patients and used by several therapists simultaneously. Modeling techniques can also be used with groups, saving time and money in treating people with the same problem. The approach has been effective with phobias, obsessive-compulsive disorders, and sexual dysfunction and the positive effects have been reported to last for years.

Modeling techniques have been shown to affect our ability to tolerate pain. Male college students performing a pain-inducing isometric exercise were shown a videotape of models doing the same exercise. Some of the models appeared to tolerate the pain well, while others did not. Subjects who saw the pain-tolerant models continued to exercise for a significantly longer period of time and reported significantly less discomfort than did subjects whose models seemed more adversely affected by the pain. In addition, those who viewed pain-intolerant models experienced the onset of pain sooner during the exercise period as well as an accelerated heart rate (Symbaluk, Heth, Cameron, & Pierce, 1997).

Considerable research has been conducted on self-efficacy during and after behavior modification therapy. The results have shown that as the subjects' self-efficacy improved during treatment, they were increasingly able to deal with the source of the fear. It was the therapeutic procedure itself that enhanced self-efficacy.

Anxiety

We noted that many behaviors can be modified through the modeling approach. We will consider two instances: fear of medical treatment and test anxiety.

Fear of medical treatment. Some people have such an intense fear of medical situations that they are prevented from seeking treatment. One early study dealt with children who were scheduled for surgery and had never been in a hospital before. They were divided into two groups: an experimental group that watched a film about a boy's experience in the hospital, and a control group that saw a film about a boy taking a trip (Melamed & Siegel, 1975). The child in the hospital film was an exemplary model. Despite some initial anxiety, he coped well with the doctors and the medical procedures.

The children's anxiety was assessed by several techniques including direct observation of behavior, responses on self-report inventories, and physiological measures. These assessments were made the night before surgery and were repeated a few weeks later. The results showed that the modeling film had been effective in reducing anxiety. Subjects who had seen the hospital film had fewer behavior problems after hospitalization than did those in the control group.

Similar procedures have been used to reduce fear of hospitalization in adults as well as fear of dental treatment. One study involved a medical procedure considered so stressful that more than 80 percent of patients initially refused to undergo it or quit it prematurely (Allen, Danforth, & Drabman, 1989). Subjects who watched a video of a model having the procedure and describing how he coped with his distress were more likely to complete the treatment with less anxiety and a shorter hospital stay.

Test anxiety. For some college students, test anxiety is so serious that their examination performance does not accurately reflect their knowledge of the material being tested. In the classic research, a sample of college students was divided into groups based on their personality test scores: those high in test anxiety and those low in test anxiety (Sarason, 1975).

Some of the students saw a filmed model talking about her anxiety when taking tests and her ways of dealing with it. Other students saw a film of the same model who talked about test anxiety but not about coping mechanisms. Under a third condition, students watched the filmed model talking about other college activities.

Then the subjects were given a list of nonsense syllables to memorize and were tested on their ability to recall them. The results showed that subjects high in test anxiety were most strongly affected by the model who talked about coping mechanisms. They performed significantly better on the recall test than did high-anxiety subjects who had been exposed to the other two conditions.

Ethical Issues in Behavior Modification

Although the results of behavior modification are impressive, the techniques have drawn criticism from educators, politicians, and even psychologists. They have suggested that behavior modification exploits people, manipulating and controlling them against their will. Bandura argues that these charges are misleading. Behavior modification does not occur without the client's awareness. Indeed, self-awareness and self-regulation are vital for the effectiveness of any program to change or relearn behaviors. In other words, behavior modification techniques will not be successful unless the person is able to understand what behaviors are being reinforced.

Further, the clients themselves decide what they want to change; they are not being controlled by anyone else. People come to a therapist to eliminate specific fears and anxieties that inhibit their ability to function or to cope with daily life. Bandura notes that the client–therapist relationship is a contract between two consenting individuals, not a relationship between a sinister master-controller and a spineless puppet.

reciprocal determinism
The idea that behavior is controlled or determined by the individual, through cognitive processes, and by the environment, through external social stimulus events.

Bandura also explained that far from manipulating or enslaving, modeling techniques actually increase personal freedom. People who are afraid to leave the house or who have a compulsion to wash their hands continually are not truly free. They are living within the constraints imposed by their phobic or compulsive behavior. Those constraints allow little choice. Removing the constraints through behavior modification techniques can increase freedom and the opportunity for personal growth.

Many such techniques have derived from Bandura's work and are popular alternatives to psychoanalysis and other therapeutic approaches.

Questions About Human Nature

Bandura's position is clear on the issue of free will versus determinism. Behavior is controlled by the person through the cognitive processes, and by the environment through external social situations. Bandura calls this view **reciprocal determinism**.

triadic reciprocality
The idea that behavior is determined through the interaction of behavioral, cognitive, and environmental or situational variables.

He noted that people are neither "powerless objects controlled by environmental forces nor free agents who can become whatever they choose. Both people and their environments are reciprocal determinants of each other" (1977, p. vii). He later introduced the notion of **triadic reciprocality**, in which three factors—behavior, cognitive processes, and environmental variables—interact (Bandura, 1986).

Although human behavior is influenced by external social and environmental forces, we are not helpless with respect to them. Our reactions to stimuli are self-activated in accordance with our learned expectations. Following Bandura's rules for observational learning, we observe and interpret the potential effects of our actions and determine which behaviors are appropriate for a given situation. We encode and represent these external events symbolically and anticipate that a certain behavior will bring a certain response. Thus, we choose and shape our behavior to gain reinforcement and avoid punishment.

This viewpoint accepts self-awareness, self-reinforcement, and other internal forms of the regulation of behavior. Reinforcement does not automatically change behavior. When it does effect a change, it is usually because the individual is aware of what is being reinforced and expects the same reward for behaving that way again. Some degree of self-direction interacts with past and present events. Thus, we are influenced by external forces and in turn guide the extent and direction of such influences. The notion of self-direction of behavior represents an optimistic view of human nature. Bandura believes that individuals create their own environments. He suggests that abnormal behaviors, which he sees as little more than bad habits, can be changed by behavior modification techniques.

On the nature–nurture issue, Bandura proposes that most behaviors (except basic reflexes) are learned and that genetic factors play a minor role. However, he recognizes that hereditary factors such as body type, physical maturation, and appearance can influence the reinforcers people receive, particularly in childhood. For example, clumsy, unattractive children will receive different reinforcers than children who are graceful and attractive.

Childhood experiences are important in Bandura's theory. Childhood learning may be more influential than learning in adulthood. Our internal performance standards, which affect our self-efficacy, are established in childhood, along with a set of ideal behaviors. However, childhood experiences can be unlearned later in life, and new performance standards and behaviors may be substituted. We are not captives of the reinforcers we received in our early years. Because at least some behavior results from experience, it may be inferred that Bandura accepts the uniqueness of personality. Also, our ultimate and necessary goal in life is to set realistic performance standards to maintain an adequate level of self-efficacy.

Assessment in Bandura's Theory

Like Skinner, Bandura focuses on behavior rather than on internal motivating variables. He did not use assessment measures such as free association, dream analysis, or projective techniques. Unlike Skinner, Bandura accepted the operation of cognitive variables. It is these cognitive variables, as well as behavior, that can be assessed.

For example, in the modeling study we described involving children about to undergo surgery, assessment techniques included direct observation, self-report inventories, and physiological measurements. In studies of self-efficacy, behavioral and cognitive variables were assessed quantitatively. Self-efficacy with regard to phobias was assessed by the subjects' self-ratings of the number of tasks on a behavioral-avoidance test they expected to be able to complete. College students' test anxiety was assessed by personality inventories. Thus, the assessment of behavioral and cognitive variables is important in the social-learning approach to personality.

Research on Bandura's Theory

Bandura favors well-controlled laboratory investigations in the rigorous tradition of experimental psychology. We noted his use of experimental and control groups and the precise measurement of independent and dependent variables. He studies large subject groups and compares their average performance by statistical analysis. The people he has selected to study have shown diverse behavioral disorders, such as phobias, alcoholism, fetishism, and sexual dysfunctions. Their ages range from preschool through adult. Thus, his social-learning theory is based on a broad cross-section of the population. This approach increases the generalizability and applicability of his research findings.

To illustrate further the kind of research that has proceeded from Bandura's theory, we consider representative work on self-efficacy and on the effect of televised models on aggressive behavior.

Self-Efficacy

Age and gender differences. Self-efficacy differs as a function of gender and age. Research with children and adults shows that on the average, men score higher than women in self-efficacy. These gender differences peak during the 20s and then decline in later years. For both men and women, self-efficacy increases through childhood and early adulthood, peaks in middle age, and then declines after age 60 (Gecas, 1989; Lachman, 1985).

However, even though self-efficacy appears to decline with age, there exists a wide range of individual differences in our beliefs about our capabilities. For example, in a study of 557 adults in the Netherlands, average age 66, the people who believed that their memory was worsening performed significantly less well on tests of memory functioning, which were administered 6 years later, than did people whose sense of self-efficacy included the belief that their memory capabilities were high (Valentijn, Hill, Van Hooren, Bosma, Van Boxtel, Jolles, & Ponds, 2006). This research provides further support that our belief in our own abilities may, indeed, affect those abilities.

Physical appearance. We noted Bandura's suggestion that physical appearance can influence the reinforcers people receive from others and, thus, how they feel about themselves. A study of 210 adult men and women ages 25–76 showed that physical appearance had a greater effect on their feelings of being in control of their lives than did their level of self-esteem or their health (Andreoletti, Zebrowitz, & Lachman, 2001).

For example, having a round face, large eyes, small nose bridge, and small chin ("baby-faceness") was found to be strongly related to low control beliefs in young and middle adulthood. Older baby-faced adults reported stronger feelings of control, perhaps because people reacted to them differently since they looked younger than did thin-faced people of the same age. The findings were stronger for women; a more youthful appearance later in life was shown to have definite advantages both socially and in the workplace.

Another major finding in this study was the significant effect of physical attractiveness on control beliefs. People who were rated less attractive reported lower feelings of control in both job and social situations. In addition, shorter people reported lower feelings of control in young adulthood than did taller people or those of average height.

Academic performance. Research demonstrates a significant positive relationship between self-efficacy and academic performance. Teachers with a high degree of self-efficacy or confidence in their teaching abilities create more opportunities for their students to achieve at a high level. Self-efficacy in students has also been positively related to motivation, level of effort, level of aspiration, and persistence in classroom situations (see, for example, Bassi, Steca, Fave, & Caprara, 2007; Gibson & Dembo, 1984; Multon, Brown, & Lent, 1991; Zimmerman, 1995).

Bandura also found differences in the ways schools inculcate self-efficacy in their students. In high-achieving schools, principals were more concerned with education than with implementing policies and regulations, and teachers set high expectations and standards for their students. In low-achieving schools principals functioned more as administrators and disciplinarians than as educators, and teachers expected little in the way of academic performance from their students (Bandura, 1997).

Cultural differences have been shown to influence self-efficacy in children. A study was conducted with 800 elementary school students in grades two to six in East and West Germany, before those nations were reunified. Students in the East German communist-collectivist culture scored lower in self-efficacy than did children in the West German capitalist-individualist culture. The East German children had less confidence in their ability to perform well in school and considered themselves to be less intelligent than West German students (Oettingen & Maier, 1999).

Career choice and job performance. Gender differences in self-efficacy can influence our choice of career. Research has shown that men perceive themselves to be high in self-efficacy for so-called traditional "male" as well as traditional "female" occupations. In contrast, women perceive themselves high in self-efficacy for so-called female occupations but low in self-efficacy for traditional male occupations. The men and women subjects in this research performed at comparable levels on standardized tests of verbal and quantitative skills. Thus, they possessed similar measurable abilities but perceived these abilities differently. Their feelings about their own competence for various careers differed as a function of gender (Hackett, 1995).

The higher the level of self-efficacy, the wider the range of career possibilities and the stronger the interest taken in them. Low self-efficacy may restrict the careers a person considers and contribute to indecisiveness about the options believed to be viable (Bores-Rangel, Church, Szendre, & Reeves, 1990). In one study, first-year women college students were found to be lower in self-efficacy than first-year men with regard to perceived ability to perform well in math courses (Lapan, Boggs, & Morrill, 1989). This affected the choice of college major and led women to avoid such programs as engineering and science, which in turn limited their career options.

Self-efficacy can affect the amount of time spent job hunting as well as future job success. Employees high in self-efficacy set higher personal goals and are more committed to them than employees low in self-efficacy. Those high in self-efficacy tend to focus on analyzing and solving problems on the job, whereas those low in self-efficacy focus on personal deficiencies and the fear of failure, which can undermine their productivity (Locke & Latham, 1990).

The significant positive relationship between self-efficacy and job performance was supported by a meta-analysis of 114 research studies involving more than 21,600 subjects. The higher the level of a person's self-efficacy, the better is his or her performance on the job (Stajkovic & Luthans, 1998). An update of this research found that self-efficacy was a better predictor of performance for jobs of low complexity than it was for jobs of medium or high complexity (Judge, Jackson, Shaw, Scott, & Rich, 2007).

Other research has demonstrated that people high in self-efficacy are more successful in job training programs and report higher levels of job satisfaction, organizational commitment, and job performance than do people who are low in self-efficacy (Salas & Cannon-Bowers, 2001).

Physical health. Self-efficacy also affects several aspects of physical well-being. In one study, pregnant women who had been taught relaxation and breathing exercises to reduce pain during childbirth believed they had greater control over that pain than did women who had not been taught relaxation techniques. The higher the women's self-efficacy and feeling of control, the longer they were able to tolerate the discomfort experienced during delivery before requesting pain medication. In addition, the higher their perceived self-efficacy, the less pain medication they required (Manning & Wright, 1983).

Other research supports the positive relationship between self-efficacy and pain tolerance. Coping techniques that improve self-efficacy produce substantial increases in endorphins, which are the body's natural painkillers. In a study on chronic pain, 45 patients suffering low back pain were given a pain-rating scale and a self-efficacy rating scale. Their progress in a 3-week rehabilitation program was monitored. After 6 months it was found that patients higher in self-efficacy reported better physical functioning and less back pain than did patients lower in self-efficacy (Altmaier, Russell, Kao, Lehmann, & Weinstein, 1993).

Self-efficacy is also related to the maintenance of healthy behaviors.

> Life-style habits can enhance or impair health. This enables people to exert some behavioral control over their vitality and quality of health. Efficacy beliefs affect every phase of personal change—whether people even consider changing their health habits; whether they enlist the motivation and perseverance needed to succeed should they choose to do so; and how well they maintain the habit changes they have achieved. (Bandura, 1995, p. 28)

A study of 114 Native American and Native Alaskan adults showed a clear relationship between self-efficacy and alcohol use: The lower the level of self-efficacy, the greater the alcohol consumption (Taylor, 2000). In the case of cigarette smoking, studies of adolescents show that the higher their self-efficacy, the more resistant they are to peer pressure to start smoking. Among college student smokers, high self-efficacy was found to be the best predictor of an expressed intention to reduce the number of cigarettes smoked or to quit (Schwarzer & Fuchs, 1995; Stacy, Sussman, Dent, Burton, & Floy, 1992).

Other studies show that people high in self-efficacy are more likely to stop smoking because they are confident of success whereas people low in self-efficacy are unlikely even to try (Becona, Frojan, & Lista, 1988; DiClemente, Prochaska, & Gilbertini, 1985). In additional research, self-efficacy measured before attempting to quit smoking was significantly related to smoking behavior a month after quitting. The higher the initial self-efficacy, the fewer cigarettes smoked during the month. Subjects who resisted smoking during that time period had greater self-efficacy than did those who resumed smoking (Garcia, Schmitz, & Doerfler, 1990). High self-efficacy has also been related to other health-enhancing behaviors such as exercise, weight control, and safe sex practices.

Self-efficacy can affect recovery from physical illness. For example, one study found that people high in self-efficacy responded better to cognitive and behavioral treatment for pulmonary disease than did patients low in self-efficacy. Men who suffered heart attacks showed a higher rate of return to normal activities and less fear and depression when both they and their spouses believed in their cardiac fitness. The higher the patients' self-efficacy, the more likely they were to follow prescribed exercise programs and the more they improved (Kaplan, Atkins, & Reinsch, 1984; McLeod, 1986).

A study of 105 adult patients recovering from orthopedic surgery (hip or knee replacement) showed that those high in self-efficacy performed significantly better in rehabilitation therapy programs than did those low in self-efficacy (Waldrop, Lightsey, Ethington, Woemmel, & Coke, 2001). And a study of 69 breast cancer patients found that the higher the expectation of remaining cancer-free in the future, the better the emotional adjustment to the disease (Carver, Harris, Lehman, Durel, Anton, Spencer, & Pozo-Kaderman, 2000).

Mental health. In Italy, a study of 282 boys and girls whose average age was 11.5 years found that children who rated themselves low in social and academic efficacy were significantly more likely to experience depression than were children who rated themselves high in efficacy. Low social efficacy has also been significantly related to depression in a sample of adolescents in the United States (Bandura,

Pastorelli, Barbaranelli, & Caprara, 1999). In a study of adolescents in the Netherlands, low social efficacy was related to high levels of anxiety, neuroticism, and symptoms of depression (Muris, 2002).

A similar relationship was documented with adults. Low social efficacy was found to contribute to feelings of depression, partly because a lack of coping skills inhibited the development of a social support network (Holahan & Holahan, 1987). These findings may indicate a circular relationship rather than simple cause-and-effect. Low self-efficacy can lead to depression, and depression can reduce self-efficacy. People who are depressed believe that they are far less capable than others of performing effectively in many areas of life and that they have little control over their situations (Bandura, 1997).

A study of 185 college students in the United States related self-efficacy to several of the characteristics of mental health proposed by the neopsychoanalytic theorist Alfred Adler. Students who scored high in self-efficacy also scored higher in social interest, the desire to strive for perfection, and a sense of belonging than did students who scored low in self-efficacy (Dinter, 2000).

Research conducted in Canada and in the United States showed that adults who scored high on a measure of self-efficacy were likely also to score high in self-esteem. They were less likely to procrastinate or to give up trying when dealing with an obstacle than were subjects low in self-efficacy (Lightsey, Burke, Ervin, Henderson, & Yee, 2006; Steel, 2007).

Coping with stress. Enhanced self-efficacy and a sense of control over life events are positively related to the ability to cope with stress and to minimize its harmful effects on biological functioning. Bandura wrote, "A strong sense of coping efficacy reduces vulnerability to stress and depression in taxing situations and strengthens resiliency to adversity" (Bandura, 2001, p. 10). High self-efficacy has been associated with strengthening the body's immune system, lowering the release of stress-related hormones, and reducing susceptibility to respiratory infections.

Studies have shown that high self-efficacy can help women cope with the stress of abortion. A sample of 291 women completed questionnaires to rate perceived self-efficacy and to assess their mood immediately after the procedure and again 3 weeks later. Subjects higher in self-efficacy adjusted more satisfactorily with significantly less depression and higher mood states than did those lower in self-efficacy (Cozzarelli, 1993). Another study dealt with stress experienced following the birth of one's first child. Self-report inventories assessed self-efficacy, psychological distress, and background variables such as income, age, education, and marital satisfaction. Women higher in self-efficacy coped better with the demands than did those lower in self-efficacy (Ozer, 1995).

A study of refugees migrating from East to West Germany after the destruction of the Berlin Wall in 1990 showed that people higher in self-efficacy adapted significantly better to the change from an economically disadvantaged lifestyle under a communist system to an affluent lifestyle under a capitalist system.

> Perceived self-efficacy proved to be a powerful personal resource regarding the impact of migration stress on cognitive appraisals as well as on psychological and physical

wellbeing. . . . Highly self-efficacious migrants perceived the demands in their new life more as challenges and less as threats. They experienced lower anxiety, better health, and fewer health complaints than low self-efficacious migrants. (Jerusalem & Mittag, 1995, p. 195)

Research was conducted on 76 adults in the Netherlands who had suffered facial disfigurement as a result of treatment for cancers of the head or neck. Those who measured lower in self-efficacy experienced higher levels of stress in response to unpleasant or rejecting behaviors of other people. Those who scored higher in self-efficacy experienced less stress because they believed they could exercise some control over how other people reacted to them (Hagedoorn & Molleman, 2006).

Collective Efficacy

Just as an individual may develop a sense of self-efficacy, a group of people working together in a common enterprise to achieve common goals may develop a sense of collective efficacy. For example, a baseball or football team, a department within a large organization, a military combat unit, or a group of neighbors uniting to fight a developer can engender the strong feeling that they can and will achieve their goals and overcome all obstacles.

The value of collective efficacy has been studied in college basketball teams. It was demonstrated that a high sense of collective efficacy arose in teams that had highly competent leaders early in the season and that had won most of their games in the previous season. Teams with the highest collective efficacy at the beginning of the new season placed better in end-of-season standings than did teams that scored low in collective efficacy (Watson, Chemers, & Preiser, 2001).

The Relationship between Aggressive Behavior and Television and Video Games

Bandura and many other researchers have demonstrated convincingly that in laboratory situations and in the real world, seeing violence begets violence whether on television, in movies, or in our homes, streets, and schools.

For example, a group of delinquent boys displayed significantly more violent behavior toward their peers after watching violent films than did a control group of boys who saw nonviolent films. The kinds of aggressive acts the boys committed frequently duplicated those depicted in the films (Leyens, Camino, Parke, & Berkowitz, 1975). In another study, 9-year-old children who watched numerous violent television programs were found to be more aggressive 10 years later. A follow-up 20 years later showed that the same subjects still expressed a high level of aggression. Other studies report similar relationships between viewing televised violence and behaving aggressively. These results have been confirmed in many countries including the United States, England, Belgium, Finland, Poland, and Australia (Eron, 1987; Huesmann, Eron, Dubow, & Seebauer, 1987).

A large-scale literature review confirms the relationship between the viewing of violent television programs in childhood and later aggressive behavior (see Rogoff,

Paradise, Arauz, Correa-Chavez, & Angelillo, 2003). A study of 779 people in their early and mid-20s found a strong positive correlation between the amount of violence they had watched on television between the ages of 6 and 10 and their aggressive behavior as adults. In other words, the more TV violence to which they had been exposed as children, the more aggressive they were in their 20s (Huesmann, Moise-Titus, Podolski, & Eron, 2003).

In a different approach to the relationship between observed violence and aggressive behavior, researchers investigated the incidence of aggressive acts shortly after people viewed televised models committing violent acts. One analysis found a brief but sharp rise in violent actions peaking 3 to 4 days following highly publicized riots (Phillips, 1985). Murder rates in the United States were found to increase by more than 12 percent over the expected rate for the 3-day period following a televised championship boxing match, a phenomenon that was maintained over a 15-year period (Phillips, 1983). Self-directed violence also appears to increase following exposure to similar violence widely reported in the news media. The incidence of suicide tends to climb following the suicide of a movie star or other celebrity (Phillips, 1974).

Research on children, teenagers, and college students in the United States and in Germany showed that playing violent video games resulted in greater increases in aggressive and hostile behaviors than were found in people who did not play such video games. Those who played violent games were more likely to get into fights, to argue with their teachers, and to perform poorly in school. They were less likely to help others. Also, they were found to have higher levels of cardiovascular arousal. In general, the more violent the favorite games, the more violent the resulting behavior (see Anderson, 2004; Bartholow, Sestir, & Davis, 2005; Gentile, Lynch, Linder, & Walsh, 2004; Krahe & Moeller, 2004; Uhlmann & Swanson, 2004).

Additional research with college students showed significant positive correlations between time spent listening to rap music and aggressive behavior toward other people including sexually aggressive behavior toward women (see Anderson, Carnagey, & Eubanks, 2003; Barongan & Hall, 1995; Chen, Miller, Grube, & Waiters, 2006).

Reflections on Bandura's Theory

Social-learning theory focuses on overt behavior. Critics charge that this emphasis ignores distinctly human aspects of personality such as motivation and emotion. They draw an analogy with a physician whose patients have stomach pains. The physician who deals only with overt behavior may treat such patients by asking them to stop groaning and complaining and clutching their stomach. What may be required instead is medication or surgery. The physician must diagnose and treat the afflicted internal organ, the underlying cause of the pain. If just the symptom is treated and not the cause, critics say, substitute symptoms may appear.

However, the social-learning approach has several advantages. First, it is objective and amenable to laboratory methods of investigation, making it congruent with the current emphasis in experimental psychology. Most experimental psychologists reject theoretical work in personality that posits unconscious or other internal driving forces that cannot be manipulated or measured under laboratory conditions. Therefore, Bandura's approach boasts a great amount of empirical support. This is particularly true for his concept of self-efficacy; research continues to confirm its usefulness in the laboratory and in real-world situations.

Second, observational learning and behavior modification are compatible with the functional, pragmatic spirit of American psychology. More readily than other approaches, observational-learning techniques can be taken from the laboratory and applied to practical problems. The techniques also provide more immediate reinforcement for the practitioner than do other approaches. For example, in clinical situations, dramatic changes can be seen in client behavior within weeks or even days.

Behavior changes on a larger scale, and in some 60 nations, have also been demonstrated. Bandura's central idea, that people learn behaviors from role models whom they wish to emulate, has been used in radio and television programs in less well-developed nations to promote such social issues as population control, improving the status of women, and decreasing the spread of AIDS. The stories presented in these media revolved around characters who modeled behaviors designed to achieve these public health goals not only for themselves but for the greater society as well. Studies have demonstrated significant changes in safe sex practices and in family planning practices among millions of people following exposure to these models, reinforcing the notion that Bandura's ideas can be applied to the resolution of national as well as individual problems (Smith, 2002).

It is not surprising, then, that many researchers and clinicians continue to study and promote Bandura's social-learning theory. The great number of books, articles, and research studies still deriving from it attests to its continuing popularity as a way to study behavior in the laboratory and to modify behavior in the real world.

Chapter Summary

Behavior can be learned through vicarious reinforcement by observing the behavior of others and anticipating the rewards for behaving in the same way. Cognitive processes are the mediating mechanisms between stimulus and response and bring about control of behavior through self-regulation and self-reinforcement. In the classic Bobo doll study, children patterned their behavior on the model's aggressive behavior whether the model was observed live, on television, or in a cartoon. Disinhibition involves weakening an inhibition through exposure to a model. Three factors that influence modeling are the model's characteristics, the observer's characteristics, and the behavior's reward consequences.

Observational learning is governed by attentional, retention, production, and incentive and motivational processes. The self is a set of cognitive processes concerned with thought and perception. Self-reinforcement requires internal performance standards against which to evaluate behavior. Self-efficacy refers to the ability to control life events. People low in self-efficacy feel helpless and give up quickly when faced with obstacles. People who score high in self-efficacy persevere at tasks and perform at a high level. Judgments of self-efficacy are based on performance attainment, vicarious experiences, verbal persuasion, and physiological arousal.

Using these information sources, it is possible to increase self-efficacy. Infants and children are reinforced primarily by physical stimuli. Older children are reinforced more by others' approval or disapproval; this is internalized so that reinforcement becomes self-administered.

In behavior therapy, models are used to demonstrate ways of coping with threatening situations. Behavior can be modified through observation and guided participation. In covert modeling, subjects imagine how a model copes with a feared situation. Bandura's approach to behavior modification deals with overt behavior and cognitive variables, particularly self-efficacy. As self-efficacy improves during treatment, the client is increasingly able to deal with threatening situations. Behavior modification has been criticized for manipulating people against their will, but Bandura argues that with self-awareness and self-regulation, people undergoing behavior modification understand what is being reinforced.

Behavior is controlled by internal cognitive processes and external stimuli; a position Bandura calls reciprocal determinism. Triadic reciprocality refers to interaction among behavior, cognitive, and environmental variables. Most behavior is learned; genetic factors play a minor role. Learning in childhood may be more influential than learning in adulthood but adults are not victims of childhood experiences. Our ultimate goal is to set realistic performance standards to maintain an optimal level of self-efficacy. Self-efficacy varies with age and gender and can influence career choice, school performance, job performance, physical and mental health, and the ability to cope with stress. In addition, groups have been shown to develop collective efficacy.

Bandura assesses behavior and cognitive variables through direct observation, self-report inventories, and physiological measures. He favors controlled laboratory investigations using large groups of subjects and statistical analysis of data. Criticisms of Bandura's theory relate to his focus on overt behavior to the exclusion of emotions and conflicts, his treatment of symptoms rather than possible internal causes, and his failure to state precisely how cognitive variables affect behavior.

Review Questions

1. How does the observational-learning approach to personality differ from the other approaches we have discussed?

2. How does Bandura deal in his system with internal cognitive, or thought, processes, and with the unconscious?

3. What is Bandura's position on the role of reinforcement in learning?

4. Describe a typical experiment in which modeling is used to change behavior.

5. Explain disinhibition. How can the phenomenon of disinhibition explain the behavior of people in a crowd or a mob?

6. How does modeling vary as a function of the characteristics of the models, the characteristics of the observers, and the reward consequences of the behavior?

7. What are the four processes of observational learning? How are they related?

8. Explain how the production processes can be used to teach a person to play tennis.

9. How do the types of behaviors we acquire through modeling change with age?

10. What is the self, in Bandura's view? How does self-reinforcement operate to change behavior?

11. What does Bandura mean by self-efficacy? Give an example of how we can use self-efficacy to exert control over our life.

12. How do people high in self-efficacy differ from people low in self-efficacy in terms of their ability to cope with life?

13. On what sources of information do we base our judgment about our own level of efficacy?

14. Describe the developmental changes that occur in self-efficacy from infancy to old age. How can self-efficacy be increased?

15. Describe the guided participation and the covert modeling approaches to behavior modification.

16. Give an example of how modeling can be used to reduce anxiety.

17. What is the relationship between self-efficacy and physical health? Between self-efficacy and mental health?

18. What is Bandura's position on the issue of free will versus determinism? On the relative influences of heredity and environment?

19. How does self-efficacy differ as a function of gender, age, and physical attractiveness?

20. In what ways does self-efficacy influence performance in school and on the job? How does self-efficacy affect our ability to cope with stress?

21. Describe how exposure to televised violence and video game violence affects behavior.

Suggested Readings

Bandura, A. (1976). Albert Bandura. In R. I. Evans (Ed.), *The making of psychology: Discussions with creative contributors* (pp. 242–254). New York: Alfred A. Knopf. Interviews with Bandura about his life and work.

Bandura, A. (1997). *Self-efficacy: The exercise of control.* New York: W. H. Freeman. Describes 20 years of research on the idea that we can accomplish what we truly want to accomplish, that is, we are capable of consciously directing our actions to achieve success. Extends the concept of efficacy to society at large: to political beliefs, social practices, and collective action.

Bandura, A. (2001). Social cognitive theory: An agentic perspective. *Annual Review of Psychology, 52,* 1–26. Describes social cognitive theory in terms of the capacity to exercise control over the nature and quality of one's life.

Watson, C. B., Chemers, M. M., & Preiser, N. (2001). Collective efficacy: A multilevel analysis. *Personality and Social Psychology Bulletin, 27,* 1057–1068. Discusses the concept of collective efficacy, defined as the shared belief that individuals hold about the group (in this case, a college basketball team). Individual influences on collective efficacy include self-efficacy, optimism, leader effectiveness, and group performance.

PART NINE

Advances in Personality Theory

Personality theorists have usually considered completeness to be their major theoretical goal, and we have seen that some theories come closer to achieving this than others do. However, an increasing number of personality psychologists have concluded that no theory can be a truly comprehensive explanation for all aspects of our personality and behavior. It is widely accepted today that such a goal may be unrealistic. This has given rise to a number of separate theories, smaller in scope and aim. Each has a narrower range of application, focusing on a restricted aspect of personality that can be experimentally tested more thoroughly than is possible with a global theory of the total personality.

It is easy to see why the global approach to personality theory characterized the field for so long. Early personality theorists—such as Freud, Jung, and Adler—treated individual patients in a clinical setting. They were attempting to modify or cure abnormal behaviors and emotional disturbances to help people function in the real world. Of necessity, then, these theorists focused on the whole person, not just one or two traits.

The focus shifted from the whole person when personality was brought out of the clinic and into the research laboratory. Experimental psychologists typically study one variable at a time, controlling or holding constant all others. In this way, they concentrate on a limited domain or area of investigation. They collect large amounts of empirical data derived from their study of how the experimental variable relates to its antecedents and its behavioral consequences. Thus, limited-domain theories are characterized by a type of supporting data that is different from the data generated in the clinical approach.

Limited-domain theorists place less emphasis on the therapeutic value of their ideas. They typically are researchers, not clinicians, more interested in investigating personality than changing it. This does not mean that limited-domain theories have no treatment applications. Rather, it indicates that the theories were not developed specifically for use with patients, as was the case with many of the earlier personality theories.

Because personality study has become so much more experimentally oriented, we can expect the limited-domain approach to dominate the theoretical work of the 21st century. To date, more than a dozen well-formulated limited-domain theories have been proposed, and most are stimulating debate and research. Some of these theories deal with the hardy personality, the authoritarian personality, the Type A/Type B personalities, the need for achievement, altruism, cognitive dissonance, the power motive, self-disclosure, and optimal experience or flow.

We have chosen to discuss locus of control, sensation seeking, learned helplessness, optimism–pessimism, and the happy personality. They represent two contemporary approaches we have discussed in this text—the trait and the social-learning or social-cognitive approaches. Thus, each limited-domain theory we describe encompasses not only a different aspect of personality but a different approach to the ultimate explanation of personality.

Sensation seeking is one of the traits in Hans Eysenck's personality dimension E (extraversion versus introversion). It is primarily an inherited attribute and reflects the impact of behavioral genetics on personality. Locus of control and learned helplessness are learned behaviors. They have a strong cognitive component, reflecting the influence of the behaviorist, social learning, and cognitive movements in personality. The happy personality is an outgrowth of the positive psychology movement.

These theories are presented as examples of the limited-domain approach. They are not comprehensive systems, nor are they the only theories that focus on facets of personality. Our aim here is to give you the flavor of each theory and to acquaint you with the idea of studying personality in this fashion.

CHAPTER 14

Julian Rotter

Marvin Zuckerman

Martin E. P. Seligman

Facets of Personality

Julian Rotter: Locus of Control

Rotter (1916–) was born in Brooklyn, New York, the youngest of three brothers. He said they "fit quite well into Adler's descriptions of the oldest, the middle, and the 'fighting' youngest child" (1993, p. 273). The family lived comfortably until the 1929 economic depression when Rotter's father lost his business. This dramatic change in circumstances was a pivotal event for the teenage boy. He wrote, "It began in me a lifelong concern with social injustice and provided me with a powerful lesson on how personality and behavior were affected by situational conditions" (1993, p. 274).

In high school Rotter discovered books about psychoanalysis by Freud and Adler. As a game, he would interpret the dreams of his friends, and he decided he wanted to become a psychologist. Disappointed to learn that there were few jobs for psychologists, however, he chose to major in chemistry at Brooklyn College. Once there, he happened to meet Alfred Adler and switched his major to psychology after all, even though he knew it was impractical. He hoped to pursue an academic career but the widespread prejudice against Jewish faculty thwarted that goal. "At Brooklyn College and again in graduate school," he wrote, "I had been warned that Jews simply could not get academic jobs, regardless of their credentials. The warnings seemed justified" (Rotter, 1982, p. 346).

After Rotter received his Ph.D. from Indiana University in 1951, he went to work at a state mental hospital in Connecticut. He served as a psychologist with the U.S. Army during World War II and then accepted a teaching position at Ohio State University, where George Kelly was director of the clinical psychology program. (It is interesting that two personality theorists who emphasize cognition should have developed their work at the same institution. Kelly's ideas, however, were already well formulated by the time Rotter arrived.)

At Ohio State, Rotter advanced his social-learning approach to personality. His research program attracted many outstanding graduate students who went on to productive careers. One of them later referred to that time at Ohio State as the "glory days," with "Rotter and Kelly right in the midst of refining their theoretical positions and writing their magnum opuses" (Sechrest, 1984, p. 228).

In 1963 Rotter left Ohio State for the University of Connecticut at Storrs. In 1988 he received the Distinguished Scientific Contribution Award from the American Psychological Association.

Internal versus External Control of Reinforcement

internal locus of control
A belief that reinforcement is brought about by our own behavior.

Rotter sought explanations for behavior and personality outside and inside the organism, looking both to external reinforcements and internal cognitive processes. In the course of an extensive research program, he found that some people believe that their reinforcers depend on their own actions and that other people believe that their reinforcers are controlled by other people and by outside forces. He called this concept *locus of control*.

People who have been characterized as **internal locus of control** personalities believe that the reinforcement they receive is under the control of their own behaviors

external locus of control
A belief that reinforcement is under the control of other people, fate, or luck.

and attributes. Those with an **external locus of control** think that other people, fate, or luck controls the rewards they receive. In other words, they are convinced that they are powerless with respect to outside forces.

You can see how the source of our locus of control can have a considerable influence on our behavior. External locus-of-control people, who believe that their behaviors and abilities make no difference in the reinforcers they receive, may see little value in exerting any effort to improve their situation. Why should they try when they have little or no expectation of controlling present or future events?

In contrast, internal locus-of-control people believe they have a firm grip on their situation and behave accordingly. They perform at a higher level on laboratory tasks than do external locus-of-control people. In addition, internals are less susceptible to attempts to influence them, place a higher value on their skills, and are more alert to environmental cues that they use to guide behavior. They report lower anxiety and higher self-esteem, are more responsible for their actions, and enjoy greater mental and physical health.

Assessment of Locus of Control

Rotter developed self-report inventories to assess locus of control. The Internal-External (I-E) Scale (Rotter, 1966) consists of 23 forced-choice alternatives. From each pair of items, subjects select the one that best describes their beliefs (see Table 14.1). It is not difficult to determine which of each pair of alternatives represents an internal or an external locus of control. Another scale to assess locus of control is the Children's Nowicki-Strickland Internal-External Scale, a widely

Table 14.1 Sample items from the I-E Scale

1. a. Many of the unhappy things in people's lives are partly due to bad luck.
   b. People's misfortunes result from the mistakes they make.
2. a. One of the major reasons why we have wars is because people don't take enough interest in politics.
   b. There will always be wars, no matter how hard people try to prevent them.
3. a. In the long run people get the respect they deserve in this world.
   b. Unfortunately, an individual's worth often passes unrecognized no matter how hard he or she tries.
4. a. The idea that teachers are unfair to students is nonsense.
   b. Most students don't realize the extent to which their grades are influenced by accidental happenings.
5. a. Without the right breaks one cannot be an effective leader.
   b. Capable people who fail to become leaders have not taken advantage of their opportunities.
6. a. No matter how hard you try some people just don't like you.
   b. People who can't get others to like them don't understand how to get along with others.

SOURCE: J. B. Rotter, "Generalized Expectancies for Internal versus External Control of Reinforcement," *Psychological Monographs, 80* (1966):11.

used 40-item test that has been translated into two dozen languages (Nowicki & Strickland, 1973; Strickland, 1989). An adult form of the scale is available, as well as a cartoon version for use with preschool children (Nowicki & Duke, 1983). Variants of the I-E Scale measure specific behaviors such as the relationship between locus of control and factors relating to successful dieting and weight loss.

Age and Gender Differences

Studies have shown that attempts to control our external environment begin in infancy, becoming more pronounced between ages 8 to 14. A study of 223 14- and 15-year-olds in Norway found that girls scored significantly higher than boys did on internal locus of control (Manger & Ekeland, 2000). More college students have been found to show an internal rather than an external orientation. People apparently become more internally oriented as they grow older, reaching a peak in middle age (Heckhausen & Schulz, 1995; Milgram, 1971; Ryckman & Malikiosi, 1975).

In terms of overall scores on the I-E Scale, no significant differences between adult men and women subjects in the United States were documented (see, for example, DeBrabander & Boone, 1990). However, men and women respond differently to certain test items. In one study, men displayed greater internal locus of control than did women on questions relating to academic achievement (Strickland & Haley, 1980). External locus of control appears to increase in women after divorce, followed by a return to an internal locus of control (Doherty, 1983). Women who have been physically abused tend to show an external locus of control (Baron & Byrne, 1984). In China, research demonstrated that men scored higher in internal control than did women (Tong & Wang, 2006).

Racial and Socioeconomic Differences

In early research with the I-E Scale, significant racial and socioeconomic differences were found. In general, the test performance of lower social classes and minority groups showed an external locus of control. This was confirmed in a study with children. Lower-class Black children were shown to be more externally oriented than were lower- and middle-class White children or middle-class Black children (Battle & Rotter, 1963; Coleman, Campbell, Hobson, McPartland, Mood, Weinfeld, & York, 1966).

Studies conducted in Africa found that native Africans, like American-born Blacks in general, scored higher in external locus of control than did American-born Whites (Okeke, Draguns, Sheku, & Allen, 1999). In the African nation of Botswana, Black male and female adolescents scored higher in external locus of control than did White adolescents in the United States. In both countries, teens higher in socioeconomic status scored higher in internal control than did teens lower in socioeconomic status (Maqsud & Rouhani, 1991). A study of American high school students found that Hispanic American and Native American adolescents were more likely to be externally oriented than were White adolescents (Graves, 1961).

In general, Asians were shown to be more externally oriented than were Americans, a finding that may be explained in terms of cultural beliefs. Whereas American culture traditionally prizes self-reliance and individualism, Asian culture emphasizes community reliance and interdependence. Therefore, for Asians, success is viewed more as a product of external than internal factors. The more contact Asians have with Americans, the more internally oriented they seem to become. For example, Chinese residents of Hong Kong measured higher in external locus of control than did Americans of Chinese heritage, and Americans of Chinese heritage were more externally oriented than Americans of European heritage (Uba, 1994).

A study of 443 college students in South Africa and in Lebanon found that the South African students scored significantly higher in internal locus of control than did the Lebanese students. This provides another example of the difference in locus of control between an individualistic culture (South Africa) and a more collectivist and structured culture (Lebanon) (Nasser & Abouchedid, 2006).

Behavioral Differences

Internally oriented people are more likely than externally oriented people are to engage in significantly more daydreams about achievement and fewer daydreams about failure. They acquire and process more information in different situations, experience greater personal choice, and are more popular. In addition, internals are attracted to people they can manipulate, have higher self-esteem, and act in more socially skillful ways (Abdallah, 1989; Brannigan, Hauk, & Guay, 1991; Lefcourt, Martin, Fick, & Saleh, 1985).

Studies of workers in China and of athletes in Sweden found that those who measured high in internal locus of control were more able to adapt and commit to change, and also scored higher on tests of mental skills, than did those who were more externally oriented (Chen & Wang, 2007; Fallby, Hassmen, Kentta, & Durand-Burand, 2006).

People high in internal locus of control are less likely to have emotional problems or become alcoholics. They cope better with stress, as was demonstrated in a study of 361 nurses in Germany. Those who reported higher levels of work-related stress and burnout scored higher in external locus of control than did those less bothered by stress and burnout (Owen, 2006; Schmitz, Neumann, & Oppermann, 2000).

College students in Greece, a family-oriented and highly protective culture, were followed as they dealt with the social and emotional challenges of leaving home, many for the first time. Students who scored high in internal control adjusted more readily than did those high in external control (Leontopoulou, 2006). A study of first-year college students in Turkey found that those high in external locus of control were far more indecisive in new situations than were those high in internal locus of control (Bacanli, 2006).

Research also shows that people high in internal locus of control experience less anxiety and depression, and are less likely to commit suicide (see, for example, Benassi, Sweeney, & Dufour, 1988; Keltikangas-Jaruinen & Räikkönen, 1990; Kulshrestha & Sen, 2006; Lefcourt, 1982; Petrosky & Birkhimer, 1991; Spann, Molock, Barksdale, Matlin, & Puri, 2006). A study was conducted of 109 Israeli teenagers (69 males and 40 females) during the 1990 Persian Gulf War when the explosion of 40 SCUD missiles caused widespread injury and destruction. The researcher found that adolescents who scored higher on perceived control experienced significantly less anxiety and fewer stress-related symptoms than did adolescents who scored lower in perceived control (Zeidner, 1993). Other research showed that people higher in internal locus of control earned higher grades in school and scored higher on standardized tests of academic achievement. They were more resistant to attempts at persuasion and coercion, more perceptive, and more inquisitive (Findley & Cooper, 1983; Lefcourt, 1982).

Physical Health Differences

Internally oriented people may be physically healthier than externally oriented people are. Research showed that internals tend to have lower blood pressure and fewer heart attacks. When they do develop cardiac problems, they cooperate better with the hospital staff and are released earlier than patients who are externally oriented.

A study of more than 1,000 patients recovering from coronary artery bypass surgery found that those high in internal control had achieved a higher level of physical functioning at 6 weeks and 6 months after surgery than had those low in internal control (Barry, Kasl, Lichtman, Vaccarino, & Krumholz, 2006).

Internals tend to be more cautious about their health and are more likely to wear seat belts, to exercise, and to quit smoking (Phares, 1993; Seeman, Seeman, & Sayles, 1985; Segall & Wynd, 1990). Overall, the evidence seems clear that people who think they have control over their lives pay more attention to their health.

One study delineated four aspects of locus of control as it relates to physical health: self-mastery, illness prevention, illness management, and self-blame. The factor most closely associated with physical well-being was self-mastery, defined as a belief in one's ability to overcome illness (Marshall, 1991).

Developing Locus of Control in Childhood

Evidence suggests that locus of control is learned in childhood and is directly related to parental behavior. External control beliefs were likely to be expressed by children reared in homes without an adult male role model. Also, external control beliefs tended to increase with the number of siblings. This researcher concluded that children in large single-parent families headed by women are more likely to develop an external locus of control (Schneewind, 1995). Parents of children who possessed an internal locus of control were found to be highly supportive, to offer praise (positive reinforcement) for achievements, and to be consistent in their discipline. They were not authoritarian. As their children grew older, these parents continued to foster an internal orientation by encouraging independence (Wichern & Nowicki, 1976).

Reflections on Locus of Control

A large-scale research program conducted on 1,689 college students and 175 sales representatives for a pharmaceutical firm reported a strong relationship between Rotter's concept of locus of control and Bandura's concept of self-efficacy (Judge, Erez, Bono, & Thoresen, 2002). Thus, it can be suggested that both ideas deal with our perception or belief about the degree of control we have over the events in our life and our ability to cope with them. A major difference between the two concepts is that locus of control can be generalized over many situations whereas self-efficacy tends to be specific to a particular situation. However, Bandura insisted there was little overlap between the concepts of self-efficacy and locus of control. He wrote,

> Beliefs about whether one can produce certain actions (perceived self-efficacy) cannot, by any stretch of the imagination, be considered the same as beliefs about whether actions affect outcomes (locus of control). (1997, p. 20)

Nevertheless, it is clear that Rotter's research has been highly rigorous and well controlled and that he used objective measures wherever possible. Studies have provided considerable empirical support. The I-E Scale has generated a wealth of research and has been applied in clinical and educational settings. Rotter noted that locus of control has become "one of the most studied variables in psychology" (1990, p. 489).

 LOG ON

The Social Learning Theory of Julian B. Rotter

An overview of Rotter's life and work plus a list of his publications.

For a direct link to this site, log on to the student companion site for this book at http://www.academic.cengage.com/psychology/Schultz and choose Chapter 14.

Marvin Zuckerman: Sensation Seeking

sensation seeking
The need for varied, novel, and complex sensations and experiences.

Beginning in the 1970s, psychologist Marvin Zuckerman (1928–), at the University of Delaware, has conducted research on a limited-domain aspect of personality that he calls **sensation seeking**. This trait has a large hereditary component initially noted by Eysenck. Zuckerman describes sensation seeking as a desire for "varied, novel, complex, and intense sensations and experience, and the willingness to take physical, social, legal, and financial risks for the sake of such experience" (Zuckerman, 1994a, p. 27).

Assessing Sensation Seeking

To measure sensation seeking, Zuckerman constructed the Sensation Seeking Scale (SSS), a 40-item paper-and-pencil questionnaire. When developing this test, he administered it to many people whose behavior corresponded to his definition of sensation seeking. These included people who volunteered for psychological experiments that exposed them to novel experiences, people whose jobs involved physical danger (police officers and race-car drivers), and people who admitted to experimenting with drugs or varied sexual experiences. Their SSS scores were compared

Table 14.2 Sample items from the Sensation Seeking Scale, Form V

Choose the statement in each pair that you prefer.
1. a. I like wild uninhibited parties.
   b. I prefer quiet parties with good conversation.
2. a. I get bored seeing the same old faces.
   b. I like the comfortable familiarity of everyday friends.
3. a. A sensible person avoids activities that are dangerous.
   b. I sometimes like to do things that are a little frightening.
4. a. I would like to take off on a trip with no preplanned or definite routes or timetables.
   b. When I go on a trip I like to plan my route and timetable fairly carefully.
5. a. I would like to try parachute jumping.
   b. I would never want to try jumping out of a plane with or without a parachute.
6. a. There is altogether too much portrayal of sex in movies.
   b. I enjoy watching many of the sexy scenes in movies.
7. a. I am not interested in experience for its own sake.
   b. I like new, exciting experiences and sensations even if they are a bit frightening, unconventional, or illegal.
8. a. People should dress according to some standard of taste, neatness, and style.
   b. People should dress in individual ways, even if the effects are sometimes strange.

SOURCE: *Behavioral Expressions and Biosocial Bases of Sensation Seeking,* by M. Zuckerman, 1994, pp. 389–392. Cambridge, England: Cambridge University Press.

with the scores of people who chose to avoid novel or risky activities. Those people who deliberately sought unusual activities scored high on the SSS, and those who preferred less venturesome activities scored low. Sample items from the test are shown in Table 14.2.

Using the method of factor analysis, Zuckerman (1983) identified four components of sensation seeking.

- Thrill and adventure seeking: a desire to engage in physical activities involving speed, danger, novelty, and defiance of gravity such as parachuting, scuba diving, or bungee jumping.
- Experience seeking: the search for novel experiences through travel, music, art, or a nonconformist lifestyle with similarly inclined persons.
- Disinhibition: the need to seek release in uninhibited social activities.
- Boredom susceptibility: an aversion to repetitive experiences, routine work, and predictable people, and a reaction of restless discontent when exposed to such situations.

Zuckerman later proposed good and bad kinds of sensation seeking. The so-called good type, or *non-impulsive socialized sensation seeking*, involves the thrill and adventure-seeking component. The bad kind, *impulsive unsocialized sensation seeking*, consists of high scores on the disinhibition, experience seeking, and boredom susceptibility components as well as high scores on Eysenck's psychoticism scale (Roberti, 2004; Zuckerman, 1994b).

LOG ON

Sensation Seeking Scale

Take the Sensation Seeking Scale for yourself and see how adventurous you are.

Sensation Seeking Scale

Another version of the Sensation Seeking Scale developed by Zuckerman for use as part of the driver's license testing in Australia.

For direct links to these sites, log on to the student companion site for this book at http://www.academic.cengage.com/psychology/Schultz and choose Chapter 14.

Characteristics of Sensation Seekers

Zuckerman and his associates found that sensation seeking varies as a function of age. Younger people are more inclined to seek adventure, risk, and novel experiences than are older people. For example, studies of high school and college students in the United States and in Canada found that those who scored high in sensation seeking were far more likely to engage in various kinds of reckless behaviors as well as un-controlled gambling than were those who scored low (George, Baechtold, Frost, & Campbell, 2006; Gupta, Derevensky, & Ellenbogen, 2006). Test scores on subjects ranging from adolescents to 60-year-olds showed that sensation seeking begins to decrease in one's 20s.

In a personal comment on his own sensation-seeking behavior Zuckerman noted that when he was a college student, he "reached my full sensation-seeking potential through drinking, sex, and hitch-hiking around the country." At the age of 74, he wrote,

> When I was a young sensation seeker I imagined that after I retired I would do all kinds of adventurous things like hang gliding, parachute jumping, and learning to fly an air-plane. But whereas thrill and adventure seeking and disinhibition fall rapidly with age, experience seeking does not change. (Zuckerman, 2004, pp. 13, 21)

Zuckerman continues to seek new experiences, but they are less physically adventurous than before.

Significant gender differences were found in the four components of sensa-tion seeking. Men scored higher on thrill and adventure seeking, disinhibition, and boredom susceptibility. Women scored higher on experience seeking. Similar results were obtained from subjects in the United States, England, Scotland, Japan, and Thailand. Researchers also found significant racial and cultural differences. Asians scored lower on the SSS than did people in Western countries. White subjects scored higher in sensation seeking than did non-Whites. No significant differences were re-ported as a function of educational level. College students did not score significantly higher or lower on the SSS than those who did not attend college.

The need for sensation seeking manifests itself in the desire for novel and sometimes dangerous activities such as bungee jumping.

© Andy Belcher/ImageState/Jupiterimages

Behavioral Differences

Although some people high in measured sensation seeking enjoy activities such as mountain climbing, hang gliding, auto racing, skiing, scuba diving, and parasailing, whereas those low in sensation seeking generally do not, the behavioral differences are not always so dramatic. Some high sensation seekers do prefer a variety of activities but not necessarily dangerous ones. These people may opt for encounter groups, meditation training, and other novel experiences. Once the initial excitement has subsided, however, high sensation seekers usually discontinue the activities because they no longer provide the optimal level of stimulation.

Research showed that high sensation seekers were more likely than low sensation seekers to experiment with illicit drugs. Studies of more than 500 cocaine abusers and opiate addicts in the United States found that those who scored higher on the SSS exhibited more severe symptoms of drug abuse, including psychological impairment and the use of more than one drug, than did those who scored low on the SSS. High-scoring addicts started using drugs at an earlier age than low-scoring addicts did (Ball, Carroll, & Rounsaville, 1994; Kosten, Ball, & Rounsaville, 1994).

Research conducted with several large groups confirmed the relationship between high SSS scores and drug, alcohol, and marijuana use, as well as the behaviors of drug selling and shoplifting. The subjects in these studies included 383 African Americans (9–15 years old), 799 university students in South Africa (16–49 years old), and 360 adolescents in Norway (12–16 years old) (Hansen & Breivik, 2001; Peltzer, Malaka, & Phaswana, 2001; Stanton, Li, Cottrell, & Kaljee, 2001).

Studies on groups in the United States found that high sensation seekers were more likely to smoke cigarettes, drink alcohol, drive fast, have more car accidents and convictions for reckless or drunken driving, and engage in frequent sex. A study of African-American women ages 15–21 found that those who scored high on a measure of sexual sensation seeking reported greater sexual risk-taking behaviors such as more instances of intercourse with more partners and less use of condoms than those who scored low (Spitalnick, DiClemente, Wingood, Crosby, Milhausen, Sales, McCarty, Rose, & Younger, 2007).

In Zuckerman's research, 16 percent of the high sensation seekers reported homosexual encounters, as compared with 7 percent of low sensation seekers. Among college men, high sensation-seeking scores correlated positively with risky sexual behavior the men knew could expose them to AIDS (Zuckerman, 1994b). These findings were confirmed by research on older subjects. The correlation between sensation seeking scores and risky sexual behavior among gay men (both Blacks and Whites) was so strong that the researchers concluded that high-sensation-seeking males constitute a high-risk group for AIDS (Fisher & Misovich, 1990; Kalichman, Johnson, Adair, Rompa, Multhauf, & Kelly, 1994).

Physical risk-taking behavior has been related to sensation seeking. Skydivers, firefighters, riot-control police officers, and race-car drivers scored higher on the SSS than did groups not engaged in these activities. Research on male college undergraduate students in Israel found that high sensation seekers were more likely than low sensation seekers to participate in risky sports and to volunteer for army combat units (Hobfoll, Rom, & Segal, 1989).

Other findings describe different types of risk takers. Those identified as antisocial risk takers (drug addicts) or as adventurous risk takers (mountain climbers) showed significantly higher SSS scores than those identified as pro-social risk takers (police officers and firefighters). The researcher suggested that the motives of the pro-social group are related to factors other than thrill and adventure seeking (Levenson, 1990). High sensation seekers appear more willing than low sensation seekers to relocate from familiar to unfamiliar surroundings and to travel to exotic places, even when the journey involves physical hazards.

There are a number of other ways in which high sensation seekers behave differently from low sensation seekers. Studies in Israel showed that high sensation seekers are more likely to cross a street on foot against a stoplight. They also show a preference for so-called arousing or hot colors such as red and orange rather than pastels such as light blue (Rosenbloom, 2006a, 2006b). A study of young people in Germany, ages 14–24, found that significantly more high sensation seekers had tattoos and body piercings than did low sensation seekers (Stirn, Hinz, & Braehler, 2006). Adults in the United States who measured high in sensation seeking were found to go to the movies far more often than did low sensation seekers (Hall, 2005).

Studies of high school and college students in China demonstrated that high sensation seekers were more likely to become obsessed with computer games and Internet use (Qing-Xin, Rong-Gang, & Yan, 2005; Zheng, Ming-Yi, Chun-Li, Jing, Jing, & Xiao-Yun, 2006). Research on workers in the United States showed that high sensation seekers were much more likely to use their workplace computers for personal reasons such as sending emails, playing computer games, and viewing Web sites with sexual content (Everton, Mastrangelo, & Jolton, 2005).

A study of 233 low-level employees in the United States found that high sensation seekers scored lower on job performance than did low sensation seekers. High sensation seekers were also less likely to establish social relationships at work or to try to obtain information from co-workers or supervisors. The researchers suggested that such lower level jobs might not be sufficiently stimulating for high sensation seekers (Reio & Sanders-Reio, 2006).

Personality Differences

Zuckerman and his colleagues correlated SSS scores with measures of other personality factors. One study showed that SSS scores, particularly on disinhibition, were related to Eysenck's factor of extraversion and to the asocial tendencies associated with psychoticism. Zuckerman suggested that high sensation seekers are egocentrically extraverted, which means they are concerned with other people only as an audience or source of stimulation. They do not relate to other people in a dependent or nurturing way. High sensation-seeking scores also correlate positively with extraversion as described by Jung and measured by the Myers-Briggs Type Indicator (Morehouse, Farley, & Youngquist, 1990). However, investigations of sensation seeking and neuroticism as determined by psychological test scores showed no correlation. Zuckerman suggested that SSS scores did not point to abnormal or neurotic behavior but that neuroses such as phobias and obsessive-compulsive behaviors might be related to low sensation seeking.

High scores on the SSS correlate with a high degree of autonomy. High scorers openly express their emotions, are assertive in relating to others, are nonconforming, and are confirmed risk takers. They act independently of social conventions and of other people's needs and attitudes. Governed primarily by their own needs, they order their lives to maximize opportunities for self-fulfillment. High scores on the SSS were also positively correlated with the openness to experience and the agreeableness dimensions of the Five-Factor model of personality (Roberti, 2004).

Cognitive Processes

Additional research related sensation seeking to cognitive processes of thought, perception, and intelligence. High sensation seekers were found to recognize symbols and figures more quickly than did low sensation seekers, which suggests that high sensation seekers process information more rapidly. High sensation seekers preferred greater complexity in visual stimulation, whereas low sensation seekers preferred stability, simplicity, and symmetry. High sensation seekers can focus their attention better than low sensation seekers. This was demonstrated in a study of 108 men and women college students who listened with headsets as different stimuli were presented to each ear simultaneously. When asked to repeat the words presented in one ear and to ignore the words presented in the other ear, high sensation seekers performed significantly better than did low sensation seekers on this task (Ball & Zuckerman, 1992).

Correlations between sensation seeking and intelligence test scores are generally positive but not high. A study of 1,795 children in the island nation of Mauritius found that those who scored high in sensation seeking at age 3 scored 12 points higher on intelligence tests at age 11 than did children who scored low in sensation seeking at age 3. The results were similar for boys and for girls and were not affected by the parents' type of occupation or level of education (Raine, Reynolds, Venables, & Mednick, 2002).

Other research showed that high sensation seekers did not earn better grades in school. Zuckerman suggested that because high sensation seekers were more involved in recreational pursuits, they used less time for study. Tests of creativity and originality revealed that high sensation seekers have a greater capacity for original thinking but do not always express it in their schoolwork. High SSS scorers seem to be attracted to speculative, bizarre, pseudoscientific ideas. They tended to engage in primary-process thought (to use Freudian terminology). They may have images, dreams, and daydreams so vivid that the distinction blurs between these internal stimuli and the real world. Zuckerman suggested that because high sensation seekers continually search for novel experiences, if they cannot find them in external situations they look inward and create a fantasy world.

Occupational Preferences

Because high sensation seekers have a greater need for stimulating and varied experiences, they select different jobs than do low sensation seekers. On tests of vocational interests, such as the Kuder Preference Record, high and low sensation seekers showed significant differences. High SSS scores correlated positively with scientific interests and negatively with clerical interests. Men with high SSS scores also scored high on the Strong Vocational Interest Blank scales showing interest in the helping professions such as psychologist, physician, psychiatrist, social worker, and minister. Their scores correlated negatively with business sector jobs such as accountant, purchasing agent, and banker. Women with high SSS scores had high interest test scores for the profession of lawyer and low interest test scores for elementary school teacher, home economics teacher, and dietician. High sensation seekers of both sexes who were interested in the helping professions expressed a preference for risky, cutting-edge jobs such as crisis intervention work or paramedic duty on emergency response teams.

Attitudes

High sensation seekers were shown to be more liberal in political and religious attitudes than were low sensation seekers. Those with high SSS scores are more likely to express atheistic views rather than belief in any conventional faith. High scorers on the SSS express more permissive attitudes toward sexual behavior, whether their own or that of other people. Low sensation seekers are more likely to be frequent churchgoers. They scored high on measures of authoritarianism, which is a personality style characterized by rigid opinions and prejudiced attitudes. Low sensation seekers also show a low tolerance for ambiguity. They believe ambiguous ideas and situations are threats rather than challenges (Zuckerman, 1994a).

Physiological Differences

Zuckerman and his colleagues found that high and low sensation seekers showed different physiological responses to stimuli. High sensation seekers demonstrated stronger or more highly aroused physiological responses and higher tolerance thresholds for pain, loud noise, and other stressful stimuli (Zuckerman, 1990). Because high sensation seekers are better able to tolerate increases in arousal, Zuckerman suggested that they should cope better with stress than can low sensation seekers, who have a lower tolerance for arousal. This was confirmed in a study of 425 male and female high school varsity athletes. The students completed questionnaires assessing sensation seeking, emotional stability, coping skills, positive and negative life events, and positive and negative personal sports events such as injuries on the playing field. Low sensation seekers were found to have a significantly reduced ability to cope with stress (Smith, Ptacek, & Smoll, 1992).

In studies of high sensation seekers exposed to novel stimuli, researchers detected increases in the electrical activity of the brain and the level of sex hormones. The level of monoamine oxidase (an enzyme that controls the neurotransmitters, which produces rapid emotional swings) showed a decrease, which heightened feelings of excitement and euphoria (Zuckerman, Buchsbaum, & Murphy, 1980).

Heredity versus Environment

Research using the twin-comparison approach shows a strong hereditary basis for the sensation-seeking personality factor. A study by Eysenck suggested that 58 percent of this trait could be accounted for by genetic factors (Eysenck, 1983). A twin study conducted jointly by Zuckerman and Sybil Eysenck found an even greater genetic component (Zuckerman, 1993). Although sensation seeking is primarily inherited, Zuckerman also recognizes the influence of situational or environmental factors. One such factor is parental sensation seeking. Low-sensation-seeking parents may be overly fearful, protective, and inhibiting of their children, forbidding them to engage in adventurous behaviors. High-sensation-seeking parents may encourage and reinforce their children for engaging in unusual activities, thus promoting additional sensation-seeking behaviors.

Scores on the SSS in early studies also supported the idea that first-borns and only-borns of both sexes were higher in sensation seeking than are later-borns. Because first-borns and only-borns receive more stimulation and attention from their parents at an early age, they are likely to be exposed to a greater optimal level of stimulation, which predisposes them to sensation seeking behavior as adults (Zuckerman, 1979). However, later research conducted in England failed to find any correlation between birth order and sensation seeking (Crozier & Birdsey, 2003).

Reflections on Sensation Seeking

Zuckerman's focus on the sensation-seeking personality trait has stimulated a great deal of research. Sensation seeking has been related to a wide range of behavioral, cognitive, personality, and physiological variables. Zuckerman's emphasis on the

Table 14.3 **Self-descriptions of high and low sensation seekers**

High sensation seekers	Low sensation seekers
Enthusiastic	Frightened
Playful	Panicky
Adventurous	Tense
Elated	Nervous
Imaginative	Shaky
Daring	Fearful
Zany	Worried
Mischievous	Upset

SOURCE: From "Sensation Seeking" by M. Zuckerman. In *Dimensions of Personality* by H. London and J. E. Exner, Jr. (Eds.), 1978, New York: Wiley.

heritability of sensation seeking places his work in a different category from the behavioral and social-learning approaches to personality, which focus on the influences of situational factors and of learning.

Sensation-seeking theory has a commonsense appeal. It is easy to accept the idea that people differ in their need for excitement and risk, change and adventure. We can describe our own level of sensation seeking and make fairly accurate judgments about the levels of our friends and relatives by considering the activities they enjoy or avoid. Zuckerman asked high and low sensation seekers to choose from a list of adjectives those that best described themselves. Compare your own characteristics with the results shown in Table 14.3.

Martin E. P. Seligman: Learned Helplessness and the Optimistic/Pessimistic Explanatory Style

learned helplessness
A condition resulting from the perception that we have no control over our environment.

In the mid-1960s, psychologist Martin Seligman (1943–) at the University of Pennsylvania began research on a limited-domain aspect of personality he calls **learned helplessness**. He observed this phenomenon in a laboratory experiment on dogs on his first day as a graduate student. The dogs were subjects in a two-part conditioning experiment. In the first part, they were being conditioned to associate a high-pitched sound with an electric shock. This was a simple Pavlovian classical conditioning situation involving respondent behavior (the pairing of the tone with the shock).

In the second part of the experiment, the dogs were put individually in a large box that contained two compartments divided by a low wall. A shock was delivered through the floor of the compartment in which the dog was placed. To escape the shock, the dog needed to emit the appropriate operant behavior—simply to jump over the low barrier into the other compartment where there was no electric shock. Once the dogs learned to jump the wall—something dogs can be expected to do quickly—they would be tested to see if the high-pitched tone without the electric shock would bring about the same response. The experiment's goal was to determine whether learning in the first situation (pairing the tone with the shock) carried over to the second situation (pairing the tone with the escape behavior).

The research did not work out the way it was planned. The dogs did not cross the barrier to escape the shock. Instead, when the shock was administered through the floor of their compartment, they lay down, whimpered, and made no effort to escape. The experimenters were baffled, but Seligman thought he had a clue. He suggested that during the first part of the experiment, the dogs had learned that they were helpless. When the tone sounded, there was nothing they could do to avoid the paired shock. Why even try? This learned reaction apparently generalized to the second part of the experiment, even though a means of escape was available. Seligman wrote,

> I was stunned by the implications. If dogs could learn something as complex as the futility of their actions, here was an analogy to human helplessness, one that could be studied in the laboratory. Helplessness was all around us—from the urban poor to the newborn child to the despondent patient with his face to the wall. Was this a laboratory model of human helplessness, one that could be used to understand how it comes about, how to cure it, how to prevent it, what drugs worked on it, and who was particularly vulnerable to it? (1990, p. 20)

Determined to find the answers to these questions, Seligman launched an intensive research program on learned helplessness, a condition he described as resulting from the perception that we have no control over our environment, that there is nothing we can do to change our circumstances. Later, Seligman expanded his research interests to include the larger personality issue of optimism versus pessimism.

Early Research

In Seligman's initial experiments, dogs were harnessed and exposed to painful, though not physically harmful, electric shock. There was no action the dogs could take to escape or avoid the shock. After a series of shocks, the dogs were placed in a two-compartment shuttle box. As in the first experiment Seligman had witnessed, a shock was administered through the floor of the compartment in which the dogs had been placed. The behavior of these dogs was then compared with that of a control group of dogs that had not been exposed to the first series of electric shocks.

When the dogs in the control group were placed in the box and given the shock through the floor, they raced about the compartment until they accidentally leaped the barrier into the safe compartment. On succeeding trials, they jumped the barrier more quickly each time, having learned that this was the way to escape. The dogs in the experimental group, who had received electric shocks before being placed in the shuttle box, behaved differently. After getting the shock through the compartment floor, they raced around for about 30 seconds and then gave up, dropping to the floor and whimpering. They never learned to escape, not even when experimenters tried to entice them over the barrier with food. These dogs had become passive and helpless and could make no attempt to alter their situation (Overmier & Seligman, 1967; Seligman & Maier, 1967).

Learned helplessness was similarly demonstrated in humans. In one study, subjects in the experimental group were exposed to a loud, irritating noise and told they could turn it off if they pressed a series of buttons in the correct sequence.

The conditions were arranged so that there was no correct sequence. No matter what action the subjects took, the noise continued. In the control group, the subjects could turn off the noise by pressing buttons in a sequence that was relatively easy to learn. In the next step, the experimental subjects were placed in a situation in which all they had to do to stop the noise was move their hand from one side of a box to the other in response to a light signal. Control-group subjects rapidly learned this series of behaviors but experimental-group subjects did not. They sat passively, making no effort to turn off the irritating noise (Hiroto, 1974).

Other studies with human subjects confirmed and extended these findings. Learned helplessness was found to occur after subjects observed helpless models, especially when the subjects recognized similarities between themselves and the models. The experimenters suggested that the subjects were saying, in effect, "If the models can't do anything about this, neither can I."

A meta-analysis of 132 studies involving several thousand subjects found that the effects of inescapable shock were even stronger in human than in animal subjects. Learned helplessness effects have been found in adult men and women, college students, adolescents, children, elderly persons, and patients in psychiatric hospitals (see, for example, Villanova & Peterson, 1991).

It has also been suggested that learned helplessness may occur in everyday life in situations where we are subjected to continuous intrusive stimuli such as noise over which we have no control (see, for example, Evans & Stecker, 2004; Rabinowitz, 2005).

Learned Helplessness in Elderly Persons

Applying the concept of learned helplessness to a real-world situation, psychologists investigated whether elderly residents of nursing homes, residing in a setting in which they had little control or choice, might learn to be helpless (Langer & Rodin, 1976). The researchers designed an experiment to determine whether offering nursing home residents greater control would affect their feelings of lethargy and their lack of motivation and activity. Perhaps the common listlessness stemmed from ceding control to the nursing home staff and from learning that their own behaviors and wishes had little effect on their living conditions.

Residents of one floor in the facility were given the opportunity to make decisions about their daily lives—for example, choosing what they wanted for breakfast, caring for the plants in their room, arranging their furniture. They were told that they would assume more responsibility for their care and make many decisions formerly controlled by the staff. Residents of the other floor of the nursing home remained under the authority of the staff. Their quarters, food, and recreational activities were identical to those on the experimental floor, but they had no personal influence or responsibility.

Behavioral differences became apparent within a few weeks. Residents who had been given a degree of personal control were happier and more physically active. They spent more time in social activities and less time alone in their room. The nursing staff reported that 93 percent of these residents showed enhanced social and emotional adjustment. Of the residents living under the old system, with no increase in personal control, only 21 percent showed positive changes. A follow-up visit 18 months later confirmed that the differences persisted. Also, of the residents given personal responsibility, 15 percent had died since the beginning of the study; in the more helpless group, 30 percent had died (Baltes & Bates, 1986).

Learned Helplessness and Emotional Health

The beneficial effects on psychological health of having control over one's life have been widely documented. For example, researchers studied 71 men and women cancer patients, ages 29 to 80. They interviewed the patients and gave questionnaires to assess marital satisfaction, psychological adjustment, and perception of control. Patients with the highest perception of control were better adjusted than patients who believed they had little control over their situation. This finding held even for patients severely debilitated by their physical condition. People who believed they could exert some influence over their illness and their emotions showed greater psychological adjustment than did people in better physical condition but with a low perception of control (Thompson, Sobolew-Shubin, Galbraith, Schwankovsky, & Cruzen, 1993).

Another study found that it was possible for people to learn to increase their feeling of control. A sample of 110 men and women (average age 55) scheduled for extensive dental work were assessed prior to treatment for their level of anxiety and their desire for control in a dental setting. Half the patients were shown a stress inoculation training video; the other half, the control group, was shown a video about the local sights. The results showed that patients with low control in a dental setting but with a strong desire for greater control benefited the most from seeing the stress training video. They believed they felt more control and less pain during the actual treatment than did similar patients in the control group who had received no stress training (Law, Logan, & Baron, 1994).

Animal Research on Learned Helplessness and Health

The results of the nursing home study raised the possibility that learned helplessness could affect physical health. To test this hypothesis, Seligman and his associates designed a study in which rats were injected with malignant tumor cells. The rats were exposed to one of three conditions: an electric shock from which they could escape, a shock from which they could not escape, and no shock (Visintainer, Volpicelli, & Seligman, 1982). Under normal circumstances, based on the number of cells injected, half the rats would be expected to reject the cells and survive. In the control group (no electric shock), 50 percent rejected the tumor as expected. Among the rats that received a shock but could escape, thus having some control over their situation, 70 percent rejected the tumor and survived. But in the learned helplessness group that could not escape the shock, only 27 percent of the rats rejected the malignant cells and survived.

These results were supported in a similar study of young rats. When the rats reached adulthood, they received injections of malignant cells and were exposed to the same three experimental conditions. The majority of the rats who had learned to be helpless when young failed as adults to reject the tumor. In contrast, the majority of the rats who had learned control when young rejected the tumor as adults (Seligman & Visintainer, 1985). Seligman concluded, "Childhood experiences proved to be crucial in tumor rejection by adults. Childhood mastery immunized, and early helplessness put adult rats at risk for cancer" (1990, p. 170).

Learned helplessness was also shown to weaken the rats' immune system (Maier, Laudenslager, & Ryan, 1985). The immune system forms a major part of the body's defense against illness. It contains several kinds of cells, including T-cells and NK (natural killer) cells, which resist viruses, bacteria, and tumor cells. In rats subjected to inescapable shock, T-cells no longer multiplied rapidly in response to specific invaders, and NK cells lost their ability to destroy other infections. These findings may provide a physiological explanation for the result that the helpless rats were unable to reject their tumor.

Explanatory Style: Optimism and Pessimism

Seligman later expanded his theory to encompass the factor of optimism versus pessimism. He argued that it is not only the lack of control under conditions of learned helplessness that affects our health. Also important is how we explain this lack of control to ourselves. He proposed the concept of explanatory style to account for this factor. An **optimistic explanatory style** prevents helplessness; a **pessimistic explanatory style** spreads helplessness to all facets of life.

explanatory style
A way of explaining to ourselves our relative lack of control over our environment. An optimistic explanatory style can prevent learned helplessness; a pessimistic explanatory style spreads helplessness to all facets of life.

You already know from your own experience the basic difference between optimists and pessimists. Put simply, "optimists are people who expect good things to happen to them; pessimists are people who expect bad things to happen to them" (Carver & Scheier, 2002, p. 231). According to Seligman, people with an optimistic explanatory style tend to be healthier than are people with a pessimistic explanatory style. Pessimists tend to believe that their actions are of little consequence. For this reason, they are unlikely to try to prevent illness by changing their behavior with regard to smoking, diet and exercise, or timely medical attention. A study of 72 young adults found that optimistic people were less likely than pessimistic people were to get sick. However, when optimists did fall ill, they were far more likely to take responsibility for their care, such as resting, consulting a physician, or drinking appropriate fluids (Peterson, Maier, & Seligman, 1993).

In another investigation of explanatory style and physical health, researchers found that among college undergraduates, pessimists had twice as many infectious illnesses over a 1-year period than did optimists. Among breast cancer patients experiencing a recurrence, the optimists lived longer over a 5-year period of study, independent of the severity of their illness. Optimists were also shown to develop stronger immune systems and to be more likely to recover from heart attacks (Peterson & Seligman, 1987; Peterson, Maier, & Seligman, 1993).

A study of 105 first-semester law school students found that those who scored high for an optimistic explanatory style had a significantly greater number of T-cells and NK cells, which protect against infections, than did those who scored low on optimism (Segerstrom & Taylor, 1998). Research on 100 adult men and women ages 30 to 45 found that those who scored high for a pessimistic explanatory style held more negative beliefs about their life and had higher blood pressure readings than did those who scored low on pessimism (Räikkönen, Matthews, Flory, Owens, & Gump, 1999).

The health of a group of 200 men was monitored from age 25 to their late 60s (Peterson, Seligman, & Vaillant, 1988). At the beginning of the study, the subjects wrote essays that were analyzed for themes indicating an optimistic or a pessimistic explanatory style. The men were interviewed periodically and given questionnaires about life events. Every 5 years they were given a physical exam. No differences in health were reported up to age 45. By age 60, however, it was clear that the optimists were in far better health than were the pessimists. Those subjects with an optimistic explanatory style evidenced fewer and less severe symptoms of the diseases of middle age than did the pessimists.

Optimists might also live longer than pessimists. A long-range study of 180 nuns in the United States found that those who displayed optimism in the life stories they were asked to write while in their early 20s had a significantly lower death rate when they were surveyed 60 years later than did those who displayed pessimism in their early writings (Danner, Snowdon, & Friesen, 2001). A study of 839 patients under treatment for a variety of medical conditions showed that the optimists had 19 percent greater longevity than the pessimists when both groups were surveyed 30 years later (Maruta, Colligan, Malinchoc, & Offord, 2000). A study of 128 elderly men and women in England found that those who scored high in optimism were in far better physical health than were those who scored low (Steptoe, Wright, Kunz-Ebrecht, & Lliffe, 2006).

Optimism has also been shown to be beneficial in coping with AIDS. In a study of 550 homosexual and bisexual men, some were diagnosed as HIV-negative and others as HIV-positive and thus likely to develop AIDS. The men were given questionnaires to assess their degree of optimism or pessimism as well as psychological adjustment, feeling of control, and concern about the disease. Those who scored high on optimism scored lower on psychological distress, had fewer worries about illness, believed they were at lower risk for developing AIDS, and believed they would have a higher degree of control over the disease than did those who scored low on optimism. Those who were already HIV-positive were found to be more optimistic about not developing AIDS than were those who were HIV-negative. The researchers explained,

> They believe that they are safe from AIDS because they have probably developed an immunity. They believe that they can eliminate the virus from their system and that their immune systems are better able to accomplish this than those of other gay men. They believe that staying healthy and in good physical condition can prevent the development of AIDS. (Taylor, Kemeny, Aspinwall, Schneider, Rodriguez, & Herbert, 1992, p. 469)

Although such beliefs may be illusory, they also helped the subjects cope with a serious health threat and minimize the depression that accompanies a major illness. Further, the men highest in optimism were no more likely to engage in high-risk sexual behaviors than were those lowest in optimism. In general, those highest in optimism took better care of their health.

Among a group of 165 women in Norway diagnosed with breast cancer those who scored high on pessimism were far more likely to be anxious and depressed one year following treatment than were those who scored low on pessimism (Schou, Ekeberg, Ruland, Sandvik, & Karesen, 2004). Another study of these same women found that their levels of optimism and pessimism remained stable for the year following treatment regardless of whether their prognosis was favorable or unfavorable (Schou, Ekeberg, Sandvik, & Ruland, 2005). A study of more than 5,000 adults in Finland found that those who scored high in optimism recovered a positive attitude more quickly following the severe illness or death of a family member than did those low in optimism (Kivimaki, Vahtera, Elovainio, Helenius, Singh-Manoux, & Pentti, 2005).

A study of 280 adults in the United States found that older subjects had more optimistic explanatory styles and scored higher in subjective well-being than did younger subjects. Research on elderly people in China also showed that those who were more optimistic reported greater subjective well-being (Isaacowitz, 2005a, 2005b; Leung, Moneta, & McBride-Chang, 2005).

Optimism has been found to vary with the intensity of one's religious beliefs. Members of fundamentalist Jewish, Muslim, and Calvinist faiths scored higher on measures of optimism than did more moderate religious groups such as Conservative Jews, Lutherans, and Methodists. Similarly, the moderate group scored higher on optimism than did members of more liberal faiths such as Reform Jews and Unitarians. The researchers suggested that the greater optimism among fundamentalists was its association with "more hopefulness and less hopelessness. Fundamentalism is also associated with less personal blame for negative events" (Sethi & Seligman, 1994, p. 58).

Cultural differences in explanatory style have been investigated. Optimism-pessimism measures were taken from 257 college students in the United States, 312 college students in China, and 44 college students of Chinese-American heritage. It was found that the American subjects were more optimistic than were the Chinese Americans, and that the Chinese Americans were more optimistic than were the mainland Chinese (Lee & Seligman, 1997). College students in Kuwait scored significantly lower on optimism than did college students in the United States (Abdel-Khalek & Lester, 2006). A study of 348 college students in Italy found that men demonstrated more optimism than did women (Colombo, Balbo, & Baruffi, 2006).

A comparison of college students in the United States and Japan found that Japanese students were more pessimistic than were American students. The American students were far more likely to predict that positive events would happen to them rather than to other people. In contrast, the Japanese students believed that positive events were much more likely to happen to other people (Chang, Asakawa, & Sanna, 2001).

Not surprisingly, research has shown that stressful life experiences can affect one's level of optimism. A group of adult subjects who were primary caregivers for relatives with Alzheimer's disease were compared on measures of optimism-pessimism with a group of adults who were not acting as caregivers. The caregivers grew increasingly pessimistic over a 4-year period and experienced greater anxiety, stress, and physical health complaints (Robinson-Whelen, Kim, MacCallum, & Kiecolt-Glaser, 1997).

A study of 89 college students showed that those who scored higher on optimism at the beginning of their first semester experienced significantly less stress and depression during that semester than did those who scored lower on optimism (Brissette, Scheier, & Carver, 2002). Similarly, a study of 237 middle-aged adults found that those who scored high in optimism reported fewer symptoms of depression than those who scored high in pessimism (Chang & Sanna, 2001). Research on 204 children from 3rd to 6th grade found that those highest in optimism had fewer symptoms of depression and fewer behavioral problems than children low in optimism (Ey, Hadley, Allen, Palmer, Klosky, Deptula, Thomas, & Cohen, 2005).

Research conducted on 639 college students in the United States found that, in general, optimists earned better grades than pessimists. This was also found in a study of 400 men and women college students in Kuwait; optimists earned higher grades (El-Anzi, 2005). In addition, when pessimists received lower grades than their peers, they reported greater feelings of depression than did optimists who received lower grades than their peers (Gibbons, Blanton, Gerrard, Buunk, & Eggleston, 2000).

Optimism has even been shown to affect how well a person can dribble a basketball, at least in France. When 14- to 16-year-old boys and girls were led to believe that they had failed a dribbling test, those who had scored high in optimism were less anxious, more confident, and performed better in a second test than those high in pessimism (Martin-Krumm, Sarrazin, Peterson, & Famose, 2003).

Optimism and pessimism may also affect our cognitive functioning. This was demonstrated in research on college student responses to positive and negative stimuli. Students who scored high on pessimism were more likely to pay attention to negative stimuli; students who scored high on optimism attended to both positive and negative stimuli (Segerstrom, 2001). A study of more than 600 college students in Germany found that optimists were flexible and adaptable in their cognitive activities whereas pessimists were more often inflexible, rigid, and likely to give up in the pursuit of their goals (Weber, Vollmann, & Renner, 2007).

There is some suggestion that an optimistic explanatory style may not always be of value (see, for example, Schneider, 2001). Some optimists may hold unrealistic views about their vulnerability to the effects of their behavior. For example, they may overindulge in cigarette smoking, drinking, or drug use and tell themselves that such behaviors cannot harm them because their attitude is so positive, despite evidence to the contrary.

Research on college students who were gambling at a casino near their university showed that the optimists among them were far more likely to continue gambling in the face of consistent losses whereas the pessimists were more likely to stop. The researchers concluded that the optimists maintained their positive expectations about winning even during a losing streak (Gibson & Sanbonmatsu, 2004). This type of unrealistic optimism—the belief that good things are much more likely to happen to oneself than to others—is more widespread in individualistic cultures such as the United States than in collectivist cultures such as China, and is more prevalent among men than women (see, for example, Lin & Raghubir, 2005).

On the other hand, unrealistic pessimism in the face of adversity, such as a serious illness, may also be harmful. Telling yourself that you will never be able to cope or overcome the situation (thus exhibiting low self-efficacy) may lead to a lack of effort and, thus, a lack of success (see Blanton, Axsom, McClive, & Price, 2001).

People who are severely depressed believe they are helpless. They generalize their failure in one situation, such as a poor grade in one course, to all other aspects of life.

© Arthur Tress/Photo Researchers, Inc.

Depression

Seligman's research program revealed an association between learned helplessness and depression. A major symptom of depression is the feeling of being unable to control life events. Seligman referred to depression as the "ultimate pessimism." People who are severely depressed believe they are helpless. They see little point in trying to do anything because they do not expect that anything will work out well for them. Seligman observed several similarities between the symptoms of depression and the characteristics of learned helplessness (Seligman, 1990).

All of us experience occasional feelings of helplessness when we fail in some situation or when family or job pressures seem overwhelming. No matter how unhappy or angry we may feel at the moment, however, most people usually recover after a period of time. But some people do not recover quickly or easily. They may generalize their failure in one activity (say, earning a poor grade or failing to get a promotion) to other areas of life and to their personal sense of self-worth. Consequently, they can become helpless and depressed in all situations and lose their impetus to strive.

As you can see from Table 14.4, depression is associated with symptoms of poor health such as ulcers, stress, and norepinephrine deficiency. Depression also puts people at risk for physical illness by reducing the effectiveness of the immune system, suppressing NK cell activity and altering white blood cell count, findings confirmed by more than 40 studies over a 10-year period (Herbert & Cohen, 1993; Weisse, 1992).

According to Seligman, the important difference between people who recover from temporary depression and those who do not is their explanatory style. "A pessimistic explanatory style changes learned helplessness from brief and local to long-lasting

Table 14.4 **Similarity of symptoms of learned helplessness and depression**

Learned helplessness	Depression
Passivity	Passivity
Difficulty learning that responses produce relief	Difficulty learning that responses produce outcomes
Lack of aggression	Introjected hostility
Weight loss and anorexia	Loss of libido
Norepinephrine depletion*	Norepinephrine depletion
Ulcers and stress	Ulcers and stress, feelings of helplessness

*Norepinephrine acts as a neurotransmitter; severe depression is associated with norepinephrine deficiency.
SOURCE: Adapted from *Learned Helplessness and Depression in Animals and Men*, by M. E. P. Seligman. Copyright © 1976 by General Learning Press, Morristown, NJ.

and general," he wrote. "Learned helplessness becomes full-blown depression when the person who fails is a pessimist. In optimists, a failure produces only brief demoralization" (1990, p. 76). In addition, pessimists formulate explanations about negative situations in personal and pervasive terms, saying, for example, "It's all my fault," "It's always going to be this way," or "It's going to affect every aspect of my life."

Seligman's research on his undergraduate students supports the hypothesis that learned helplessness leads to depression in people with a pessimistic explanatory style. At the beginning of the semester, students were tested to determine their explanatory style and were asked to state the course grade they believed would represent personal failure. After the midterm exam, the students took a personality test to measure their level of depression. The results showed that 30 percent of those with an optimistic explanatory style and who received grades they considered a personal failure showed symptoms of depression. Among those with a pessimistic explanatory style who received disappointing grades, 70 percent became depressed. Similar results were found in other research with college students and in studies of third-grade elementary school students. In both cases, explanatory style predicted the incidence of depression (Nolen-Hoeksema, Girgus, & Seligman, 1987; Zullow & Seligman, 1985).

The Attribution Model

The concept of explanatory style describes how people differ in the way they explain to themselves their feelings of learned helplessness or lack of control. Some people are devastated by learned helplessness. They appear to give up, become depressed, and experience health problems. Others facing similar situations recover after a period of time. Seligman proposed a cognitive explanation for these differences, a revised concept of learned helplessness called the **attribution model**. The key word is *attribution*. When we fail at something, we attribute that failure to some cause. This is how we explain to ourselves the source of our failure and our lack of control.

Seligman suggested that pessimists attribute personal failure to internal, stable, and global causes whereas optimists attribute failure to external, unstable, and

attribution model
The idea that we attribute our lack of control or failure to some cause.

specific causes. For example, if you fail a course and make an *internal attribution*, you are saying there is something wrong with you. Maybe you are not smart enough to pass. If you make an *external attribution*, you are saying that the cause lies elsewhere. Maybe the professor doesn't like you or your job doesn't leave you enough time to study.

If the cause of your failure cannot be changed, it is considered *stable*. If it can be modified, such as reducing your work hours so you have more time to study, it is considered *unstable*. If you make a *global* attribution, you are saying that whatever caused you to fail that course is likely to cause you to fail other courses. By making a *specific* attribution you are limiting your failure to one course. That failure does not transfer to other courses of study or areas of life.

Seligman and his colleagues developed a test to measure explanatory or attributional style (Peterson, Semmel, Von Baeyer, Abramson, Metalsky, & Seligman, 1982). The Attributional Style Questionnaire (ASQ) presents 12 hypothetical situations. Six are positive events, such as becoming wealthy, and six are negative events, such as a disappointing social experience. Some events deal with achievement in school or on the job; other events involve getting along with people. When you take the test, you are asked to suggest a cause for each situation and to rate that cause on the three dimensions: internal versus external, stable versus unstable, and global versus specific.

In one study, the ASQ was given to first-year college students who had experienced negative events. Students who made internal, stable, and global attributions for their situations (the pessimistic style) received lower grades in their courses than those who made external, unstable, and specific attributions (the optimistic style) (Peterson & Barrett, 1987). Because both groups were of similar intelligence, that was not a factor in explaining the difference in grades. The researchers concluded that the pessimists responded to negative events and problems passively and made few attempts to alter their circumstances.

Research on college students in Canada found that those who had a stable and global attributional style for negative events also showed symptoms of hopelessness and depression (Sturman, Mongrain, & Kohn, 2006). Among college students in China, those with an external attributional approach scored higher on a measure of subjective well-being than did those with making internal attributions (Yu & Shu-hua, 2005).

The Development of Learned Helplessness in Childhood

Although learned helplessness can occur throughout life, Seligman believes we are particularly vulnerable to those feelings in infancy and early childhood. During these formative years the experience of learned helplessness can predispose us to the pessimistic explanatory style (Seligman, 1975). Infants begin life in a state of total helplessness, with no control over their environment. As they mature, they become increasingly able to exercise control. They can cry, which brings parents or caregivers to tend to their needs. They can crawl, walk, and speak, and the mastery of each skill brings greater possibilities for control—and for failure. Through these early interactions with the physical and social environments, a child's sense of helplessness, or of mastery and control, will be determined.

When infants make a response, that activity may lead to some change in their environment, such as food, a toy, or a hug or it may have no effect whatever. At a primitive level, infants form associations between responses and outcomes. If the responses do not lead to successful outcomes, the result is the condition of learned helplessness. Infants learn that particular responses don't work, and they may generalize this idea to other responses, believing that none of them will work. This generalized learned helplessness accompanies a sense of having no control over life. In contrast, a high correlation between responses and outcomes provides positive feedback that leads to feelings of mastery and control. A consistent explanatory style develops by about age 8 and is strongly affected by the parents' explanatory style. Seligman remarked, "pessimistic parents also have pessimistic children" (Peterson, Maier, & Seligman, 1993, p. 293). However, it is important to note that research on more than 1,300 twins and non-twin sibling adolescents found that their attributional style was influenced by *both* genetic factors and by learning (Lau, Rijsdijk, & Eley, 2006).

Learned helplessness can also develop later in childhood in response to brutality from peers, a harsh school environment, or other negative experiences. Race and poverty are also factors in the development of learned helplessness. Students who are treated by teachers and peers as though they are less intelligent or skilled than other students may develop learned helplessness.

Reflections on Learned Helplessness

The concepts of learned helplessness and optimism-versus-pessimism have generated hundreds of research studies. Seligman and his associates have applied the concepts to sports, politics, religion, child rearing, and job performance. However, some critics suggest that there is little difference between learned helplessness and Rotter's concept of external locus of control. Both appear to express the idea that there are some people who believe there is little they can do to influence their lives and therefore cease to try. Seligman admits the two concepts overlap but sees an important distinction.

> The difference is that locus of control is a belief about the nature of reinforcement—that is, about rewards and punishments in the world. Causal attributions are judgments about the causes of events. Although related, these are not the same. (Peterson, Maier, & Seligman, 1993, p. 145)

The learned helplessness limited-domain theory of personality leaves several questions unanswered. For example, does a person's explanatory style cause depression, or does depression cause a particular explanatory style? Is the effect of prolonged failure on self-esteem more important than its relationship to learned helplessness? Is the Attributional Style Questionnaire used to measure explanatory style truly valid?

Overall, a large, impressive body of data supports the learned helplessness concept. Seligman has lately turned his attention to a related idea called learned optimism. He has developed a program of exercises to teach optimism to adults and to children, thus applying his findings beyond the laboratory to the home and the workplace. Let us now turn to Seligman's latest extension of this work, the idea of a positive psychology and the factors that influence our subjective well-being. In other words, what makes us happy?

Positive Psychology

Positive psychology was advanced in the late 1990s by Seligman during his term as president of the American Psychological Association. Positive psychology deals with happiness, excellence, and optimal human functioning. He criticized older approaches to personality that ignored human strengths and virtues, focusing instead on abnormalities, defensiveness, weaknesses, and negative motivations—on what's wrong with people rather than on what's good. Does this emphasis on the positive sound familiar to you? Yes, it is what Maslow and other humanistic psychologists were calling for decades ago. There is, however, an important difference between humanistic psychology and positive psychology. Instead of using the highly subjective approach Maslow adopted in his study of self-actualizing people, positive psychology relies on rigorous experimental research.

What can positive psychology tell us about the happy personality? You know from your own experience that some people you meet are more optimistic, open, and full of energy and vitality than are others. What causes them to be this way even when you know they are facing social or job or financial problems? Even if you are not one of these joyful people, we hope you have at least known temporary periods of happiness, when you have fallen in love, aced a tough exam, or gotten the job you really wanted, making you feel on top of the world.

Psychologists have variously labeled the happy personality in terms such as *subjective well-being* or *life satisfaction* and define it as encompassing a cognitive evaluation of the quality of one's life experience and the possession of positive affect (McGregor & Little, 1998). (The word *affect* refers to moods and emotions.) Thus, happiness has both rational and emotional aspects.

Who are these happy personalities? As you might expect, research has uncovered a variety of factors that can influence our happiness. Is money, or financial stability, the first one you thought of? It turns out that the old adage is true; money does not buy happiness. However, the absence of money can lead to unhappiness. Research shows that an income adequate to fund basic needs is a necessary, though not sufficient, prerequisite for happiness. Surveys show that people who lack the money to provide for essentials are unhappy, but having money significantly beyond what is actually needed has little measurable effect on happiness. Even winning a huge amount in a lottery usually results in only a temporary increase in subjective well-being (DeNeve & Cooper, 1998; Diener, Suh, Lucas, & Smith, 1999; King & Napa, 1998).

So if you think all you need to be happy is a bigger house or a flashier car, think again. Surveys show consistently that more and expensive possessions do not guarantee happiness. One researcher concluded: "The more people endorse materialistic goals, the less happy and satisfied they are with life" (Van Boven, 2005, p. 133). Other research has shown that high-income people tend to experience greater stress and to devote less of their time to relaxation and leisure activities than those with lower incomes (Kahneman, Krueger, Schkade, Schwartz, & Stone, 2006).

Is health related to happiness? Like money, the absence of good health can diminish happiness but being healthy does not necessarily mean a happy personality. Thus, health appears to be a necessary but not sufficient condition for subjective well-being. Age and gender generally have little bearing on happiness. Studies show that life satisfaction does not decline with age and that men and women do not differ significantly in reported subjective well-being (Diener, Suh, Lucas, & Smith, 1999; DeNeve & Cooper, 1998; Myers, 2000).

However, the relationship between age and happiness is inconsistent. Some studies suggest that happiness improves with age; others fail to support that connection. Among adolescents, many are not happy but those who are have certain factors in common. For example, studies of teenagers in the United States have found that the ones who score high in subjective well-being are far more likely to have parents who value them, show interest in them, and express concern about their future. This relationship appears to be stronger for girls than for boys (Rayle, 2005).

Adolescents who measured high in life satisfaction had more positive relationships with peers and parents, reported lower levels of anxiety and depression, and had greater hope for the future. They also expressed a feeling of greater personal control over their life than did adolescents scoring low in life satisfaction (Gilman & Huebner, 2006). Teenagers in China who scored high in subjective well-being had better educated parents who rarely quarreled than did teenagers who scored low (Guo-Xing & Hai, 2006).

As we noted, some studies of older people suggest that happiness does not decline with advancing age. When two groups of subjects were compared—one with an average age of 31, the other 68—the results showed that happiness increased with age (Lacey, Smith, & Ubel, 2006). Another study suggested that happiness peaks at age 65 and decreases thereafter (Mroczek & Spiro, 2005).

Research on more than 3,000 managers in the United States (ages 25 to 74) found a strong positive relationship between life satisfaction and an orientation toward the future (which includes actively planning for the future). That relationship was greater for older managers than for younger managers (Prenda & Lachman, 2001).

A study of older adults in Germany (ages 70–103) supports the research showing that old age, by itself, is not a cause of decline in subjective well-being. In this study, however, people who experienced health problems and physical limitations in old age did suffer a decline in subjective well-being (Kunzmann, Little, & Smith, 2000). Another study on older Germans who were hospitalized with various disabilities found that it was not the physical impairment that lowered feelings of subjective well-being as much as the person's attitude toward the infirmity. People with more positive attitudes scored higher in subjective well-being than those who expressed negative attitudes (Schneider, Driesch, Kruse, Nehen, & Heuft, 2006).

Research with elderly subjects in Slovakia also demonstrated the relationship between attitude and happiness. Those who scored high in what the researchers called "a belief in a just world" reported greater happiness than those who did not subscribe to such a belief (Dzuka & Dalbert, 2006).

Physical exercise is an important component of subjective well-being in older people. An analysis of 36 studies revealed that both aerobic exercise and resistance or strength training showed a strong positive correlation with happiness (Netz, Wu, Becker, & Tenenbaum, 2005).

A meta-analysis of 286 studies of older people also confirmed the idea that subjective well-being does not automatically decline with age. The elderly subjects in these studies reported levels of life satisfaction, well-being, and happiness that were as high as those of younger people. However, older people who had stronger social networks and supportive friends reported higher levels of happiness than did those who were more socially isolated (Pinquart & Soerensen, 2000).

If social support is important for subjective well-being in old age, does it follow that older persons who are married are happier than those who are not? Yes. The evidence is clear from research conducted in more than 40 countries, involving some 60,000 people, that married people report higher levels of happiness than do people who are divorced, separated, widowed, or who have never married (Diener, Gohm, Suh, & Oishi, 2000). Married women have been found to be happier than unmarried women, and married men are happier than unmarried men (Mastekaasa, 1995).

Social support in general correlates highly with subjective well-being in most of the Western cultures in which it has been studied. For example, research in Israel found that life satisfaction was higher in people with strong social support networks, and that this was particularly important for new immigrants (Litwin, 2005). Studies in Finland showed that among recent immigrants, active social support was critical to their psychological well-being (Jasinskaja-Lahti, Liebkind, Jaakkola, & Reuter, 2006).

Studies in more collectivist Eastern cultures such as China and Turkey revealed little or no relationship between social support and subjective well-being (Dan, Jun, & Ji-Liang, 2006; Turkum, 2005). Research with college students in Turkey found that the chance to provide social support to other people was significantly related to psychological well-being but receiving social support from others had no effect on psychological well-being (Gencoz & Ozlale, 2004).

Happiness appears to vary across cultures, with a nation's relative wealth being of major importance. Countries marked by such poverty that satisfying basic needs is difficult have much lower reported levels of happiness among the population than do more economically advanced countries (Diener, Diener, & Diener, 1995; Veenhoven, 2005). Evidence also suggests that subjective well-being is markedly higher in individualistic societies such as the United States than in collectivist or group-oriented cultures such as China (Diener, Suh, Smith, & Shao, 1995). For example, a comparison between 472 Korean and 432 American adolescents showed that the Koreans reported lower overall life satisfaction. They were also less satisfied with their families, friends, schools, and environment than were the U.S. teenagers (Park & Huebner, 2005).

In related research it has been found that descendants of immigrants from other cultures tend to reflect the level of subjective well-being characteristic of those cultures, even in the absence of direct contact. A study of several thousand Americans who had immediate ancestors from other countries found that their level of happiness corresponded to that of the nation of origin of their ancestors. For example, people in Denmark and in Sweden reported high subjective well-being, as did Americans whose ancestors came from these countries. Americans whose ancestors came from cultures with lower levels of subjective well-being, such as Hungary and Lithuania, had similar levels of subjective well-being. The researchers noted that:

> different cultures seem to produce people with different levels of subjective well-being. . . . The socialization agents most responsible for the transmission of subjective well-being across time to space are probably the family and other social networks. (Rice & Steele, 2004, pp. 641, 643).

The characteristics of subjective well-being also vary among regions of the same country. A nationwide survey of 3,485 Americans ages 25 to 75 found different criteria for happiness in various sectors of the country (Plaut, Markus, & Lachman, 2002). For example, people in New England included physical well-being, autonomy, and not feeling constrained as necessary conditions for subjective well-being. People in western south-central states (Texas, Oklahoma, Arkansas, and Louisiana) showed a greater concern with personal growth and feelings of cheerfulness and happiness as criteria for subjective well-being. People in eastern south-central states (Kentucky, Tennessee, Mississippi, and Alabama) focused more on social responsibility and contributing to the welfare and well-being of others as necessary for their own feelings of subjective well-being and happiness. Consistencies throughout the country were also found. Overall, subjective well-being was typified by feelings of autonomy and being in control, by a sense of purpose, and by an absence of negative emotions such as pessimism.

The impact of race was suggested by a study of 312 African-American adults asked to rate their life satisfaction. Those who had experienced discrimination reported lower levels of life satisfaction than did those who had experienced no discrimination. Those who attended predominantly White schools had higher life satisfaction levels than those who went to predominantly Black or mixed-race schools (Broman, 1997). A study of 127 older African-American adults (ages 55 to 93) also found lower levels of life satisfaction among those who reported the stress of racial discrimination (Utsey, Payne, Jackson, & Jones, 2002).

Similar results were found in a study of 135 African-American college students. Those who reported higher levels of perceived racial discrimination had lower levels of life satisfaction as well as more symptoms of depression (Prelow, Mosher, & Bowman, 2006).

Research on 240 African-American students attending college in Kansas found that those who felt a greater sense of identification with and acceptance by the Black community at their college reported higher levels of psychological well-being than did those who felt less of an identification with and acceptance by fellow African Americans (Postmes & Branscombe, 2002).

Considerable research has been conducted on the personality correlates of the happy personality, particularly the facets of the five-factor model. For example, several studies note that people who score low on neuroticism and high on extraversion and conscientiousness report high levels of subjective well-being (DeNeve & Cooper, 1998; Hayes & Joseph, 2003; Keyes, Shmotkin, & Ryff, 2002; Siegler & Brummett, 2000).

A study of Eysenck's three personality factors conducted in 39 countries, and of the Big Five factors conducted in 26 countries, found that low neuroticism and high extraversion correlated significantly with national levels of subjective well-being (Steel & Ones, 2002). A comparison of more than 4,000 adults in the United States and in Germany found that low neuroticism was the strongest predictor of subjective well-being (Staudinger, Fleeson, & Baltes, 1999). Other studies conducted in more than 30 countries confirm that low neuroticism and high extraversion are major correlates of subjective well-being (see, for example, Libran & Howard, 2006; Lynn & Steel, 2006).

A similar finding was obtained in a population of apes. The happiest orangutans in zoos in the United States, Canada, and Australia were those rated by zoo employees as being high in extraversion, low in neuroticism, and high in agreeableness (Weiss, King, & Perkins, 2006).

Overall, the importance of these primarily inherited factors of neuroticism, extraversion, and agreeableness in well-being in so many different cultures suggests that life satisfaction and happiness may have a strong genetic component.

Other personality variables have been found to contribute to subjective well-being. A study of 474 college students in the United States and 200 college students in South Korea identified four factors contributing to happiness: autonomy, competence, relatedness, and self-esteem. These factors were consistent over both cultures (Sheldon, Elliot, Kim, & Kasser, 2001).

You have probably already concluded that self-efficacy and internal locus of control are positively related to life satisfaction. In general, we are happiest when we feel competent in coping with life and in control of the reinforcers that are important to us. A study of 480 adults in Germany, ages 20 to 90, confirmed that the feeling of being in control of one's life was strongly related to subjective well-being (Lang & Heckhausen, 2001).

A study of more than 350 adults ages 44 to 65 linked three additional variables to life satisfaction: self-acceptance, environmental mastery, and autonomy. Self-acceptance includes making positive evaluations about oneself and one's life. Environmental mastery refers to the ability to deal effectively with challenges and problems. Autonomy implies a strong sense of self-determination (Schmutte & Ryff, 1997). A study of older adults confirmed the role of autonomy as a significant contributor to happiness (Sheldon, Kasser, Houser-Marko, Jones, & Turban, 2005).

A meta-analysis of 148 studies involving more than 42,000 subjects found that trust, internal locus of control, emotional stability, self-esteem, and the ability to deal positively with stress all correlated with high subjective well-being (DeNeve & Cooper, 1998).

Not surprisingly, having positive emotions—such as joy, interest, love, and enthusiasm—is linked to subjective well-being (see, for example, Frederickson, 2001). And the reverse seems to hold as well: negative emotions detract from a sense of well-being. A study of 283 college students found that the factor of vengefulness (the desire to seek vengeance against someone else) led to lower life satisfaction (McCullough, Bellah, Kilpatrick, & Johnson, 2001). A study of Holocaust survivors living in Israel found that even 60 years after the tragedy the traumatic effects lingered in the form of negative emotions and low levels of subjective well-being (Ben-Zur & Zimmerman, 2005).

A study of nearly 48,000 eighth- and ninth-graders in Finland found that having opportunities for self-fulfillment and social relationships in and out of the school environment correlated highly with subjective well-being (Konu, Lintonen, & Rimpelae, 2002).

What about social relationships developed through Internet chat rooms and blogs? A study of 192 adolescents in China found no significant effects on happiness of participation in online social interactions. However, research with 101 college students in Italy showed an increase in subjective well-being and a greater feeling of closeness to their own social group and to society in general after forming social relationships through the Internet (Biao-Bin, Man-Na, Bi-Qun, & Yong-Hong, 2006; Contarello & Sarrica, 2007).

People high in subjective well-being differ from people low in subjective well-being in terms of their motivations and goals. One research review concluded that life satisfaction was enhanced when the goals people set for themselves were concerned with personal growth and with community contributions and were considered feasible, realistic, and of value to the culture. People rated high in life satisfaction were found to be intensely committed to achieving their goals and believed they were making progress toward those ends (Lyubomirsky, 2001).

Two studies—one involving more than 13,000 college students from 31 countries, and the other involving more than 7,000 students from 41 countries—found significant differences in the ways in which happy and unhappy people perceive, judge, or construe events in their lives.

> In assessing their life satisfaction, unhappy individuals appear to give greater weight than happy individuals to what might be wrong in their lives. . . . In contrast, happy individuals see through the proverbial rose-colored glasses and weigh the positive aspects of their lives more heavily than do unhappy individuals. (Diener, Lucas, Oishi, & Suh, 2002, p. 444)

 ## Log On

Positive Psychology Center

The Web site for Seligman's Positive Psychology Center offers the chance to participate in positive psychology research studies as well as links to related sites.

Authentic Happiness

Seligman's Authentic Happiness site has more than 700,000 registered users worldwide; it offers information about research projects as well as questionnaires you can take on various aspects of optimism and happiness.

Reflective Happiness

Seligman's Positive Psychotherapy site contains exercises to overcome depression, increase positive emotions, and build happiness as well as newsletters, a book club, self-assessment tests, and a contact link to send questions directly to Seligman.

For direct links to these sites, log on to the student companion site for this book at http://www.academic.cengage.com/psychology/Schultz and choose Chapter 14.

Is there a relationship between happiness and success? And, if so, which comes first? Research tends to show that happiness, or subjective well-being, leads to the kinds of behaviors that bring about success. People high in subjective well-being "are more likely to secure job interviews, to be evaluated more positively by supervisors once they obtain a job, [and] to show superior performance and productivity" (Lyubomirsky, King, & Diener, 2005, p. 8).

Comment

How would you rate yourself on subjective well-being, life satisfaction, and happiness? What about your family members and friends? And what about Martin Seligman, the psychologist who founded the positive psychology movement? A few years ago, Seligman and a colleague, Ed Diener, studied 222 college students, some identified as happy, others as unhappy. They found clear differences between the two groups. The happier students (those who scored in the top 10 percent on several measures of happiness) were more extraverted and agreeable, less neurotic, and more social than were the unhappier students. The happy personalities reported having strong, positive relationships with friends, family, and romantic partners. They were highly satisfied with their lives, recalled many more good events than bad ones, and experienced more positive emotions daily than negative ones (Diener & Seligman, 2002).

When Seligman was asked by a reporter for the *New York Times* to comment on the results, he joked that he was dismayed by the characteristics of the happy students, particularly their highly sociable nature. "These were not the findings I was hoping for. As an introverted intellectual who spends a lot of time reading [rather than socializing], it tells me that I'm not going to be a good candidate for the upper 10 percent!" (Goode, 2002).

But there's more to the happiness issue. Seligman suspected that there can be different kinds of happiness, different ways of finding satisfaction in life. To the newspaper reporter, Seligman suggested that the key to happiness in his own case was a deep commitment to his work. If a research questionnaire had asked, for example, "How often are you immersed in what you are doing?" then he might have made it into the top 10 percent of happy people.

To prove his point about different kinds of happiness Seligman proposed three distinct components or types:

- Positive emotion: the pleasant life
- Engagement: the engaged life
- Meaning: the meaningful life

The pleasant life consists of a great deal of positive emotion such as job satisfaction, contentment, serenity, and optimism. This could be applied the happy college student described above as highly sociable, extraverted, and agreeable.

The engaged life consists of engagement, involvement, commitment, and absorption in work. As Seligman noted, "time passes quickly" for this type of person. "Attention is completely focused on the activity. The sense of self is lost" (Seligman, Rashid, & Parks, 2006, p. 777). The engaged life proposed by Seligman appears similar to Rogers's notion of the fully functioning person, Maslow's concept of self-actualization, and the self-determination theory proposed by Ryan and Deci as an outgrowth of Maslow's work.

The meaningful life involves using one's talents, abilities, and strengths to belong to, serve, or commit completely to some enterprise larger than the self. This could be a religion, organization, political party, ideal, or anything else that transcends the self. Living a meaningful life, Seligman wrote, "produces a sense of satisfaction and the belief that one has lived well" (Seligman, Rashid, & Parks, 2006, p. 777). His research has shown that the pursuit of meaning and engagement were much more strongly correlated with happiness than the pursuit of pleasure.

Seligman's appeal for a positive psychology has received an enthusiastic response. A laudatory article in *Newsweek* (2002) described positive psychology as a "whole new age in research psychology." A large number of studies, publications, and symposia have been forthcoming, and research on happiness and other positive emotions has increased substantially. In 2002, Seligman wrote *Authentic Happiness: Using the New Positive Psychology to Realize Your Potential for Lasting Fulfillment*, a book that has received wide popular recognition. In 2005 *Time* published a special issue devoted to the work of Seligman and his colleagues. When Harvard University first offered a course on positive psychology in 1999, only 20 students signed up; by 2006 it had become the most popular course on campus, with an enrollment of 854! Course work on positive psychology is now offered at many colleges and dozens of books on the subject are available (see, for example, Compton, 2006; Lambert, 2007). In less than a decade, then, positive psychology has come to be considered a new approach to the study of personality.

Chapter Summary

Rotter found that people who believe that the reinforcement they receive is under their control are internal locus of control personalities; those who believe they have no control over the reinforcements they receive are external locus of control personalities. Internals feel a stronger sense of personal choice, are in better physical and mental health, are less bothered by stress, earn higher grades in school, and have higher self-esteem than do externals. Research has shown that people become more internally oriented as they grow older, reaching a peak in middle age. People in lower socioeconomic classes, in some minority groups, and in some cultural groups, tend to be externals. Parents of internally oriented children tend to be supportive and consistent in their discipline, encouraging their child's independence.

According to Zuckerman, sensation seeking is an inherited trait concerned with the need for novel and complex sensations and experiences. The Sensation Seeking Scale is designed to assess this aspect of personality. Four components of sensation seeking are thrill and adventure seeking, experience seeking, disinhibition, and boredom susceptibility. Zuckerman later distinguished between good sensation seeking, which is socialized and non-impulsive, and bad sensation seeking, which is unsocialized, impulsive, and characterized by high scores on measures of psychoticism.

Research has shown higher levels of sensation seeking among White subjects, males, people from Western cultures, and young people from adolescence to their early 20s. High sensation seekers are more likely to use drugs, smoke cigarettes, drink alcohol, drive fast, engage in frequent sex, gamble, take physical risks, and travel to dangerous places. In terms of personality, high sensation seekers tend to be egocentrically extraverted, autonomous, assertive, nonconforming, and uninhibited in expressing emotions. In cognitive functioning, high sensation seekers recognize symbols and figures more quickly and prefer complexity in visual stimulation.

Vocational interests of high-sensation-seeking males are oriented toward science and the helping professions. Low-sensation-seeking males are more oriented toward clerical and business concerns. High sensation seekers tend to hold more liberal religious and political attitudes. They are higher in tolerance for ambiguity, more permissive in sexual attitudes, and lower in authoritarianism. They display stronger physiological responses to novel stimuli. Sensation seeking is primarily inherited but can be influenced by environmental factors such as birth order and parental level of sensation seeking.

Learned helplessness, investigated by Seligman, results from our perception that we have no control over our environment. An optimistic explanatory style can prevent learned helplessness; a pessimistic style spreads helplessness to all facets of life and can lead to physical illness and depression. Pessimists make personal, permanent, and pervasive explanations to themselves about negative events. Thus, helplessness changes from brief and localized to long lasting and generalized.

The attribution model of learned helplessness involves attributing a failure to some cause. Pessimists attribute their failures to internal, stable, and global causes. Optimists attribute their failures to external, unstable, and specific causes. Optimists tend to live longer, enjoy better health, and experience less stress and depression than do pessimists. The Attributional Style Questionnaire measures these causal dimensions. Although learned helplessness can occur at any age, infants and young children are particularly vulnerable. Infants learn that a correspondence exists between their responses and outcomes when responses bring changes in their environment; they learn helplessness when these responses do not bring about desired changes. Major causes of learned helplessness are maternal deprivation and an environment that provides a low level of stimulation and feedback.

Positive psychology focuses on characteristics of the happy personality; that is, those people who score high on measures of subjective well-being or life satisfaction. High subjective well-being is associated with social support and positive relations with others, a positive attitude, physical activity, not being a member of a minority group that experiences discrimination, and living in an economically advanced individualistic society. Characteristics of the happy personality include low neuroticism, high extraversion, autonomy, self-esteem, self-efficacy, an internal locus of control, and a sense of being in control of one's life. These people also tend to be successful in their careers.

Seligman posited three components or types of happiness: the pleasant life consisting of a great deal of positive emotion, the engaged life consisting of engagement, commitment, and absorption in work, and the meaningful life consisting of committing one's talents and abilities in the service of a cause or purpose larger than oneself.

Review Questions

1. What are the differences between the global and the limited-domain approaches to personality?

2. How do internal and external locus-of-control people differ in terms of their views of the source of the reinforcements they receive?

3. Give examples of how internal locus-of-control people behave differently from external locus-of-control people.

4. If external locus-of-control people learned that a tornado was approaching, would they be likely to believe there was nothing they could do about their situation, or would they be likely to take some action to protect themselves, their family, and their property? Why?

5. What parental behaviors foster a child's internal locus of control?

6. Describe the racial, social class, and cultural differences found in research on internal versus external locus of control.

7. How do the concepts of locus of control and self-efficacy differ? In what ways are they similar?

8. Define sensation seeking and describe its four components.

9. How does Zuckerman distinguish between good and bad sensation seeking. Which type are you?

10. What does research show about differences in sensation seeking as a function of age, gender, culture, and race?

11. How do people high in sensation seeking differ from people low in sensation seeking in terms of personality and cognitive functioning?

12. Give examples of ways in which high sensation seekers behave differently from low sensation seekers.

13. Describe the occupational interests and political attitudes of high sensation seekers.

14. Discuss the relative importance of heredity and environment in determining sensation seeking.

15. Define learned helplessness and describe Seligman's early research with dogs.

16. In the study on elderly residents of nursing homes, how did having greater control over their lives affect the residents' behavior and attitudes?

17. How can learned helplessness affect physical health? How does it relate to depression?

18. Distinguish between optimistic and pessimistic explanatory styles. How can they affect health?

19. How does the attribution model of learned helplessness differ from Seligman's earlier version of learned helplessness?

20. Explain how learned helplessness can develop in childhood.

21. Discuss the similarities and differences between Seligman's contemporary version of positive psychology and the earlier humanistic psychology of Maslow and Rogers.

22. Describe the effect on subjective well-being of each of these four factors: financial status, health, race, and culture.

23. In what ways do the personalities of people who score high in subjective well-being differ from those who score low?

24. Describe the three components or types of happiness, according to Seligman. Which one corresponds most closely to Maslow's concept of self-actualization?

Suggested Readings

Locus of Control

Judge, T. A., Erez, A., Bono, J. E., & Thoresen, C. J. (2002). Are measures of self-esteem, neuroticism, locus of control, and generalized self-efficacy indicators of a common core construct? *Journal of Personality and Social Psychology, 83,* 693–710. Describes a meta-analysis of studies on these four traits and suggests that they indicate a single personality factor.

Rotter, J. B. (1993). Expectancies. In C. E. Walker (Ed.), *The history of clinical psychology in autobiography*

(Vol. 2, pp. 273–284). Pacific Grove, CA: Brooks/Cole. Covers Rotter's graduate training, academic experience, and the early work on locus of control. Describes the growth of academic clinical psychology programs and related political controversies.

Strickland, B. R. (1989). Internal–external control expectancies: From contingency to creativity. *American Psychologist, 44,* 1–12. Reviews the research literature on internal versus external locus of control beliefs and relates the findings to measures of physical and psychological health.

Sensation Seeking

Brannigan, G. G., & Merrens, M. R. (Eds.). (1993). *The undaunted psychologist: Adventures in research.* Philadelphia: Temple University Press. Essays by academic psychologists on the origins of their research interests. Includes a chapter by Zuckerman about personal and intellectual approaches to research.

Raine, A., Reynolds, C., Venables, P. H., & Mednick, S. A. (2002). Stimulation seeking and intelligence: A prospective longitudinal study. *Journal of Personality and Social Psychology, 82,* 663–674. Documents a link between high sensation-seeking behaviors at age 3 (such as exploration and active play) and cognitive abilities and school performance at age 11, suggesting that young sensation-seekers create for themselves an enriched environment that stimulates intellectual development.

Zuckerman, M. (1990). The psychophysiology of sensation seeking. *Journal of Personality, 58,* 313–345. Summarizes research on the differences in psychophysiological response of high and low sensation seekers to novel or intense stimuli.

Zuckerman, M. (2004). The shaping of personality: Genes, environments, and chance encounters. *Journal of Personality Assessment, 82,* 11–22. An autobiographical sketch tracing Zuckerman's career in personality assessment, particularly his research on the biological basis of sensation seeking.

Zuckerman, M. (2007). *Sensation seeking and risky behavior.* Washington, DC: American Psychological Association. Reviews the role of sensation seeking in a variety of behaviors including auto racing, sports, risky sex practices, and antisocial behaviors such as substance abuse and crime. Offers insights into prevention and treatment of maladaptive forms of sensation seeking.

Learned Helplessness

Robinson-Whelen, S., Kim, C., MacCallum, R. C., & Kiecolt-Glaser, J. K. (1997). Distinguishing optimism from pessimism in older adults. Is it more important to be optimistic or not to be pessimistic? *Journal of Personality and Social Psychology, 73,* 1345–1353. Describes longitudinal research on the persistence of optimism and pessimism among a sample of adults (mid-50s through 60s) facing significant life challenges and stresses, such as caring for a terminally ill relative.

Segerstrom, S. C., & Taylor, S. E. (1998). Optimism is associated with mood, coping, and immune change in response to stress. *Journal of Personality and Social Psychology, 74,* 1646–1655. Uses questionnaires and physiological measurements to study the effects of optimism on mood, expectations, coping behaviors, health behaviors, and changes in immune system among first-year law school students.

Seligman, M. E. P. (1975). *Helplessness: On depression, development, and death.* San Francisco: W. H. Freeman. Describes the early research on learned helplessness, its development in childhood, and its impact on depression and physical health.

Seligman, M. E. P. (1990). *Learned optimism.* New York: Alfred A. Knopf. Describes differences in explanatory style between optimists and pessimists and relates these styles to physical and mental health. Offers techniques for changing pessimism to optimism.

Seligman, M. E. P. (2006). Distinguished Scientific Contribution Award. *American Psychologist, 61,* 772–788. A biographical sketch of Seligman, an extensive research bibliography, and the formal citation from the American Psychological Association.

Positive Psychology

Csikszentmihalyi, M., & Csikszentmihalyi, I. S. (Eds.). (2006). *A life worth living: Contributions to positive psychology.* Oxford: Oxford University Press. Reviews ideas associated with positive psychology such as personal autonomy, character, peak experiences, spirituality, coping with trauma and stress, and personal goals.

Diener, E., Oishi, S., & Lucas, R. E. (2003). Personality, culture, and subjective well-being: Emotional and cognitive evaluations of life. *Annual Review of Psychology, 54,* 403–425. Discusses the influences of personality, culture, and life circumstances on subjective well-being (described as happiness, peace, fulfillment, and life satisfaction).

Lyubomirsky, S. (2001). Why are some people happier than others? The role of cognitive and motivational processes in well-being. *American Psychologist, 56,* 239–249. Shows how self-described happy and unhappy people differ in the cognitive and motivational strategies they use in coping with life.

Ryan, R. M., & Deci, E. L. (2001). On happiness and human potentials. *Annual Review of Psychology, 52,* 141–166. Reviews research on well-being from two perspectives: happiness (that is, well-being defined as attaining pleasure and avoiding pain) and self-realization (that is, well-being defined in terms of the degree to which a person is fully functioning).

Schneider, S. L. (2001). In search of realistic optimism: Meaning, knowledge, and warm fuzziness. *American Psychologist, 56,* 250–263. Suggests differences between realistic and unrealistic optimism and their relationship to the control we can exert over our life experiences.

Seligman, M. E. P. (2002). *Authentic happiness: Using the new positive psychology to realize your potential for lasting fulfillment.* New York: Free Press. A guide to developing positive emotions, positive character, and personal satisfaction.

Wallace, B. A., & Shapiro, S. L. (2006). Mental balance and well-being: Building bridges between Buddhism and Western psychology. *American Psychologist, 61,* 690–701. Draws a relationship between the study of subjective well-being, as promoted by the positive psychology movement, and the Buddhist tradition of cultivating exceptional states of mental well-being.

Weiss, A., King, J. E., & Perkins, L. (2006). Personality and subjective well-being in orangutans. *Journal of Personality and Social Psychology, 90,* 501–511. Describes research to assess personality factors, moods, and behaviors in great apes.

Personality in Perspective

In the Introduction, we stated that our purpose was to explore the forces and factors that shape personality, to attempt to discover what makes us the way we are. We have discussed nearly two dozen theories, ranging from Sigmund Freud's work at the turn of the 20th century to contemporary developments in the 21st century. Because we have covered so many diverse approaches, you may be tempted to conclude that the field of personality is marked more by chaos than certainty, more by differences than agreements.

Which theory is correct? Which solves the puzzle of personality? The most complete answer we can suggest is that all theories discuss factors that are influential, to some degree, in shaping our personality. Each theorist has contributed vital pieces to the puzzle. Now it is time to examine those pieces to try to see the whole picture. We will summarize these viewpoints in a brief and broad overview of the themes, or factors, that have emerged from the work of the various theorists.

- The genetic factor
- The environmental factor
- The learning factor
- The parental factor
- The developmental factor
- The consciousness factor
- The unconscious factor

The Genetic Factor

There is increasingly strong evidence that many personality traits or dimensions are inherited (see, for example, Caspi, Roberts, & Shiner, 2005). These include the following:

- Eysenck's dimensions of psychoticism, neuroticism, and extraversion (the latter derived from the work of Jung)
- McCrae and Costa's five-factor model of personality including neuroticism, extraversion, openness to experience, agreeableness, and conscientiousness
- Buss and Plomin's three temperaments of emotionality, activity, and sociability.

In addition, Zuckerman's proposed trait of sensation seeking is primarily influenced by genetic factors. Thus, the trait approach, with its emphasis on the impact of heredity, remains a useful and growing area of personality research. What remains to be determined is precisely how many inherited factors, traits, or temperaments there are. Would it be Cattell's 16, Eysenck's 3, McCrae and Costa's 5, Buss and Plomin's 3, or some as yet undiscovered number?

Recent research involving more than 1,700 pairs of twins from Canada, Germany, and Japan, has provided support for the genetic basis of the five-factor model. The principal author of the study suggests that this may "represent the common heritage of the human species" (Yamagata et al., 2006, p. 96). Studies done in Belgium on more than 1,000 twins and non-twin siblings found a high stability in traits during childhood and adolescence, which also reinforces the importance of genetic factors in personality (DeFruyt, Bartels, Van Leeuwen, DeClercq, Decuyper, & Mervielde, 2006).

A study of 1,090 adolescent twins (both fraternal and identical) in Sweden found a strong genetic component in the psychopathic personality prone to violent antisocial behavior (Larsson, Andershed, & Lichtenstein, 2006). Future research in behavior genetics may yield even more facets of personality that are shaped by inherited factors.

No matter what number of traits there may be, however, not even the most ardent proponent of the genetics approach argues that personality can be completely explained by heredity. What we inherit are dispositions, not destinies; tendencies, not certainties. Whether our genetic predispositions are ever realized depends on social and environmental conditions, particularly those of childhood.

The Environmental Factor

Every personality theorist we have discussed acknowledged the importance of the social environment. Adler spoke of the impact of birth order, arguing that personality is influenced by our position in the family relative to our siblings. We are exposed to varying parental and social situations as a function of the extent of the age difference between siblings or whether we have siblings at all. In Adler's view, these different home environments can result in different personalities.

Horney believed that the culture and time period in which we are reared shows its effects, such as those she recorded in the neuroses exhibited by German and by American patients. She also pointed out the vastly different social environments to which boys and girls are exposed as children. She spoke of female inferiority developing from the way girls are treated in a male-dominated culture. She suggested that women raised in a matriarchal culture might have higher self-esteem and different personality characteristics.

Even Allport and Cattell, who inaugurated the trait approach to the study of personality, agreed on the importance of the environment. Allport noted that although genetics supplies the basic raw material of personality, it is the social environment that shapes the material into the finished product. Cattell argued that heredity is more important for some of his 16 personality factors than for others, but that environmental influences will ultimately affect every factor to some extent.

Erikson's eight stages of psychosocial development are innate, but the environment determines the ways in which those genetically based stages are realized. He believed that social and historical forces influence the formation of ego identity. Maslow and Rogers contended that self-actualization was innate but recognized that environmental factors could inhibit or promote the self-actualization need.

Large-scale societal events such as wars and economic recessions can restrict life choices and influence the formation of self-identity. More ordinary life changes (such as becoming parents, getting a divorce, or changing jobs) can also affect personality.

Even the time period in which you were born and reared can influence your personality. In effect, societal standards and attitudes, likes and dislikes, as well as the nature of external threats, are different for each generation. "A large number of theorists have suggested that birth cohort—as a proxy for the larger sociocultural environment—can have substantial effects on personality" (Twenge, 2000, p. 2).

This was demonstrated in a large-scale study comparing personality data of 40,192 college students and 12,056 young people ages 9 to 17. These two birth cohort groups, one from the 1950s and one from the 1980s, showed highly significant differences on two personality dimensions: anxiety and neuroticism. The 1980s group demonstrated substantially higher anxiety and neuroticism. These differences were attributed to decreases in social connectedness from the 1950s to the 1980s, as evidenced by a higher divorce rate, lower birth rate, later age at first marriage, and more people living alone during the 1980s (Twenge, 2000).

Our jobs can also influence our personality. This was shown in a study of 910 people ages 18 to 26 living in New Zealand. Personality measures given at 18, and again at 26, showed that those subjects in satisfying, high-status jobs at 26 had increased in positive emotionality (well-being, social closeness, and feelings of achievement) and decreased in negative emotionality (aggressiveness, alienation, and stress) since age 18. The researchers concluded that "work experiences have the potential to modify basic personality dispositions" (Roberts, Caspi, & Moffitt, 2003, p. 13).

Ethnic background and whether we are part of a minority or majority culture, helps determine personality. We saw examples of ethnic differences in such variables as sensation seeking, locus of control, and the need for achievement. We also learned that members of minority groups develop an ethnic identity as well as an ego identity and have to adapt to both cultures. The success of this adaptation affects personality and psychological health.

We also saw that culture is an important aspect of the environment that can shape personality. Western cultures tend to be more individualistic than Eastern cultures. In addition, people in Western cultures tend to score higher on extraversion, sensation seeking, and subjective well-being. People in Eastern cultures tend to score lower on these personality characteristics.

For all these reasons, then, it is impossible to deny the impact of diverse environmental and social forces on personality. The most significant way in which that impact is exerted is through learning.

The Learning Factor

Evidence is overwhelming that learning plays a major role in influencing virtually every aspect of behavior. All of the social and environmental forces that shape personality do so by the techniques of learning. Even inherited facets of personality can be modified, disrupted, prevented, or allowed to flourish by the process of learning. Skinner (based on earlier work by Watson and Pavlov) taught us the value of positive reinforcement, successive approximation, superstitious behavior, and other learning variables in shaping what others call personality, but which he described as simply an accumulation of learned responses.

Bandura introduced the idea that we learn from watching models (observational learning) and through vicarious reinforcement. Bandura agreed with Skinner that most behaviors are learned and that genetics plays only a limited role.

We discussed many aspects of personality that have scientific evidence to show that they are learned, such as McClelland's need for achievement (originally proposed by Murray). In addition, considerable research has documented that learning will influence self-efficacy (Bandura), locus of control (Rotter), learned helplessness, and optimism versus pessimism (Seligman). These concepts appear to be related to a broader notion: level of control. People who believe they have control over their lives are high in self-efficacy, have an internal locus of control, and are not characterized by learned helplessness (which involves lack of control). In Seligman's terms, people who believe they are in control are optimistic rather than pessimistic.

Control is beneficial to many aspects of life. A high degree of control has been related to better coping mechanisms, fewer stress effects, greater mental and physical health, perseverance, higher aspirations and self-esteem, lower anxiety, higher grades, and greater social skills and popularity. By whatever name—self-efficacy, internal locus of control, or optimism—control is determined by social and environmental factors. It is learned in infancy and childhood, though it can change later in life. We saw that specific parental behaviors can foster a child's feeling of being in control. Thus, the notion of control is a learned dimension of personality for which parental behavior is paramount.

The Parental Factor

Although Freud was the first theorist to emphasize parental influences on the formation of personality, virtually every theorist echoed his views. Recall Adler's focus on the consequences for a child who feels unwanted or rejected by his or her parents. Such parental rejection can lead to insecurity, leaving the person angry, and deficient in self-esteem. Horney wrote from her own experience about how lack of parental warmth and affection can undermine a child's security and result in feelings of helplessness.

Allport and Cattell, whose work was based on the importance of traits, also recognized the parental factor in personality formation. Allport considered the infant's relationship with the mother to be the primary source of affection and security, conditions crucial to later personality development. Cattell saw infancy as the major formative period, with the behavior of parents and siblings shaping the child's character. Erikson held that the child's relationship with the mother in the first year of life was vital in promoting a trusting attitude. Maslow commented on how necessary it was for parents to satisfy their child's physiological and safety needs in the first 2 years of life. This was a prerequisite for the emergence of higher-order needs. Rogers spoke of the parents' responsibility for supplying unconditional positive regard to their children.

We have also seen examples of how parental behaviors can determine specific aspects of personality, such as the need for achievement, self-efficacy, locus of control, learned helplessness or optimism, and subjective well-being. Parental behaviors can influence primarily inherited traits such as sensation seeking. You can easily imagine how uncaring and punitive parents could stifle the emergence of inherited traits such as extraversion, sociability, agreeableness, and openness to experience.

There is a great deal of evidence showing that children of parents who are described as authoritative (that is, warm but firm in their child-rearing practices) are more competent and mature than children of parents described as permissive, harsh, or indifferent. Researchers have noted that

> authoritative parenting is associated with a wide range of psychological and social advantages in adolescence, just as it is in early and middle childhood. . . . the combination of parental responsiveness and demandingness is consistently related to adolescent adjustment, school performance, and psychosocial maturity. (Steinberg & Morris, 2001, p. 88)

A study of 548 adolescents in Singapore found that those whose parents were authoritative had greater confidence in their abilities and were better adjusted socially than were teenagers whose parents were authoritarian (that is, strict, harsh, and demanding obedience) (Ang, 2006).

We have also discussed cultural differences in parental style. Parents in Arab cultures tend to be more authoritarian than authoritative. A study of mothers who had immigrated with their children to Canada showed that the women from collectivist cultures such as Egypt, Iran, India, and Pakistan were more authoritarian than women from individualistic countries in Western Europe (Rudy & Grusec, 2006).

Considerable research also suggests that praise from parents can promote a child's sense of autonomy, realistic standards and expectations, competence, and self-efficacy, and can enhance intrinsic motivation to achieve (see Henderlong & Lepper, 2002). And just as positive parental behaviors have positive effects on children, negative parental behaviors have detrimental effects.

A review of research on the relationship between early childhood experiences and adult psychopathology showed consistently that the childhood of depressed and anxious adults was related to inadequate parenting. The parents were found to be more rejecting and abusive, and less caring and affectionate, than parents of less troubled adults (Brewin, Andrews, & Gotlib, 1993). A study of more than 100 mothers rated them on the factors of emotionality and agreeableness. Mothers characterized by negative emotions and disagreeableness had children who scored higher in defiance, anger, disobedience, and other behavior problems than did mothers who did not exhibit negative emotional qualities (Kochanska, Clark, & Goldman, 1997).

A 12-year study of 439 children in Finland showed that when mothers had hostile attitudes toward child rearing (attitudes measured when their children were 3 and 6 years old), the children were highly likely to have hostile attitudes when they became 15. Thus, hostile mothers were found to rear children who also became hostile (Räikkönen, Katainen, Keskivaara, & Keltikangas-Jarvinen, 2000). A longitudinal study in the United States comparing subjects at ages 5 and 31 found that restrictive, cold, and strict parenting of the 5-year-olds produced adults who scored high in conformity and low in self-direction (Kasser, Koestner, & Lekes, 2002).

What happens when parents are not the primary caregivers, that is, when parents share child-rearing responsibilities with day care workers, friends, or family members while they work outside the home? In a national longitudinal survey of more than 15,000 children ages 3 to 12, no significant problems with behavior or self-esteem were found when the mothers took a job outside the home. The researcher concluded that care-giving by someone other than the child's mother had no negative impact on the variables studied (Harvey, 1999).

A unique real-world laboratory in which to explore the issue of surrogate caregivers is the collective child-care arrangement in kibbutzim in Israel. In that situation, mothers attend to their infants' needs for the first few months of life. Then the primary responsibility for child care is assigned to professional caregivers. Children typically spend more time with these surrogate mothers and fathers than they do with their parents.

Overall, kibbutz children were found to function and adapt well, assuming they established a secure relationship with their parents during infancy. Indeed, the strength of that bond was the strongest predictor of children who became dominant, independent, and achievement oriented. However, the barracks style sleeping arrangements (like summer camp or boarding school) in early childhood could lead to a more anxious, restrained, and emotionally flat personality. Adults reared on a kibbutz who failed to bond with their parents or caregivers showed introversion, diminished capacity for friendship, and reduced emotional intensity in interpersonal relations (Aviezer, Van Ijzendoorn, Sagi, & Schuegel, 1994).

A major controversy erupted in the late 1990s when it was suggested that parental attitudes and behaviors have no long-term effects on their child's personality outside the home (Harris, 1995, 1998). According to this idea, peers influence a child's personality much more than do parents. Children adopt the behaviors, attitudes, values, and characteristics of their classmates and friends in an effort to win their acceptance and approval.

Proponents of this view do not completely deny the influence of parents on their child's personality. What they do dispute is the idea that parental influence is maintained outside the home environment.

> Parents do influence their children's behavior. Of course they do. But the influence is in context, specific to the home. When children go out, they leave behind the behavior they acquired at home. They cast it off like the dorky sweater their mother made them wear. (Harris, quoted in Sleek, 1998, p. 9)

Modest support for this proposal was provided by a study of 839 pairs of twins in late adolescence. The results showed that twins who had more friends in common were more alike in personality than were twins who had fewer friends in common. This suggests that friends, rather than the home environment, had a greater impact on their personality (Loehlin, 1997).

Researchers who subscribe to the primacy of genetic factors in personality also tend to reject or minimize the parental effect, suggesting that the family environment contributes little to personality (Matthews & Deary, 1998). However this controversy is eventually resolved—whether personality is determined by parents, peers, genes, or some combination of factors—it leads us to another question. Is personality fixed in early life by these influences or can it be changed in later years? That question leads us to a consideration of the developmental factor.

The Developmental Factor

Freud believed that personality was shaped and fixed by the age of 5 and that it was difficult thereafter to alter any aspect of it. We accept that the childhood years are crucial to personality formation, but it is also clear that personality continues to develop well beyond childhood, perhaps throughout the entire life span. Theorists such as Cattell, Allport, Erikson, and Murray viewed childhood as important but agreed that personality could be modified in later years. Some theorists suggested that personality development is ongoing in adolescence. Jung, Maslow, Erikson, and Cattell noted middle age as a time of major personality change.

The question is, how long does our personality continue to change and grow? Does your self at age 20 indicate what you will be like at 40? As with most questions about personality, this has become a highly complex issue. Perhaps it is not even the right question to ask.

It may not surprise you to learn that empirical evidence supports diverse viewpoints. Does personality change? Well, yes. Does personality also remain stable? Uh, probably, yes. But if we were to refine the question and ask whether some personality characteristics remain stable over a lifetime while other characteristics change, then we would be able to answer with an unqualified yes.

What has emerged from research is the suggestion that our basic foundation of enduring personality dispositions (such as the traits described in McCrae and Costa's five-factor model) remains stable over many years. According to the evidence, these basic traits and capacities appear to be enduring from age 30 on. Some research shows that the factors of neuroticism, extraversion, and openness decline from college age to middle age, whereas the factors of agreeableness and conscientiousness increase with age. Cross-cultural comparisons have demonstrated this consistency in such diverse countries as the United States, Germany, Italy, Portugal, Croatia, and South Korea (Costa & McCrae, 1997; McCrae et al., 1999).

Other research has led to different results. For example, a 40-year study of several hundred people found that scores on dominance and independence peaked in middle age, and that personality did not stop evolving and changing after age 20 (Helson, Jones, & Kwan, 2002). A meta-analysis of 152 longitudinal studies involving more than 55,000 subjects showed a high level of consistency in personality traits at all ages. The highest level of consistency was found in adulthood (Roberts & Delvecchio, 2000). According to these findings, then, traits are consistent over the life span, with consistency reaching its highest level after age 50.

Additional research has focused on personality change in childhood and adolescence. A study of 876 teenagers, ages 12–18, in Estonia showed that their personalities, as measured by the five-factor model, remained stable over the 2-year period of the research (Pullmann, Raudsepp, & Allik, 2006). Research with 392 U.S. college students over 30 months showed that they became more open, agreeable, and conscientious during that time. The researchers noted, "These results are consistent with the notion that personality changes more in early adulthood than after the age of 30. We found this to be true even over a relatively short period of 2.5 years" (Vaidya, Gray, Haig, & Watson, 2002, p. 19).

A study of 32,515 people ages 21–60, conducted over the Internet, showed that conscientiousness and agreeableness increased through early and middle adulthood. Conscientiousness increased most strongly in the 20s; agreeableness increased most strongly during the 30s (Srivastava, John, Gosling, & Potter, 2003). Other research suggests that people tend to become more dominant in social situations and more conscientious and emotionally stable, as they grow from young adulthood to middle age (Roberts, Walton, & Viechtbauer, 2006). Large-scale studies also support the notion that personality remains generally stable after age 30 and into late adulthood (Johnson, McGue, & Krueger, 2005; Terracciano, Costa, & McCrae, 2006).

A study of 921 people in New Zealand (ages 18–26) showed that personality changes during those years demonstrated an increasing level of psychological maturity. The subjects became more self-controlled, more confident in social situations, and less angry and alienated. Women showed a higher level of psychological maturity overall than men did (Roberts, Caspi, & Moffitt, 2001). In a study of 205 children ages 8–12, who were surveyed again 10 years later, personality changes between the ages of 18 and 22 could be predicted to a significant extent by their personality characteristics in childhood (Shiner, Masten, & Tellegen, 2002). What all these studies confirm is that personality changes as we grow into adolescence and early adulthood, a finding you may already have observed in yourself.

What brings about personality change in adulthood? Theorists who favor the overriding influence of genetic factors suggest that any personality change is independent of environmental factors. Other theorists believe that the answer is rooted in social and environmental influences and in the adaptations we make to them. Changes in economic circumstances, leaving college, marriage and parenthood, divorce, job loss or advancement, midlife crises, aging parents—all create problems to which adults must adjust.

A 3-year study in the Netherlands of men and women in their forties found that those who had successfully adapted to their expected social roles, such as success in a career and in family life, scored higher on the five-factor personality dimensions than did those who had not adapted successfully. Thus, personality change was found to be associated with the successful adaptation to various midlife concerns (Van Aken, Denisson, Branje, Dubas, & Goossens, 2006).

In other instances of adjustment, people who have lost their jobs have shown significant increases in neuroticism and decreases in conscientiousness and extraversion. Adults who were actively dating and maintaining social relationships scored lower in neuroticism and higher in extraversion, conscientiousness, and self-esteem than people who were not dating (Costa, Herbst, McCrae, & Siegler, 2000; Neyer & Asendorpf, 2001).

Two longitudinal studies of women examined the social factor of the women's liberation movement of the 1970s and its impact from the college years into middle age. Significant increases were found over time in the personality traits of dominance, self-acceptance, empathy, achievement, and self-focus. Decreases were noted in adherence to rules or norms (Agronick & Duncan, 1998; Roberts & Helson, 1997).

These cultural and personal challenges leave their impact on the personality. One theorist suggested that personality continues to develop on three levels: dispositional traits, personal concerns, and life narrative (McAdams, 1994). *Dispositional traits* are inherited traits of the kind discussed by McCrae and Costa, those characteristics found to remain stable and relatively unchanging from age 30 on. *Personal concerns* refer to conscious feelings, plans, and goals; what we want, how we try to achieve it, and how we feel about the people in our life. These may change often over the life span as a result of the diverse situations and influences to which we are exposed. Although these situations can alter our feelings and intentions, our underlying dispositional traits (such as our basic level of neuroticism or extraversion) with which we confront these life situations remain relatively stable. *Life narrative* implies shaping the self, attaining an identity, and finding a unified purpose in life. We are constantly writing our life story, creating who we are and how we fit into the world. Like personal concerns, the life narrative changes in response to social and environmental situations. As adults we may adjust our narrative to adapt to each stage of life and its needs, challenges, and opportunities. In sum, then, this view holds that the underlying dispositional traits of personality remain largely constant, while our conscious judgments about who we are and who we would like to be are subject to change. That idea leads to another factor the theorists have considered: consciousness.

The Consciousness Factor

Almost every personality theory we have described deals explicitly or implicitly with conscious (cognitive) processes. Even Freud and Jung, who focused on the unconscious, wrote of an ego or conscious mind that perceives, thinks, feels, and remembers, enabling us to interact with the real world. Through the ego we are able to perceive stimuli and later recall an image of them. Jung wrote about rational functioning, making conscious judgments and evaluations of our experiences. Adler described humans as conscious, rational beings capable of planning and directing the course of our life. We formulate hopes, plans, and dreams and delay gratification, and we consciously anticipate future events.

Allport believed that people who are not neurotic will function in a conscious, rational way, aware and in control of the forces that motivate them. Rogers thought people were primarily rational beings, governed by a conscious perception of themselves and their world of experience. Maslow also recognized the role of consciousness; he proposed cognitive needs to know and to understand.

Kelly offered the most complete theory based on cognitive factors. He argued persuasively that we form constructs about our environment and about other people and that we make predictions (anticipations) about them based on these constructs. We formulate hypotheses about our social world and test them against the reality of our experience. Based on everyday evidence, it is difficult to deny that people construe, predict, and anticipate how others will behave and then modify or adapt their behavior accordingly.

Bandura credits people with the ability to learn through example and vicarious reinforcement. To do so, we must be able to anticipate and appreciate the consequences of the actions we observe in others. We visualize or imagine the results of our reinforcements for behaving the same way a model does, even though we may never have experienced those consequences personally. Thus, there is widespread agreement that consciousness exists and is an influence on personality. However, there is less agreement on the role or even the existence of another influence, that of the unconscious.

The Unconscious Factor

Sigmund Freud introduced us to the world of the unconscious, that murky repository of our darkest fears and conflicts, forces that affect our conscious thoughts and behaviors. Psychologists have found some evidence to support Freud's notion that thoughts and memories are repressed in the unconscious, and that repression (as well as other defense mechanisms) may operate at the unconscious level. Along with the cognitive movement in psychology has come not only an interest in conscious processes but also a renewed interest in the unconscious. Recent research confirms that the unconscious is a powerful force, perhaps even more pervasive in its influence than Freud suggested. However, the modern depiction of the unconscious is not the same as Freud's view. Contemporary researchers focus on unconscious cognitive processes and describe them as more rational than emotional.

The rational unconscious is often referred to as the non-conscious, to distinguish it from Freud's unconscious, his so-called dark cauldron of repressed wishes and desires. One method for studying the non-conscious involves subliminal activation, in which various stimuli are presented to subjects below their level of conscious awareness. Despite the subjects' inability to perceive the stimuli, their conscious processes and behaviors can be activated by those stimuli. The obvious conclusion to be drawn from such research is that people can be influenced by stimuli they can neither see nor hear. We also discussed the "Mommy and I are one" study about how subliminal presentation of certain stimuli influenced cognitive as well as emotional responses (Silverman & Weinberger, 1985). The subliminal stimuli had therapeutic value even though the subjects had no conscious awareness of the actual messages. Thus, the unconscious may have both a rational and an emotional component.

Although the unconscious is an ongoing research topic in psychology today, many of the personality theorists who followed Freud ignored it. We may suggest that the emotional unconscious as Freud envisioned it—the startling idea that signaled the formal beginning of the study of personality—remains the least understood factor and still very much what it was in Freud's time, mysterious and inaccessible.

And so it is with the study of personality, as we have seen throughout this book. There are diverse ways to define and describe personality, and each theory we have discussed has contributed another part of the answer to that vital question. We have spanned the viewpoints from Sigmund Freud and his emphasis on anxiety, the unconscious, and a life of fear and repression to positive psychology and the characteristics of the happy personality. And we have covered many other ideas in between, all of which have added to our understanding. But there are more possibilities to consider, more to be learned, and no doubt new approaches will be presented, new theories as yet unimagined.

Your formal course work in this field may be ending, but the attempt to understand personality is not. Although it is true that enormous progress has been made in charting personality and detailing the factors that shape it, the challenges of the field remain active and dynamic. Perhaps the question, "What is personality?" is the most important of all, for it reflects the attempt to understand ourselves.

Review Questions

1. Six questions about human nature were posed in the Introduction. We asked you to write down your own thoughts on these issues. Now that you have studied the approaches to personality presented in this book, reconsider your answers to see how your views may have changed.

2. Think about the similarities and differences between your personality and the personality of your mother, father, or siblings. What factors do you see in common?

3. Which of the approaches to personality discussed in this text did you find most helpful in understanding yourself? Which was of the least value to you?

4. Think back to what you were like in your early adolescence. Who do you believe influenced you more at that time, your parents or your peers? Now that you are older, is your answer to that question the same?

5. What changes have you seen in your personality from childhood to the present? Have there been periods in your life when you deliberately tried to alter your personality? Were you successful? If so, what techniques did you use?

6. Do you think it is possible to evaluate personality accurately enough to predict whether certain people will be happy, emotionally stable, or perform well on the job?

7. Summarize in a few sentences what you have learned about your own personality from this course.

ability traits Traits that describe our skills and how efficiently we will be able to work toward our goals.

actualization tendency The basic human motivation to actualize, maintain, and enhance the self.

aggressive drive The compulsion to destroy, conquer, and kill.

aggressive personality Behaviors and attitudes associated with the neurotic trend of moving against people, such as a domineering and controlling manner.

analytical psychology Jung's theory of personality.

anima archetype; animus archetype Feminine aspects of the male psyche; masculine aspects of the female psyche.

anxiety To Freud, a feeling of fear and dread without an obvious cause: reality anxiety is a fear of tangible dangers; neurotic anxiety involves a conflict between id and ego; moral anxiety involves a conflict between id and superego.

archetypes Images of universal experiences contained in the collective unconscious.

attitudes To Allport, attitudes are similar to traits. However, attitudes have specific objects of reference and involve either positive or negative evaluations. To Cattell, attitudes are our interests in and emotions and behaviors toward some person, object, or event. This is a broader definition than typically used in psychology.

attribution model The idea that we attribute our lack of control or failure to some cause.

basic anxiety A pervasive feeling of loneliness and helplessness; the foundation of neurosis.

basic strengths To Erikson, motivating characteristics and beliefs that derive from the satisfactory resolution of the crisis at each developmental stage.

basic weaknesses Motivating characteristics that derive from the unsatisfactory resolution of developmental crises.

behavior modification A form of therapy that applies the principles of reinforcement to bring about desired behavioral changes.

behavioral genetics The study of the relationship between genetic or hereditary factors and personality traits.

behaviorism The school of psychology, founded by John B. Watson, that focused on psychology as the study of overt behavior rather than of mental processes.

cardinal traits The most pervasive and powerful human traits.

case study A detailed history of an individual that contains data from a variety of sources.

castration anxiety A boy's fear during the Oedipal period that his penis will be cut off.

catharsis The expression of emotions that is expected to lead to the reduction of disturbing symptoms.

cathexis An investment of psychic energy in an object or person.

central traits The handful of outstanding traits that describe a person's behavior.

cognitive complexity A cognitive style or way of construing the environment characterized by the ability to perceive differences among people.

cognitive needs Innate needs to know and to understand.

cognitive simplicity A cognitive style or way of construing the environment characterized by a relative inability to perceive differences among people.

collective unconscious The deepest level of the psyche containing the accumulation of inherited experiences of human and pre-human species.

common traits Traits possessed in some degree by all persons.

compensation A motivation to overcome inferiority, to strive for higher levels of development.

complex To Jung, a core or pattern of emotions, memories, perceptions, and wishes in the personal unconscious organized around a common theme, such as power or status. To Murray, a normal pattern of childhood development that influences the adult personality; childhood developmental stages include the claustral, oral, anal, urethral, and genital complexes.

compliant personality Behaviors and attitudes associated with the neurotic trend of moving toward people, such as a need for affection and approval.

conditional positive regard Approval, love, or acceptance granted only when a person expresses desirable behaviors and attitudes.

conditions of worth To Rogers, a belief that we are worthy of approval only when we express desirable behaviors and attitudes and refrain from expressing those that bring disapproval from others; similar to the Freudian superego.

conflict To Horney, the basic incompatibility of the neurotic trends.

conscience A component of the superego that contains behaviors for which the child has been punished.

constitutional traits Source traits that depend on our physiological characteristics.

construct An intellectual hypothesis that we devise and use to interpret or explain life events. Constructs are bipolar, or dichotomous, such as tall versus short or honest versus dishonest.

constructive alternativism The idea that we are free to revise or replace our constructs with alternatives as needed.

control group In an experiment, the group that does not receive the experimental treatment.

coping behavior Consciously planned behavior determined by the needs of a given situation and designed for a specific purpose, usually to bring about a change in one's environment.

correlational method A statistical technique that measures the degree of the relationship between two variables, expressed by the correlation coefficient.

creative power of the self The ability to create an appropriate style of life.

crisis To Erikson, the turning point faced at each developmental stage.

death instincts The unconscious drive toward decay, destruction, and aggression.

defense mechanisms Strategies the ego uses to defend itself against the anxiety provoked by conflicts of everyday life. Defense mechanisms involve denials or distortions of reality.

deficit (deficiency) needs The lower needs; failure to satisfy them produces a deficiency in the body.

denial A defense mechanism that involves denying the existence of an external threat or traumatic event.

dependent variable In an experiment, the variable the experimenter desires to measure, typically the subjects' behavior or response to manipulation of the independent variable.

detached personality Behaviors and attitudes associated with the neurotic trend of moving away from people, such as an intense need for privacy.

disinhibition The weakening of inhibitions or constraints by observing the behavior of a model.

displacement A defense mechanism that involves shifting id impulses from a threatening object or from one that is unavailable to an object that is available; for example, replacing hostility toward one's boss with hostility toward one's child.

dream analysis A technique involving the interpretation of dreams to uncover unconscious conflicts. Dreams have a manifest content (the actual events in the dream) and a latent content (the symbolic meaning of the dream events).

dynamic lattice The representation in a chart or diagram of the relationships among ergs, sentiments, and attitudes.

dynamic traits Traits that describe our motivations and interests.

early recollections A personality assessment technique in which our earliest memories, whether of real events or fantasies, are assumed to reveal the primary interest of our life.

ego To Freud, the rational aspect of the personality, responsible for directing and controlling the instincts according to the reality principle. To Jung, the conscious aspect of personality. To Murray, the conscious organizer of behavior; this is a broader conception than Freud's.

ego identity The self-image formed during adolescence that integrates our ideas of what we are and what we want to be.

ego-ideal A component of the superego that contains the moral or ideal behaviors for which a person should strive.

Electra complex During the phallic stage (ages 4 to 5), the unconscious desire of a girl for her father, accompanied by a desire to replace or destroy her mother.

encounter groups A group therapy technique in which people learn about their feelings and about how they relate to (or encounter) one another.

entropy principle A tendency toward balance or equilibrium within the personality; the ideal is an equal distribution of psychic energy over all structures of the personality.

environmental-mold traits Source traits that are learned from social and environmental interactions.

epigenetic principle of maturation The idea that human development is governed by a sequence of stages that depend on genetic or hereditary factors.

equivalence principle The continuing redistribution of energy within a personality; if the energy expended on certain conditions or activities weakens or disappears, that energy is transferred elsewhere in the personality.

ergs Permanent constitutional source traits that provide energy for goal-directed behavior. Ergs are the basic innate units of motivation.

experimental group In an experiment, the group that is exposed to the experimental treatment.

explanatory style A way of explaining to ourselves our relative lack of control over our environment. An optimistic explanatory style can prevent learned helplessness; a pessimistic explanatory style spreads helplessness to all facets of life.

expressive behavior Spontaneous and seemingly purposeless behavior, usually displayed without our conscious awareness.

external locus of control A belief that reinforcement is under the control of other people, fate, or luck.

externalization A way to defend against the conflict caused by the discrepancy between an idealized and a real self-image by projecting the conflict onto the outside world.

extinction The process of eliminating a behavior by withholding reinforcement.

extraversion An attitude of the psyche characterized by an orientation toward the external world and other people.

factor analysis A statistical technique based on correlations between several measures, which may be explained in terms of underlying factors.

feminine psychology To Horney, a revision of psychoanalysis to encompass the psychological conflicts inherent in the traditional ideal of womanhood and women's roles.

fictional finalism The idea that there is an imagined or potential goal that guides our behavior.

fixation A condition in which a portion of libido remains invested in one of the psychosexual stages because of excessive frustration or gratification.

fixed role therapy A psychotherapeutic technique in which the client acts out constructs appropriate for a fictitious person. This shows the client how the new constructs can be more effective than the old ones he or she has been using.

free association A technique in which the patient says whatever comes to mind. In other words, it is a kind of daydreaming out loud.

fully functioning person Rogers's term for self-actualization, for developing all facets of the self.

functional analysis An approach to the study of behavior that involves assessing the frequency of a behavior, the situation in which it occurs, and the reinforcers associated with it.

functional autonomy of motives The idea that motives in the normal, mature adult are independent of the childhood experiences in which they originally appeared.

growth (being) needs The higher needs; although growth needs are less necessary than deficit needs for survival, they involve the realization and fulfillment of human potential.

habits Specific, inflexible responses to specific stimuli; several habits may combine to form a trait.

hierarchy of needs   An arrangement of innate needs, from strongest to weakest, that activates and directs behavior.

historical determinism   The view that personality is basically fixed in the early years of life and subject to little change thereafter.

id   To Freud, the aspect of personality allied with the instincts; the source of psychic energy, the id operates according to the pleasure principle. To Murray, the id contains the primitive, amoral, and lustful impulses described by Freud, but it also contains desirable impulses, such as empathy and love.

idealized self-image   For normal people, the self-image is an idealized picture of oneself built on a flexible, realistic assessment of one's abilities. For neurotics, the self-image is based on an inflexible, unrealistic self-appraisal.

identity crisis   The failure to achieve ego identity during adolescence.

idiographic research   The intensive study of a relatively small number of subjects using a variety of assessment techniques.

incongruence   A discrepancy between a person's self-concept and aspects of his or her experience.

independent variable   In an experiment, the stimulus variable or condition the experimenter manipulates to learn its effect on the dependent variable.

individual psychology   Adler's theory of personality.

individuation   A condition of psychological health resulting from the integration of all conscious and unconscious facets of the personality.

inferiority complex   A condition that develops when a person is unable to compensate for normal inferiority feelings.

inferiority feelings   The normal condition of all people; the source of all human striving.

instinctive drift   The substitution of instinctive behaviors for behaviors that had been reinforced.

instinctoid needs   Maslow's term for the innate needs in his needs-hierarchy theory.

instincts   In Freud's system, mental representations of internal stimuli, such as hunger, that drive a person to take certain actions.

internal locus of control   A belief that reinforcement is brought about by our own behavior.

introversion   An attitude of the psyche characterized by an orientation toward one's own thoughts and feelings.

Jonah complex   The fear that maximizing our potential will lead to a situation with which we will be unable to cope.

latency period   To Freud, the period from approximately age 5 to puberty, during which the sex instinct is dormant, sublimated in school activities, sports, and hobbies, and in developing friendships with members of the same sex.

L-data   Life-record ratings of behaviors observed in real-life situations, such as the classroom or office.

learned helplessness   A condition resulting from the perception that we have no control over our environment.

libido   To Freud, the form of psychic energy, manifested by the life instincts, that drives a person toward pleasurable behaviors and thoughts. To Jung, a broader and more generalized form of psychic energy.

life instincts   The drive for ensuring survival of the individual and the species by satisfying the needs for food, water, air, and sex.

life-history reconstruction   Jung's type of case study that involves examining a person's past experiences to identify developmental patterns that may explain present neuroses.

maldevelopment   A condition that occurs when the ego consists solely of a single way of coping with conflict.

metamotivation   The motivation of self-actualizers, which involves maximizing personal potential rather than striving for a particular goal object.

metaneeds   States of growth or being toward which self-actualizers evolve.

metapathology   A thwarting of self-development related to failure to satisfy the metaneeds.

modeling   A behavior-modification technique that involves observing the behavior of others (the models) and participating with them in performing the desired behavior.

Myers-Briggs Type Indicator (MBTI)   An assessment test based on Jung's psychological types and the attitudes of introversion and extraversion.

need for achievement   The need to achieve, overcome obstacles, excel, and live up to a high standard.

negative reinforcement   The strengthening of a response by the removal of an aversive stimulus.

neurotic competitiveness   An indiscriminate need to win at all costs.

neurotic needs   Ten irrational defenses against anxiety that become a permanent part of personality and that affect behavior.

neurotic trends   Three categories of behaviors and attitudes toward oneself and others that express a person's needs; Horney's revision of the concept of neurotic needs.

nomothetic research   The study of the statistical differences among large groups of subjects.

object relations theories   Outgrowths of psychoanalytic theory that focus more on relationships with the objects (such as the mother) that satisfy instinctual needs, rather than on the needs themselves.

observational learning   Learning new responses by observing the behavior of other people.

Oedipus complex   During the phallic stage (ages 4 to 5), the unconscious desire of a boy for his mother, accompanied by a desire to replace or destroy his father.

operant behavior   Behavior emitted spontaneously or voluntarily that operates on the environment to change it.

operant conditioning   The procedure by which a change in the consequences of a response will affect the rate at which the response occurs.

opposition principle   Jung's idea that conflict between opposing processes or tendencies is necessary to generate psychic energy.

organismic valuing process   The process by which we judge experiences in terms of their value for fostering or hindering our actualization and growth.

peak experience   A moment of intense ecstasy, similar to a religious or mystical experience, during which the self is transcended.

penis envy   The envy the female feels toward the male because the male possesses a penis; this is accompanied by a sense of loss because the female does not have a penis.

permeability   The idea that constructs can be revised and extended in light of new experiences.

perseverative functional autonomy   The level of functional autonomy that relates to low-level and routine behaviors.

persona archetype   The public face or role a person presents to others.

personal construct theory   Kelly's description of personality in terms of cognitive processes. We are capable of interpreting behaviors and events and of using this understanding to guide our behavior and to predict the behavior of other people.

personal dispositions   Traits that are peculiar to an individual, as opposed to traits shared by a number of people.

personal unconscious   The reservoir of material that was once conscious but has been forgotten or suppressed.

personal-document technique   A method of personality assessment that involves the study of a person's written or spoken records.

personality   The unique, relatively enduring internal and external aspects of a person's character that influence behavior in different situations.

person-centered therapy   Rogers's approach to therapy in which the client (not the "patient") is assumed to be responsible for changing his or her personality.

personology   Murray's system of personality.

play constructions   A personality assessment technique for children in which structures assembled from dolls, blocks, and other toys are analyzed.

pleasure principle   The principle by which the id functions to avoid pain and maximize pleasure.

positive regard   Acceptance, love, and approval from others.

positive self-regard   The condition under which we grant ourselves acceptance and approval.

press   The influence of the environment and past events on the current activation of a need.

primary needs   Survival and related needs arising from internal bodily processes.

primary-process thought   Childlike thinking by which the id attempts to satisfy the instinctual drives.

proactive needs Needs that arise spontaneously.

proceeding A basic segment of behavior; a time period in which an important behavior pattern occurs from beginning to end.

projection A defense mechanism that involves attributing a disturbing impulse to someone else.

projective test A personality assessment device in which subjects are presumed to project personal needs, fears, and values onto their interpretation or description of an ambiguous stimulus.

propriate functional autonomy The level of functional autonomy that relates to our values, self-image, and lifestyle.

proprium Allport's term for the ego or self.

psyche Jung's term for personality.

psychoanalysis Sigmund Freud's theory of personality and system of therapy for treating mental disorders.

psychohistorical analysis The application of Erikson's life-span theory, along with psychoanalytic principles, to the study of historical figures.

psychological types To Jung, eight personality types based on interactions of the attitudes (introversion and extraversion) and the functions (thinking, feeling, sensing, and intuiting).

psychosexual stages of development To Freud, the oral, anal, phallic, and genital stages through which all children pass. In these stages, gratification of the id instincts depends on the stimulation of corresponding areas of the body.

psychosocial stages of development To Erikson, eight successive stages encompassing the life span. At each stage, we must cope with a crisis in either an adaptive or a maladaptive way.

punishment The application of an aversive stimulus following a response in an effort to decrease the likelihood that the response will recur.

Q-data Self-report questionnaire ratings of our characteristics, attitudes, and interests.

Q-sort technique A self-report technique for assessing aspects of the self-concept.

range of convenience The spectrum of events to which a construct can be applied. Some constructs are relevant to a limited number of people or situations; other constructs are broader.

rationalization A defense mechanism that involves reinterpreting our behavior to make it more acceptable and less threatening to us.

reaction formation A defense mechanism that involves expressing an id impulse that is the opposite of the one that is truly driving the person.

reactive needs Needs that involve a response to a specific object.

reality principle The principle by which the ego functions to provide appropriate constraints on the expression of the id instincts.

reciprocal determinism The idea that behavior is controlled or determined by the individual, through cognitive processes, and by the environment, through external social stimulus events.

regression A defense mechanism that involves retreating to an earlier, less frustrating period of life and displaying the usually childish behaviors characteristic of that more secure time.

reinforcement The act of strengthening a response by adding a reward, thus increasing the likelihood that the response will be repeated.

reinforcement schedules Patterns or rates of providing or withholding reinforcers.

reliability The consistency of response to a psychological assessment device. Reliability can be determined by the test-retest, equivalent-forms, and split-halves methods.

repression A defense mechanism that involves unconscious denial of the existence of something that causes anxiety.

resistance In free association, a blockage or refusal to disclose painful memories.

respondent behavior Responses made to or elicited by specific environmental stimuli.

reversal experimental design A research technique that involves establishing a baseline, applying an experimental treatment, and withdrawing the experimental treatment to determine whether the behavior returns to its baseline value or whether some other factor is responsible for the observed behavior change.

safety need A higher-level need for security and freedom from fear.

secondary needs Emotional and psychological needs, such as achievement and affiliation.

secondary traits   The least important traits, which a person may display inconspicuously and inconsistently.

secondary-process thought   Mature thought processes needed to deal rationally with the external world.

self archetype   To Jung, the archetype that represents the unity, integration, and harmony of the total personality.

self-actualization   The fullest development of the self.

self-characterization sketch   A technique designed to assess a person's construct system; that is, how a person perceives himself or herself in relation to other people.

self-control   The ability to exert control over the variables that determine our behavior.

self-efficacy   Our feeling of adequacy, efficiency, and competence in coping with life.

self-reinforcement   Administering rewards or punishments to oneself for meeting, exceeding, or falling short of one's own expectations or standards.

self-report inventory   A personality assessment technique in which subjects answer questions about their behaviors and feelings.

self-sentiment   The self-concept, which is the organizer of our attitudes and motivations.

sensation seeking   The need for varied, novel, and complex sensations and experiences.

sentiments   To Cattell, environmental-mold source traits that motivate behavior.

serial   A succession of proceedings related to the same function or purpose.

shadow archetype   The dark side of the personality; the archetype that contains primitive animal instincts.

sign-versus-sample approach   In the sign approach to assessing *personality*, character types, traits, or unconscious conflicts are inferred from questionnaires and other self-report inventories. In the sample approach to assessing *behavior*, test responses are interpreted as directly indicative of present behavior, not of traits, motives, or childhood experiences.

social interest   Our innate potential to cooperate with other people to achieve personal and societal goals.

source traits   Stable, permanent traits that are the basic factors of personality, derived by the method of factor analysis.

striving for superiority   The urge toward perfection or completion that motivates each of us.

style of life   A unique character structure or pattern of personal behaviors and characteristics by which each of us strives for perfection. Basic styles of life include the dominant, getting, avoiding, and socially useful types.

sublimation   A defense mechanism that involves altering or displacing id impulses by diverting instinctual energy into socially acceptable behaviors.

subliminal perception   Perception below the threshold of conscious awareness.

subsidiation   To Murray, a situation in which one need is activated to aid in the satisfaction of another need. To Cattell, the relationships among ergs, sentiments, and attitudes, in which some elements are subordinate to others.

successive approximation   An explanation for the acquisition of complex behavior. Behavior such as learning to speak will be reinforced only as it comes to approximate or approach the final desired behavior.

superego   To Freud, the moral aspect of personality; the internalization of parental and societal values and standards. To Murray, the superego is shaped not only by parents and authority figures, but also by the peer group and culture.

superiority complex   A condition that develops when a person overcompensates for normal inferiority feelings.

superstitious behavior   Persistent behavior that has a coincidental and not a functional relationship to the reinforcement received.

surface traits   Traits that show a correlation but do not constitute a factor because they are not determined by a single source.

symptom analysis   Similar to catharsis, the symptom analysis technique focuses on the symptoms reported by the patient and attempts to interpret the patient's free associations to those symptoms.

T-data   Data derived from personality tests that are resistant to faking.

temperament traits   Traits that describe our general behavioral style in responding to our environment.

thema   A combination of press (the environment) and need (the personality) that brings order to our behavior.

token economy   A behavior-modification technique in which tokens, which can be exchanged for valued objects or privileges, are awarded for desirable behaviors.

traits   To Allport, distinguishing characteristics that guide behavior. Traits are measured on a continuum and are subject to social, environmental, and cultural influences. To Cattell, reaction tendencies, derived by the method of factor analysis, that are relatively permanent parts of the personality.

triadic reciprocality   The idea that behavior is determined through the interaction of behavioral, cognitive, and environmental or situational variables.

tyranny of the shoulds   An attempt to realize an unattainable idealized self-image by denying the true self and behaving in terms of what we think we should be doing.

unconditional positive regard   Approval granted regardless of a person's behavior. In Rogers's person-centered therapy, the therapist offers the client unconditional positive regard.

unique traits   Traits possessed by one or a few persons.

validity   The extent to which an assessment device measures what it is intended to measure. Types of validity include predictive, content, and construct.

vicarious reinforcement   Learning or strengthening a behavior by observing the behavior of others, and the consequences of that behavior, rather than experiencing the reinforcement or consequences directly.

womb envy   The envy a male feels toward a female because she can bear children and he cannot. Womb envy was Horney's response to Freud's concept of penis envy in females.

word association test   A projective technique in which a person responds to a stimulus word with whatever word comes to mind.

References

Abdallah, T. M. (1989). Self-esteem and locus of control of college men in Saudi Arabia. *Psychological Reports, 65*(3, Pt. 2), 1323–1326.

Abdel-Khalek, A., & Lester, D. (2006). Optimism and pessimism in Kuwaiti and American college students. *International Journal of Social Psychiatry, 52,* 110–126.

Abma, R. (2004). Madness and mental health. In J. Janz & P. Van Drunnen (Eds.), *A social history of psychology* (pp. 93–128). Malden, MA: Blackwell.

Achenbach, T., & Zigler, E. (1963). Social competence and self-image disparity in psychiatric and nonpsychiatric patients. *Journal of Abnormal and Social Psychology, 67,* 197–205.

Adams, D. (1954). *The anatomy of personality.* Garden City, NY: Doubleday.

Adams, G. R., & Fitch, S. A. (1982). Ego stage and identity status development: A cross-sequential analysis. *Journal of Personality and Social Psychology, 43,* 574–583.

Adams-Webber, J. R. (2001). Cognitive complexity and role relationships. *Journal of Constructivist Psychology, 14*(1), 43–50.

Adler, A. (1930). Individual psychology. In C. Murchison (Ed.), *Psychologies of 1930* (pp. 395–405). Worcester, MA: Clark University Press.

Adler, A. (1939). *Social interest: A challenge to mankind.* J. Linton, & R. Vaughan (Trans.). New York: Putnam. (Original work published 1933)

Adler, A. (1963). *The practice and theory of individual psychology.* P. Radin (Trans.). Paterson, NJ: Littlefield, Adams. (Original work published 1924)

Adler, J. (2006, March 27). Freud in our midst. *Newsweek,* pp. 43–49.

Agronick, G., & Duncan, L. E. (1998). Individual differences, life path, and importance attributed to the women's movement. *Journal of Personality and Social Psychology, 74,* 1545–1555.

Alansari, B. M. (2006). Gender differences in anxiety among undergraduates from 16 Islamic countries. *Social Behavior and Personality, 34,* 651–660.

Albright, L., Malloy, T. E., Dong, Q., Kenny, D. A., Fang, X., Winquist, L., & Yu, D. (1997). Cross-cultural consensus in personality judgments. *Journal of Personality and Social Psychology, 72,* 558–569.

Allemand, M., Zimprich, D., & Hertzog, C. (2007). Cross-sectional age differences and longitudinal age changes of personality in middle adulthood and old age. *Journal of Personality, 75,* 323–328.

Allen, J., & Dana, R. (2004). Methodological issues in cross-cultural and multicultural Rorschach research. *Journal of Personality Assessment, 82,* 189–206.

Allen, K. D., Danforth, J. S., & Drabman, R. C. (1989). Videotaped modeling and film distraction for fear reduction in adults undergoing hyperbaric oxygen therapy. *Journal of Consulting and Clinical Psychology, 57,* 554–558.

Allik, J., & McCrae, R. (2004). Toward a geography of personality traits: Patterns of profiles across 36 cultures. *Journal of Cross-Cultural Psychology, 35,* 13–28.

Allport, G. W. (1937). *Personality: A psychological interpretation.* New York: Holt.

Allport, G. W. (1955). *Becoming: Basic considerations for a psychology of personality.* New Haven, CT: Yale University Press.

Allport, G. W. (1961). *Pattern and growth in personality.* New York: Holt.

Allport, G. W. (Ed.). (1965). *Letters from Jenny.* New York: Harcourt, Brace & World.

Allport, G. W. (1966). Traits revisited. *American Psychologist, 21,* 1–10.

Allport, G. W. (1967). Autobiography. In E. G. Boring & G. Lindzey (Eds.), *A history of psychology in autobiography* (Vol. 5, pp. 1–25). New York: Appleton-Century-Crofts.

Allport, G. W., & Cantril, H. (1934). Judging personality from voice. *Journal of Social Psychology, 5,* 37–55.

Allport, G. W., & Vernon, P. (1933). *Studies in expressive movement.* New York: Macmillan.

Allport, G. W., Vernon, P., & Lindzey, G. (1960). *A study of values* (3rd ed.). Boston: Houghton Mifflin.

489

Altmaier, E. M., Russell, D. W., Kao, C. F., Lehmann, T. R., & Weinstein, J. N. (1993). Role of self-efficacy in rehabilitation outcomes among chronic low back pain patients. *Journal of Counseling Psychology, 40,* 335–339.

Ambody, N., & Rosenthal, R. (1992). Thin slices of expressive behavior as predictors of interpersonal consequences: A meta-analysis. *Psychological Bulletin, 111,* 256–274.

Amirkhan, J. H., Risinger, R. T., & Swickert, R. J. (1995). Extraversion: A "hidden" personality factor in coping? *Journal of Personality, 63,* 189–212.

Andersen, D. C., & Friedman, L. J. (1997). Erik Erikson on revolutionary leadership [Retrospective review of four books by Erikson]. *Contemporary Psychology, 42,* 1063–1067.

Anderson, C. (2004). An update on the effects of playing violent video games. *Journal of Adolescence, 27,* 113–122.

Anderson, C., Carnagey, N., & Eubanks, J. (2003). Exposure to violent media: The effects of songs with violent lyrics on aggressive thoughts and feelings. *Journal of Personality and Social Psychology, 84,* 960–971.

Anderson, C., John, O., Keltner, D., & Kring, A. (2001). Who attains social status? Effects of personality and physical attractiveness in social groups. *Journal of Personality and Social Psychology, 81,* 116–132.

Anderson, J. W. (1988). Henry A. Murray's early career: A psychobiographical exploration. *Journal of Personality, 56,* 139–171.

Anderson, J. W. (1990). The life of Henry A. Murray: 1893–1988. In A. I. Rabin, R. A. Zucker, R. A. Emmons, & S. Frank (Eds.), *Studying persons and lives* (pp. 304–334). New York: Springer.

Andreoletti, C., Zebrowitz, L. A., & Lachman, M. E. (2001). Physical appearance and control beliefs in young, middle-aged, and older adults. *Personality and Social Psychology Bulletin, 27,* 969–981.

Ang, R. (2006). Effects of parenting style on personal and social variables for Asian adolescents. *American Journal of Orthopsychiatry, 76,* 503–511.

Anthis, K., & LaVoie, J. (2006). Readiness to change: A longitudinal study of changes in adult identity. *Journal of Research in Personality, 40,* 209–219.

Apostal, R. A. (1991). College students' career interests and sensing-intuition personality. *Journal of College Student Development, 32,* 4–7.

Appignanesi, L., & Forrester, J. (1992). *Freud's women.* New York: Basic Books.

Arbisi, P., Ben-Porath, Y., & McNulty, J. (2002). A comparison of MMPI-2 validity in African-American and Caucasian psychiatric inpatients. *Psychological Assessment, 14*(1), 3–15.

Archer, S. L. (1982). The lower age boundaries of identity development. *Child Development, 53,* 1551–1556.

Aries, E., & Moorehead, K. (1989). The importance of ethnicity in the development of identity of Black adolescents. *Psychological Reports, 65,* 75–82.

Arnett, J. J. (1999). Adolescent storm and stress, reconsidered. *American Psychologist, 54,* 317–326.

Arnold, E. (2005). A voice of their own: Women moving into their fifties. *Health Care for Women International, 26,* 630–651.

Arokach, A. (2006). Alienation and domestic abuse: How abused women cope with loneliness. *Social Indicators Research, 78,* 327–340.

Asendorpf, J. B., & Wilpers, S. (1998). Personality effects on social relationships. *Journal of Personality and Social Psychology, 74,* 1531–1544.

Ashton, M., Lee, K., & Paunonen, S. (2002). What is the central feature of extraversion? Social attention versus reward sensitivity. *Journal of Personality and Social Psychology, 83,* 245–252.

Assor, A., Roth, G., & Deci, E. (2004). The emotional costs of parents' conditional regard: A self-determination theory analysis. *Journal of Personality, 72,* 47–87.

Atkinson, J. W., Lens, W., & O'Malley, P. M. (1976). Motivation and ability: Interactive psychological determinants of intellectual performance, educational achievement, and each other. In W. H. Sewell, R. H. Hanser, & D. L. Featherman (Eds.), *Schooling and achievement in American society.* New York: Academic Press.

Aviezer, A., Van Ijzendoorn, M. H., Sagi, A., & Schuegel, C. (1994). "Children of the Dream" revisited: 70 years of collective early child care in Israeli kibbutzim. *Psychological Bulletin, 116,* 99–116.

Ayllon, T., & Azrin, N. (1968). *The token economy.* New York: Appleton-Century-Crofts.

Baars, B. J. (1986). *The cognitive revolution in psychology.* New York: Guilford Press.

Bacanli, F. (2006). Personality characteristics as predictors of personal indecisiveness. *Journal of Career Development, 32,* 320–332.

Back, M., Schmukle, S., & Egloff, B. (2006). Who is late and who is early? Big Five personality factors and punctuality in attending psychological experiments. *Journal of Research in Personality, 40,* 841–848.

Bair, D. (2003). *Jung: A biography.* Boston: Little Brown.

Baldwin, A. L. (1949). The effect of home environment on nursery school behavior. *Child Development, 20,* 49–61.

Balistreri, E., Busch-Rossnagel, N. A., & Geisinger, K. F. (1995). Development and preliminary validation of the Ego Identity Process Questionnaire. *Journal of Adolescence, 18,* 179–182.

Ball, S. A., Carroll, K. M., & Rounsaville, B. J. (1994). Sensation seeking, substance abuse, and psychopathology in treatment-seeking and community cocaine abusers. *Journal of Consulting and Clinical Psychology, 62,* 1053–1057.

Ball, S. A., & Zuckerman, M. (1992). Sensation seeking and selective attention: Focused and divided attention on a dichotic listening task. *Journal of Personality and Social Psychology, 63,* 825–831.

Baltes, M. M., & Bates, P. B. (1986). *Psychology of control and aging.* Hillsdale, NJ: Erlbaum.

Bandura, A. (1965). Influence of models' reinforcement contingencies on the acquisition of imitative responses. *Journal of Personality and Social Psychology, 1,* 589–595.

Bandura, A. (1973). *Aggression: A social learning analysis.* Englewood Cliffs, NJ: Prentice-Hall.

Bandura, A. (1977). *Social learning theory.* Englewood Cliffs, NJ: Prentice-Hall.

Bandura, A. (1986). *Social foundations of thought and action: A social cognitive theory.* Englewood Cliffs, NJ: Prentice-Hall.

Bandura, A. (1995). Exercise of personal and collective efficacy in changing societies. In A. Bandura (Ed.), *Self-efficacy in changing societies* (pp. 1–45). Cambridge, England: Cambridge University Press.

Bandura, A. (1997). *Self-efficacy: The exercise of control.* New York: W. H. Freeman.

Bandura, A. (2001). Social cognitive theory: An agentic perspective. *Annual Review of Psychology, 52,* 1–26.

Bandura, A., Blanchard, E. B., & Ritter, B. (1969). The relative efficacy of desensitization and modeling approaches for inducing behavioral, affective, and attitudinal changes. *Journal of Personality and Social Psychology, 13,* 173–199.

Bandura, A., Grusec, J. E., & Menlove, F. L. (1967). Vicarious extinction of avoidance behavior through symbolic modeling. *Journal of Personality and Social Psychology, 5,* 16–22.

Bandura, A., Pastorelli, C., Barbaranelli, C., & Caprara, G. V. (1999). Self-efficacy pathways to childhood depression. *Journal of Personality and Social Psychology, 76,* 258–269.

Bandura, A., Ross, D., & Ross, S. A. (1963). Imitation of film-mediated aggressive models. *Journal of Abnormal and Social Psychology, 66,* 3–11.

Bandura, A., & Walters, R. (1963). *Social learning and personality development.* New York: Holt, Rinehart & Winston.

Bannister, D., Fransella, F., & Agnew, J. (1971). Characteristics and validity of the grid test on thought disorder. *British Journal of Social and Clinical Psychology, 10,* 144–151.

Bannister, D., & Salmon, P. (1966). Schizophrenic thought disorder: Specific or diffuse? *British Journal of Medical Psychology, 39,* 215–219.

Barelds, D. (2005). Self and partner personality in intimate relationships. *European Journal of Personality, 19,* 501–518.

Barger, S. D., Kircher, J. C., & Croyle, R. T. (1997). The effects of social context and defensiveness on the physiological responses of repressive copers. *Journal of Personality and Social Psychology, 73,* 1118–1128.

Bargh, J. A., & Chartrand, T. L. (1999). The unbearable automaticity of being. *American Psychologist, 54,* 462–479.

Bargh, J. A., Gollwitzer, P., Lee-Chai, A., Barndollar, K., & Troetschel, R. (2001). The automated will: Nonconscious activation and pursuit of behavioral goals. *Journal of Personality and Social Psychology, 81,* 1014–1027.

Baron, R., & Byrne, D. (1984). *Social psychology: Understanding human interaction* (4th ed.). Newton, MA: Allyn & Bacon.

Barongan, C., & Hall, G. (1995). The influence of misogynous rap [music] on sexual aggression against women. *Psychology of Women Quarterly, 19,* 195–207.

Baroun, K., & Al-Ansari, B. (2005). The impact of anxiety and gender on perceiving the Mueller-Lyer illusion. *Social Behavior and Personality, 33,* 33–42.

Barrett, A. (2005). Gendered experiences in midlife: Implications for age identity. *Journal of Aging Studies, 19,* 163–183.

Barrett, L., Lane, R., Sechrest, L., & Schwartz, G. (2000). Sex differences in emotional awareness. *Personality and Social Psychology Bulletin, 26,* 1027–1035.

Barrick, M. R., & Mount, M. K. (1996). Effects of impression management and self-deception on the predictive validity of personality constructs. *Journal of Applied Psychology, 81,* 261–272.

Barrick, M. R., Mount, M. K., & Strauss, J. P. (1993). Conscientiousness and performance of sales representatives. Test of the mediating effects of goal setting. *Journal of Applied Psychology, 78,* 715–722.

Barrineau, P. (2005). Personality types among undergraduates who withdraw from liberal arts college. *Journal of Psychological type, 65,* 27–32.

Barron, K., & Harackiewicz, J. (2001). Achievement goals and optimal motivation: Testing multiple goal models. *Journal of Personality and Social Psychology, 80,* 706–722.

Barry, L., Kasl, S., Lichtman, J., Vaccarino, V., & Krumholz, H. (2006). Perceived control and change in physical functioning after coronary artery bypass grafting. *International Journal of Behavioral Medicine, 13,* 229–236.

Bartholow, B., Sestir, M., & Davis, E. (2005). Correlates and consequences of exposure to videogame violence: Hostile personality, empathy, and aggressive behavior. *Personality and Social Psychology Bulletin, 31,* 1573–1586.

Bassi, M., Steca, P., Fave, A., & Caprara, G. (2007). Academic self-efficacy and quality of experience in learning. *Journal of Youth and Adolescence, 36,* 301–312.

Battle, E., & Rotter, J. B. (1963). Children's feelings of personal control as related to social class and ethnic group. *Journal of Personality, 31,* 482–490.

Beaumont, S., & Zukanovic, R. (2005). Identity development in men and its relation to psychosocial distress and self-worth. *Canadian Journal of Behavioural Science, 37,* 70–81.

Beck, E., Burnet, K., & Vosper, J. (2006). Birth order effects on facets of extraversion. *Personality and Individual Differences, 40,* 953–959.

Becona, E., Frojan, M. J., & Lista, M. J. (1988). Comparison between two self-efficacy scales in maintenance of smoking cessation. *Psychological Reports, 62,* 359–362.

Begue, L., & Roche, S. (2005). Birth order and youth delinquency behaviour: Testing the differential parental control hypothesis in a French representative sample. *Psychology, Crime and Law, 11,* 73–85.

Belmont, L., & Marolla, F. A. (1973). Birth order, family size and intelligence. *Science, 182,* 1096–1101.

Benassi, V. A., Sweeney, P. D., & Dufour, C. L. (1988). Is there a relationship between locus of control orientation and depression? *Journal of Abnormal Psychology, 97,* 357–367.

Benet-Martinez, V., Lee, F., & Leu, J. (2006). Biculturalism and cultural complexity: Expertise in cultural representations. *Journal of Cross-Cultural Psychology, 37,* 386–407.

Ben-Zur, H., & Zimmerman, M. (2005). Aging holocaust survivors' well-being and adjustment: Association with ambivalence over emotional expression. *Psychology and Aging, 20,* 710–713.

Berg, M. B., Janoff-Bulman, P., & Cotter, J. (2001). Perceiving value in obligations and goals: Wanting to do what should be done. *Personality and Social Psychology Bulletin, 27,* 982–995.

Bergeman, C. S., Chipeur, H. M., Plomin, R., Pedersen, N. L., McClearn, G. E., Nesselroade, J. R., Costa, P. T., Jr., & McCrae, R. R. (1993). Genetic and environmental effects on openness to experience, agreeableness, and conscientiousness: An adoption-twin study. *Journal of Personality, 61,* 159–179.

Bergin, A. E., & Strupp, H. H. (1972). *Changing frontiers in the science of psychotherapy.* New York: Aldine-Atherton.

Berry, D. S. (1990). Taking people at face value: Evidence for the kernel of truth hypothesis. *Social Cognition, 8,* 343–361.

Berry, D. S., & Wero, J. L. F. (1993). Accuracy in face perception: A view from ecological psychology. *Journal of Personality, 61,* 497–520.

Berzonsky, M. (2004). Identity style, parental authority, and identity commitment. *Journal of Youth and Adolescence, 33,* 213–220.

Bettelheim, B. (1984). *Freud and man's soul.* New York: Vintage Books.

Biao-Bin, V., Man-Na, H., Bi-Qun, Q., & Yong-Hong, H. (2006). Relationship between Internet behavior and subjective well-being of teenagers. *Chinese Journal of Clinical Psychology, 14,* 68–69.

Bilsker, D., & Marcia, J. E. (1991). Adaptive regression and ego identity. *Journal of Adolescence, 14,* 75–84.

Birnbaum, M. (2004). Human research on data collection via the Internet. *Annual Review of Psychology, 55,* 803–832.

Bjork, D. W. (1993). *B. F. Skinner: A life.* New York: Basic Books.

Blackman, D. E. (1995). B. F. Skinner (1904–1990). In R. Fuller (Ed.), *Seven pioneers of psychology: Behaviour and mind* (pp. 107–129). London: Routledge.

Blanton, H., Axsom, D., McClive, K., & Price, S. (2001). Pessimistic bias in comparative evaluations: A case of perceived vulnerability to the effects of negative life events. *Personality and Social Psychology Bulletin, 27,* 1627–1636.

Blanton, S. (1971). *Diary of my analysis with Sigmund Freud.* New York: Hawthorn Books.

Block, J., & Block, J. (1980). The role of ego-control and ego-resiliency in the organization of behavior. In W. A. Collins (Ed.), *The Minnesota symposium on child psychology* (Vol. 13, pp. 39–101). Hillsdale, NJ: Erlbaum.

Block, J., & Block, J. (2006). Venturing a 30-year longitudinal study. *American Psychologist, 61,* 315–327.

Bloland, S. (2005). In the shadow of fame: A memoir by the daughter of Erik H. Erikson. New York: Viking Press.

Blustein, D. L., Devenis, L. E., & Kidney, B. A. (1989). Relationship between the identity formation process and career development. *Journal of Counseling Psychology, 36,* 196–202.

Boden, J., & Baumeister, R. (1997). Repressive coping: Distraction using pleasant thoughts and memories. *Journal of Personality and Social Psychology, 73,* 45–62.

Bodin, M., & Romelsjo, A. (2006). Predictors of abstinence and nonproblem drinking after 12-step treatment in Sweden. *Journal of Studies on Alcohol, 67,* 139–146.

Bogaert, A. (2003). Number of older brothers and social orientation: New tests and the attraction/behavior distinction in two national probability samples. *Journal of Personality and Social Psychology, 84,* 644–652.

Bolger, N., Davis, A., & Rafaeli, E. (2003). Diary methods: Capturing life as it is lived. *Annual Review of Psychology, 54,* 579–616.

Booth-Kewley, S., & Vickers, R. R., Jr. (1994). Associations between major domains of personality and health behavior. *Journal of Personality, 62,* 281–298.

Bores-Rangel, E., Church, A. T., Szendre, D., & Reeves, C. (1990). Self-efficacy in relation to occupational consideration and academic performance in high school equivalency students. *Journal of Counseling Psychology, 37,* 407–418.

Borkenau, P., Riemann, R., Angleitner, A., & Spinath, F. (2001). Genetic and environmental influences on observed personality: Evidence from the German Observational Study of Adult Twins. *Journal of Personality and Social Psychology, 80,* 655–668.

Bornstein, R. F. (2001). The impending death of psychoanalysis. *Psychoanalytic Psychology, 18,* 2–20.

Bornstein, R. F. (2002). The impending death of psychoanalysis: From destructive obfuscation to constructive dialogue. *Psychoanalytic Psychology, 19,* 580–590.

Bornstein, R. F., & Masling, J. M. (1998). Introduction: The psychoanalytic unconscious. In R. F. Bornstein & J. M. Masling (Eds.), *Empirical perspectives on the psychoanalytic unconscious* (pp. xiii–xxviii). Washington, DC: American Psychological Association.

Bottome, P. (1939). *Alfred Adler: A biography.* New York: Putnam.

Bouchard, T. J. (1985). Twins reared together and apart: What they tell us about human diversity. In S. W. Fox (Ed.), *Individuality and determinism: Chemical and biological bases* (pp. 147–184). New York: Plenum Press.

Bourne, E. (1978a). The state of research on ego identity: A review and appraisal. Part I. *Journal of Youth and Adolescence, 7,* 223–257.

Bourne, E. (1978b). The state of research on ego identity: A review and appraisal. Part II. *Journal of Youth and Adolescence, 7,* 371–392.

Bowker, A. (2006). The relationship between sports participation and self-esteem during early adolescence. *Canadian Journal of Behavioural Science, 38,* 214–229.

Bracey, J., Bamaca, M., & Umana-Taylor, A. (2004). Examining ethnic identity and self-esteem among biracial and monoracial adolescents. *Journal of Youth and Adolescence, 33,* 123–132.

Brannigan, G. G., Hauk, P. A., & Guay, J. A. (1991). Locus of control and daydreaming. *Journal of Genetic Psychology, 152,* 29–33.

Breger, L. (2000). *Freud: Darkness in the midst of vision.* New York: Wiley.

Breger, L., Hunter, I., & Lane, R. W. (1971). *The effect of stress on dreams.* New York: International Universities Press.

Breland, H. M. (1974). Birth order, family configuration and verbal achievement. *Child Development, 45,* 1011–1019.

Breland, K., & Breland, M. (1961). The misbehavior of organisms. *American Psychologist, 16,* 681–684.

Brewin, C. R., Andrews, B., & Gotlib, I. H. (1993). Psychopathology and early experience: A reappraisal of retrospective reports. *Psychological Bulletin, 113,* 82–98.

Briggs, K. C., & Myers, I. B. (1943, 1976). *Myers-Briggs Type Indicator.* Palo Alto, CA: Consulting Psychologists Press.

Brissette, I., Scheier, M., & Carver, C. (2002). The role of optimism in social network development, coping, and psychological adjustment during a life transition. *Journal of Personality and Social Psychology, 82,* 102–111.

Brody, L. R., Rozek, M. K., & Muten, E. O. (1985). Age, sex, and individual differences in children's defensive styles. *Journal of Clinical Child Psychology, 14,* 132–138.

Brody, N. (1997). Dispositional paradigms: Comment on Eysenck (1997) and the biosocial science of individual differences. *Journal of Personality and Social Psychology, 73,* 1242–1245.

Broman, C. L. (1997). Race-related factors and life satisfaction among African Americans. *Journal of Black Psychology, 23,* 36–49.

Brome, V. (1981). *Jung: Man and myth.* New York: Atheneum.

Bronstein, P. (1988). Personality from a sociocultural perspective. In P. Bronstein & K. Quina (Eds.), *Teaching a psychology of people: Resources for gender and sociocultural awareness* (pp. 60–68). Washington, DC: American Psychological Association.

Brown, C., Matthews, K., & Bromberger, J. (2005). How do African-American and Caucasian women view themselves at midlife? *Journal of Applied Social Psychology, 35,* 2057–2075.

Brown, L. L., Tomarkin, A., Orth, D., Loosen, P., Kalin, N., & Davidson, R. (1996). Individual differences in repressive-defensiveness predict basal salivary cortisol levels. *Journal of Personality and Social Psychology, 70,* 362–371.

Bruhn, A. R. (1992a). The early memories procedure: A projective test of autobiographical memory. Part 1. *Journal of Personality Assessment, 58,* 1–15.

Bruhn, A. R. (1992b). The early memories procedure: A projective test of autobiographical memory. Part 2. *Journal of Personality Assessment, 58,* 326–346.

Bryant, B. L. (1987). Birth order as a factor in the development of vocational preferences. *Individual Psychology, 43,* 36–41.

Buchanan, L. P., Kern, R., & Bell-Dumas, J. (1991). Comparison of content in created versus actual early recollections. *Individual Psychology, 47,* 348–355.

Buchanan, T., Johnson, J., & Goldberg, L. (2005). Implementing a five-factor personality inventory for use on the Internet. *European Journal of Psychological Assessment, 21,* 115–127.

Bullard, A. (2005). The critical impact of Franz Fanon and Henri Collomb: Race, gender, and personality testing of North and West Africans. *Journal of the History of the Behavioral Sciences, 41,* 225–248.

Bullock, W. A., & Gilliland, K. (1993). Eysenck's arousal theory of introversion-extraversion: A converging measures investigation. *Journal of Personality and Social Psychology, 64,* 113–123.

Burger, J., & Lynn, A. (2005). Superstitious behavior among American and Japanese professional baseball players. *Basic and Applied Social Psychology, 27,* 71–76.

Busch, F. N., Shear, M. K., Cooper, A. M., Shapiro, T., & Leon, A. (1995). An empirical study of defense mechanisms in panic disorder. *Journal of Nervous and Mental Disease, 183,* 299–303.

Bushman, B. J. (2002). Does venting anger feed or extinguish the flame? Catharsis, rumination, distraction, anger, and aggressive responding. *Personality and Social Psychology Bulletin, 28,* 724–731.

Bushman, B. J., Baumeister, R. F., & Stack, A. D. (1999). Catharsis, aggression, and persuasive influence: Self-fulfilling or self-defeating prophecies? *Journal of Personality and Social Psychology, 76,* 367–376.

Bushman, B., Bonacci, A., Pedersen, W., Vasquez, E., & Miller, N. (2005). Chewing on it can chew you up: Effects of rumination on triggered displaced aggression. *Journal of Personality and Social Psychology, 88,* 969–983.

Buss, A. H. (1988). *Personality: Evolutionary heritage and human distinctiveness.* Hillsdale, NJ: Erlbaum.

Buss, A. H., & Plomin, R. (1975). *A temperament theory of personality development.* New York: Wiley.

Buss, A. H., & Plomin, R. (1984). *Temperament: Early developing personality traits.* Hillsdale, NJ: Erlbaum.

Buss, A. H., & Plomin, R. (1986). The EAS approach to temperament. In R. Plomin & J. Dunn (Eds.), *The study of temperament: Changes, continuities and challenges* (pp. 67–79). Hillsdale, NJ: Erlbaum.

Butcher, J. (2004). Personality assessment without borders: Adaptation of the MMPI-2 across cultures. *Journal of Personality Assessment, 83,* 90–104.

Butler, J. M., & Haigh, G. V. (1954). Changes in the relationship between self-concepts and ideal concepts consequent upon client-centered counseling. In C. R. Rogers & R. F. Dymond (Eds.), *Psychotherapy and personality change.* Chicago: University of Chicago Press.

Bynum, M., Burton, E., & Best, C. (2007). Racism experiences and psychological functioning in African-American college freshmen: Is racial socialization a buffer? *Cultural Diversity and Ethnic Minority Psychology, 13,* 64–71.

Caldwell, R., Beutler, L., Ross, S., & Silver, N. (2006). An examination of the relationships between parental monitoring, self-esteem and delinquency among Mexican-American adolescents. *Journal of Adolescence, 29,* 459–464.

Campbell, W. K., Rudich, E. A., & Sedikides, C. (2002). Narcissism, self-esteem, and the positivity of self views: Two portraits of self-love. *Personality and Social Psychology Bulletin, 28,* 358–368.

Camras, L. (1998). Production of emotional facial expressions in European American, Japanese, and Chinese infants. *Developmental Psychology, 34,* 616–628.

Camras, L., Bakeman, R., Chen, Y., Norris, K., & Cain, T. (2006). Culture, ethnicity, and children's facial expressions: A study of European, American, Mainland Chinese, Chinese American, and adopted Chinese girls. *Emotion, 6,* 103–114.

Camras, L., Oster, H., Campos, J. J., Miyake, K., & Bradshaw, D. (1997). Japanese and American infants' responses to arm restraint. In P. Ekman & E. L. Rosenberg (Eds.), *What the face reveals* (pp. 289–299). New York: Oxford University Press.

Cann, D. R., & Donderi, D. C. (1986). Jungian personality typology and the recall of everyday and archetypal dreams. *Journal of Personality and Social Psychology, 50,* 1021–1030.

Caplan, P. J. (1979). Erikson's concept of inner space: A data-based reevaluation. *American Journal of Orthopsychiatry, 49,* 100–108.

Capron, E., (2004). Types of pampering and the narcissistic personality trait. *Journal of Individual Psychology, 60,* 76–83.

Carlson, R. (1980). Studies of Jungian typology: II. Representations of the personal world. *Journal of Personality and Social Psychology, 38,* 801–810.

Carlson, R., & Levy, N. (1973). Studies of Jungian typology: I. Memory, social perception, and social action. *Journal of Personality, 41,* 559–576.

Carmichael, C. M., & McGue, M. (1994). A longitudinal family study of personality change and stability. *Journal of Personality, 62,* 1–20.

Carr, D. (2004). "My daughter has a career; I just raised babies." The psychological consequences of women's intergenerational social comparison. *Social Psychology Quarterly, 67,* 132–154.

Carskadon, T. G. (1978). Use of the Myers-Briggs Type Indicator in psychology courses and discussion groups. *Teaching of Psychology, 5,* 140–142.

Carver, C., & Scheier, M. (2002). Optimism. In C. Snyder & S. Lopez (Eds.), *Handbook of positive psychology* (pp. 231–243). New York: Oxford University Press.

Carver, C. S., Harris, S. D., Lehman, J. H., Durel, L. A., Anton, M. H., Spencer, S. M., & Pozo-Kaderman, C. (2000). How important is the perception of personal control? Studies of early stage breast cancer patients. *Personality and Social Psychology Bulletin, 26,* 139–149.

Caspi, A., Bem, D. J., & Elder, G. H. (1989). Continuities and consequences of interactional styles across the life course. *Journal of Personality, 57,* 375–406.

Caspi, A., Elder, G. H., & Bem, D. J. (1987). Moving against the world: Life course patterns of explosive children. *Developmental Psychology, 23,* 308–313.

Caspi, A., Elder, G. H., & Bem, D. J. (1988). Moving away from the world: Life course patterns of shy children. *Developmental Psychology, 24,* 824–831.

Caspi, A., Roberts, B., & Shiner, R. (2005). Personality development: Stability and change. *Annual Review of Psychology, 56,* 453–484.

Caspi, A., & Silva, P. (1994). Temperamental qualities at age 3 predict personality traits in young adulthood: Longitudinal evidence from a birth cohort. *Child Development, 65.*

Cattell, R. B. (1950). *Personality: A systematic theoretical and factual study.* New York: McGraw-Hill.

Cattell, R. B. (1959). Foundations of personality measurement theory in multivariate expression. In B. M. Bass & I. A. Berg (Eds.), *Objective approaches to personality assessment* (pp. 42–65). Princeton, NJ: Van Nostrand.

Cattell, R. B. (1965, 1970). *The scientific analysis of personality.* Baltimore: Penguin Books.

Cattell, R. B. (1973). *Personality and mood by questionnaire.* San Francisco: Jossey-Bass.

Cattell, R. B. (1974a). Autobiography. In G. Lindzey (Ed.), *A history of psychology in autobiography* (Vol. 6, pp. 59–100). Englewood Cliffs, NJ: Prentice-Hall.

Cattell, R. B. (1974b). Travels in psychological hyperspace. In T. S. Krawiec (Ed.), *The psychologists* (Vol. 2, pp. 85–133). New York: Oxford University Press.

Cattell, R. B. (1982). *The inheritance of personality and ability: Research methods.* New York: Academic Press.

Cattell, R. B. (1990). Advances in Cattellian personality theory. In L. A. Pervin (Ed.), *Handbook of personality: Theory and research* (pp. 101–110). New York: Guilford Press.

Cattell, R. B. (1993). Planning basic clinical research. In C. E. Walker (Ed.), *The history of clinical psychology in autobiography* (Vol. 2, pp. 101–111). Pacific Grove, CA: Brooks/Cole.

Cattell, R. B., & Kline, P. (1977). *The scientific analysis of personality and motivation.* New York: Academic Press.

Cattell, R. B., & Nesselroade, J. R. (1967). Likeness and completeness theories examined by Sixteen Personality Factor measures by stably and unstably married couples. *Journal of Personality and Social Psychology, 7,* 351–361.

Ceci, S. J., & Bruck, M. (1993). Suggestibility of the child witness: A historical review and synthesis. *Psychological Bulletin, 113,* 403–439.

Chamorro-Premuzic, T., Furnham, A., & Petrides, K. (2006). Personality and intelligence: The relationship of Eysenck's Giant Three with verbal and numerical ability. *Journal of Individual Differences, 27,* 147–150.

Chang, E., & Sanna, L. (2001). Optimism, pessimism, and positive and negative affectivity in middle-aged adults: A test of a cognitive-affective model of psychological adjustment. *Psychology and Aging, 16,* 524–531.

Chang, E., Asakawa, K., & Sanna, L. (2001). Cultural variations in optimistic and pessimistic bias: Do Easterners really expect the worst and Westerners really expect the best when predicting future life events? *Journal of Personality and Social Psychology, 81,* 476–491.

Chen, J., & Wang, L. (2007). Locus of control and the three components of commitment to change. *Personality and Individual Differences, 42,* 503–512.

Chen, M., Miller, B., Grube, J., & Waiters, E. (2006). Music, substance use, and aggression. *Journal of Studies on Alcohol, 67,* 373–381.

Cherry, R., & Cherry, L. (1973, August 26). The Horney heresy. *The New York Times Magazine,* pp. 12ff.

Chesney, M. A., Ekman, P., Friesen, W. V., Black, G. W., & Hecker, M. H. L. (1997). Type A behavior pattern: Facial behavior and speech components. In P. Ekman & E. L. Rosenberg (Eds.), *What the face reveals* (pp. 456–466). New York: Oxford University Press.

Chodorkoff, B. (1954). Self-perception, perceptual defense, and adjustment. *Journal of Abnormal and Social Psychology, 49,* 508–512.

Chowdhury, M., & Amin, M. (2006). Personality and students' academic achievement: Interactive effects of conscientiousness and agreeableness on students' performance in Principles of Economics. *Social Behavior and Personality, 34,* 381–388.

Christensen, A., Ehlers, S., Wiebe, J., Moran, P., Raichle, K., Ferneyhough, K., & Lawton, W. (2002). Patient personality and mortality: A 4-year prospective study of chronic renal insufficiency. *Health Psychology, 21,* 315–320.

Chuah, S., Drasgow, F., & Roberts, B. (2006). Personality assessment: Does the medium matter? No. *Journal of Research in Personality, 40,* 359–376.

Church, A. T., & Lonner, W. J. (1998). The cross-cultural perspective in the study of personality. *Journal of Cross-Cultural Psychology, 29,* 32–62.

Ciaccio, N. (1971). A test of Erikson's theory of ego epigenesis. *Developmental Psychology, 4,* 306–311.

Ciarrochi, J., & Heaven, P. (2007). Longitudinal examination of the impact of Eysenck's psychoticism dimension on emotional well-being in teenagers. *Personality and Individual Differences, 42,* 597–608.

Clark, A. (2005). An early recollection of Albert Einstein: Perspectives on its meaning and his life. *Journal of Individual Psychology, 61,* 126–136.

Clemmens, E. R. (1987). Karen Horney, a reminiscence. In K. Horney, *Final lectures* (pp. 107–115). New York: Norton.

Coan, R. W. (1972). Measurable components of openness to experience. *Journal of Consulting and Clinical Psychology, 39,* 346.

Cohen, J. B. (1967). An interpersonal orientation to the study of consumer behavior. *Journal of Marketing Research, 4,* 270–278.

Cohen, S., & Wills, T. A. (1985). Stress, social support, and the buffering hypothesis. *Psychological Bulletin, 98,* 310–357.

Cokley, K. (2002). Testing Cross's racial identity model: An examination of the relationship between racial identity and internalized racialism. *Journal of Counseling Psychology, 49,* 476–483.

Coleman, J. S., Campbell, E. Q., Hobson, C. J., McPartland, J., Mood, A. M., Weinfeld, F. D., & York, R. L. (1966). *Equality of educational opportunity.* Washington, DC: U.S. Office of Education.

Coles, R. (1998). Psychoanalysis: The American experience. In M. S. Roth (Ed.), *Conflict and culture* (pp. 140–151). New York: Knopf.

Colombo, F., Balbo, M., & Baruffi, M. (2006). Subjective well-being in a sample of Italian students. *Homeostasis in Health and Disease, 44,* 34–39.

Combs, D., Penn, D., & Fenigstein, A. (2002). Ethnic differences in subclinical paranoia: An expansion of norms of the paranoia scale. *Cultural Diversity and Ethnic Minority Psychology, 8,* 248–256.

Compton, W. (2006). *An introduction to positive psychology.* Belmont, CA: Thomson Wadsworth.

Conner, M., & Abraham, C. (2001). Conscientiousness and the theory of planned behavior: Toward a more complete model of the antecedents of intentions and behavior. *Personality and Social Psychology Bulletin, 27,* 1547–1561.

Constantine, M., Alleyne, V., Wallace, B., & Franklin-Jackson, D. (2006). Africentric cultural values: Their relation to positive mental health in African-American adolescent girls. *Journal of Black Psychology, 32,* 141–154.

Constantinople, A. (1969). An Eriksonian measure of personality development in college students. *Developmental Psychology, 1,* 357–372.

Contarello, A., & Sarrica, M. (2007). ICTs, social thinking and subjective well-being: The Internet and its representations in everyday life. *Computers in Human Behavior, 23,* 1016–1032.

Conway, M., & Holmes, A. (2004). Psychosocial stages and the accessibility of autobiographical memories across the life cycle. *Journal of Personality, 72,* 461–480.

Coolidge, F., Moor, C. J., Yamazaki, T. G., Stewart, S. E., & Segal, D. L. (2001). On the relationship between Karen

Horney's tripartite neurotic type theory and personality disorder features. *Personality and Individual Differences, 30,* 1387–1400.

Coolidge, F., Segal, D., Benight, C., & Danielian, J. (2004). The predictive power of Horney's psychoanalytic approach. *American Journal of Psychoanalysis, 64,* 363–374.

Coopersmith, S. (1967). *The antecedents of self-esteem.* New York: W. H. Freeman.

Corby, B., Hodges, E., & Perry, D. (2007). Gender identity and adjustment in Black, Hispanic, and White preadolescents. *Developmental Psychology, 43,* 261–266.

Costa, P. T., Jr., & McCrae, R. R. (1984). Personality as a lifelong determinant of well-being. In C. Z. Malatesta & C. E. Izard (Eds.), *Emotion in adult development* (pp. 141–158). Beverly Hills, CA: Sage.

Costa, P. T., Jr., & McCrae, R. R. (1988). Personality in adulthood: A six-year longitudinal study of self-reports and spouse ratings on the NEO Personality Inventory. *Journal of Personality and Social Psychology, 54,* 853–863.

Costa, P. T., Jr., & McCrae, R. R. (1997). Longitudinal stability of adult personality. In R. Hogan, J. Johnson, & S. Briggs (Eds.), *Handbook of personality psychology* (pp. 269–290). San Diego: Academic Press.

Costa, P., Herbst, P., McCrae, R. R., & Siegler, I. (2000). Personality at midlife: Stability, intrinsic maturation, and response to life events. *Assessment, 7,* 365–378.

Cote, J. E., & Levine, C. (1988). The relationship between ego identity status and Erikson's notions of institutionalized moratoria, value orientation stage, and ego dominance. *Journal of Youth and Adolescence, 17,* 81–99.

Couturier, J., & Lock, J. (2006). Denial and minimization in adolescents with anorexia nervosa. *International Journal of Eating Disorders, 39,* 212–216.

Cowan, D. A. (1989). An alternative to the dichotomous interpretation of Jung's psychological functions: Developing more sensitive measurement technology. *Journal of Personality Assessment, 53,* 459–471.

Cozzarelli, C. (1993). Personality and self-efficacy as predictors of coping with abortion. *Journal of Personality and Social Psychology, 65,* 1224–1236.

Cramer, P. (1987). The development of defense mechanisms. *Journal of Personality, 54,* 597–614.

Cramer, P. (1990). *The development of defense mechanisms: Theory, research and assessment.* New York: Springer-Verlag.

Cramer, P. (2007). Longitudinal study of defense mechanisms: Late childhood to late adolescence. *Journal of Personality, 75,* 1–24.

Cramer, P., & Block, J. (1998). Preschool antecedents of defense mechanism use in young adults: A longitudinal study. *Journal of Personality and Social Psychology, 74,* 159–169.

Crandall, J. E. (1981). *Theory and measurement of social interest: Empirical tests of Alfred Adler's concept.* New York: Columbia University Press.

Crandall, J. E. (1984). Social interest as a moderator of life stress. *Journal of Personality and Social Psychology, 47,* 164–174.

Crawford, T., Cohen, P., Johnson, J., Sneed, J., & Brook, J. (2004). The course and psychological correlates of personality disorder symptoms in adolescence: Erikson's developmental theory revisited. *Journal of Youth and Adolescence, 33,* 373–387.

Crewsdon, J. (1988). *By silence betrayed: Sexual abuse of children in America.* Boston: Little, Brown.

Crocker, J., & Luhtanen, R. (2003). Level of self-esteem and contingencies of self-worth: Unique effects on academic, social, and financial problems in college students. *Personality and Social Psychology Bulletin, 29,* 701–712.

Crocker, J., & Park, L. (2004). The costly pursuit of self-esteem. *Psychological Bulletin, 130,* 392–414.

Crockett, W. H. (1982). The organization of construct systems: The organization corollary. In J. C. Mancuso & J. R. Adams-Webber (Eds.), *The construing person.* New York: Praeger.

Crook, T., Raskin, A., & Eliot, J. (1981). Parent–child relationships and adult depression. *Child Development, 52,* 950–957.

Crowe, M., Andel, R., Pedersen, N., Fratiglioni, L., & Gatz, M. (2006). Personality and risk of cognitive impairment 25 years later. *Psychology and Aging, 21,* 573–580.

Crozier, W., & Birdsey, N. (2003). Shyness, sensation seeking and birth-order position. *Personality and Individual Differences, 35,* 127–134.

Curry, C. (1998). Adolescence. In K. Trew & J. Kremer (Eds.), *Gender and psychology* (pp. 107–117). New York: Oxford University Press.

Dallery, J., Glenn, I., & Raiff, B. (2007). An Internet-based abstinence reinforcement treatment for cigarette smoking. *Drug and Alcohol Dependence, 86,* 230–238.

Dan, T., Jun, Z., & Ji-Liang, S. (2006). The influence factors of subjective well-being in older adults. *Chinese Mental Health Journal, 20,* 160–162.

Dana, R. (2002). Mental health services for African Americans: A cultural/racial perspective. *Cultural Diversity and Ethnic Minority Psychology, 8,* 3–18.

Daniels, D., & Plomin, R. (1985). Origins of individual differences in infant shyness. *Developmental Psychology, 21,* 118–121.

Danner, D., Snowdon, D., & Friesen, W. (2001). Positive emotions in early life and longevity: Findings from the nun study. *Journal of Personality and Social Psychology, 80,* 804–813.

Daugherty, D. A., Murphy, M. J., & Paugh, J. (2001). An examination of the Adlerian construct of social interest with criminal offenders. *Journal of Counseling and Development, 79,* 465–471.

Davidow, S., & Bruhn, A. R. (1990). Earliest memories and the dynamics of delinquency: A replication study. *Journal of Personality Assessment, 54,* 601–616.

Davis, P. J. (1987). Repression and the inaccessibility of affective memories. *Journal of Personality and Social Psychology, 53,* 585–593.

DeBrabander, B., & Boone, C. (1990). Sex differences in perceived locus of control. *Journal of Social Psychology, 130,* 271–272.

DeCarvalho, R. J. (1999). Otto Rank, the Rankian circle in Philadelphia, and the origin of Carl Rogers' person-centered psychotherapy. *History of Psychology, 2,* 132–148.

DeFruyt, F., Bartels, M., Van Leeuwen, K., DeClercq, B., Decuyper, M., & Mervielde, I. (2006). Five types of personality continuity in childhood and adolescence. *Journal of Personality and Social Psychology, 91,* 538–552.

Delmonte, M. M. (2000). Retrieved memories of childhood sexual abuse. *British Journal of Medical Psychology, 73,* 1–13.

Dement, W. C., & Wolpert, E. A. (1958). The relationship of eye movements, body motility, and external stimuli to dream content. *Journal of Experimental Psychology, 55,* 543–553.

DeNeve, K., & Cooper, H. (1998). The happy personality: A meta-analysis of 137 personality traits and subjective well-being. *Psychological Bulletin, 124,* 197–229.

DePaulo, B. M. (1993). The ability to judge others from their expressive behaviors. In K. H. Craik, R. Hogan, & R. N. Wolfe (Eds.), *Fifty years of personality psychology* (pp. 197–206). New York: Plenum Press.

DeRaad, B. (2000). *The big five personality factors: The psycholexical approach to personality.* Seattle: Hogrefe & Huber.

Derks, D., Bos, A., & Von Grumbkow, J. (2007). Emoticons and social interaction on the Internet: The importance of social context. *Computers in Human Behavior, 23,* 842–849.

DeVito, A. J. (1985). Review of Myers-Briggs Type Indicator. In J. V. Mitchell, Jr. (Ed.), *Ninth mental measurements yearbook* (Vol. 2, pp. 1030–1032). Lincoln: University of Nebraska Press.

DiClemente, C. C., Prochaska, J. O., & Gilbertini, M. (1985). Self-efficacy and the stages of self-change of smoking. *Cognitive Therapy and Research, 9,* 181–200.

Diener, E., & Seligman, M. E. P. (2002). Very happy people. *Psychological Science, 13,* 81–84.

Diener, E., Diener, M., & Diener, C. (1995). Factors predicting the subjective well-being of nations. *Journal of Personality and Social Psychology, 69,* 851–864.

Diener, E., Gohm, C., Suh, E. M., & Oishi, S. (2000). Similarity of the relations between marital status and subjective well-being across cultures. *Journal of Cross Cultural Psychology, 31,* 419–436.

Diener, E., Lucas, R., Oishi, S., & Suh, E. M. (2002). Looking up and looking down: Weighting good and bad information in life satisfaction judgments. *Personality and Social Psychology Bulletin, 28,* 437–445.

Diener, E., Oishi, S., & Lucas, R. E. (2003). Personality, culture, and subjective well-being: Emotional and cognitive evaluations of life. *Annual Review of Psychology, 54,* 403–425.

Diener, E., Suh, E. M., Lucas, R. E., & Smith, H. L. (1999). Subjective well-being: Three decades of progress. *Psychological Bulletin, 125,* 276–302.

Diener, E., Suh, E. M., Smith, H. L., & Shao, L. (1995). National differences in reported subjective well-being. *Social Indicators Research, 34,* 7–32.

Digman, J. M. (1990). Personality structure: Emergence of the five-factor model. *Annual Review of Psychology, 41,* 417–440.

Digman, J. M. (1997). Higher-order factors of the Big Five. *Journal of Personality and Social Psychology, 73,* 1246–1256.

Dignan, M. (1965). Ego identity and maternal identification. *Journal of Personality and Social Psychology, 1,* 476–483.

Dingfelder, S. (2005). Closing the gap for Latino patients. *Monitor on Psychology, 36*(1), 58–61.

Dinter, L. (2000). The relationship between self-efficacy and lifestyle patterns. *Journal of Individual Psychology, 56,* 462–473.

Distinguished Scientific Contribution Award. (1958). *American Psychologist, 13,* 729–738. [B. F. Skinner]

Distinguished Scientific Contribution Award. (1981). *American Psychologist, 36,* 27–42. [A. Bandura]

Doherty, W. (1983). Impact of divorce on locus of control orientation in adult women: A longitudinal study. *Journal of Personality and Social Psychology, 44,* 834–840.

Donaldson, G. (1996). Between practice and theory: Melanie Klein, Anna Freud, and the development of child analysis. *Journal of the History of the Behavioral Sciences, 32,* 160–176.

Donnellan, B., Trzesniewski, K., Robins, R., Moffitt, T., & Caspi, A. (2005). Low self-esteem is related to aggression, antisocial behavior, and delinquency. *Psychological Science, 16,* 328–335.

Douglas, C. (1993). *Translate this darkness: The life of Christiana Morgan.* New York: Simon & Schuster.

Downey, D. B. (2001). Number of siblings and intellectual development: The resource dilution explanation. *American Psychologist, 56,* 497–504.

Dru, V. (2003). Relationships between an ego orientation scale and a hypercompetitive scale: Their correlates with dogmatism and authoritarianism factors. *Personality and Individual Differences, 35,* 1509–1524.

Duck, S. W., & Spencer, C. (1972). Personal constructs and friendship formation. *Journal of Personality and Social Psychology, 23,* 40–45.

Duncan, L. E., & Agronick, G. W. (1995). The intersection of life stage and social events: Personality and life outcomes. *Journal of Personality and Social Psychology, 69,* 558–568.

Dwairy, M. (2004). Parenting styles and psychological adjustment of Arab adolescents. *Transcultural Psychiatry, 41,* 275–286.

Dwairy, M., Achoui, M., Abouserie, R., & Farah, A. (2006). Parenting styles, individuation, and mental health of Arab adolescents. *Journal of Cross-Cultural Psychology, 37,* 262–272.

Dzuka, J., & Dalbert, C. (2006). The belief in a just world and subjective well-being in old age. *Aging and Mental Health, 10,* 439–444.

Eagle, M. N. (1988). How accurate were Freud's case histories? [Review of *Freud and the Rat Man*]. *Contemporary Psychology, 33,* 205–206.

Eaves, L. J., Eysenck, H. J., & Martin, N. G. (1989). *Genes, culture, and personality: An empirical approach.* New York: Academic Press.

Eccles, J. S., Barber, B., & Jozefowicz, D. (1999). Linking gender to educational, occupational, and recreational choices. In W. B. Swann, Jr., J. H. Langlois, & L. A. Gilbert (Eds.), *Sexism and stereotypes in modern society* (pp. 153–192). Washington, DC: American Psychological Association.

Eckardt, M. (2006). Karen Horney: A portrait. *American Journal of Psychoanalysis, 66,* 105–108.

Eissler, K. R. (1971). *Talent and genius: The fictitious case of Tausk contra Freud.* New York: Quadrangle Books.

Ekman, P., Matsumoto, D., & Friesen, W. V. (1997). Facial expressions in affective disorders. In P. Ekman & E. L. Rosenberg (Eds.), *What the face reveals* (pp. 331–341). New York: Oxford University Press.

El-Anzi, F. (2005). Academic achievement and its relationship with anxiety, self-esteem, optimism, and pessimism in Kuwaiti students. *Social Behavior and Personality, 33,* 95–104.

Ellenberger, H. F. (1970). *The discovery of the unconscious: The history and evolution of dynamic psychiatry.* New York: Basic Books.

Ellenberger, H. F. (1978). Carl Gustav Jung: His historical setting. In H. Reise (Ed.), *Historical explorations in medicine and psychiatry* (pp. 142–150). New York: Springer.

Elliot, A. J., & Church, M. A. (1997). A hierarchical model of approach and avoidance achievement motivation. *Journal of Personality and Social Psychology, 72,* 218–232.

Elliot, A. J., & Sheldon, K. M. (1997). Avoidance achievement motivation: A personal goals analysis. *Journal of Personality and Social Psychology, 73,* 171–185.

Elliot, A. J., Faler, J., McGregor, H. A., Campbell, W. K., Sedikides, C., & Harackiewicz, J. M. (2000). Competence valuation as a strategic intrinsic motivation process. *Personality and Social Psychology Bulletin, 26,* 780–794.

Ellis, R. A., & Taylor, M. S. (1983). Role of self-esteem within the job search process. *Journal of Applied Psychology, 68,* 632–640.

Elms, A. C. (1994). *Uncovering lives: The uneasy alliance of biography and psychology.* New York: Oxford University Press.

Endo, Y., Heine, S. J., & Lehman, D. R. (2000). Culture and positive illusions in close relationships: How my relationships are better than yours. *Personality and Social Psychology Bulletin, 26,* 1571–1586.

Erikson, E. H. (1950). *Childhood and society.* New York: Norton.

Erikson, E. H. (1959). Identity and the life cycle: Selected papers. *Psychological Issues, 1* (Monograph 1).

Erikson, E. H. (1968). *Identity: Youth and crisis.* New York: Norton.

Erikson, E. H. (1975). *Life history and the historical moment.* New York: Norton.

Erikson, E. H., Erikson, J. M., & Kivnick, H. Q. (1986). *Vital involvement in old age.* New York: Norton.

Eron, L. (1987). The development of aggressive behavior from the perspective of a developing behaviorism. *American Psychologist, 42,* 435–442.

Evans, G., & Stecker, R. (2004). Motivational consequences of environmental stress. *Journal of Environmental Psychology, 24,* 143–165.

Evans, R. I. (1968). *B. F. Skinner: The man and his ideas.* New York: Dutton.

Everton, W., Mastrangelo, P., & Jolton, J. (2005). Personality correlates of employees' personal use of work computers. *Cyberpsychology and Behavior, 8,* 143–153.

Exner, J. E., Jr. (1993). *The Rorschach: A comprehensive system: Vol. 1. Basic foundations* (3rd ed.). New York: Wiley.

Ey, S., Hadley, W., Allen, D., Palmer, S., Klosky, J., Deptula, D., Thomas, J., & Cohen, R. (2005). A new measure of children's optimism and pessimism: The Youth Life Orientation Test. *Journal of Child Psychology and Psychiatry, 46,* 548–558.

Eysenck, H. J. (1980). Autobiography. In G. Lindzey (Ed.), *A history of psychology in autobiography* (Vol. 7, pp. 153–187). San Francisco: W. H. Freeman.

Eysenck, H. J. (1983). A biometrical-genetical analysis of impulsive and sensation seeking behavior. In M. Zuckerman (Ed.), *Biological bases of sensation seeking, impulsivity, and anxiety* (pp. 1–27). Hillsdale, NJ: Erlbaum.

Eysenck, H. J. (1990a). Genetic and environmental contributions to individual differences: The three major dimensions of personality. *Journal of Personality, 58,* 245–261.

Eysenck, H. J. (1990b). Biological dimensions of personality. In L. A. Pervin (Ed.), *Handbook of personality: Theory and research* (pp. 244–276). New York: Guilford Press.

Eysenck, H. J. (1997). Personality and experimental psychology: The unification of psychology and the possibility of a paradigm. *Journal of Personality and Social Psychology, 73,* 1224–1237.

Eysenck, H. J., & Eysenck, M. W. (1985). *Personality and individual differences: A natural science approach.* New York: Plenum Press.

Eysenck, H. J., & Eysenck, S. (1963). *Eysenck Personality Inventory.* San Diego, CA: Educational and Industrial Testing Service.

Eysenck, H. J., & Gudjonsson, G. H. (1989). *The causes and cures of criminality.* New York: Plenum Press.

Faith, M. S., Wong, F. Y., & Carpenter, K. M. (1995). Group sensitivity training: Update, meta-analysis, and recommendations. *Journal of Counseling Psychology, 3,* 390–399.

Falbo, T. (1978). Only children and interpersonal behavior: An experimental and survey study. *Journal of Applied Social Psychology, 8,* 244–253.

Falbo, T., & Polit, D. F. (1986). Quantitative review of the only child literature: Research evidence and theory development. *Psychological Bulletin, 100,* 176–189.

Fallby, J., Hassmen, P., Kentta, G., & Durand-Burand, N. (2006). Relationship between locus of control, sense of coherence, and mental skills in Swedish elite athletes. *International Journal of Sport and Exercise Psychology, 4,* 111–120.

Fancher, R. (2000). Snapshots of Freud in America, 1899–1999. *American Psychologist, 55,* 1025–1028.

Farley, F. (2000). Obituary: Hans J. Eysenck (1916–1997). *American Psychologist, 55,* 674–675.

Feldman-Summers, S., & Pope, K. S. (1994). The experience of "forgetting" childhood abuse: A national survey of psychologists. *Journal of Consulting and Clinical Psychology, 62,* 636–639.

Ferguson, E. (2000). Hypochondriacal concerns and the five factor model of personality. *Journal of Personality, 68,* 705–724.

Fiebert, M. S. (1997). In and out of Freud's shadow: A chronology of Adler's relationship with Freud. *Individual Psychology, 53,* 241–269.

Findley, M. J., & Cooper, H. M. (1983). Locus of control and academic achievement: A literature review. *Journal of Personality and Social Psychology, 44,* 419–427.

Fisher, J. D., & Misovich, S. J. (1990). Social influence and AIDS-preventive behavior. In J. Edwards, R. S. Tindale, & E. J. Posavac (Eds.), *Social influence processes and prevention* (pp. 39–70). New York: Plenum Press.

Fisher, S. P., & Greenberg, R. P. (1977). *The scientific credibility of Freud's theories and therapy.* New York: Basic Books.

Fisher, S. P., & Greenberg, R. P. (1996). *Freud scientifically reappraised: Testing the theories and therapy.* New York: Wiley.

Fiske, K., & Pillemer, D. (2006). Adult recollections of earliest childhood dreams: A cross-cultural study. *Memory, 14,* 57–67.

Floderus-Myrhed, B., Pedersen, N., & Rasmuson, I. (1980). Assessment of heritability for personality, based on a short form of the Eysenck Personality Inventory: A study of 12,898 twin pairs. *Behavior Genetics, 10,* 153–162.

Ford, J. G. (1991). Inherent potentialities of actualization: An initial exploration. *Journal of Humanistic Psychology, 31*(3), 65–88.

Foster, C. (2007, Sept./Oct.). Confidence man [Albert Bandura]. *Stanford Magazine* [online, pp. 1–4].

Frable, D. E. S. (1997). Gender, racial, ethnic, sexual, and class identities. *Annual Review of Psychology, 48,* 139–162.

Frable, D. E. S., Wortman, C., & Joseph, J. (1997). Predicting self-esteem, well-being, and distress in a cohort of gay men: The importance of cultural stigma, personal visibility, community networks, and positive identity. *Journal of Personality, 65,* 599–624.

Franklin-Jackson, D., & Carter, R. (2007). The relationships between race-related stress, racial identity, and mental health for Black Americans. *Journal of Black Psychology, 33,* 5–26.

Fransella, F., & Neimeyer, R. (2003). George Alexander Kelly: The man and his theory. In F. Fransella (Ed.), *International handbook of personal construct psychology* (pp. 21–31). Chichester, England: Wiley.

Franz, C. E., McClelland, D. C., & Weinberger, J. (1991). Childhood antecedents of conventional social accomplishment in midlife adults: A 36–year prospective study. *Journal of Personality and Social Psychology, 60,* 586–595.

Frederickson, B. (2001). The role of positive emotions in positive psychology: The broaden-and-build theory of positive emotions. *American Psychologist, 56,* 218–226.

Freedman, D. G. (1974). *Human infancy: An evolutionary perspective.* Hillsdale, NJ: Erlbaum.

French, S., Seidman, E., Allen, L., & Aber, J. (2006). The development of ethnic identity during adolescence. *Developmental Psychology, 42,* 1–10.

Freud, A. (1936). *The ego and the mechanisms of defense.* New York: International Universities Press.

Freud, S. (1901). The psychopathology of everyday life. In *The standard edition of the complete psychological works of Sigmund Freud* (Vol. 6). J. Strachey (Ed. & Trans.). London: Hogarth Press.

Freud, S. (1914). On the history of the psychoanalytic movement. In *Standard edition* (Vol. 14, pp. 3–66). London: Hogarth Press.

Freud, S. (1925). An autobiographical study. In *Standard edition* (Vol. 20). London: Hogarth Press.

Freud, S. (1940). An outline of psychoanalysis. In *Standard edition* (Vol. 23, pp. 141–207). London: Hogarth Press.

Freud, S. (1954). *The origins of psychoanalysis: Letters to Wilhelm Fliess, drafts and notes: 1887–1902.* M. Bonaparte, A. Freud, & E. Kris (Eds.). New York: Basic Books.

Freud, S. (1963). *Psychoanalysis and faith: The letters of Sigmund Freud and Oskar Pfister.* H. Meng & E. Freud (Eds.). New York: Basic Books.

Freud, S. (1985). *The complete letters of Sigmund Freud to Wilhelm Fliess, 1887–1904.* J. M. Masson (Ed.). Cambridge, MA: Belknap Press of Harvard University.

Freud, S., & Jung, C. G. (1974). *The Freud/Jung letters.* W. McGuire (Ed.). Princeton, NJ: Princeton University Press.

Frick, W. B. (2000). Remembering Maslow: Reflections on a 1968 interview. *Journal of Humanistic Psychology, 40,* 128–147.

Friedman, H. S., Schwartz, J. E., Tomlinson-Keasey, C., Tucker, J. S., Martin, L. R., Wingard, D. L., & Criqui, M. H. (1995). Childhood conscientiousness and longevity: Health behaviors and cause of death. *Journal of Personality and Social Psychology, 68,* 696–703.

Friedman, H. S., Tucker, J. S., Tomlinson-Keasey, C., Schwartz, J. E., Wingard, D. L., & Criqui, M. H. (1993). Does childhood personality predict longevity? *Journal of Personality and Social Psychology, 65,* 176–185.

Friedman, L. J. (1996). Psychological advice in the public realm in America, 1940–1970 [Review of the book *The Romance of American Psychology*]. *Contemporary Psychology, 41,* 219–222.

Friedman, L. J. (1999). *Identity's architect: A biography of Erik H. Erikson.* New York: Simon & Schuster.

Funder, D. C. (2001). Personality. *Annual Review of Psychology, 52,* 83–110.

Gaines, S. O., Jr., et al. (1997). Links between race/ethnicity and cultural values as mediated by racial/ethnic identity and moderated by gender. *Journal of Personality and Social Psychology, 72,* 1460–1476.

Galambos, N., Barker, E., & Krahn, H. (2006). Depression, self-esteem, and anger in emerging adulthood: Seven-year trajectories. *Developmental Psychology, 42,* 350–365.

Ganellan, R. J. (2002). Calming the storm: Contemporary use of the Rorschach. [Review of the book *Essentials of Rorschach Assessment*]. *Contemporary Psychology, 47,* 325–327.

Garcia, M. E., Schmitz, J. M., & Doerfler, L. A. (1990). A fine-grained analysis of the role of self-efficacy in self-initiated attempts to quit smoking. *Journal of Consulting and Clinical Psychology, 58,* 317–322.

Gardner, H. (1993). *Creating minds.* New York: Basic Books.

Gardner, W. L., Pickett, C. L., & Brewer, M. B. (2000). Social exclusion and selective memory: How the need to belong influences memory for social events. *Personality and Social Psychology Bulletin, 26,* 486–496.

Gates, L., Lineberger, M. R., Crockett, J., & Hubbard, J. (1988). Birth order and its relationship to depression, anxiety, and self-concept test scores in children. *Journal of Genetic Psychology, 149,* 29–34.

Gay, P. (1988). *Freud: A life for our time.* New York: Norton.

Gecas, V. (1989). The social psychology of self-efficacy. *Annual Review of Sociology, 15,* 291–316.

Gencoz, T., & Ozlale, Y. (2004). Direct and indirect effects of social support on psychological well-being. *Social Behavior and Personality, 32,* 449–458.

Gendlin, E. T., & Tomlinson, T. M. (1967). The process conception and its measurement. In C. R. Rogers, E. T. Gendlin, D. J. Kiesler, & C. B. Truax (Eds.), *The therapeutic relationship and its impact: A study of psychotherapy with schizophrenics.* Madison: University of Wisconsin Press.

Gentile, D., Lynch, P., Linder, J., & Walsh, D. (2004). The effects of violent video game habits on adolescent hostility, aggressive behaviors, and school performance. *Journal of Adolescence, 27,* 5–22.

George, K., Baechtold, J., Frost, R., & Campbell, J. (2006). Sensation seeking, aggression, and reckless behavior in high school students, college students, and adults. *Perceptual and Motor Skills, 103,* 801–802.

Gibbons, F., Blanton, H., Gerrard, M., Buunk, B., & Eggleston, T. (2000). Does social comparison make a difference? Optimism as a moderator of the relation between comparison level and academic performance. *Personality and Social Psychology Bulletin, 26,* 637–648.

Gibson, B., & Sanbonmatsu, D. (2004). Optimism, pessimism, and gambling: The downside of optimism. *Personality and Social Psychology Bulletin, 30,* 149–160.

Gibson, S., & Dembo, M. H. (1984). Teacher efficacy: A construct validation. *Journal of Educational Psychology, 76,* 569–582.

Gilman, R. (2001). The relationship between life satisfaction, social interest, and frequency of extracurricular activities among adolescent students. *Journal of Youth and Adolescence, 30,* 749–767.

Gilman, R., & Huebner, E. (2006). Characteristics of adolescents who report very high life satisfaction. *Journal of Youth and Adolescence, 35,* 311–319.

Gladwell, M. (2004, Sept. 20). Annals of psychology: Personality plus. *The New Yorker,* pp. 42–48.

Glucksberg, S., & King, L. J. (1967). Motivated forgetting mediated by implicit verbal chaining: A laboratory analog of repression. *Science, 158,* 517–519.

Goby, V. (2006). Personality and online/offline choices: MBTI profiles and favored communication modes in a Singapore study. *Cyberpsychology and Behavior, 9,* 5–13.

Gold Medal Award for Life Achievement in Psychological Science. (1997). *American Psychologist, 52,* 797–799. [Cattell]

Goleman, D. (1987, August 31). B. F. Skinner: On his best behavior. *The New York Times.*

Goode, E. (2002, July 2). Researchers find that those who are happiest are less neurotic, more extroverted. *The New York Times.*

Gosling, S., Vazire, S., Srivastava, S., & John, O. (2004). Should we trust Web-based studies? A comparative analysis of six preconceptions. *American Psychologist, 59,* 93–104.

Gough, H. G., Fioravanti, M., & Lazzari, R. (1983). Some implications of self versus idealized self-congruence on the Revised Adjective Check List. *Journal of Personality and Social Psychology, 44,* 1214–1220.

Gough, H. G., Lazzari, R., & Fioravanti, M. (1978). Self versus ideal self: A comparison of five Adjective Check List indices. *Journal of Consulting and Clinical Psychology, 35,* 1085–1091.

Graham, W., & Balloun, J. (1973). An empirical test of Maslow's need hierarchy theory. *Journal of Humanistic Psychology, 13,* 97–108.

Gram, P., Dunn, B., & Ellis, D. (2005). Relationship between EEG and psychological type. *Journal of Psychological Type, 65,* 33–46.

Graves, T. D. (1961). *Time perspective and the deferred gratification pattern in a tri-ethnic community.* Boulder: University of Colorado Institute of Behavioral Science.

Graziano, W. G., Jensen-Campbell, L. A., & Sullivan-Logan, G. M. (1998). Temperament, activity, and expectations for later personality development. *Journal of Personality and Social Psychology, 74,* 1266–1277.

Green, A., Rafaeli, E., Bolger, N., Shrout, P., & Reis, H. (2006). Paper or plastic? Data equivalence in paper and electronic diaries. *Psychological Methods, 11,* 87–105.

Greever, K., Tseng, M., & Friedland, B. (1973). Development of the Social Interest Index. *Journal of Consulting and Clinical Psychology, 41,* 454–458.

Grey, L. (1998). *Alfred Adler, the forgotten prophet: A vision for the 21st century.* Westport, CT: Praeger.

Grieser, C., Greenberg, R., & Harrison, R. H. (1972). The adaptive function of sleep: The differential effects of sleep and dreaming on recall. *Journal of Abnormal Psychology, 80,* 280–286.

Grubrich-Simitis, I. (1998). "Nothing about the totem meal!" On Freud's notes. In M. S. Roth (Ed.), *Freud: Conflict and culture* (pp. 17–31). New York: Knopf.

Guo-Xing, S., & Hai, Y. (2006). Subjective well-being of middle-school children. *Chinese Mental Health Journal, 20,* 238–241.

Gupta, R., Derevensky, J., & Ellenbogen, S. (2006). Personality characteristics and risk-taking tendencies among adolescent gamblers. *Canadian Journal of Behavioural Science, 38,* 201–213.

Hackett, G. (1995). Self-efficacy in career choice and development. In A. Bandura (Ed.), *Self-efficacy in changing societies* (pp. 232–258). Cambridge, England: Cambridge University Press.

Hafner, J. L., Fakouri, M. E., & Labrentz, H. L. (1982). First memories of "normal" and alcoholic individuals. *Individual Psychology, 38,* 238–244.

Hagedoorn, M., & Molleman, E. (2006). Facial disfigurement in patients with head and neck cancer: The role of social self-efficacy. *Health Psychology, 25,* 643–647.

Hall, A. (2005). Sensation seeking and the use and selection of media materials. *Psychological Reports, 97,* 236–244.

Hall, C., & Van de Castle, R. (1965). An empirical investigation of the castration complex in dreams. *Journal of Personality, 33,* 20–29.

Hall, E. (1983, June). A conversation with Erik Erikson. *Psychology Today,* pp. 22–30.

Hall, M. H. (1967, September). An interview with "Mr. Behaviorist" B. F. Skinner. *Psychology Today,* pp. 21–23, 68–71.

Hall, M. H. (1968, July). A conversation with Abraham H. Maslow. *Psychology Today,* pp. 35–37, 54–57.

Hamberger, L. K., & Hastings, J. E. (1992). Racial differences on the MCMI in an outpatient clinical sample. *Journal of Personality Assessment, 58,* 90–95.

Hamm, J. (2000). Do birds of a feather flock together? The variable bases for African American, Asian American, and European American adolescents' selection of similar friends. *Developmental Psychology, 36,* 209–219.

Hampson, S., Andrews, J., Barckley, M., Lichtenstein, E., & Lee, M. (2000). Conscientiousness, perceived risk, and risk-reduction behaviors; A preliminary study. *Health Psychology, 19,* 496–500.

Hampson, S., & Goldberg, L. (2006). A first large cohort study of personality trait stability over the 40 years between elementary school and midlife. *Journal of Personality and Social Psychology, 91,* 763–779.

Handel, R. W., & Ben-Porath, Y. S. (2000). Multicultural assessment with the MMPI-2: Issues for research and practice. In R. H. Dana (Ed.), *Handbook of cross-cultural and multicultural personality assessment* (pp. 229–245). Mahwah, NJ: Erlbaum.

Hanewitz, W. B. (1978). Police personality: A Jungian perspective. *Crime and Delinquency, 24,* 152–172.

Hankoff, L. D. (1987). The earliest memories of criminals. *International Journal of Offender Therapy and Comparative Criminology, 31,* 195–201.

Hansen, E., & Breivik, G. (2001). Sensation-seeking as a predictor of positive and negative risk behaviour among adolescents. *Personality and Individual Differences, 30,* 627–640.

Hanson, R. K. (1992). Thematic analysis of daily events as a method of personality assessment. *Journal of Personality Assessment, 58,* 606–620.

Harber, K. D. (1998). Feedback to minorities: Evidence of a positive bias. *Journal of Personality and Social Psychology, 73,* 622–628.

Harker, L., & Keltner, D. (2001). Expressions of positive emotion in women's college yearbook pictures and their relationship to personality and life outcomes across adulthood. *Journal of Personality and Social Psychology, 80,* 112–124.

Harrington, D. M., Block, J. H., & Block, J. (1987). Testing aspects of Carl Rogers' theory of creative environments: Child-rearing antecedents of creative potential in young adolescents. *Journal of Personality and Social Psychology, 52,* 851–856.

Harrington, R., & Loffredo, D. A. (2001). The relationship between life satisfaction, self-consciousness, and the Myers-Briggs Type Inventory dimensions. *Journal of Psychology, 135,* 439–450.

Harris, J. R. (1995). Where is the child's environment? A group socialization theory of development. *Psychological Review, 102,* 458–489.

Harris, J. R. (1998). *The nurture assumption: Why children turn out the way they do.* New York: Free Press.

Harris, D., & Kuba, I. (1997). Ethnocultural identity and eating disorders in women of color. *Professional Psychology, 28,* 341–347.

Harter, S., Marold, D. B., Whitesell, N. R., & Cobbs, G. (1996). A model of the effects of perceived parent and peer support on adolescent false-self behavior. *Child Development, 67,* 360–374.

Harvey, E. (1999). Short-term and long-term effects of early parental employment on children of the National Longitudinal Survey of Youth. *Developmental Psychology, 35,* 445–459.

Hawkins, R. P., Peterson, R. F., Schweid, E., & Bijou, S. W. (1966). Behavior therapy in the home: Amelioration of problem parent–child relations with the parent in a therapeutic role. *Journal of Experimental Child Psychology, 4,* 99–107.

Hayes, H., & Joseph, S. (2003). Big five correlates of three measures of subjective well-being. *Personality and Individual Differences, 34,* 723–727.

Heaven, P., & Ciarrochi, J. (2006). Perceptions of parental styles and Eysenckian psychoticism in youth. *Personality and Individual Differences, 41,* 61–70.

Heckhausen, J., & Schulz, R. (1995). A life-span theory of control. *Psychological Review, 102,* 284–304.

Heine, S., Lehman, D., Markus, H., & Kitayama, S. (1999). Is there a universal need for positive self-regard? *Psychological Review, 106,* 766–794.

Heine, S., & Renshaw, K. (2002). Inter-judge agreement, self-enhancement, and liking: Cross-cultural divergences. *Personality and Social Psychology Bulletin, 28,* 578–587.

Heine, S., Takata, T., & Lehman, D. R. (2000). Beyond self-presentation: Evidence for self-criticisms among Japanese. *Personality and Social Psychology Bulletin, 26,* 71–78.

Heller, D., Watson, D., & Hies, R. (2004). The role of person versus situation in life satisfaction. *Psychological Bulletin, 130,* 574–600.

Heller, M., & Haynal, V. (1997). Depression and suicide faces. In P. Ekman & E. L. Rosenberg (Eds.), *What the face reveals* (pp. 398–407). New York: Oxford University Press.

Helms, J. (1990). *Black and white racial identity: Theory, research, and practice.* New York: Greenwood Press.

Helson, R. (1992). Women's difficult times and the rewriting of the life story. *Psychology of Women Quarterly, 16,* 331–347.

Helson, R., & Klohnen, E. C. (1998). Affective coloring of personality from young adulthood to midlife. *Personality and Social Psychology Bulletin, 24,* 241–252.

Helson, R., & Srivastava, S. (2001). Three paths of adult development: Conservers, seekers, and achievers. *Journal of Personality and Social Psychology, 80,* 995–1010.

Helson, R., Jones, C., & Kwan, V. (2002). Personality change over 40 years of adulthood: Hierarchical linear modeling analyses of two longitudinal samples. *Journal of Personality and Social Psychology, 83,* 752–766.

Helson, R., Stewart, A., & Ostrove, J. (1995). Identity in three cohorts of midlife women. *Journal of Personality and Social Psychology, 69,* 544–557.

Henderlong, J., & Lepper, M. (2002). The effects of praise on children's intrinsic motivation: A review and synthesis. *Psychological Bulletin, 128,* 774–795.

Herbert, T. B., & Cohen, S. (1993). Depression and immunity: A meta-analytic review. *Psychological Bulletin, 113,* 472–486.

Herrera, N., Zajonc, R., Wieczorkowska, G., & Cichomski, B. (2003). Beliefs about birth rank and their reflection in reality. *Journal of Personality and Social Psychology, 85,* 142–150.

Hilgard, E. (1987). *Psychology in America: A historical survey.* San Diego: Harcourt Brace Jovanovich.

Hiroto, D. S. (1974). Locus of control and learned helplessness. *Journal of Experimental Psychology, 102,* 187–193.

Hobfoll, S. E., Rom, T., & Segal, B. (1989). Sensation seeking, anxiety, and risk taking in the Israeli context. In S. Einstein (Ed.), *Drug and alcohol use: Issues and factors* (pp. 53–59). New York: Plenum Press.

Hoffman, E. (1988). *The right to be human: A biography of Abraham Maslow.* Los Angeles: Tarcher.

Hoffman, E. (1994). *The drive for self: Alfred Adler and the founding of individual psychology.* Reading, MA: Addison-Wesley.

Hoffman, E. (Ed.) (1996). *Future visions: The unpublished papers of Abraham Maslow.* Thousand Oaks, CA: Sage.

Holahan, C. K., & Holahan, C. J. (1987). Self-efficacy, social support, and depression in aging: A longitudinal analysis. *Journal of Gerontology, 42,* 65–68.

Holmgren, S., Molander, B., & Nilsson, K. (2006). Intelligence and executive functioning in adult age: Effects of sibship size and birth order. *European Journal of Cognitive Psychology, 18,* 138–158.

Holtgraves, T. (2004). Social desirability and self-reports: Testing models of socially desirable responding. *Personality and Social Psychology Bulletin, 30,* 161–172.

Holzman, P. S. (1994). Hilgard on psychoanalysis as a science. *Psychological Science, 5,* 190–191.

Horn, J. (2001). Obituary: Raymond Bernard Cattell, 1905–1998. *American Psychologist, 56,* 71–72.

Horney, K. (1926). The flight from womanhood. *International Journal of Psychoanalysis, 7.*

Horney, K. (1937). *The neurotic personality of our time.* New York: Norton.

Horney, K. (1939). *New ways in psychoanalysis.* New York: Norton.

Horney, K. (1942). *Self-analysis.* New York: Norton.

Horney, K. (1945). *Our inner conflicts.* New York: Norton.

Horney, K. (1967). The flight from womanhood: The masculinity-complex in women as viewed by men and by women. In H. Kelman (Ed.), *Feminine psychology.* New York: Norton.

Horney, K. (1980). *The adolescent diaries of Karen Horney.* New York: Basic Books. [Diaries written 1899–1911]

Horney, K. (1987). *Final lectures.* D. H. Ingram (Ed.). New York: Norton. [Lectures delivered 1952]

Howell, L., & Beth, A. (2004). Pioneers in our own lives: Grounded theory of lesbians' midlife development. *Journal of Women and Aging, 16,* 133–147.

Huesmann, L., Eron, L., Dubow, E., & Seebauer, E. (1987). Television viewing habits in childhood and adult aggression. *Child Development, 58,* 357–367.

Huesmann, L., Moise-Titus, J., Podolski, C., & Eron, L. (2003). Longitudinal relations between children's exposure to TV violence and their aggressive and violent behavior in young adulthood: 1977–1992. *Developmental Psychology, 39,* 201–221.

Huifang, Y., & Shuming, Z. (2004, July). A research on the personality types of business managers. *Psychological Science (China),* 983–985.

Hunt, C., Keogh, E., & French, C. (2006). Anxiety sensitivity: The role of conscious awareness and selective attentional bias to physical threat. *Emotion, 6,* 418–428.

Huo-Liang, G. (2006). Personality and crime: A meta-analysis of studies on criminals' behavior. *Chinese Mental Health Journal, 20,* 465–468.

Hwang, W. (2006). The psychotherapy adaptation and modification framework: Application to Asian Americans. *American Psychologist, 61,* 702–715.

Ibanez, G., Kuperminc, G., Jurkovic, G., & Perilla, J. (2004). Cultural attributes and adaptations linked to achievement motivation among Latino adolescents. *Journal of Youth and Adolescence, 33,* 559–568.

Isaacowitz, D. (2005a). Correlates of well-being in adulthood and old age: A tale of two optimisms. *Journal of Research in Personality, 39,* 224–244.

Isaacowitz, D. (2005b). The gaze of the optimist. *Personality and Social Psychology Bulletin, 31,* 407–415.

Jackson, M., & Sechrest, L. (1962). Early recollections in four neurotic diagnostic categories. *Journal of Individual Psychology, 18,* 52–56.

Jacobson, J. L., & Wille, D. E. (1986). The influence of attachment patterns on developmental changes in peer interaction from the toddler to the preschool period. *Child Development, 57,* 338–347.

Jaffé, A. (1971). *The myth of meaning: Jung and the expansion of consciousness.* New York: Putnam.

Jasinskaja-Lahti, I., Liebkind, K., Jaakkola, M., & Reuter, A. (2006). Perceived discrimination, social support networks, and psychological well-being among three immigrant groups. *Journal of Cross-Cultural Psychology, 37,* 293–311.

Jensen-Campbell, L., & Graziano, W. G. (2000). Beyond the school yard: Relationships as moderators of daily interpersonal conflict. *Personality and Social Psychology Bulletin, 26,* 923–935.

Jensen-Campbell, L., & Malcolm, K. (2007). The importance of conscientiousness in adolescent and interpersonal relationships. *Personality and Social Psychology Bulletin, 33,* 368–383.

Jerusalem, M., & Mittag, W. (1995). Self-efficacy in stressful life transitions. In A. Bandura (Ed.), *Self-efficacy in changing societies* (pp. 177–201). Cambridge, England: Cambridge University Press.

Jiao, S., Ji, G., & Jing, Q. (1986). Comparative study of behavioral qualities of only children and sibling children. *Child Development, 57,* 357–361.

John, O. P. (1990). The big five factor taxonomy: Dimensions of personality in the natural language and in questionnaires. In L. A. Pervin (Ed.), *Handbook of personality: Theory and research* (pp. 66–100). New York: Guilford Press.

John, O. P., Pals, J. L., & Westenberg, P. M. (1998). Personality prototypes and ego development: Conceptual similarities and relations in adult women. *Journal of Personality and Social Psychology, 74,* 1093–1108.

Johnson, R. C. (1980). Summing up [Review of the book *Personality and learning theory,* Vol. 1: The structure of personality in its environment]. *Contemporary Psychology, 25,* 299–300.

Johnson, W., McGue, M., & Krueger, R. (2005). Personality stability in late adulthood: A behavioral genetic analysis. *Journal of Personality, 73,* 523–552.

Jones, E. (1953, 1955, 1957). *The life and work of Sigmund Freud* (3 vols.). New York: Basic Books.

Jones, R. L. (1994). An empirical study of Freud's penis-baby equation. *Journal of Nervous and Mental Disease, 182*(3), 127–135.

Joormann, J., & Gotlib, I. (2006). Is this happiness I see? Biases in the identification of emotional facial expressions in depression and social phobia. *Journal of Abnormal psychology, 115,* 705–714.

Jorm, A. F. (1987). Sex differences in neuroticism: A quantitative synthesis of published research. *Australian and New Zealand Journal of Psychiatry, 21,* 501–506.

Joseph, S., & Linley, P. (2005). Positive adjustment to threatening events: An organismic valuing theory of growth through adversity. *Review of General Psychology, 9,* 262–280.

Judge, T., Erez, A., Bono, J., & Thoresen, C. (2002). Are measures of self-esteem, neuroticism, locus of control, and generalized self-efficacy indicators of a common core construct? *Journal of Personality and Social Psychology, 83,* 693–710.

Judge, T., Jackson, C., Shaw, J., Scott, J., & Rich, B. (2007). Self-efficacy and work-related performance: The integral role of individual differences. *Journal of Applied Psychology, 92,* 107–127.

Jung, C. G. (1909). The association method. In H. Read, M. Fordham, & G. Adler (Eds.), *The collected works of C. G. Jung* (Vol. 2, pp. 442, 444). Princeton, NJ: Princeton University Press.

Jung, C. G. (1923). Psychological types. In *Collected works* (Vol. 6). Princeton, NJ: Princeton University Press.

Jung, C. G. (1927). The structure of the psyche. In *Collected works* (Vol. 8, pp. 139–158). Princeton, NJ: Princeton University Press.

Jung, C. G. (1928). On psychic energy. In *Collected works* (Vol. 8, pp. 3–66). Princeton, NJ: Princeton University Press.

Jung, C. G. (1930). The stages of life. In *Collected works* (Vol. 8, pp. 387–403). Princeton, NJ: Princeton University Press.

Jung, C. G. (1947). On the nature of the psyche. In *Collected works* (Vol. 8, pp. 159–234). Princeton, NJ: Princeton University Press.

Jung, C. G. (1953). *Two essays on analytical psychology.* New York: Pantheon.

Jung, C. G. (1961). *Memories, dreams, reflections.* New York: Vintage Books.

Kagan, J. (1984). *The nature of the child.* New York: Basic Books.

Kagan, J. (1989). Temperamental contributions to social behavior. *American Psychologist, 44,* 668–674.

Kagan, J. (1999). *Three seductive ideas.* Cambridge, MA: Harvard University Press.

Kagan, J., Kearsley, R., & Zelazo, P. (1978). *Infancy.* Cambridge, MA: Harvard University Press.

Kagan, J., Snidman, N., & Arcus, D. (1992). Initial reactions to unfamiliarity. *Current Directions in Psychological Science, 1,* 171–174.

Kahneman, D., Krueger, A., Schkade, D., Schwartz, N., & Stone, A. (2006). Would you be happier if you were richer? A focusing illusion. *Science, 312,* 1908–1910.

Kalichman, S. C., Johnson, J. R., Adair, V., Rompa, D., Multhauf, K., & Kelly, J. A. (1994). Sexual sensation seeking: Scale development and predicting AIDS-risk behavior among homosexually active men. *Journal of Personality Assessment, 62,* 385–397.

Kanagawa, C., Cross, S. E., & Markus, H. R. (2001). "Who am I?" The cultural psychology of the conceptual self. *Personality and Social Psychology Bulletin, 27,* 90–103.

Kaplan, R., Atkins, C. J., & Reinsch, S. (1984). Specific efficacy expectations mediate exercise compliance in patients with COPD. *Health Psychology, 3,* 223–242.

Kaplan, R., & Saccuzzo, D. (2005). *Psychological testing: Principles, applications, and issues.* Belmont, CA: Thomson Wadsworth.

Kashima, Y., Kokubo, T., Kashima, E., Boxall, D., Yamaguchi, S., & Macrae, K. (2004). Cultural and self: Are there within-culture differences in self between metropolitan areas and regional cities? *Personality and Social Psychology Bulletin, 30,* 816–823.

Kasler, J., & Nevo, O. (2005). Early recollections as predictors of study area choice. *Journal of Individual Psychology, 61,* 217–232.

Kasser, T., Koestner, R., & Lekes, N. (2002). Early family experiences and adult values: A 26-year prospective longitudinal study. *Personality and Social Psychology Bulletin, 28,* 826–835.

Kaufman, M. T. (2002, Sept. 8). Face it: Your looks are revealing. *The New York Times.*

Kazdin, A. E. (1989). *Behavior modification in applied settings* (4th ed.). Pacific Grove, CA: Brooks/Cole.

Kazdin, A. E., & Bootzin, R. (1972). The token economy: An evaluative review. *Journal of Applied Behavioral Analysis, 5,* 343–372.

Kelly, G. A. (1955). *The psychology of personal constructs.* New York: Norton.

Kelly, G. A. (1958). The theory and technique of assessment. *Annual Review of Psychology, 9,* 323–352.

Kelly, G. A. (1969). *Clinical psychology and personality: The selected papers of George Kelly.* B. Maher (Ed.) New York: Wiley.

Keltikangas-Jaruinen, L., & Raikkonen, K. (1990). Healthy and maladjusted Type A behavior in adolescents. *Journal of Youth and Adolescence, 19,* 1–18.

Keltner, D. (1997). Facial expression, personality, and psychopathology. In P. Ekman & E. L. Rosenberg (Eds.), *What the face reveals* (pp. 450–452). New York: Oxford University Press.

Keniston, K. (1983, June). Remembering Erikson at Harvard. *Psychology Today,* p. 29.

Kerestes, G. (2006). Birth order and maternal ratings of infant temperament. *Studia Psychologica, 48,* 95–106.

Kernis, M. H., Paradise, A. W., Whitaker, D. J., Wheatman, S. R., & Goldman, B. N. (2000). Master of one's psychological domain? Not likely if one's self-esteem is unstable. *Personality and Social Psychology Bulletin, 26,* 1297–1305.

Keyes, C., Shmotkin, D., & Ryff, D. (2002). Optimizing well-being: The empirical encounter of two traditions. *Journal of Personality and Social Psychology, 82,* 1007–1022.

Kidwell, J. (1982). The neglected birth order: Middle-borns. *Journal of Marriage and the Family, 44,* 225–235.

Kihlstrom, J. F. (1994). Psychodynamics and social cognition. *Journal of Personality, 62,* 681–696.

King, L. A., & Napa, C. K. (1998). What makes a life good? *Journal of Personality and Social Psychology, 75,* 156–165.

Kirschenbaum, H., & Jourdan, A. (2005). The current status of Carl Rogers and the person-centered approach.

Psychotherapy: Theory, Research, Practice, Training, 42, 37–51.

Kivimaki, M., Vahtera, J., Elovainio, M., Helenius, H., Singh-Manoux, A., & Pentti, J. (2005). Optimism and pessimism as predictors of change in health after death or onset of severe illness in family. *Health Psychology, 24,* 413–421.

Klein, M. H., Malthieu, P. L., Gendlin, E. T., & Kiesler, D. J. (1969). *The Experiencing Scale: A research and training manual.* Madison: Wisconsin Psychiatric Institute.

Kochanska, G., Clark, L. A., & Goldman, M. S. (1997). Implications of mothers' personality for their parenting and their young children's developmental outcomes. *Journal of Personality, 65,* 387–420.

Konu, A., Lintonen, T., & Rimpelae, M. (2002). Factors associated with schoolchildren's general subjective well-being. *Health Education Research, 17,* 155–165.

Kopp, R., & Eckstein, D. (2004). Using early memory metaphors and client-generated metaphors in Adlerian therapy. *Journal of Individual Psychology, 60,* 163–174.

Kosten, T. A., Ball, S. A., & Rounsaville, B. J. (1994). A sibling study of sensation seeking and opiate addiction. *Journal of Nervous and Mental Disease, 182,* 284–289.

Krahe, B., & Moeller, I. (2004). Playing violent electronic games, hostile attributional style, and aggression-related norms in German adolescents. *Journal of Adolescence, 27,* 53–69.

Kristensen, P., & Bjerkedal, T. (2007). Explaining the relation between birth order and intelligence. *Science, 316,* 1717.

Kruger, J. (1999). Lake Wobegon be gone! The "below-average" effect and the egocentric nature of comparative ability judgments. *Journal of Personality and Social Psychology, 77,* 221–232.

Krüll, M. (1986). *Freud and his father.* New York: Norton.

Kulshrestha, U., & Sen, C. (2006). Subjective well-being in relation to emotional intelligence and locus of control among executives. *Journal of the Indian Academy of Applied Psychology, 32,* 129–134.

Kunzmann, U., Little, T., & Smith, J. (2000). Is age-related stability of subjective well-being a paradox? Cross-sectional and longitudinal evidence from the Berlin Aging Study. *Psychology and Aging, 15,* 511–526.

Kurman, J. (2001). Self-enhancement: Is it restricted to individualistic cultures? *Personality and Social Psychology Bulletin, 27,* 1705–1716.

Lacey, H., Smith, D., & Ubel, P. (2006). Hope I die before I get old: Mispredicting happiness. *Journal of Happiness Studies, 7,* 167–182.

Lachman, M. E. (1985). Personal efficacy in middle and old age: Differential and normative patterns of change. In G. H. Elder, Jr. (Ed.), *Life course dynamics* (pp. 188–216). Ithaca, NY: Cornell University Press.

Laird, T., & Shelton, A. (2006). From an Adlerian perspective: Birth order, dependency, and binge drinking on a historically Black university campus. *Journal of Individual Psychology, 62,* 18–35.

Lambert, C. (2007, Jan.–Feb.). The science of happiness. *Harvard Magazine, 109,* 26–30, 94.

Lang, F., & Heckhausen, J. (2001). Perceived control over development and subjective well-being: Differential benefits across adulthood. *Journal of Personality and Social Psychology, 81,* 509–523.

Langan-Fox, J., & Roth, S. (1995). Achievement motivation and female entrepreneurs. *Journal of Occupational and Organizational Psychology, 68,* 209–218.

Langer, E. J., & Rodin, J. (1976). The effects of choice and enhanced personal responsibility for the aged: A field experiment in an institutional setting. *Journal of Personality and Social Psychology, 34,* 191–198.

Lapan, R. T., Boggs, K. R., & Morrill, W. H. (1989). Self-efficacy as a mediator of investigative and realistic general occupational themes on the Strong-Campbell Interest Inventory. *Journal of Counseling Psychology, 36,* 176–182.

Larsen, R. J., & Kasimatis, M. (1991). Day-to-day symptoms: Individual differences in the occurrence, duration, and emotional concomitants of minor daily illness. *Journal of Personality, 59,* 387–423.

Larsson, H., Andershed, H., & Lichtenstein, P. (2006). A genetic factor explains most of the variation in the psychopathic personality. *Journal of Abnormal Personality, 115,* 221–230.

Lau, J., Rijsdijk, F., & Eley, C. (2006). I think, therefore I am: A twin study of attributional style in adolescents. *Journal of Child Psychology and Psychiatry, 47,* 696–703.

Laursen, B., Pulkkinen, L., & Adams, R. (2002). The antecedents and correlates of agreeableness in adulthood. *Developmental Psychology, 38,* 591–603.

Law, A., Logan, H., & Baron, R. S. (1994). Desire for control, felt control, and stress inoculation training during dental treatment. *Journal of Personality and Social Psychology, 67,* 926–936.

Leak, G. (2006a). Development and validation of a revised measure of Adlerian social interest. *Social Behavior and Personality, 34,* 443–450.

Leak, G. (2006b). An empirical assessment of the relationship between social interest and spirituality. *Journal of Individual Psychology, 62,* 59–69.

Leak, G., & Leak, K. (2006). Adlerian social interest and positive psychology. *Journal of Individual Psychology, 62,* 207–223.

Lee, M., Okazaki, S., & Yoo, H. (2006). Frequency and intensity of social anxiety in Asian Americans and European Americans. *Cultural Diversity and Ethnic Minority Psychology, 12,* 291–305.

Lee, Y. T., & Seligman, M. E. P. (1997). Are Americans more optimistic than the Chinese? *Personality and Social Psychology Bulletin, 23,* 32–40.

Lefcourt, H. M. (1982). *Locus of control: Current trends in theory and research* (2nd ed.). Hillsdale, NJ: Erlbaum.

Lefcourt, H. M., Martin, R. A., Fick, C. M., & Saleh, W. E. (1985). Locus of control for affiliation in social interactions. *Journal of Personality and Social Psychology, 48,* 755–759.

Lefkowitz, M. M., & Tesiny, E. P. (1984). Rejection and depression: Prospective and contemporaneous analysis. *Developmental Psychology, 20,* 776–785.

Leonard, R., & Burns, A. (2006). Turning points in the lives of midlife and older women: Five-year follow-up. *Australian Psychologist, 41,* 28–36.

Leontopoulou, S. (2006). Resilience of Greek youth at an educational transition point: The role of locus of control and coping strategies as resources. *Social Indicators Research, 76,* 95–126.

Lester, D. (1990). Maslow's hierarchy of needs and personality. *Personality and Individual Differences, 11,* 1187–1188.

Letzring, T., Block, J., & Funder, D. (2005). Ego-control and ego-resiliency: Generalization of self-report scales based on personality descriptions from acquaintances, clinicians, and the self. *Journal of Research in Personality, 39,* 395–422.

Leung, B., Moneta, G., & McBride-Chang, C. (2005). Think positively and feel positively: Optimism and life satisfaction in late life. *International Journal of Aging and Human Development, 61,* 335–365.

Levenson, M. R. (1990). Risk taking and personality. *Journal of Personality and Social Psychology, 58,* 1073–1080.

Levinson, D. J. (1978). *The seasons of a man's life.* New York: Knopf.

Levinson, D. J. (1996). *The seasons of a woman's life.* New York: Knopf.

Leyens, J., Camino, L., Parke, R., & Berkowitz, L. (1975). Effects of movie violence on aggression in a field setting as a function of group dominance and cohesion. *Journal of Personality and Social Psychology, 32,* 346–360.

Li, F., McAuley, E., Harmer, P., Duncan, T., & Chaumeton, N. (2001). Tai Chi enhances self-efficacy and exercise behavior in older adults. *Journal of Aging and Physical Activity, 9,* 161–171.

Libran, E., & Howard, V. (2006). Personality dimensions and subjective well-being. *Spanish Journal of Psychology, 9,* 38–44.

Lightsey, O., Burke, M., Ervin, A., Henderson, D., & Yee, C. (2006). Generalized self-efficacy, self-esteem, and negative affect. *Canadian Journal of Behavioural Science, 38,* 72–80.

Lin, Y., & Raghubir, P. (2005). Gender differences in unrealistic optimism about marriage and divorce. *Personality and Social Psychology Bulletin, 31,* 198–207.

Lippa, R. A., Martin, L. R., & Friedman, H. S. (2000). Gender related individual differences and mortality in the Terman longitudinal study: Is masculinity hazardous to your health? *Personality and Social Psychology Bulletin, 26,* 1560–1570.

Lischetzke, T., & Eid, M. (2006). Why extraverts are happier than introverts: The role of mood regulation. *Journal of Personality, 74,* 1127–1162.

Litwin, H. (2005). Correlates of successful aging: Are they universal? *International Journal of Aging and Human Development, 61,* 313–333.

Liu, W., Rochlen, A., & Mohr, J. (2005). Real and ideal gender-role conflict: Exploring psychological distress among men. *Psychology of Men and Masculinity, 6,* 137–148.

Locke, E. A., & Latham, G. P. (1990). *A theory of goal setting and task performance.* Englewood Cliffs, NJ: Prentice-Hall.

Loehlin, J. C. (1997). A test of J. R. Harris's theory of peer influences on psychology. *Journal of Personality and Social Psychology, 72,* 1197–1201.

Loehlin, J. C., Horn, J. M., & Willerman, L. (1990). Heredity, environment, and personality change: Evidence from the Texas adoption project. *Journal of Personality, 58,* 221–243.

Loehlin, J. C., & Nichols, R. C. (1976). *Heredity, environment, and personality: A study of 850 sets of twins.* Austin: University of Texas Press.

Loevinger, J. (1976). *Ego development.* San Francisco: Jossey-Bass.

Loffredo, D., & Opt, S. (2006). Argumentativeness and Myers-Briggs Type Indicator preferences. *Journal of Psychological Type, 66,* 59–68.

Loftus, E., & Davis, D. (2006). Recovered memories. *Annual Review of Clinical Psychology, 2,* 469–498.

Loftus, E., & Ketcham, K. (1994). *False memories and allegations of sexual abuse.* New York: St. Martin's Press.

Loftus, E., Polonsky, S., & Fullilove, M. T. (1994). Memories of childhood sexual abuse. *Psychology of Women Quarterly, 18,* 67–84.

Londerville, S., & Main, M. (1981). Security of attachment, compliance, and maternal training methods in the second year of life. *Developmental Psychology, 17,* 289–299.

Loo, C. M. (1998). *Chinese America: Mental health and quality of life in the inner city.* Thousand Oaks, CA: Sage.

Lucas, R., & Diener, E. (2001). Understanding extraverts' enjoyment of social situations: The importance of pleasantness. *Journal of Personality and Social Psychology, 81,* 343–356.

Lucas, R., & Fujita, F. (2000). Factors influencing the relation between extraversion and pleasant affect. *Journal of Personality and Social Psychology, 79,* 1039–1056.

Luce, K., Winzelberg, A., Das, S., Osborne, M., Bryson, S., & Taylor, C. (2007). Reliability of self-report: Paper versus online administration. *Computers in Human Behavior, 23,* 1384–1389.

Luyckx, K., Goossens, L., Soenens, B., Beyers, W., & Vansteenkiste, M. (2005). Identity statuses based on four rather than two identity dimensions: Extending and refining Marcia's paradigm. *Journal of Youth and Adolescence, 34,* 605–618.

Lynn, M., & Steel, P. (2006). National differences in subjective well-being: The interactive effects of extraversion and neuroticism. *Journal of Happiness Studies, 7,* 155–165.

Lyons, D. (2002). Freer to be me: The development of executives at midlife. *Consulting Psychology Journal: Practice and Research, 54,* 15–27.

Lyubomirsky, S. (2001). Why are some people happier than others? The role of cognitive and motivational processes in well-being. *American Psychologist, 56,* 239–249.

Lyubomirsky, S., King, L., & Diener, E. (2005). The benefits of frequent positive affect: Does happiness lead to success? *Psychological Bulletin, 131,* 803–855.

Mackavey, W. R., Malley, J. E., & Stewart, A. J. (1991). Remembering autobiographically consequential experiences: Content analysis of psychologists' accounts of their lives. *Psychology and Aging, 6,* 50–59.

Maddux, J. E. (2002). The power of believing you can. In C. R. Snyder & S. J. Lopez (Eds.), *Handbook of positive psychology* (pp. 277–287). New York: Oxford University Press.

Magnus, K., Diener, E., Fujita, F., & Pavot, W. (1993). Extraversion and neuroticism as predictors of objective life events: A longitudinal analysis. *Journal of Personality and Social Psychology, 65,* 1046–1053.

Mahalik, J. R., Cournoyer, R. J., DeFrank, W., Cherry, M., & Napolitano, J. M. (1998). Men's gender role conflict and use of psychological defenses. *Journal of Counseling Psychology, 45,* 247–255.

Mahoney, J., & Hartnett, J. (1973). Self-actualization and self-ideal discrepancy. *Journal of Psychology, 85,* 37–42.

Mahoney, P. J. (1986). *Freud and the Rat Man.* New Haven: Yale University Press.

Mahoney, P. (1992). Freud as a family therapist: Reflections. In T. Gelfand & J. Kerr (Eds.), *Freud and the history of psychoanalysis* (pp. 307–317). Hillsdale, NJ: Analytic Press.

Maier, S. F., Laudenslager, M., & Ryan, S. M. (1985). Stressor controllability, immune function, and endogenous opiates. In F. R. Brush and J. B. Overmier (Eds.), *Affect, conditioning, and cognition: Essays on the determinants of behavior* (pp. 203–210). Hillsdale, NJ: Erlbaum.

Maier, S. J., & Seligman, M. E. P. (1976). Learned helplessness: Theory and evidence. *Journal of Experimental Psychology, 105,* 3–46.

Maio, G. R., Fincham, F. D., & Lycett, E. J. (2000). Attitudinal ambivalence toward parents and attachment style. *Personality and Social Psychology Bulletin, 26,* 1451–1464.

Malcolm, J. (1984). *In the Freud archives.* New York: Knopf.

Malloy, T., Albright, L., Diaz-Loving, R., Dong, Q., & Lee, Y. (2004). Agreement in personality judgments within and between nonoverlapping social groups in collectivist cultures. *Personality and Social Psychology Bulletin, 30,* 106–117.

Manaster, G. (2006). *Adlerian Lifestyle Counseling* by W. Rule & M. Bishop [book review]. *PsycCritiques: APA Review of Books, 51.*

Manaster, G., & Mays, M. (2004). Early recollections: A conversation. *Journal of Individual Psychology, 60,* 107–114.

Manger, T., & Ekeland, O. (2000). On the relationship between locus of control, level of ability and gender. *Scandinavian Journal of Psychology, 41,* 225–229.

Manning, M. M., & Wright, T. L. (1983). Self-efficacy expectancies, outcome expectancies, and the persistence of pain control in childbirth. *Journal of Personality and Social Psychology, 45,* 421–431.

Maqsud, M., & Rouhani, S. (1991). Relationships between socioeconomic status, locus of control, self-concept, and academic achievement of Botswana adolescents. *Journal of Youth and Adolescence, 20,* 107–114.

Marcia, J. E. (1966). Development and validation of ego-identity status. *Journal of Personality and Social Psychology, 3,* 551–558.

Marcia, J. E. (1967). Ego identity status: Relationship to change in self-esteem, general maladjustment and authoritarianism. *Journal of Personality, 35,* 118–133.

Marcia, J. E. (1980). Identity in adolescence. In J. Adelson (Ed.), *Handbook of adolescent psychology* (pp. 159–187). New York: Wiley.

Marcia, J. E., & Friedman, M. L. (1970). Ego identity status in college women. *Journal of Personality, 38,* 249–263.

Marcus, B., & Schutz, A. (2005). Why are people reluctant to participate in research? Personality correlates of four different types of nonresponse as inferred from self- and observer ratings. *Journal of Personality, 73,* 959–984.

Marcus-Newhall, A., Pedersen, W., Miller, N., & Carlson, M. (2000). Displaced aggression is alive and well: A meta-analytic review. *Journal of Personality and Social Psychology, 78,* 670–689.

Markstrom, C., Li, X., Blackshire, S., & Wilfong, J. (2005). Ego strength development of adolescents involved in adult-sponsored structured activities. *Journal of Youth and Adolescence, 34,* 85–95.

Markstrom, C., & Marshall, S. (2007). The psychological inventory of ego strength: Examination of theory and psychometric properties. *Journal of Adolescence, 30,* 63–79.

Marshall, G. N. (1991). A multidimensional analysis of internal health locus of control beliefs: Separating the wheat from the chaff? *Journal of Personality and Social Psychology, 61,* 483–491.

Marshall, G. N., Wortman, C. B., Vickers, R. R., Jr., Kusulas, J. W., & Hervig, L. K. (1994). The five-factor model of personality as a framework for personality-health research. *Journal of Personality and Social Psychology, 67,* 278–286.

Martin, C. M. (1999). A developmental perspective on gender effects and gender concepts. In W. B. Swann, Jr., J. H. Langlois, & L. A. Gilbert (Eds.), *Sexism and stereotypes in modern society* (pp. 45–73). Washington, DC: American Psychological Association.

Martin, N., & Jardine, R. (1986). Eysenck's contributions to behaviour genetics. In S. Modgill & L. Modgill (Eds.), *Hans Eysenck: Consensus and controversy* (pp. 13–47). London: Falmer.

Martin-Krumm, C., Sarrazin, P., Peterson, C., & Famose, J. (2003). Explanatory style and resilience after sports failure. *Personality and Individual Differences, 35,* 1685–1695.

Maruta, T., Colligan, R., Malinchoc, M., & Offord, K. (2000). Optimists versus pessimists: Survival rate among medical patients over a 30-year period. *Mayo Clinic Proceedings, 75,* 140–143.

Masling, J. M., Rabie, L., & Blondheim, S. H. (1967). Obesity, level of aspiration, and Rorschach and TAT measures of oral dependence. *Journal of Consulting Psychology, 31,* 233–239.

Maslow, A. H. (1957). A philosophy of psychology: The need for a mature science of human nature. *Main Currents in Modern Thought, 13,* 27–32.

Maslow, A. H. (1968). *Toward a psychology of being* (2nd ed.). New York: Van Nostrand Reinhold.

Maslow, A. H. (1970a). Tribute to Alfred Adler. *Journal of Individual Psychology, 26,* 13.

Maslow, A. H. (1970b). *Motivation and personality* (2nd ed.). New York: Harper & Row.

Maslow, A. H. (1971). *The farther reaches of human nature.* New York: Viking Press.

Maslow, A. H. (1979). *The journals of A. H. Maslow.* [R. J. Lowry (Ed.).] Pacific Grove, CA: Brooks/Cole.

Maslow, A. H. (1987). *Motivation and personality* (3rd ed.). New York: Harper & Row.

Masson, J. M. (1984). *The assault on truth: Freud's suppression of the seduction theory.* New York: Farrar, Straus & Giroux.

Mastekaasa, A. (1995). Age variations in the suicide rates and self-reported subjective well-being of married and never married persons. *Journal of Community and Applied Social Psychology, 5,* 21–39.

Matheny, A. P. (1983). A longitudinal twin study of the stability of components from Bayley's Infant Behavior Record. *Child Development, 54,* 356–360.

Mathew, P., & Bhatewara, S. (2006). Personality differences and preferred styles of conflict management among managers. *Abhigyan* [Asian journal of management], *23*(4), 38–45.

Matthews, G., & Deary, I. J. (1998). *Personality traits.* Cambridge, England: Cambridge University Press.

Matthews, K. A., Batson, C. D., Horn, J., & Rosenman, R. H. (1981). "Principles in his nature which interest him in the fortune of others . . .": The heritability of empathic concern for others. *Journal of Personality, 49,* 237–247.

Matula, K. E., Huston, T. L., Grotevant, H. D., & Zamutt, A. (1992). Identity and dating commitment among women and men in college. *Journal of Youth and Adolescence, 21,* 339–356.

Mayes, R., & Horwitz, A. (2005). DSM-III and the revolution in the classification of mental illness. *Journal of the History of the Behavioral Sciences, 41,* 249–267.

Mazzoni, G. A. L., Lombardo, P., Malvagia, S., & Loftus, E. (1999). Dream interpretations and false beliefs. *Professional Psychology, 30,* 45–50.

McAdams, D. P. (1994). Can personality change? Levels of stability and growth in personality across the life span. In T. F. Heatherton & J. L. Weinberger (Eds.), *Can personality change?* (pp. 299–313). Washington, DC: American Psychological Association.

McAdams, D. P. (2001). The psychology of life stories. *Review of General Psychology, 5,* 100–122.

McAdams, D. P., & de St. Aubin, E. (1992). A theory of generativity and its assessment through self-report, behavior acts, and narrative themes in autobiography. *Journal of Personality and Social Psychology, 62,* 1003–1015.

McAdams, D. P., Diamond, A., de St. Aubin, E., & Mansfield, E. (1997). Stories of commitment: The psychosocial construction of generative lives. *Journal of Personality and Social Psychology, 72,* 678–694.

McAdams, D. P., Hart, H. M., & Maruna, S. (1998). The anatomy of generativity. In D. P. McAdams & E. de St. Aubin (Eds.), *Generativity and adult development* (pp. 7–43). Washington, DC: American Psychological Association.

McAdams, D. P., Reynolds, J., Lewis, M., Patten, A. H., & Bowman, P. J. (2001). When bad things turn good and good things turn bad: Sequences of redemption and contamination in life narratives and their relation to psychosocial adaptation in midlife adults and in students. *Personality and Social Psychology Bulletin, 27,* 474–485.

McAdams, D. P., Ruetzel, K., & Foley, J. M. (1986). Complexity and generativity at midlife: Relations among social motives, ego development, and adults' plans for the future. *Journal of Personality and Social Psychology, 50,* 800–807.

McCann, S., Stewin, L., & Short, R. (1990). Frightening dream frequency and birth order. *Individual Psychology, 46,* 304–310.

McClelland, D. C. (1965a). *N* achievement and entrepreneurship: A longitudinal study. *Journal of Personality and Social Psychology, 1,* 389–392.

McClelland, D. C. (1965b). Toward a theory of motive acquisition. *American Psychologist, 20,* 321–333.

McClelland, D. C. (1985). *Human motivation.* Glenview, IL: Scott, Foresman.

McClelland, D. C. (1987). Characteristics of successful entrepreneurs. *Journal of Creative Behavior, 3,* 219–233.

McClelland, D. C., Atkinson, J. W., Clark, R. A., & Lowell, E. L. (1953). *The achievement motive.* New York: Appleton-Century-Crofts.

McClelland, D. C., & Boyatzis, R. E. (1982). The leadership motive pattern and long-term success in management. *Journal of Applied Psychology, 67,* 737–743.

McClelland, D. C., & Franz, C. E. (1992). Motivational and other sources of work accomplishments in midlife: A longitudinal study. *Journal of Personality, 60,* 679–707.

McClelland, D. C., Koestner, R., & Weinberger, J. (1989). How do self-attributed and implicit motives differ? *Psychological Review, 96,* 690–702.

McCrae, R. R., & Costa, P. T., Jr. (1985a). Openness to experience. In R. Hogan & W. H. Jones (Eds.), *Perspectives in personality* (Vol. 1, pp. 145–172).

McCrae, R. R., & Costa, P. T., Jr. (1985b). Updating Norman's "adequate taxonomy": Intelligence and personality dimensions in natural language and questionnaires. *Journal of Personality and Social Psychology, 49,* 710–721.

McCrae, R. R., & Costa, P. T., Jr. (1987). Validation of the five-factor model of personality across instruments and observers. *Journal of Personality and Social Psychology, 52,* 81–90.

McCrae, R. R., & Costa, P. T., Jr. (1989). Reinterpreting the Myers-Briggs Type Indicator from the perspective of the five-factor model of personality. *Journal of Personality, 57,* 17–40.

McCrae, R. R., & Costa, P. T., Jr. (1991). Adding *Liebe und Arbeit*: The full five-factor model and well-being. *Personality and Social Psychology Bulletin, 17,* 227–232.

McCrae, R. R., & Costa, P. T., Jr. (1997). Personality trait structure as a human universal. *American Psychologist, 52,* 509–516.

McCrae, R. R., Costa, P. T., Jr., Hrebickova, M., Urbanek, T., Martin, T., Oryol, V., Rukavishnikov, A., & Senin, I. (2004a). Age differences in personality traits across cultures: Self-report and observer perspectives. *European Journal of Personality, 18,* 143–157.

McCrae, R. R., Costa, P. T., Jr., Martin, T., Oryol, V., Rukavishnikov, A., Senin, I., Hrebickova, M., & Urbanek, T. (2004b). Consensual validation of personality traits across cultures. *Journal of Research in Personality, 38,* 179–201.

McCrae, R. R., Costa, P. T., Jr., Terracciano, A., Parker, W. D., Mills, C. J., DeFruyt, F., & Mervielde, I. (2002). Personality trait development from age 12 to age 18: Longitudinal, cross-sectional, and cross-cultural analyses. *Journal of Personality and Social Psychology, 83,* 1456–1468.

McCrae, R. R., & Terracciano, A. (2005). Universal features of personality traits from the observer's perspective:

Data from 50 cultures. *Journal of Personality and Social Psychology, 88,* 547–561.

McCrae, R. R., Yi, M. S. M., Trapnell, P. D., Bond, M. H., & Paulhus, D. L. (1998). Interpreting personality profiles across cultures: Bilingual, acculturation, and peer rating studies of Chinese undergraduates. *Journal of Personality and Social Psychology, 74,* 1041–1055.

McCrae, R. R., et al. (1999). Age differences in personality across the adult life span: Parallels in five cultures. *Developmental Psychology, 35,* 466–477.

McCrae, R. R., et al. (2000). Nature over nurture: Temperament, personality, and life span development. *Journal of Personality and Social Psychology, 78,* 173–186.

McCullough, M. (2001). Freud's seduction theory and its rehabilitation: A saga of one mistake after another. *Review of General Psychology, 5,* 3–22.

McCullough, M., Bellah, C., Kilpatrick, S., & Johnson, J. (2001). Vengefulness: Relationships with forgiveness, rumination, well-being, and the Big Five. *Personality and Social Psychology Bulletin, 27,* 601–610.

McGregor, I., & Little, B. R. (1998). Personal projects, happiness, and meaning. *Journal of Personality and Social Psychology, 74,* 494–512.

McHale, S., Updegraff, K., Helms-Erikson, H., & Crouter, A. (2001). Sibling influences on gender development in middle childhood and early adolescence: A longitudinal study. *Developmental Psychology, 37,* 115–125.

McLaughlin, N. G. (1998). Why do schools of thought fail? Neo-Freudianism as a case study in the sociology of knowledge. *Journal of the History of the Behavioral Sciences, 34,* 113–134.

McLeod, B. (1986, October). Rx for health: A dose of self-confidence. *Psychology Today,* pp. 46–50.

McNally, R., Clancy, S., Schacter, D., & Pitman, R. (2000). Personality profiles, dissociation, and absorption in women reporting repressed, recovered, or continuous memories of childhood sexual abuse. *Journal of Consulting and Clinical Psychology, 68,* 1033–1037.

McNally, R., Perlman, C., Ristuccia, C., & Clancy, S. (2006). Clinical characteristics of adults reporting repressed, recovered, or continuous memories of childhood sexual abuse. *Journal of Consulting and Clinical Psychology, 74,* 237–242.

McNulty, J. L., Graham, J. R., Ben-Porath, Y. S., & Stein, L. A. R. (1997). Comparative validity of MMPI-2 scores of African Americans and Caucasian mental health center clients. *Psychological Assessment, 9,* 464–470.

Medinnus, G., & Curtis, F. (1963). The relation between maternal self-acceptance and child acceptance. *Journal of Counseling Psychology, 27,* 542–544.

Melamed, B. G., & Siegel, L. J. (1975). Reduction of anxiety in children facing hospitalization and surgery by use of filmed modeling. *Journal of Consulting and Clinical Psychology, 43,* 511–521.

Mellor, S. (1989). Gender differences in identity formation as a function of self–other relationships. *Journal of Youth and Adolescence, 18,* 361–375.

Mellor, S. (1990). How do only children differ from other children? *Journal of Genetic Psychology, 151,* 221–230.

Meyer, G. N. (2001). Introduction to the final special section in the special series on the utility of the Rorschach for clinical assessment. *Psychological Assessment, 13,* 419–422.

Miletic, M. P. (2002). The introduction of feminine psychology to psychoanalysis: Karen Horney's legacy. *Contemporary Psychoanalysis, 38,* 287–299.

Milgram, N. A. (1971). Locus of control in Negro and white children at four age levels. *Psychological Reports, 29,* 459–465.

Milton, J. (2002). *The road to malpsychia: Humanistic psychology and our discontents.* San Francisco: Encounter Books.

Mindess, H. (1988). *Makers of psychology: The personal factor.* New York: Human Sciences Press.

Miner-Rubino, K., Winter, D., & Stewart, A. (2004). Gender, social class, and the subjective experience of aging: Self-perceived personality change from early adulthood to late midlife. *Personality and Social Psychology Bulletin, 30,* 1599–1610.

Miranda, A. O., Frevert, E. S., & Kern, R. M. (1998). Lifestyle differences between bicultural and low- and high-acculturation level Latino adults. *Individual Psychology, 54,* 119–134.

Mischel, W. (1968). *Personality and assessment.* New York: Wiley.

Mischel, W. (1973). Toward a cognitive social-learning reconceptualization of personality. *Psychological Review, 80,* 252–283.

Morehouse, R. E., Farley, F., & Youngquist, J. V. (1990). Type T personality and the Jungian classification system. *Journal of Personality Assessment, 54,* 231–235.

Moretti, M. M., & Higgins, E. T. (1990). Relating self-discrepancy to self-esteem: The contribution of discrepancy beyond actual-self ratings. *Journal of Experimental Social Psychology, 26,* 108–123.

Morgan, C. D., & Murray, H. A. (1935). A method for investigating fantasies. *Archives of Neurology and Psychiatry, 34,* 289–306.

Morling, B., Kitayama, S., & Miyamoto, Y. (2002). Cultural practices emphasize influence in the United States and adjustment in Japan. *Personality and Social Psychology Bulletin, 28,* 311–323.

Moskowitz, D. S., & Schwartzman, A. E. (1989). Life paths of aggressive and withdrawn children. In D. M. Buss & N. Cantor (Eds.), *Personality psychology: Recent trends and emerging directions* (pp. 99–114). New York: Springer-Verlag.

Motley, M. T. (1987, February). What I meant to say. *Psychology Today,* pp. 24–28.

Mroczek, D., & Almeida, D. (2004). The effect of daily stress, personality, and age on daily negative affect. *Journal of Personality, 72,* 355–378.

Mroczek, D., & Spiro, A. (2005). Change in life satisfaction during adulthood: Findings from the Veterans Affairs Normative Aging Study. *Journal of Personality and Social Psychology, 88,* 189–202.

Multon, K. D., Brown, S. D., & Lent, R. W. (1991). Relation of self-efficacy beliefs to academic outcomes: A meta-analytic investigation. *Journal of Counseling Psychology, 38,* 30–38.

Muris, P. (2002). Relationships between self-efficacy and symptoms of anxiety disorders and depression in a normal adolescent sample. *Personality and Individual Differences, 32,* 337–348.

Murray, H. A. (1938). *Explorations in personality: A clinical and experimental study of fifty men of college age.* New York: Oxford University Press.

Murray, H. A. (1940). What should psychologists do about psychoanalysis? *Journal of Abnormal and Social Psychology, 35,* 150–175.

Murray, H. A. (1967). Autobiography. In E. G. Boring & G. Lindzey (Eds.), *A history of psychology in autobiography.* (Vol. 5, pp. 283–310). New York: Appleton-Century-Crofts.

Murray, K. M., & Johnson, W. B. (2001). Personality type and success among female naval academy midshipmen. *Military Medicine, 166,* 889–893.

Myers, D. G. (2000). The funds, friends, and faith of happy people. *American Psychologist, 55,* 56–67.

Myers, D. G., & Diener, E. (1995). Who is happy? *Psychological Science, 6,* 10–19.

Myers, L., & Derakshan, N. (2004). Do childhood memories colour social judgements of today? The case of repressors. *European Journal of Personality, 18,* 321–330.

Nakamura, M. (2002). Relationship between anxiety and physical traits of facial expression. *Japanese Journal of Psychology, 73,* 140–147.

Nasser, R., & Abouchedid, K. (2006). Locus of control and attribution for poverty: Comparing Lebanese and South African university students. *Social Behavior and Personality, 34,* 777–796.

Needs, A. (1988). Psychological investigations of offending behaviour. In F. Fransella & L. Thomas (Eds.), *Experimenting with personal construct psychology* (pp. 493–506). London: Routledge & Kegan Paul.

Neimeyer, G. J. (1984). Cognitive complexity and marital satisfaction. *Journal of Social and Clinical Psychology, 2,* 258–263.

Nelson, D. L., & Burke, R. J. (2000). Women executives. *Academy of Management Executive, 14,* 107–121.

Netz, Y., Wu, M., Becker, B., & Tenenbaum, G. (2005). Physical activity and psychological well-being in advanced age: A meta-analysis of intervention studies. *Psychology and Aging, 20,* 272–284.

Newman, D. L., Tellegen, A., & Bouchard, T. J. (1998). Individual differences in adult ego development: Sources of influence in twins reared apart. *Journal of Personality and Social Psychology, 74,* 985–995.

Newman, L. S., & McKinney, L. C. (2002). Repressive coping and threat-avoidance: An idiographic Stroop study. *Personality and Social Psychology Bulletin, 28,* 409–422.

Newman, L. S., Duff, K. J., & Baumeister, R. F. (1997). A new look at defensive projection: Thought suppression, accessibility, and biased person perception. *Journal of Personality and Social Psychology, 72,* 980–1001.

Newman, L. S., Higgins, E. T., & Vookles, J. (1992). Self-guide strength and emotional vulnerability: Birth order as a moderator of self-affect relations. *Personality and Social Psychology Bulletin, 18,* 402–411.

Neyer, F., & Asendorpf, J. (2001). Personality-relationship transactions in young adulthood. *Journal of Personality and Social Psychology, 81,* 1190–1204.

Nezlek, J., & Allen, M. (2006). Social support as a moderator of day-to-day relationships between daily negative events and daily psychological well-being. *European Journal of Personality, 20,* 53–68.

Nezlek, J., Kowalski, R. M., Leary, M. R., Blevins, T., & Holgate, S. (1997). Personality moderators of reactions to interpersonal rejection: Depression and trait self-esteem. *Personality and Social Psychology Bulletin, 23,* 1235–1244.

Nghe, L., & Mahalik, J. (2001). Examining racial identity statuses as predictors of psychological defenses in African American college students. *Journal of Counseling Psychology, 48,* 10–16.

Nguyen, S. (2006). The role of cultural factors affecting the academic achievement of Vietnamese refugee students. *Dissertation Abstracts International A: Humanities & Social Sciences, 67,* 495.

Nicholson, I. A. M. (2003). *Inventing personality: Gordon Allport and the science of selfhood.* Washington, DC: American Psychological Association.

Nigg, J., John, O., Blaskey, L., Huang-Pollock, C., Willicut, E., Hinshaw, S., & Pennington, B. (2002). Big Five dimensions and ADHD symptoms: Links between personality traits and clinical symptoms. *Journal of Personality and Social Psychology, 83,* 451–469.

Nikelly, A. (2005). Positive health outcomes of social interest. *Journal of Individual Psychology, 61,* 329–342.

Nolen-Hoeksema, S., Girgus, J., & Seligman, M. E. P. (1987). Learned helplessness in children: A longitudinal study of depression, achievement, and explanatory style. *Journal of Personality and Social Psychology, 51,* 435.

Noll, R. (1994). *The Jung cult: Origins of a charismatic movement.* Princeton, NJ: Princeton University Press.

Noll, R. (1997). *The Aryan Christ: The secret life of Carl Jung.* New York: Random House.

Novy, D., Stanley, M., Averill, P., & Daza, P. (2001). Psychometric comparability of English- and Spanish-language measures of anxiety and related affective symptoms. *Psychological Assessment, 13,* 347–355.

Nowicki, S., & Duke, M. P. (1983). The Nowicki-Strickland life-span locus of control scales: Construct validation. In H. M. Lefcourt (Ed.), *Research with the locus of control construct* (Vol. 2, pp. 13–51). Orlando, FL: Academic Press.

Nowicki, S., & Strickland, B. R. (1973). A locus of control scale for children. *Journal of Consulting Psychology, 40,* 148–154.

Oettingen, G., & Maier, H. (1999). Where political system meets culture: Effects on efficacy appraisal. In Y. T. Lee, C. R. McCauley, & J. G. Draguns (Eds.), *Personality and person perception across cultures* (pp. 163–190). Mahwah, NJ: Erlbaum.

Ofshe, R., & Watters, E. (1994). *False memories, psychotherapy, and sexual hysteria.* New York: Scribner's.

Oishi, S., & Diener, E. (2001). Goals, culture, and subjective well-being. *Personality and Social Psychology Bulletin, 27,* 1674–1682.

Okeke, B. I., Draguns, J. G., Sheku, B., & Allen, W. (1999). Culture, self, and personality in Africa. In Y. T. Lee, C. R. McCauley, & J. G. Draguns (Eds.), *Personality and person perception across cultures* (pp. 139–162). Mahwah, NJ: Erlbaum.

Olioff, M., & Aboud, F. E. (1991). Predicting postpartum dysphoria in primiparous mothers: Roles of perceived parenting self-efficacy and self-esteem. *Journal of Cognitive Psychotherapy, 5,* 3–14.

O'Neill, R. M., & Bornstein, R. F. (1990). Oral-dependence and gender: Factors in help-seeking response set and self-reported pathology in psychiatric inpatients. *Journal of Personality Assessment, 55,* 28–40.

Orgler, H. (1963). *Alfred Adler, the man and his work: Triumph over the inferiority complex.* New York: New American Library.

Orlofsky, J. L., Marcia, J. E., & Lesser, I. M. (1973). Ego identity status and the intimacy versus isolation crisis of young adulthood. *Journal of Personality and Social Psychology, 27,* 211–219.

Ormel, J., & Wohlfarth, T. (1991). How neuroticism, long-term difficulties, and life situation changes influence psychological distress: A longitudinal model. *Journal of Personality and Social Psychology, 60,* 744–755.

OSS Assessment Staff. (1948). *Assessment of men: Selection of personnel for the U.S Office of Strategic Services.* New York: Rinehart.

Overmier, J. B., & Seligman, M. E. P. (1967). Effects of inescapable shock upon subsequent escape and avoidance learning. *Journal of Comparative and Physiological Psychology, 63,* 28–33.

Owen, S. (2006). Occupational stress among correctional supervisors. *Prison Journal, 86,* 164–181.

Ozer, E. M. (1995). The impact of childcare responsibility and self-efficacy on psychological health of professional working mothers. *Psychology of Women Quarterly, 19,* 315–335.

Pace, T., Robbins, R., Choney, S., Hill, J., Lacey, K., & Blair, G. (2006). A cultural-contextual perspective on the validity of the MMPI-2 with American Indians. *Cultural Diversity and Ethnic Minority Psychology, 12,* 320–333.

Paige, J. M. (1966). Letters from Jenny: An approach to the clinical analysis of personality structure by computer. In P. J. Stone (Ed.), *The general inquirer: A computer approach to context analysis.* Cambridge, MA: MIT Press.

Pals, J. L. (1999). Identity consolidation in early adulthood: Relations with ego-resiliency, the context of marriage, and personality change. *Journal of Personality, 67,* 295–329.

Pancer, S., Hunsberger, B., Pratt, M., & Alisat, S. (2000). Cognitive complexity of expectations and adjustment to university in the first year. *Journal of Adolescent Research, 15,* 38–57.

Paris, B. J. (1994). *Karen Horney: A psychoanalyst's search for self-understanding.* New Haven, CT: Yale University Press.

Paris, R., & Helson, R. (2002). Early mothering experience and personality change. *Journal of Family Psychology, 16,* 172–185.

Park, C., Armeli, S., & Tennen, H. (2004). Appraisal-coping goodness of fit: A daily Internet study. *Personality and Social Psychology Bulletin, 30,* 558–569.

Park, N., & Huebner, E. (2005). A cross-cultural study of the levels and correlates of life satisfaction among adolescents. *Journal of Cross-Cultural Psychology, 36,* 444–456.

Parkes, K. R. (1986). Coping in stressful episodes. *Journal of Personality and Social Psychology, 51,* 1277–1292.

Parkham, T., & Helms, J. (1985a). Attitudes of racial identity and self-esteem of black students: An exploratory investigation. *Journal of College Student Personnel, 26,* 143–147.

Parkham, T., & Helms, J. (1985b). Relation of racial identity and attitudes to self-actualization and affective states of black students. *Journal of Counseling Psychology, 32,* 431–440.

Patterson, R. (2006). The child within: Karen Horney on vacation. *American Journal of Psychoanalysis, 66,* 109–112.

Patterson, T., & Joseph, S. (2007). Person-centered personality theory: Support from self-determination theory and positive psychology. *Journal of Humanistic Psychology, 47,* 117–139.

Paunonen, S. V. (1998). Hierarchical organization of personality and prediction of behavior. *Journal of Personality and Social Psychology, 74,* 538–556.

Paunonen, S. V., & Ashton, M. C. (2001). Big Five factors and facets and the prediction of behavior. *Journal of Personality and Social Psychology, 81,* 524–539.

Pedersen, N. L., Plomin, R., McClearn, G. E., & Friberg, L. (1988). Neuroticism, extraversion, and related traits in adult twins reared apart and reared together. *Journal of Personality and Social Psychology, 55,* 950–957.

Peltzer, K., Malaka, D., & Phaswana, N. (2001). Psychological correlates of substance use among South African university students. *Social Behavior and Personality, 29,* 799–806.

Peluso, P., Peluso, J., Buckner, J., Curlette, W., & Kern, R. (2004). An analysis of the reliability of the BASIS-A Inventory using a northeastern and southeastern U.S. sample. *Journal of Individual Psychology, 60,* 294–307.

Pervin, L. A. (1984). *Current controversies and issues in personality* (2nd ed.). New York: Wiley.

Pervin, L. A. (2003). *The science of personality* (2nd ed.). New York: Oxford University Press.

Pesant, N., & Zadra, A. (2006). Dream content and psychological well-being: A longitudinal study of the continuity hypothesis. *Journal of Clinical Psychology, 62,* 111–121.

Peter, J., & Valkenburg, P. (2006). Individual differences in perceptions of Internet communication. *European Journal of Communication, 21,* 213–226.

Peterson, B. E. (2002). Longitudinal analysis of midlife generativity, intergenerational roles, and caregiving. *Psychology and Aging, 17,* 161–168.

Peterson, B. E., Smirles, K. A., & Wentworth, P. A. (1997). Generativity and authoritarianism: Implications for personality, political involvement, and parenting. *Journal of Personality and Social Psychology, 72,* 1202–1216.

Peterson, B. E., & Stewart, A. J. (1990). Using personal and fictional documents to assess psychosocial development: A case study of Vera Brittain's generativity. *Psychology and Aging, 5,* 400–411.

Peterson, C., & Barrett, L. C. (1987). Explanatory style and academic performance among college freshmen. *Journal of Personality and Social Psychology, 53,* 603–607.

Peterson, C., Maier, S. F., & Seligman, M. E. P. (1993). *Learned helplessness: A theory for the age of personal control.* New York: Oxford University Press.

Peterson, C., & Seligman, M. E. P. (1987). Explanatory style and illness. Special issue: Personality and physical health. *Journal of Personality, 55,* 237–265.

Peterson, C., Seligman, M. E. P., & Vaillant, G. (1988). Pessimistic explanatory style as a risk factor for physical illness: A 35-year longitudinal study. *Journal of Personality and Social Psychology, 55,* 23–27.

Peterson, C., Semmel, A., Von Baeyer, C., Abramson, L. Y., Metalsky, G. I., & Seligman, M. E. P. (1982). The Attributional Style Questionnaire. *Cognitive Therapy and Research, 6,* 287–300.

Petrosky, M. J., & Birkhimer, J. C. (1991). The relationship among locus of control coping styles and psychological symptom reporting. *Journal of Clinical Psychology, 47,* 336–345.

Phares, E. J. (1993). From therapy to research: A patient's legacy. In G. G. Brannigan & M. R. Merrens (Eds.), *The undaunted psychologist: Adventures in research* (pp. 157–171). Philadelphia: Temple University Press.

Phillips, D. P. (1974). The influence of suggestion on suicide: Substantive and theoretical implications of the Werther effect. *American Sociological Review, 39,* 340–354.

Phillips, D. P. (1983). The impact of mass media violence on U.S homicides. *American Sociological Review, 48,* 560–568.

Phillips, D. P. (1985). The found experiment: A new technique for assessing impact of mass media violence on real-world aggressive behavior. In G. Comstock (Ed.), *Public communication and behavior* (Vol. 1). New York: Academic Press.

Phinney, J. S., & Chavira, V. (1992). Ethnic identity and self-esteem: An exploratory longitudinal study. *Journal of Adolescence, 15,* 271–281.

Phipps, S., & Steele, R. (2002). Repressive adaptive style in children with chronic illness. *Psychosomatic Medicine, 64,* 34–42.

Piedmont, R. L. (1988). The relationship between achievement motivation, anxiety, and situational characteristics on performance on a cognitive task. *Journal of Research in Personality, 22,* 177–187.

Pierre, M., & Mahalik, J. (2005). Examining African self-consciousness and Black racial identity as predictors of Black men's psychological well-being. *Cultural Diversity and Ethnic Minority Psychology, 11,* 28–40.

Pilkington, B., & Lenaghan, M. (1998). Psychopathology. In K. Trew & J. Kremer (Eds.), *Gender and psychology* (pp. 179–191). New York: Oxford University Press.

Pillay, Y. (2005). Racial identity as a predictor of the psychological health of African-American students at a predominantly White university. *Journal of Black Psychology, 31,* 46–66.

Pinquart, M., & Soerensen, S. (2000). Influences of socioeconomic status, social network, and competence on subjective well-being in later life: A meta-analysis. *Psychology and Aging, 15,* 187–224.

Plaut, V., Markus, H., & Lachman, M. (2002). Place matters: Consensual features and regional variation in American well-being and self. *Journal of Personality and Social Psychology, 83,* 160–184.

Plomin, R., Chipeur, H. M., & Loehlin, J. C. (1990). Behavioral genetics and personality. In L. A. Pervin (Ed.), *Handbook of personality: Theory and research* (pp. 225–243). New York: Guilford Press.

Podd, M. H., Marcia, J. E., & Rubin, R. (1968). The effects of ego identity status and partner perception on a prisoner's dilemma game. *Journal of Social Psychology, 82,* 117–126.

Pole, N., Best, S., Metzler, T., & Marmar, C. (2005). Why are Hispanics at greater risk for PTSD? *Cultural Diversity and Ethnic Minority Psychology, 11,* 144–161.

Pollak, S., & Sinha, P. (2002). Effects of early experience on children's recognition of facial displays of emotion. *Developmental Psychology, 38,* 784–791.

Porcerelli, J. H., Thomas, S., Hibbard, S., & Cogan, R. (1998). Defense mechanisms development in children, adolescents, and late adolescents. *Journal of Personality Assessment, 71,* 411–420.

Postmes, T., & Branscombe, N. (2002). Influence of long-term racial environmental composition on subjective well-being in African Americans. *Journal of Personality and Social Psychology, 83,* 735–751.

Prelow, H., Mosher, C., & Bowman, M. (2006). Perceived racial discrimination, social support, and psychological adjustment among African-American college students. *Journal of Black Psychology, 32,* 442–454.

Prenda, K., & Lachman, M. (2001). Planning for the future: A life management strategy for increasing control and life satisfaction in adulthood. *Psychology and Aging, 16,* 206–216.

Prochnik, G. (2006). *Putnam camp: Sigmund Freud, James Jackson Putnam, and the purpose of American psychology.* New York: Other Press.

Puca, R. M., & Schmalt, H. (2001). The influence of the achievement motive on spontaneous thoughts in pre- and post-decisional action phases. *Personality and Social Psychology Bulletin, 27,* 302–308.

Pullmann, H., Raudsepp, L., & Allik, J. (2006). Stability and change in adolescents' personality: A longitudinal study. *European Journal of Personality, 20,* 447–459.

Pyszczynski, T., Greenberg, J., Solomon, S., Arndt, J., & Schimel, J. (2004). Why do people need self-esteem? A theoretical and empirical review. *Psychological Bulletin, 130,* 435–468.

Qing-Xin, S., Rong-Gang, Z., & Yan, G. (2005). Internet addiction disorder and sensation seeking of middle school and high school students. *Chinese Mental Health Journal, 19,* 453–456.

Quiery, N. (1998). Parenting the family. In K. Trew & J. Kremer (Eds.), *Gender and psychology* (pp. 129–140). New York: Oxford University Press.

Quinn, S. (1987). *A mind of her own: The life of Karen Horney.* New York: Summit Books.

Rabinowitz, P. (2005). Is noise bad for your health? *Lancet, 365*(9475), 1908–1909.

Räikkönen, K., Katainen, S., Keskivaara, P., & Keltikangas-Jaervinen, L. (2000). Temperament, mothering, and hostile attitudes: A 12-year longitudinal study. *Personality and Social Psychology Bulletin, 26,* 3–12.

Räikkönen, K., Matthews, K. A., Flory, J. D., Owens, J. F., & Gump, B. B. (1999). Effects of optimism, pessimism, and trait anxiety on ambulatory blood pressure and mood during everyday life. *Journal of Personality and Social Psychology, 76,* 104–113.

Raine, A., Reynolds, C., Venables, P., & Mednick, S. (2002). Stimulation seeking and intelligence: A prospective longitudinal study. *Journal of Personality and Social Psychology, 82,* 663–674.

Rainey, N. (1998). Old age. In K. Trew & J. Kremer (Eds.), *Gender and psychology* (pp. 153–164). New York: Oxford University Press.

Rayle, A. (2005). Adolescent gender differences in mattering and wellness. *Journal of Adolescence, 28,* 753–763.

Reimanis, G. (1974). Personality development, anomie, and mood. *Journal of Personality and Social Psychology, 29,* 355–357.

Reio, T., & Sanders-Reio, J. (2006). Sensation seeking as an inhibitor of job performance. *Personality and Individual Differences, 40,* 631–642.

Rendon, D. (1987). Understanding social roles from a Horneyan perspective. *American Journal of Psychoanalysis, 47,* 131–142.

Repucci, N. D., & Saunders, J. T. (1974). Social psychology of behavior modification: Problems of implementation in natural settings. *American Psychologist, 29,* 649–660.

Resnicow, K., Soler, R. E., Braithwaite, R. L., Ben Selassie, M., & Smith, M. (1999). Development of a racial and ethnic identity scale for African American adolescents: The Survey of Black Life. *Journal of Black Psychology, 25,* 171–188.

Reuman, D. A., Alwin, D. F., & Veroff, J. (1984). Assessing the validity of the achievement motive in the presence of random measurement error. *Journal of Personality and Social Psychology, 47,* 1347–1362.

Rice, B. (1968, March 17). Skinner agrees he is the most important influence in psychology. *The New York Times Magazine,* p. 27ff.

Rice, T., & Steele, B. (2004). Subjective well-being and culture across time and space. *Journal of Cross-Cultural Psychology, 35,* 633–647.

Richelle, M. N. (1993). *B. F. Skinner: A reappraisal.* Hillsdale, NJ: Erlbaum.

Riggio, R. E., & Friedman, H. S. (1986). Impression formation: The role of expressive behavior. *Journal of Personality and Social Psychology, 50,* 421–427.

Riggio, R. E., Lippa, R., & Salinas, C. (1990). The display of personality in expressive movement. *Journal of Research in Personality, 24,* 16–31.

Roazen, P. (1975). *Freud and his followers.* New York: Knopf.

Roazen, P. (1993). *Meeting Freud's family.* Amherst, MA: University of Massachusetts Press.

Roberti, J. (2004). A review of behavioral and biological correlates of sensation seeking. *Journal of Research in Personality, 38,* 256–279.

Roberts, B. W., & Delvecchio, W. F. (2000). The rank-order consistency of personality traits from childhood to old age: A quantitative review of longitudinal studies. *Psychological Bulletin, 126,* 3–25.

Roberts, B. W., & Helson, R. (1997). Changes in culture, changes in personality: The influence of individualism in a longitudinal study of women. *Journal of Personality and Social Psychology, 72,* 641–651.

Roberts, B. W., Caspi, A., & Moffitt, T. (2001). The kids are all right: Growth and stability in personality development from adolescence to adulthood. *Journal of Personality and Social Psychology, 81,* 670–683.

Roberts, B. W., Caspi, A., & Moffitt, T. (2003). Work experiences and personality development in young adulthood. *Journal of Personality and Social Psychology, 84,* 582–593.

Roberts, B. W., & Robins, R. W. (2000). Brood dispositions, brood aspirations: The intersection of personality traits and major life goals. *Personality and Social Psychology Bulletin, 26,* 1284–1296.

Roberts, B., Walton, K., & Viechtbauer, W. (2006). Patterns of mean-level change in personality traits across the life course: A meta-analysis of longitudinal studies. *Psychological Bulletin, 132,* 1–25.

Robins, R. W., Trzesniewski, K., Tracy, J., Gosling, S., & Potter, J. (2002). Global self-esteem across the life span. *Psychology and Aging, 17,* 423–434.

Robinson, F. G. (1992). *Love's story told: A life of Henry A. Murray.* Cambridge, MA: Harvard University Press.

Robinson-Whelen, S., Kim, C., MacCallum, R. C., & Kiecolt-Glaser, J. K. (1997). Distinguishing optimism from pessimism in older adults. *Journal of Personality and Social Psychology, 73,* 1345–1353.

Roccas, S., Sagiu, L., Schwartz, S. H., & Knafo, A. (2002). The Big Five personality factors and personal values. *Personality and Social Psychology Bulletin, 28,* 789–801.

Rodgers, J. L. (2001). What causes birth order— intelligence patterns? The admixture hypothesis, revised. *American Psychologist, 56,* 505–510.

Rodriguez-Mosquera, P. M., Manstead, A. S. R., & Fischer, A. H. (2000). The role of honor-related values in the elicitation, experience, and communication of pride, shame, and anger: Spain and the Netherlands compared. *Personality and Social Psychology Bulletin, 26,* 833–844.

Rofe, Y. (2006). Affiliation tendencies on the eve of the Iraq War: A utility theory perspective. *Journal of Applied Social Psychology, 36,* 1781–1789.

Rogers, C. R. (1954). The case of Mrs. Oak: A research analysis. In C. R. Rogers & R. F. Dymond (Eds.), *Psychotherapy and personality change.* Chicago: University of Chicago Press.

Rogers, C. R. (1961). *On becoming a person: A therapist's view of psychotherapy.* Boston: Houghton Mifflin.

Rogers, C. R. (1967). Autobiography. In E. G. Boring & G. Lindzey (Eds.), *A history of psychology in autobiography* (Vol. 5, pp. 341–384). New York: Appleton-Century-Crofts.

Rogers, C. R. (1970). *Carl Rogers on encounter groups.* New York: Harper & Row.

Rogers, C. R. (1974). In retrospect: Forty-six years. *American Psychologist, 29,* 115–123.

Rogers, C. R. (1980). *A way of being.* Boston: Houghton Mifflin.

Rogers, C. R. (1987). An interview with Carl Rogers. In A. O. Ross, *Personality: The scientific study of complex human behavior* (pp. 118–119). New York: Holt, Rinehart & Winston.

Rogoff, B., Paradise, R., Arauz, R. M., Correa-Chavez, M., & Angelillo, C. (2003). First-hand learning through intent participation. *Annual Review of Psychology, 54,* 175–203.

Rose, R. J. (1995). Genes and human behavior. *Annual Review of Psychology, 46,* 625–654.

Rosenbloom, T. (2006a). Color preferences of high and low sensation seekers. *Creativity Research Journal, 18,* 229–235.

Rosenbloom, T. (2006b). Sensation seeking pedestrian crossing compliance. *Social Behavior and Personality, 34,* 113–122.

Rosenthal, D. R., Gurney, M. R., & Moore, S. M. (1981). From trust to intimacy: A new inventory for examining Erikson's stages of psychosocial development. *Journal of Youth and Adolescence, 10,* 525–536.

Rosenzweig, S. (1985). Freud and experimental psychology: The emergence of idiodynamics. In S. Koch & D. Leary (Eds.), *A century of psychology as science* (pp. 135–207). New York: McGraw-Hill.

Rotter, J. B. (1966). Generalized expectancies for internal versus external control of reinforcement. *Psychological Monographs, 80* (Whole No. 609).

Rotter, J. B. (1982). *The development and applications of social learning theory: Selected papers.* New York: Praeger.

Rotter, J. B. (1990). Internal versus external control of reinforcement: A case history of a variable. *American Psychologist, 45,* 489–493.

Rotter, J. B. (1993). Expectancies. In C. E. Walker (Ed.), *History of clinical psychology in autobiography* (Vol. 2, pp. 273–284). Pacific Grove, CA: Brooks/Cole.

Rubins, J. L. (1978). *Karen Horney: Gentle rebel of psychoanalysis.* New York: Dial Press.

Rucker, D. D., & Pratkanis, A. R. (2001). Projection as an interpersonal influence tactic: The effects of the pot calling the kettle black. *Personality and Social Psychology Bulletin, 27,* 1494–1507.

Rudolph, K., & Conley, C. (2005). The socioeconomic costs and benefits of social-evaluative concerns: Do girls care too much? *Journal of Personality, 73,* 115–138.

Rudy, D., & Grusec, J. (2006). Authoritarian parenting in individualistic and collectivist groups: Associations with maternal emotion and cognition and children's self-esteem. *Journal of Family Psychology, 20,* 68–78.

Rushton, J. P., Fulker, D. W., Neale, M. C., Blizard, R. A., & Eysenck, H. J. (1984). Altruism and genetics. *Acta Geneticae et Gemellologiae, 33,* 265–271.

Russell, J. A., Bachorowski, J. A., & Fernandez-Dols, J. M. (2003). Facial and vocal expressions of emotion. *Annual Review of Psychology, 54,* 329–349.

Ryan, R. M., & Deci, E. L. (2000). Self-determination theory and the facilitation of intrinsic motivation, social development, and well-being. *American Psychologist, 55,* 68–78.

Ryan, R. M., & Frederick, C. (1997). On energy, personality, and health: Subjective vitality as a dynamic reflection of well-being. *Journal of Personality, 65,* 529–565.

Ryckman, R. M., Hammer, M., Kaczor, L. M., & Gold, J. A. (1990). Construction of a Hypercompetitive Attitude Scale. *Journal of Personality Assessment, 55,* 630–639.

Ryckman, R. M., & Malikiosi, M. X. (1975). Relationship between locus of control and chronological age. *Psychological Reports, 36,* 655–658.

Ryckman, R. M., Thornton, B., & Butler, J. C. (1994). Personality correlates of the Hypercompetitive Attitude Scale: Validity tests of Horney's theory of neurosis. *Journal of Personality Assessment, 62,* 84–94.

Ryckman, R. M., Thornton, B., Gold, J., & Burckle, M. (2002). Romantic relationships of hypercompetitive individuals. *Journal of Social and Clinical Psychology, 21,* 517–530.

Ryckman, R. M., Van Den Borne, H., & Syroit, J. (1992). Differences in hypercompetitive attitude between American and Dutch university students. *Journal of Social Psychology, 132,* 331–334.

Salas, E., & Cannon-Bowers, J. A. (2001). The science of training: A decade of progress. *Annual Review of Psychology, 52,* 471–499.

Salili, F. (1994). Age, sex, and cultural differences in the meaning and dimensions of need achievement. *Personality and Social Psychology Bulletin, 20,* 635–648.

Sammallahti, P., & Aalberg, V. (1995). Defense style in personality disorders. *Journal of Nervous and Mental Disease, 183,* 516–521.

Sanna, L. J., & Pusecker, P. A. (1994). Self-efficacy, valence of self-evaluation, and performance. *Personality and Social Psychology Bulletin, 20,* 82–92.

Sarason, I. G. (1975). Test anxiety and the self-disclosing coping model. *Journal of Consulting and Clinical Psychology, 43,* 148–153.

Saudino, K. J., Pedersen, N. L., Lichtenstein, P., McClearn, G. E., & Plomin, R. (1997). Can personality explain genetic influences on life events? *Journal of Personality and Social Psychology, 72,* 196–206.

Sayers, J. (1991). *Mothers of psychoanalysis: Helene Deutsch, Karen Horney, Anna Freud, Melanie Klein.* New York: Norton.

Scarr, S. (1968). Environmental bias in twin studies. *Eugenics Quarterly, 15,* 34–40.

Schachter, S. (1959). *The psychology of affiliation.* Stanford, CA: Stanford University Press.

Schachter, S. (1963). Birth order, eminence, and higher education. *American Sociological Review, 28,* 757–767.

Schachter, S. (1964). Birth order and sociometric choice. *Journal of Abnormal and Social Psychology, 68,* 453–456.

Schimmack, U., & Hartmann, K. (1997). Individual differences in the memory representation of emotional episodes. *Journal of Personality and Social Psychology, 73,* 1064–1079.

Schimmack, U., Oishi, S., Furr, R., & Funder, D. (2004). Personality and life satisfaction: A facet-level analysis. *Personality and Social Psychology Bulletin, 30,* 1062–1075.

Schmitz, N., Neumann, W., & Oppermann, R. (2000). Stress, burnout and locus of control in German nurses. *International Journal of Nursing Studies, 37,* 95–99.

Schmutte, P. S., & Ryff, C. D. (1997). Personality and wellbeing. *Journal of Personality and Social Psychology, 73,* 549–559.

Schneewind, K. A. (1995). Impact of family processes on control beliefs. In A. Bandura (Ed.), *Self-efficacy in changing societies* (pp. 114–148). Cambridge, England: Cambridge University Press.

Schneider, G., Dreisch, G., Kruse, A., Nehen, H., & Heuft, G. (2006). Old and ill and still feeling well? Determinants of subjective well-being in 60-year-olds: The role of the sense of coherence. *American Journal of Geriatric Psychiatry, 14,* 850–859.

Schneider, S. (2001). In search of realistic optimism: Meaning, knowledge, and warm fuzziness. *American Psychologist, 56,* 250–263.

Schneidman, E. S. (2001). My visit with Christiana Morgan. *History of Psychology, 4,* 289–296.

Schou, I., Ekeberg, O., Ruland, C., Sandvik, L., & Karesen, R. (2004). Pessimism as a predictor of emotional morbidity one year following breast cancer surgery. *Psychooncology, 13,* 309–320.

Schou, I., Ekeberg, O., Sandvik, L., & Ruland, C. (2005). Stability in optimism-pessimism in relation to bad news: A study of women with breast cancer. *Journal of Personality Assessment, 84,* 148–154.

Schredl, M. (2006). Factors affecting the continuity between waking and dreaming: Emotional intensity and emotional tone of the waking-life event. *Sleep and Hypnosis, 8,* 1–5.

Schredl, M., Funkhouser, A., & Arn, N. (2006). Dreams of truck drivers: A test of the continuity hypothesis of dreaming. *Imagination, Cognition, and Personality, 25,* 179–186.

Schredl, M., & Piel, E. (2006). War-related dream themes in Germany from 1956 to 2000. *Political Psychology, 27,* 299–307.

Schul, Y., & Vinokur, A. D. (2000). Projection in person perception among spouses as a function of the similarity in their shared experiences. *Personality and Social Psychology Bulletin, 26,* 987–1001.

Schultz, D. P. (1990). *Intimate friends, dangerous rivals: The turbulent relationship between Freud and Jung.* Los Angeles: Jeremy Tarcher.

Schur, M. (1972). *Freud: Living and dying.* New York: International Universities Press.

Schwartz, J., Buboltz, W., Seemann, E., & Flye, A. (2004). Personality styles: Predictors of masculine gender role conflict in male prison inmates. *Psychology of Men and Masculinity, 5,* 59–64.

Schwarz, N. (1999). Self-reports: How the questions shape the answers. *American Psychologist, 54,* 93–105.

Schwarzer, R., & Fuchs, R. (1995). Changing risk behaviors and adopting health behaviors: The role of self-efficacy beliefs. In A. Bandura (Ed.), *Self-efficacy in changing societies* (pp. 259–315). Cambridge, England: Cambridge University Press.

Schwitzgebel, E., Huang, C., & Zhou, Y. (2006). Do we dream in color? Cultural variations and skepticism. *Dreaming, 16,* 35–42.

Scollon, C., & Diener, E. (2006). Love, work, and changes in extraversion and neuroticism over time. *Journal of Personality and Social Psychology, 91,* 1152–1165.

Sechrest, L. (1968). Personal constructs and personal characteristics. *Journal of Individual Psychology, 24,* 162–166.

Sechrest, L. (1984). Review of J. B. Rotter's *The development and applications of social learning theory: Selected papers. Journal of the History of the Behavioral Sciences, 20,* 228–230.

Sechrest, L., & Jackson, D. N. (1961). Social intelligence and accuracy of interpersonal predictions. *Journal of Personality, 29,* 169–182.

Seeman, M., Seeman, T., & Sayles, M. (1985). Social networks and health status: A longitudinal analysis. *Social Psychology Quarterly, 48,* 237–248.

Segall, M., & Wynd, C. A. (1990). Health conception, health locus of control, and power as predictors of smoking behavior change. *American Journal of Health Promotion, 4,* 338–344.

Segerstrom, S. C. (2001). Optimism and attentional bias for negative and positive stimuli. *Personality and Social Psychology Bulletin, 27,* 1334–1343.

Segerstrom, S. C., & Taylor, S. E. (1998). Optimism is associated with mood, coping, and immune change in response to stress. *Journal of Personality and Social Psychology, 74,* 1646–1655.

Seidah, A., & Bouffard, T. (2007). Being proud of oneself as a person or being proud of one's physical appearance: What matters for feeling well in adolescence? *Social Behavior and Personality, 35,* 255–268.

Seligman, M. E. P. (1975). *Helplessness: On depression, development, and death.* San Francisco: W. H. Freeman.

Seligman, M. E. P. (1990). *Learned optimism.* New York: Knopf.

Seligman, M. E. P. (2002). *Authentic happiness: Using the new positive psychology to realize your potential for lasting fulfillment.* New York: Free Press.

Seligman, M. E. P., & Maier, S. F. (1967). Failure to escape traumatic shock. *Journal of Experimental Psychology, 74,* 1–9.

Seligman, M. E. P., Rashid, T., & Parks, A. (2006). Positive psychotherapy. *American Psychologist, 61,* 774–788.

Seligman, M. E. P., & Visintainer, M. (1985). Tumor rejection and early experience of uncontrollable shock in the rat. In F. R. Brush & J. B. Overmier (Eds.), *Affect, conditioning, and cognition: Essays on the determinants of behavior* (pp. 203–210). Hillsdale, NJ: Erlbaum.

Sellers, R. M., Chavous, T. M., & Cooke, D. Y. (1998). Racial ideology and racial centrality as predictors of African American college students' academic performance. *Journal of Black Psychology, 24,* 8–27.

Sellers, R. M., Rowley, S. A. J., Chavous, T. M., Shelton, J. N., & Smith, M. A. (1997). Multidimensional Inventory of Black Identity: A preliminary investigation of reliability and construct validity. *Journal of Personality and Social Psychology, 73,* 805–815.

Sethi, S., & Seligman, M. E. P. (1994). The hope of fundamentalists. *Psychological Science, 5,* 58.

Shamir, B. (1986). Self-esteem and the psychological impact of unemployment. *Social Psychology Quarterly, 49,* 61–72.

Shatz, S. (2004). The relationship between Horney's three neurotic types and Eysenck's PEN model of personality. *Personality and Individual Differences, 37,* 1255–1261.

Sheldon, K., Arndt, J., & Houser-Marko, L. (2003). In search of the organismic valuing process: The human tendency to move towards beneficial goal choices. *Journal of Personality, 71,* 835–886.

Sheldon, K., Elliot, A., Kim, Y., & Kasser, T. (2001). What is satisfying about satisfying events? Testing ten candidate psychological needs. *Journal of Personality and Social Psychology, 80,* 325–339.

Sheldon, K., & Kasser, T. (2001). Getting older, getting better? Personal strivings and psychological maturity across the life span. *Developmental Psychology, 37,* 491–501.

Sheldon, K., Kasser, T., Houser-Marko, L., Jones, T., & Turban, D. (2005). Doing one's duty: Chronological age, felt autonomy, and subjective well-being. *European Journal of Personality, 19,* 97–115.

Sheldon, W. (1942). *The varieties of temperament: A psychology of constitutional differences.* New York: Harper & Row.

Sher, K., Bartholow, B., & Wood, M. (2000). Personality and substance abuse disorders: A prospective study. *Journal of Consulting and Clinical Psychology, 68,* 818–829.

Shevrin, H. (1977). Some assumptions of psychoanalytic communication: Implications of subliminal research for psychoanalytic method and technique. In N. Freedman & S. Grand (Eds.), *Communicative structures and psychic structures.* New York: Plenum Press.

Shiner, R. L. (1998). How shall we speak of children's personalities in middle childhood? A preliminary taxonomy. *Psychological Bulletin, 124,* 308–332.

Shiner, R. L., Masten, A., & Tellegen, A. (2002). A developmental perspective on personality in emerging adulthood: Childhood antecedents and concurrent adaptation. *Journal of Personality and Social Psychology, 83,* 1165–1177.

Shirachi, M., & Spirrison, C. (2006). Repressive coping style and substance use among college students. *North American Journal of Psychology, 8,* 99–114.

Shostrom, E. L. (1964). An inventory for the measurement of self-actualization. *Educational and Psychological Measurement, 24,* 207–218.

Shostrom, E. L. (1974). *Manual for the Personal Orientation Inventory.* San Diego: Educational and Industrial Testing Service.

Shull, R., & Grimes, J. (2006). Resistance to extinction following variable-interval reinforcement. *Journal of the Experimental Analysis of Behavior, 85,* 23–29.

Siegel, A. M. (2001). An antidote to misconceptions about self psychology. [Review of *Kohut's Freudian vision*]. *Contemporary Psychology, 46,* 316–317.

Siegelman, M. (1988). "Origins" of extroversion–introversion. *Journal of Psychology, 69,* 85–91.

Siegler, I., & Brummett, B. (2000). Associations among NEO personality assessments and well-being at midlife: Facet level analysis. *Psychology and Aging, 15,* 710–714.

Silvera, D., & Seger, C. (2004). Feeling good about ourselves: Unrealistic self-evaluations and their relation to self-esteem in the United States and Norway. *Journal of Cross-Cultural Psychology, 35,* 571–585.

Silverman, L. H., & Weinberger, I. (1985). Mommy and I are one: Implications for psychotherapy. *American Psychologist, 40,* 1296–1308.

Simon, L. (1998). *Genuine reality: A life of William James.* New York: Harcourt Brace.

Skinner, B. F. (1938). *The behavior of organisms: An experimental analysis.* New York: Appleton-Century.

Skinner, B. F. (1948). *Walden Two.* New York: Macmillan.

Skinner, B. F. (1953). *Science and human behavior.* New York: Free Press.

Skinner, B. F. (1967). Autobiography. In E. G. Boring & G. Lindzey (Eds.), *A history of psychology in autobiography* (Vol. 5, pp. 385–413). New York: Appleton-Century-Crofts.

Skinner, B. F. (1971). *Beyond freedom and dignity.* New York: Knopf.

Skinner, B. F. (1979). *The shaping of a behaviorist.* New York: Knopf.

Skinner, B. F. (1983). *A matter of consequences.* New York: Knopf.

Skinner, T., Hampson, S., & Fife-Schau, C. (2002). Personality, personal model beliefs, and self-care in adolescents and young adults with Type I diabetes. *Health Psychology, 21,* 61–70.

Skitka, L., & Sargis, E. (2006). The Internet as psychological laboratory. *Annual Review of Psychology, 57,* 529–555.

Sleek, S. (1998, October). Blame your peers, not your parents. *APA Monitor,* p. 9.

Slugoski, B. F., & Ginsburg, G. P. (1989). Ego identity and explanatory speech. In J. Shotter & K. F. Gergen (Eds.), *Texts of identity* (pp. 36–55). London: Sage.

Smillie, L., Yeo, G., Furnham, A., & Jackson, C. (2006). Benefits of all work and no play: The relationship between neuroticism and performance as a function of resource allocation. *Journal of Applied Psychology, 91,* 139–155.

Smith, A., & Williams, K. (2004). R U there? Ostracism by cell phone text messages. *Group Dynamics, 8,* 291–301.

Smith, D. (2002). The theory heard 'round the world. *Monitor on Psychology, 33*(9), 30–32.

Smith, J. E., Stefan, C., Kovaleski, M., & Johnson, G. (1991). Recidivism and dependency in a psychiatric population: An investigation with Kelly's dependency grid. *International Journal of Personal Construct Psychology, 4,* 157–173.

Smith, M. B. (1990). Henry A. Murray (1893–1988): Humanistic psychologist. *Journal of Humanistic Psychology, 30*(1), 6–13.

Smith, R. E., Ptacek, J. T., & Smoll, F. L. (1992). Sensation seeking, stress, and adolescent injuries: A test of stress-buffering, risk-taking, and coping skills hypotheses. *Journal of Personality and Social Psychology, 62,* 1016–1024.

Solnit, A. J. (1992). Freud's view of mental health and fate. In E. E. Garcia (Ed.), *Understanding Freud: The man and his ideas* (pp. 64–77). New York: New York University Press.

Spangler, W. D. (1992). Validity of questionnaire and TAT measures of need for achievement: Two meta-analyses. *Psychological Bulletin, 112,* 140–154.

Spann, M., Molock, S., Barksdale, C., Matlin, S., & Puri, R. (2006). Suicide and African-American teenagers: Risk factors and coping mechanisms. *Suicide and Life-Threatening Behavior, 36,* 553–568.

Spitalnick, J., DiClemente, R., Wingood, G., Crosby, R., Milhausen, R., Sales, J., McCarty, F., Rose, E., & Younger, S. (2007). Sexual sensation seeking and its relationship to risky sexual behavior among African-American adolescents. *Journal of Adolescence, 30,* 165–173.

Srivastava, S., John, O., Gosling, S., & Potter, J. (2003). Development of personality in early and middle adulthood: Set like plaster or persistent change? *Journal of Personality and Social Psychology, 84,* 1041–1053.

Sroufe, L. A., Fox, N. E., & Pancake, V. R. (1983). Attachment and dependency in developmental perspective. *Child Development, 54,* 1615–1627.

Stacy, A. W., Sussman, S., Dent, C. W., Burton, D., & Floy, B. R. (1992). Moderators of peer social influence in adolescent smoking. *Personality and Social Psychology Bulletin, 18,* 163–172.

Stajkovic, A., & Luthans, F. (1998). Self-efficacy and work-related performance: A meta-analysis. *Psychological Bulletin, 124,* 240–261.

Stanton, B., Li, X., Cottrell, L., & Kaljee, J. (2001). Early initiation of sex, drug-related risk behaviors, and sensation seeking among urban low-income African-American adolescents. *Journal of the National Medical Association, 93*(4), 129–138.

Statton, J. E., & Wilborn, B. (1991). Adlerian counseling and the early recollections of children. *Individual Psychology, 47,* 338–347.

Staudinger, U. M. (2001a). Life reflection: A social-cognitive analysis of life review. *Review of General Psychology, 5,* 148–160.

Staudinger, U. M. (2001b). More than pleasure? Toward a psychology of growth and strength? [Review of *Wellbeing: The foundations of hedonic psychology*]. *Contemporary Psychology, 46,* 552–554.

Staudinger, U. M., Fleeson, W., & Baltes, P. B. (1999). Predictors of subjective physical health and global well-being: Similarities and differences between the United States and Germany. *Journal of Personality and Social Psychology, 76,* 305–319.

Steel, P. (2007). The nature of procrastination: A meta-analytic and theoretical review of quintessential self-regulatory failure. *Psychological Bulletin, 133,* 65–94.

Steel, P., & Ones, D. (2002). Personality and happiness: A national-level analysis. *Journal of Personality and Social Psychology, 83,* 767–781.

Steinberg, L., & Morris, A. S. (2001). Adolescent development. *Annual Review of Psychology, 52,* 83–110.

Stelmack, R. M. (1997). Toward a paradigm in personality: Comment on Eysenck's (1997) view. *Journal of Personality and Social Psychology, 73,* 1238–1241.

Stepansky, P. E. (1983). *In Freud's shadow: Adler in context.* New York: Analytic Press.

Stephen, J., Fraser, E., & Marcia, J. E. (1992). Moratorium achievement (MAMA) cycles in lifespan identity development: Value orientations and reasoning system correlates. *Journal of Adolescence, 15,* 283–300.

Stephenson, W. (1953). *The study of behavior: Q-technique and its methodology.* Chicago: University of Chicago Press.

Steptoe, A., Wright, C., Kunz-Ebrecht, S., & Lliffe, S. (2006). Dispositional optimism and health behaviour in community-dwelling older people: Associations with healthy ageing. *British Journal of Health Psychology, 11,* 71–84.

Sterba, R. F. (1982). *Reminiscences of a Viennese psychoanalyst.* Detroit, MI: Wayne State University Press.

Stewart, A. J., & Ostrove, J. M. (1998). Women's personality in middle age: Gender, history, and midcourse corrections. *American Psychologist, 53,* 1185–1194.

Stewart, A. J., & Vandewater, E. A. (1999). "If I had it to do over again . . . ." Midlife review, midcourse corrections, and women's well-being in midlife. *Journal of Personality and Social Psychology, 76,* 270–283.

Stewart, G. L., Carson, K. P., & Cardy, R. L. (1996). The joint effects of conscientiousness and self-leadership training on employee self-directed behavior in a service setting. *Personnel Psychology, 49,* 143–164.

Stilwell, N. A., Wallick, M. M., Thal, S. E., & Burleson, J. A. (2000). Myers-Briggs Type and medical specialty choice: A new look at an old question. *Teaching and Learning in Medicine, 12,* 14–20.

Stirn, A., Hinz, A., & Braehler, E. (2006). Prevalence of tattooing and body piercing in Germany and perception of health, mental disorders, and sensation seeking among tattooed and body-pierced individuals. *Journal of Psychosomatic Research, 60,* 531–534.

Story, A. L. (1998). Self-esteem and memory for favorable and unfavorable personality feedback. *Personality and Social Psychology Bulletin, 24,* 51–64.

Strano, D., & Petrocelli, J. (2005). A preliminary examination of the role of inferiority feelings in the academic achievement of college students. *Journal of Individual Psychology, 61,* 80–89.

Straumann, T. J., Vookles, J., Berenstein, V., Chaiken, S., & Higgins, E. T. (1991). Self-discrepancies and vulnerability to body dissatisfaction and disordered eating. *Journal of Personality and Social Psychology, 61,* 946–956.

Streitmatter, J. (1993). Identity status and identity style: A replication study. *Journal of Adolescence, 16,* 211–215.

Stricker, L. J., & Ross, J. (1962). *A description and evaluation of the Myers-Briggs Type Indicator.* Princeton, NJ: Educational Testing Service.

Strickland, B. R. (1989). Internal-external control expectancies: From contingency to creativity. *American Psychologist, 44,* 1–12.

Strickland, B. R., & Haley, W. E. (1980). Sex differences on the Rotter I-E Scale. *Journal of Personality and Social Psychology, 39,* 930–939.

Strumpfer, D. (1970). Fear and affiliation during a disaster. *Journal of Social Psychology, 82,* 263–268.

Sturman, E., Mongrain, M., & Kohn, P. (2006). Attributional style as a predictor of hopelessness depression. *Journal of Cognitive Psychotherapy, 20,* 447–458.

Suedfeld, P., Soriano, E., McMurtry, D., Paterson, H., Weiszbeck, T., & Krell, R. (2005). Erikson's components of a healthy personality among Holocaust survivors immediately and forty years after the war. *International Journal of Aging and Human Development, 60,* 229–248.

Suinn, R. (1999, March). Scaling the summit: Valuing ethnicity. *APA Monitor,* p. 2.

Sulloway, F. J. (1979). *Freud, biologist of the mind: Beyond the psychoanalytic legend.* New York: Basic Books.

Sulloway, F. J. (1992). Reassessing Freud's case histories: The social construction of psychoanalysis. In T. Gelfand & J. Kerr (Eds.), *Freud and the history of psychoanalysis* (pp. 153–192). Hillsdale, NJ: Analytic Press.

Sulloway, F. J. (1995). Birth order and evolutionary psychology: A meta-analytic overview. *Psychological Inquiry, 6*(1).

Sulloway, F. J. (2007). Birth order and intelligence. *Science, 317,* 1711.

Suls, J., Green, P., & Hillis, S. (1998). Emotional reactivity to everyday problems, affective inertia, and neuroticism. *Personality and Social Psychology Bulletin, 24,* 127–136.

Susskind, J., Littlewort, G., Bartlett, M., Movellan, J., & Anderson, A. (2007). Human and computer recognition of facial expressions of emotion. *Neuropsychologia, 45,* 152–162.

Sutton-Smith, B., & Rosenberg, B. C. (1970). *The sibling.* New York: Holt, Rinehart & Winston.

Swann, W., Chang-Schneider, C., & McClarty, K. (2007). Do people's self-views matter? Self-concept and self-esteem in everyday life. *American Psychologist, 62,* 84–94.

Swenson, R., & Prelow, H. (2005). Ethnic identity, self-esteem, and perceived efficacy as mediators of the relation of supportive parenting to psychosocial outcomes among urban adolescents. *Journal of Adolescence, 28,* 465–477.

Symbaluk, D. G., Heth, C. D., Cameron, J., & Pierce, W. D. (1997). Social modeling, monetary incentives, and pain endurance: The role of self-efficacy in pain perception. *Personality and Social Psychology Bulletin, 23,* 258–269.

Taft, L. B., & Nehrke, M. F. (1990). Reminiscences, life review, and ego integrity in nursing home residents. *International Journal of Aging and Human Development, 30,* 189–196.

Tangney, J., Baumeister, R., & Boone, A. (2004). High self-control predicts good adjustment, less pathology, better grades, and interpersonal success. *Journal of Personality, 72,* 271–324.

Tavris, C. (1992). *The mismeasure of woman.* New York: Simon & Schuster.

Taylor, M. (2000). The influence of self-efficacy on alcohol use among American Indians. *Cultural Diversity and Ethnic Minority Psychology, 6,* 152–167.

Taylor, S. E., Kemeny, M. E., Aspinwall, L. G., Schneider, S. C., Rodriguez, R., & Herbert, M. (1992). Optimism, coping, psychological distress, and high-risk sexual behavior among men at risk for acquired immunodeficiency syndrome (AIDS). *Journal of Personality and Social Psychology, 63,* 460–473.

Tellegen, A., Lykken, D. T., Bouchard, T. J., Wilcox, K., Segal, N., & Rich, S. (1988). Personality similarity in twins reared apart and together. *Journal of Personality and Social Psychology, 54,* 1031–1039.

Tennen, H., Affleck, G., & Armeli, S. (2005). Personality and daily experience revisited. *Journal of Personality, 73,* 1–19.

Terracciano, A., Costa, P., & McCrae, R. (2006). Personality plasticity after age 30. *Personality and Social Psychology Bulletin, 32,* 999–1009.

Teti, D. M., & Gelfand, D. M. (1991). Behavioral competence among mothers of infants in the first year: The mediational role of maternal self-efficacy. *Child Development, 62,* 918–929.

Tetlock, P. E. (1983). Cognitive style and political ideology. *Journal of Personality and Social Psychology, 45,* 118–126.

Tetlock, P. E. (1984). Cognitive style and political belief systems in the British House of Commons. *Journal of Personality and Social Psychology, 46,* 365–375.

Thomas, A. (1986). The New York Longitudinal Study: From infancy to early adult life. In R. Plomin & J. Dunn (Eds.), *The study of temperament* (pp. 39–52). Hillsdale, NJ: Erlbaum.

Thomas, A., Chess, S., & Korn, S. (1982). The reality of difficult temperament. *Merrill-Palmer Quarterly, 28,* 1–20.

Thompson, S. C., Sobolew-Shubin, A., Galbraith, M. E., Schwankovsky, L., & Cruzen, D. (1993). Maintaining perception of control: Finding perceived control in low-control circumstances. *Journal of Personality and Social Psychology, 64,* 293–304.

Thompson, T. (1988). Benedictus behavior analysis: B. F. Skinner's magnum opus at fifty [Review of *The behavior of organisms: An experimental analysis*]. *Contemporary Psychology, 33,* 397–402.

Thompson, V., & Alexander, H. (2006). Therapists' race and African-American clients' reactions to therapy. *Psychotherapy: Theory, Research, Practice, Training, 43,* 99–110.

Tobey, L. H., & Bruhn, A. R. (1992). Early memories and the criminally dangerous. *Journal of Personality Assessment, 59,* 137–152.

Tong, J., & Wang, L. (2006). Validation of locus of control scale in Chinese organizations. *Personality and Individual Differences, 41,* 941–950.

Torges, C., Stewart, A., & Miner-Rubino, K. (2005). Personality after prime of life: Men and women coming to terms with regrets. *Journal of Research in Personality, 39,* 148–165.

Tori, C., & Bilmes, M. (2002). Multiculturalism and psychoanalytic psychology: The validation of a defense mechanism measure in an Asian population. *Psychoanalytic Psychology, 19,* 701–721.

Tran, X., & Ralston, L. (2006). Tourist preferences: Influence of unconscious needs. *Annals of Tourism Research, 33,* 424–441.

Triandis, H. C., & Suh, E. M. (2002). Cultural influences on personality. *Annual Review of Psychology, 53,* 133–160.

Tribich, D., & Messer, S. (1974). Psychoanalytic character type and states of authority as determiners of suggestibility. *Journal of Consulting and Clinical Psychology, 42,* 842–848.

Triplet, R. G. (1993). Book review of *Love's story told: A life of Henry A. Murray. Journal of the History of the Behavioral Sciences, 29,* 384–386.

Trull, T. J., Widiger, T. A., Useda, J. D., Holcomb, J., Doan, B., Axelrod, S. R., Stern, B. L., & Gershuny, B. S. (1998). A structured interview for the assessment of the five-factor model of personality. *Psychological Assessment, 10,* 229–240.

Trzesniewski, K. H., Donnellan, M. B., Moffitt, B., Robins, R. W., Poulton, R., & Caspi, A. (2006). Low self-esteem during adolescence predicts poor health, criminal behavior, and limited economic prospects during adulthood. *Developmental Psychology, 42,* 381–390.

Trzesniewski, K. H., Donnellan, M. B., & Robins, R. W. (2003). Stability of self-esteem across the life span. *Journal of Personality and Social Psychology, 84,* 205–220.

Tucker, J., Elliott, M., & Klein, D. (2006). Social control of health behavior: Associations with conscientiousness and neuroticism. *Personality and Social Psychology Bulletin, 32,* 1143–1152.

Tuerlinckx, F., DeBoeck, P., & Lens, W. (2002). Measuring needs with the Thematic Apperception Test: A psychometric study. *Journal of Personality and Social Psychology, 82,* 448–461.

Turkle, S. (1995). *Life on the screen: Identity in the age of the Internet.* New York: Simon & Schuster.

Turkum, A. (2005). Do optimism, social network richness, and submissive behaviors predict well-being? Study with a Turkish sample. *Social Behavior and Personality, 33,* 619–628.

Twenge, J. (2000). The age of anxiety? The birth cohort change in anxiety and neuroticism, 1952–1993. *Journal of Personality and Social Psychology, 79,* 1007–1021.

Uba, L. (1994). *Asian Americans: Personality patterns, identity, and mental health.* New York: Guilford Press.

Uhlmann, E., & Swanson, J. (2004). Exposure to violent video games increases automatic aggressiveness. *Journal of Adolescence, 27,* 41–52.

Umana-Taylor, A. (2004). Ethnic identity and self-esteem: Examining the role of social context. *Journal of Adolescence, 27,* 139–146.

Utsey, S., Payne, Y., Jackson, E., & Jones, A. (2002). Race-related stress, quality of life indicators, and life satisfaction among elderly African Americans. *Cultural Diversity and Ethnic Minority Psychology, 8,* 7–17.

Utz, S. (2003). Social identification and interpersonal attraction in MUDs [multi-user dungeons]. *Swiss Journal of Psychology, 62,* 91–101.

Vaidya, J. G., Gray, E. K., Haig, J., & Watson, D. (2002). On the temporal stability of personality: Evidence for differential stability and the role of life experiences. *Journal of Personality and Social Psychology, 83,* 1469–1484.

Valentijn, S., Hill, R., Van Hooren, S., Bosma, H., Van Boxtel, M., Jolles, J., & Ponds, R. (2006). Memory self-efficacy predicts memory performance: Results from a 6-year follow-up study. *Psychology and Aging, 21,* 165–172.

Valli, K., Revonsuo, A., Palkas, O., & Punamaki, R. (2006). The effect of trauma on dream content: A field study of Palestinian children. *Dreaming, 16,* 63–87.

Van Aken, M., Denisson, J., Branje, S., Dubas, J., & Goossens, L. (2006). Midlife concerns and short-term personality change in middle adulthood. *European Journal of Personality, 20,* 497–513.

Van Boven, L. (2005). Experientialism, materialism, and the pursuit of happiness. *Review of General Psychology, 9,* 132–142.

van den Boom, D. C., & Hoeksma, J. B. (1994). The effect of infant irritability on mother-infant interaction: A growth-curve analysis. *Developmental Psychology, 30,* 581–590.

Van de Water, D. A., & McAdams, D. P. (1989). Generativity and Erikson's "belief in the species." *Journal of Research in Personality, 23,* 435–449.

Vandewater, E. A., Ostrove, J. M., & Stewart, A. J. (1997). Predicting women's well-being in midlife: The importance of personality development and social role involvements. *Journal of Personality and Social Psychology, 72,* 1147–1160.

Vandiver, B., Cross, W., Worrell, F., & Fhagen-Smith, P. (2002). Validating the Cross Racial Identity Scale. *Journal of Counseling Psychology, 49,* 71–85.

Van Hiel, A., Mervielde, I., & DeFruyt, F. (2006). Stagnation and generativity: Structure, validity, and differential relationships with adaptive and maladaptive personality. *Journal of Personality, 74,* 543–573.

Van Yperen, N. (2006). A novel approach to assessing achievement goals in the context of the 2 × 2 framework: Identifying distinct profiles of individuals with different dominant achievement goals. *Personality and Social Psychology Bulletin, 32,* 1432–1445.

Veenhoven, R. (2005). Is life getting better? How long and happily do people live in modern society? *European Psychologist, 10,* 330–343.

Vetere, A., & Myers, L. (2002). Repressive coping style and adult romantic attachment style. *Personality and Individual Differences, 32,* 799–807.

Viken, R. J., Rose, R. J., Kaprio, J., & Koskenvuo, M. (1994). A developmental genetic analysis of adult personality: Extraversion and neuroticism from 18 to 59 years of age. *Journal of Personality and Social Psychology, 66,* 722–730.

Villanova, P., & Peterson, C. (1991). Meta-analysis of human helplessness experiments. Unpublished data. Cited in Peterson, Maier, & Seligman, 1993.

Viner, R. (1996). Melanie Klein and Anna Freud: The discourse of the early dispute. *Journal of the History of the Behavioral Sciences, 32,* 4–15.

Visintainer, M., Volpicelli, J., & Seligman, M. E. P. (1982). Tumor rejection in rats after inescapable or escapable shock. *Science, 216,* 437–439.

Vleioras, G., & Bosma, H. (2005). Are identity styles important for psychological well-being? *Journal of Adolescence, 28,* 397–409.

Von Dras, D. D., & Siegler, I. C. (1997). Stability in extraversion and aspects of social support at midlife. *Journal of Personality and Social Psychology, 72,* 233–241.

Wagerman, S., & Funder, D. (2007). Acquaintance reports of personality and academic achievement: A case for conscientiousness. *Journal of Research in Personality, 41,* 221–229.

Waldrop, D., Lightsey, O., Ethington, C., Woemmel, C., & Coke, A. (2001). Self-efficacy, optimism, health competence, and recovery from orthopedic surgery. *Journal of Counseling Psychology, 48,* 233–238.

Walker, B., & Winter, D. (2007). The elaboration of personal construct psychology. *Annual Review of Psychology, 58,* 453–477.

Walters, R. H., Bowen, N. V., & Parke, R. D. (1963). Experimentally induced disinhibition of sexual responses. Cited in Bandura & Walters, 1963.

Walton, K., & Roberts, B. (2004). On the relationship between substance use and personality traits: Abstainers are not maladjusted. *Journal of Research in Personality, 38,* 515–535.

Wang, Q., & Conway, M. (2004). The stories we keep: Autobiographical memory in American and Chinese middle-aged adults. *Journal of Personality, 72,* 911–938.

Want, V., Parham, T., Baker, R., & Sherman, M. (2004). African-American students' ratings of Caucasian and African-American counselors varying in racial consciousness. *Cultural Diversity and Ethnic Minority Psychology, 10,* 123–136.

Warburton, J., McLaughlin, D., & Pinsker, D. (2006). Generative acts: Family and community involvement of older Australians. *International Journal of Aging and Human Development, 63,* 115–137.

Waterman, A. S. (1982). Identity development from adolescence to adulthood: An extension of theory and a review of research. *Developmental Psychology, 18,* 341–358.

Waterman, C. K., Buebel, M. E., & Waterman, A. S. (1970). Relationship between resolution of the identity crisis and outcomes of previous psychosocial crises. Proceedings of the 78th Annual Convention of the American Psychological Association, 5, 467–468.

Watkins, C. E., Jr. (1994). Measuring social interest. *Individual Psychology, 50,* 69–96.

Watkins, C. E., Jr., & St. John, C. (1994). Validity of the Sulliman scale of social interest. *Individual Psychology, 50,* 166–169.

Watson, C. B., Chemers, M. M., & Preiser, N. (2001). Collective efficacy: A multilevel analysis. *Personality and Social Psychology Bulletin, 27,* 1057–1068.

Watson, D., Clark, L. A., McIntyre, C. W., & Hamaker, S. (1992). Affect, personality, and social activity. *Journal of Personality and Social Psychology, 63,* 1011–1025.

Watson, D., & Humrichouse, J. (2006). Personality development in emerging adulthood: Integrating evidence from self-ratings and spouse ratings. *Journal of Personality and Social Psychology, 91,* 959–974.

Watson, M. W., & Getz, K. (1990). The relationship between Oedipal behaviors and children's family role concepts. *Merrill-Palmer Quarterly, 36,* 487–505.

Watts, R., & Holden, J. (1994). Why continue to use "fictional finalism"? *Individual Psychology, 50,* 161–163.

Weber, H., Vollmann, M., & Renner, B. (2007). The spirited, the observant, and the disheartened: Social concepts of optimism, realism, and pessimism. *Journal of Personality, 75,* 169–197.

Webster, R. (1995). *Why Freud was wrong: Sin, science, and psychoanalysis.* New York: Basic Books.

Wegner, D. M., & Wheatley, T. (1999). Apparent mental causation: Sources of the experience of will. *American Psychologist, 54,* 480–492.

Wehr, G. (1987). *Jung: A biography.* Boston: Shambhala.

Weinberger, D. (1995). The content validity of the repressive coping style. In J. Singer (Ed.), *Repression and dissociation* (pp. 337–386). Chicago: University of Chicago Press.

Weinberger, I., & Silverman, L. H. (1990). Testability and empirical validation of psychoanalytic dynamic propositions through subliminal psychodynamic activation. *Psychoanalytic Psychology, 7,* 299–339.

Weiss, A., King, J., & Perkins, L. (2006). Personality and subjective well-being in orangutans. *Journal of Personality and Social Psychology, 90,* 501–511.

Weisse, C. S. (1992). Depression and immunocompetence: A review of the literature. *Psychological Bulletin, 111,* 475–489.

Weitlauf, J. C., Cervone, D., Smith, R. E., & Wright, P. M. (2001). Assessing generalizations in perceived self-efficacy: Multi-domain and global assessments of the effects of self-defense training for women. *Personality and Social Psychology Bulletin, 27,* 1683–1691.

Westen, D. (1990). Psychoanalytic approaches to personality. In L. A. Pervin (Ed.), *Handbook of personality* (pp. 21–65). New York: Guilford Press.

Westen, D. (1998). The scientific legacy of Sigmund Freud. *Psychological Bulletin, 124,* 333–371.

Westermeyer, J. (2004). Predictors and characteristics of Erikson's life cycle model among men: A 32-year longitudinal study. *International Journal of Aging and Human Development, 58,* 29–48.

Westkott, M. (1986). *The feminist legacy of Karen Horney.* New Haven, CT: Yale University Press.

Whitbourne, S. K., Elliot, L. B., Zuschlag, M. K., & Waterman, A. S. (1992). Psychosocial development in adulthood: A 22-year sequential study. *Journal of Personality and Social Psychology, 63,* 260–271.

White, J., Campbell, L., Stewart, A., Davies, M., & Pilkington, L. (1997). The relationship of psychological birth order to career interests. *Individual Psychology, 53,* 89–103.

Wichern, F., & Nowicki, S. (1976). Independence training practices and locus of control orientation in children and adolescents. *Developmental Psychology, 12,* 77.

Williams, D. E., & Page, M. M. (1989). A multidimensional measure of Maslow's hierarchy of needs. *Journal of Research in Personality, 23,* 192–213.

Williams, L. M. (1994). Recall of childhood trauma: A prospective study of women's memories of child sexual abuse. *Journal of Consulting and Clinical Psychology, 62,* 1167–1176.

Wills, T., Murry, V., Brody, G., Gibbons, F., Gerrard, M., Walker, C., & Ainette, M. (2007). Ethnic pride and self-control related to protective and risk factors. *Health Psychology, 26,* 50–59.

Wilson, C. (1972). *New pathways in psychology.* New York: Taplinger.

Wilson, G. (1977). Introversion–extroversion. In T. Blass (Ed.), *Personality variables in social behavior.* Hillsdale, NJ: Erlbaum.

Winkielman, P., Berridge, K., & Wilbarger, J. (2005). Unconscious affective reactions to masked happy versus angry faces influence consumption behavior and judgments of value. *Personality and Social Psychology Bulletin, 31,* 121–135.

Winter, D. A. (1992). *Personal construct psychology in clinical practice.* London: Routledge.

Winter, D. G. (1973). *The power motive.* New York: Free Press.

Winter, D. G. (1993a). Gordon Allport and Letters from Jenny. In K. H. Craik, R. Hogan, & R. N. Wolfe (Eds.), *Fifty years of personality psychology* (pp. 147–163). New York: Plenum Press.

Winter, D. G. (1993b). Power, affiliation, and war: Three tests of a motivational model. *Journal of Personality and Social Psychology, 65,* 532–545.

Winterbottom, M. R. (1958). The relation of need for achievement to learning experiences in independence and mastery. In J. W. Atkinson (Ed.), *Motives in fantasy, action, and society.* Princeton, NJ: Van Nostrand.

Wittels, F. (1924). *Sigmund Freud: His personality, his teaching, and his school.* London: Allen & Unwin.

Wood, J. M., Garb, H. N., Lilienfeld, S. O., & Nezworski, M. T. (2002). Clinical assessment. *Annual Review of Psychology, 53,* 519–543.

Xian-Li, A., & Guang-Xing, X. (2006). Dream contents of modern undergraduate students. *Chinese Mental Health Journal, 14,* 57–67.

Yamagata, S., Suzuki, A., Ando, J., Ono, Y., Kijima, N., Yoshimura, K., Ostendorf, F., Angleitner, A., Riemann, R., Spinath, F., Livesley, W., & Jang, K. (2006). Is the genetic structure of human personality universal? A cross-cultural twin study from North America, Europe, and Asia. *Journal of Personality and Social Psychology, 90,* 987–998.

Ying, Y., Lee, P., Tsai, J., Yeh, J., & Huang, J. (2000). The concept of depression in Chinese American college students. *Cultural Diversity and Ethnic Minority Psychology, 6,* 183–185.

Young-Bruehl, E. (1988). *Anna Freud: A biography.* New York: Summit Books.

Yu, P., & Shu-Hua, L. (2005). The relationship between college students' attributional style, self-efficacy and subjective well-being. *Chinese Journal of Clinical Psychology, 13,* 43–44.

Zajonc, R. B. (2001). The family dynamics of intellectual development. *American Psychologist, 56,* 490–496.

Zajonc, R. B., Markus, H., & Markus, G. B. (1979). The birth order puzzle. *Journal of Personality and Social Psychology, 37,* 1325–1341.

Zaretsky, E. (2004). *Secrets of the soul: A social and cultural history of psychoanalysis.* New York: Knopf.

Zeidner, M. (1993). Coping with disaster: The case of Israeli adolescents under threat of missile attack. *Journal of Youth and Adolescence, 22,* 89–108.

Zheng, H., Ming-Yi, Q., Chun-Li, Y., Jing, N., Jing, D., & Xiao-Yun, Z. (2006). Correlated factors comparison: The trends of computer game addiction and Internet relationship addiction. *Chinese Journal of Clinical Psychology, 14,* 244–247.

Zimmerman, B. J. (1995). Self-efficacy and educational development. In A. Bandura (Ed.), *Self-efficacy in changing societies* (pp. 202–231). Cambridge, England: Cambridge University Press.

Zucker, A., Ostrove, J., & Stewart, A. (2002). College educated women's personality development in adulthood: Perceptions and age differences. *Psychology and Aging, 17,* 236–244.

Zuckerman, M. (1979). *Sensation seeking: Beyond the optimal level of arousal.* Hillsdale, NJ: Erlbaum.

Zuckerman, M. (1983). *Biological bases of sensation seeking, impulsivity, and anxiety.* Hillsdale, NJ: Erlbaum.

Zuckerman, M. (1990). The psychophysiology of sensation seeking. *Journal of Personality, 58,* 313–345.

Zuckerman, M. (1993). Out of sensory deprivation and into sensation seeking: A personal and scientific journey. In G. G. Brannigan & M. R. Merrens (Eds.), *The undaunted psychologist: Adventures in research* (pp. 45–57). Philadelphia: Temple University Press.

Zuckerman, M. (1994a). *Behavioral expressions and biosocial bases of sensation seeking.* Cambridge, England: Cambridge University Press.

Zuckerman, M. (1994b). Impulsive unsocialized sensation seeking: The biological foundations of a basic dimension of personality. In J. E. Bates & T. D. Wachs (Eds.), *Temperament: Individual differences at the interface of biology and behavior* (pp. 219–255). Washington, DC: American Psychological Association.

Zuckerman, M. (2004). The shaping of personality: Genes, environments, and chance encounters. *Journal of Personality Assessment, 82,* 11–22.

Zuckerman, M., Buchsbaum, M. S., & Murphy, D. L. (1980). Sensation seeking and its biological correlates. *Psychological Bulletin, 88,* 187–214.

Zuckerman, M., Eysenck, S., & Eysenck, H. J. (1978). Sensation seeking in England and America: Cross-cultural, age and sex comparisons. *Journal of Consulting and Clinical Psychology, 46,* 139–149.

Zullow, H., & Seligman, M. E. P. (1985). Pessimistic ruminations predict increase in depressive symptoms. Unpublished manuscript. [Cited in D. L. Rosenhan & M. E. P. Seligman, *Abnormal psychology* (2nd ed.). New York: Norton.]

Zurbriggen, E. L., & Sturman, T. S. (2002). Linking motives and emotions: A test of McClelland's hypothesis. *Personality and Social Psychology Bulletin, 28,* 521–535.

Author Index

Subject Index